Computer Accounting with QuickBooks® 2018

Eighteen Edition

Donna Kay, MBA, PhD, CPA, CITP

QuickBooks Pro 2018
QuickBooks Premier 2018
QuickBooks Accountant 2018

Mc Graw Hill Education

COMPUTER ACCOUNTING WITH QUICKBOOKS® 2018

Published by McGraw-Hill Education, 2 Penn Plaza, New York, NY 10121.

Some ancillaries, including electronic and print components, may not be available to customers outside the United States.

This book is printed on acid-free paper.

2 3 4 5 6 7 8 9 GPC 21 20

ISBN 978-1-260-08473-3
MHID 1-260-08473-6

Cover Image: © *manttek/Shutterstock*

mheducation.com/highered

Computer Accounting with QuickBooks

18th Edition by Donna Kay

Why QuickBooks?

World's No. 1 Accounting Software
Millions of Users

Are you Ready?

What's New? New Chapters!

New Chapter 3, *QuickBooks Transactions,* provides an overview of all QuickBooks transactions, including banking, customer, vendor and employee transactions.

Chapter 6, *Vendors and Expenses,* and Chapter 7, *Inventory,* divide vendor tasks into two chapters to make the material more manageable. Chapter 6 covers vendor transactions related to services, such as how to record entering bills and paying bills. Chapter 7 covers vendor transactions related to inventory and the purchase of products, such as creating purchase orders, receiving inventory, entering bills, and paying bills.

Chapter 9, *QuickBooks Adjustments,* is a new chapter addressing adjusting entries in more depth. Reports are covered in a separate chapter, Chapter 10, *QuickBooks Reports.*

Chapter 12, *QuickBooks Service Company Case,* is a new chapter covering a comprehensive QuickBooks case study, Mookie The Beagle™ Spa.

Chapter 14, *QuickBooks Merchandising Company Case,* is a new chapter covering a comprehensive QuickBooks case study, Mookie The Beagle™ Spa Supplies.

What's New?
Streamlined Learning!

Computer Accounting with QuickBooks 2018 uses a highly effective three-step approach to streamline learning. Simplify and streamline learning QuickBooks with **XPM:**

1. **eXplore**
2. **Practice**
3. **Master**

eXplore QuickBooks using the chapter with numerous screen shots and detailed instructions. While we eXplore, we will focus on learning how to navigate and use QuickBooks. Chapters in *Computer Accounting with QuickBooks* are designed as tutorials to introduce the accounting software features. All chapters are based on realistic, virtual company scenarios to enhance your understanding of QuickBooks in the business environment.

Practice entering information and transactions into QuickBooks with end-of-chapter exercises. Exercises are designed with fewer instructions to test your understanding and, when needed, to develop your skills at quickly seeking out additional information to complete tasks. The ability to seek out information as needed, is an increasingly important skill in a rapidly changing business environment. *Computer Accounting with QuickBooks* is designed to facilitate your development of this crucial skill.

Master QuickBooks with projects and case studies. The projects and cases cover QuickBooks tasks from setting up a new company and entering transactions to generating QuickBooks reports. To improve long-term retention of your software skills and mastery of QuickBooks, the virtual projects and cases challenge you to apply and develop both software and problem-solving skills. Two additional mastery opportunities, Chapter 12 and Chapter 14, are comprehensive case studies to integrate your knowledge and QuickBooks skills.

What's New?

New! Hot Dots Make Learning QuickBooks Even Easier

Matching step-by-step instructions, **Hot Dots** on screen captures make learning QuickBooks even faster and easier. For example:

Recording a credit sale in QuickBooks requires three steps:

1. **Create Invoices.** Create an invoice to bill the customer for the product or service provided. QuickBooks records accounts receivable and the sales amount.
2. **Receive Payments.** Receive payment from the customer. QuickBooks reduces accounts receivable and increases undeposited funds.
3. **Record Deposits.** Deposit the customer's payment in the bank.

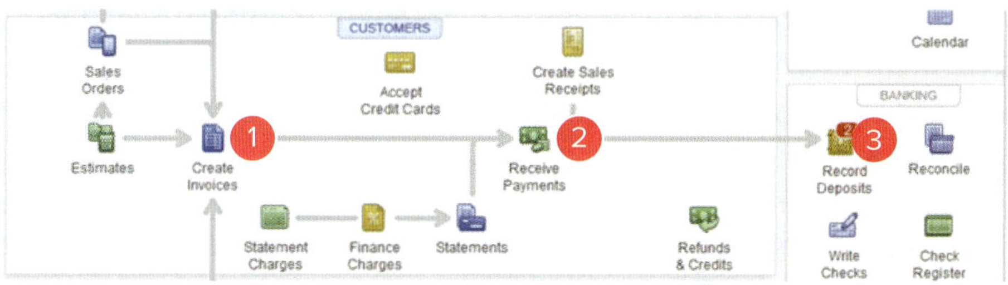

Why Choose the Leading Text to Learn the World's Leading Financial Software for Entrepreneurs?

- **By design, this text makes learning QuickBooks efficient and effective.** Designed using research-based pedagogy, this text facilitates learning QuickBooks in the most effective way.
- **QuickBooks Accountant 2018 software free with a new text.** See www.mhhe.com/kay2018 for information on how to download and install.
- **Student Starter files save you time.** QuickBooks Starter files are provided with your text to make it easy to start chapters.
- **www.mhhe.com/kay2018 website.** www.mhhe.com/kay2018 offers useful resources to make learning QuickBooks easier including Excel report templates, updates, help and support links, video links, assistance with QuickBooks troubleshooting, and more.
- **Go Digital** with Excel templates and instructions for your QuickBooks assignments, available at www.mhhe.com/kay2018.
- **Expanded assignments** using virtual company projects and cases to enhance your learning.
- **QuickBooks Issue Resolution** for assistance in navigating software issues and correcting errors (Chapter 17 and www.My-QuickBooks.com).
- **Quick Review Guide** (Chapter 17) summarizes easy step-by-step explanations covering frequently used tasks.
- **QuickBooks Consulting Project** (Chapter 18) guides you through the development of a QuickBooks consulting project to put your QuickBooks knowledge into practice.
- **Connect Homework.** Enter assignments into Connect, view interactive feedback to facilitate learning, and receive auto-graded homework. Ask your instructor if you are using Connect with *Computer Accounting with QuickBooks.*

What kind of study tools does *Connect* offer?

- **SmartBook.** As a student engages with SmartBook, the reading experience continually adapts by highlighting content based on what the student knows and doesn't know. This means students are more engaged with course content, can better prioritize their time, and come to class prepared.
- **Assignment Materials.** After completing assignments in QuickBooks 2018 students can enter key elements of their solution into Connect for grading. Based on instructor settings, they can receive instant feedback either while working on the assignment or after the assignment is submitted for grade. Assignable materials include: exercises, projects, practice quizzes, and test bank materials.
- **Insight.** The analytic tools within Connect provide at-a-glance information regarding class performance and assignment effectiveness.

How Do I Learn More about Becoming a QuickBooks Certified User?

QuickBooks User Certification is certification that is obtained by passing the QuickBooks User Certification Examination. See Chapter 17 for more detailed information about developing your action plan to review for QuickBooks User Certification.

What is the QuickBooks User Certification examination?

The QuickBooks User Certification examination is an online exam that is proctored at authorized testing centers. The QuickBooks User Certification is a certification focused on QuickBooks users. The QuickBooks ProAdvisor certification is a different certification that is focused more on accountants who provide advisory services to QuickBooks clients.

Why consider the QuickBooks User Certification?

Passing the QuickBooks User Certification examination adds another credential to your resume. Employers often value credentials that indicate skill and a knowledge level as a baseline for employment.

How do I obtain more information about the QuickBooks User Certification exam?

For more information about the QuickBooks User Certification examination, see:

- www.certiport.com
- www.My-QuickBooks.com, QB Certified User
- *Computer Accounting with QuickBooks* Chapter 17

How Is this Text Mapped to the QuickBooks User Certification?

Computer Accounting with QuickBooks offers a Quick Review Guide to streamline your review for the QuickBooks User Certification examination.

The QuickBooks User Certification exam covers the 10 domains listed in the following table. Each section of Chapter 17 of *Computer Accounting with QuickBooks* is mapped to one of the 10 domains of the QuickBooks User Certification.

Chapter 17 Section No.	QuickBooks User Certification Domain
17.1	QuickBooks Setup
17.2	QuickBooks Utilities and General Product Knowledge
17.3	List Management
17.4	Items
17.5	Sales
17.6	Purchases
17.7	Payroll
17.8	Reports
17.9	Basic Accounting
17.10	Customization and Saving Time

Chapter 17 Quick Review Guide streamlines your review since it is mapped to the 10 domains covered by the QuickBooks User Certification exam. While Chapters 1 through 16 of this text use a tutorial approach for learning QuickBooks effectively, the Quick Review Guide in Chapter 17 is designed to guide you in quickly reviewing targeted key material efficiently.

For more information regarding the QuickBooks User Certification, see the Quick Review Guide in Chapter 17.

Dear QuickBooks Student

Welcome To Learning QuickBooks!

Give yourself a competitive advantage – learn the leading financial software for entrepreneurs using *Computer Accounting with QuickBooks.* Designed using the most effective way to learn QuickBooks, this text streamlines learning QuickBooks because it focuses on you—the learner.

Proven instructional techniques are incorporated throughout the text to make your mastery of QuickBooks as effortless as possible. Using a hands-on approach, this text integrates understanding accounting with mastery of QuickBooks. Designed for maximum flexibility to meet your needs, *Computer Accounting with QuickBooks* can be used either in a QuickBooks course or independently at your own pace.

To streamline your learning, this text uses a highly effective three-step approach (XPM).

1. *eXplore.* Providing numerous screen shots and detailed instructions, chapters in *Computer Accounting with QuickBooks* are designed as tutorials for you to explore and learn QuickBooks features.
2. *Practice.* Designed with fewer instructions, the end-of-chapter exercises provide opportunities for you to practice and test your understanding.
3. *Master.* Virtual company projects and case studies provide mastery opportunities for you to apply and integrate your QuickBooks skills.

A Quick Review Guide in Chapter 17 provides a handy resource to seek out additional information as needed. In addition, Chapter 17 streamlines review for the QuickBooks User Certification Exam.

Good luck with QuickBooks and best wishes for your continued success,

Donna Kay

connect®

McGraw-Hill Connect® is a highly reliable, easy-to-use homework and learning management solution that utilizes learning science and award-winning adaptive tools to improve student results.

Homework and Adaptive Learning

- Connect's assignments help students contextualize what they've learned through application, so they can better understand the material and think critically.
- Connect will create a personalized study path customized to individual student needs through SmartBook®.
- SmartBook helps students study more efficiently by delivering an interactive reading experience through adaptive highlighting and review.

Over **7 billion questions** have been answered, making McGraw-Hill Education products more intelligent, reliable, and precise.

Connect's Impact on Retention Rates, Pass Rates, and Average Exam Scores

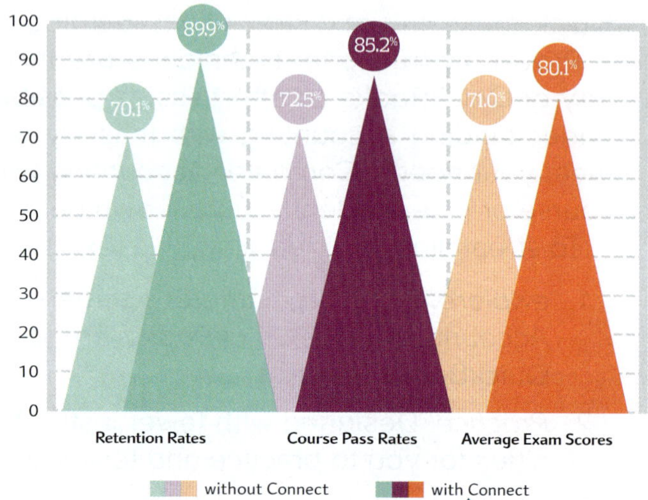

Using **Connect** improves retention rates by **19.8** percentage points, passing rates by **12.7** percentage points, and exam scores by **9.1** percentage points.

73% of instructors who use **Connect** require it; instructor satisfaction **increases** by 28% when **Connect** is required.

Quality Content and Learning Resources

- Connect content is authored by the world's best subject matter experts, and is available to your class through a simple and intuitive interface.
- The Connect eBook makes it easy for students to access their reading material on smartphones and tablets. They can study on the go and don't need internet access to use the eBook as a reference, with full functionality.
- Multimedia content such as videos, simulations, and games drive student engagement and critical thinking skills.

Robust Analytics and Reporting

- Connect Insight® generates easy-to-read reports on individual students, the class as a whole, and on specific assignments.
- The Connect Insight dashboard delivers data on performance, study behavior, and effort. Instructors can quickly identify students who struggle and focus on material that the class has yet to master.
- Connect automatically grades assignments and quizzes, providing easy-to-read reports on individual and class performance.

©Hero Images/Getty Images

Impact on Final Course Grade Distribution

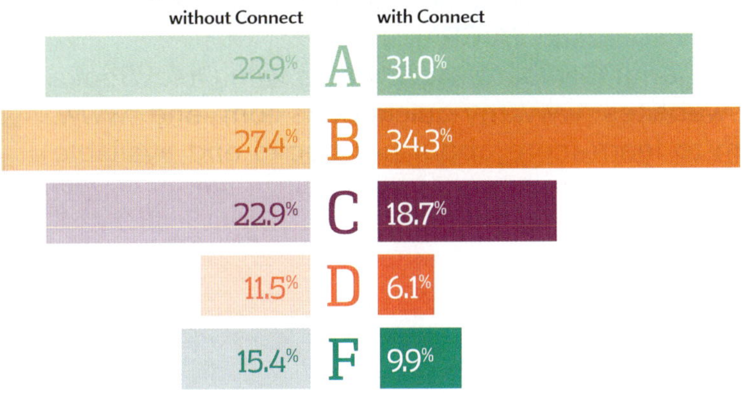

More students earn **As** and **Bs** when they use **Connect**.

Trusted Service and Support

- Connect integrates with your LMS to provide single sign-on and automatic syncing of grades. Integration with Blackboard®, D2L®, and Canvas also provides automatic syncing of the course calendar and assignment-level linking.
- Connect offers comprehensive service, support, and training throughout every phase of your implementation.
- If you're looking for some guidance on how to use Connect, or want to learn tips and tricks from super users, you can find tutorials as you work. Our Digital Faculty Consultants and Student Ambassadors offer insight into how to achieve the results you want with Connect.

Meet the Author

Donna Kay is a former professor of Accounting and Accounting Systems and Forensics, teaching both undergraduate and graduate accounting. Dr. Kay earned B.S. and MBA degrees from Southern Illinois University at Edwardsville before receiving a Ph.D. from Saint Louis University, where she conducted action research on the perceived effectiveness of instructional techniques for learning technology. Dr. Kay designs her textbooks to incorporate the most effective instructional techniques based on research findings, making your learning journey as productive as possible. Named to Who's Who Among American Women, Dr. Kay holds certifications as both a Certified Public Accountant (CPA) and Certified Informational Technology Professional (CITP) and is an active member of the American Institute of Certified Public Accountants (AICPA).

Donna Kay is also the author of *Computer Accounting with QuickBooks Online*. Visit Dr. Kay's websites www.my-quickbooks.com and www.my-quickbooksonline.com to learn more about her books and available resources.

Acknowledgments

Thanks to all who have helped in advancing this text through 18 editions, especially feedback from students and instructors. Special thanks to:

- The MHE QuickBooks team Steve, Kevin, Allie, Dana, and Daryl
- Sandy Roman for her cheerful, careful accuracy checking and editing
- Brian Behrens for always being in my corner with greatly appreciated support
- Matt, Steve and Sherry
- Faust and Silvia
- Graziella, Voitek, Alice, Marco, Anjela and Michael
- Maria, Julie, Kathy, Karen, Eugene, Gerry, Eddie, Frank and Nancy
- Carole, Mimi, Kelly, Herb, and Maureen
- Andre, Lynne, Tony, Paulny, Jean, Lumenes, Bichotte and William
- All the QuickBooks educators who share ideas, comments, suggestions, and encouragement. Special recognition to:
    - Teri Grimmer, Portland Community College
    - Mike Fritz, Portland Community College
    - Amy Browning, Ivy Tech Distance Education
    - Michael Goldfine, Brooklyn College
    - Miriam Lefkowitz, Brooklyn College
    - Paige Paulsen, Salt Lake Community College
    - Nancy Schrumpf, Parkland College
    - Mary Ann Hurd, Sauk Valley Community College
    - Jennifer Johnson, University of Texas at Dallas
    - Craig Miller University of Minnesota, Crookston
    - James Capone, Kean University
    - Carol Thomas, West Virginia University Parkersburg
    - W. Brian Voss, Austin Community College – Eastview
    - Joel Peralto, Hawaii Community College
    - Vicki Williams, University of Alaska – Juneau
    - Larry Herring, Texas State University – San Marcos

- David Packard, Elgin Community College
- Daniel Jenkins, Albany Technical College
- Cecile Roberti, Community College of Rhode Island – Warwick
- Natalie Waddell, Central Georgia Technical College
- Rebecca Butler, City College of San Francisco
- Deborah Hudson, Gaston College
- John Kelly, Manchester Community College
- Amy Chataginer, Mississippi Gulf Coast Community College – Jackson County
- Donna Parker, Mississippi Gulf Coast Community College – Jefferson Davis
- Linda Kropp, Modesto Junior College
- Cathy Scott, Navarro College
- Sara Barritt, Northeast Community College
- Sophia Ju, Edmonds Community College
- Jeanette Ramos-Alexander, New Jersey City University
- Susan C. Robbins, Pensacola State College
- Stephanie Swaim, North Lake College
- James Tappen, SUNY Rockland Community College
- Laurence Zuckerman, SUNY Fulton Montgomery Community College
- Crystal Cleary, Terra State Community College
- Jennifer Oliver, Quinebaug Valley Community College

Get Started

To get started, go to **www.mhhe.com/Kay2018** > **QuickBooks 2018 Software** for directions on how to download, install, and register QuickBooks 2018 Software which is needed for use with this textbook.

1. QuickBooks 2018 Software. Follow the step-by-step instructions to download and install the QuickBooks 2018 software. Then register/activate the software using the License and Product Number Code Card provided with your new copy of this textbook.

   If your text did not come with a License and Product Number Code Card, you can go to the following website and register for a free license.
   http://www.intuiteducationprogram.com/students/

   Note: It may take up to 3 business days for Intuit to process License requests.

2. QBB Starter Files. You will need QBB Starter Files to start using Chapters 1 through 10, 15, and 17. Go to www.mhhe.com/Kay2018 (or www.My-QuickBooks.com) to find links to download the QBB Starter Files.

3. Excel Report Templates. To organize your answers and reports, use the Excel Report Templates. Go to www.mhhe.com/Kay2018 to download the Excel Report Templates for Chapters 1 through 16.

To organize your downloaded files, consider setting up folders on your computer Desktop. For example, set up one folder for QBB Starter Files and another folder for Excel Report Templates. You can think of these files as *input* to QuickBooks.

- QBB Starter Files (for downloaded files)
- Excel Report Templates (for downloaded files)

Later, you will need folders for your *output* from QuickBooks: QBB Backup Files and Excel Reports.

- QBB Backup Files (for your QBB backups)
- Excel Reports (for your assignment reports and answers)

Chapter 1 provides you with step-by-step instructions on how to use the QuickBooks and Excel files.

QuickBooks® and QuickBooks® Online are registered trademarks of Intuit Inc.

iPad® and iPhone® are registered trademarks of Apple Inc.

Android™ is a registered trademark of Google Inc.

Microsoft®, Windows®, and Microsoft Excel® are registered trademarks of Microsoft, Inc.

Contents

Computer Accounting with QuickBooks

18th Edition by Donna Kay

Contents Overview

Designed as hands-on tutorials for learning QuickBooks, *Computer Accounting with QuickBooks* chapters provide screen captures with step-by-step, detailed instructions. To improve long-term retention of your QuickBooks skills, end-of-chapter learning activities are designed with fewer instructions to test your understanding and, when needed, to develop your skills to quickly seek out additional information to complete the task. The ability to find information as needed is an increasingly important skill in a rapidly changing business environment. The design of *Computer Accounting with QuickBooks* seamlessly facilitates your development of this crucial skill.

Chapters 1 through 10 focus on learning the basics of entering transactions and generating reports using the sample company, Rock Castle Construction.

Chapters 11 through 15 build upon the first ten chapters, covering the entire accounting cycle, including new company setup as well as QuickBooks advanced features for accountants. Chapter 11 and 12 cover sole proprietor service businesses, and Chapter 13, 14 and 15 cover a merchandising corporation. Using a progressive approach, the text gradually introduces advanced features while maintaining continuity and interest.

Chapters 16 provides insights into the differences between QuickBooks Desktop covered in this text and QuickBooks Online, including user and accountant versions of each.

Chapter 17 provides assistance in reviewing for the QuickBooks User Certification. Chapter 17 can also be used as a Quick Review Guide, providing step-by-step instructions for frequently used customer, vendor, and employee tasks in a convenient, user-friendly resource.

Chapter 18 offers a framework of seven milestones for conducting a QuickBooks consulting project.

Chapter 1 QuickBooks Quick Tour: Navigation and Settings

This chapter provides a guided tour of the QuickBooks Desktop software using QuickBooks Navigation tools and introduces the QuickBooks sample company, Rock Castle Construction. Other topics include how to restore starter files and how to create backup files.

Chapter 2 QuickBooks Chart of Accounts

This chapter introduces how to customize QuickBooks Chart of Accounts to meet specific business needs.

Chapter 3 QuickBooks Transactions

Chapter 3 provides an introduction to the various types of transactions entered in QuickBooks, including banking, customer, vendor, and employee transactions.

Chapter 4 Banking

This chapter focuses on the checking account and check register for a small business. Topics include making deposits, writing checks, matching bank transactions, and reconciling bank statements.

Chapter 5 Customers and Sales

Chapter 5 demonstrates how to record customer transactions. Topics include how to create invoices and record customer payments.

Chapter 6 Vendors and Expenses

Chapter 6 focuses on recording vendor transactions, such as recording expenses.

Chapter 7 Inventory

Chapter 7 focuses on recording transactions related to inventory, including creating purchase orders, entering bills for inventory and paying bills.

Chapter 8 Employees and Payroll

Chapter 8 covers time tracking, billing tracked time, and processing payroll using QuickBooks payroll service.

Chapter 9 QuickBooks Adjustments

Chapter 9 covers how to create a trial balance and enter adjusting entries.

Chapter 10 QuickBooks Reports

Chapter 10 completes the accounting cycle, covering a variety of QuickBooks reports, including memorized reports.

Chapter 11 QuickBooks Service Company

Chapter 11 covers how to set up a new company in QuickBooks, create customer, vendor, and item lists, and enter transactions for a service company.

Chapter 12 QuickBooks Service Company Case

Chapter 12 is a QuickBooks Service Company Case that provides an opportunity to integrate QuickBooks skills and knowledge covered thus far in a comprehensive fashion for a service company.

Chapter 13 QuickBooks Merchandising Company

Chapter 13 covers how to set up a new merchandising corporation with inventory in QuickBooks, create customer, vendor, and item lists, and enter transactions for a merchandising company.

Chapter 14 QuickBooks Merchandising Company Case

Chapter 14 is a QuickBooks Merchandising Company Case that provides an opportunity to integrate QuickBooks skills and knowledge in a comprehensive fashion for a company that sells products.

Chapter 15 Advanced QuickBooks Features for Accountants

This chapter covers the advanced features of QuickBooks software including budgets, estimates, progress billing, credit card sales, accounting for bad debts, the audit trail, and accountant's copy.

Chapter 16 QuickBooks Desktop Versus QuickBooks Online

Chapter 16 compares and contrasts QuickBooks Desktop and QuickBooks Online. QuickBooks user options and QuickBooks accountant options are presented.

Chapter 17 Quick Review Guide

Chapter 17 provides step-by-step instructions for frequently used customer, vendor, and employee tasks in a convenient, user-friendly resource that can also be used in preparing for QuickBooks Certification.

Chapter 18 QuickBooks Consulting Project

This chapter outlines the project management milestones for development of a QuickBooks accounting system. Providing you with an opportunity to apply QuickBooks software to a consulting project gives you hands-on professional experience for your resume.

Virtual Learning Activity Mapping

What is the most effective way to learn QuickBooks?

Virtual company cases provide you with a realistic context and business environment to enhance your understanding of QuickBooks. Related learning activities mapping follows.

Rock Castle Construction

- **Chapter 1* and Exercises 1**
- **Chapter 2* and Exercises 2**
- **Chapter 3* and Exercises 3**
- **Chapter 4* and Exercises 4**
- **Chapter 5* and Exercises 5**
- **Chapter 6* and Exercises 6**
- **Chapter 7* and Exercises 7**
- **Chapter 8* and Exercises 8**
- **Chapter 9* and Exercises 9**
- **Chapter 10* and Exercises 10**

For Rock Castle Construction learning activities, we will restore a Starter file at the beginning of each chapter that will be used to complete the chapter and exercises.

Larry's Landscaping

- **Project 1.1***
- **Project 2.1**
- **Project 3.1**
- **Project 4.1**

---

*QuickBooks Starter files are provided for these learning activities.

- **Project 5.1**
- **Project 6.1**
- **Project 7.1**
- **Project 8.1**
- **Project 9.1**
- **Project 10.1**

For Larry's Landscaping projects, we will restore a Project 1.1 Starter file and then use our own QuickBooks files after that to complete the remaining projects. The projects provide an opportunity to practice QuickBooks. Since you will be using your own file, you will want to be check and cross check your work to avoid entering errors. If you find you have an issue with your QuickBooks file that you are unable to resolve, contact your instructor.

Paint Palette

- **Chapter 11 and Exercises 11**
- **Chapter 15* and Exercises 15**

Paint Palette is a new service company so we do not need a Starter file for Chapter 11. We will be creating a new QuickBooks company. For Chapter 15 a Starter file is provided.

Paint Palette Store

- **Chapter 13 and Exercises 13**

Paint Palette Store is a new merchandising company so we do not need a Starter file for Chapter 13. We will be creating a new QuickBooks company.

Germain Consulting

- **Project 11.1**
- **Project 15.1**

Project 11.1 is a new service company so we do not need a Starter file. We will be creating a new QuickBooks company. Project 15.1 is a continuation of Project 11.1 so you will need to use your Project 11.1 QBB backup file to start Project 15.1.

Raphael LLC

- **Project 11.2**

Project 11.2 is a new service company so we do not need a Starter file. We will be creating a new QuickBooks company.

Ella's Knittery

- **Project 13.1**

Project 13.1 is a new merchandising company so we do not need a Starter file. We will be creating a new QuickBooks company.

Dragon Enterprises

- **Project 13.2**

Project 13.2 is a new merchandising company so we do not need a Starter file. We will be creating a new QuickBooks company.

Your Name Floral Design

- **Project 15.2**

Project 15.2 is a new company so we do not need a Starter file. We will be creating a new QuickBooks company.

Mookie The Beagle™ Spa

- **Chapter 12**

Mookie The Beagle™ Spa is a new service company so we do not need a Starter file for Chapter 12. We will be creating a new QuickBooks company.

Mookie The Beagle™ Spa Supplies

- **Chapter 14**

Mookie The Beagle™ Spa Supplies is a new merchandising company so we do not need a Starter file for Chapter 14. We will be creating a new QuickBooks company.

Chapter 1

QuickBooks Quick Tour: Navigation and Settings

BACKSTORY

Rock Castle, owner of Rock Castle Construction, called to hire you as his accountant. His former accountant unexpectedly accepted a job offer in Hawaii, and Rock Castle Construction needs someone immediately to maintain its accounting records. Mr. Castle indicates they use QuickBooks to maintain the company's accounting records. When you tell him that you are not familiar with QuickBooks, Mr. Castle reassures you, *"No problem! QuickBooks is easy to learn. Stop by my office this afternoon."*

When you arrive at Rock Castle Construction, Mr. Castle leads you to a desk as he rapidly explains Rock Castle's accounting.

"Rock Castle needs to keep records of transactions with customers, vendors, and employees. We must keep a record of our customers and the sales and services we provide to those customers. Also, it is crucial for the company to be able to bill customers promptly and keep a record of cash collected from them. If we don't know who owes Rock Castle money, we can't collect it.

"Rock Castle also needs to keep track of the supplies, materials, and inventory we purchase from vendors. We need to track all purchase orders, the items received, the invoices or bills received from vendors, and the payments made to vendors. If we don't track bills, we can't pay our vendors on time. And if Rock Castle doesn't pay its bills on time, the vendors don't like to sell to us.

"Also, we like to keep our employees happy. One way to do that is to pay them the right amount at the right time. So Rock Castle must keep track of the time worked by its employees, the amounts owed to the employees, and the wages and salaries paid to them.

"QuickBooks permits Rock Castle to keep a record of all of these transactions. Also, we need records so we can prepare tax returns, financial reports for bank loans, and reports to evaluate the company's performance and make business decisions.

"Your first assignment is to learn more about QuickBooks." Mr. Castle tosses you a QuickBooks training manual as he rushes off to answer a phone call.

Slightly overwhelmed by Mr. Castle's rapid-fire delivery, you sink into a chair. As you look around your cubicle, you notice for the first time the leaning tower of papers stacked beside the computer, waiting to be processed. No wonder Mr. Castle wanted you to start right way.

Mr. Castle bursts back into your cubicle quickly tossing something onto your cluttered desk. *"And here's your new company smartphone—that way I can reach you anytime I need you!"*

Noticing your startled expression, Mr. Castle pauses and then reassuringly says, *"Don't worry—IT has already set up security for your new phone so that all financial communications will be secure."*

Opening the QuickBooks training manual, you see the following.

Section 1.1

INSTALL QUICKBOOKS

QuickBooks® Desktop (QBDT) is a software-based financial system for entrepreneurs. QuickBooks Accountant software accompanies new texts of *Computer Accounting with Quickbooks 2018*.

To download and install the QuickBooks software:

1. Go to **www.mhhe.com/kay2018**
2. Select the **Quickbooks 2018 Software** menu item
3. Follow the instructions to **Download the QuickBooks 2018 Software**
4. Follow the instructions to **Install the QuickBooks 2018 Software**
5. Follow the instructions to **Register / Activate the QuickBooks 2018 Software**

! **Register / Activate QuickBooks software** with Intuit after installing or you will be locked out of the software. If registered, you will be able to use the QuickBooks software for up to 5 months. If you fail to register the software, you will be locked out of the software and unable to use it.

! **QuickBooks Accountant** software comes with new texts. If you purchase a used text, be aware that the QuickBooks software codes may already have been used and expired.

QuickBooks Accountant software that comes with your text is Windows-based software. If you have a Mac, see your instructor. Also, go to www.My-QuickBooks.com. Select QB & My Mac for options.

Section 1.2

START QUICKBOOKS

To start QuickBooks software, click the **QuickBooks** icon on your desktop. If a QuickBooks icon does not appear on your desktop, from Microsoft® Windows® click **Start** button > **Programs** > **QuickBooks** > **QuickBooks Premier Accountant Edition.**

> **QuickBooks Accountant** includes all the features of QuickBooks Pro plus features for client services. If you use QuickBooks Pro, your screens may appear slightly different than those appearing in this text.

Section 1.3

RESTORE A QUICKBOOKS FILE

QuickBooks uses several different types of files. Two types of QuickBooks files that you will be using throughout this text are:

1. **QBW file.** The QuickBooks working file in which you can enter accounting data and transactions.
2. **QBB file.** The QuickBooks backup file used to move a QuickBooks file to another computer or if the working file (QBW) fails. The starter files provided for you with this text are QBB files. Because QBB files are compressed, the QBB file must be restored (unzipped) using QuickBooks software. Unlike Excel files, for example, QBB files cannot be opened by clicking on the file.

The QBW file is the only QuickBooks file in which you can enter data and transactions. When you enter transactions into a QBW file, the information is automatically saved. The typical workflow for a business is to use the QBW file to record transactions and periodically back up to a QBB (backup) file.

RESTORE STARTER FILES

For purposes of this text, we will use QuickBooks Starter files that are QBB files containing the company data needed to complete the assignments in this text. The QBB Starter files are compressed files that must be unzipped, or restored, into QBW files before the files can be used.

For your convenience, QuickBooks (QBB) Starter files accompany Computer *Accounting with QuickBooks 2018*.

Go to www.My-QuickBooks.com or www.mhhe.com/kay2018 to download the Starter files from the Online Learning Center.

To stay organized, consider adding a folder to your Desktop: QBB STARTER FILES. Then copy the QBB STARTER files to that folder.

For Connect users, the Starter Files are accessible through your Connect Chapter Assignments.

! QuickBooks Desktop (QBDT) QBB Files are compressed backup files that can be restored and used. To use QBB Starter files, the compressed file must be restored following the instructions here. Since it is a compressed file, you cannot open and use the QuickBooks Starter files by simply clicking on the file. Instead you must follow the instructions here to unzip and restore the data file before using it.

To restore the Starter File for Chapter 1 from a QBB file to a QBW file:

1. From the No Company Open window, select **Open or restore an existing company.** (If the Let's get your business set up quickly! window appears first, select **Other Options > Open Existing File.**)
2. Select **Restore a backup copy**
3. Click **Next**
4. When the Open or Restore Company window appears, select **Local backup**
5. Click **Next**
6. Identify the location of the **CHAPTER 1 STARTER.QBB** file. If you copied the CHAPTER 1 STARTER file to your desktop, select the **Look in** field to find the location of the .QBB file on your desktop.
7. Select the file: **CHAPTER 1 STARTER.QBB**
8. The Files of type field should automatically display: **QBW Backup (*.QBB)**
9. Click **Open**
10. When the Open or Restore window appears, click **Next**
11. Identify the file name and location of the QBW company file. To save the QBW (working file) on your desktop, select the location to save in: **Desktop.** (Another option is to save your QBW files to Users > Public > Public Documents > Intuit > QuickBooks > Company Files. Be sure you have permissions to save to a folder.)
12. Enter QBW File name: **YourName Chapter 1.** (Insert your name in the QBW file name so you can identify your files.)
13. The Save as type field should automatically appear as **QuickBooks Files (*.QBW).**
14. Click **Save**
15. Click **OK** when the QuickBooks Desktop Information window appears notifying you that **You're opening a QuickBooks sample file**

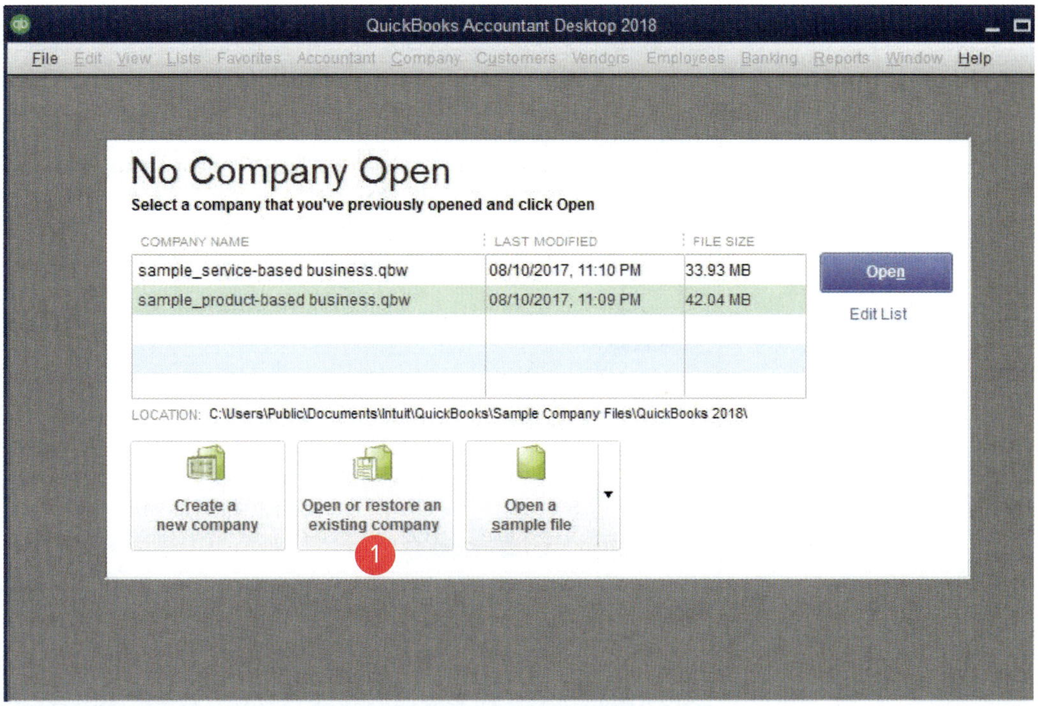
QuickBooks Accountant Desktop 2018
File Edit View Lists Favorites Accountant Company Customers Vendors Employees Banking Reports Window Help
No Company Open
Select a company that you've previously opened and click Open
COMPANY NAME
LAST MODIFIED
FILE SIZE
sample_service-based business.qbw
08/10/2017, 11:10 PM
33.93 MB
sample_product-based business.qbw
08/10/2017, 11:09 PM
42.04 MB
Open
Edit List
LOCATION: C:\Users\Public\Documents\Intuit\QuickBooks\Sample Company Files\QuickBooks 2018\
Create a new company
Open or restore an existing company
Open a sample file
1

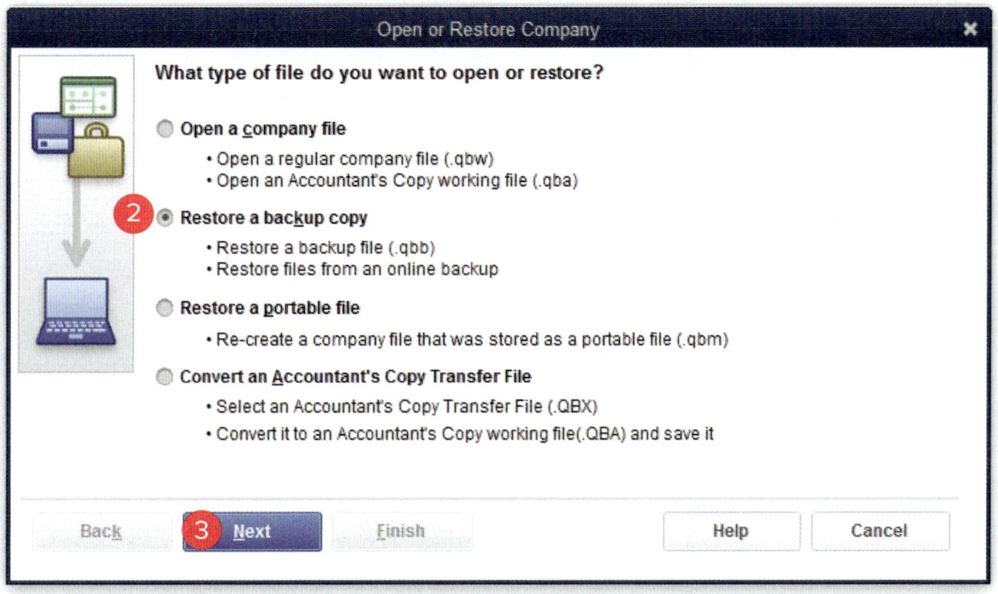
Open or Restore Company
What type of file do you want to open or restore?
Open a company file
• Open a regular company file (.qbw)
• Open an Accountant's Copy working file (.qba)
2
Restore a backup copy
• Restore a backup file (.qbb)
• Restore files from an online backup
Restore a portable file
• Re-create a company file that was stored as a portable file (.qbm)
Convert an Accountant's Copy Transfer File
• Select an Accountant's Copy Transfer File (.QBX)
• Convert it to an Accountant's Copy working file(.QBA) and save it
Back
3
Next
Finish
Help
Cancel

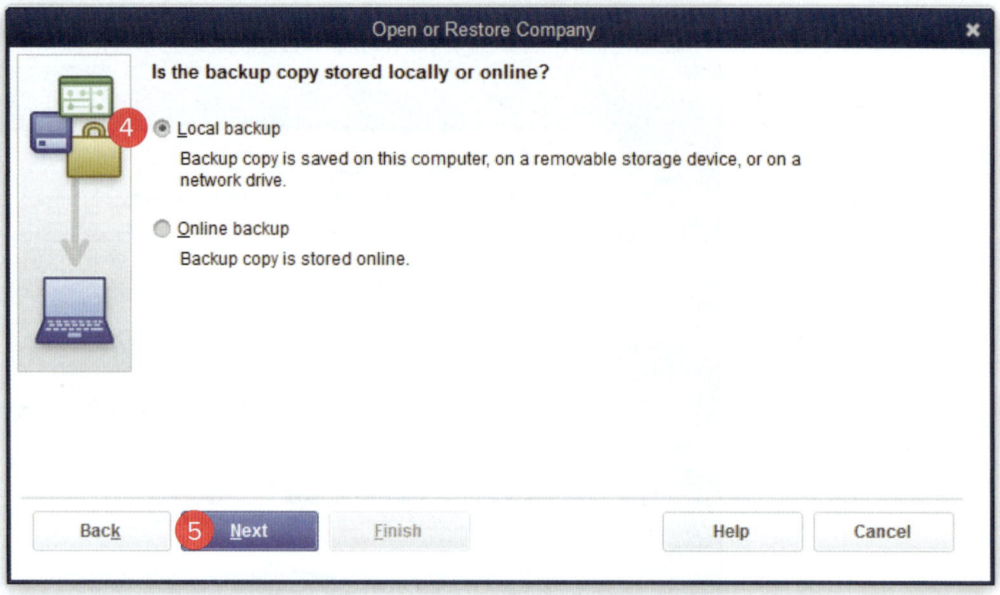
Open or Restore Company
Is the backup copy stored locally or online?
4
Local backup
Backup copy is saved on this computer, on a removable storage device, or on a network drive.
Online backup
Backup copy is stored online.
Back
5
Next
Finish
Help
Cancel

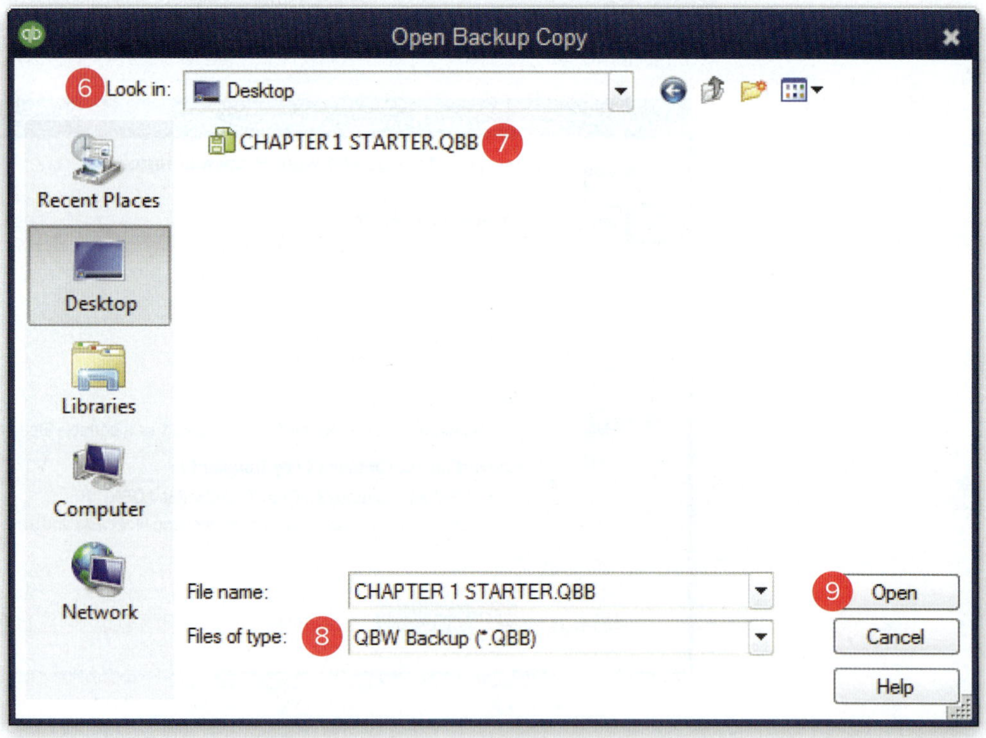
Open Backup Copy
6
Look in:
Desktop
CHAPTER 1 STARTER.QBB
7
Recent Places
Desktop
Libraries
Computer
Network
File name:
CHAPTER 1 STARTER.QBB
Files of type:
8
QBW Backup (*.QBB)
9
Open
Cancel
Help

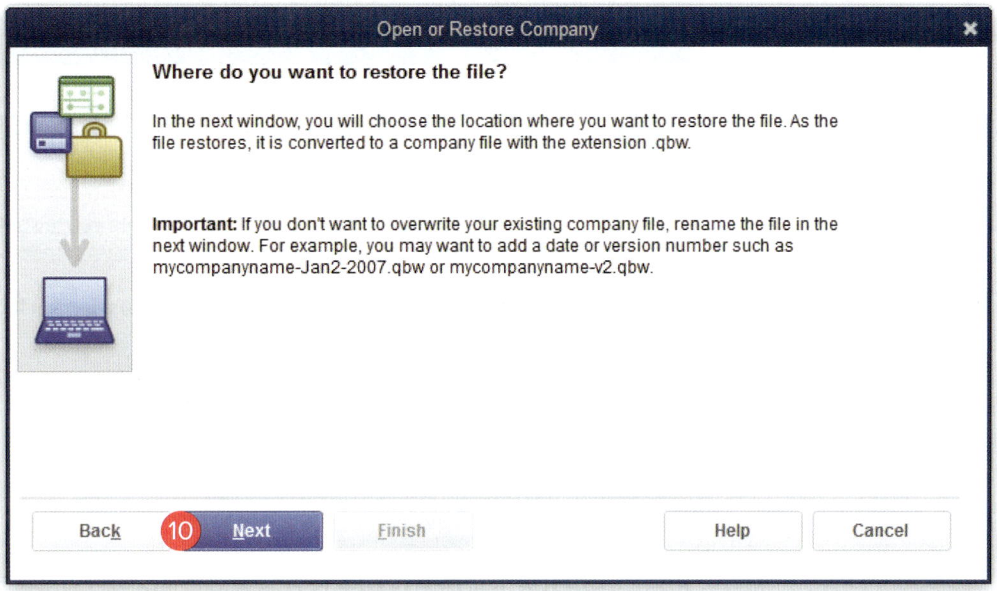
Open or Restore Company
Where do you want to restore the file?
In the next window, you will choose the location where you want to restore the file. As the file restores, it is converted to a company file with the extension .qbw.
Important: If you don't want to overwrite your existing company file, rename the file in the next window. For example, you may want to add a date or version number such as mycompanyname-Jan2-2007.qbw or mycompanyname-v2.qbw.
Back
10
Next
Finish
Help
Cancel

Save Company File as
11
Save in:
Desktop
Recent Places
Desktop
Libraries
Computer
Network
File name:
12
Chapter 1.qbw
Save as type:
13
QuickBooks Files (*.QBW)
14
Save
Cancel
Help

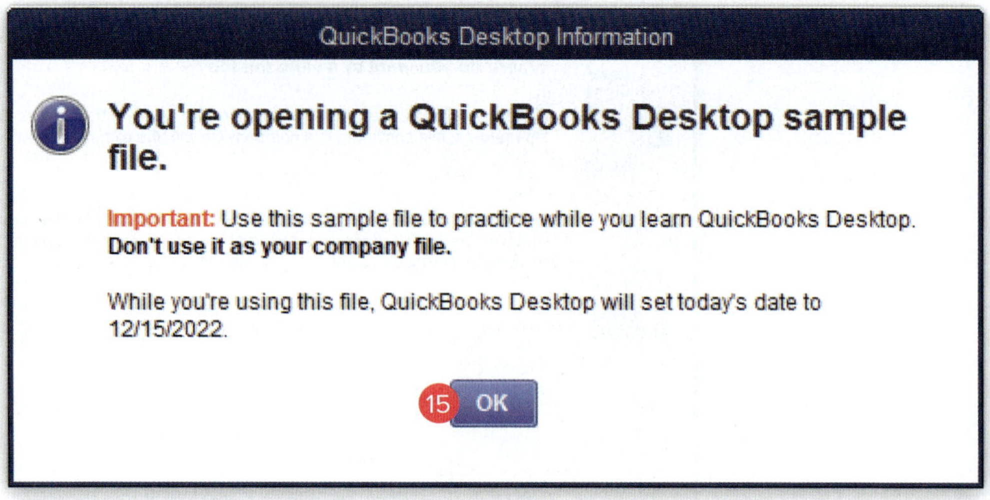

Now that we have restored the QBB file (CHAPTER 1 STARTER.QBB) to a QBW file (Chapter 1.QBW), we can use the QBW file to update settings, enter transactions, and create reports.

CHANGE COMPANY NAME

So that your name automatically appears on reports and checks, update the Company Name setting to add your name to the company name.

To change a company name in QuickBooks, complete the following:

1. From My Shortcuts on the Navigation Bar, select **My Company**
2. When the My Company window appears, select **Edit**
3. When the Company Information window appears, update the Company Name field to: **YourName Chapter 1 Rock Castle Construction**
4. Select **OK** to close the Company Information window
5. **Close** the My Company window

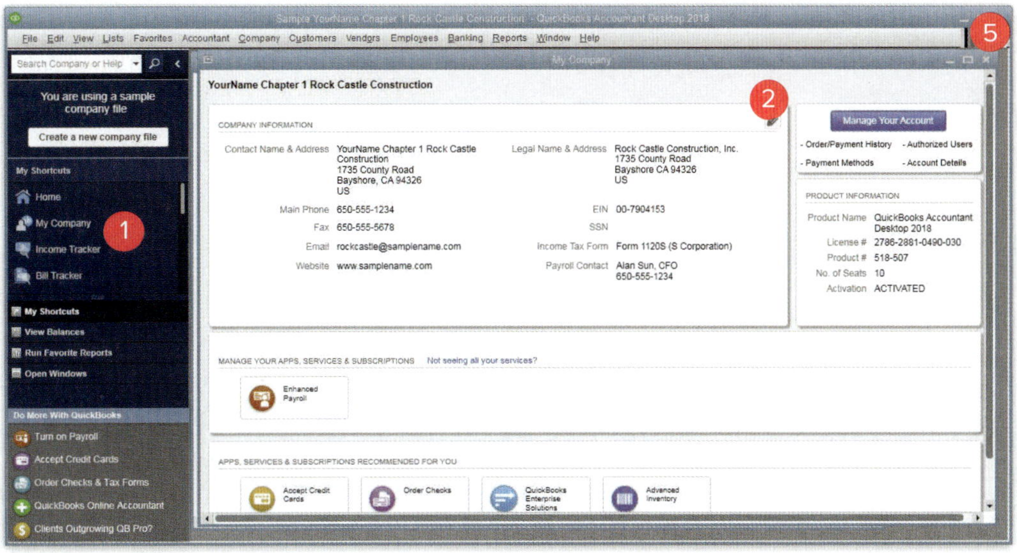
YourName Chapter 1 Rock Castle Construction
You are using a sample company file
Create a new company file
My Shortcuts
Home
My Company
Income Tracker
Bill Tracker
View Balances
Run Favorite Reports
Open Windows
Do More With QuickBooks
Turn on Payroll
Accept Credit Cards
Order Checks & Tax Forms
QuickBooks Online Accountant
Clients Outgrowing QB Pro?
COMPANY INFORMATION
Contact Name & Address
YourName Chapter 1 Rock Castle Construction
1735 County Road
Bayshore, CA 94326
US
Legal Name & Address
Rock Castle Construction, Inc.
1735 County Road
Bayshore CA 94326
US
Main Phone 650-555-1234
Fax 650-555-5678
Email rockcastle@samplename.com
Website www.samplename.com
EIN 00-7904153
SSN
Income Tax Form Form 1120S (S Corporation)
Payroll Contact Alan Sun, CFO 650-555-1234
Manage Your Account
- Order/Payment History
- Authorized Users
- Payment Methods
- Account Details
PRODUCT INFORMATION
Product Name QuickBooks Accountant Desktop 2018
License # 2786-2881-0490-030
Product # 518-507
No. of Seats 10
Activation ACTIVATED
MANAGE YOUR APPS, SERVICES & SUBSCRIPTIONS
Not seeing all your services?
Enhanced Payroll
APPS, SERVICES & SUBSCRIPTIONS RECOMMENDED FOR YOU
Accept Credit Cards
Order Checks
QuickBooks Enterprise Solutions
Advanced Inventory
1
2
5

Company Information
Contact Information
Legal Information
Company Identification
Report Information
Payroll Tax Form Information
CONTACT INFORMATION
Company Name YourName Chapter 1 Rock Castle Construction
Address 1735 County Road
Bayshore, CA 94326
Country US
Phone No. 650-555-1234
Fax No. 650-555-5678
E-mail rockcastle@samplename.cc
Web Site www.samplename.com
OK
Cancel
Help
Ship To Address...
Attach...
3
4

Section 1.4

QuickBooks SatNav

QuickBooks SatNav is your satellite navigation for QuickBooks, assisting you in navigating QuickBooks

Learning QuickBooks will be easier if you have an overview of the entire QuickBooks system. Just like you use your smartphone to zoom in for detail and zoom out for the big picture, when learning Quickbooks you may find that you also need to adjust your thinking to zoom out to see the big picture of the entire financial system or at other times adjust your thinking to zoom in to view details.

QuickBooks SatNav is designed to assist you in zooming out and zooming in. QuickBooks SatNav divides QuickBooks into three processes:

1. **QuickBooks Settings.** This includes Company Settings and the Company Chart of Accounts. Company Settings include setting up a new company and selecting company preferences. QuickBooks uses an EasyStep Interview that asks us questions about our business. QuickBooks then automatically creates a company file for our business. In Chapters 1 through 10 of this text, we will use Rock Castle Construction, a sample company data file, that has already been created for us. In Chapters 11, 12, 13 and 14, we will set up a new QuickBooks company. To learn how to set up a company file, see Chapter 11.

   Another aspect of QuickBooks Settings is the Company Chart of Accounts, a list of all the accounts for a company. Accounts are used to sort and track accounting information. For example, a business needs one account for cash, another account to track amounts customers owe (Accounts Receivable), and yet another account to track inventory. QuickBooks automatically creates a Chart of Accounts in the EasyStep Interview. QuickBooks permits us to modify the Chart of Accounts later, after completing the EasyStep Interview.

   QuickBooks Settings are discussed in Chapters 1, 2, 11, 12, 13, and 14.

2. **QuickBooks Transactions.** This includes recording transactions in QuickBooks. Transaction types can be categorized as Banking, Customers and Sales, Vendors and Expenses, and Employees and

Payroll. In basic terms, recording transactions involves recording money in and money out.

Transactions are exchanges between the QuickBooks company and other parties, such as customers, vendors, and employees. QuickBooks Home Page is an overview of the most frequently used transactions in a flowchart form.

Typically in a transaction, the company gives something and receives something in exchange. QuickBooks is used to keep a record what is given and what is received in the transaction. We can enter transaction information into QuickBooks using the onscreen Journal or onscreen forms, such as onscreen invoices and onscreen checks.

QuickBooks Transactions are covered in Chapters 3 through 8, 11, 12, 13, and 14.

3. **QuickBooks Reports.** QuickBooks reports are the output of the system. Reports typically provide information to decision makers. For example, accounting information is used to prepare:

   - Financial statements for external users, such as creditors and investors. Internal users, such as managers, also may use financial statements. Financial statements are standardized financial reports that summarize information about past transactions. The primary financial statements for a business are:
     - **Balance Sheet:** summarizes what a company owns and owes on a particular date.
     - **Profit & Loss Statement** (or **Income Statement**): summarizes what a company has earned and the expenses incurred to earn the income.
     - **Statement of Cash Flows:** summarizes cash inflows and cash outflows for operating, investing, and financing activities of a business.
   - Tax returns for federal and state tax agencies.
   - Management reports for company managers and owners to use when making business decisions. Such decisions include: Will we have enough cash to pay our bills on time? Are we collecting customer payments when due? An example of such a report is a cash budget that projects amounts of cash that will be collected and spent in the future.

   Quickbooks Reports are covered in several chapters with a focus on reports in Chapters 9, 10, 11, 12, 13, and 14.

This QuickBooks SatNav will be used in the first 15 chapters to illustrate which aspect of QuickBooks the chapter will focus on. If you start to feel lost in QuickBooks, return to this QuickBooks SatNav to assist you in navigating QuickBooks. In later chapters and projects, the focus of the chapter is highlighted in yellow on the QuickBooks SatNav.

> **Learning QuickBooks** requires integrating knowledge of accounting, financial systems, and financial technology. Don't become discouraged if you find that you need to go over the same material more than once. That is normal. Learning how accounting and financial tech is interrelated takes repetition.

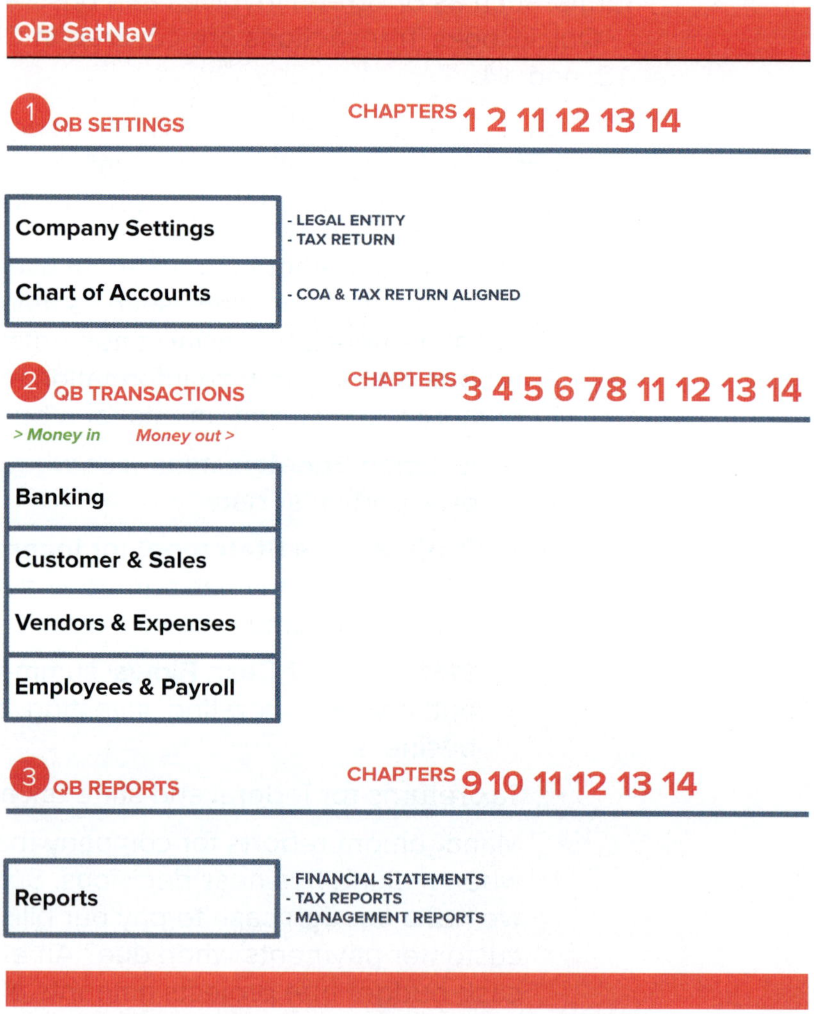

Section 1.5

QUICKBOOKS NAVIGATION

Taking a few minutes to learn QuickBooks navigation will make learning QuickBooks easier. QuickBooks offers three different ways to navigate QuickBooks software:

1. Home Page. Click the Home icon on the Navigation Bar (Icon Bar) to reveal flowcharts of frequently used tasks.
2. Navigation Bar. Click on the Navigation Bar (Icon Bar) to display customer, vendor, and employee centers and frequently used windows, such as customer invoices.
3. Menu Bar. Click on the Menu Bar to reveal a drop-down menu for each area.

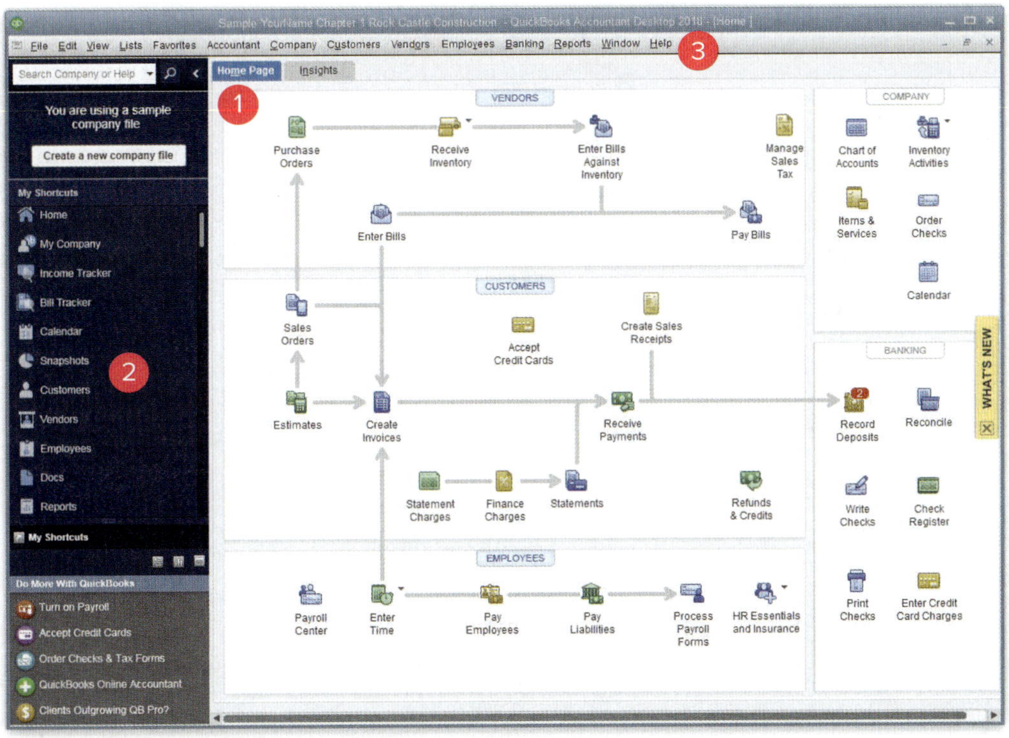

> **What's New** may appear on the right side of your Home Page. Open What's New to view the new features in the 2018 version of QuickBooks Desktop. Click the X beside What's New if you wish to remove it from your Home Page.

Next, we explore navigation in greater detail.

Section 1.6

QUICKBOOKS HOME PAGE

To view the QuickBooks Home Page, click the **Home** icon in the Navigation Bar. The Home Page contains the following main categories of transactions and tasks:

1. Customer or sales transactions
2. Vendor or expense transactions
3. Employee or payroll transactions
4. Banking and credit card transactions
5. Company tasks

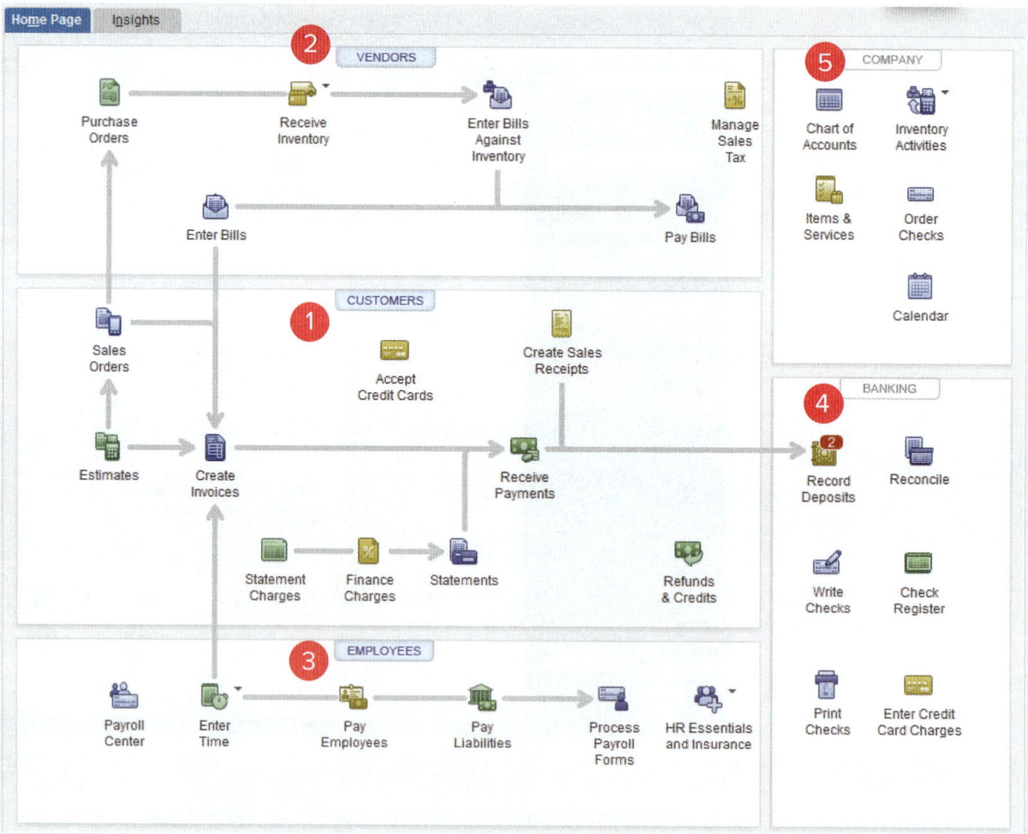

CUSTOMERS

The Customers section is a flowchart of the main activities associated with sales and customers. For example, we can:

1. Create estimates
2. Create invoices to bill customers
3. Record payments received from customers (cash, check, and credit card payments)

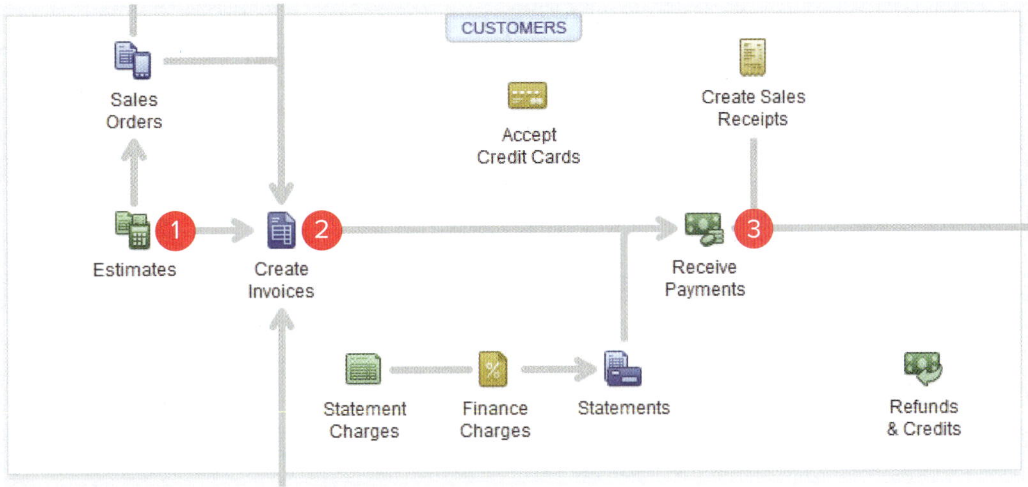

VENDORS

From the Vendors flowchart, we can record:

1. Purchase orders (orders placed to purchase items)
2. Inventory received
3. Bills received for inventory
4. Bills received for services
5. Bills paid
6. Sales tax paid

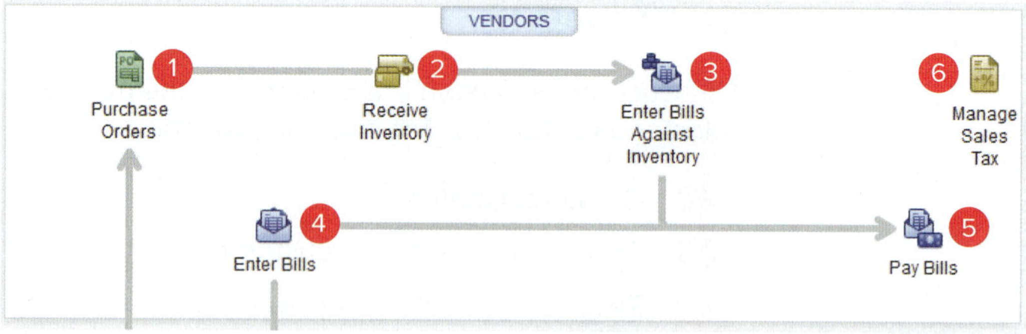

EMPLOYEES

From the Employees flowchart, we can:

1. Enter time worked
2. Pay employees
3. Pay payroll tax liabilities
4. Process payroll forms

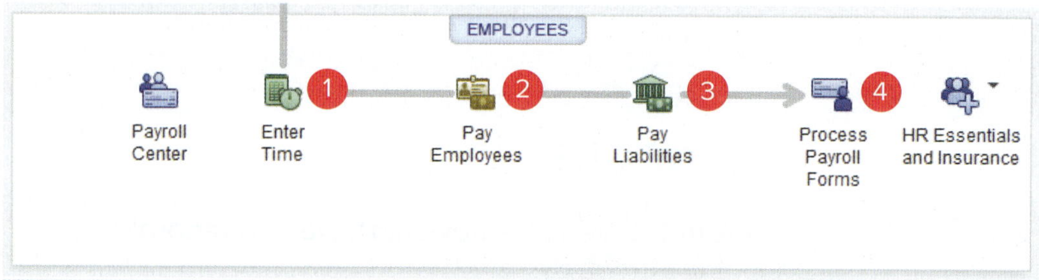

BANKING

From the Banking section, we can:

1. Record deposits
2. Write checks
3. Reconcile a bank statement
4. View the check register

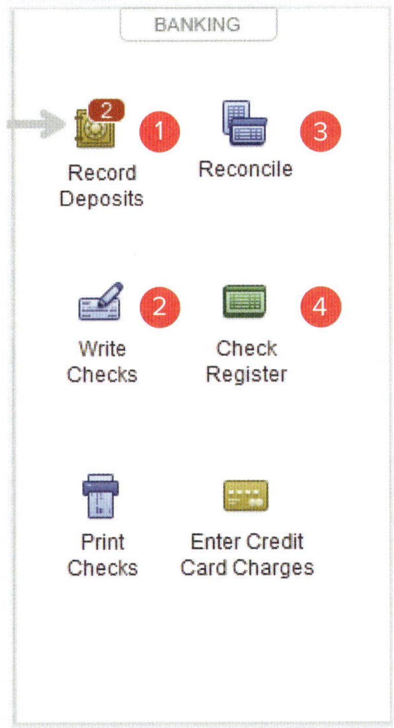

COMPANY

From the Company section, we can access:

1. Chart of Accounts. A list of accounts a company uses to track accounting information.
2. Items & Services. A list of items and services that a company buys and/or sells.
3. Inventory Activities. Perform inventory activities including accessing the Inventory Center or adjusting the quantity of inventory on hand.
4. Calendar. View your to do list and reminders in a calendar form.

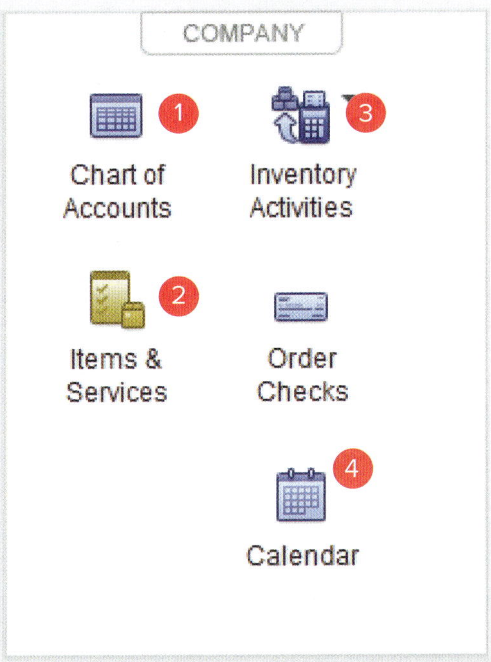

Section 1.7

QUICKBOOKS NAVIGATION BAR

QuickBooks Navigation Bar (or Icon Bar) is located on the left side of your screen. The Navigation Bar permits you to quickly access various QuickBooks screens. The Navigation Bar can be displayed either at the top beneath the Menu Bar or on the left side of the QuickBooks window.

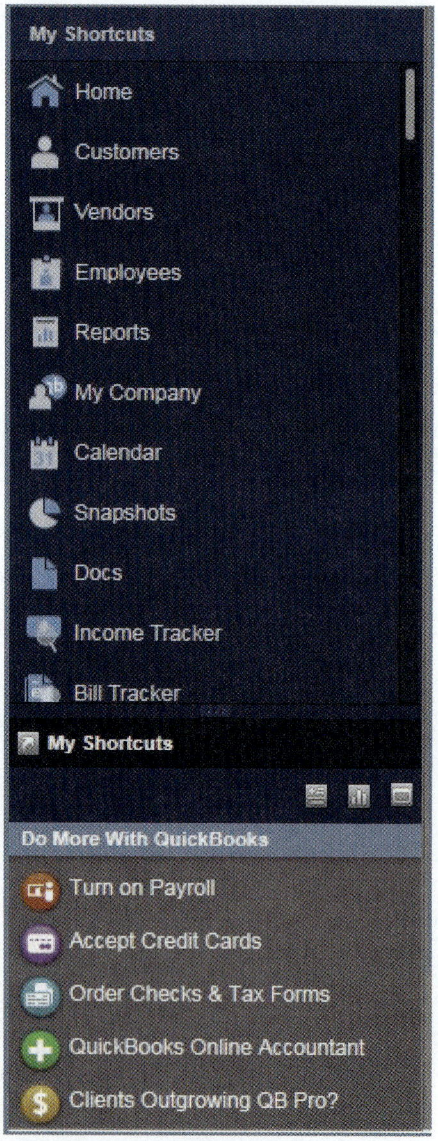

To display the Navigation Bar if it does not appear on your screen:

1. Select **View** on the Menu Bar
2. Select **Left Icon Bar**

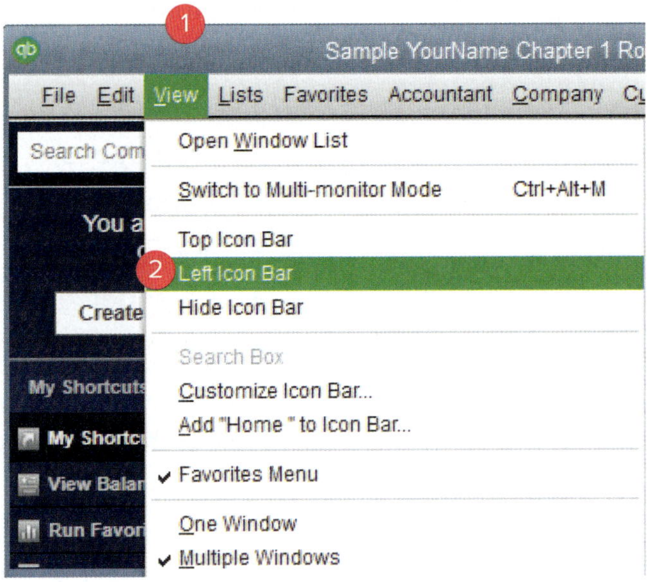

The Navigation Bar, or Icon Bar, can be customized to display the tasks that are used most frequently. To customize the Navigation Bar:

1. Select **View** on the Menu Bar
2. Select **Customize Icon Bar**

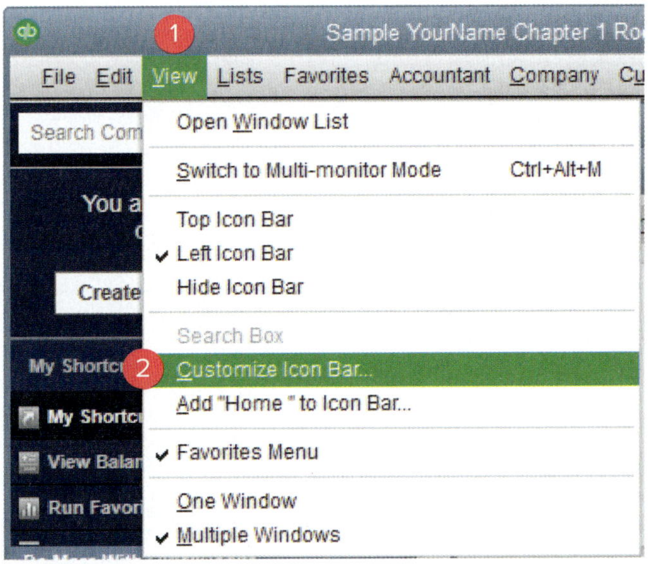

3 **Drag and drop** to reorder the tasks in the following order:

- Home
- Customers
- Vendors
- Employees
- Reports
- My Company
- Calendar
- Snapshots
- Docs

4 Select the **OK** button to close

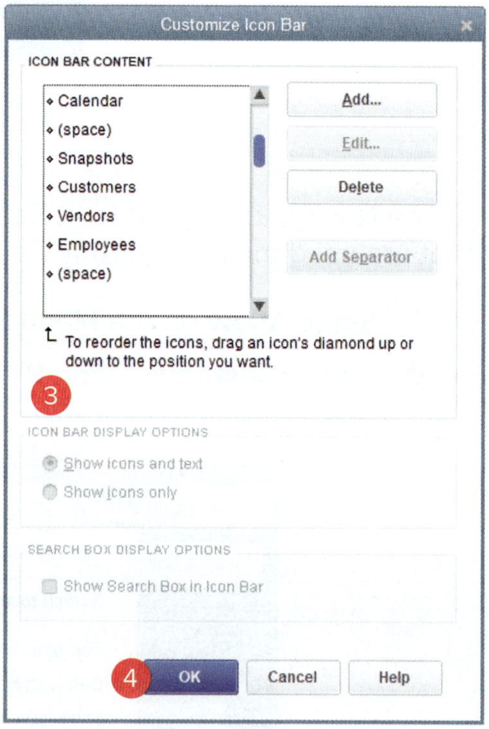

Section 1.8

QUICKBOOKS MENUS

We can also access tasks using the Menu Bar across the top of the QuickBooks window.

1. Select **File** on the Menu Bar to display the drop-down File Menu

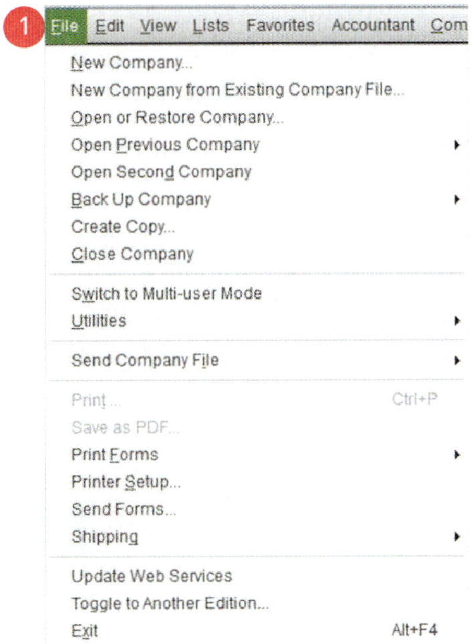

From the drop-down File Menu, you can perform tasks including the following:

- Create a new company file
- Create a new company from an existing company file
- Open or restore an existing company file
- Open a previous company file
- Open a second company file, permitting you to have two QuickBooks company files open at the same time
- Back up your company file

- Create a copy of your company file
- Close a company file
- Switch to multi-user mode when QuickBooks is used on a network
- Use utilities such as importing and exporting files
- Send a copy of your QuickBooks company file to your accountant

QuickBooks output tasks include:

- Print or save as a Portable Document Format (PDF) file
- Print Forms for printing forms, such as invoices, sales receipts, and tax forms
- Printer Setup to select a printer as well as fonts and margins
- Send Forms to email various QuickBooks forms, such as sending invoices to customers
- Ship using FedEx, UPS, and USPS

In QuickBooks Accountant Edition, the File Menu displays Toggle to Another Edition. This command allows you to switch to another QuickBooks edition, such as QuickBooks Pro.

To remove the drop-down File Menu from the screen, click anywhere outside the drop-down menu or press the **Esc** (Escape) key.

2 Select **Edit** on the Menu Bar to display the drop-down Edit Menu

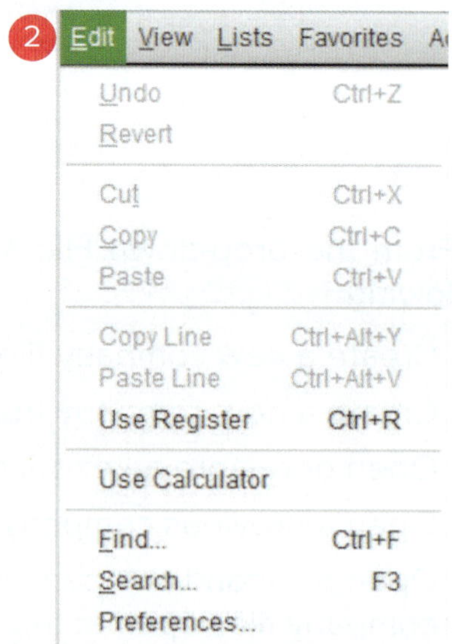

From the drop-down Edit Menu, you can undo, cut, copy, paste, and edit information entered in QuickBooks.

The Edit Menu changes based upon which windows are open. For example:

3. Click the **Home** icon to display the Home Page
4. Click the **Purchase Orders** icon in the Vendors section of the Home Page to display the purchase order form

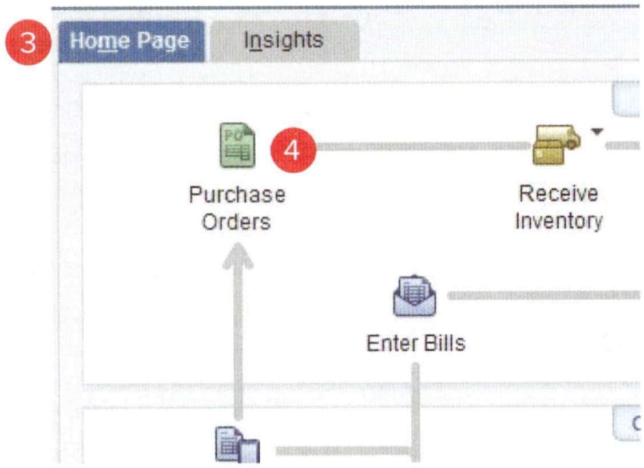

5. Select **Edit** on the Menu Bar to display the drop-down Edit Menu again. Notice that the Edit Menu now contains: New Purchase Order, Duplicate Purchase Order, Memorize Purchase Order, and Change Account Color.

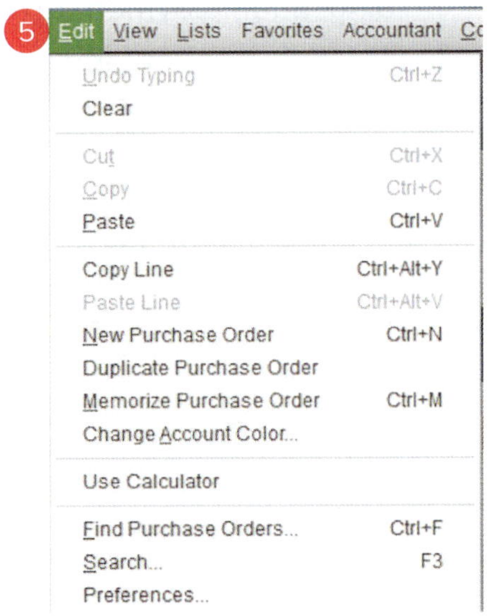

6 Click **Lists** on the Menu Bar to display the drop-down Lists Menu

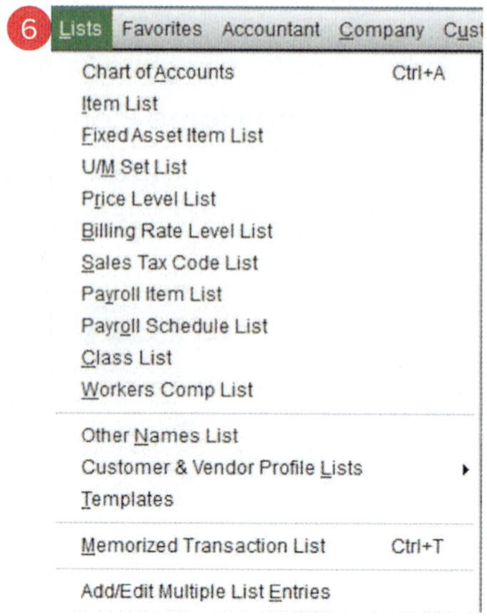

From the drop-down Lists Menu, you can access various lists of information.

- **Chart of Accounts.** A list of accounts used to record transactions.
- **Item List.** A list of inventory items that you buy and sell or a list of services provided to customers.
- **Payroll Item List.** A list of items related to payroll checks and company payroll expense such as salary, hourly wages, federal and state withholding, unemployment taxes, Medicare, and Social Security.
- **Templates.** A list of templates for business forms, such as invoices and purchase orders.
- **Memorized Transaction List.** A list of recurring transactions that are memorized or saved. For example, if your company pays $900 in rent each month, then the rent payment transaction can be memorized to eliminate the need to reenter it each month.

7 Click **Accountant** on the Menu Bar to display the drop-down Accountant Menu

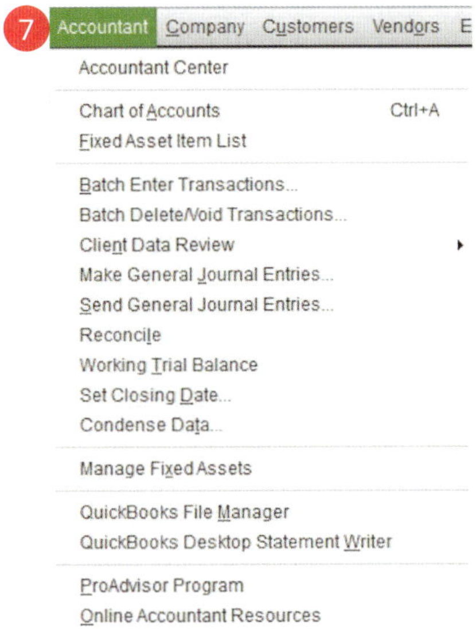

From the drop-down Accountant Menu, you can access features accountants use for client services.

- **Accountant Center.** A central location to organize accountant tools in QuickBooks.
- **Chart of Accounts.** A list of accounts used to record transactions.
- **Client Data Review.** This tool streamlines client file cleanup tasks.
- **Make General Journal Entries.** An onscreen journal for the accountant to make correcting and adjusting entries.
- **Reconcile.** The accountant can reconcile client bank statements.
- **Working Trial Balance.** The accountant can use this to review beginning balances, adjustments, and ending balances.
- **Set Closing Date.** The accountant can set the closing date for the accounting period.
- **Condense Data.** This feature permits the accountant to create a period copy of a client's QuickBooks files. For example, an accountant might create a period copy of a client's 2018 accounting year to provide to the IRS.
- **Online Accountant Resources.** QuickBooks offers desktop and online accounting solutions. See Chapter 17 of this text for more information about QuickBooks Online Accountant.

8 Click **Company** on the Menu Bar to display the drop-down Company Menu

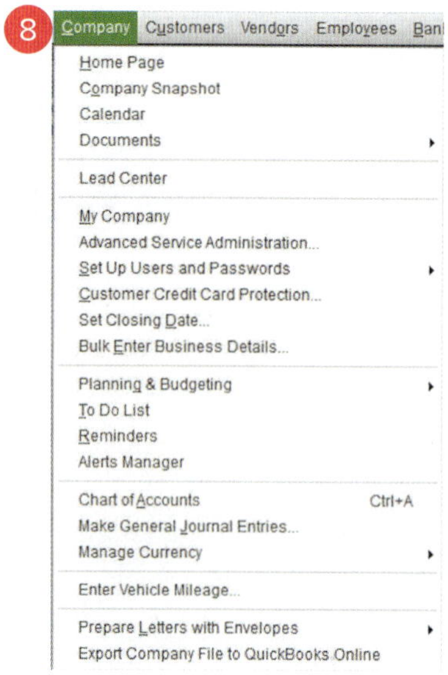

From the Company Menu, you can:

- Access company information and, for example, change the company name
- Set up users and restrict access to certain parts of QuickBooks
- Change your password
- Set up budgets and use planning decision tools
- Create a To Do List and Reminders
- Access the Chart of Accounts and onscreen Journal
- Enter vehicle mileage
- Export Company File to QuickBooks Online

9 Click **Customers** on the Menu Bar to display the drop-down Customers Menu

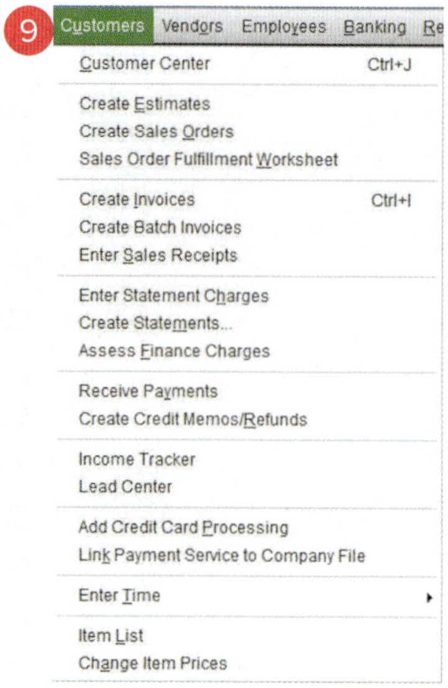

Customers and sales transactions are one of four major types of transactions in QuickBooks. The Customers Menu lists the various activities related to Customers and Sales, including the following. Notice that some of the customer activities on the drop-down Customers Menu can also be accessed from the Home Page.

- Access the Customer Center
- Create estimates
- Create invoices
- Create batch invoices
- Receive payments from customers
- Enter credit memos or refunds
- Access the Item List
- Change item prices

10 Click **Vendors** on the Menu Bar to display the drop-down Vendors Menu

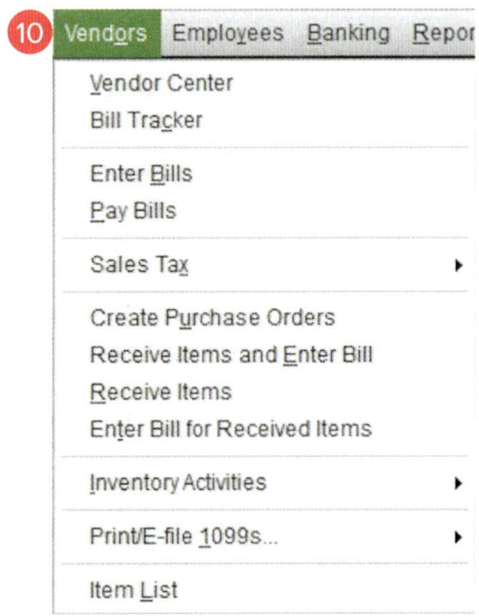

Vendors and expenses transactions are one of four major types of transactions in QuickBooks. The Vendors Menu lists the various activities related to Vendors and Expenses, including the following. Notice that some of the vendor activities on the drop-down Vendors Menu can also be accessed from the Home Page.

- Access the Vendor Center
- Enter Bills
- Pay Bills
- Create Purchase Orders

- Receive Items and Enter Bill
- Receive Items
- Print/E-file 1099s
- Access the Item List

11 Click **Employees** on the Menu Bar to display the drop-down Employee Menu

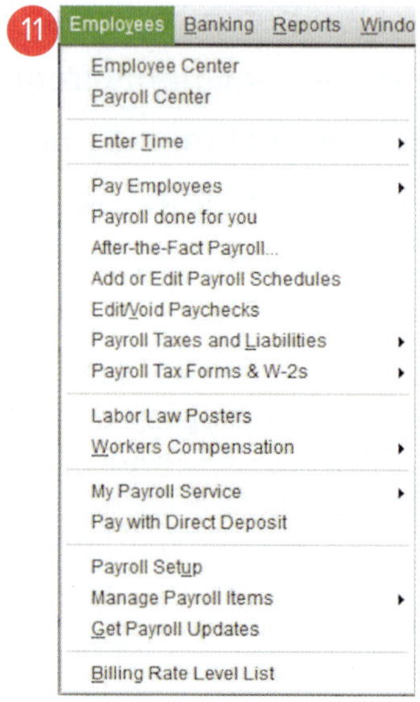

Employees or payroll transactions are one of four major types of transactions in QuickBooks. The Employees Menu lists the various activities related to employees and payroll, including the following. Notice that some of the employee activities on the drop-down Employees Menu can also be accessed from the Home Page.

- Access the Employee Center
- Access the Payroll Center
- Enter time
- Pay employees
- Add or edit payroll schedules
- Edit or void paychecks
- Pay payroll taxes and liabilities
- Prepare payroll tax forms and W-2s
- Pay with direct deposit

12 Click **Banking** on the Menu Bar to display the drop-down Banking Menu

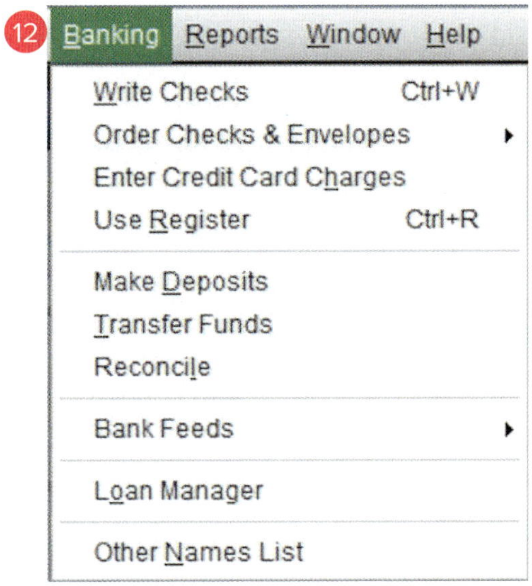

Banking transactions are one of four major types of transactions in QuickBooks. The Banking Menu lists the various activities related to banking, including the following. Notice that some of the banking activities on the drop-down Banking Menu can also be accessed from the Home Page.

- Write checks
- Enter credit card charges
- Use Check Register
- Make deposits
- Transfer funds
- Reconcile bank statements

13 Click **Reports** on the Menu Bar to display the list of reports that QuickBooks can create for your company

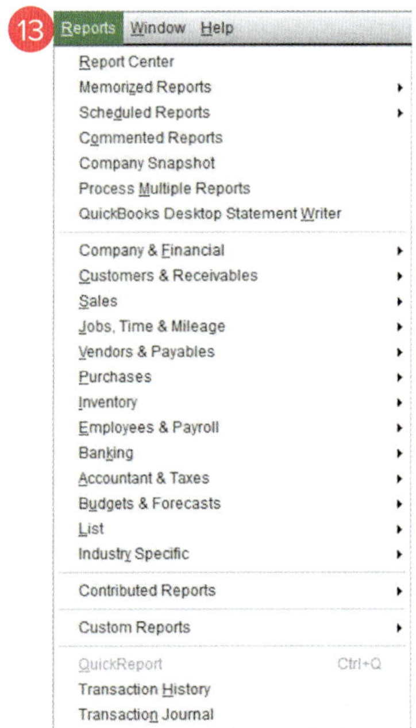

The Reports Menu lists the various activities related to preparing reports, including the following.

- Access the Report Center
- Access memorized reports that have been saved to reuse
- Access scheduled reports that are to be run at specific times
- Access different types of reports, such as company reports, customer reports, sales reports, vendor reports, and employee and payroll reports
- Access the transaction journal

Notice that reports can also be accessed from the Report Center by selecting Reports on the Navigation Bar.

14 Click **Window** on the Menu Bar to display the drop-down Window Menu. From this menu we can switch between windows to display onscreen.

15 If not already selected, select **Create Purchase Orders** window from the drop-down menu. Then **close** the Create Purchase Orders window by clicking the **X** in the upper right corner of the Create Purchase Orders window.

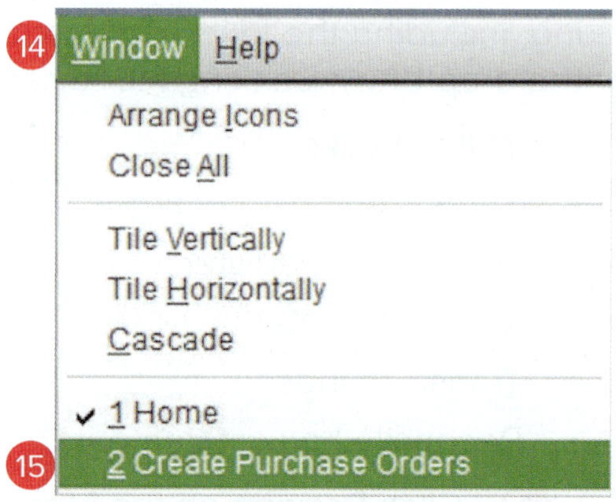

Section 1.9

QUICKBOOKS REPORTS

Preparing reports is an important aspect of an accountant's role. QuickBooks offers many different types of reports that can be customized to meet business needs.

CREATE REPORTS

To prepare a QuickBooks report, such as a Trial Balance, for Rock Castle Construction:

1. To view the Report Center, select **Reports** in the My Shortcuts section of the Navigation Bar
2. Select **Accountant & Taxes** from the report categories on the left of the window
3. Select **Carousel View**
4. Select **Trial Balance** report
5. Select the date range: **11/01/2022 To 11/30/2022**
6. Select **Run** icon to display the Trial Balance report. (Optional) If you would like to print the Trial Balance report, with the Trial Balance displayed on your QuickBooks screen, select Print to print the report. Leave the report displayed on your screen.

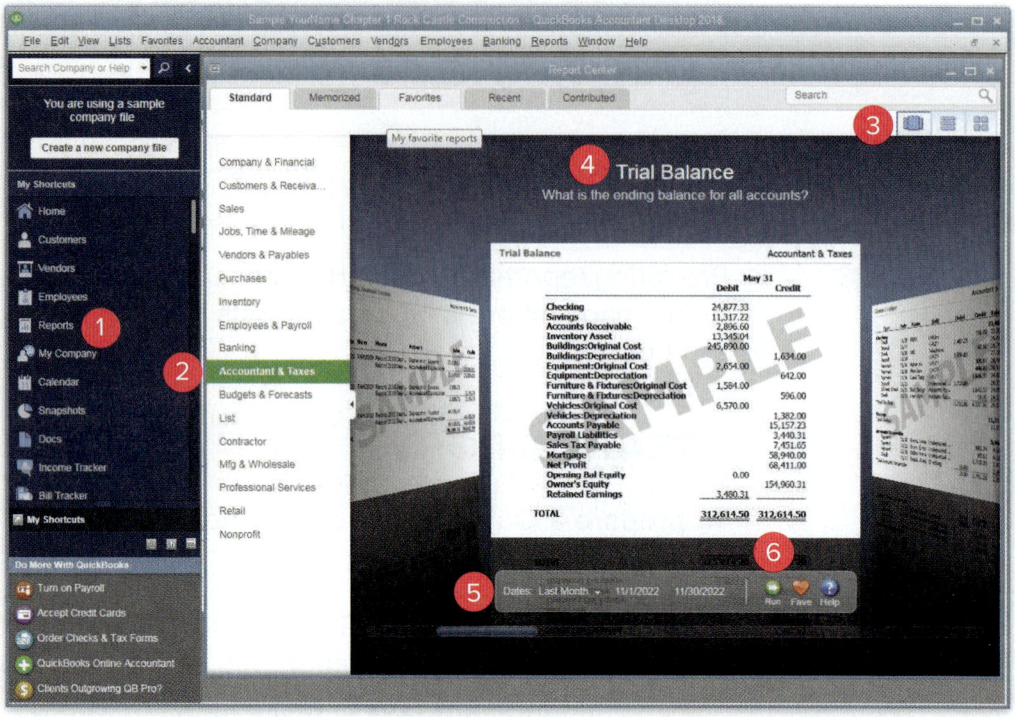

EXPORT REPORTS TO EXCEL

QuickBooks offers the option of exporting reports to Microsoft Excel® or PDF format.

To organize your text assignments, first we will download Excel Report Templates so all of your chapter assignments can be exported into one Excel file instead of separate Excel files.

To download Excel Report Templates for QuickBooks assignments:

1. Go to **www.My-QuickBooks.com**
2. Select the **QB2018** link
3. Scroll down to the section **Excel Report Templates**
4. Download the **Excel Report Template** for **Chapter 1** to your Desktop
5. **Open** the Excel workbook. (If you receive a Protected Mode message, click Enable Editing.)
6. Select **File** > **Save As**
7. Enter file name: **YourLastName FirstName CH1 REPORTS**

8. The filename extension should be: **.xls or .xlsx**
9. **Close** the Excel workbook

C1.9.1 Trial Balance. To export the Trial Balance QuickBooks report to the Excel Report Template:

1. To export the Trial Balance from the QuickBooks software, with the Trial Balance report displayed on your screen, select **Excel**
2. Select **Create New Worksheet**
3. When the Send Report to Excel window appears, select **Replace an existing worksheet**
4. Click the **Browse** button and select your **CH1 REPORTS Excel file.** Select **Open.**
5. From the drop-down list, select the sheet: **C1.9.1 TB**
6. Click the **Advanced** button
7. Uncheck **Space between columns**
8. Uncheck **Include QuickBooks Export Guide worksheet with helpful advice**
9. Select **On printed report and screen**
10. Click **OK**
11. Click **Export**
12. When the Export Report Alert window appears, select **Do not display this message in the future**
13. Select **Yes**
14. Click the **X** in the upper right corner of the Trial Balance window to close this report. If asked if you would like to memorize the report, select **No.**

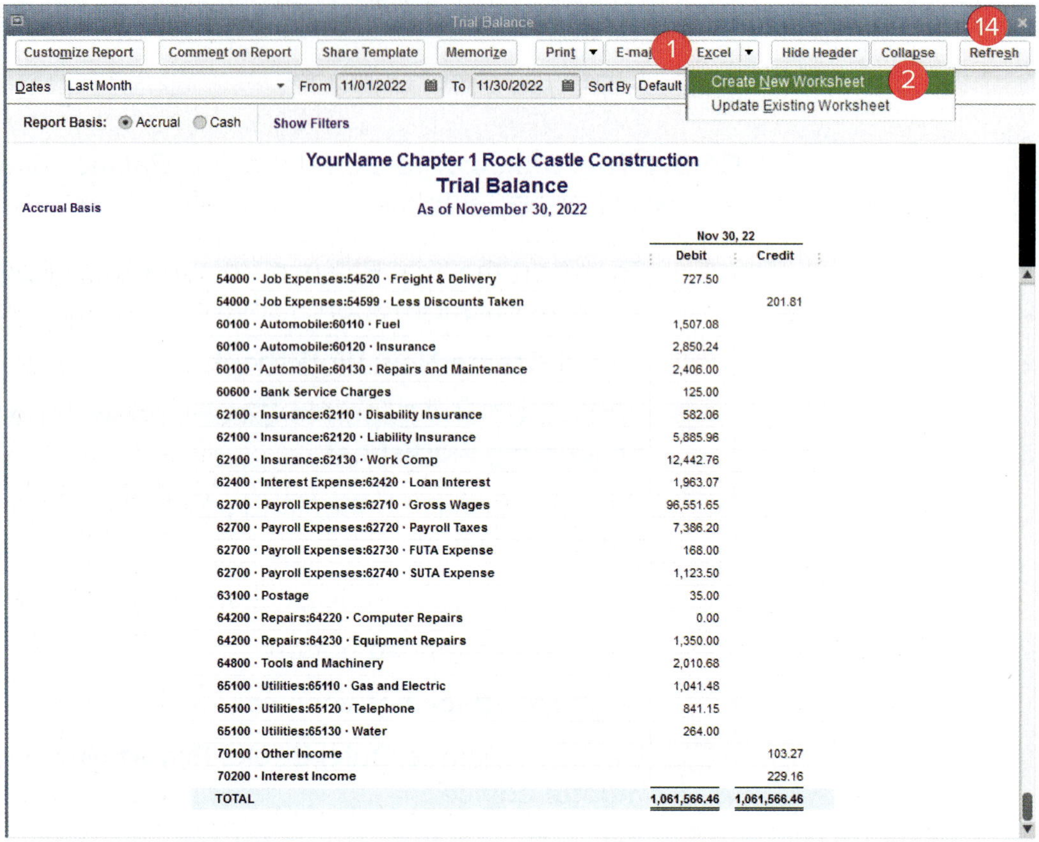
Trial Balance
Customize Report
Comment on Report
Share Template
Memorize
Print
E-mail
Excel
Hide Header
Collapse
Refresh
Create New Worksheet
Update Existing Worksheet
Dates
Last Month
From 11/01/2022
To 11/30/2022
Sort By Default
Report Basis: Accrual Cash
Show Filters
YourName Chapter 1 Rock Castle Construction
Trial Balance
Accrual Basis
As of November 30, 2022
Nov 30, 22
Debit Credit
54000 · Job Expenses:54520 · Freight & Delivery 727.50
54000 · Job Expenses:54599 · Less Discounts Taken 201.81
60100 · Automobile:60110 · Fuel 1,507.08
60100 · Automobile:60120 · Insurance 2,850.24
60100 · Automobile:60130 · Repairs and Maintenance 2,406.00
60600 · Bank Service Charges 125.00
62100 · Insurance:62110 · Disability Insurance 582.06
62100 · Insurance:62120 · Liability Insurance 5,885.96
62100 · Insurance:62130 · Work Comp 12,442.76
62400 · Interest Expense:62420 · Loan Interest 1,963.07
62700 · Payroll Expenses:62710 · Gross Wages 96,551.65
62700 · Payroll Expenses:62720 · Payroll Taxes 7,386.20
62700 · Payroll Expenses:62730 · FUTA Expense 168.00
62700 · Payroll Expenses:62740 · SUTA Expense 1,123.50
63100 · Postage 35.00
64200 · Repairs:64220 · Computer Repairs 0.00
64200 · Repairs:64230 · Equipment Repairs 1,350.00
64800 · Tools and Machinery 2,010.68
65100 · Utilities:65110 · Gas and Electric 1,041.48
65100 · Utilities:65120 · Telephone 841.15
65100 · Utilities:65130 · Water 264.00
70100 · Other Income 103.27
70200 · Interest Income 229.16
TOTAL 1,061,566.46 1,061,566.46
1
2
14

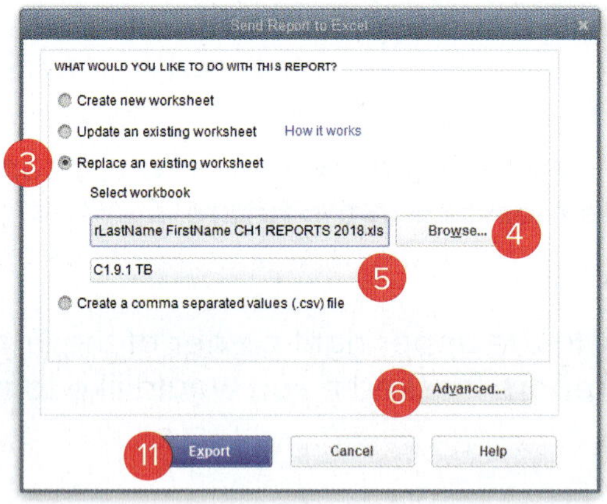
Send Report to Excel
WHAT WOULD YOU LIKE TO DO WITH THIS REPORT?
Create new worksheet
Update an existing worksheet
How it works
Replace an existing worksheet
Select workbook
rLastName FirstName CH1 REPORTS 2018.xls
Browse...
C1.9.1 TB
Create a comma separated values (.csv) file
Advanced...
Export
Cancel
Help
3
4
5
6
11

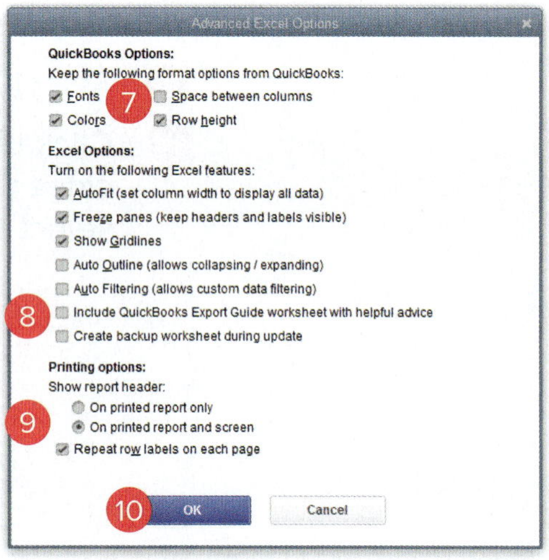
Advanced Excel Options
QuickBooks Options:
Keep the following format options from QuickBooks:
Fonts
Space between columns
Colors
Row height
Excel Options:
Turn on the following Excel features:
AutoFit (set column width to display all data)
Freeze panes (keep headers and labels visible)
Show Gridlines
Auto Outline (allows collapsing / expanding)
Auto Filtering (allows custom data filtering)
Include QuickBooks Export Guide worksheet with helpful advice
Create backup worksheet during update
Printing options:
Show report header:
On printed report only
On printed report and screen
Repeat row labels on each page
OK
Cancel
7
8
9
10

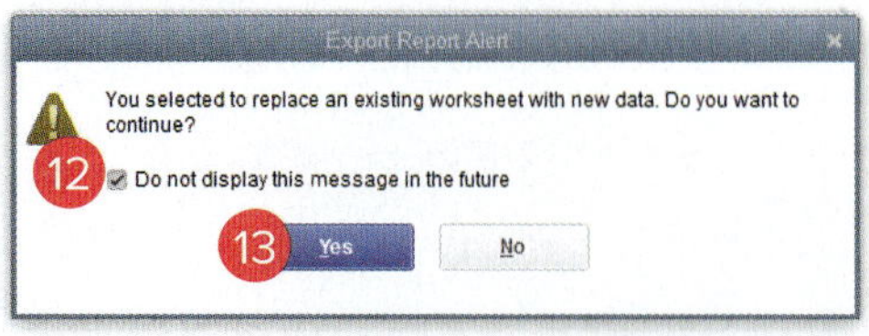
Export Report Alert
You selected to replace an existing worksheet with new data. Do you want to continue?
Do not display this message in the future
Yes
No
12
13

Excel should open on your screen with your QuickBooks Trial Balance inserted.

1. Select the **1 REPORTS** sheet tab
2. Mark the report sheet you completed by inserting an "**X**"
3. Save your **CH1 REPORTS** Excel workbook using the filename: **YourLastName FirstName CH1 REPORTS**
4. (Optional) If you would like to print the Trial Balance report, with the Trial Balance displayed on your QuickBooks screen, select **Print** to print the report

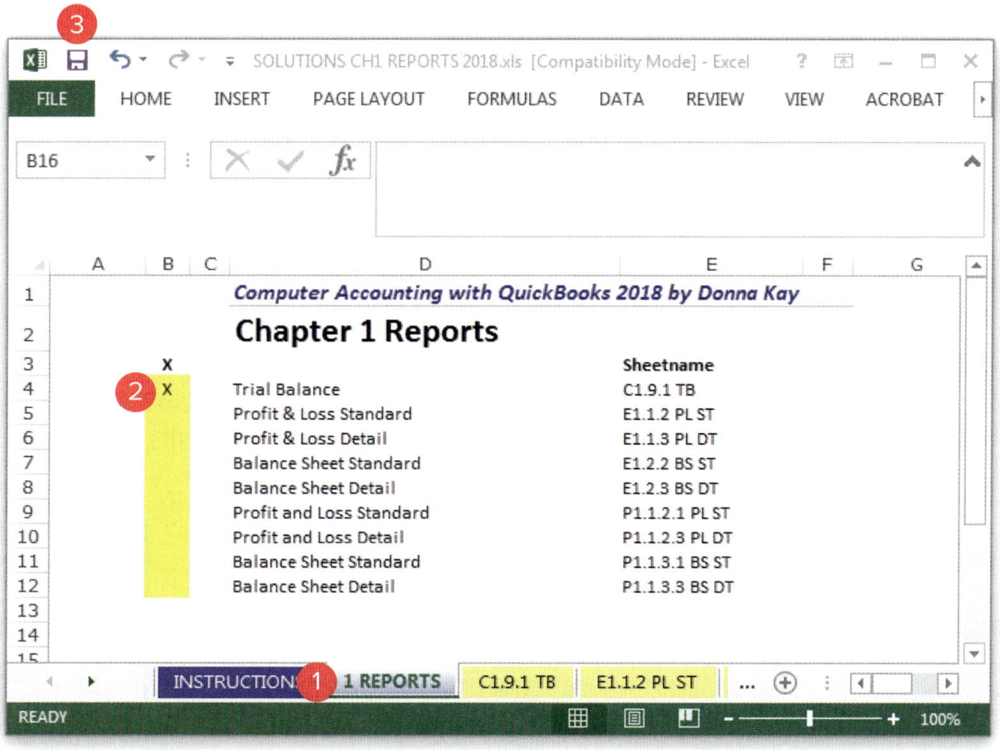

Section 1.10

QUICKBOOKS HELP AND SUPPORT

If you need assistance with a QuickBooks issue:

- Go to http://www.quickbooks.com/support
- See Correcting Errors section of Chapter 17
- Use the Intuit Community
- Go to www.My-QuickBooks.com, Issue Resolution link
- Contact your instructor
- Use the QuickBooks Help Menu, described as follows

To use the Quickbooks Help Menu:

1. Select **Help** on the Menu Bar to display the drop-down menu of Help features
2. Select **QuickBooks Desktop Help** from the Help Menu, and the Have a Question? window will appear
3. At the top of the Have a Question? window, you can type in your question and then view the results

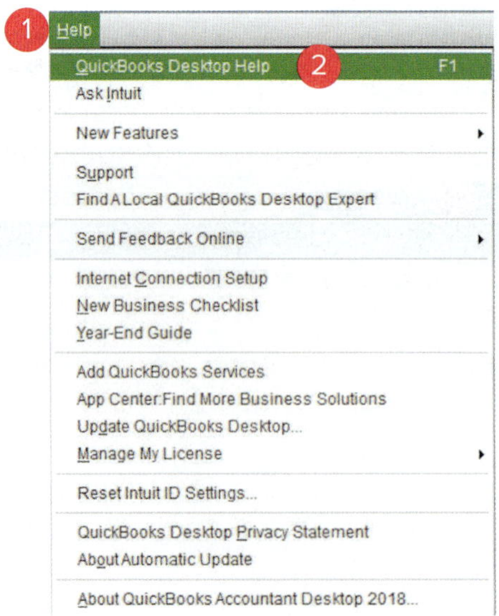

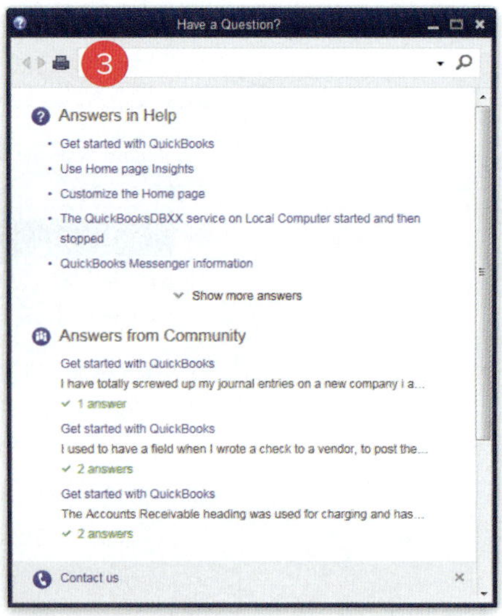

Section 1.11

BACK UP QUICKBOOKS FILES

As mentioned previously, there are two types of QuickBooks files that we will be using in this text.

1. **QBW file.** The QuickBooks working file in which you can enter accounting data and transactions.
2. **QBB file.** The QuickBooks backup file is a compressed file used to move a QuickBooks file to another computer or if the working file (QBW) fails.

QBB Files. We will be using two different types QBB files with this text: 1. QBB Starter Files that are provided to us to start an activity 2. QBB Backup Files that we create at the end of an activity.

The QBW file is the only QuickBooks file in which we can enter data and transactions. When we enter transactions into a QBW file, the information is automatically saved. The typical workflow for a business is to use the QBW file to record transactions and periodically back up to a QBB (backup) file.

A sound disaster recovery plan includes a backup system. For example, a good backup system is to have a different backup for each business day: Monday backup, Tuesday backup, Wednesday backup, and so on. Then if it is necessary to use the backup file and the Wednesday backup, for example, fails, the company has a Tuesday backup to use. Furthermore, it is recommended that a business store at least one backup at a remote location.

Typically, the backup file is used only if the company's working file (QBW) fails. Then the backup file (QBB) can be restored and used. So it is important that the backup copy is as up to date as possible in case it must be used to replace lost company data. The backup file (QBB) is compressed and must be restored to a working file (QBW) before you can use it to enter data or transactions.

The backup schedule used with this text is to create a backup QBB file at the end of each chapter, exercise or project.

To save a backup (QBB) file:

1. With your QuickBooks file (*.QBW) open, click **File**
2. Select **Back Up Company**
3. Select **Create Local Backup**
4. When the Create Backup window appears, select **Local backup**
5. Select **Next**
6. If asked where to save your files, to make it easier to find your backup files, click the **Browse** button
7. Select **Desktop**
8. Click **OK** to close the Browse for Folder window. Click **OK** again to close the Backup Options window. Select **Use this Location** if a QuickBooks warning window appears.
9. Select **Save it now**
10. Select **Next**
11. When the Save Backup Copy window appears, the Save in field should automatically show: **Desktop**
12. Update the File name field as shown to: **YourName Chapter 1 (Backup).** Depending on your operating system settings, the file extension .QBB may appear automatically. If the .QBB extension does not appear, ***do not type it.***
13. The Save as type field should automatically appear as **QBW Backup (*.QBB)**
14. Select **Save.** If a QuickBooks Information message appears, click **OK.**

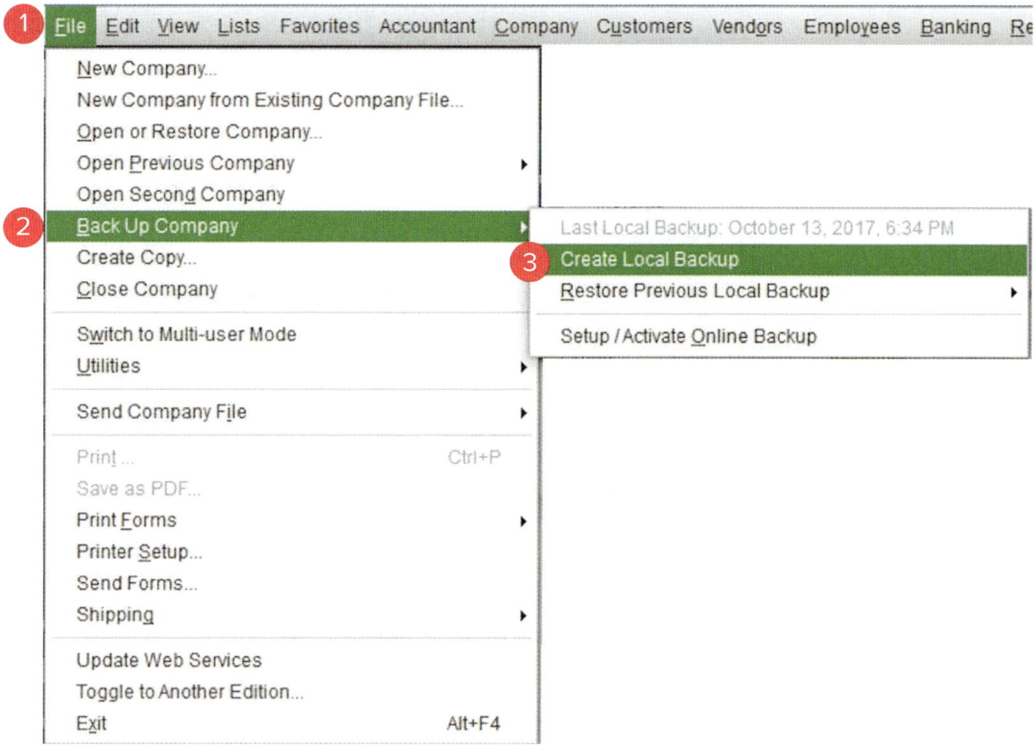
1
File Edit View Lists Favorites Accountant Company Customers Vendors Employees Banking Re
New Company...
New Company from Existing Company File...
Open or Restore Company...
Open Previous Company
Open Second Company
2
Back Up Company
Create Copy...
Close Company
Switch to Multi-user Mode
Utilities
Send Company File
Print ... Ctrl+P
Save as PDF...
Print Forms
Printer Setup...
Send Forms...
Shipping
Update Web Services
Toggle to Another Edition...
Exit Alt+F4
Last Local Backup: October 13, 2017, 6:34 PM
3
Create Local Backup
Restore Previous Local Backup
Setup / Activate Online Backup

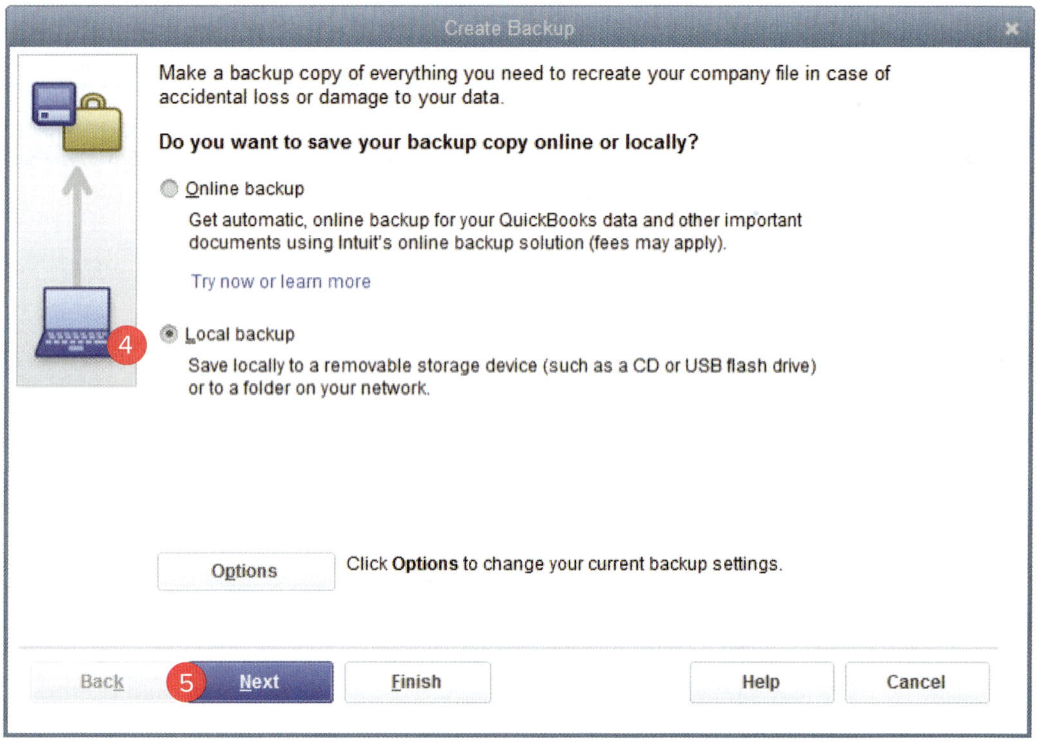
Create Backup
Make a backup copy of everything you need to recreate your company file in case of accidental loss or damage to your data.
Do you want to save your backup copy online or locally?
Online backup
Get automatic, online backup for your QuickBooks data and other important documents using Intuit's online backup solution (fees may apply).
Try now or learn more
4
Local backup
Save locally to a removable storage device (such as a CD or USB flash drive) or to a folder on your network.
Options
Click Options to change your current backup settings.
Back
5
Next
Finish
Help
Cancel

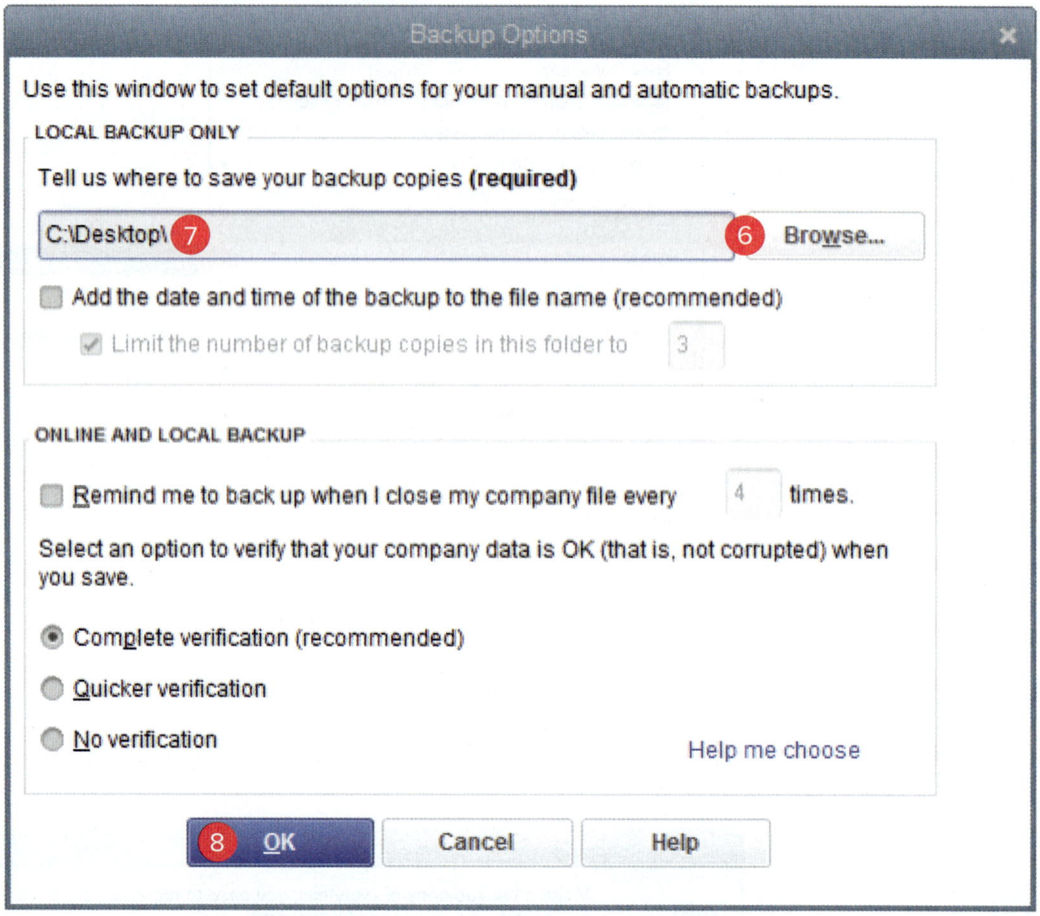
Backup Options
Use this window to set default options for your manual and automatic backups.
LOCAL BACKUP ONLY
Tell us where to save your backup copies (required)
C:\Desktop\
7
6
Browse...
Add the date and time of the backup to the file name (recommended)
Limit the number of backup copies in this folder to
3
ONLINE AND LOCAL BACKUP
Remind me to back up when I close my company file every
4
times.
Select an option to verify that your company data is OK (that is, not corrupted) when you save.
Complete verification (recommended)
Quicker verification
No verification
Help me choose
8
OK
Cancel
Help

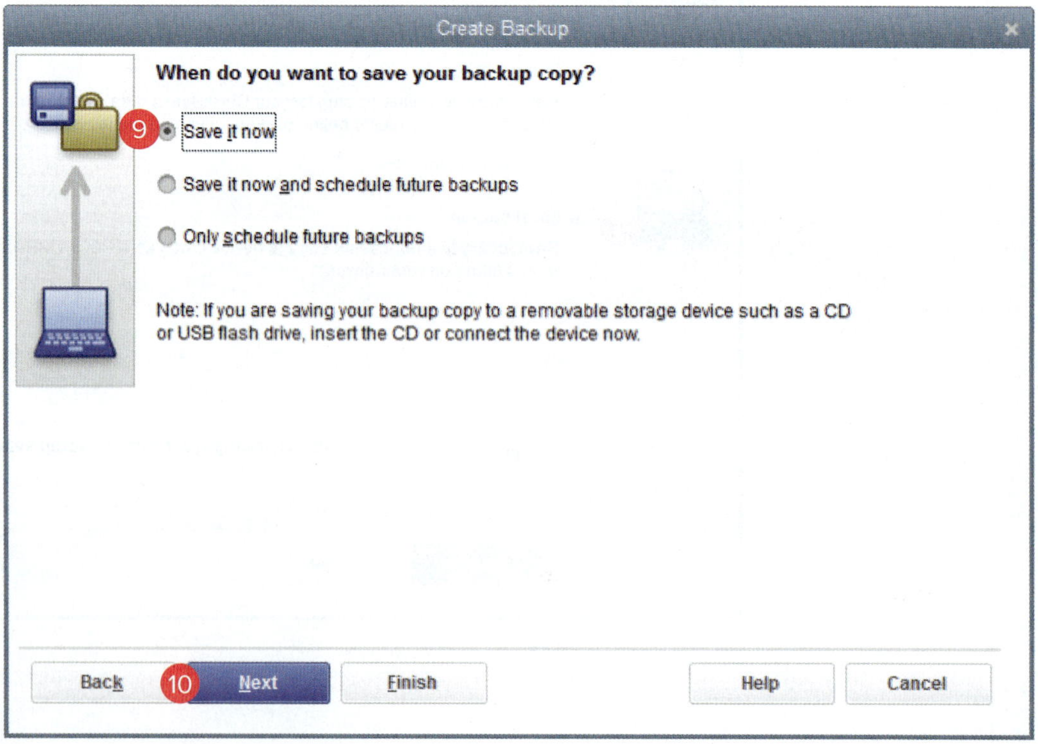
Create Backup
When do you want to save your backup copy?
9
Save it now
Save it now and schedule future backups
Only schedule future backups
Note: If you are saving your backup copy to a removable storage device such as a CD or USB flash drive, insert the CD or connect the device now.
Back
10
Next
Finish
Help
Cancel

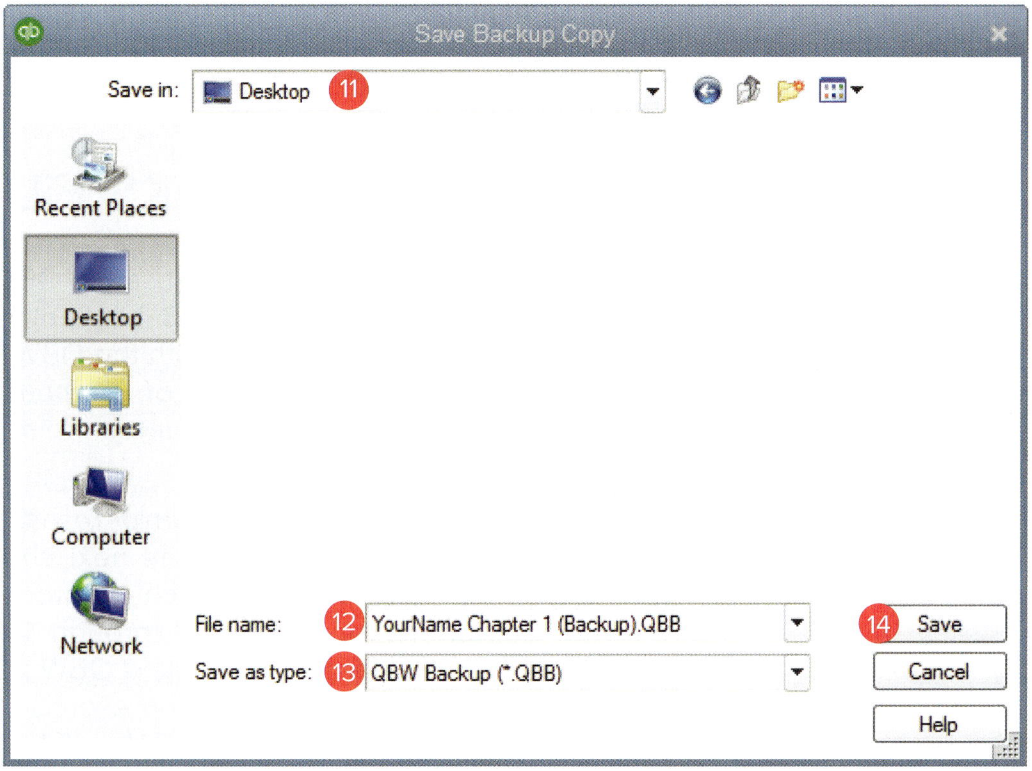
Save Backup Copy
Save in:
Desktop
11
Recent Places
Desktop
Libraries
Computer
Network
File name:
12
YourName Chapter 1 (Backup).QBB
Save as type:
13
QBW Backup (*.QBB)
14
Save
Cancel
Help

Section 1.12

RESTORE QUICKBOOKS FILE OPTIONS

The typical workflow for a business is to use the QBW file to record transactions and periodically back up to a QBB (backup) file. The QBB (backup) file is only restored if there is an issue with the QBW file.

For our QuickBooks assignments of *Computer Accounting with QuickBooks,* there are two options for our restore schedule.

1. **Chapters and Exercises.** Chapters and exercises provide opportunities to *explore* and *practice*. If an error results while we are exploring or practicing, it will not affect the next chapter because a new QBB Starter File is provided for each chapter when needed. There is a QBB Starter File for Chapters 1 through 10, 15 and 17. We will restore the QBB Starter File to create a QBW file. Then we will complete the activities in the chapter and exercises. After we complete the activities, we will create a QBB Backup File.
2. **Projects.** Projects provide *mastery* opportunities. We are provided a QBB Starter File for Project 1. After that we will continue to use our own files to complete subsequent Projects 2 through 10. Just as in a business workflow, since we are using the same computer, we can continue to use the same QBW file. We will make backups at the end of each project. However, we will only use our QBB Backup File if our QBW file fails or we need to switch to a different computer. When completing the projects, errors will carry forward, so it is important to check and cross check work as well as track down and resolve errors.

If your QuickBooks Project file has an issue that you are unable to fix, contact your instructor for assistance.

QUICKBOOKS CHAPTER & EXERCISES		
QBW	**QBB STARTER FILES**	**QBB BACKUP FILES**
Start		
↓		
Restore QBB STARTER FILE	← CHAPTER 1 QBB STARTER FILE	
↓		
Complete Chapter 1		
↓		
Back Up		→ **QBB BACKUP FILE**
↓		
Complete Exercise 1.1		
↓		
Back Up		→ **QBB BACKUP FILE**
↓		
Repeat		
↓		
Restore QBB STARTER FILE	← CHAPTER 2 QBB STARTER FILE	
↓		
Complete Chapter 2		
↓		
Back Up		→ **QBB BACKUP FILE**
↓		
Repeat		
↓		
End		

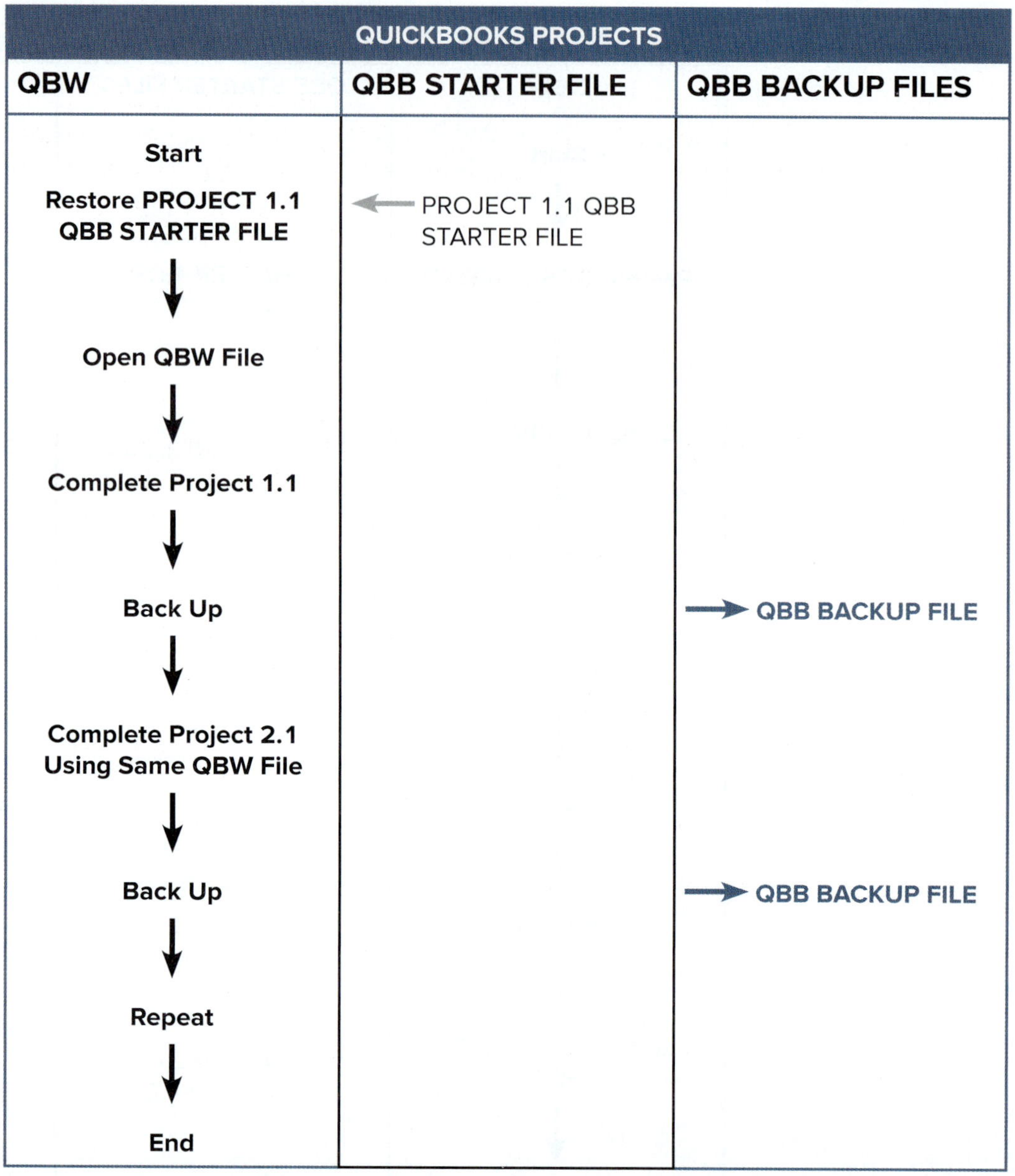
QUICKBOOKS PROJECTS
QBW
QBB STARTER FILE
QBB BACKUP FILES
Start
Restore PROJECT 1.1 QBB STARTER FILE
PROJECT 1.1 QBB STARTER FILE
Open QBW File
Complete Project 1.1
Back Up
QBB BACKUP FILE
Complete Project 2.1 Using Same QBW File
Back Up
QBB BACKUP FILE
Repeat
End

QBW WORKFLOW

If you will be using the same computer to complete Chapter 1 QuickBooks exercises, just as in a business workflow, you can continue to use the same QBW file. You will make backups at the end of each chapter, exercise, or project. However, you will only use the backup if your QBW file fails.

If you are using the QBW approach, **leave your QBW file open and proceed directly to Exercise 1.1.**

QBB RESTORE

If you will be switching computers, after you finish your QuickBooks work session, you will back up to a QBB file in order to move your QuickBooks file to another computer. When you restart your work session on another computer, you will restore the backup (QBB) file.

If you are using the QBB approach, and are ending your computer session now, use the following directions to **close** the company file and **exit** QuickBooks. When you restart, you will **restore your backup file** to complete Exercise 1.1.

Section 1.13

CLOSE AND EXIST QUICKBOOKS

After you have backed up your QuickBooks file, you can close the QuickBooks QBW file and exit QuickBooks software.

CLOSE QUICKBOOKS QBW COMPANY FILE

To close a QuickBooks company file:

1. From the Menu Bar, select **File**
2. Click **Close Company**

If the company QBW file is left open when you exit QuickBooks, the next time anyone uses the QuickBooks software, the company file might still be open, permitting access to your company accounting records.

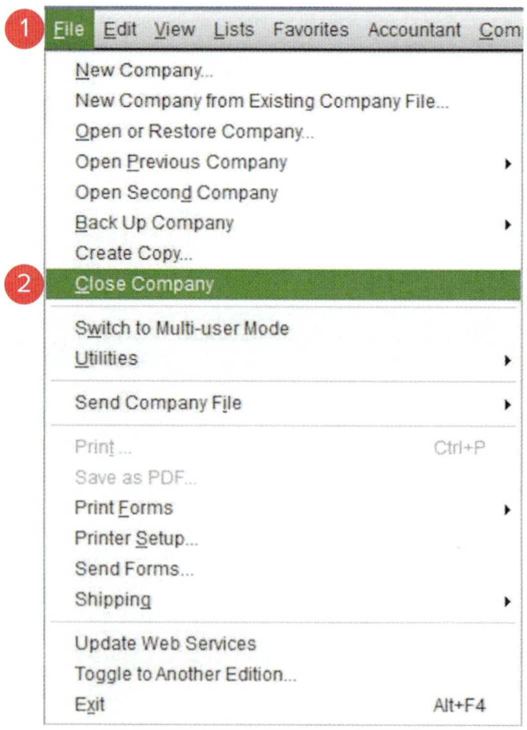

EXIT QUICKBOOKS SOFTWARE

To exit QuickBooks software:

1. From the Menu Bar, select **File**
2. Select **Exit**

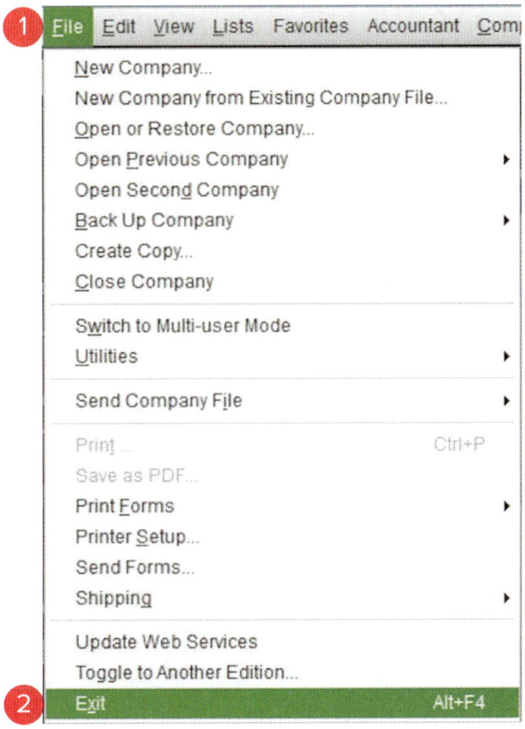

! It is important to periodically exit QuickBooks software because QuickBooks updates may be downloaded but are only installed when QuickBooks software is reopened. Periodically exiting QuickBooks software and reopening it will ensure that the latest updates have been installed.

Section 1.14

ACCOUNTING ESSENTIALS

Accounting Systems

Accounting Essentials summarize important foundational accounting knowledge that may be useful when using QuickBooks

What's the language of business?

Accounting is the language of business. Learning accounting is similar to learning a new language, such as Spanish or French. As you use this text, you will learn terms and definitions that are unique to accounting.

What's the objective of an accounting system?

The objective of an accounting system is to collect, summarize, and communicate information to decision makers. Accounting information is used to:

- Prepare tax returns for federal and state tax agencies.
- Prepare financial statements for banks and investors.
- Prepare reports for managers and owners to use when making decisions. Such decisions include: Are our customers paying their bills on time? Which of our products are the most profitable? Will we have enough cash to pay our bills next month?

What are the main components to an accounting system?

Most accounting systems consist of three components:

- Input, such as entering transactions
- Processing, such as the processing that QuickBooks does for you automatically, sorting and posting appropriate accounts when you enter transactions
- Output, such as the QuickBooks report you generate

What are the main advantages of a computerized accounting system?

Before computerized accounting systems, the process component had to be performed manually consuming numerous hours of work to sort, post, calculate balances, and so on. With a computerized accounting system, most of the processing is done automatically saving hours of manual work.

www.my-quickbooks.com

Go to **www.My-QuickBooks.com** to view additional QuickBooks resources including:

- **Excel Report Templates** to organize QuickBooks reports exported to Excel
- ***Computer Accounting with QuickBooks* updates,** sometimes required when there is a software update that affects the text
- **QuickBooks Video links**
- **QuickBooks Help and Support links**
- **Other QuickBooks Resources** to make learning QuickBooks easier and more effective
- **QuickBooks Issue Resolution** offers a guided approach to troubleshooting QuickBooks

Troubleshooting QuickBooks and Correcting Errors are crucial QuickBooks skill to acquire. See www.My-QuickBooks.com > QB Issue Resolution for Troubleshooting QuickBooks tips. See Chapter 17, Quick Review Guide, for tips on Correcting Errors.

Bookmark www.My-QuickBooks.com for future use.

Note that the exercises contain instructions but fewer screen captures than the chapter. The screen captures are included in the chapter when we are exploring. In the exercises, the focus is on practicing, so there are instructions included but fewer screen captures. This learning approach increases retention of material and results in deeper learning.

EXERCISE 1.1: Profit and Loss Statement

BACKSTORY

While working at your computer, you notice Mr. Castle heading toward you. Adding another stack of papers to your overflowing inbox, he says, *"I need a profit & loss statement and a balance sheet for November as soon as possible. I haven't seen any financial statements since our former accountant left."*

As he walks away, Mr. Castle calls over his shoulder, *"From now on I'd like a P&L and balance sheet by the first of each month."*

E1.1.1 QuickBooks File

If you will be using the same computer and the same Chapter 1.QBW file:

1. If your Chapter 1.QBW file is not already open, open it by selecting **File > Open Previous Company.** Select your **Chapter 1.QBW file.** If a QuickBooks Information window appears with a message about the sample company file, click **OK.**
2. Add **YourName Exercise 1.1** to the company name by selecting **Company Menu > My Company.**

> **Note that the company name** appears on reports and can differ from the file name. See Chapter 16 for additional instructions for changing the company name.

> **If you are not using the same computer that you used for Chapter 1,** you will need to restore your Chapter 1 Backup.QBB file using the instructions in Appendix B: Back Up & Restore QuickBooks. After restoring, add YourName Exercise 1.1 to the company name.

E1.1.2 Profit and Loss, Standard

The Profit & Loss Statement (also called the Income Statement) lists income earned and expenses incurred to generate income. Summarizing the amount of profit or loss a company has earned, the Profit & Loss Statement is one of the primary financial statements given to bankers and investors.

Prepare the QuickBooks Profit & Loss Standard for Rock Castle Construction by completing the following steps:

1. Click **Reports** in the Navigation Bar
2. Select type of report: **Company & Financial**
3. Select report: **Profit & Loss Standard**
4. Select the date range: **Last Month.** The Dates field will now be: **11/01/2022 To 11/30/2022.** Select the **Run** icon.
5. Export the report to **Excel** or **print** the Profit and Loss Standard. (If your Chapter 1 Excel Report workbook is already open, you may receive an error message. Close the Chapter 1 Excel Report workbook. Then export the report again.)

6. **Close** the Profit & Loss Standard window
7. **Highlight** the amount of the single largest income item appearing on the Profit & Loss Statement for the month of November
8. **Highlight** the amount of the single largest expense item appearing on the Profit & Loss Statement for the month of November

E1.1.3 Profit and Loss, Detail

Prepare the QuickBooks Profit & Loss Detail for Rock Castle Construction by completing the following steps:

1. Click **Reports** in the Navigation Bar
2. Select type of report: **Company & Financial**
3. Select report: **Profit & Loss Detail**
4. Select the date range: **Last Month.** The Dates field will now be: **11/01/2022 To 11/30/2022.** Select the **Run** icon.
5. Export the report to **Excel** or **print** the Profit and Loss Detail
6. **Close** the Profit & Loss Detail window
7. **Highlight** the amount of the single largest Subcontractors Expense item appearing on the Profit & Loss Detail for the month of November
8. **Highlight** the amount of the single largest Utilities Expense item appearing on the Profit & Loss Detail for the month of November

E1.1.4 Back Up Exercise 1.1

Save a backup of your Exercise file using the file name: YourName Exercise 1.1 Backup.QBB. See *Appendix B: Back Up & Restore QuickBooks Files* for instructions.

EXERCISE 1.2: Balance Sheet

E1.2.1 QuickBooks File

If you will be using the same computer and the same QBW file:

1. Select your **QBW file.**
2. Add **YourName Exercise 1.2** to the company name by selecting **Company Menu > My Company.**

> **If you are not using the same computer that you used for Chapter 1 and Exercise 1.1,** you will need to restore your latest prior Backup.QBB file using the instructions in Appendix B: Back Up & Restore QuickBooks. After restoring, add YourName Exercise 1.2 to the company name.

E1.2.2 Balance Sheet, Standard

The Balance Sheet is the financial statement that summarizes the financial position of a business. Listing assets, liabilities, and equity, the Balance Sheet reveals what a company owns and what it owes.

To prepare the Balance Sheet Standard for Rock Castle Construction at November 30, 2022, complete the following steps:

1. From the Report Center window, select type of report: **Company & Financial**
2. Select report: **Balance Sheet Standard**
3. Select date range: **Last Month** with Dates field **From 11/01/2022 To 11/30/2022.** Select the **Run** icon.
4. Export the report to **Excel** or **print** the Balance Sheet Standard
5. **Highlight** the amount of the single largest asset listed on Rock Castle Construction's November 30, 2022 Balance Sheet
6. **Highlight** the amount of Total Checking/Savings listed on Rock Castle Construction's November 30, 2022 Balance Sheet

E1.2.3 Balance Sheet, Detail

To prepare the Balance Sheet Detail for Rock Castle Construction at November 30, 2022, complete the following steps:

1. From the Report Center window, select type of report: **Company & Financial**
2. Select report: **Balance Sheet Detail**
3. Select date range: **Last Month** with Dates field **From 11/01/2022 To 11/30/2022.** Select the **Run** icon.
4. Export the report to **Excel** or **print** the Balance Sheet Detail
5. **Highlight** the ending balance for Undeposited Funds listed on Rock Castle Construction's November 30, 2022 Balance Sheet Detail

E1.1.4 Back Up Exercise 1.2

Save a backup of your Exercise file using the file name: YourName Exercise 1.2 Backup.QBB. See *Appendix B: Back Up & Restore QuickBooks Files* for instructions.

PROJECT 1.1

Larry's Landscaping

BACKSTORY

Larry's Landscaping just hired you as an accounting consultant to maintain its accounting records using QuickBooks financial software. The QuickBooks company file for Larry's Landscaping has already been created and transactions have been entered. Your assignment is to complete the following steps to export reports to Excel and then email them to the finance director at Larry's.

QB SatNav

The objective of Project 1.1 is to facilitate your mastery of QuickBooks Desktop. As shown in the following QB SatNav, Project 1.1 focuses on QB Reports.

QB SatNav

1 QB SETTINGS

- Company Settings
- Chart of Accounts

2 QB TRANSACTIONS

> Money in *Money out >*

- Banking
- Customers & Sales
- Vendors & Expenses
- Employees & Payroll

3 QB REPORTS

- Reports

P1.1.1 Restore Starter File

Restore the Project 1 Starter file. (.QBB file) for Larry's Landscaping. *See Appendix B: Back Up & Restore QuickBooks Files for instructions.*

1. Restore the **PROJECT 1.1 STARTER.QBB** for Larry's Landscaping
2. Update the Company Name to: **YourName Project 1.1 Larry's Landscaping**

P1.1.2 Profit and Loss

1. Using the Chapter 1 Excel Report Template, export to **Excel** the Profit & Loss Standard for Larry's Landscaping for the Last Fiscal Year, October 1, 2021 through September 30, 2022.

! When exporting to Excel, remember to select Advanced Excel Options:

- **Uncheck Space between columns**
- **Uncheck Include QuickBooks Export Guide worksheet with helpful advice**
- **Select On printed report and screen**

2. **Highlight** the single largest expense item
3. Export to **Excel** the Profit & Loss Detail for Larry's Landscaping for the Last Fiscal Year, October 1, 2021 through September 30, 2022
4. Which type of landscaping service produces more revenue for Larry's: Installation or Maintenance & Repairs? **Highlight** your answer.

P1.1.3 Balance Sheet

1. Export to **Excel** the Balance Sheet Standard for Larry's Landscaping for the Last Fiscal Year ending September 2022
2. **Highlight** the largest single liability on the balance sheet
3. Export to **Excel** the Balance Sheet Detail for Larry's Landscaping for the Last Fiscal Year, ending September 2022
4. **Highlight** the largest asset

P1.1.4 Back Up Project 1.1

Save a backup of your Project file using the file name: YourName Project 1.1 Backup.QBB. See *Appendix B: Back Up & Restore QuickBooks Files* for instructions.

Chapter 2

QuickBooks Chart of Accounts

BACKSTORY

The next morning when you arrive at work, Mr. Castle is waiting for you, pacing in the aisle outside your cubicle.

He looks at you over the top of his glasses, his voice tense when he asks, *"Do you have the P&L and balance sheet ready?"*

"Yes sir!" you reply, handing him the financial statements.

You hit the Send button on your smartphone. *"And I'm sending you a link so you can also view the financials in a spreadsheet."*

The creases in Mr. Castle's brow disappear as his eyes run down the statements, murmuring to himself as he walks away, *"The creditor waiting in my office should like this. . . ."*

As he rounds the corner, he calls back to you, *"See your inbox for account changes we need to make. And we haven't gotten around to password protecting our QuickBooks file yet. But I'm confident you'll be able to figure that out."*

Opening the QuickBooks training manual, you dive into learning how to update the Chart of Accounts and password protect QuickBooks files.

Section 2.1

QuickBooks SatNav

QuickBooks SatNav is your satellite navigation for QuickBooks, assisting you in navigating QuickBooks

In Chapter 2, we will see how to customize a company's Chart of Accounts, a list of all the accounts used by a company to collect accounting information. In addition, we will learn how to restrict access to our QuickBooks accounting records using passwords to improve security and controls.

QuickBooks SatNav is designed to assist in seeing how all the QuickBooks pieces we learn fit together. As mentioned in Chapter 1, QuickBooks SatNav divides QuickBooks into three processes:

1. **QuickBooks Settings.** This includes Company Settings when setting up a new QuickBooks company and the Company Chart of Accounts.
2. **QuickBooks Transactions.** This includes recording transactions in QuickBooks. Transaction types can be categorized as Banking, Customers and Sales, Vendors and Expenses, and Employees and Payroll. In basic terms, recording transactions involves recording money in and money out.
3. **QuickBooks Reports.** QuickBooks reports are the output of the system, such as commonly used financial statements of Balance Sheet, Income Statement, and Statement of Cash Flows.

In this chapter we focus on customizing:

- QuickBooks Company settings, such as passwords for security, and
- Company Chart of Accounts

QB SatNav

1 QB SETTINGS — CHAPTERS 1 2 11 12 13 14

- Company Settings
- Chart of Accounts

2 QB TRANSACTIONS — CHAPTERS 3 4 5 6 7 8 11 12 13 14

> Money in *Money out >*

- Banking
- Customers & Sales
- Vendors & Expenses
- Employees & Payroll

3 QB REPORTS — CHAPTERS 9 10 11 12 13 14

- Reports

Section 2.2

START QUICKBOOKS AND OPEN QUICKBOOKS COMPANY

START QUICKBOOKS

To start QuickBooks software, click the **QuickBooks** icon on your desktop. If a QuickBooks icon does not appear on your desktop, from Microsoft® Windows® click **Start** button > **Programs** > **QuickBooks** > **QuickBooks Premier Accountant Edition.**

> **QuickBooks Accountant** includes all the features of QuickBooks Pro plus features for client services. If you use QuickBooks Pro, your screens may appear slightly different than those appearing in this text.

QBB STARTER FILE

The typical workflow for a business is to use the QBW file to record transactions and periodically back up to a QBB (backup) file. The QBB (backup) file is only restored if there is an issue with the QBW file.

To complete our *Computer Accounting with QuickBooks* assignments for chapters and exercises, we will restore the QBB Starter File for the chapter. There is a QBB Starter File for Chapters 1 through 10, 15 and 17. Then we will complete the chapter and exercise assignments, making backups at the end of the chapter or exercise. However, we will only use our QBB Backup File if our QBW file fails or we need to change to a different computer.

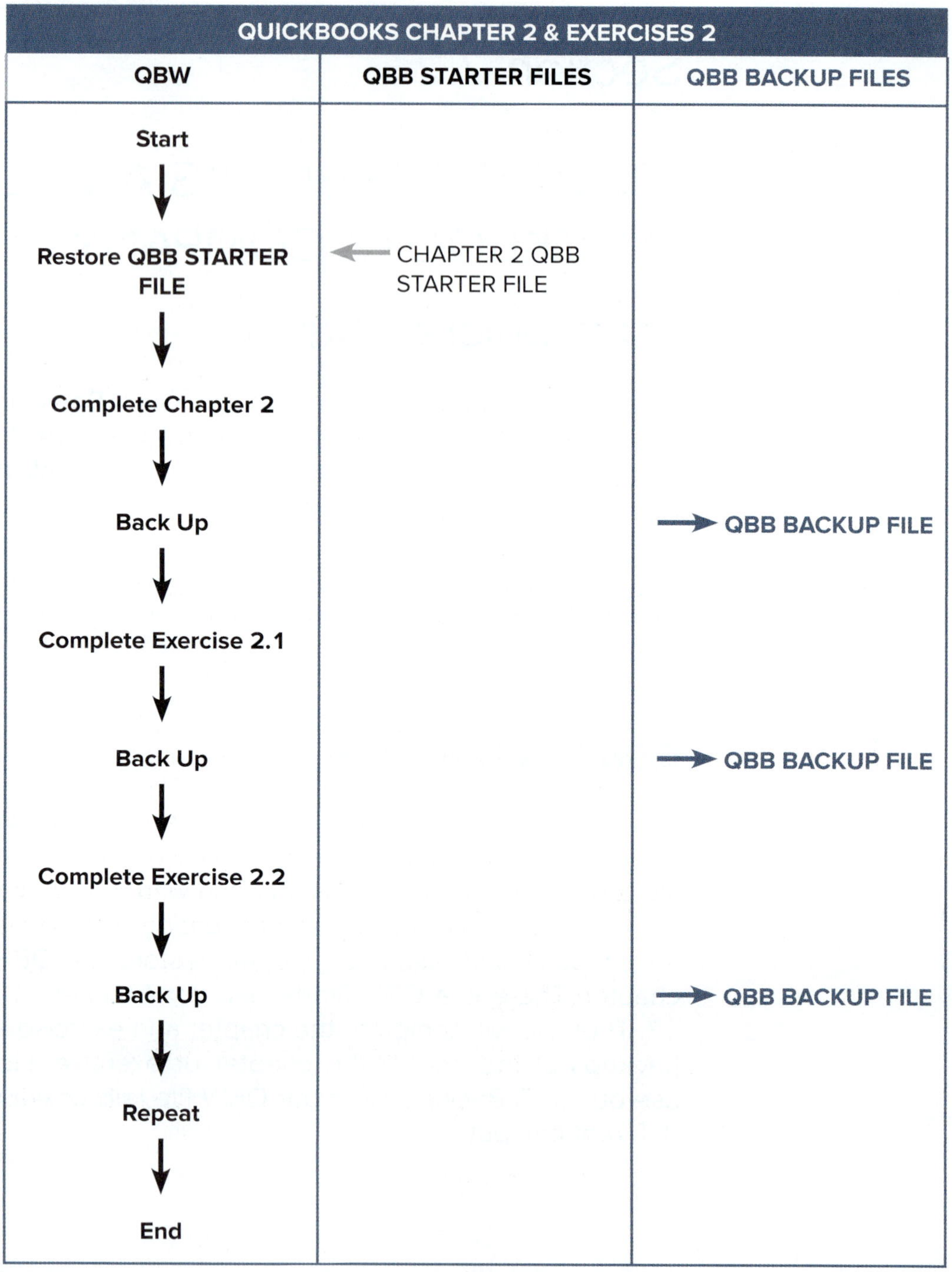

RESTORE QBB STARTER FILE

For purposes of this text, we will use QuickBooks Starter files that are QBB files containing the company data needed to complete the assignments in this text. The QBB Starter files are compressed files that must be unzipped, or restored, into QBW files before the files can be used.

For your convenience, QuickBooks (.QBB) Starter files accompany *Computer Accounting with QuickBooks 2018.*

Go to www.My-QuickBooks.com or www.mhhe.com/kay2018 to download the Starter files from the Online Learning Center.

To stay organized, consider adding a folder to your Desktop: QBB STARTER FILES. Then copy the QBB STARTER files to that folder.

For Connect users, the Starter Files are accessible through your Connect Chapter Assignments.

! **QuickBooks Desktop (QBDT)** Data Files are compressed backup files that can be restored and used. To use Starter Files, the compressed file must be restored following the instructions here. Since it is a compressed file, you cannot open and use the QuickBooks data files by simply clicking on the file. Instead you must follow the instructions here to unzip and restore the data file before using it.

To restore the Chapter 2 QBB Starter file from a QBB file to a QBW file:

1. From the No Company Open window, select **Open or restore an existing company**
2. Select **Restore a backup copy**
3. Click **Next**
4. When the Open or Restore Company window appears, select **Local backup**
5. Click **Next**
6. Identify the location of the **CHAPTER 2 STARTER.QBB** file. If you copied the CHAPTER 2 STARTER.QBB file to your desktop, select the **Look in** field to find the location of the .QBB file on your desktop.
7. Select the file: **CHAPTER 2 STARTER.QBB**
8. The Files of type field should automatically display: **QBW Backup (*.QBB)**
9. Click **Open**
10. When the Open or Restore window appears, click **Next**
11. Identify the file name and location of the QBW company file. To save the QBW (working file) on your desktop, select the location to save in: **Desktop.** (Another option is to save your QBW files to Users > Public > Public Documents > Intuit > QuickBooks > Company Files. Be sure you have permissions to save to a folder.)
12. Enter QBW File name: **YourName Chapter 2.** (Insert your name in the QBW file name so you can identify your files.)

13 The Save as type field should automatically appear as **QuickBooks Files (*.QBW)**

14 Click **Save**

15 Click **OK** when the QuickBooks Desktop Information window appears notifying you that **You're opening a QuickBooks sample file**

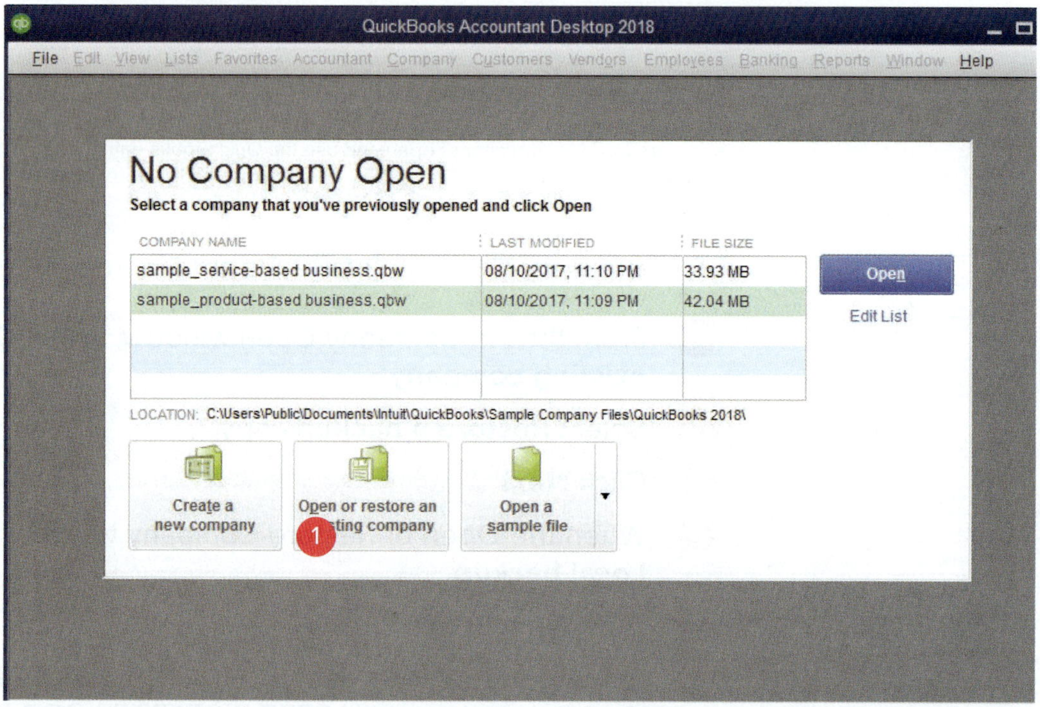

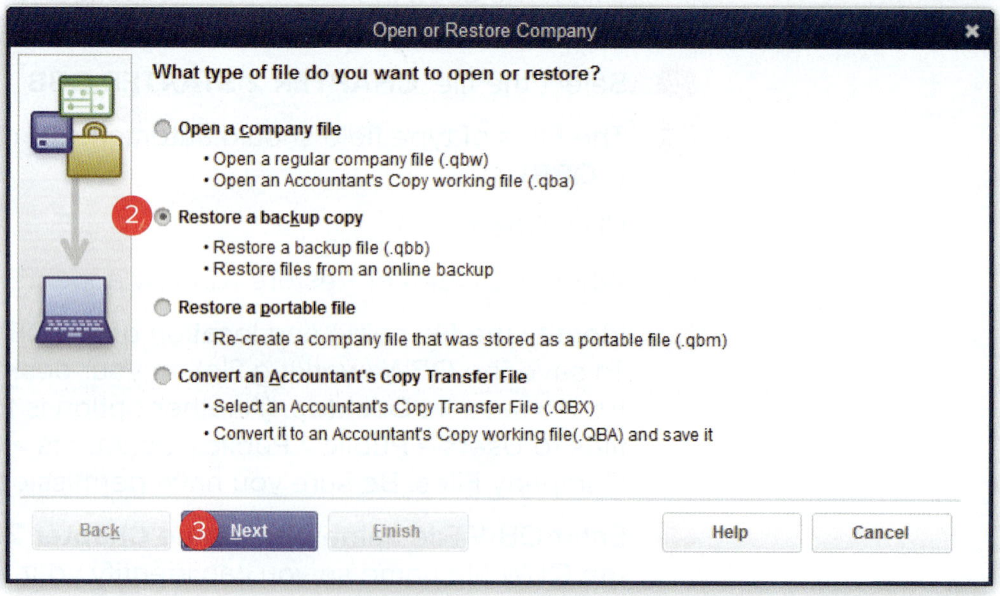

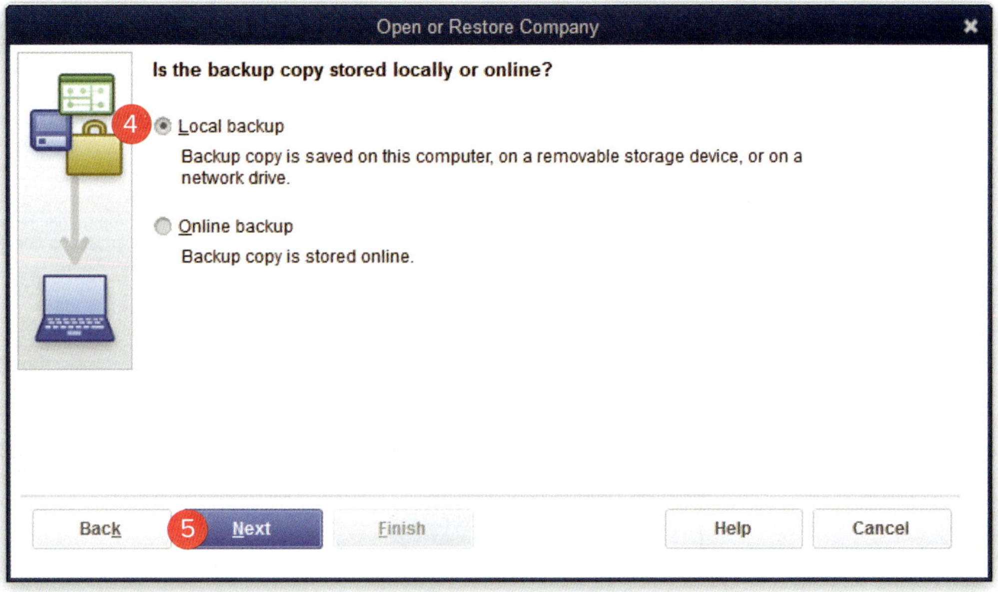
Open or Restore Company
Is the backup copy stored locally or online?
4
Local backup
Backup copy is saved on this computer, on a removable storage device, or on a network drive.
Online backup
Backup copy is stored online.
Back
5
Next
Finish
Help
Cancel

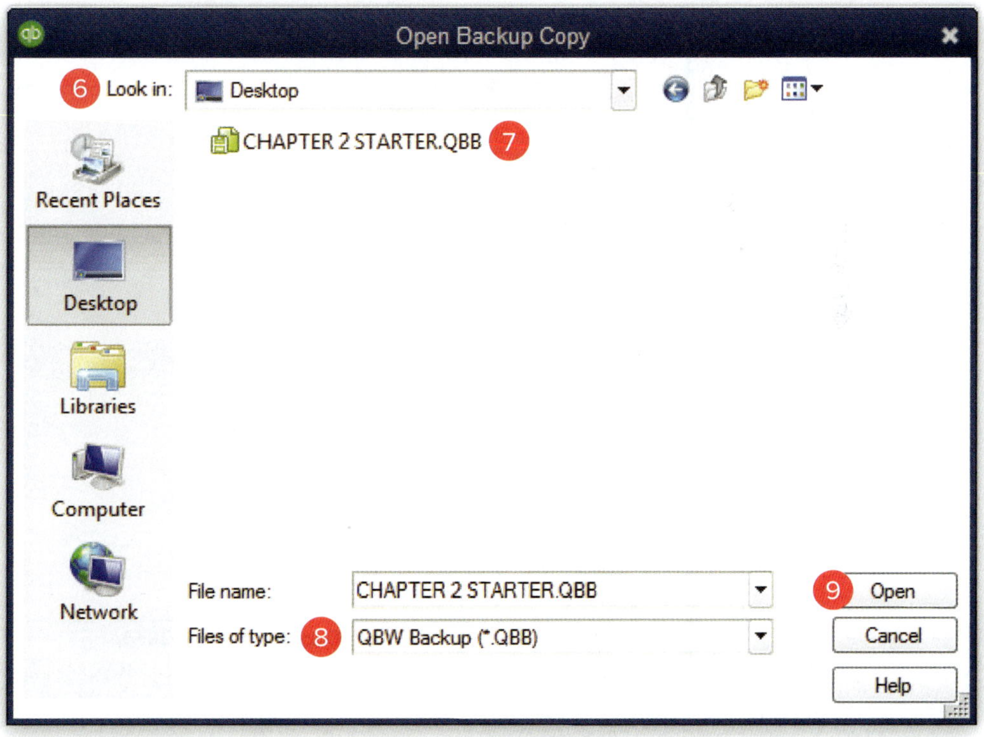
Open Backup Copy
6
Look in:
Desktop
CHAPTER 2 STARTER.QBB
7
Recent Places
Desktop
Libraries
Computer
Network
File name:
CHAPTER 2 STARTER.QBB
9
Open
Files of type:
8
QBW Backup (*.QBB)
Cancel
Help

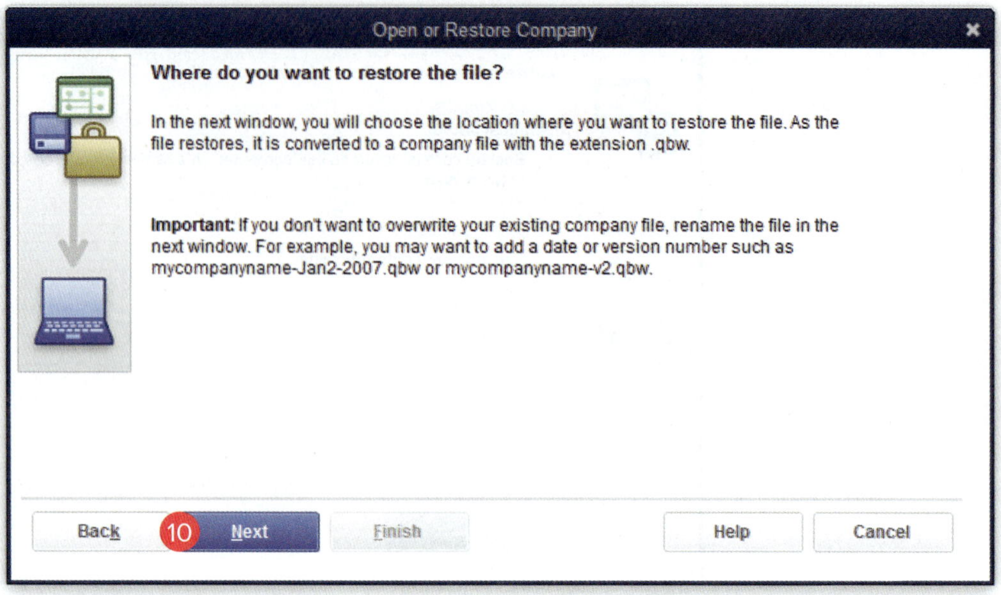
Open or Restore Company
Where do you want to restore the file?
In the next window, you will choose the location where you want to restore the file. As the file restores, it is converted to a company file with the extension .qbw.
Important: If you don't want to overwrite your existing company file, rename the file in the next window. For example, you may want to add a date or version number such as mycompanyname-Jan2-2007.qbw or mycompanyname-v2.qbw.
Back
10
Next
Finish
Help
Cancel

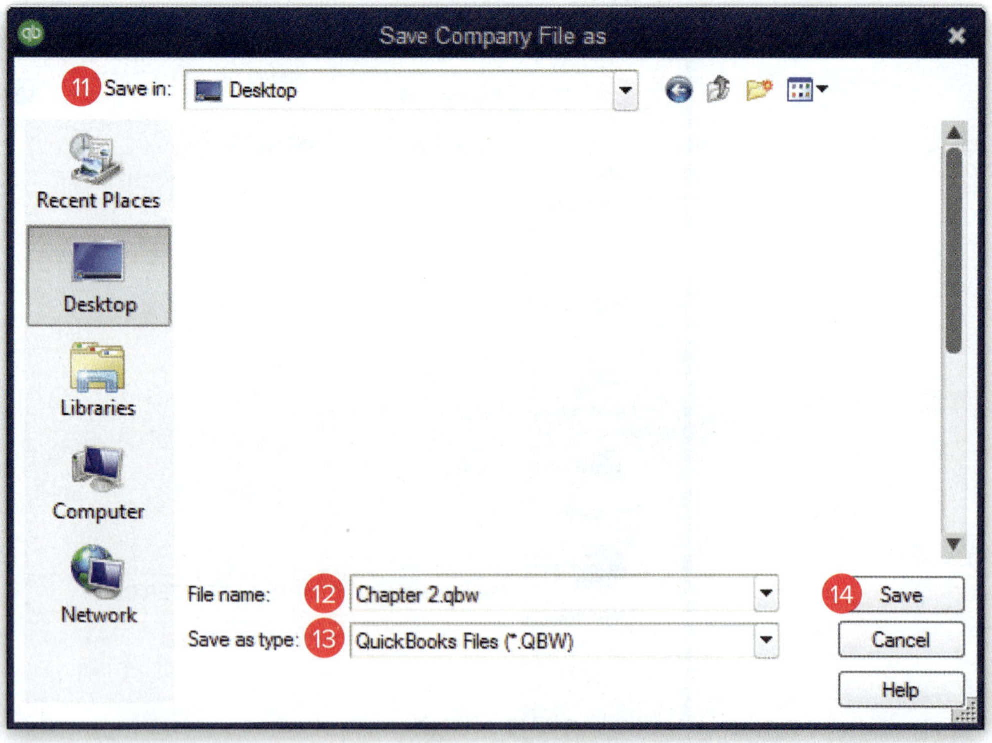
Save Company File as
11
Save in:
Desktop
Recent Places
Desktop
Libraries
Computer
Network
File name:
12
Chapter 2.qbw
Save as type:
13
QuickBooks Files (*.QBW)
14
Save
Cancel
Help

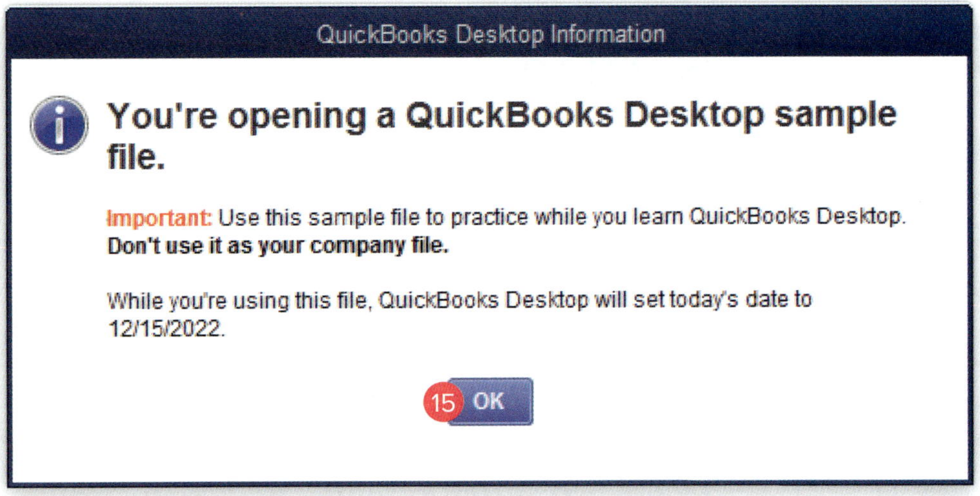

CHANGE COMPANY NAME

So that your name automatically appears on reports and checks, update the Company Name setting to add your name to the company name.

To change a company name in QuickBooks, complete the following:

1. From My Shortcuts on the Navigation Bar, select **My Company**
2. When the My Company window appears, select **Edit**
3. When the Company Information window, update Company Name field to: **YourName Chapter 2 Rock Castle Construction.** Select **OK** to close the Company Information window.
4. **Close** the My Company window

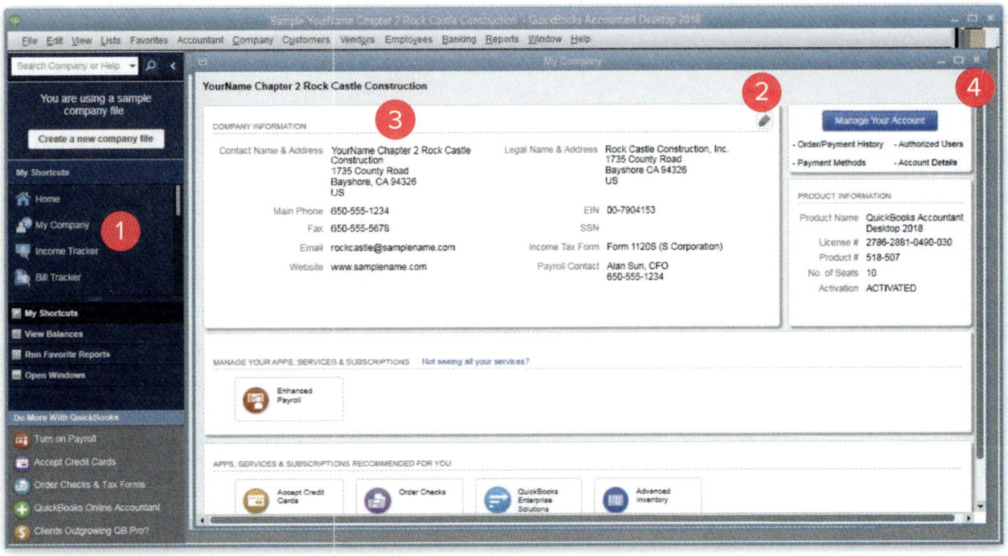

Section 2.3

CUSTOMIZING CHART OF ACCOUNTS (COA)

When we set up a new company, QuickBooks automatically creates a Chart of Accounts. Then we can customize the Chart of Accounts to suit our specific needs by adding, deleting, and editing accounts. By adding, editing, and deleting accounts, we can customize the QuickBooks chart of accounts to align with the business tax return. This can save countless hours when preparing tax reports, reduce errors, and streamline tax return preparation.

> **Customize the Chart of Accounts** to track the information needed for the company's tax return. Obtain a copy of the tax form for the business at www.irs.gov. Then modify the COA to track information needed for the tax return.

Section 2.4

DISPLAY CHART OF ACCOUNTS (COA)

We can display the Chart of Accounts in different ways:

1. From the Company Menu
2. From the Navigation Bar
3. From the Company section of the Home Page

To view the Chart of Accounts for Rock Castle Construction from the Home Page, complete the following steps:

1. Click the **Chart of Accounts** icon in the Company section of the Home Page
2. For each account, the account name, type of account, and the balance of the account are listed. The **Account** button at the bottom of the window displays a drop-down menu for adding, editing, and deleting accounts.
3. Another option is to right-click in the Chart of Accounts window to display a pop-up menu to add and edit accounts.

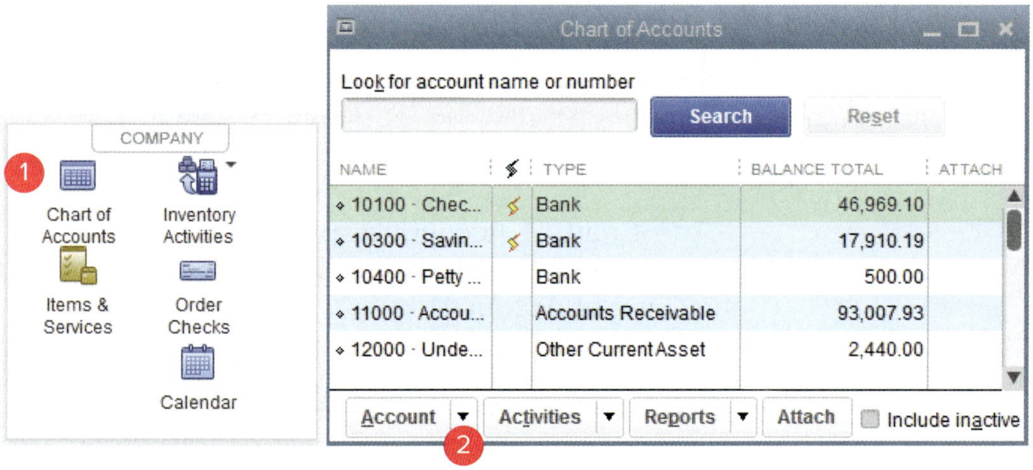

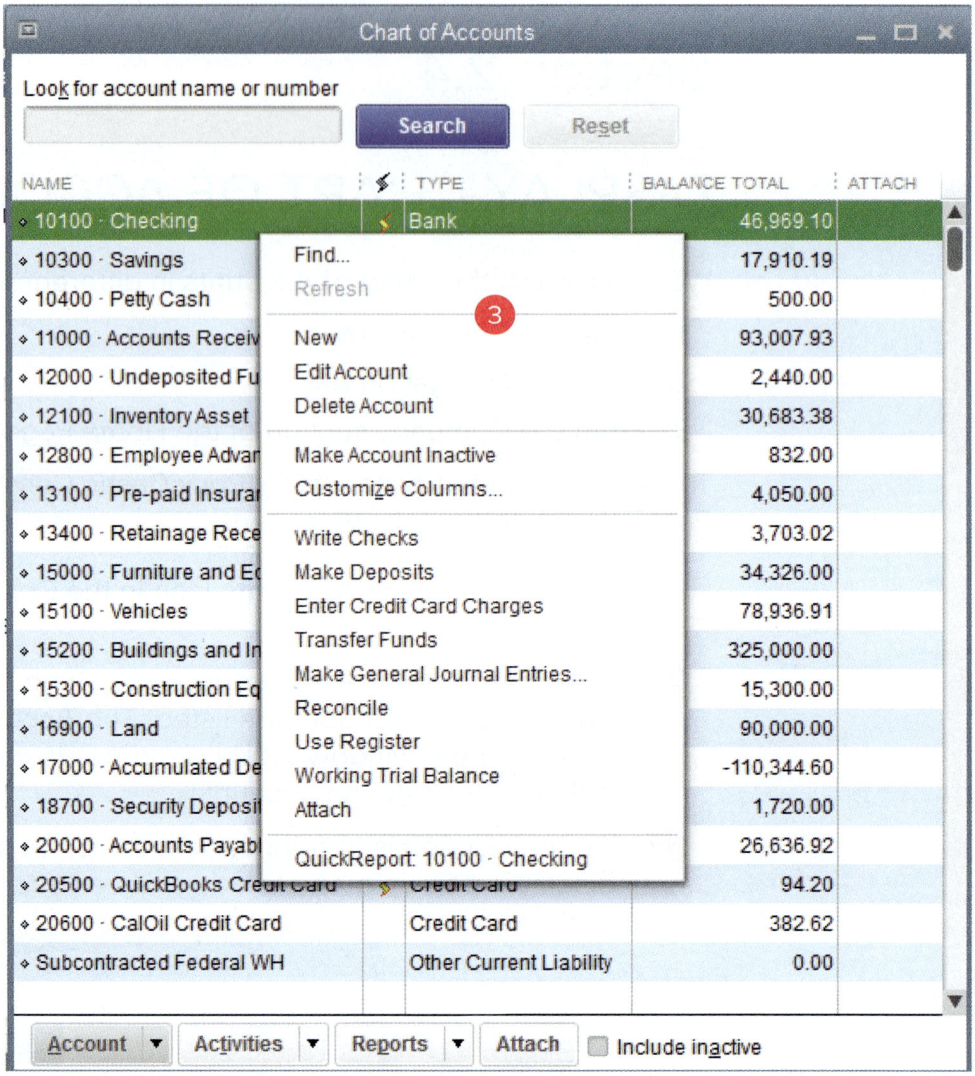

The Chart of Account displays account titles. In addition, sometimes companies prefer to also display account numbers for accounts listed in the Chart of Accounts.

DISPLAY ACCOUNT NUMBERS

Account numbers are used to uniquely identify accounts. Usually account numbers are used as a coding system to also identify the account type. For example, a typical numbering system for accounts might be as follows.

Account Type	Account No.
Asset accounts	10000 – 19999
Liability accounts	20000 – 29999
Equity accounts	30000 – 39999
Revenue (income) accounts	40000 – 49999
Expense accounts	50000 – 59999

Account type determines whether the account appears on the Balance Sheet or Income Statement.

QuickBooks preferences will determine whether the account number is displayed in the Chart of Accounts. If account numbers are not displayed in Rock Castle Construction's Chart of Accounts, select the QuickBooks preference to view account numbers as follows.

1. Select **Edit Menu**
2. Select **Preferences**
3. When the Preferences window appears, click the **Accounting** icon in the left scrollbar
4. Then select the **Company Preferences** tab
5. Select **Use account numbers** to display the account numbers in the Chart of Accounts
6. Then click **OK.** (If the Chart of Accounts does not appear on your screen, click **Window Menu** > **Chart of Accounts.**)

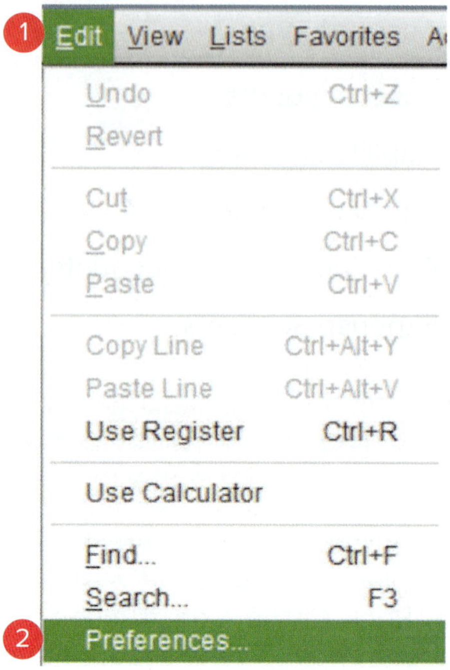

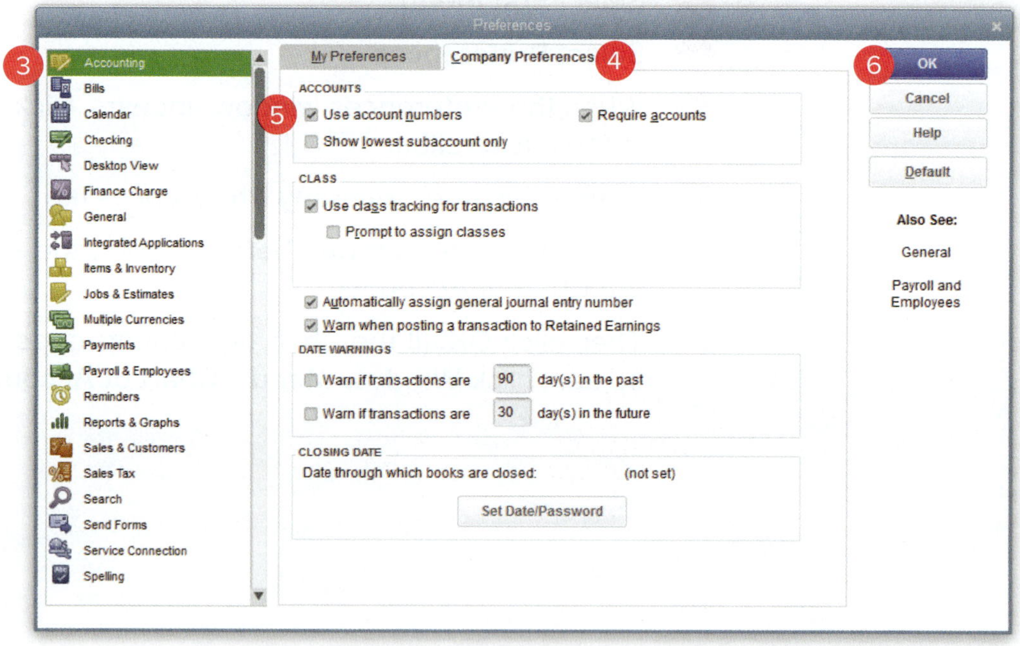

The Chart of Accounts should now list account numbers preceding the account name.

Section 2.5

ADD NEW ACCOUNTS

We can customize the Chart of Accounts by adding, deleting, and editing accounts as needed to meet our company's specific and changing needs.

Rock Castle Construction has decided to begin advertising and would like to add an Advertising Expense account to the Chart of Accounts.

To add a new account to the Chart of Accounts:

1. Click the **Account** button at the bottom of the Chart of Accounts window to display a drop-down menu
2. Select **New**
3. Select Account Type: **Expense**
4. Click **Continue**
5. In the Add New Account window, verify the Account Type: **Expense**
6. Enter the new Account Number: **60400**
7. Enter the Account Name: **Advertising Expense**
8. Leave **Subaccount unchecked.** Subaccounts are subcategories of an account.
9. Select Tax-Line Mapping: **Deductions: Advertising.** This indicates the Advertising Expense account balance will appear as a deduction on Rock Castle Construction's tax return. Selecting the appropriate Tax Line ensures that QuickBooks provides the information needed to complete your tax return.
10. Click **Save & Close** to save the changes and close the Add New Account window

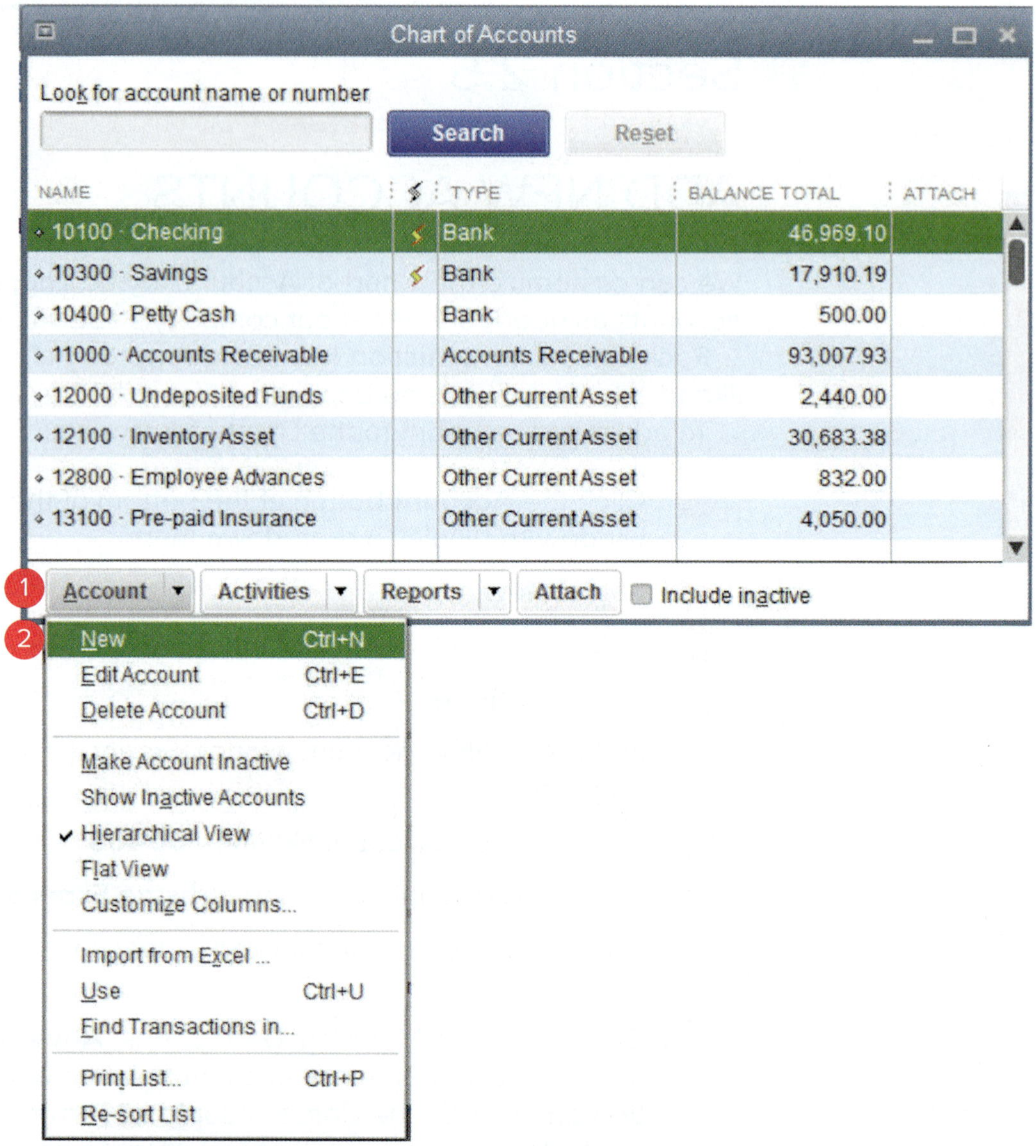
Chart of Accounts
Look for account name or number
Search
Reset
NAME
TYPE
BALANCE TOTAL
ATTACH
10100 · Checking
Bank
46,969.10
10300 · Savings
Bank
17,910.19
10400 · Petty Cash
Bank
500.00
11000 · Accounts Receivable
Accounts Receivable
93,007.93
12000 · Undeposited Funds
Other Current Asset
2,440.00
12100 · Inventory Asset
Other Current Asset
30,683.38
12800 · Employee Advances
Other Current Asset
832.00
13100 · Pre-paid Insurance
Other Current Asset
4,050.00
1
Account
Activities
Reports
Attach
Include inactive
2
New Ctrl+N
Edit Account Ctrl+E
Delete Account Ctrl+D
Make Account Inactive
Show Inactive Accounts
Hierarchical View
Flat View
Customize Columns...
Import from Excel ...
Use Ctrl+U
Find Transactions in...
Print List... Ctrl+P
Re-sort List

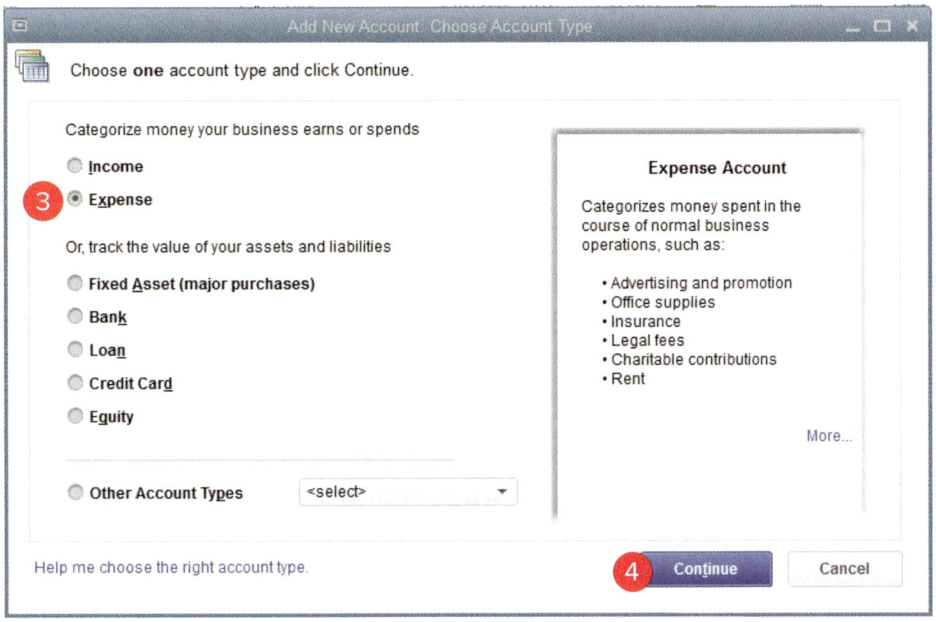

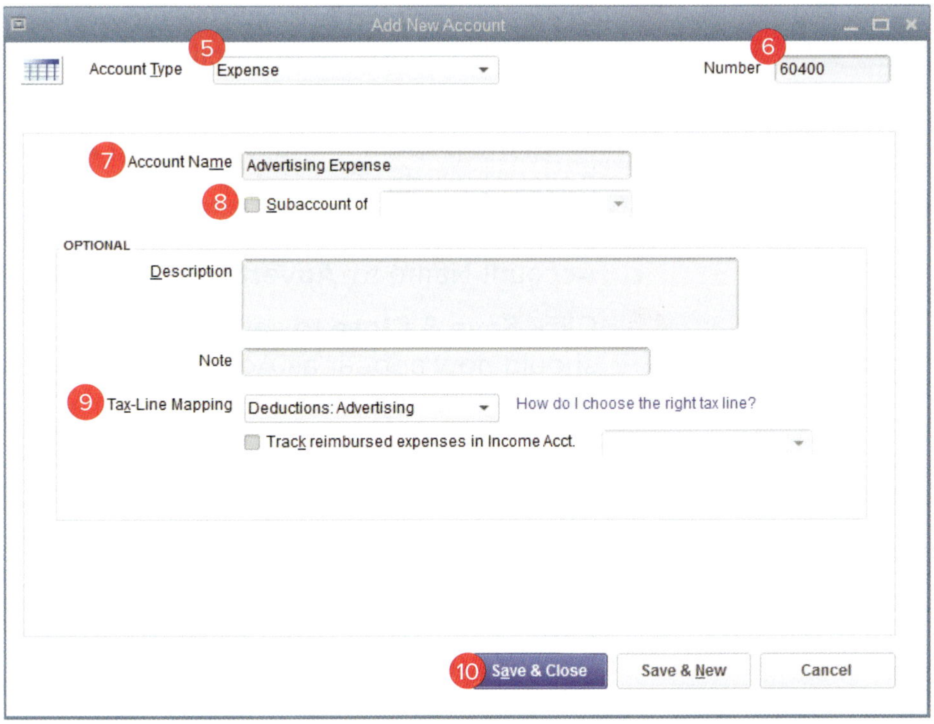

Notice that Account 60400 Advertising Expense now appears on the Chart of Accounts.

If the new account had been a Balance Sheet account (an asset, liability, or equity account), QuickBooks would ask you for the opening account balance as of your QuickBooks start date. Since Advertising Expense is an Expense account that appears on the Income Statement and not the Balance Sheet, QuickBooks did not ask for the opening balance.

Section 2.6

EDIT ACCOUNTS

Next, we will edit an account. Rock Castle Construction would like to change the name of the Advertising Expense account to Advertising & Promotion.

To change the name of the Advertising Expense account to Advertising & Promotion:

1. Select **View Menu > Open Window List** to display all open windows. From the Open Window List, select the Chart of Accounts window. From the Chart of Accounts window, select the account to edit: **60400 Advertising Expense.**
2. Click the **Account** button in the lower left corner of the Chart of Accounts window or **right-click** the mouse to display the pop-up menu
3. From the pop-up menu, select **Edit Account** to open the Edit Account window
4. Make changes to the account information. In this case, change Account Name to: **Advertising & Promotion.**
5. Click **Save & Close** to save the changes. Advertising Expense should now appear as Advertising & Promotion in the Chart of Accounts window.

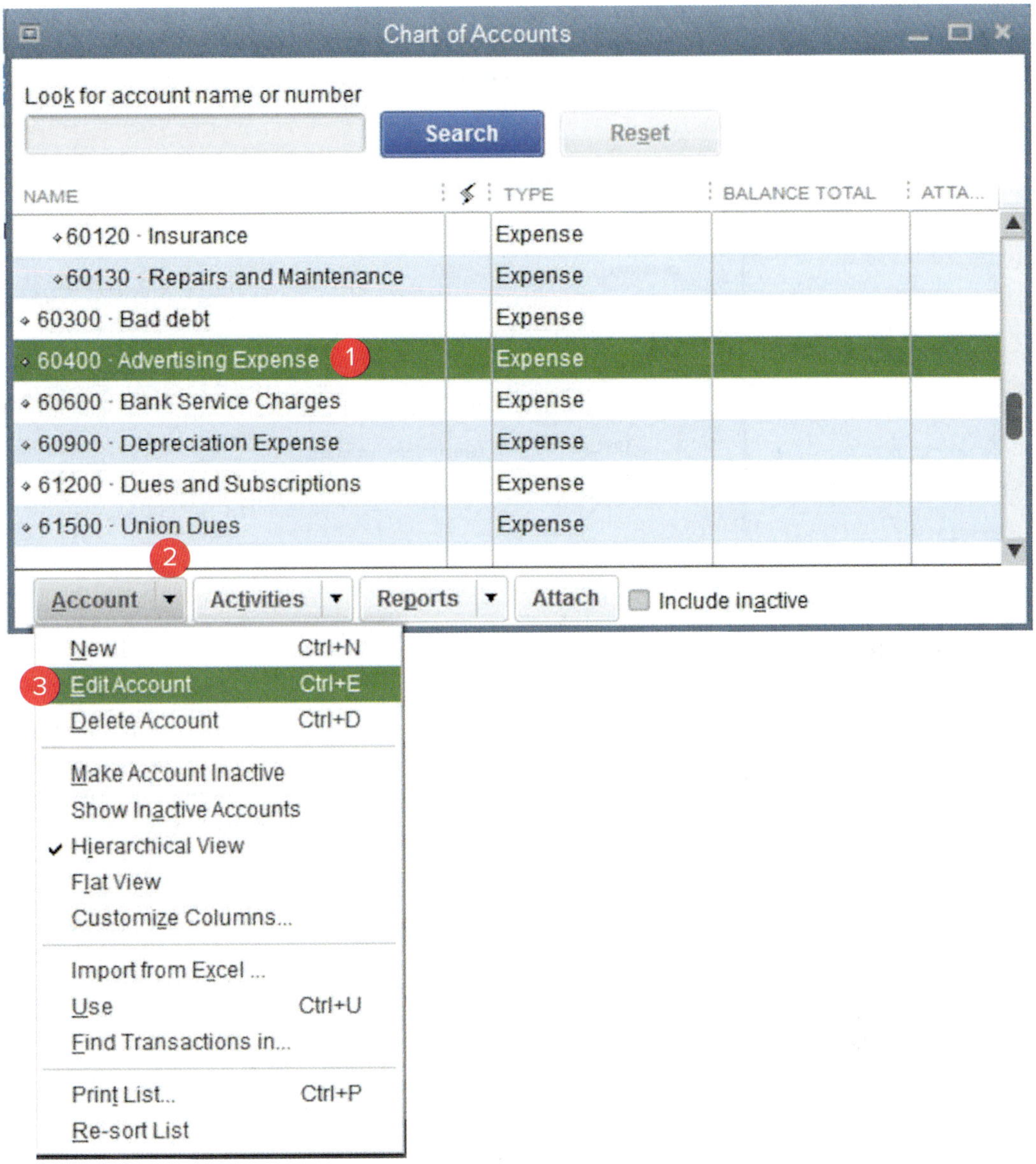
Chart of Accounts
Look for account name or number
Search
Reset
NAME
TYPE
BALANCE TOTAL
ATTA...
60120 · Insurance
Expense
60130 · Repairs and Maintenance
Expense
60300 · Bad debt
Expense
60400 · Advertising Expense
1
Expense
60600 · Bank Service Charges
Expense
60900 · Depreciation Expense
Expense
61200 · Dues and Subscriptions
Expense
61500 · Union Dues
Expense
2
Account
Activities
Reports
Attach
Include inactive
New Ctrl+N
3
Edit Account Ctrl+E
Delete Account Ctrl+D
Make Account Inactive
Show Inactive Accounts
Hierarchical View
Flat View
Customize Columns...
Import from Excel ...
Use Ctrl+U
Find Transactions in...
Print List... Ctrl+P
Re-sort List

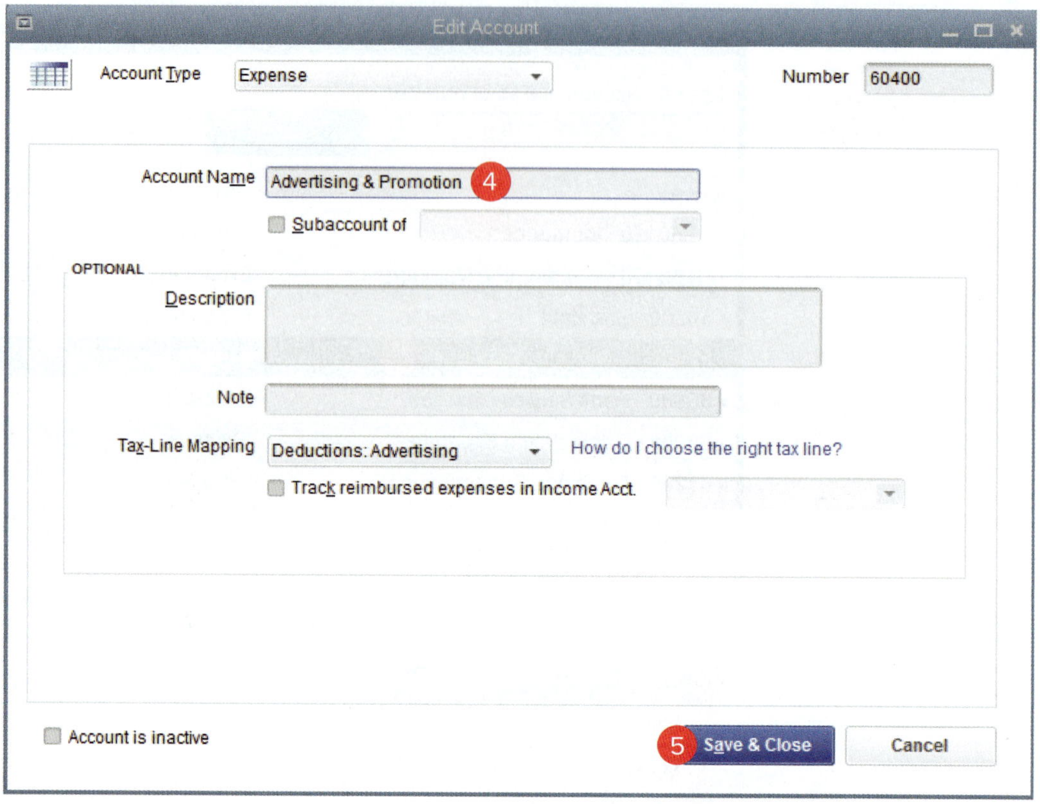
Edit Account
Account Type
Expense
Number
60400
Account Name
Advertising & Promotion
4
Subaccount of
OPTIONAL
Description
Note
Tax-Line Mapping
Deductions: Advertising
How do I choose the right tax line?
Track reimbursed expenses in Income Acct.
Account is inactive
5
Save & Close
Cancel

Section 2.7

DELETE ACCOUNTS

Occasionally we may want to delete unused accounts from the Chart of Accounts. We can only delete accounts that are not being used. For example, if an account has been used to record a transaction and has a balance, it cannot be deleted. If an account has subaccounts associated with it, that account cannot be deleted.

Rock Castle Construction would like to delete an account it does not plan to use, the Printing and Reproduction Expense account.

To delete an account:

1. From the Chart of Accounts window, select the account to delete. In this case, click **63300: Printing and Reproduction.**
2. Click the **Account** button at the bottom of the Chart of Accounts window
3. Click **Delete Account**
4. Click **OK** to confirm that you want to delete the account

Section 2.8

CREATE CHART OF ACCOUNTS REPORT

QuickBooks provides an Account Listing report that lists the Chart of Accounts plus the account balances.

First, re-sort the Chart of Accounts list as follows:

1. From the Chart of Accounts window, select the **Account** button
2. Select **Re-sort List**
3. When the Re-sort List? Window appears, select **OK**
4. **Close** the Chart of Accounts window

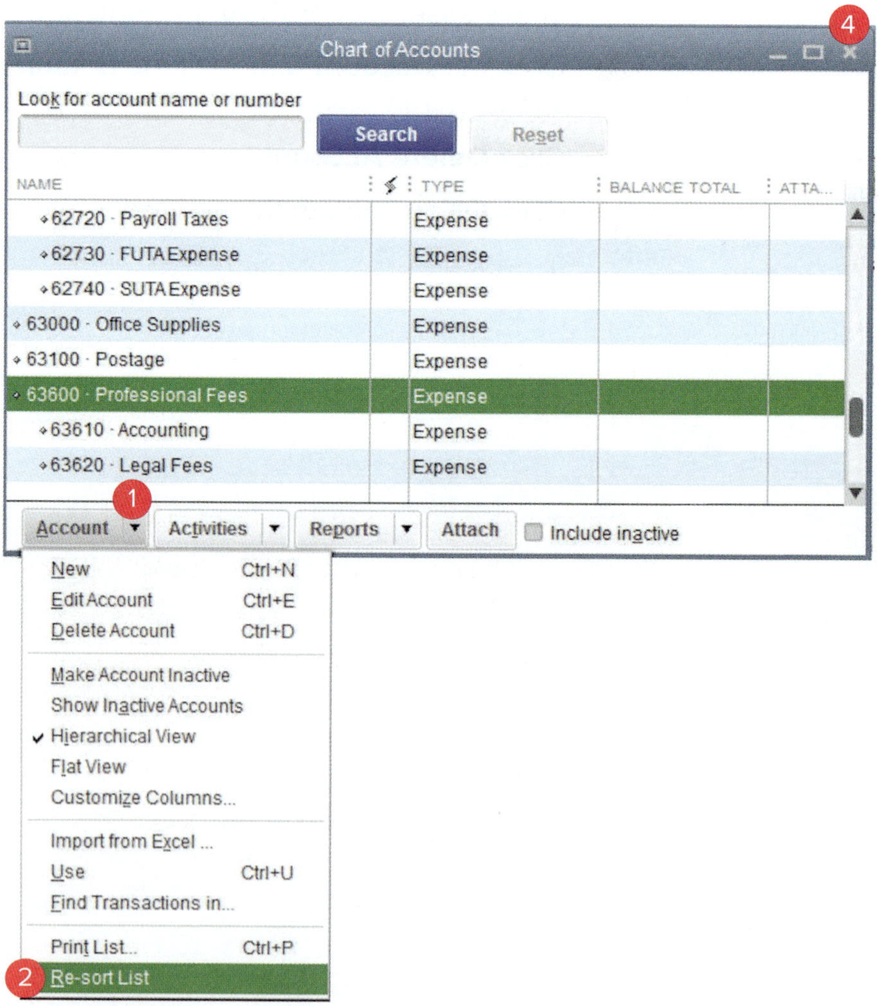

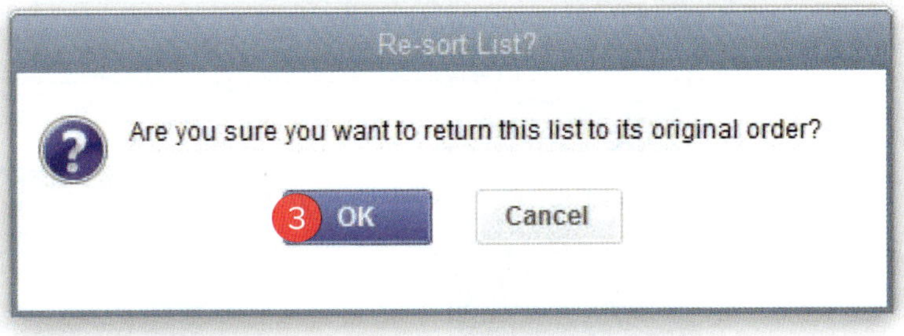

C2.8.1 Chart of Accounts. To create the Chart of Accounts (Account Listing) report:

1. Select **Reports** in the My Shortcuts section of the Navigation Bar
2. Select **Accountants & Taxes**
3. Select **Account Listing**
4. Select Date: **12/15/2022**
5. Select **Run**
6. To export the Account Listing report to Excel, at the top of the Account Listing window select **Excel**
7. Select **Create New Worksheet**
8. When the Send Report to Excel window appears, select **Replace an existing worksheet**
9. Browse for **YourLastName FirstName CH2 REPORTS** Excel file
10. From the drop-down list, select the sheet: **C2.8.1 COA**
11. Select the **Advanced** button
12. **Uncheck Space between columns**
13. **Uncheck Include QuickBooks Export Guide worksheet with helpful advice**
14. Select Show report header: **On printed report and screen**
15. Click **OK**
16. Click **Export**

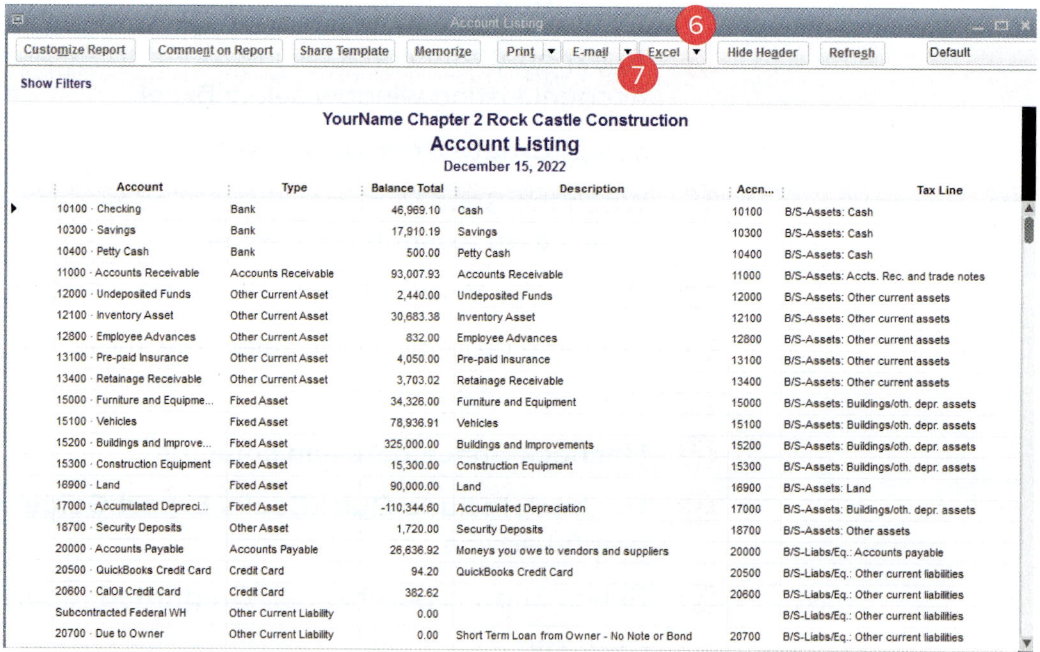

YourName Chapter 2 Rock Castle Construction
Account Listing
December 15, 2022

Account	Type	Balance Total	Description	Accn...	Tax Line
10100 · Checking	Bank	46,969.10	Cash	10100	B/S-Assets: Cash
10300 · Savings	Bank	17,910.19	Savings	10300	B/S-Assets: Cash
10400 · Petty Cash	Bank	500.00	Petty Cash	10400	B/S-Assets: Cash
11000 · Accounts Receivable	Accounts Receivable	93,007.93	Accounts Receivable	11000	B/S-Assets: Accts. Rec. and trade notes
12000 · Undeposited Funds	Other Current Asset	2,440.00	Undeposited Funds	12000	B/S-Assets: Other current assets
12100 · Inventory Asset	Other Current Asset	30,683.38	Inventory Asset	12100	B/S-Assets: Other current assets
12800 · Employee Advances	Other Current Asset	832.00	Employee Advances	12800	B/S-Assets: Other current assets
13100 · Pre-paid Insurance	Other Current Asset	4,050.00	Pre-paid Insurance	13100	B/S-Assets: Other current assets
13400 · Retainage Receivable	Other Current Asset	3,703.02	Retainage Receivable	13400	B/S-Assets: Other current assets
15000 · Furniture and Equipme...	Fixed Asset	34,326.00	Furniture and Equipment	15000	B/S-Assets: Buildings/oth. depr. assets
15100 · Vehicles	Fixed Asset	78,936.91	Vehicles	15100	B/S-Assets: Buildings/oth. depr. assets
15200 · Buildings and Improve...	Fixed Asset	325,000.00	Buildings and Improvements	15200	B/S-Assets: Buildings/oth. depr. assets
15300 · Construction Equipment	Fixed Asset	15,300.00	Construction Equipment	15300	B/S-Assets: Buildings/oth. depr. assets
16900 · Land	Fixed Asset	90,000.00	Land	16900	B/S-Assets: Land
17000 · Accumulated Depreci...	Fixed Asset	-110,344.60	Accumulated Depreciation	17000	B/S-Assets: Buildings/oth. depr. assets
18700 · Security Deposits	Other Asset	1,720.00	Security Deposits	18700	B/S-Assets: Other assets
20000 · Accounts Payable	Accounts Payable	26,636.92	Moneys you owe to vendors and suppliers	20000	B/S-Liabs/Eq.: Accounts payable
20500 · QuickBooks Credit Card	Credit Card	94.20	QuickBooks Credit Card	20500	B/S-Liabs/Eq.: Other current liabilities
20600 · CalOil Credit Card	Credit Card	382.62		20600	B/S-Liabs/Eq.: Other current liabilities
Subcontracted Federal WH	Other Current Liability	0.00			B/S-Liabs/Eq.: Other current liabilities
20700 · Due to Owner	Other Current Liability	0.00	Short Term Loan from Owner - No Note or Bond	20700	B/S-Liabs/Eq.: Other current liabilities

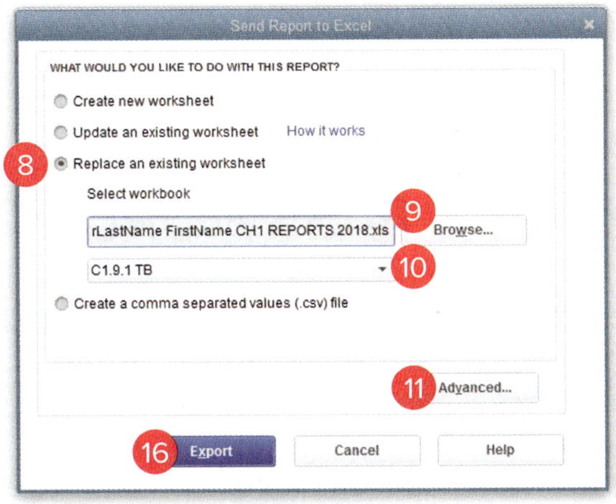

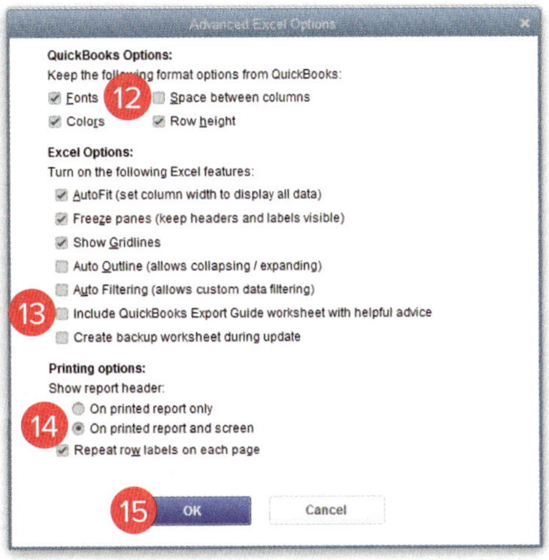

Excel software should open on your screen with your QuickBooks report.

1. Select the **2 REPORTS** sheet tab
2. Mark the report you have completed by inserting an "**X**"
3. Save your **CH2 REPORTS** Excel workbook using the filename: **YourLastName FirstName CH2 REPORTS**
4. **Close** the Account Listing window

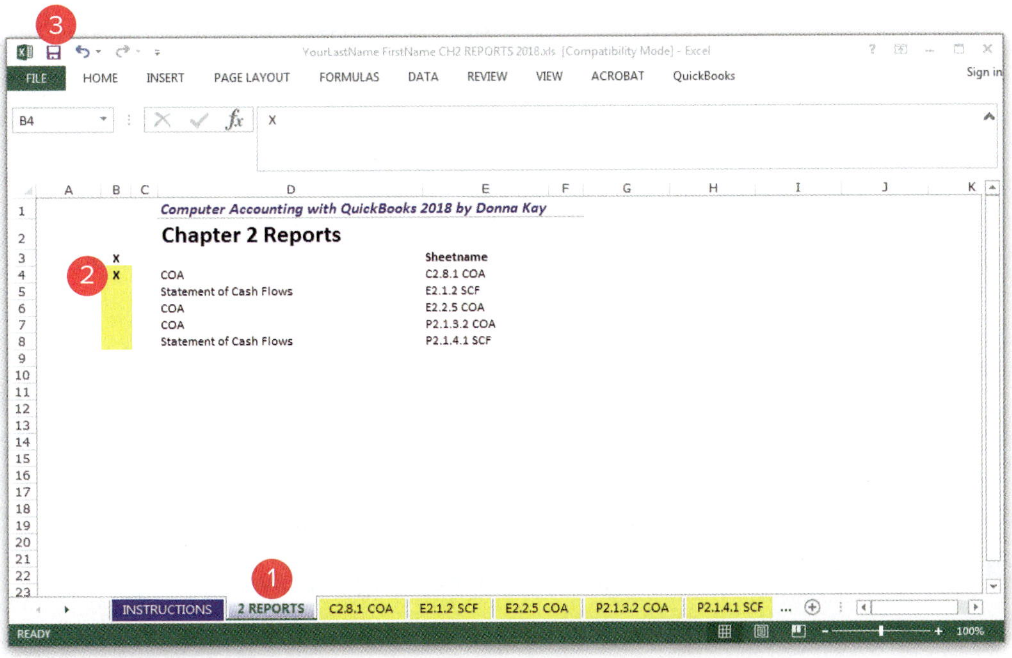

Section 2.9

QUICKBOOKS PASSWORD PROTECTION

QuickBooks permits a company to conveniently collect accounting information and store it in a single file. Much of the accounting information stored in QuickBooks is confidential, however, and a company often wants to limit employee access.

Password protection can be used to customize and limit access to company data and improve security and control.

Two ways to restrict access to accounting information stored in a QuickBooks company data file are:

1. Password protect the company file so individuals must enter a user ID and password to open the company file.
2. Limit access to selected areas of the company's accounting data. For example, a user may access accounts receivable to view customer balances but not be able to access payroll or check writing.

Only the QuickBooks Administrator can add users with passwords and grant user access to selected areas of QuickBooks. The QuickBooks Administrator is an individual who has access to all areas of QuickBooks.

To add a new user and password protection to your company file:

1. Select **Company Menu**
2. Select **Set Up Users and Passwords**
3. Select **Set Up Users**
4. First, set up a QuickBooks Administrator who has access to all areas of QuickBooks. The Administrator can then add new users. To add the Administrator password, from the User List window, select **Admin.**
5. Select **Edit User**
6. On the Change user password and access window, enter and confirm a **Password** of your choice. ***Write the password on the inside cover of your text.***
7. Select a **Challenge Question**
8. Enter your **Challenge Answer**
9. Click **Next**
10. Click **Finish**

11 Only the QuickBooks Administrator can add new users. To add another user, click **Add User.**

12 In the following Set up user password and access window, enter **YourName** in the User Name field

13 At this point, if you were adding another employee as a user, you would ask the employee to enter and confirm his or her password. In this instance, enter and confirm a **password** of your choice. ***Write the password on the inside cover of your book.***

14 Click **Next**

15 In the following window, you can restrict user access to selected areas of QuickBooks or give the user access to all areas of QuickBooks. Select: **All areas of QuickBooks.**

16 Click **Next**

17 Select **Yes** to confirm that you want to give access to all areas of QuickBooks

18 The next window summarizes the user's access for each QuickBooks area, indicating access to create documents, print, and view reports. Click **Finish.**

19 Two names (Admin and YourName) should appear on the User List

20 Click **Close** to close the User List window

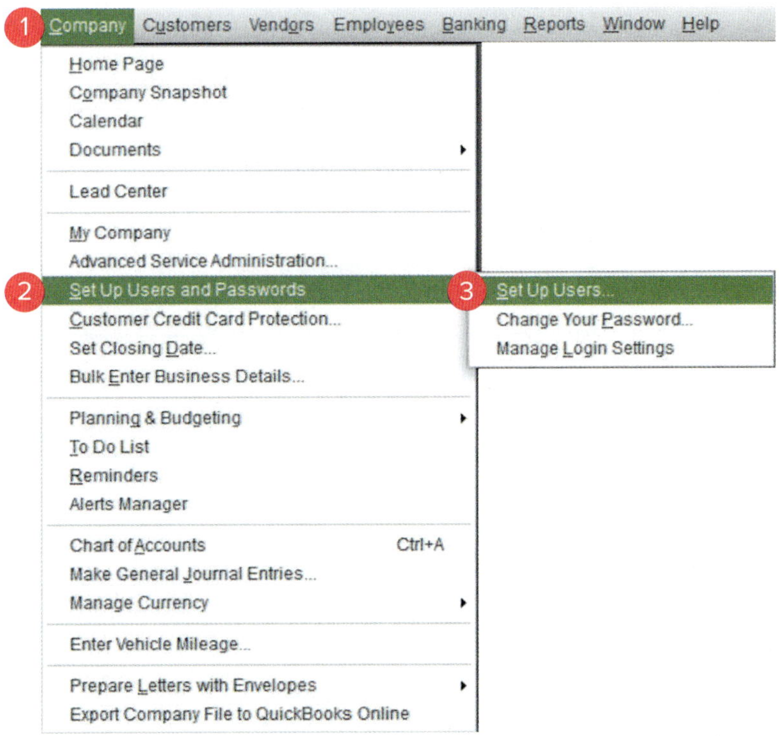

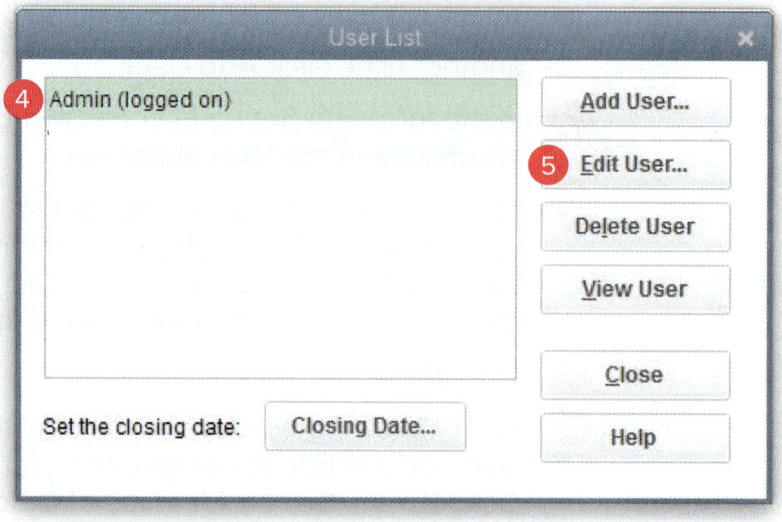
User List
4
Admin (logged on)
Add User...
5
Edit User...
Delete User
View User
Close
Set the closing date:
Closing Date...
Help

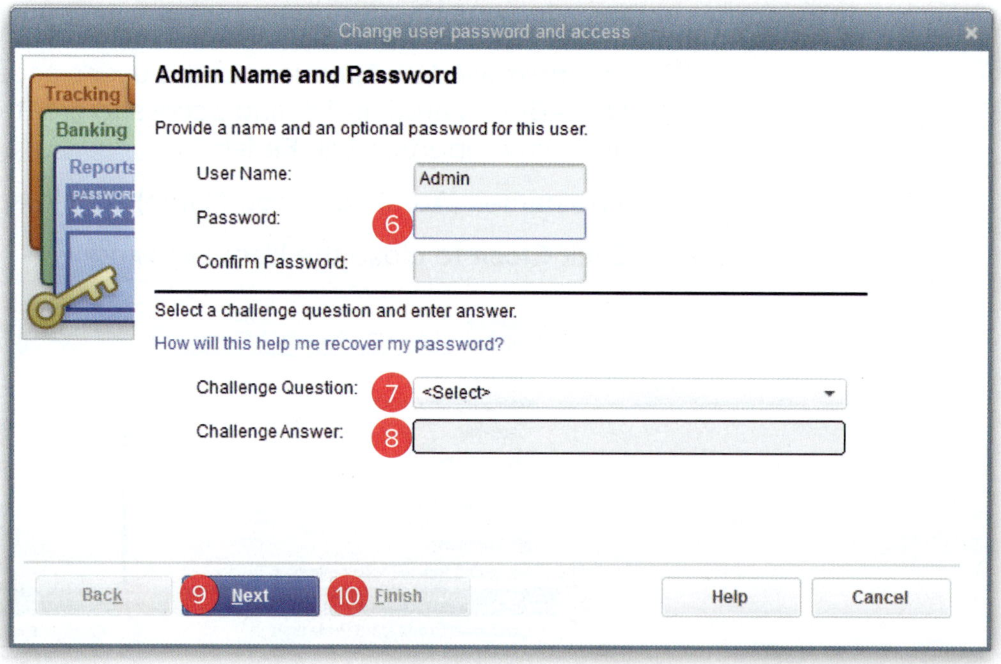
Change user password and access
Tracking
Banking
Reports
PASSWORD
Admin Name and Password
Provide a name and an optional password for this user.
User Name:
Admin
Password:
6
Confirm Password:
Select a challenge question and enter answer.
How will this help me recover my password?
Challenge Question:
7
<Select>
Challenge Answer:
8
Back
9
Next
10
Finish
Help
Cancel

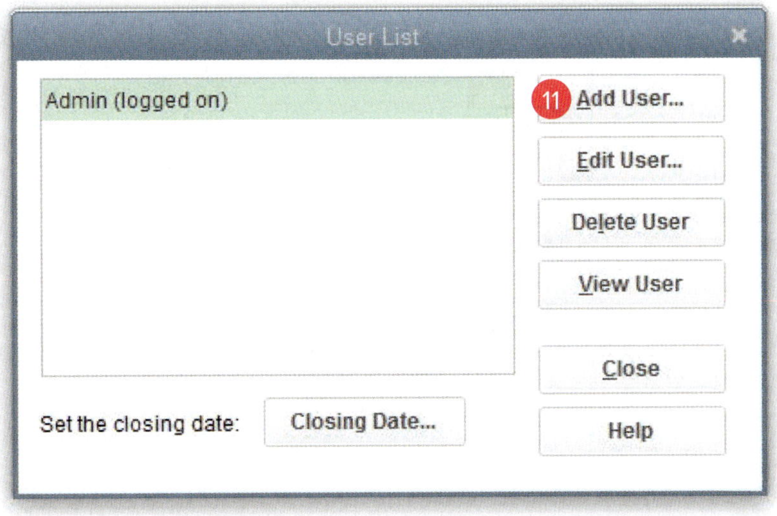
User List
Admin (logged on)
11 Add User...
Edit User...
Delete User
View User
Close
Set the closing date:
Closing Date...
Help

Set up user password and access
User Name and Password
Provide a name and an optional password for this user.
User Name:
12 YourName
Password:
13
Confirm Password:
Tracking
Banking
Reports
Back
14 Next
Finish
Help
Cancel

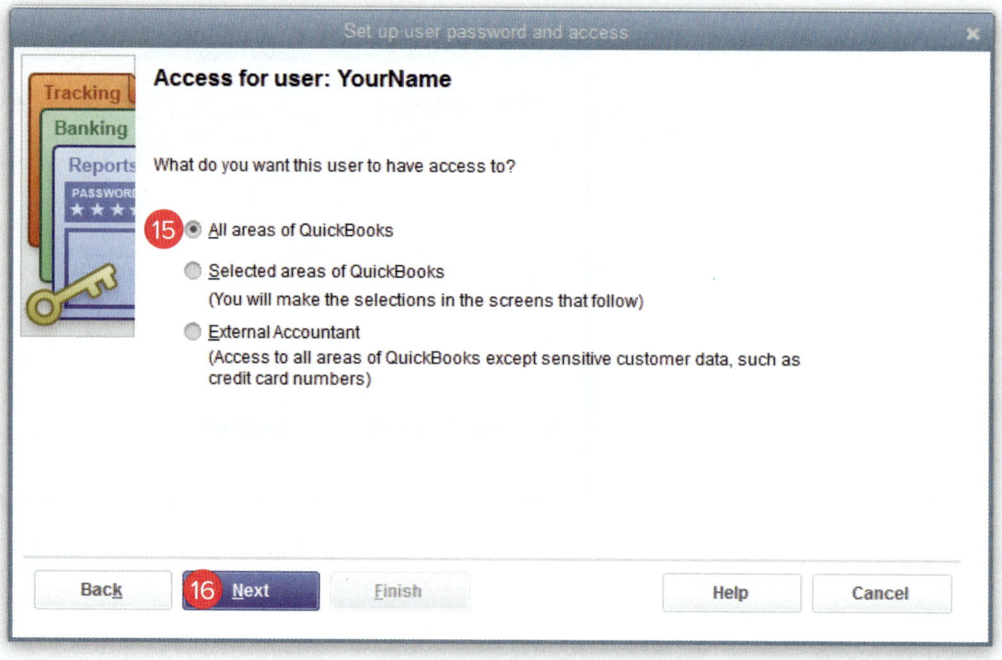
Set up user password and access
Tracking
Banking
Reports
PASSWORD
Access for user: YourName
What do you want this user to have access to?
15
All areas of QuickBooks
Selected areas of QuickBooks
(You will make the selections in the screens that follow)
External Accountant
(Access to all areas of QuickBooks except sensitive customer data, such as credit card numbers)
Back
16
Next
Finish
Help
Cancel

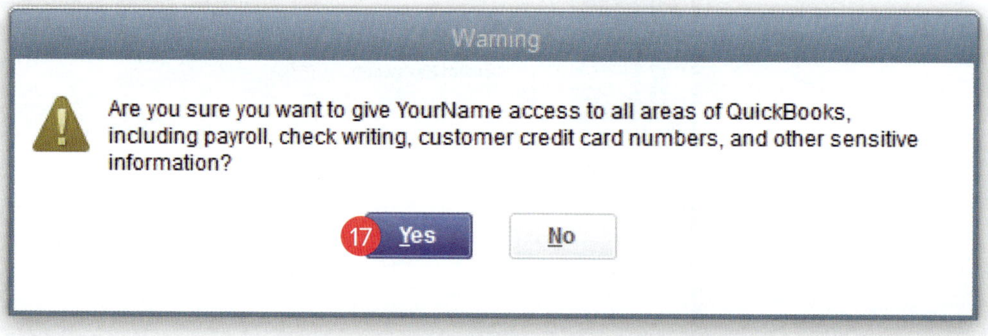
Warning
Are you sure you want to give YourName access to all areas of QuickBooks, including payroll, check writing, customer credit card numbers, and other sensitive information?
17
Yes
No

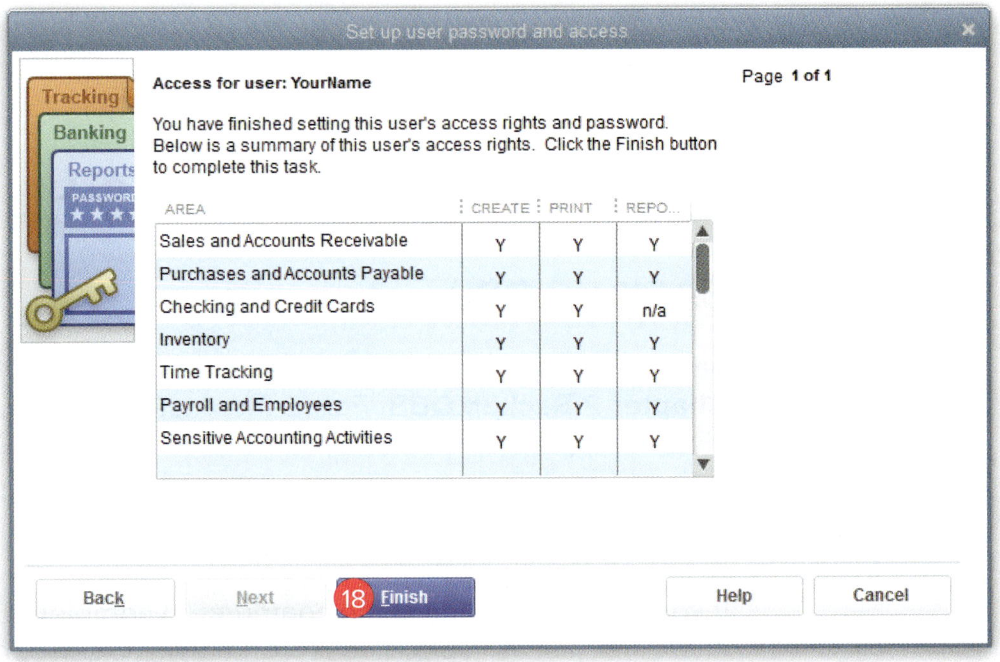

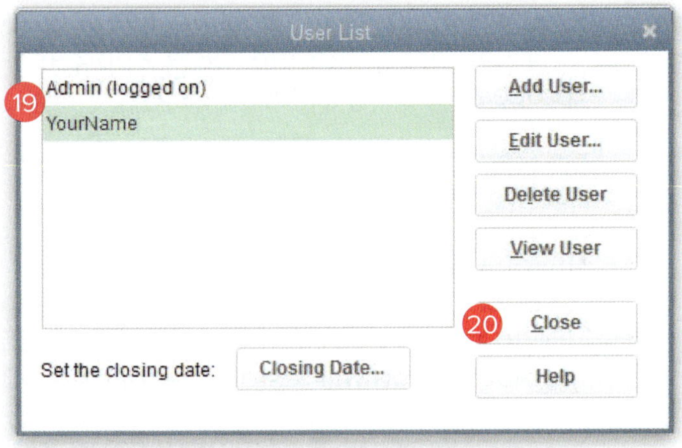

Notice User Access Rights are set by Areas: Create, Print, Reports.

Now whenever you open the company file for Rock Castle Construction, you will be asked to enter your user name and password.

! **Write your password** on the inside of your book cover. You will not be able to access your company file without your password.

! **If you use QBB STARTER FILES** provided with the text and a password screen appears, use log in Admin and leave the password blank. If that does not work, see www.My-QuickBooks.com for more information or contact your instructor.

Section 2.10

BACK UP QUICKBOOKS FILES

BACK UP QBB

Save a backup of your Chapter 2 file using the file name: **YourName Chapter 2 Backup.QBB.** For further instructions on how to back up your file, *see Appendix B: Back Up & Restore QuickBooks Files.*

QBW WORKFLOW

If you will be using the same computer to complete Chapter 2 QuickBooks exercises, just as in a business workflow, you can continue to use the same QBW file. You will make backups at the end of each exercise. However, you will only use the backup if your QBW file fails.

If you are using the QBW approach, leave your .QBW file open and proceed directly to Exercise 2.1.

QBB RESTORE

If you will be switching computers, after you finish your QuickBooks work session, you will back up to a QBB file in order to move your QuickBooks file to another computer. When you restart your work session on another computer, you will restore the backup (QBB) file.

If you are using the QBB approach, and are ending your computer session now, close your QBW file and exit QuickBooks. When you restart, you will restore your backup file to complete Exercise 2.1.

Section 2.11

ACCOUNTING ESSENTIALS

Chart of Accounts

Accounting Essentials summarize important foundational accounting knowledge that may be useful when using QuickBooks

What is the primary objective of accounting?

- The primary objective of accounting is to provide information for decision making. Businesses use a financial system, such as QuickBooks Online, to capture, track, sort, summarize, and communicate financial information.

How is financial information for decision making provided?

- Financial reports summarize and communicate information about a company's financial position and business operations.

What is the difference between financial reports and financial statements?

- Financial statements are standardized financial reports that summarize information about past transactions. Financial statements are provided to external users and internal users for decision making. External users include bankers, creditors, and investors.
- Internal users include managers and employees of the business.

What are the main financial statements for a business?

- The primary financial statements for a business are:
- **Balance Sheet** summarizes what a company owns and owes on a particular date.
- **Profit & Loss Statement** (also referred to as P & L or Income Statement) summarizes the income a company has earned and the expenses incurred to earn the income.
- **Statement of Cash Flows** summarizes cash inflows and cash outflows for operating, investing, and financing activities of a business.

What is a Chart of Accounts?

- **Chart of Accounts (COA)** is a list of all the accounts and account numbers for a business. Accounts are used to sort and track accounting information. For example, a business needs one account for cash, another account to track amounts customers owe (Accounts Receivable), and yet another account to track inventory.

Why Use Accounts?

- We use **accounts** to record transactions in our accounting system. Accounts (such as the Checking account or Insurance Expense account) permit us to sort, organize, summarize, and track information.
- We can add **subaccounts** for even better tracking. Example: We could add subaccounts Rental Insurance Expense and Liability Insurance Expense as subaccounts to our Insurance Expense account. (It's the best of both worlds. We have additional detail of subaccounts Rental Insurance and Liability Insurance Expense and the subaccounts roll up into the total for the parent account, Insurance Expense.)

What are the Different Types of Accounts?

- We can group accounts into the following different account types:

Balance Sheet accounts			**Profit and Loss accounts**	
Assets	**Liability**	**Equity**	**Income**	**Expense**
Bank account	Accounts Payable	Capital Investment	Sales	Supplies Expense
Accounts Receivable	Credit Cards Payable	Retained Earnings	Consulting Fees	Rent Expense
Equipment	Loans Payable		Interest Income	Utilities Expense

What are Balance Sheet Accounts?

- The Balance Sheet is a financial statement that summarizes what a company owns and what it owes.
- Balance Sheet accounts are accounts that appear on the company's Balance Sheet.

- Three types of accounts appear on the Balance Sheet:
    1. Assets
    2. Liabilities
    3. Owners' (or Stockholders') Equity

1. **Assets** are resources that a company owns. These resources are expected to have future benefit.

    Asset accounts include:

    - Cash.
    - Accounts receivable (amounts to be *received* from customers in the future).
    - Inventory.
    - Other current assets (assets likely to be converted to cash or consumed within one year).
    - Fixed assets (property used in the operations of the business, such as equipment, buildings, and land).
    - Intangible assets (such as copyrights, patents, trademarks, and franchises).

How Do We Know if an Account is an Asset?

Ask:

Will our enterprise receive a *future benefit* from the item? (For example, prepaid insurance has future benefit.)

Answer:

If we will receive *future benefit,* the account is probably an *asset.*

2. **Liabilities** are amounts a company owes to others. Liabilities are obligations. For example, if a company borrows $10,000 from the bank, the company has an obligation to repay the $10,000 to the bank. Thus, the $10,000 obligation is shown as a liability on the company's Balance Sheet.

   Liability accounts include:

   - Accounts payable (amounts that are owed and will be paid to suppliers in the future).
   - Sales taxes payable (sales tax owed and to be paid in the future).
   - Interest payable (interest owed and to be paid in the future).
   - Other current liabilities (liabilities due within one year).
   - Loan payable (also called notes payable).
   - Mortgage payable. (The difference between a note payable and a mortgage payable is that a mortgage payable has real estate as collateral.)
   - Other long-term liabilities (liabilities due after one year).

How Do We Know if an Account is a Liability?

Ask:

Is our enterprise *obligated* to do something, such as pay a bill or provide a service?

Answer:

If we have an *obligation,* the account is probably a *liability.*

3. **Equity accounts** (or stockholders' equity for a corporation) represent the net worth of a business. Equity is calculated as assets (resources owned) minus liabilities (amounts owed).

   Different types of business ownership include:

   - Sole proprietorship (an unincorporated business with one owner).
   - Partnership (an unincorporated business with more than one owner).
   - Corporation (an incorporated business with one or more owners).

   Owners' equity is increased by:

   - Investments by owners. For a corporation, owners invest by buying stock.

- Net profits retained in the business rather than distributed to owners.

Owners' equity is decreased by:

- Amounts paid to owners as a return for their investment. For a sole proprietorship or partnership, these are called withdrawals or distributions. For a corporation, they are called dividends.
- Losses incurred by the business.

How Do We Calculate Equity?

Equity = Assets − Liabilities

Assets
− Liabilities
= Equity

What we *own* minus what we *owe* leaves equity.

What are Profit and Loss Accounts?

- The Profit and Loss Statement (also called the Income Statement or P&L Statement) reports the results of a company's operations, listing income and expenses for a period of time.
- Profit and Loss accounts are accounts that appear on a company's Profit and Loss Statement.
- QuickBooks uses two different types of Profit and Loss accounts:
  1. Income accounts
  2. Expense accounts

1. **Income** accounts record sales to customers and other revenues earned by the company. Revenues are the prices charged customers for products and services provided.

   Examples of Income accounts include:

   - Sales or revenues.
   - Fees earned.
   - Interest income.
   - Rental income.
   - Gains on sale of assets.

2. **Expense** accounts record costs that have expired or been consumed in the process of generating income. Expenses are the costs of providing products and services to customers.

   Examples of Expense accounts include:

   - Cost of goods sold expense.
   - Salaries expense.
   - Insurance expense.
   - Rent expense.
   - Interest expense.

How Do We Calculate Net Income?

Net Income = *Income* (*Revenue*) − *Expenses* (*including CGS*)

Income (Revenue)
− *Expenses (including CGS)*
= *Net Income* (*Net Profit or Net Earnings*)

Net income is calculated as income (or revenue) less cost of goods sold and other expenses. Net income is an attempt to match or measure efforts (expenses) against accomplishments (revenues).

Three Names for the Same Thing: Net Income is also referred to as Net Profit or Net Earnings.

What are Permanent Accounts?

- In general, Balance Sheet accounts are considered **permanent accounts** (with the exception of the Withdrawals or Distributions account which is closed out each year).
- Balances in permanent accounts are carried forward from year to year. Thus, for a Balance Sheet account, such as Checking, the balance at December 31 is carried forward and becomes the opening balance on January 1 of the next year.

What are Temporary Accounts?

- Profit and Loss accounts are called **temporary accounts** because they are used to track account data for a temporary period of time, usually one year.
- At the end of each year, temporary accounts are closed (the balance reduced to zero). For example, if a Profit and Loss account, such as Advertising Expense, had a $13,000 balance at December 31,

the $13,000 balance would be closed or transferred to owners' equity at year-end. The opening balance on January 1 for the Advertising Expense account would be $0.00.

What are Non-Posting Accounts?

- Non-posting accounts are accounts that do not appear on the Balance Sheet or Income Statement. However, these accounts are needed to track information necessary for the accounting system.
- Examples of non-posting accounts include:
  - Purchase orders: documents that track items that have been ordered from suppliers.
  - Estimates: bids or proposals submitted to customers.

www.my-quickbooks.com

Go to **www.My-QuickBooks.com** to view additional QuickBooks resources including:

- **Excel Report Templates** to organize QuickBooks reports exported to Excel
- ***Computer Accounting with QuickBooks*** **updates,** sometimes required when there is a software update that affects the text
- **QuickBooks Video links**
- **QuickBooks Help and Support links**
- **Other QuickBooks Resources** to make learning QuickBooks easier and more effective
- **QuickBooks Issue Resolution** offers a guided approach to trouble-shooting QuickBooks

Troubleshooting QuickBooks and Correcting Errors are crucial QuickBooks skill to acquire. See www.My-QuickBooks.com > QB Issue Resolution for Troubleshooting QuickBooks tips. See Chapter 17, Quick Review Guide, for tips on Correcting Errors.

Bookmark www.My-QuickBooks.com for future use.

Note that the exercises contain instructions but fewer screen captures than the chapter. The screen captures are included in the chapter when we are exploring. In the exercises, the focus is on practicing, so there are instructions included but fewer screen captures. This learning approach increases retention of material and results in deeper learning.

EXERCISE 2.1: Statement of Cash Flows

BACKSTORY

When you return to your cubicle after lunch, you find the following note stuck to your computer screen.

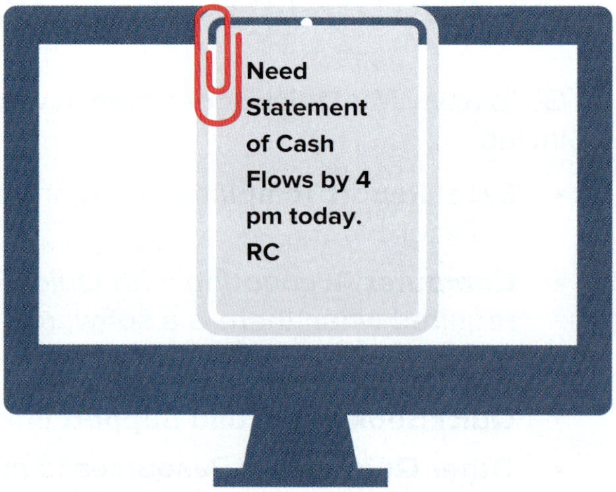

E2.1.1 QuickBooks File

If you will be using the same computer and the same Chapter 2.QBW file:

1. If your Chapter 2.QBW file is not already open, open it by selecting **File > Open Previous Company.** Select your **Chapter 2.QBW file.** If a QuickBooks Information window appears with a message about the sample company file, click **OK.**
2. Add **YourName Exercise 2.1** to the company name by selecting **Company Menu > My Company.**

If you are not using the same computer that you used for Chapter 2, you will need to restore your Chapter 2 Backup.QBB file using the instructions in Appendix B: Back Up & Restore QuickBooks Files. After restoring, add YourName Exercise 2.1 to the company name.

E2.1.2 Print Statement of Cash Flows

The Statement of Cash Flows summarizes a company's cash inflows and cash outflows. The cash flows are grouped by activity:

- Cash flows from operating activities. Cash flows related to the operations of the business—providing goods and services to customers.
- Cash flows from investing activities. Cash flows that result from investing (buying and selling) long-term assets, such as investments and property.
- Cash flows from financing activities. Cash flows that result from borrowing or repaying principal on debt or from transactions with owners.

Print the Statement of Cash Flows for Rock Castle Construction by completing the following steps:

1. Click **Reports** in the Navigation Bar
2. Select type of report: **Company & Financial**
3. Select report: **Statement of Cash Flows**
4. Select the date range: **Last Month.** The Dates field will now be: **11/01/2022 To 11/30/2022.** Select the **Run** icon.
5. Export the report to **Excel** or **print** the Statement of Cash Flows
6. **Close** the Statement of Cash Flows window
7. **Close** the Report Center window
8. **Highlight** the net change in cash for the period on the Statement of Cash Flows

E2.1.3 Back Up Exercise 2.1

Save a backup of your Exercise file using the file name: YourName Exercise 2.1 Backup.QBB. See *Appendix B: Back Up & Restore QuickBooks Files* for instructions.

EXERCISE 2.2: Chart of Accounts

BACKSTORY

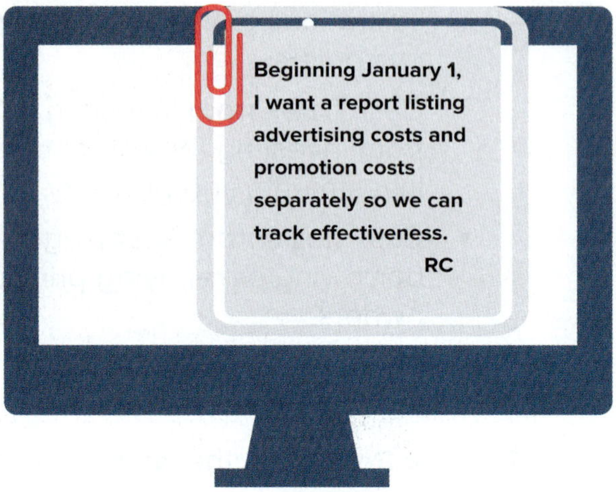

When you return to your cubicle after your afternoon break, another note is stuck to your computer screen.

In order to track advertising costs separately from promotion costs, you decide to make the following changes to the Chart of Accounts.

- Rename Account 60400 Advertising & Promotion account to: Selling Expense
- Add two subaccounts: 60410 Advertising Expense and 60420 Promotion Expense

After these changes, the Chart of Accounts should list the following accounts:

- Account 60400: Selling Expense
- Subaccount 60410: Advertising Expense
- Subaccount 60420: Promotion Expense

E2.2.1 QuickBooks File

If you will be using the same computer and the same QBW file:

1. Select your **QBW file.**
2. Add **YourName Exercise 2.2** to the company name by selecting **Company Menu > My Company.**

If you are not using the same computer that you used for Chapter 2 and Exercise 2.1, you will need to restore your latest prior Backup.QBB file using the instructions in Appendix B: Back Up & Restore QuickBooks files. After restoring, add YourName Exercise 2.2 to the company name.

E2.2.2 Edit Account

Edit the Chart of Accounts to change the name of Account 60400 from Advertising & Promotion to Selling Expense.

1. Open the Chart of Accounts window by clicking the **Chart of Accounts** icon in the Company section of the Home Page
2. Select account: **60400 Advertising & Promotion**
3. Click the **Account** button at the bottom of the Chart of Accounts window, then select **Edit Account** from the drop-down menu (or right-click and select Edit Account from the menu)
4. Change the account name from Advertising & Promotion to: **Selling Expense**
5. Click **Save & Close** to save the changes

E2.2.3 Add Subaccount

Add the Advertising subaccount to the Selling Expense account.

1. Click the **Account** button at the bottom of the Chart of Accounts window, then select **New** to open the Add New Account window
2. Select Account Type: **Expense.** Click **Continue.**
3. Enter Account Number: **60410**
4. Enter Account Name: **Advertising Expense**
5. **Check** the box in front of the Subaccount of field
6. From the drop-down list, select subaccount of: **60400 Selling Expense**
7. From the drop-down list for Tax-Line Mapping, select Deductions: **Advertising**
8. Click **Save & New**

E2.2.4 Add Subaccount

Add the Promotion Expense subaccount to the Selling Expense account.

1. Add the sub account: **60420 Promotion Expense**
2. Click **Save & Close**

E2.2.5 Print Chart of Accounts

Create the Chart of Accounts (Account Listing).

1. Using the Reports center, export to **Excel** or **print** the revised Chart of Accounts
2. **Highlight** the accounts that you changed or added in this exercise

E2.2.6 Back Up Exercise 2.2

Save a backup of your Exercise file using the file name: YourName Exercise 2.2 Backup.QBB. See *Appendix B: Back Up & Restore QuickBooks Files* for instructions.

PROJECT 2.1

Larry's Landscaping

As an accounting consultant for Larry's Landscaping complete the following to customize QuickBooks for the company and create reports.

QB SatNav

The objective of Project 2.1 is to facilitate your mastery of QuickBooks Desktop. As shown in the following QB SatNav, Project 2.1 focuses on the first and last of the three process: QB Settings and QB Reports.

QB SatNav

1 QB SETTINGS

- Company Settings
- Chart of Accounts

2 QB TRANSACTIONS

> Money in *Money out >*

- Banking
- Customers & Sales
- Vendors & Expenses
- Employees & Payroll

3 QB REPORTS

- Reports

P2.1.1 QuickBooks File

1. Use either your QuickBooks Company file (QBW) or restore the backup file (QBB) that you completed for Project 1.1. (If you have issues with your QuickBooks file, contact your instructor.)
2. Update the Company Name to: **YourName Project 2.1 Larry's Landscaping**

P2.1.2 QuickBooks Preferences

1. Using QuickBooks preferences, select **Use the last entered date as default**
2. Using QuickBooks preferences, select **Use account numbers** to display account numbers in the Chart of Accounts

P2.1.3 Chart of Accounts

Customize Larry's Chart of Accounts as follows.

1. Enter the following accounts and **re-sort** the Chart of Accounts

Account	**Supplies**
Account No.	**7310**
Account Type	**Expense**
Account Description	**Cleaning Supplies**
Tax Line	**Schedule C: Supplies (not from COGS)**

Account	**Computer Supplies**
Account No.	**7320**
Account Type	**Expense**
Account Description	**Computer Supplies**
Tax Line	**Schedule C: Supplies (not from COGS)**

Account	**Professional Design Fees**
Account No.	**7430**
Account Type	**Expense**
Account Description	**Professional Design Fees**
Subaccount of	**7400 Professional Fees**
Tax Line	**Schedule C: Legal and professional fees**

Account	**Section 179**
Account No.	**6710**
Account Type	**Expense**
Account Description	**Section 179**
Subaccount of	**6700 Depreciation**
Tax Line	**Schedule C: Other business expenses**

Account	**Internet Provider**
Account No.	**7754**
Account Type	**Expense**
Account Description	**Internet Provider**
Subaccount of	**7750 Utilities**
Tax Line	**Schedule C: Office expenses**

2. Export to **Excel** the Chart of Accounts for Larry's Landscaping using the Account Listing report at December 15, 2022
3. **Highlight** the accounts that you added

P2.1.4 Financial Reports

1. Export to **Excel** the Statement of Cash Flows for Larry's Landscaping for the Last Fiscal Year, October 1, 2021 to September 30, 2022
2. **Highlight** any item on the statement that you might classify differently than shown on the report

P2.1.5 Back Up Project 2.1

Save a backup of your Project file using the file name: YourName Project 2.1 Backup.QBB. See *Appendix B: Back Up & Restore QuickBooks Files* for instructions.

Chapter 3

QuickBooks Transactions

BACKSTORY

As you start sorting through the random stacks of paper on your desk, you hear Mr. Castle's booming voice and rapid pace coming in your direction. You look up just in time to see Mr. Castle plant a huge stack of papers on your desk.

Smiling he says, *"Since you are getting organized I thought you'd want these papers too. And when you are finished there are more in my office. We got a little bit behind."*

Seeing the stricken look on your face, Mr. Castle pauses, putting his hands on his hips. "*Here's the way I look at it, we have all this info we have to get into QB. But it's basically about entering four, and only four, different types of transactions.*

1. *Banking and credit card transactions*
2. *Customers and sales transactions*
3. *Vendors and expenses transaction*
4. *Employees and payroll transactions*

"*And we don't need to worry about payroll for a while yet. So you can focus on three different types of transactions.*

"*So dive in!*" Mr. Castle points at the paperwork smiling.

Section 3.1

QuickBooks SatNav

QuickBooks SatNav is your satellite navigation for QuickBooks, assisting you in navigating QuickBooks

QuickBooks SatNav divides QuickBooks into three processes:

1. **QuickBooks Settings.** This includes Company Settings when setting up a new QuickBooks company and the Company Chart of Accounts.
2. **QuickBooks Transactions.** This includes recording transactions in QuickBooks. Transaction types can be categorized as Banking, Customers and Sales, Vendors and Expenses, and Employees and Payroll. In basic terms, recording transactions involves recording money in and money out.
3. **QuickBooks Reports.** QuickBooks reports are the output of the system, such as commonly used financial statements of Balance Sheet, Income Statement, and Statement of Cash Flows.

Chapter 3 provides an overview of QuickBooks transactions, shown in the following QuickBooks SatNav.

QB SatNav

1 QB SETTINGS

CHAPTERS 1 2 11 12 13 14

Company Settings
Chart of Accounts

2 QB TRANSACTIONS

CHAPTERS 3 4 5 6 7 8 11 12 13 14

> *Money in* *Money out* >

Banking
Customers & Sales
Vendors & Expenses
Employees & Payroll

3 QB REPORTS

CHAPTERS 9 10 11 12 13 14

Reports

Section 3.2

START QUICKBOOKS AND OPEN QUICKBOOKS COMPANY

START QUICKBOOKS

To start QuickBooks software, click the **QuickBooks** icon on your desktop. If a QuickBooks icon does not appear on your desktop, from Microsoft® Windows® click **Start** button > **Programs > QuickBooks > QuickBooks Premier Accountant Edition.**

QuickBooks Accountant includes all the features of QuickBooks Pro plus features for client services. If you use QuickBooks Pro, your screens may appear slightly different than those appearing in this text.

RESTORE QBB STARTER FILE

Restore the QBB Starter file for this chapter as follows.

1. Select **File** > **Restore**
2. Using the directions in *Appendix B: Back Up & Restore QuickBooks Files,* restore the **CHAPTER 3 STARTER.QBB**
3. After restoring, add **YourName Chapter 3** to the company name by selecting **Company Menu** > **My Company**

! **QuickBooks Desktop (QBDT)** Data Files are compressed backup files that can be restored and used. To use Starter Files, the compressed file must be restored following the instructions here. Since it is a compressed file, you cannot open and use the QuickBooks data files by simply clicking on the file. Instead you must follow the instructions here to unzip and restore the data file before using it.

Section 3.3

QUICKBOOKS LISTS

As a company conducts business operations, the company enters into transactions with customers, vendors, and employees. Before entering these transactions in QuickBooks, we typically want to make sure our QuickBooks Lists are up to date.

WHAT ARE QUICKBOOKS LISTS?

QuickBooks Lists are a time saving feature so that we don't have to continually re-enter the same information for accounts, customers, vendors, and so on, each time we enter a new transaction. Lists permit us to collect information that we will reuse so we don't have to re-enter it.

QuickBooks lists include:

- **Customer List.** Provides information about customers.
- **Vendor List.** Provides information about vendors.
- **Employee List.** Provides information about employees for payroll purposes.
- **Item List.** Provides information about the items or services sold to customers or purchased from vendors.
- **Payroll Item List.** Tracks detailed information about payroll, such as payroll taxes and payroll deductions. The Payroll Item List permits the use of a single or limited number of payroll accounts while more detailed information is tracked using the Item List for payroll.
- **Class List.** Permits income to be tracked according to the specific source (class) of income. An example of a class might be a department, store location, business segment, or product line.

Lists are used so that information can be entered once in a list and then reused as needed. For example, information about a customer, such as address, can be entered in the Customer List. This customer information then automatically appears on the customer invoice.

To view QuickBooks lists, select the lists as follows.

1. Select **Customers** on the Navigation Bar to view the Customers List
2. Select **Vendors** on the Navigation Bar to view the Vendors List
3. Select **Employees** on the Navigation Bar to view the Employees List
4. Select the **Items & Services** icon in the Company section of the Home Page to view the Items & Services List
5. Select the **Chart of Accounts** icon in the Company section of the Home Page to view the Chart of Accounts, a list of accounts
6. Select the **Lists Menu** to view other QuickBooks Lists, such as the Payroll Item List or the Class List

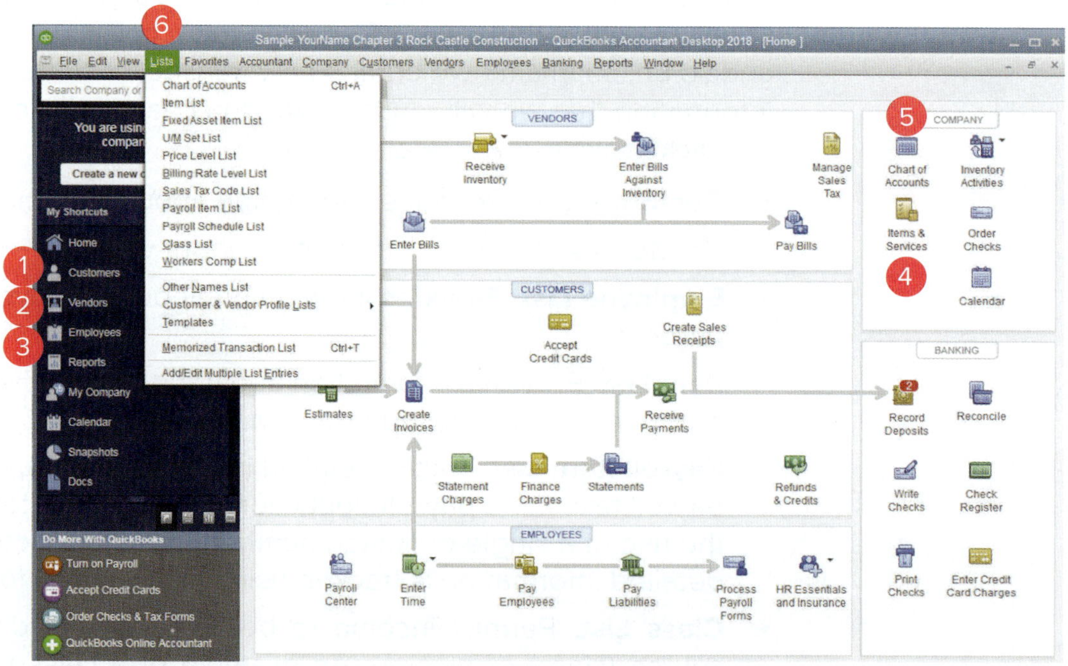

Customers List collects information about customers, such as customer name, customer number, address, and contact information.

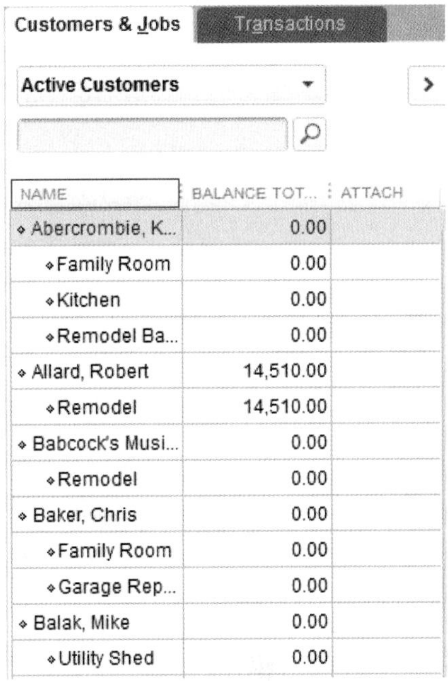

Vendors List collects information about vendors, such as vendor name, vendor number, and contact information.

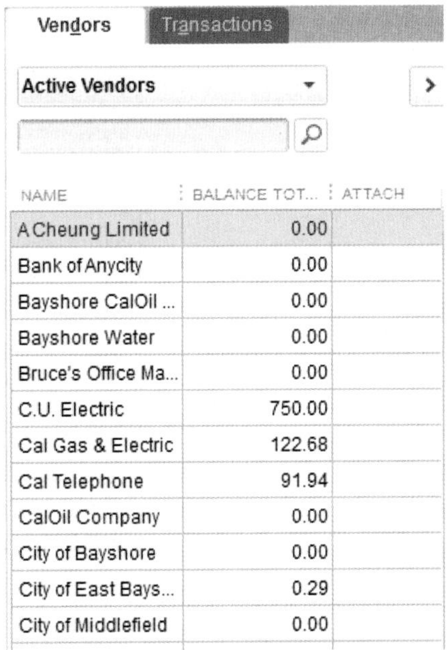

Employees List collects information about employees for payroll purposes including name, Social Security number, and address.

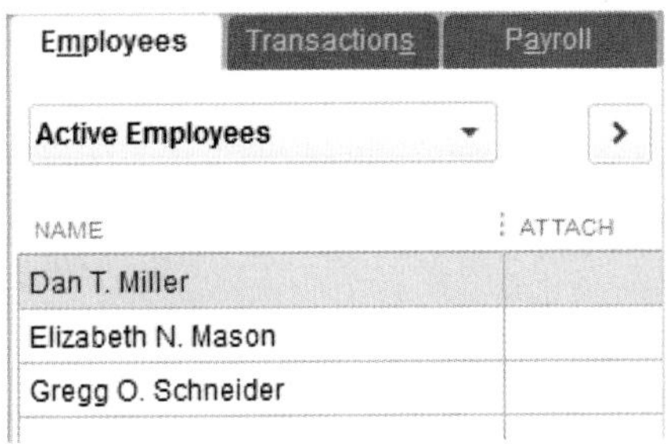

Items and Services List collects information about the products and services sold to customers, such as hours worked and types of products or services.

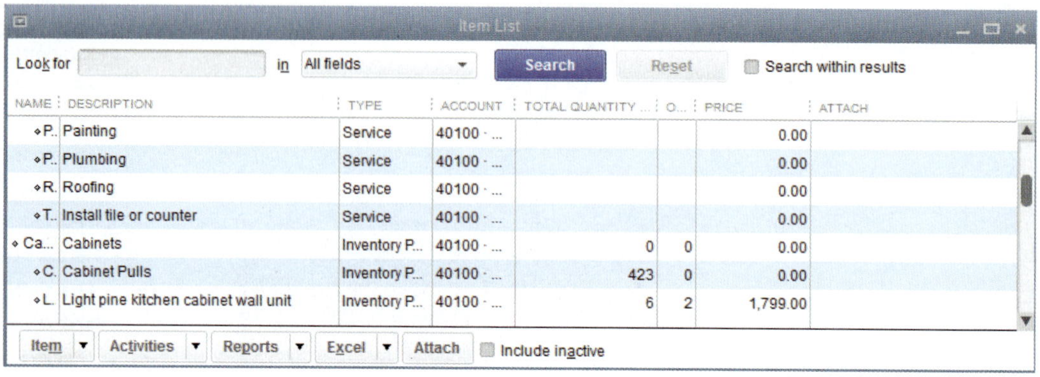

Chart of Accounts is a list of all the accounts a company uses when recording transactions. Accounts (such as the Checking account or Inventory account) permit us to sort and track accounting information.

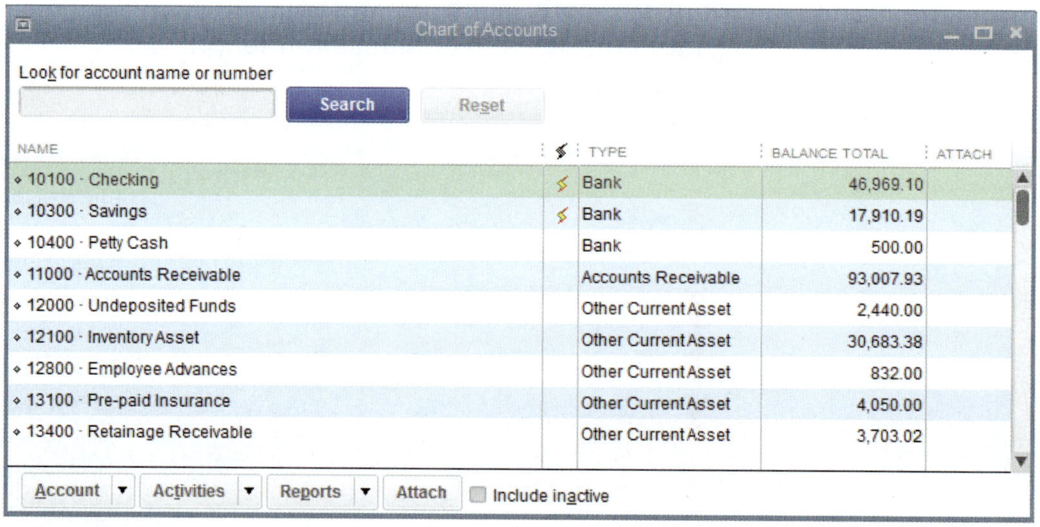

HOW DO WE UPDATE QUICKBOOKS LISTS?

There are basically two ways that we can update QuickBooks Lists.

1. *Before* entering transactions
2. *While* entering transactions

1. *Before* entering transactions, we can update QuickBooks lists as follows.

1. Select **Customers** to display and update the Customers List
2. Select **Vendors** to display and update the Vendors List
3. Select **Employees** to display and update the Employees List
4. Select the **Items & Services** icon to display and update the Items & Services List

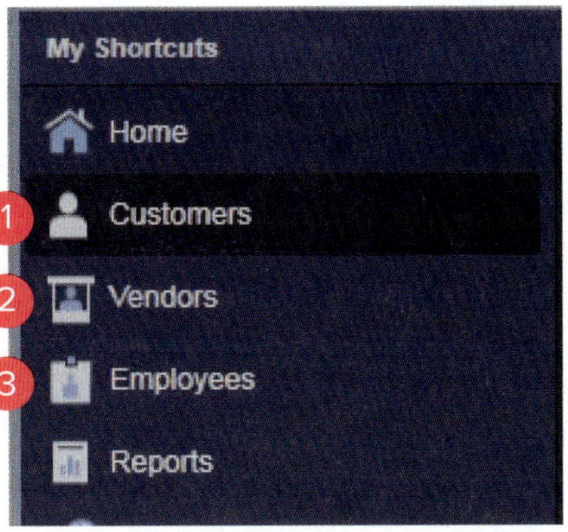

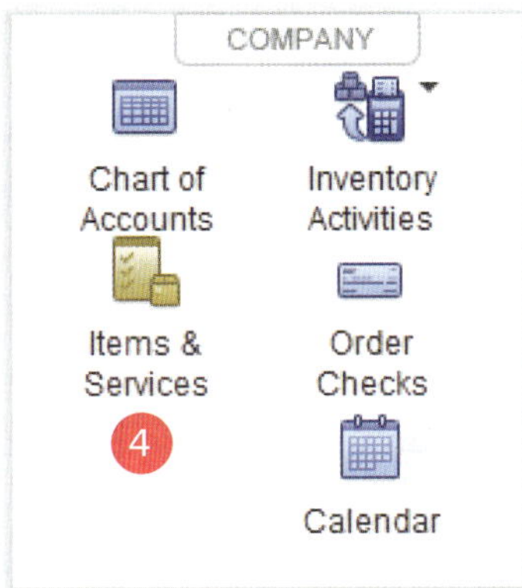

2. *While* entering transactions, we can update lists on the fly from the screen where we enter the transaction. If a customer, for example, has not been entered in the Customer List and is needed for a sales transaction, we can add the customer as follows from an onscreen Invoice form.

1. For example, to view an onscreen form such as an Invoice, select the **Create Invoices** icon to display an onscreen invoice
2. Then select **Customer:Job drop-down arrow** > **+ Add New**
3. For example, then we would enter **new customer information**
4. Normally, we would select **OK** to save the new customer information. Then we would complete and save the Invoice. In this case, select **Cancel** to leave the New Customer window.

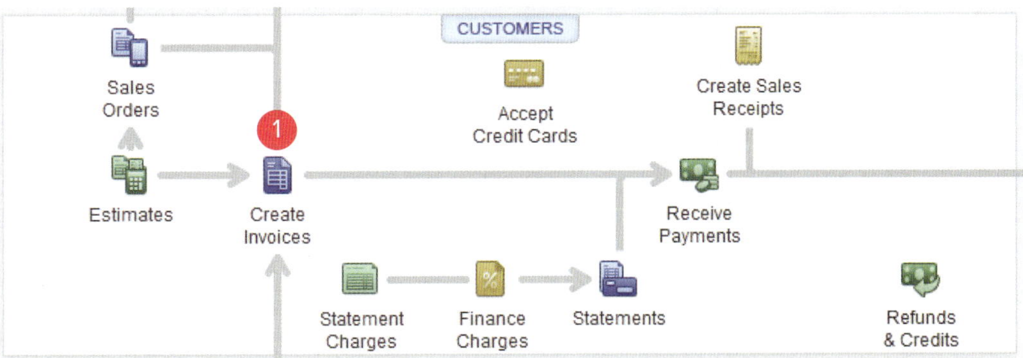

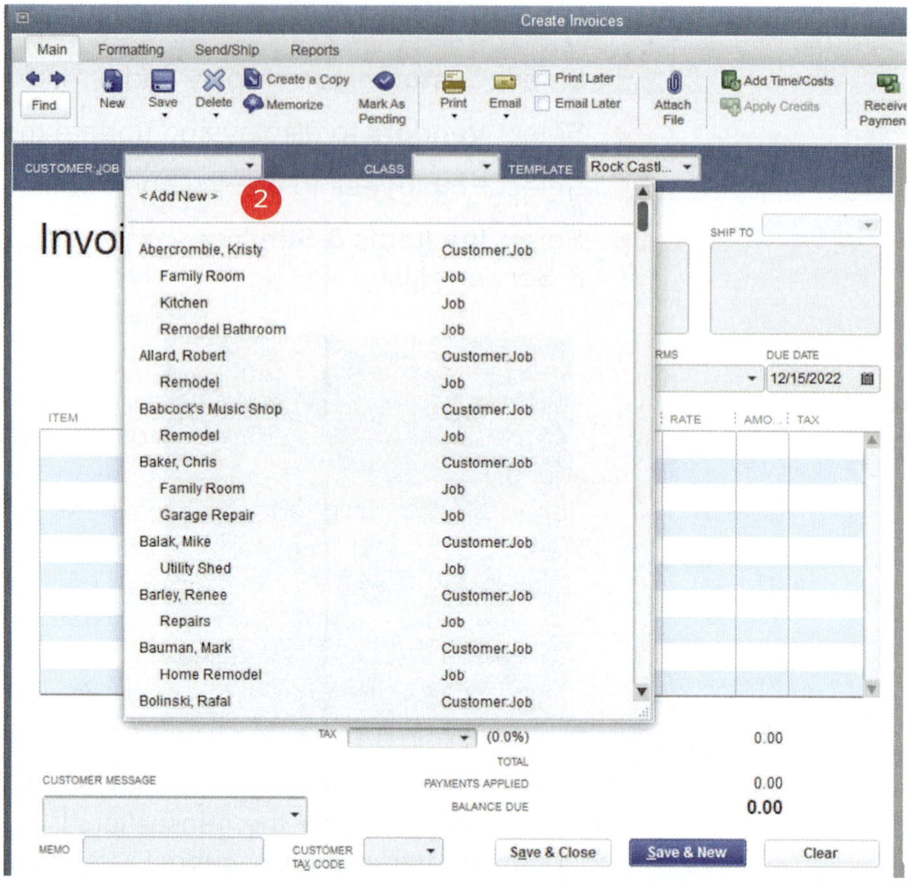
Create Invoices
Main
Formatting
Send/Ship
Reports
Find
New
Save
Delete
Create a Copy
Memorize
Mark As Pending
Print
Email
Print Later
Email Later
Attach File
Add Time/Costs
Apply Credits
Receive Paymen
CUSTOMER:JOB
CLASS
TEMPLATE
Rock Castl...
< Add New >
2
Invoi
Abercrombie, Kristy
Customer:Job
Family Room
Job
Kitchen
Job
Remodel Bathroom
Job
Allard, Robert
Customer:Job
Remodel
Job
Babcock's Music Shop
Customer:Job
Remodel
Job
Baker, Chris
Customer:Job
Family Room
Job
Garage Repair
Job
Balak, Mike
Customer:Job
Utility Shed
Job
Barley, Renee
Customer:Job
Repairs
Job
Bauman, Mark
Customer:Job
Home Remodel
Job
Bolinski, Rafal
Customer:Job
SHIP TO
DUE DATE
12/15/2022
ITEM
RATE
AMO...
TAX
TAX
(0.0%)
0.00
TOTAL
CUSTOMER MESSAGE
PAYMENTS APPLIED
0.00
BALANCE DUE
0.00
MEMO
CUSTOMER TAX CODE
Save & Close
Save & New
Clear

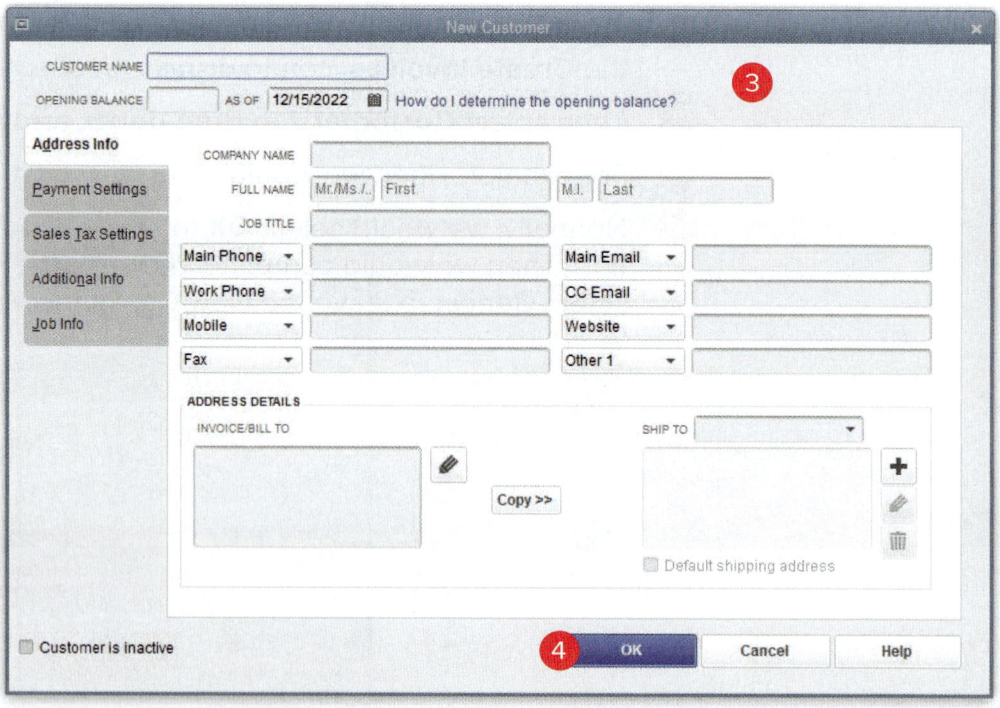
New Customer
CUSTOMER NAME
OPENING BALANCE
AS OF
12/15/2022
How do I determine the opening balance?
3
Address Info
Payment Settings
Sales Tax Settings
Additional Info
Job Info
COMPANY NAME
FULL NAME
Mr./Ms./...
First
M.I.
Last
JOB TITLE
Main Phone
Main Email
Work Phone
CC Email
Mobile
Website
Fax
Other 1
ADDRESS DETAILS
INVOICE/BILL TO
SHIP TO
Copy >>
Default shipping address
Customer is inactive
4
OK
Cancel
Help

Section 3.4

HOW DO WE ENTER TRANSACTIONS IN QUICKBOOKS?

WHAT ARE TRANSACTIONS?

Our QuickBooks financial system needs to collect information about transactions.

Transactions are exchanges. A business enters into transactions or exchanges between the business and other parties, such as customers, vendors, and employers. The business gives and receives something in an exchange.

A business can exchange services, products, cash, or a promise to pay later (Accounts Payable). A transaction must have two parts to the exchange: something must be given and something must be received.

For example, when a business sells 1 hour of consulting services to a customer, the two parts to the transaction are:

1. The business gives the customer 1 hour of consulting services.
2. In exchange, the business receives cash (or a promise to pay later) from the customer.

When we record transactions in QuickBooks we need to record what is exchanged, what is given and what is received.

ONSCREEN FORM OR ONSCREEN JOURNAL

QuickBooks offers us two different ways to enter transaction information:

1. Onscreen Journal
2. Onscreen forms

Onscreen Journal. We can make debit and credit entries in an onscreen Journal as follows.

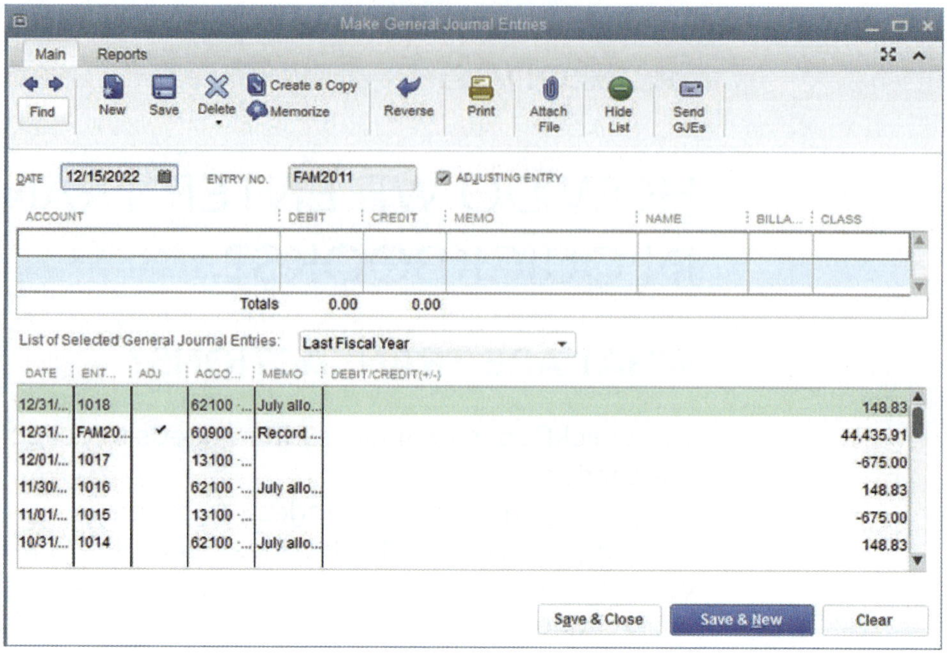

The onscreen Journal using debits and credits to enter transactions is accessed from the Accountant Menu > Make General Journal Entries.

An onscreen Journal is often used to make adjusting entries at year end to bring accounts up to date before preparing financial statements.

Instead of using the onscreen Journal, we can use onscreen forms to enter transaction information in QuickBooks.

Onscreen forms. We can enter information about transactions using onscreen forms such as the following onscreen form.

When we enter information into an onscreen form, behind the screen QuickBooks automatically converts that information into a journal entry with debits and credits. QuickBooks maintains a list of journal entries for all the transactions entered—whether entered using the onscreen Journal or onscreen forms.

For example, to view the journal entry that QuickBooks created behind the screen for a transaction entered and saved using an onscreen form, complete the following steps.

1. For example, to view an onscreen form such as an Expense, select the **Enter Bills** icon in the Vendors section of the Home Page
2. From the Enter Bills onscreen form window, select the **Main** tab at the top of the window
3. Click the back **Find** arrow until the bill for Thomas Kitchen & Bath for 12/15/2022 in the amount of $585.00 appears

4 Next select the **Reports** tab at the top of the Enter Bills window

5 Select **Transaction Journal**

6 Behind the screen, QuickBooks automatically converted the information in the Enter Bills onscreen form into a following journal entry with debits and credits. Notice that the journal entry displays a Debit to Job Materials and a Credit to Accounts Payable for $585.00.

7 **Close** the Transaction Journal window and the Enter Bills window

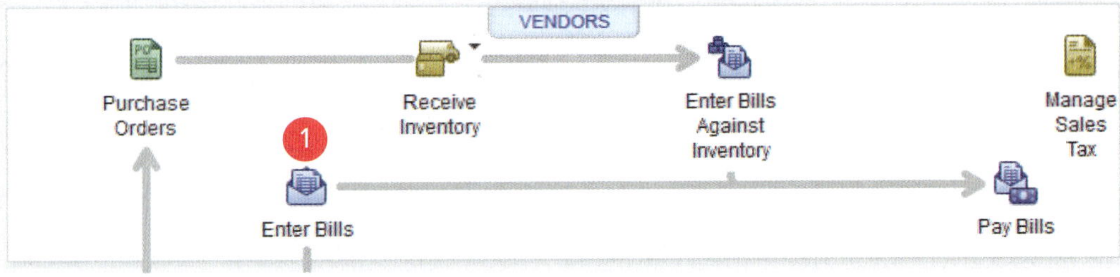

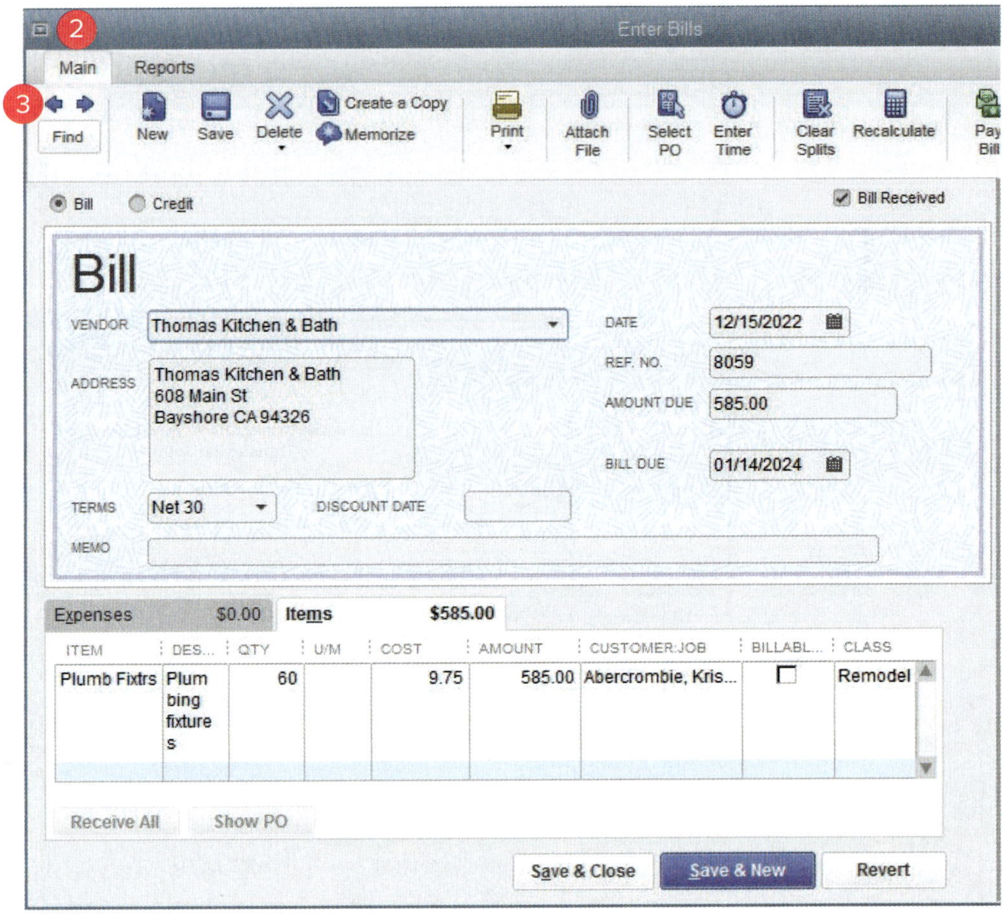

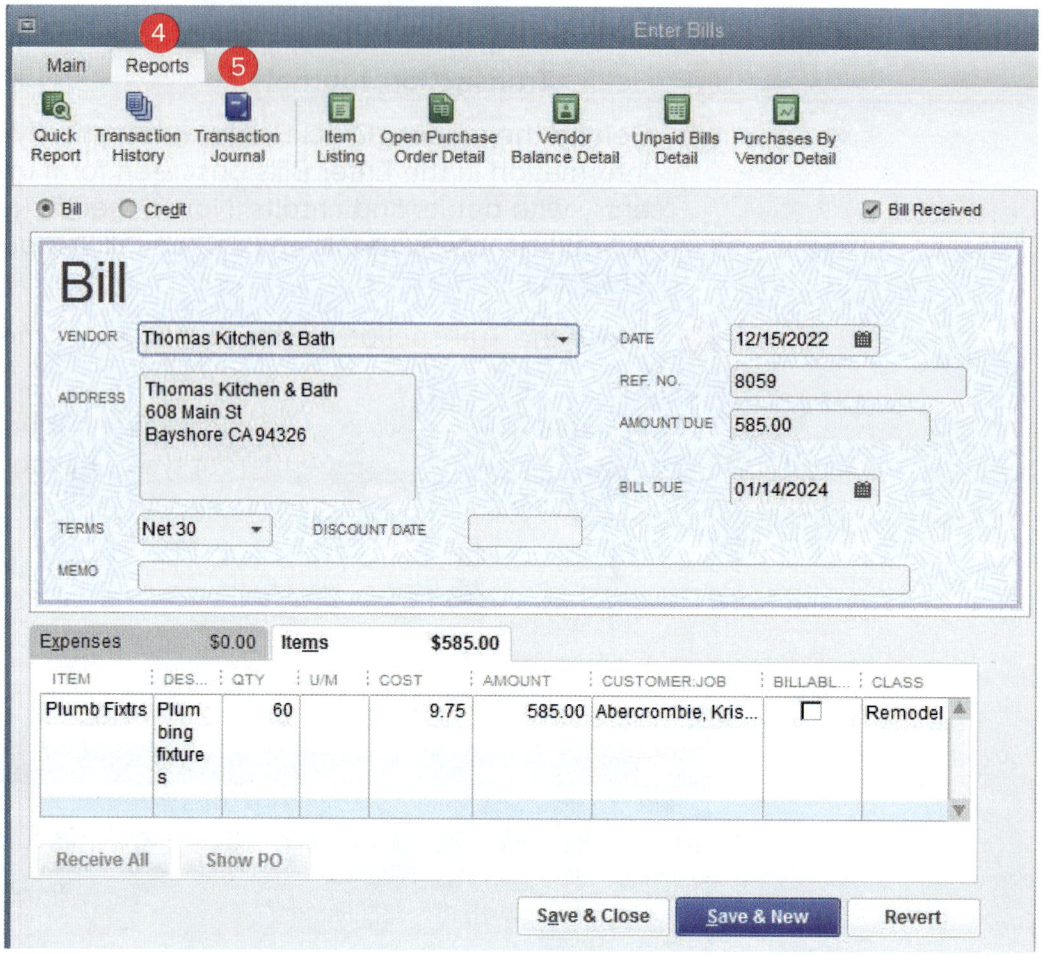
4
5
Enter Bills
Main
Reports
Quick Report
Transaction History
Transaction Journal
Item Listing
Open Purchase Order Detail
Vendor Balance Detail
Unpaid Bills Detail
Purchases By Vendor Detail
Bill
Credit
Bill Received
Bill
VENDOR
Thomas Kitchen & Bath
DATE
12/15/2022
ADDRESS
Thomas Kitchen & Bath
608 Main St
Bayshore CA 94326
REF. NO.
8059
AMOUNT DUE
585.00
BILL DUE
01/14/2024
TERMS
Net 30
DISCOUNT DATE
MEMO
Expenses $0.00
Items $585.00
ITEM
DES...
QTY
U/M
COST
AMOUNT
CUSTOMER:JOB
BILLABL...
CLASS
Plumb Fixtrs
Plum bing fixture s
60
9.75
585.00
Abercrombie, Kris...
Remodel
Receive All
Show PO
Save & Close
Save & New
Revert

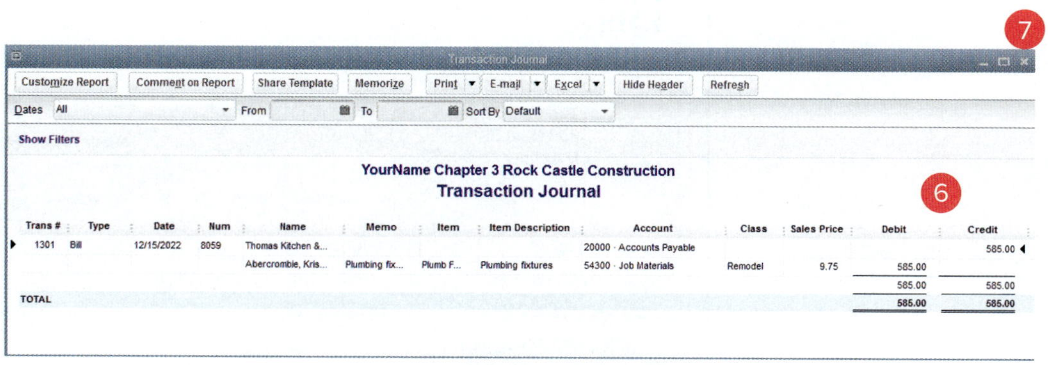
7
Transaction Journal
Customize Report
Comment on Report
Share Template
Memorize
Print
E-mail
Excel
Hide Header
Refresh
Dates All
From
To
Sort By Default
Show Filters
YourName Chapter 3 Rock Castle Construction
Transaction Journal
6
Trans #
Type
Date
Num
Name
Memo
Item
Item Description
Account
Class
Sales Price
Debit
Credit
1301
Bill
12/15/2022
8059
Thomas Kitchen &...
20000 · Accounts Payable
585.00
Abercrombie, Kris...
Plumbing fix...
Plumb F...
Plumbing fixtures
54300 · Job Materials
Remodel
9.75
585.00
585.00
585.00
TOTAL
585.00
585.00

Section 3.5

WHAT ARE THE DIFFERENT TYPES OF TRANSACTIONS?

A transaction is simply an exchange between our QuickBooks business and another party, such as a customer, vendor, or employee. Although there are many different types of transactions, generally we can group transactions into the following different types based upon the other party to the transaction:

1. Banking and Credit Card
2. Customers and Sales
3. Vendors and Expenses
4. Employees and Payroll
5. Other

QuickBooks organizes how we access entering transactions according to the type of transaction and which onscreen form we need to use to enter the transaction.

Section 3.6

BANKING AND CREDIT CARD TRANSACTIONS

QB SatNav

② **QB TRANSACTIONS** — CHAPTERS **3 4 5 6 7 8 11 12 13 14**

> Money in — Money out >

Banking
Customers/Sales
Vendors/Expenses
Employees/Payroll

Transactions that involve depositing funds or writing checks can be entered using icons in the Banking section of the Home Page.

Banking transactions include:

1. Record Deposits
2. Write Checks

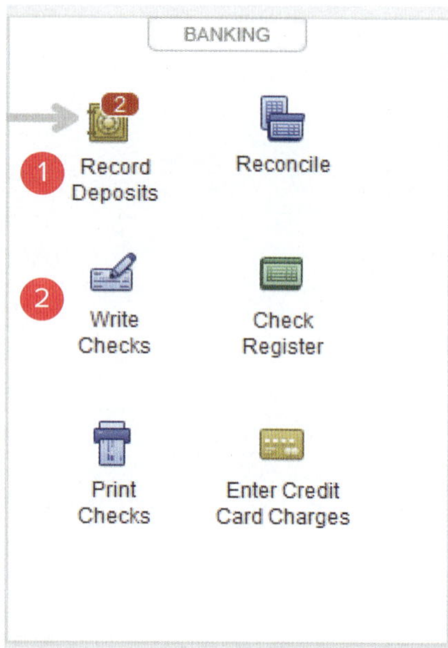

RECORD DEPOSIT

To make a deposit:

1. Select **Record Deposit** icon in the Banking section of the Home Page
2. If a Payments to Deposit window appears, confirm that none of the payments have been selected for deposit, then click **OK**
3. When the Make Deposits window appears, select Deposit To: **10100 Checking**
4. Select Date: **12/15/2022**
5. In the Received From column, enter: **YourName.** Press **Tab** key.
6. Select **Quick Add** to add YourName to the Name List
7. Select Name Type: **Other**
8. Click **OK**
9. Click in the From Account column. From the drop-down list of accounts, select **30100 Capital Stock.** Press **Tab.**
10. Enter Check No.: **999**
11. From the Payment Method drop-down list, select **Check**
12. Enter Amount: **1000.** (QuickBooks will automatically enter the comma in the amount.)
13. Select the **Save** icon to save the deposit. (To print a summary of the deposit just recorded, we would select the Print arrow at the top of the Make Deposits window. In this case, we will not print the Deposit Summary.)
14. Leave the Make Deposits window open on your screen

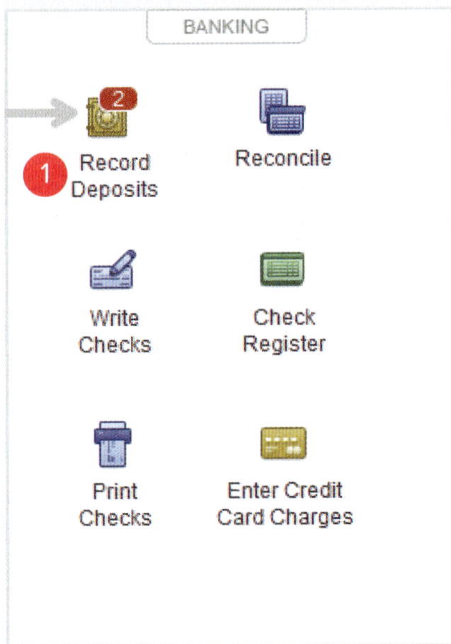

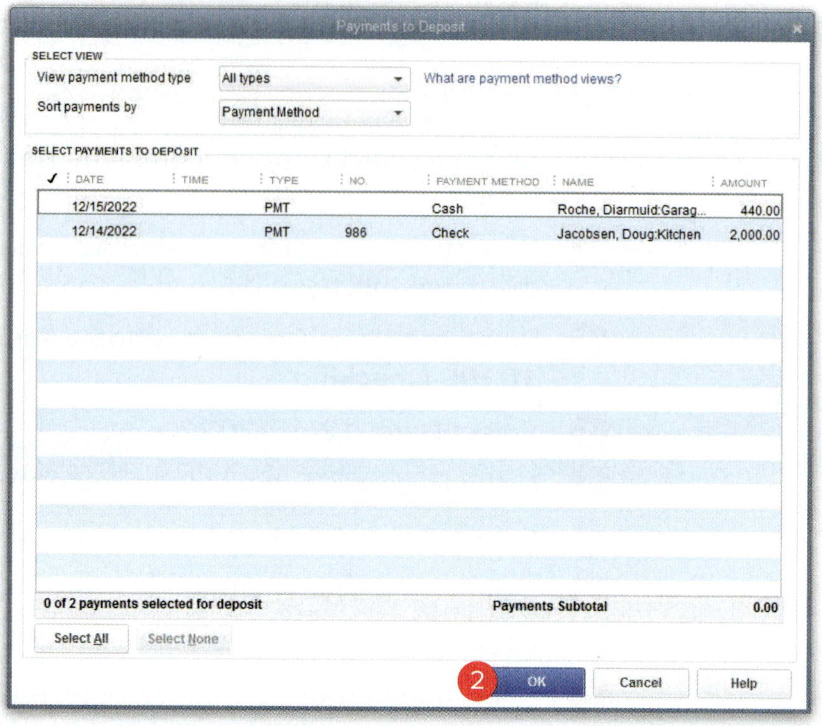
Payments to Deposit
SELECT VIEW
View payment method type
All types
What are payment method views?
Sort payments by
Payment Method
SELECT PAYMENTS TO DEPOSIT
DATE
TIME
TYPE
NO.
PAYMENT METHOD
NAME
AMOUNT
12/15/2022 PMT Cash Roche, Diarmuid:Garag... 440.00
12/14/2022 PMT 986 Check Jacobsen, Doug:Kitchen 2,000.00
0 of 2 payments selected for deposit
Payments Subtotal
0.00
Select All
Select None
2
OK
Cancel
Help

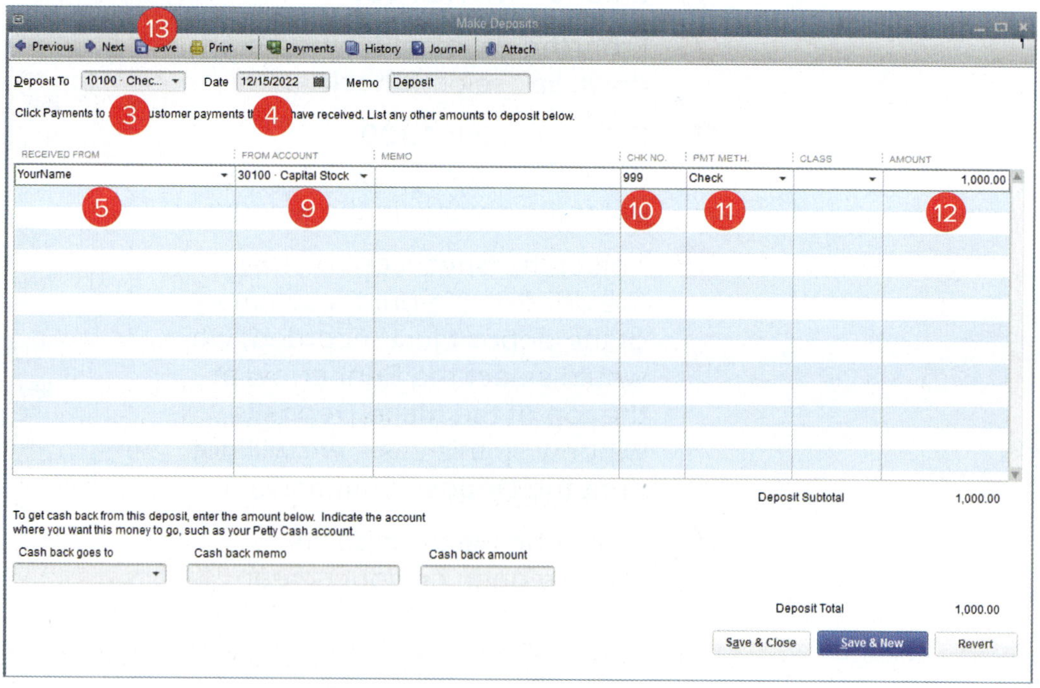
Make Deposits
13
Previous
Next
Save
Print
Payments
History
Journal
Attach
Deposit To
10100 · Chec...
Date
12/15/2022
Memo
Deposit
Click Payments to select customer payments that you have received. List any other amounts to deposit below.
3
4
RECEIVED FROM
FROM ACCOUNT
MEMO
CHK NO.
PMT METH.
CLASS
AMOUNT
YourName
30100 · Capital Stock
999
Check
1,000.00
5
9
10
11
12
Deposit Subtotal
1,000.00
To get cash back from this deposit, enter the amount below. Indicate the account where you want this money to go, such as your Petty Cash account.
Cash back goes to
Cash back memo
Cash back amount
Deposit Total
1,000.00
Save & Close
Save & New
Revert

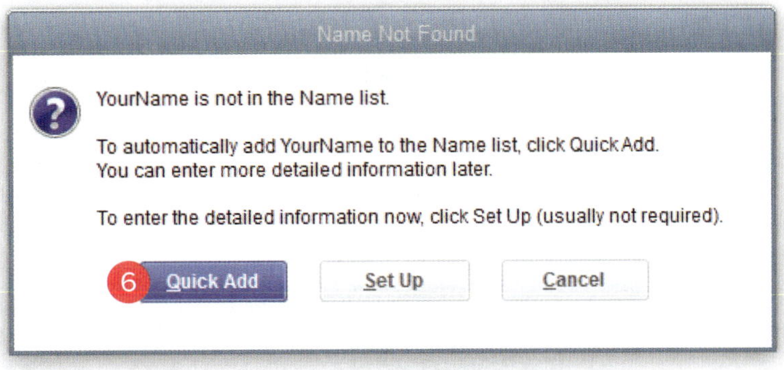

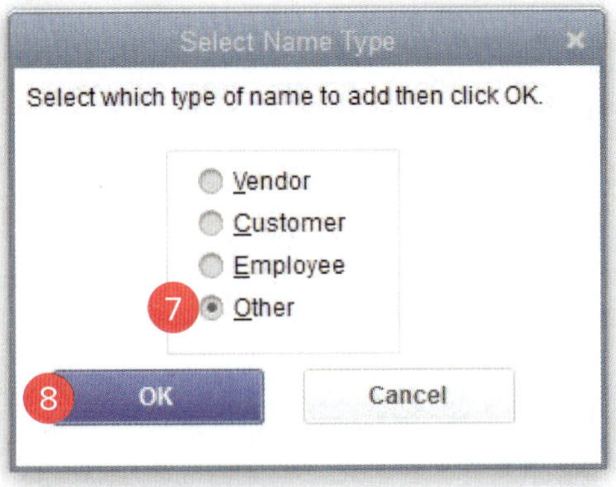

C3.6.1 Deposit Journal Entry. To view the journal entry that QuickBooks created behind the screen for the deposit entered and saved using the Make Deposits onscreen form above, complete the following steps.

1. From the Make Deposits onscreen form, select the **Journal** icon at the top of the form
2. Behind the screen, QuickBooks automatically converted the information in the Record Deposit onscreen form into a journal entry with debits and credits. Notice that the journal entry displays a Debit to 10100 Checking and a Credit to 30100 Capital Stock for $1,000.00.
3. Export the Transaction Journal report to **Excel** or **print** the report
4. **Close** the Transaction Journal window
5. Normally, we would select Save & Close to save the deposit but in this case close the Make Deposits window without saving. We will enter deposits in the exercises at the end of the chapter.

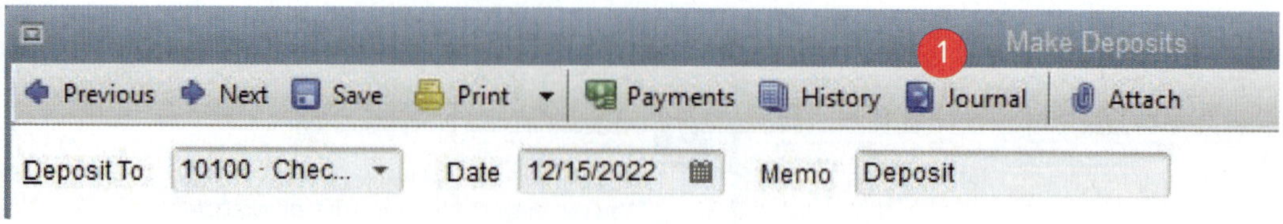

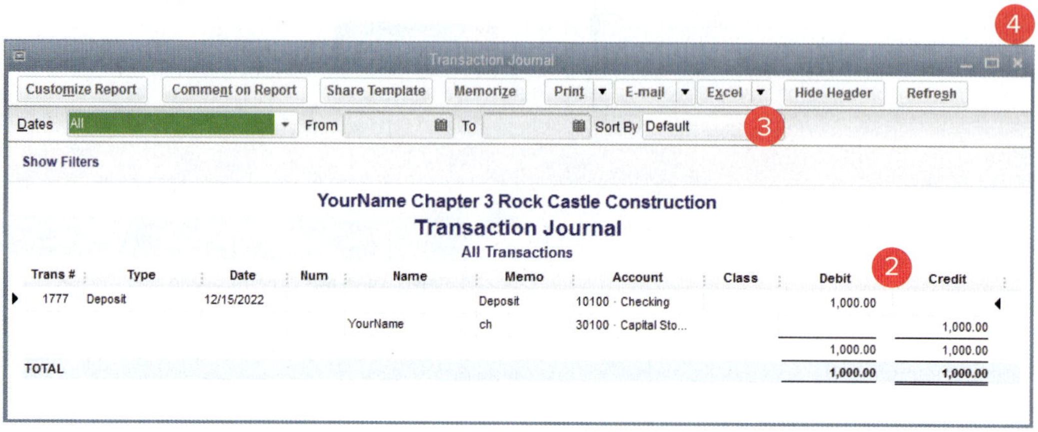

WRITE CHECK

To write a check:

1. From the Banking section of the Home Page, click the **Write Checks** icon
2. To enter the check information, select Bank Account: **10100 Checking**
3. Select Date: **12/15/2022**
4. For the Pay to the Order of field, select: **Kershaw Computer Services.** (Select Kershaw from the drop-down list or type the first few letters of the name.)
5. Enter the check amount: **300.** Press **Tab.**
6. Click the checkbox preceding **Print Later** so that a check mark appears. The Check No. field will now display: To Print. Notice there is also an option to Pay Online.
7. Next, to record the payment in the correct account using the lower portion of the Write Checks window, select the **Expenses** tab
8. If not already selected, select Account: **64220 Computer Repairs.** Account 64200 Repairs: 64220 Computer Repairs should appear

in the Account column and $300 should automatically appear in the expense Amount column.

9 If we wanted to print the check, we would select the Print button located at the top of the Write Checks window. In this case, we will not be printing the check.

10 Select **Save.** Leave the Write Checks window open on your screen.

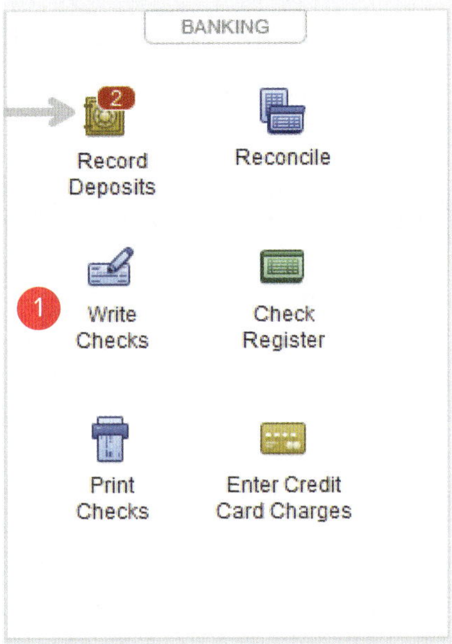

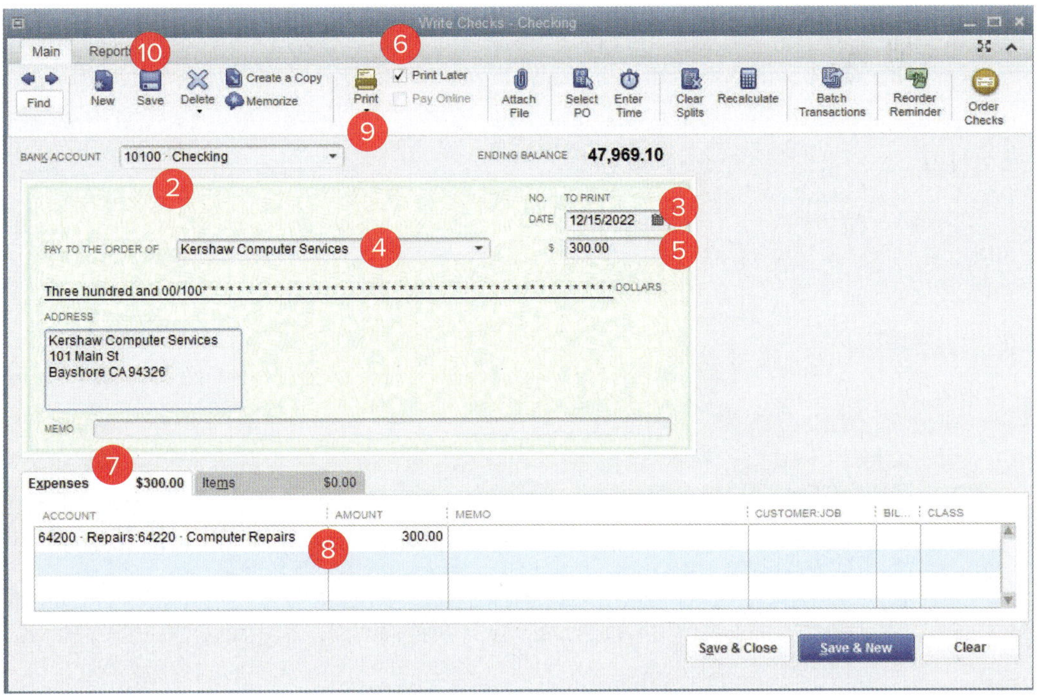

C3.6.2 Check Journal Entry. To view the journal entry that QuickBooks created behind the screen for the check entered and saved using the Write Checks onscreen form above, complete the following steps.

1. From the Write Checks onscreen form, select the **Reports** tab
2. Select the **Transaction Journal** icon
3. Export the Transaction Journal report to **Excel** or **print** the report
4. **Close** the Transaction Journal window
5. **Close** the Write Checks window

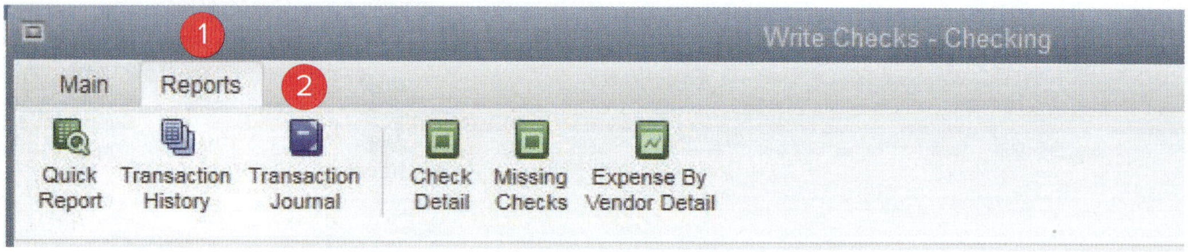

Additional banking activities are covered in the next chapter.

Section 3.7

CUSTOMER AND SALES TRANSACTIONS

QB SatNav

2 QB TRANSACTIONS — **CHAPTERS 3 4 5 6 7 8 11 12 13 14**

> Money in *Money out >*

Banking
Customers/Sales
Vendors/Expenses
Employees/Payroll

Customers transactions are exchanges between our company and customers of our company. Typically, these exchanges focus on sales transactions. Customers include parties to whom we sell products or services.

We can enter customers and sales transactions using the Customers section of the Home Page.

Customer transactions include:

1. Enter sales receipts when the customer pays at the same time a sale occurs
2. Record deposit to deposit the funds in the Checking account

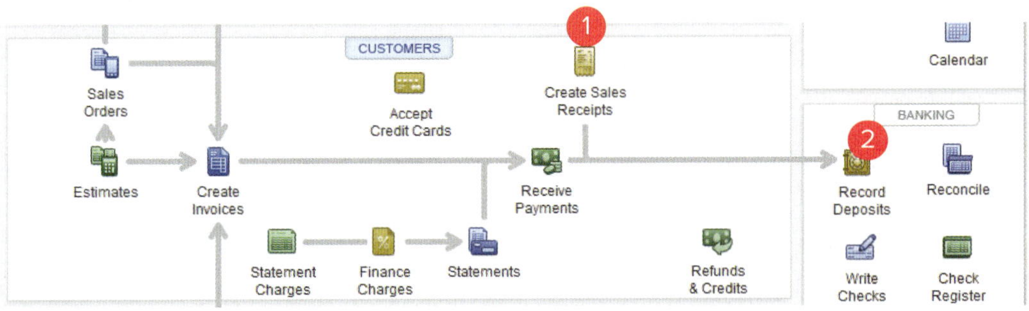

CREATE SALES RECEIPT

One of Rock Castle Construction's customers, Ernesto Natiello, wants to purchase an extra set of cabinet pulls that match the cabinets that Rock Castle Construction installed. Ernesto pays $10 in cash for the extra cabinet pulls.

To create a sales receipt for a customer sale when payment is received at the time of the sale:

1. From the Customers section of the Home Page, click **Create Sales Receipts**
2. In the Enter Sales Receipts window, select Customer: **Natiello, Ernesto**
3. Select Date: **12/15/2022**
4. Select Payment Method: **Cash**
5. Select item from the Item drop-down menu or Add New Item. In this case, select **Cabinet Pulls.**
6. Select Quantity: **1**
7. Enter Rate: **10.00**
8. Select **Print Later** checkbox
9. Select **Save.** Leave the Enter Sales Receipts window open on your screen.

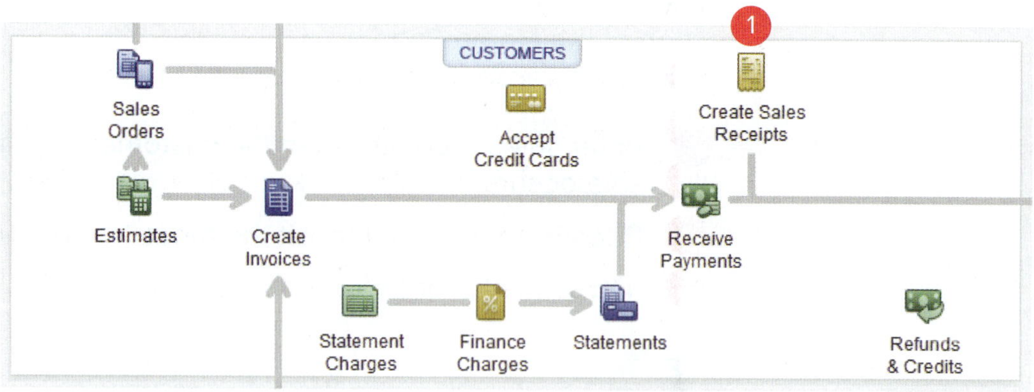

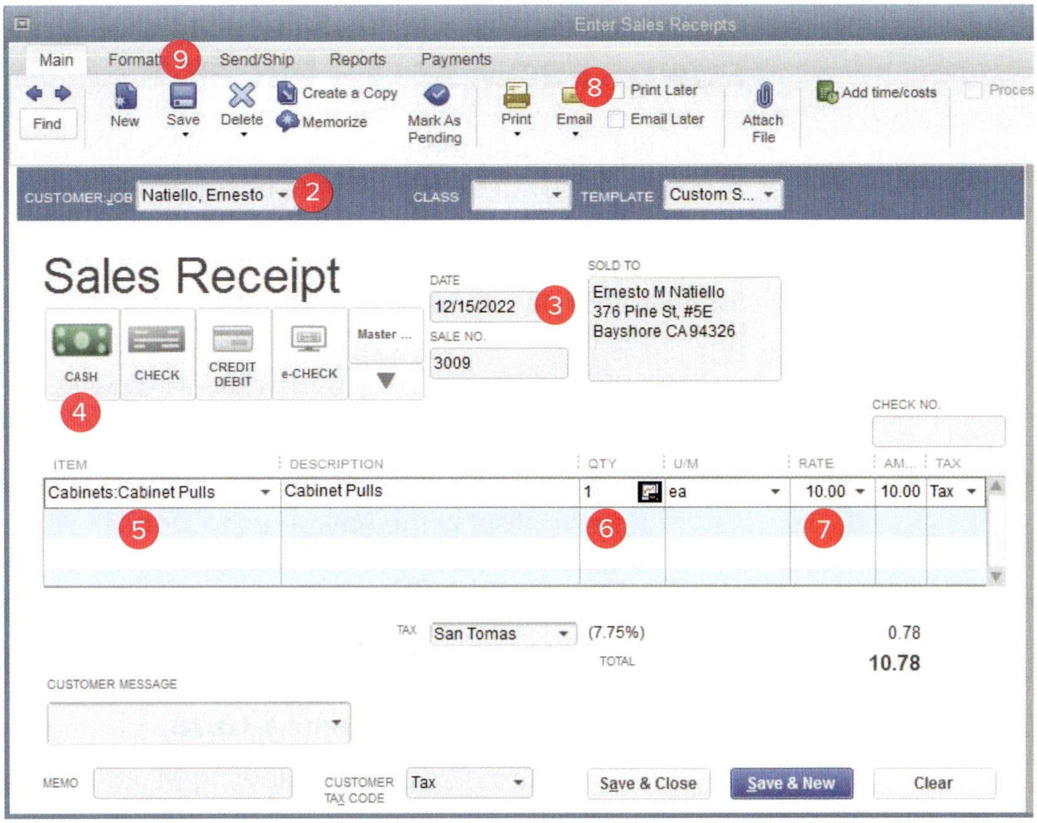

C3.7.1 Sales Receipt Journal Entry. To view the journal entry that QuickBooks created behind the screen for the sales receipt entered and saved using the Enter Sales Receipts onscreen form above, complete the following steps.

1. From the Enter Sales Receipts onscreen form, select the **Reports** tab
2. Select the **Transaction Journal** icon
3. Export the Transaction Journal report to **Excel** or **print** the report
4. **Close** the Transaction Journal window
5. **Close** the Enter Sales Receipts window

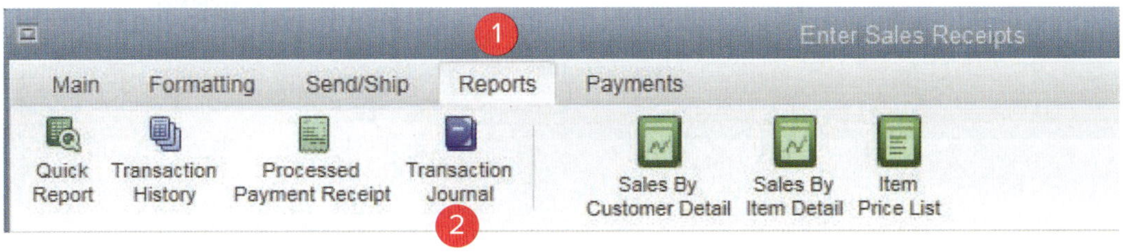

CREATE BANK DEPOSIT FOR UNDEPOSITED FUNDS FROM SALES RECEIPT

When we recorded the sales receipt, QuickBooks recorded a Debit of $10.78 in the Undeposited Funds account. Next, we must record a bank deposit to move the funds from the Undeposited Funds account to the Checking account. The process of using the Undeposited Funds account for customer payments permits a business to bundle multiple customer payments together into one bank deposit.

To record a bank deposit to transfer a customer payment from Undeposited Funds to the Checking account:

1. Click the **Record Deposits** icon in the Banking section of the Home Page to display the Payments to Deposit window. The Payments to Deposit window lists undeposited funds that have been received but not yet deposited in the bank.
2. Select the payments to transfer from the Undeposited Funds account to the Checking account. In this case select **Natiello, Ernesto** for the amount of **$10.78.**
3. Click **OK** to display the following Make Deposits window
4. Select Deposit To: **10100 Checking**
5. Select Date: **12/15/2022**
6. Verify the Amount field displays **$10.78**
7. Select **Save**

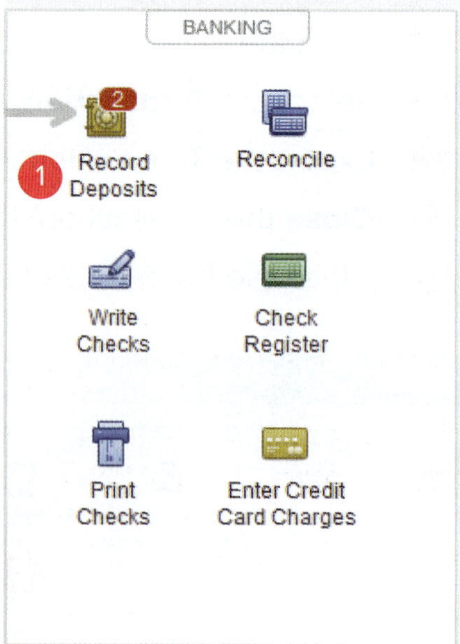

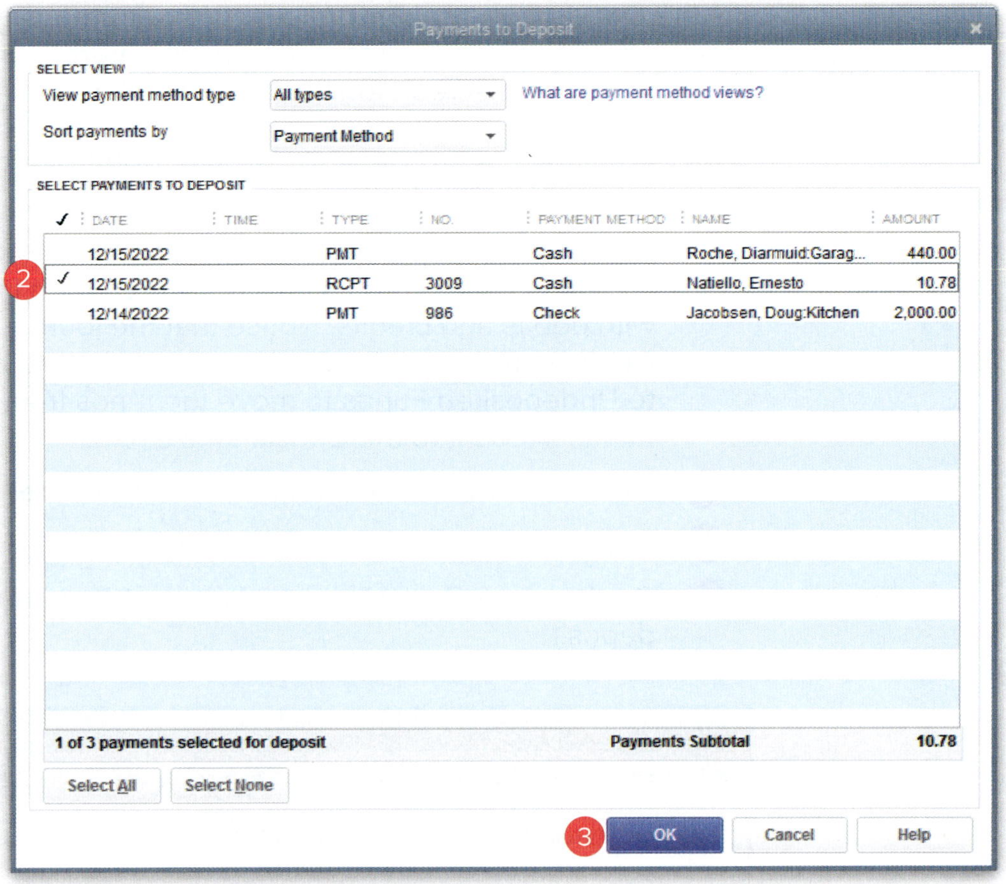
Payments to Deposit
SELECT VIEW
View payment method type
All types
What are payment method views?
Sort payments by
Payment Method
SELECT PAYMENTS TO DEPOSIT
✓ DATE TIME TYPE NO. PAYMENT METHOD NAME AMOUNT
12/15/2022 PMT Cash Roche, Diarmuid:Garag... 440.00
✓ 12/15/2022 RCPT 3009 Cash Natiello, Ernesto 10.78
12/14/2022 PMT 986 Check Jacobsen, Doug:Kitchen 2,000.00
1 of 3 payments selected for deposit
Payments Subtotal 10.78
Select All
Select None
OK
Cancel
Help
2
3

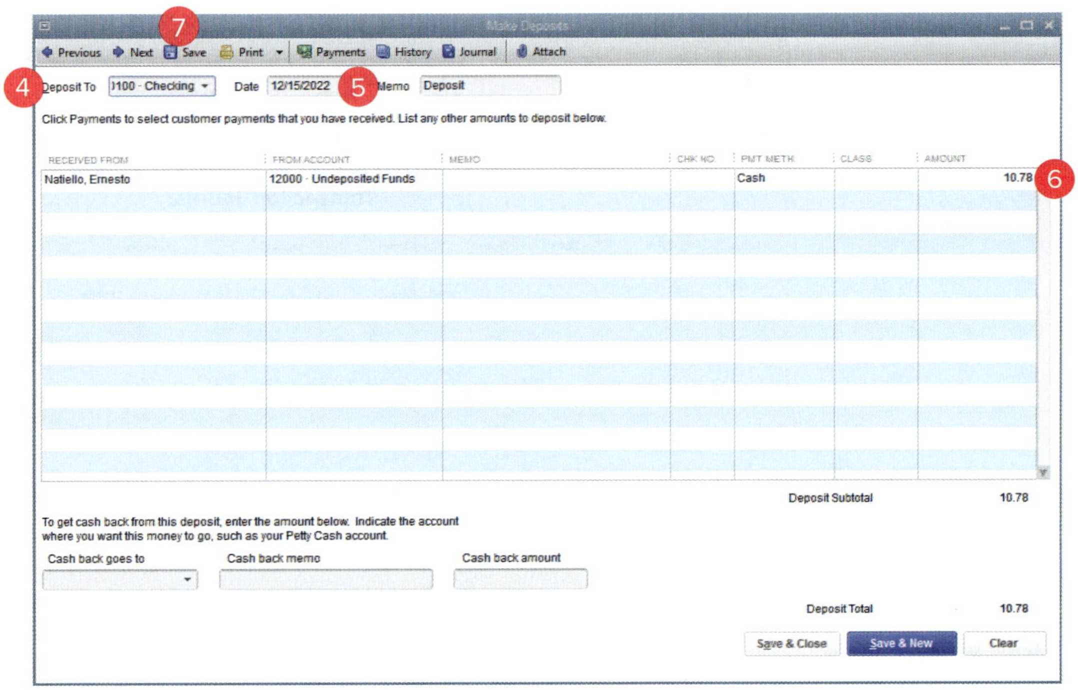
Make Deposits
Previous Next Save Print Payments History Journal Attach
Deposit To 1100 · Checking Date 12/15/2022 Memo Deposit
Click Payments to select customer payments that you have received. List any other amounts to deposit below.
RECEIVED FROM FROM ACCOUNT MEMO CHK NO. PMT METH. CLASS AMOUNT
Natiello, Ernesto 12000 · Undeposited Funds Cash 10.78
Deposit Subtotal 10.78
To get cash back from this deposit, enter the amount below. Indicate the account
where you want this money to go, such as your Petty Cash account.
Cash back goes to
Cash back memo
Cash back amount
Deposit Total 10.78
Save & Close
Save & New
Clear
4
5
6
7

C3.7.2 Deposit Journal Entry. To view the journal entry that QuickBooks created behind the screen for the deposit entered and saved using the Record Deposit onscreen form above, complete the following steps.

1. From the Record Deposit onscreen form, select the **Journal** icon at the top of the form
2. Behind the screen, QuickBooks automatically converted the information in the Record Deposit onscreen form into a journal entry with debits and credits. Notice that the journal entry displays a Debit (increase) to the Checking account and a Credit (decrease) to Undeposited Funds to move the funds from the Undeposited Funds account to the Checking account.
3. Export the Transaction Journal report to **Excel** or **print** the report
4. **Close** the Transaction Journal window
5. On the Make Deposits window, select **Save & Close** to save the deposit

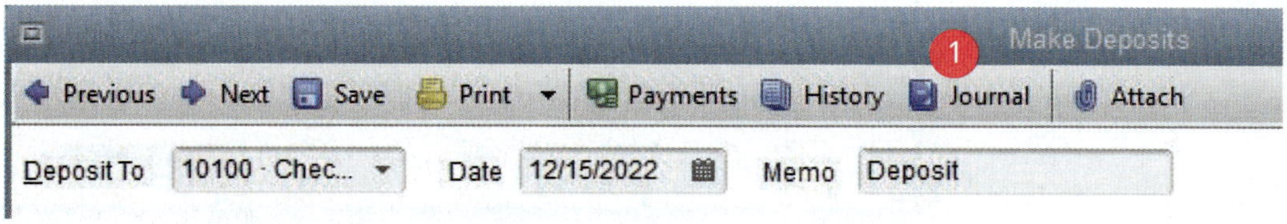

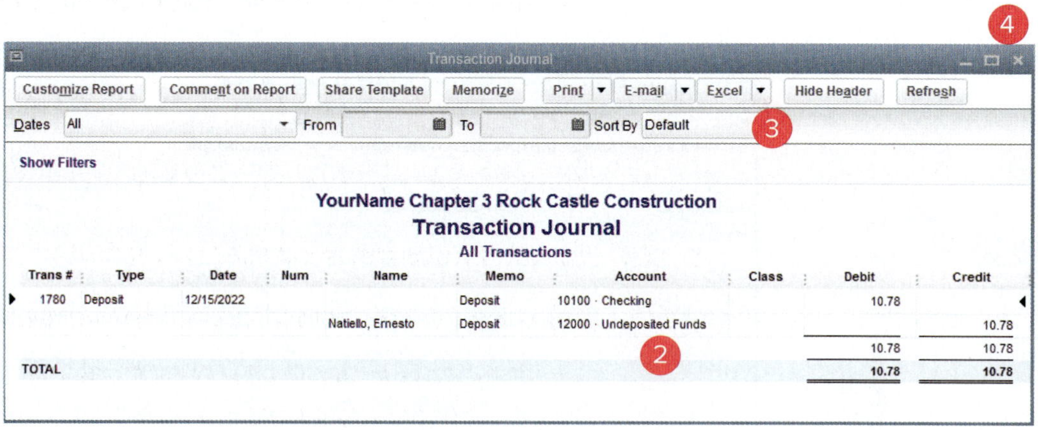

Section 3.8

VENDOR AND EXPENSE TRANSACTIONS

QB SatNav

2 **QB TRANSACTIONS** CHAPTERS 3 4 5 6 7 8 11 12 13 14

> Money in *Money out >*

Banking
Customers/Sales
Vendors/Expenses
Employees/Payroll

Vendors transactions are exchanges between our company and vendors of our company. Typically, these exchanges focus on expense transactions. Vendors include suppliers who sell products and professionals who provide services to our company.

We can enter vendors and expenses transactions using the Vendors section of the Home Page.

Vendors transactions can include:

1. Enter bills for services received
2. Pay bills

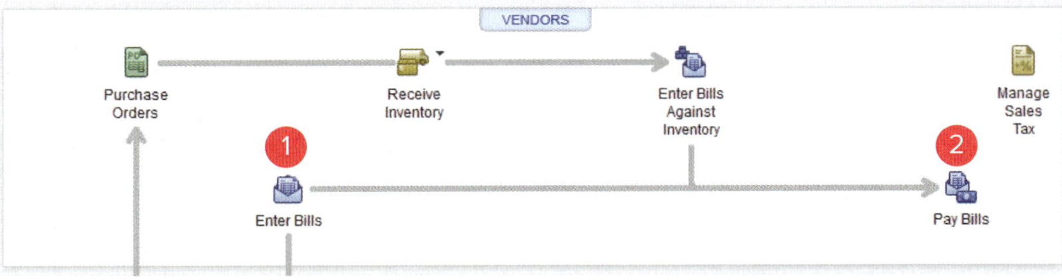

ENTER BILL

To enter bills for expenses:

1. Click the **Enter Bills** icon in the Vendors section of the Home Page
2. When the Enter Bills window appears, click the **Expenses** tab
3. Enter the following information for Rock Castle's water bill in the Enter Bills window

Vendor	**Bayshore Water**
Date	**12/15/2022**
Amount Due	**$36.00**
Terms	**Net 30**
Account	**65130: Water**

4. Select **Save**

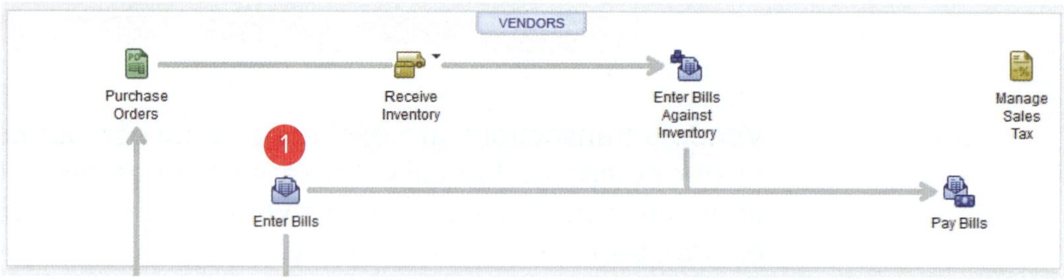

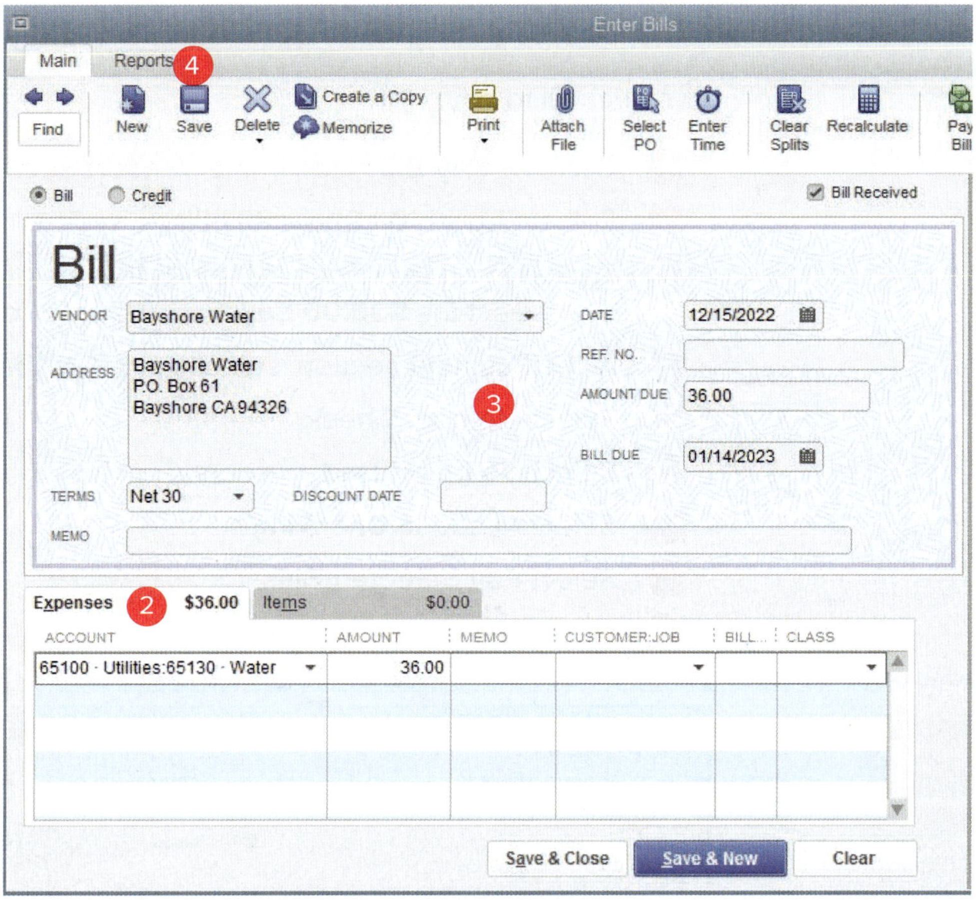

C3.8.1 Bill Journal Entry. To view the journal entry that QuickBooks created behind the screen for the bill entered and saved using the Enter Bills onscreen form above, complete the following steps.

1. From the Enter Bills onscreen form, select the **Reports** tab
2. Select the **Transaction Journal** icon
3. Export the Transaction Journal report to **Excel** or **print** the report
4. **Close** the Transaction Journal window
5. **Close** the Enter Bills window

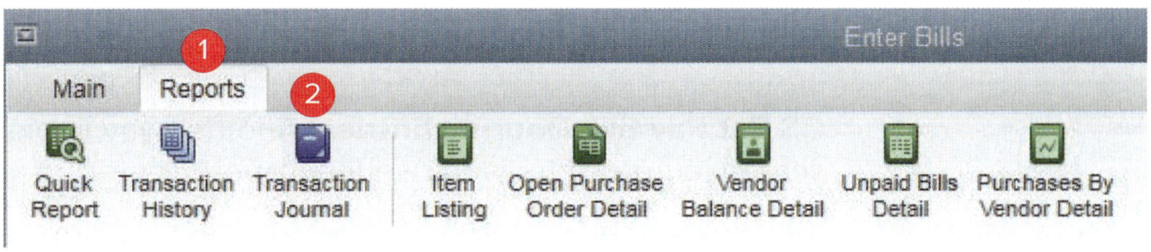

PAY BILLS

To select bill to pay:

1. Click the **Pay Bills** icon in the Vendors section of the Home Page
2. Select Show bills: **Show all bills**
3. Typically, you would select the bills that are due first. In this case, however, select the **$36.00 Bayshore Water** bill due on **01/14/2023.**
4. In the Payment section, select Date: **12/15/2022**
5. Select Method: **Check**
6. Select: **To be printed**
7. Select Account: **Checking**
8. Select **Pay Selected Bills**
9. Select **Done**

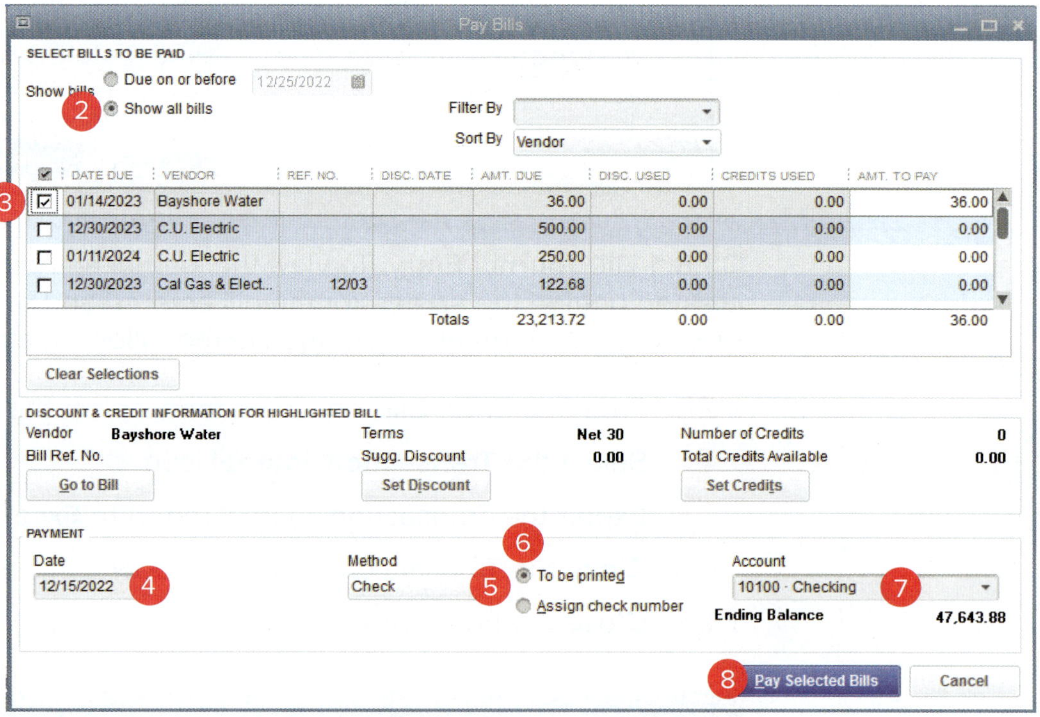

C3.8.2 Pay Bills Journal Entries. Another way to view the behind the screen journal entry is to use the Report Center. To view the journal entries that QuickBooks created behind the screen when bills were entered and selected for payment, complete the following steps.

1. From the Navigation Bar, select **Reports**
2. Select **Accountant & Taxes**
3. Select **Journal**
4. Select Date: **12/15/2022**
5. To add a filter, select **Customize Report**
6. Select **Filters** tab
7. Select Filter: **Amount**
8. Select =
9. Enter **36.00**
10. Select **OK**
11. Export the Journal report to **Excel** or **print** the report
12. Notice that the first journal entry records the expense with a debit and records an account payable of $36.00 with a credit. The second journal entry records paying the bill with a debit (decreases) Accounts Payable and a credit (decreases) the Checking account for $36.00.
13. **Close** the Journal window

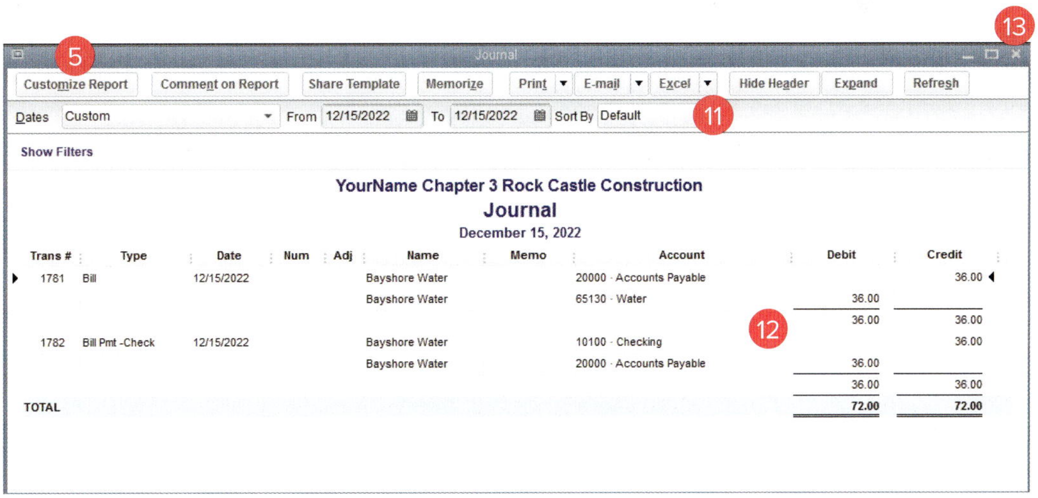

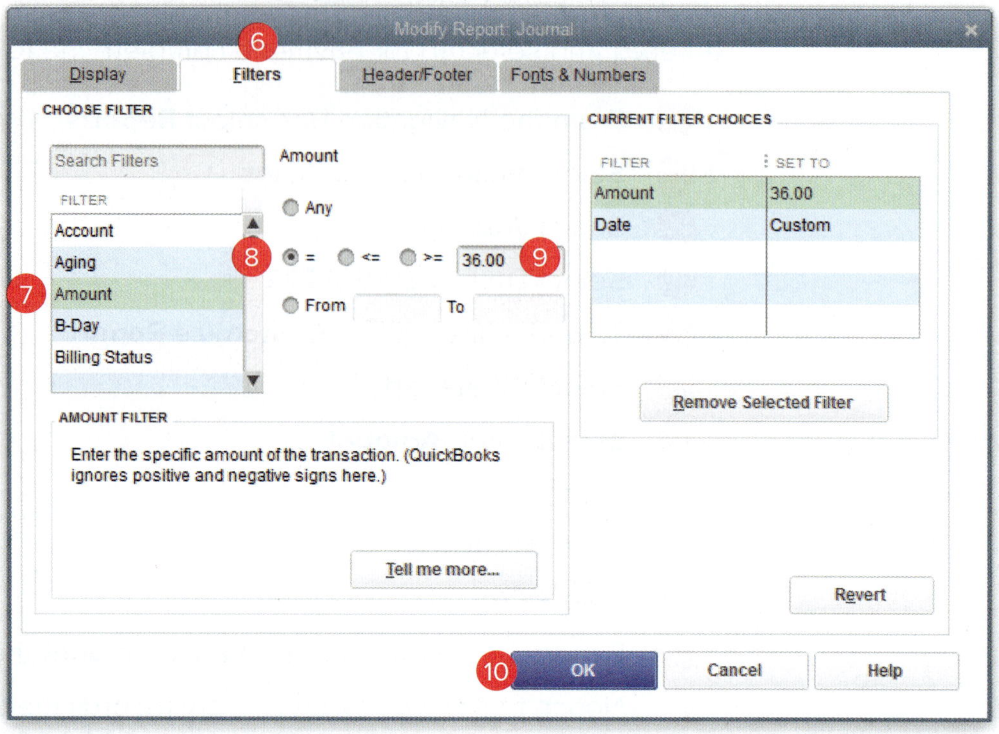
Modify Report: Journal
6
Display
Filters
Header/Footer
Fonts & Numbers
CHOOSE FILTER
Search Filters
Amount
FILTER
Account
Aging
Amount
B-Day
Billing Status
7
Any
8
= <= >=
36.00
9
From To
AMOUNT FILTER
Enter the specific amount of the transaction. (QuickBooks ignores positive and negative signs here.)
Tell me more...
CURRENT FILTER CHOICES
FILTER SET TO
Amount 36.00
Date Custom
Remove Selected Filter
Revert
10
OK
Cancel
Help

Section 3.9

EMPLOYEE AND PAYROLL TRANSACTIONS

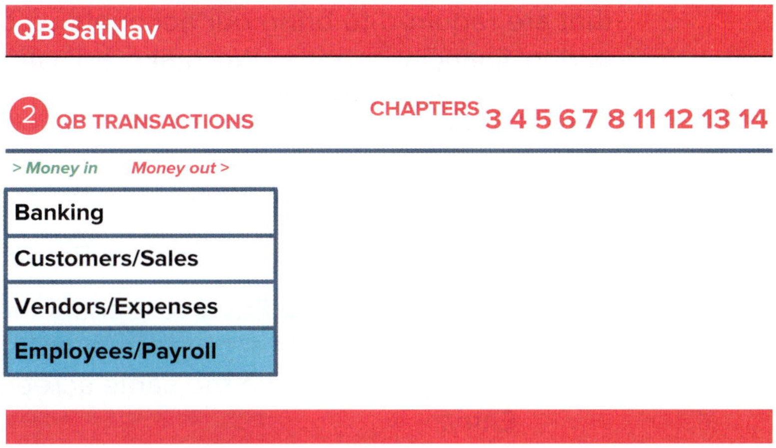

Employee transactions are exchanges between our company and the employees of our company. Typically, these exchanges focus on payroll transactions, including tracking employee time and paying employees for their services to the company.

We can enter employees and payroll transactions using either the Employees section of the Home Page or the Employees Menu.

Employee transactions can include:

1. Enter time that employees have worked
2. Pay employees wages and salaries
3. Pay payroll liabilities owed for withholdings and payroll taxes
4. Process payroll forms

Employee and payroll transactions are covered in greater depth in Chapter 8.

Section 3.10

OTHER TRANSACTIONS

If a transaction does not fall into one of the above categories, then it can be classified as other. Other transactions might include adjusting entries that are required to bring our accounts up to date at year end before preparing financial reports. We make adjusting entries using the onscreen Journal accessed as follows.

To access the Journal:

1. Select **Accountant Menu**
2. Select **Make General Journal Entries**
3. Select **Adjusting Entry** to identify the journal entry as an adjustment to accounts. If the journal entry was not an adjusting entry, then you would use the same screen except uncheck Adjusting Entry.
4. Enter the accounts and amounts for the debits and credits in the adjusting entry
5. **Close** the Make General Journal Entries window without saving

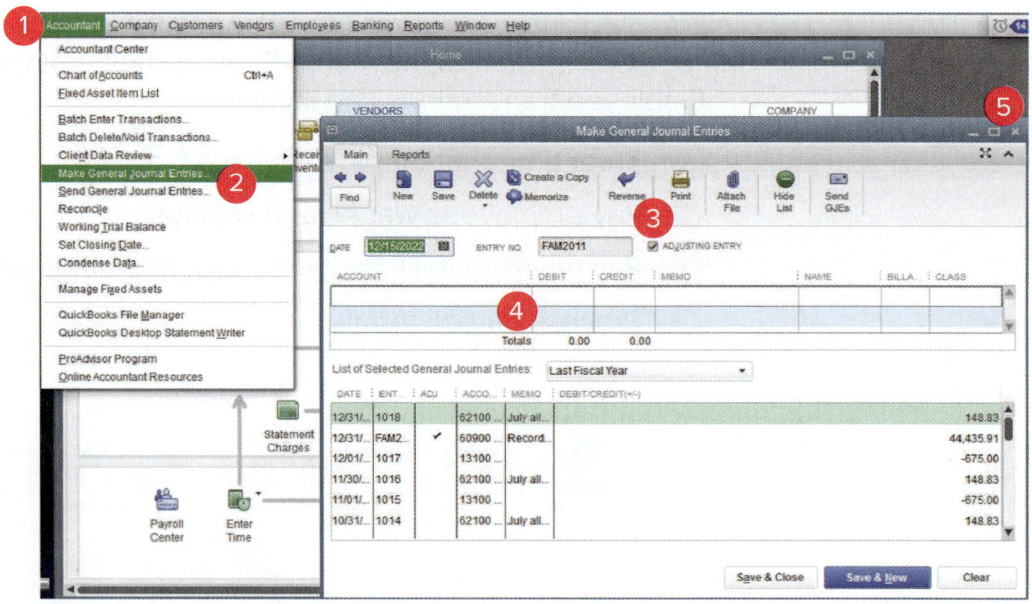

Section 3.11

MEMORIZED TRANSACTIONS

To save time entering transactions, QuickBooks offers a feature that permits us to save a transaction that will be recurring. One way we reduce errors and save time when entering transactions is to save frequently used transactions as memorized transactions.

To access the Memorized Transactions list, complete the following steps.

1. Select **Lists Menu**
2. Select **Memorized Transaction List**
3. Select **Enter Transaction** to enter a new memorized transaction
4. Select a memorized transaction in the Memorized Transaction List to use the memorized transaction to enter a new transaction
5. **Close** the Memorized Transaction List window

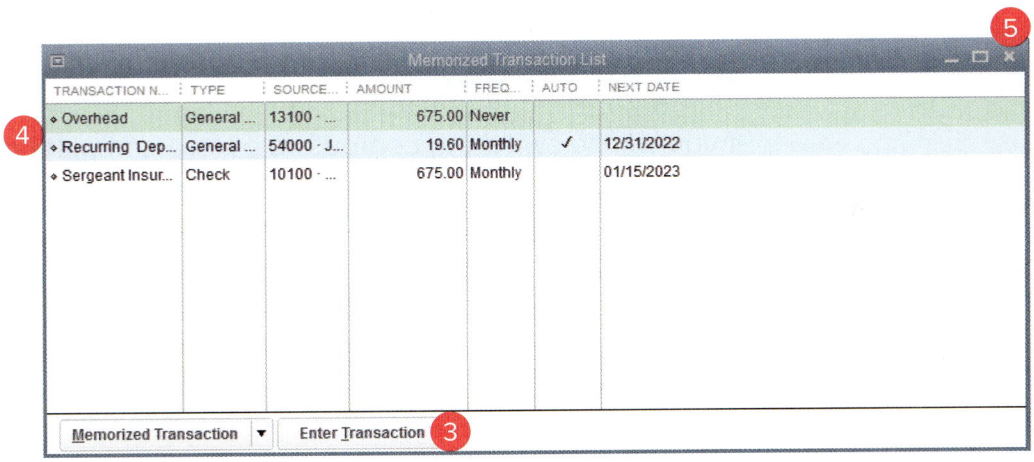

Section 3.12

BACK UP QUICKBOOKS FILES

BACK UP QBB

Save a backup of your Chapter 3 file using the file name: **YourName Chapter 3 Backup.QBB.** For further instructions on how to back up your file, *see Appendix B: Back Up & Restore QuickBooks Files.*

QBW WORKFLOW

If you will be using the same computer to complete Chapter 3 QuickBooks exercises, just as in a business workflow, you can continue to use the same QBW file.

If you are using the QBW approach, leave your .QBW file open and proceed directly to Exercise 3.1.

QBB RESTORE

If you will be switching computers before completing the exercises, after you finish your QuickBooks work session, you will back up to a QBB file in order to move your QuickBooks file to another computer. When you restart your work session on another computer, you will restore the backup (QBB) file.

If you are using the QBB approach, and are ending your computer session now, close your QBW file and exit QuickBooks. When you restart, you will restore your backup file to complete Exercise 3.1.

Section 3.13

ACCOUNTING ESSENTIALS

Double-Entry Accounting

Accounting Essentials summarize important foundational accounting knowledge that may be useful when using QuickBooks

What is double-entry accounting?

- Double-entry accounting is used with a journal to record what is exchanged in a transaction:
    1. The amount received, such as equipment purchased, is recorded with a debit.
    2. The amount given, such as cash or a promise to pay later, is recorded with a credit.
- Each journal entry must balance; debits must equal credits. This is true whether it is a manual accounting system or a computerized accounting system, such as QuickBooks.

In double-entry accounting, how do we know if a debit is an increase or a decrease to an account? How do we know if a credit is an increase or a decrease to an account?

- Whether a debit or credit increases or decreases an account depends upon the type of account.

Account Type	Debit	Credit
Assets	Increase	Decrease
Liabilities	Decrease	Increase
Equity	Decrease	Increase
Revenues (Income)	Decrease	Increase
Expenses	Increase	Decrease

What are the different types of accounts and the effect of debits and credits on the accounts?

- Five different types of accounts are listed below along with the normal balance of the account and whether debit or credit increases the account balance.

Account Type	Debit/Credit	Effect on Balance
Assets	Debit	Increase
Liabilities	Credit	Increase
Equity	Credit	Increase
Revenues (Income)	Credit	Increase
Expenses	Debit	Increase

- For example, if the transaction is the owner invests $100,000 in the business, the journal entry with debits and credits would be as follows.

Account	Account Type	Debit/ Credit	Effect on Balance	Amount
Checking	Asset	Debit	Increase	$100,000
Capital Stock	Equity	Credit	Increase	$100,000

www.my-quickbooks.com

Go to **www.My-QuickBooks.com** to view additional QuickBooks resources including:

- **Excel Report Templates** to organize QuickBooks reports exported to Excel
- ***Computer Accounting with QuickBooks* updates,** sometimes required when there is a software update that affects the text
- **QuickBooks Video links**
- **QuickBooks Help and Support links**

- **Other QuickBooks Resources** to make learning QuickBooks easier and more effective
- **QuickBooks Issue Resolution** offers a guided approach to trouble-shooting QuickBooks

Troubleshooting QuickBooks and Correcting Errors are crucial QuickBooks skill to acquire. See www.My-QuickBooks.com > QB Issue Resolution for Troubleshooting QuickBooks tips. See Chapter 17, Quick Review Guide, for tips on Correcting Errors.

Bookmark www.My-QuickBooks.com for future use.

EXERCISE 3.1: Banking Transactions

BACKSTORY

As you glance up from your work, you notice Mr. Castle tossing papers into your inbox as he charges past your cubicle. *"Here is another deposit to record."*

E3.1.1 QuickBooks File

If you will be using the same computer and the same Chapter 3.QBW file:

1. If your Chapter 3.QBW file is not already open, open it by selecting **File > Open Previous Company.** Select your **Chapter 3.QBW file.** If a QuickBooks Information window appears with a message about the sample company file, click **OK.**
2. Add **YourName Exercise 3.1** to the company name by selecting **Company Menu > My Company.**

If you are not using the same computer that you used for Chapter 3, you will need to restore your Chapter 3 Backup.QBB file using the instructions in Appendix B: Back Up & Restore QuickBooks Files. After restoring, add YourName Exercise 3.1 to the company name.

E3.1.2 Make Deposits

Rock Castle invests $2,000 in Rock Castle Construction.

1. Record the deposit for Mr. Castle's $2,000 check (No. 556). Record the deposit in Account 30100 Capital Stock with a deposit date of 12/16/2022. Use Memo: Investment.
2. Select the **Save** icon at the top of the Make Deposit window
3. Select the **Journal** icon to display the journal entry to QuickBooks created behind the screen for the deposit
4. Export to **Excel** or **print** the Transaction Journal
5. **Close** the Transaction Journal and the Make Deposits windows

E3.1.3 Write Checks

Write a check to pay the following bill.

1. Use the Write Checks window to record the following check.

Date	**12/16/2022**
Vendor	**Express Delivery Service**
Expense Account	**54520 Freight & Delivery**
Amount	**$54.00**
Check No.	**Select: Print Later**

2. Select the **Save** icon
3. Select the **Reports** tab
4. Select the **Transaction Journal** icon
5. Export the Transaction Journal report to **Excel** or **print** the report
6. **Close** the Transaction Journal and the Write Checks windows

E3.1.4 Back Up Exercise 3.1

Save a backup of your Exercise file using the file name: YourName Exercise 3.1 Backup.QBB. See *Appendix B: Back Up & Restore QuickBooks Files* for instructions.

EXERCISE 3.2: Customer and Sales Transactions

E3.2.1 QuickBooks File

If you will be using the same computer and the same QBW file:

1. Select your **QBW file.**
2. Add **YourName Exercise 3.2** to the company name by selecting **Company Menu > My Company.**

> **If you are not using the same computer that you used for Chapter 3 and Exercise 3.1,** you will need to restore your latest prior Backup.QBB file using the instructions in Appendix B: Back Up & Restore QuickBooks files. After restoring, add YourName Exercise 3.2 to the company name.

E3.2.2 Sales Receipts

1. Enter the following sales receipts for Rock Castle Construction.

Date	**12/16/2022**
Customer	**Keenan, Bridget: Storage Shed**
Item	**Lumber: Trim**
Quantity	**2**
Rate	**$15.00 each**
Payment	**Cash**
Tax	**Taxable Sales**

2. Select the **Save** icon
3. Select the **Reports** tab
4. Select the **Transaction Journal** icon
5. Export the Transaction Journal report to **Excel** or **print** the report
6. **Close** the Transaction Journal and the Enter Sales Receipts windows

E3.2.3 Make Deposits

1. Record the deposit to transfer funds from the Undeposited Funds account to the Checking account for the following sales receipt

Date	**12/16/2022**
Customer	**Keenan, Bridget: Storage Shed**
Amount	**$32.42**

2. Select the **Save** icon at the top of the Make Deposits window
3. Select the **Journal** icon to display the journal entry to QuickBooks created behind the screen for the deposit
4. Export to **Excel** or **print** the Transaction Journal
5. **Close** the Transaction Journal and the Make Deposits windows

E3.2.4 Back Up Exercise 3.2

Save a backup of your Exercise file using the file name: YourName Exercise 3.2 Backup.QBB. See *Appendix B: Back Up & Restore QuickBooks Files* for instructions.

EXERCISE 3.3: Vendors and Expense Transactions

BACKSTORY

When you arrive at work, you decide to sort through the papers stacked in the corner of your cubicle. You discover an unpaid utility bill amid the clutter.

E3.3.1 QuickBooks File

If you will be using the same computer and the same QBW file:

1. Select your **QBW file.**
2. Add **YourName Exercise 3.3** to the company name by selecting **Company Menu > My Company.**

If you are not using the same computer that you used for Chapter 3, Exercise 3.1 and Exercise 3.2, you will need to restore your latest prior Backup.QBB file using the instructions in Appendix B: Back Up & Restore QuickBooks files. After restoring, add YourName Exercise 3.3 to the company name.

E3.3.2 Enter Bills

Use the Enter Bills icon in the Vendors section of the Home Page to enter the following bills.

1. Enter the following utility bill for Rock Castle Construction.

Vendor	**Cal Gas & Electric**
Date	**12/16/2022**
Amount Due	**$81.00**
Account	**65110: Gas and Electric**

2. Select the **Save** icon at the top of the Enter Bills window
3. Select the **Reports** tab
4. Select the **Transaction Journal** icon
5. Export the Transaction Journal report to **Excel** or **print** the report
6. **Close** the Transaction Journal and the Enter Bills windows

E3.3.3 Pay Bills

1. On **12/17/2022,** pay by check the Cal Gas & Electric utility bill that you entered. (Hint: select Show all bills.)
2. From the Navigation Bar, select **Reports > Accountant & Taxes > Journal**
3. Select Dates: **12/16/2022 To 12/17/2022**
4. Customize the report to add a filter for amount equal to **$81.00**
5. Export the Journal report to **Excel** or **print** the report
6. **Close** the Journal window

E3.3.4 Back Up Exercise 3.3

Save a backup of your Exercise file using the file name: YourName Exercise 3.3 Backup.QBB. See *Appendix B: Back Up & Restore QuickBooks Files* for instructions.

PROJECT 3.1

Larry's Landscaping

As an accounting consultant for Larry's Landscaping, complete the following to enter transactions for the company.

QB SatNav

The objective of Project 3.1 is to facilitate your mastery of QuickBooks Desktop. As shown in the following QB SatNav, Project 3.1 focuses on QB Transactions.

QB SatNav

1 QB SETTINGS

- Company Settings
- Chart of Accounts

2 QB TRANSACTIONS

> Money in *Money out >*

- Banking
- Customers & Sales
- Vendors & Expenses
- Employees & Payroll

3 QB REPORTS

- Reports

P3.1.1 QuickBooks File

1. Use either your QuickBooks Company file (QBW) or restore the backup file (QBB) that you completed for Project 2.1. (If you have issues with your QuickBooks file, contact your instructor.)
2. Update the Company Name to: **YourName Project 3.1 Larry's Landscaping**

P3.1.2 Banking Transaction: Make Deposits

Enter the following banking transaction for Larry's Landscaping.

1. Record the following deposit.

Date	**12/16/2022**
Received From	**Larry Wadford**
Account	**3020 Owner's Contributions**
Memo	**Owner Investment**
Amount	**$1,300**
Cash/ Check No.	**Check No. 1558**

2. Select the **Save** icon at the top of the Make Deposit window
3. Select the **Journal** icon to display the journal entry to QuickBooks created behind the screen for the deposit
4. Export to **Excel** or **print** the Transaction Journal
5. **Close** the Transaction Journal and the Make Deposits windows

P3.1.3 Banking Transaction: Write Checks

Enter the following banking transaction for Larry's Landscaping.

1. Use the Write Checks window to record the following check.

Date	**12/16/2022**
Vendor	**Computer Services by DJ**
Account	**7552 Computer Repairs**
Memo	**Computer Repair**
Amount	**$180**
Check No.	**1464**

2. Select the **Save** icon
3. Select the **Reports** tab
4. Select the **Transaction Journal** icon
5. Export the Transaction Journal report to **Excel** or **print** the report
6. **Close** the Transaction Journal and the Write Checks windows

P3.1.4 Customers and Sales Transaction: Sales Receipts

Enter the following customers and sales transaction for Larry's Landscaping.

1. Enter the following sales receipts for Larry's Landscaping.

Template	**Sales Receipt - Retail**
Date	**12/19/2022**
Customer <Add New>	**Jean Paulny**
Item	**Pump (Fountain Pump)**
Quantity	**1**
Payment	**Cash**

2. Select the **Save** icon
3. Select the **Reports** tab
4. Select the **Transaction Journal** icon
5. Export the Transaction Journal report to **Excel** or **print** the report
6. **Close** the Transaction Journal and the Enter Sales Receipts windows

P3.1.5 Customers and Sales Transaction: Make Deposit

Enter the following customers and sales transaction for Larry's Landscaping.

1. Record the following deposits transferring funds from Undeposited Funds to the Checking account

Date	**12/21/2022**
Customer	**Jean Paulny**
Amount	**$79.88**

2. Select the **Save** icon at the top of the Make Deposit window
3. Select the **Journal** icon to display the journal entry to QuickBooks created behind the screen for the deposit
4. Export to **Excel** or **print** the Transaction Journal
5. **Close** the Transaction Journal and the Make Deposits windows

P3.1.6 Vendors and Expenses Transaction: Enter Bill

Enter the following vendors and expense transaction for Larry's Landscaping.

1. Use the Enter Bills icon to enter the following bill received by Larry's.

Date	**12/23/2022**
Vendor <Add New>	**Carole Design Media**
Account	**6000 Advertising Expense**
Terms	**Net 30**
Amount Due	**$108**

2. Select the **Save** icon at the top of the Enter Bills window
3. Select the **Reports** tab
4. Select the **Transaction Journal** icon
5. Export the Transaction Journal report to **Excel** or **print** the report
6. **Close** the Transaction Journal and the Enter Bills windows

P3.1.7 Vendors and Expenses Transaction: Pay Bill

Enter the following vendors and expense transactions for Larry's Landscaping.

1. Pay the following bills for Larry's on 12/23/2022.

Date	**12/23/2022**
Vendor	**Carole Design Media**
Account	**$108**

2. From the Navigation Bar, select **Reports** > **Accountant & Taxes** > **Journal**
3. Select Dates: **12/23/2022 To 12/23/2022**
4. Customize the report to add a filter for amount equal to **$108.00**
5. Export the Journal report to **Excel** or **print** the report
6. **Close** the Journal window

P3.1.8 Back Up Project 3.1

Save a backup of your Project file using the file name: YourName Project 3.1 Backup.QBB. See *Appendix B: Back Up & Restore QuickBooks Files* for instructions.

Chapter 4

Banking

BACKSTORY

The next morning as you pass the open door of Mr. Castle's office, you notice he is looking at the financial statements you prepared. You try to slip past his door unnoticed, but you take only a few steps when you hear him curtly call your name.

You turn to see Mr. Castle charging toward you with documents in hand.

"I need you to keep an eye on the bank accounts. Cash is the lifeblood of a business. A business can't survive if it doesn't have enough cash flowing through its veins to pay its bills. So it's very important that someone keep an eye on the cash in our bank accounts—the cash inflows into the accounts and the cash outflows from the accounts. That is your job now."

Handing you more documents, Mr. Castle continues, *"We fell behind on our bank reconciliations. Here is last month's bank statement that needs to be reconciled by the end of the workday."*

After you master QuickBooks bank reconciliations, you send Mr. Castle the following quick text.

Today, 12:57 PM

Bank reconciliation up to date by EOD

Delivered

Section 4.1

QuickBooks SatNav

QuickBooks SatNav is your satellite navigation for QuickBooks, assisting you in navigating QuickBooks

QuickBooks SatNav divides QuickBooks into three processes:

1. **QuickBooks Settings.** This includes Company Settings when setting up a new QuickBooks company and the Company Chart of Accounts.
2. **QuickBooks Transactions.** This includes recording transactions in QuickBooks. Transaction types can be categorized as Banking, Customers and Sales, Vendors and Expenses, and Employees and Payroll. In basic terms, recording transactions involves recording money in and money out.
3. **QuickBooks Reports.** QuickBooks reports are the output of the system, such as commonly used financial statements of Balance Sheet, Income Statement, and Statement of Cash Flows.

Chapter 4 focuses on banking transactions as shown in the following QuickBooks SatNav.

QB SatNav

1 QB SETTINGS — CHAPTERS 1 2 11 12 13 14

Company Settings
Chart of Accounts

2 QB TRANSACTIONS — CHAPTERS 3 4 5 6 7 8 11 12 13 14

> Money in *Money out >*

Banking
Customers & Sales
Vendors & Expenses
Employees & Payroll

3 QB REPORTS — CHAPTERS 9 10 11 12 13 14

Reports

Section 4.2

START QUICKBOOKS AND OPEN QUICKBOOKS COMPANY

START QUICKBOOKS

To start QuickBooks software, click the **QuickBooks** icon on your desktop. If a QuickBooks icon does not appear on your desktop, from Microsoft® Windows® click **Start** button > **Programs** > **QuickBooks** > **QuickBooks Premier Accountant Edition.**

QuickBooks Accountant includes all the features of QuickBooks Pro plus features for client services. If you use QuickBooks Pro, your screens may appear slightly different than those appearing in this text.

RESTORE QBB STARTER FILE

Restore the QBB Starter file for this chapter as follows.

1. Select **File** > **Restore**
2. Using the directions in *Appendix B: Back Up & Restore QuickBooks Files,* restore the **CHAPTER 4 STARTER.QBB**
3. After restoring, add **YourName Chapter 4** to the company name by selecting **Company Menu** > **My Company**

! **QuickBooks Desktop (QBDT)** Data Files are compressed backup files that can be restored and used. To use Starter Files, the compressed file must be restored following the instructions here. Since it is a compressed file, you cannot open and use the QuickBooks data files by simply clicking on the file. Instead you must follow the instructions here to unzip and restore the data file before using it.

Section 4.3

BANKING NAVIGATION

The QuickBooks Home Page contains a Banking section that displays icons used for Banking functions. If necessary click the **Home** icon in the Navigation Bar to display the Home Page.

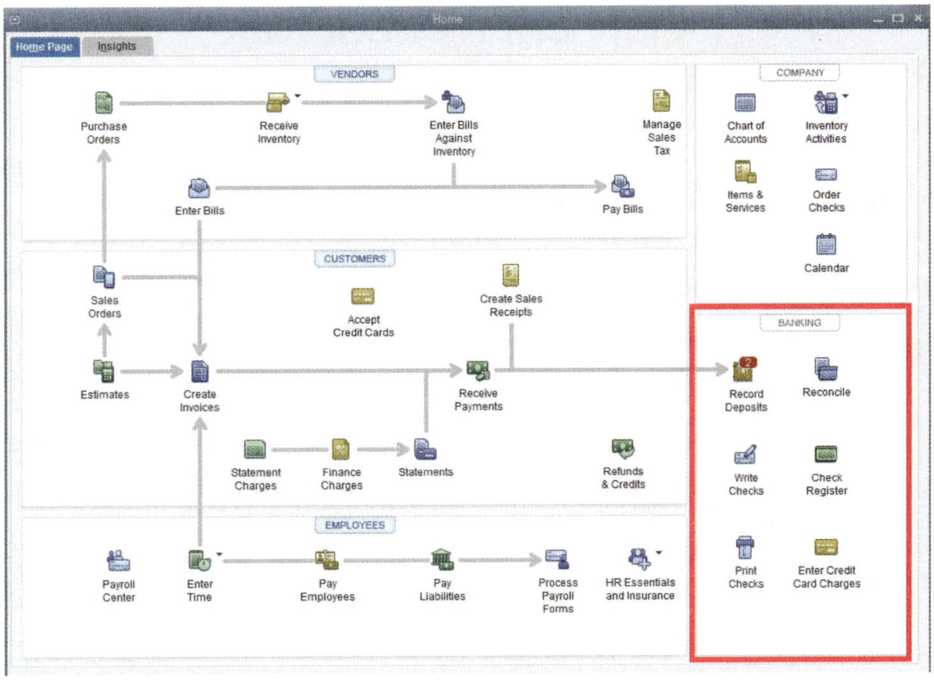

From the Banking section of the Home Page, we can:

- Record deposits (cash flowing into the Checking account)
- Write checks (cash going out of the Checking account)
- Print checks
- Reconcile bank statements
- View Check Register
- Enter credit card charges

A business should establish a *business checking account* completely separate from the owner's *personal checking account.* The company's business checking account should be used only for business transactions, such as business insurance and mortgage payments for the company's office building. An owner should maintain a completely separate checking account for personal transactions, such as mortgage payments for the owner's home.

Section 4.4

CHECK REGISTER

The Check Register is a record of all transactions affecting the Checking account. The QuickBooks onscreen Check Register looks similar to a checkbook register used to manually record deposits and checks.

VIEW CHECK REGISTER

To view the QuickBooks Check Register:

1. Click the **Check Register** icon in the Banking section of the Home Page
2. When the Use Register window appears asking us to specify a bank account, select **10100 Checking**
3. Click **OK**
4. When the Check Register window appears on the screen, notice that there is a separate column for **Payments (checks)**
5. Notice the column for **Deposits**
6. Notice the **Balance** column that automatically updates to show the Check Register balance

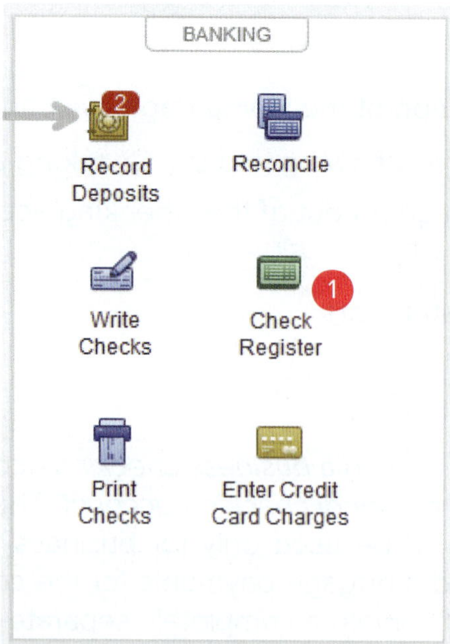

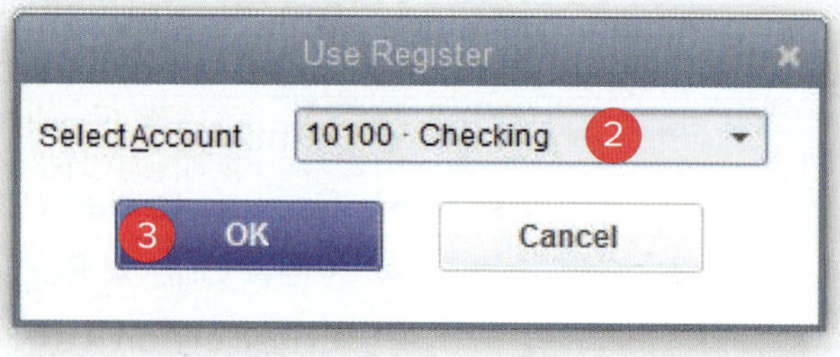

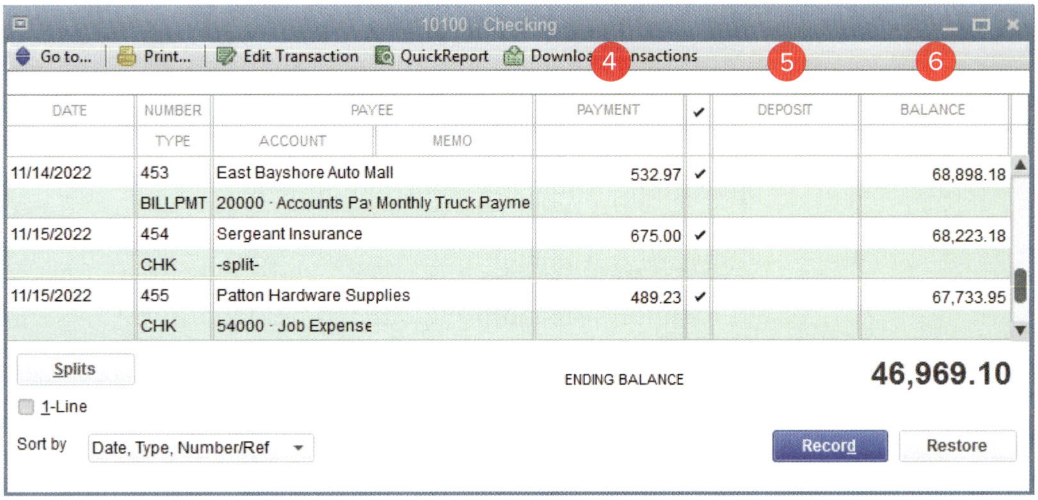

Small enterprises that have strictly cash-based operations sometimes simply use the Check Register to record all transactions. Such enterprises record payments and deposits directly into the Check Register using the Record button. However, most business enterprises require the more advanced features of the QuickBooks accounting software that are covered in the following chapters.

CHECK REGISTER DRILL DOWN

QuickBooks offers a drill-down feature from its registers. QuickBooks drill-down feature permits us to double-click and view the supporting documents. For example, from the Check Register, we can double-click on a transaction to drill down to the source document for that transaction.

To drill down and view the check for the Sergeant Insurance transaction:

1. Double-click the **Sergeant Insurance** entry on **11/15/2022** in the Check Register
2. Notice that the check is stamped **Cleared,** indicating it has already cleared the bank with funds paid to Sergeant Insurance
3. **Close** the Write Checks window by clicking on the **X** in the upper right corner of the window

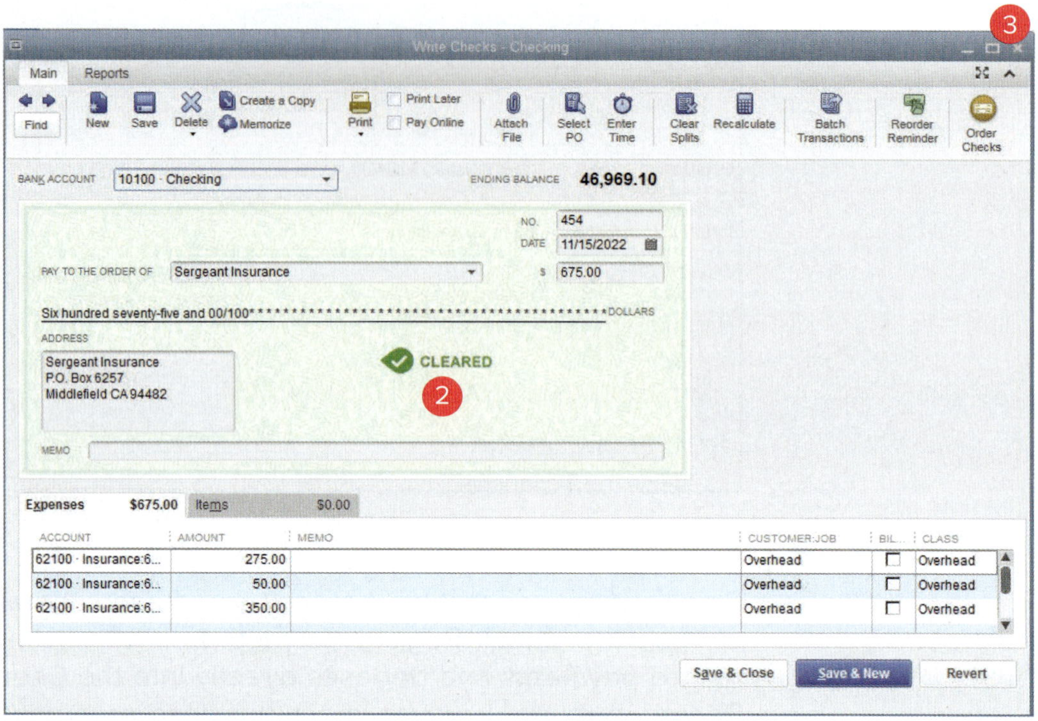

ADD NEW TRANSACTIONS TO THE CHECK REGISTER

We can record deposits and checks directly in the Check Register. Simply scroll down to the first blank line and enter the transaction information. If the new transaction is a deposit, then we enter the amount in the Deposit column. If the new transaction is a Check, then we enter the amount in the Payment column. The Balance will update automatically.

Another way to enter transactions that will appear in the Check Register is to use the Make Deposits window and the Write Checks window.

Section 4.5

MAKE DEPOSITS

Deposits are additions to the Checking account. Any cash coming into a business should be recorded as a deposit to one of the company's accounts.

QuickBooks classifies deposits into two types:

1. Payments from customers
2. Nonsales receipts (deposits other than customer payments) such as:
   - Cash received from loans
   - Investments from owners
   - Interest earned
   - Other income, such as rental income

Payments from customers are entered using the Customers section of the Home Page. For more information about recording payments from customers, see Chapter 5: Customers and Sales. Deposits other than customer payments are recorded using the Banking section of the Home Page.

QuickBooks uses a one-step or two-step process to record payments received. One-step process records the deposit directly in the Checking account. When we use the two-step process to record payments received:

1. Record the payment received but not yet deposited in an Undeposited Funds account
2. Record the deposit in the Checking account

The reason QuickBooks uses this two-step process is when our business has multiple deposits on the same day. We can record the payments received in the Undeposited Funds account when we receive the payments. Then when we make the bank deposit consisting of multiple payments, we record the transfer of the total deposit from the Undeposited Funds account to the Checking account.

Mr. Castle wants to invest an additional $72,000 in the business by depositing his $72,000 check in Rock Castle Construction's Checking account.

C4.5.1 Deposit Journal Entry. To record nonsales receipts (a deposit other than a customer payment):

1. From the Banking section of the Home Page, click the **Record Deposits** icon

2. When the Payments to Deposit window appears, notice the payments listed. These are undeposited funds that have been recorded as received but not yet deposited in the bank. Since these amounts will be deposited at a later time, confirm that none of the payments have been selected for deposit, then click **OK.**
3. When the Make Deposits window appears, record Mr. Castle's $72,000 deposit. Select Deposit To: **10100 Checking.**
4. Select Date: **12/15/2022**
5. Click in the Received From column and type: **Rock Castle.** Press the **Tab** key.
6. When prompted, select **Quick Add** to add the name to the Name List
7. Select Name Type: **Other**
8. Click **OK**
9. Click in the From Account column. From the drop-down list of accounts, select **30100 Capital Stock.** Press **Tab.**
10. Enter Memo: **Investment**
11. Enter Check No.: **555** (the number of Mr. Castle's check)
12. From the Payment Method drop-down list, select **Check**
13. Enter Amount: **72000.** (QuickBooks will automatically enter the comma in the amount.)
14. Select the **Save** icon to save the deposit. (To print a summary of the deposit just recorded, we would select the Print arrow at the top of the Make Deposits window. In this case, we will not print the Deposit Summary.)
15. Select the **Journal** icon to display the journal entry that QuickBooks created for the deposit. Notice that the journal entry to record the deposit of Mr. Castle's $72,000 check includes a debit (increase) to the Checking account and a credit (increase) to Account 30100 Capital Stock.
16. Export the Transaction Journal report to **Excel** or **print** the report
17. **Close** the Transaction Journal window and the Make Deposit window

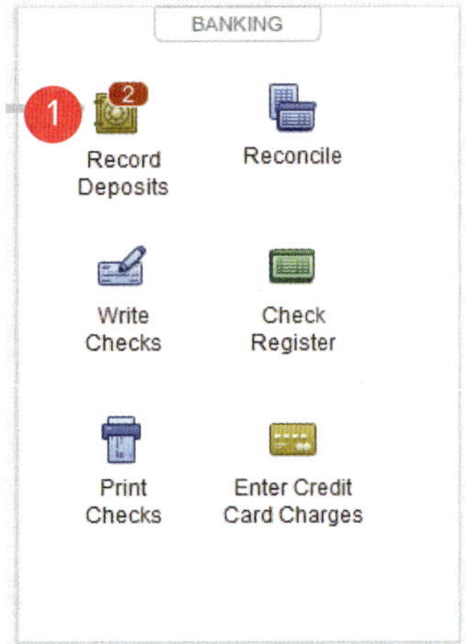
BANKING
1
2
Record Deposits
Reconcile
Write Checks
Check Register
Print Checks
Enter Credit Card Charges

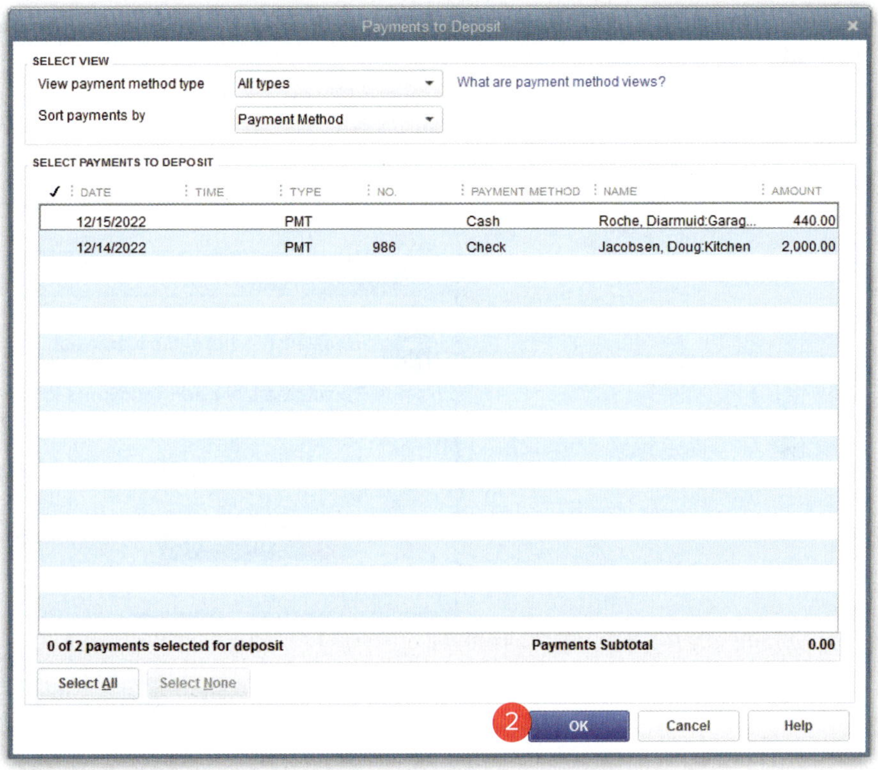
Payments to Deposit
SELECT VIEW
View payment method type
All types
What are payment method views?
Sort payments by
Payment Method
SELECT PAYMENTS TO DEPOSIT
✓ DATE TIME TYPE NO. PAYMENT METHOD NAME AMOUNT
12/15/2022 PMT Cash Roche, Diarmuid:Garag... 440.00
12/14/2022 PMT 986 Check Jacobsen, Doug:Kitchen 2,000.00
0 of 2 payments selected for deposit
Payments Subtotal 0.00
Select All
Select None
2
OK
Cancel
Help

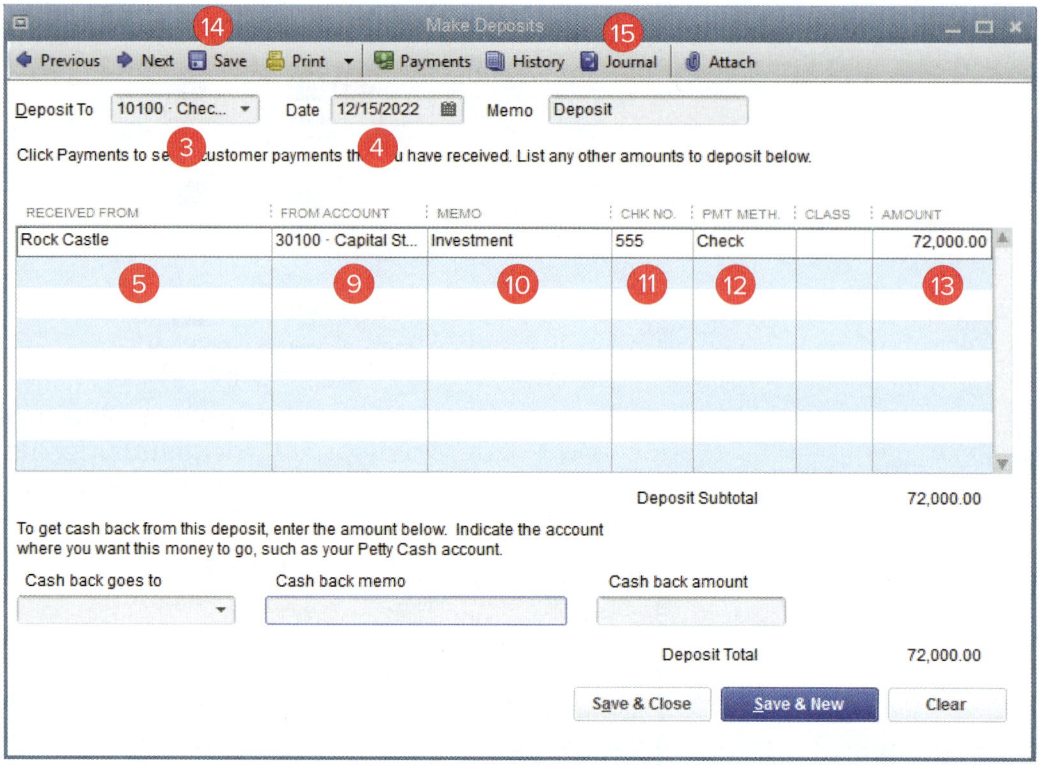

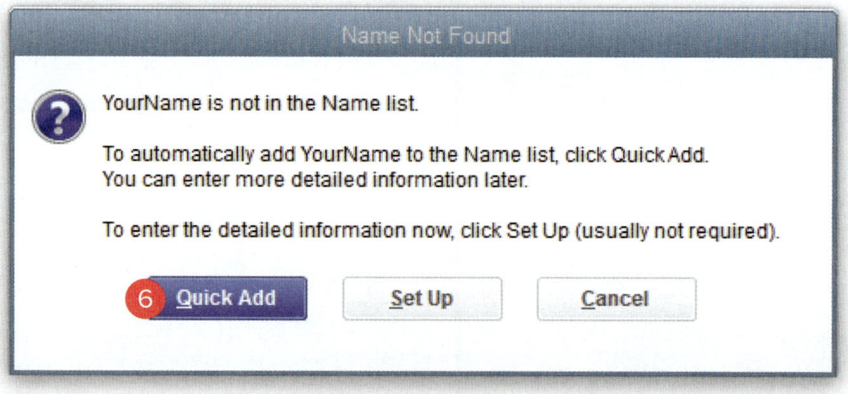

Mr. Castle's $72,000 investment in the company has now been recorded as a deposit in Rock Castle Construction's Checking account.

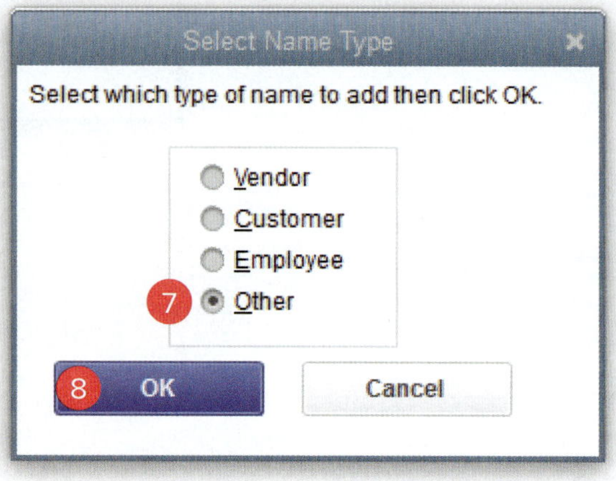

Section 4.6

ONE-STEP AND TWO-STEP APPROACHES TO BILL PAYING

A business needs to track all cash paid out of the company's checking account. Examples of payments include purchases of inventory, office supplies, employee salaries, rent payments, and insurance payments.

Supporting documents (source documents) for payments include canceled checks, receipts, and paid invoices. These source documents provide proof that the transaction occurred; therefore, source documents should be kept on file for tax purposes.

QuickBooks provides two ways to pay bills.

One-step approach to bill paying:

1. Record and pay the bill at the same time. When using this approach, the bill is paid when it is received.

Two-step approach to bill paying:

1. Record the bill when it is received
2. Pay the bill later when it is due

ONE-STEP APPROACH TO BILL PAYING

1. **Pay Bills When Received:** Record bill and print check to pay bill.

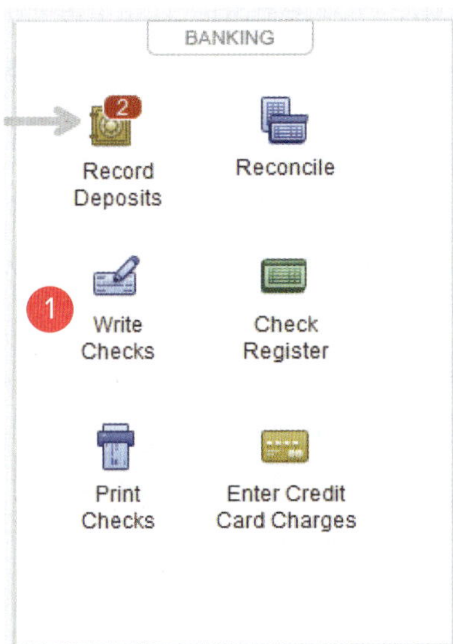

Use the Write Checks window for the one-step approach to bill paying. QuickBooks:

- Records an expense (debit)
- Reduces the Checking account (credit)

The one-step approach to bill paying is covered in this chapter.

TWO-STEP APPROACH TO BILL PAYING

1. **Enter Bills:** Record bills for services, such as utilities
2. **Pay Bills:** Select bills to pay, then print checks

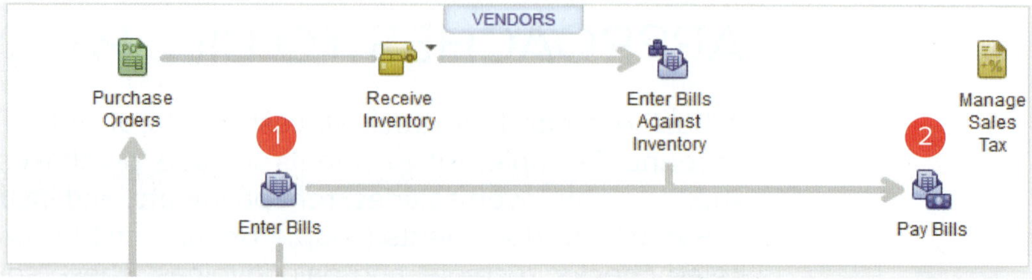

With the two-step approach to bill paying, when bills are entered QuickBooks:

- Records an expense (debit)
- Records an obligation (liability) to pay later (credit)

When the bill is paid and the obligation fulfilled, QuickBooks:

- Reduces the liability (debit)
- Reduces the Checking account (credit)

The two-step approach to bill paying is covered in Chapter 6, Vendors and Expenses.

WHEN TO USE THE ONE-STEP APPROACH

The Write Checks window (One-Step Approach) should not be used to pay:

1. Paychecks to employees for wages and salaries. Instead, from the Employees section of the Home Page, use the Pay Employees window
2. Payroll taxes and liabilities. From the Employees section, use the Pay Liabilities window
3. Sales taxes. From the Vendors section, use the Manage Sales Tax icon and the Pay Sales Tax window
4. Bills already entered in the Enter Bills window. From the Vendors section, use the Pay Bills window

The Write Checks window (One-Step Approach) can be used to pay:

1. Expenses, such as rent, utilities, and insurance
2. Non-inventory items, such as office supplies
3. Services, such as accounting or legal services

Section 4.7

WRITE CHECKS

In this chapter, you will use the Write Checks window (One-Step Approach) to pay a computer repair service bill for Rock Castle Construction.

C4.7.1 Check Journal Entry. To use the Write Checks window to pay bills:

1. From the Banking section of the Home Page, click the **Write Checks** icon and an onscreen check will appear. We can also open the Write Checks window by clicking the Check icon on the left Navigation Bar.
2. To enter the check information, select Bank Account: **10100 Checking**
3. Select Date: **12/15/2022**
4. For the Pay to the Order of field, select: **Bruce's Office Machines**
5. Enter the check amount: **100.00**
6. Click the checkbox preceding **Print Later** so that a check mark appears. This tells QuickBooks to both record and print the check. The Check No. field will now display: To Print. Notice there is also an option to Pay Online.
7. Next, to record the payment in the correct account using the lower portion of the Write Checks window, select the **Expenses** tab
8. If not already selected, select Account: **64230 Equipment Repairs.** Account 64200 Repairs: 64230 Equipment Repairs should appear in the Account column and $100 should automatically appear in the expense Amount column.

   FYI: If the payment was related to a specific customer or job, you could enter that information in the Customer: Job column and select Billable.
9. If we wanted to print the check, we would select the Print button located at the top of the Write Checks window. In this case, we will not be printing the check.

10. Select **Save.** QuickBooks automatically records the check in the Check Register. Leave the Write Checks window open on your screen.
11. From the Write Checks onscreen form, select the **Reports** tab
12. Select the **Transaction Journal** icon. The journal entry is displayed to record the check written to Bruce's Office Machines for equipment repair services. This entry debits (increases) the balance of the expense account, Equipment Repairs, and credits (decreases) the Checking account balance. If we double-click on the journal entry, we can drill down to the related source document. **Double-click** on the journal entry for the equipment repair. The Write Checks window should appear, displaying the onscreen check that we just prepared. **Close** the Write Checks window.
13. Export the Transaction Journal report to **Excel** or **print** the report
14. **Close** the Transaction Journal window and the Write Checks window

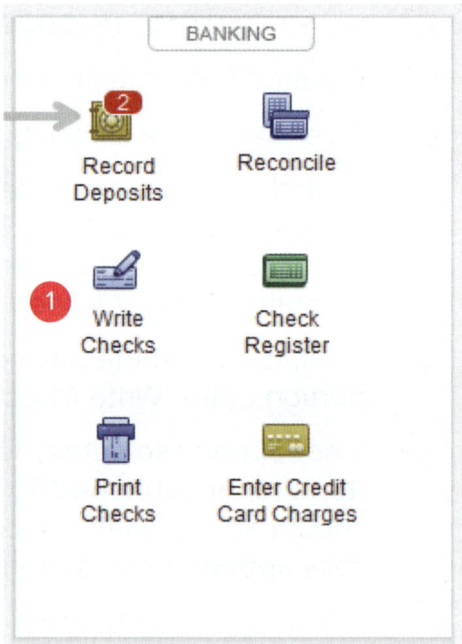

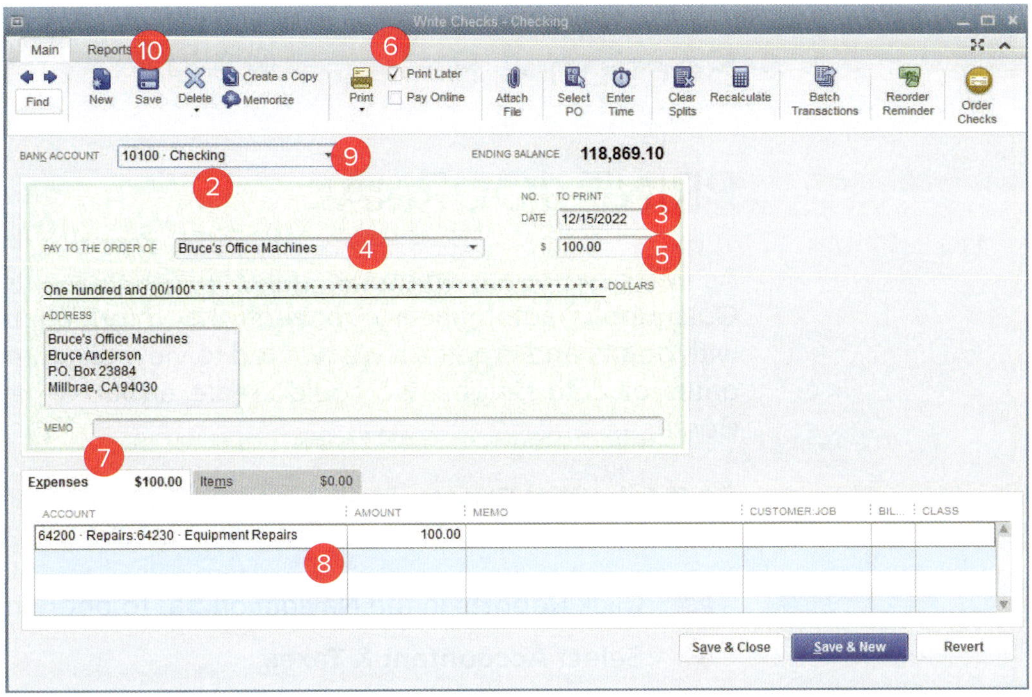
Write Checks - Checking
Main
Reports
Find
New
Save
Delete
Create a Copy
Memorize
Print
Print Later
Pay Online
Attach File
Select PO
Enter Time
Clear Splits
Recalculate
Batch Transactions
Reorder Reminder
Order Checks
BANK ACCOUNT
10100 · Checking
ENDING BALANCE
118,869.10
NO. TO PRINT
DATE 12/15/2022
PAY TO THE ORDER OF
Bruce's Office Machines
$ 100.00
One hundred and 00/100* DOLLARS
ADDRESS
Bruce's Office Machines
Bruce Anderson
P.O. Box 23884
Millbrae, CA 94030
MEMO
Expenses $100.00
Items $0.00
ACCOUNT
AMOUNT
MEMO
CUSTOMER:JOB
BIL...
CLASS
64200 · Repairs:64230 · Equipment Repairs
100.00
Save & Close
Save & New
Revert
1
2
3
4
5
6
7
8
9
10

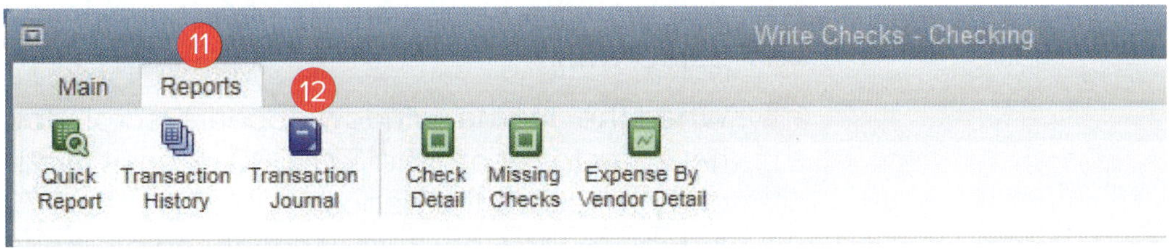
Write Checks - Checking
11
Main
Reports
12
Quick Report
Transaction History
Transaction Journal
Check Detail
Missing Checks
Expense By Vendor Detail

Section 4.8

PRINT JOURNAL

As we have seen, when we enter information into an onscreen form, QuickBooks automatically converts that information into a journal entry with debits and credits. If we wanted to view all journal entries for specific dates or date ranges, we could create a journal report from the Report Center.

C4.8.1 Journal Report. To view and print the journal entries for specific dates:

1. Click **Reports** in the Navigation bar to open the Report Center
2. Select **Accountant & Taxes**
3. Select **Journal**
4. Select Dates: From **12/15/2022** To **12/15/2022**
5. Select **Run**
6. When the Journal window appears, scroll down to find the journal entry to record the $72,000 deposit. Notice that the journal entry to record the deposit of Mr. Castle's $72,000 check includes a debit to the Checking account and a credit to Account 30100 Capital Stock.
7. **Double-click** on the journal entry for the $72,000 deposit to drill down to the related source document, the Make Deposits onscreen form
8. **Close** the Make Deposits form
9. Export to **Excel** or **print** the Journal report
10. **Close** the Journal window

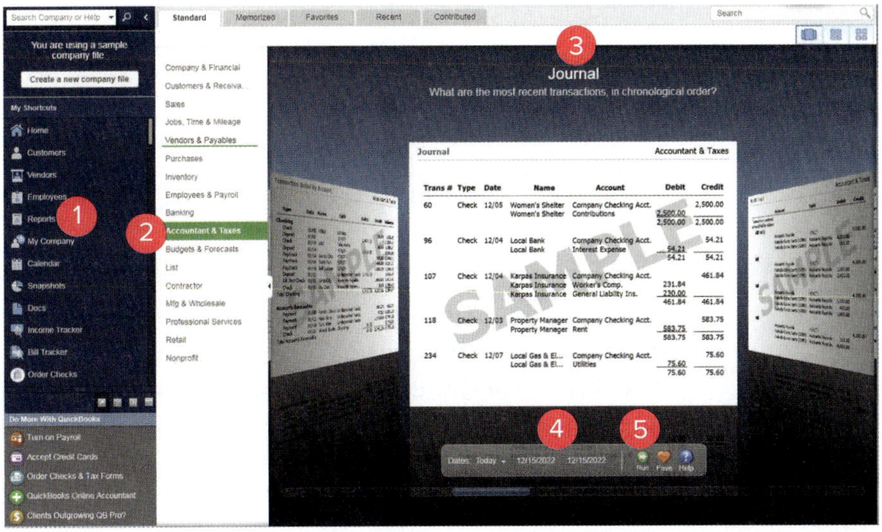
Journal
What are the most recent transactions, in chronological order?
Accountant & Taxes
1
2
3
4
5

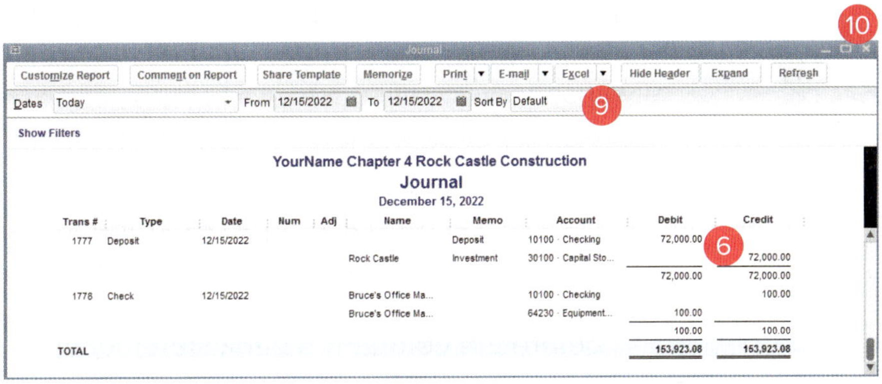
Customize Report
Comment on Report
Share Template
Memorize
Print
E-mail
Excel
Hide Header
Expand
Refresh
Dates Today
From 12/15/2022
To 12/15/2022
Sort By Default
Show Filters
YourName Chapter 4 Rock Castle Construction
Journal
December 15, 2022
TOTAL 153,923.08 153,923.08
6
9
10

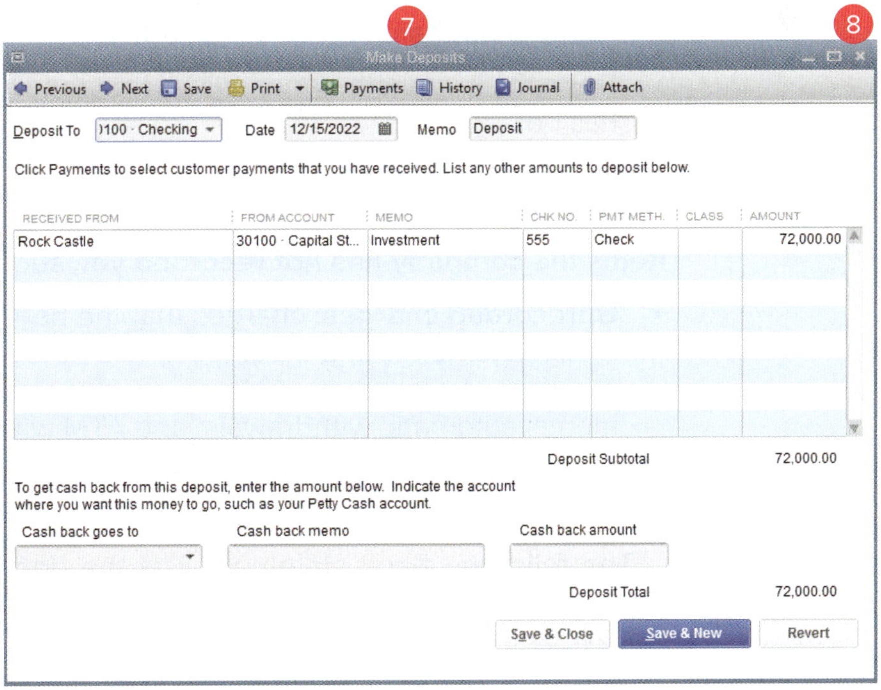
Make Deposits
Previous
Next
Save
Print
Payments
History
Journal
Attach
Deposit To
Date 12/15/2022
Memo Deposit
Click Payments to select customer payments that you have received. List any other amounts to deposit below.
Rock Castle
30100 · Capital St...
Investment
555
Check
72,000.00
Deposit Subtotal 72,000.00
To get cash back from this deposit, enter the amount below. Indicate the account where you want this money to go, such as your Petty Cash account.
Cash back goes to
Cash back memo
Cash back amount
Deposit Total 72,000.00
Save & Close
Save & New
Revert
7
8

Section 4.9

RECONCILE BANK STATEMENTS

Typically once a month, the bank sends a Checking account bank statement to you. The bank statement lists each deposit, check, and withdrawal from the account during the month.

A bank reconciliation is the process of comparing, or reconciling, the bank statement with your accounting records for the Checking account. The bank reconciliation has two objectives: (1) to detect errors and (2) to update your accounting records for unrecorded items listed on the bank statement (such as service charges).

Differences between the balance the bank reports on the bank statement and the balance the company shows in its accounting records usually arise for two reasons:

1. **Errors** (either the bank's errors or the company's errors).
2. **Timing differences.** This occurs when the company records an amount before the bank does or the bank records an amount before the company does. For example, the company may record a deposit in its accounting records, but the bank does not record the deposit before the company's bank statement is prepared and mailed.

Timing differences include:
Items the bank has not recorded yet, such as:

- **Deposits in transit:** deposits the company has recorded but the bank has not.
- **Outstanding checks:** checks the company has written and recorded but the bank has not recorded yet.

Items the company has not recorded yet, such as:

- **Unrecorded charges:** charges that the bank has recorded on the bank statement but the company has not recorded in its accounting records yet. Unrecorded charges include service charges, loan payments, automatic withdrawals, and ATM withdrawals.
- **Interest earned on the account:** interest the bank has recorded as earned but the company has not recorded yet.

The following bank statement lists the deposits and checks for Rock Castle Construction according to the bank's records as of November 20, 2022.

BANK STATEMENT

Rock Castle Construction		11-20-2022
1735 County Road		Checking
Bayshore, CA 94326		

Previous Balance	10-20-2022	$71,452.58
+ Deposits	0	0.00
− Checks	4	4,161.56
− Service Charge		10.00
+ Interest Paid		0.00
Ending Balance	11-20-2022	$67,281.02

DEPOSITS

Date	Amount
	0.00

CHECKS PAID

Date	No.	Amount
10-31-2022	**433**	**712.56**
10-31-2022	**436**	**24**
11-14-2022	**451**	**3,200**
11-19-2022	**460**	**225**

Thank you for banking with us!

C4.9.1 Bank Reconciliation. To reconcile this bank statement with Rock Castle's QuickBooks records, complete the following steps:

1. From the Banking section of the Home Page, click the **Reconcile** icon to display the Begin Reconciliation window shown below
2. Select Account to Reconcile: **Checking**
3. Enter date shown on the bank statement: **11/20/2022**
4. Compare the amount shown in the Beginning Balance field with the beginning (previous) balance of **$71,452.58** on the bank statement
5. In the Ending Balance field, enter the ending balance shown on the bank statement: **$67,281.02**
6. In the Service Charge field, enter the bank's service charge: **$10.00**
7. Change the date to **11/20/2022**
8. Select the Account: **Bank Service Charges**
9. Click **Continue**
10. To mark deposits that have been recorded by the bank as shown on the bank statement, simply **click** on the deposit in the Deposits and Other Credits section of the Reconcile window
11. To mark checks and payments that have cleared the bank as shown on the bank statement, simply **click** on the check in the Checks and Payments section of the Reconcile window. (If we use Online Banking, we would click the Matched button to reconcile online transactions and mark online transactions as cleared.)
12. After marking all deposits and checks that appear on the bank statement, **compare** the Ending Balance and the Cleared Balance at the bottom of the Reconcile window
13. If the Difference amount in the lower right corner of the Reconcile window equals **$0.00,** click **Reconcile Now.** If there is a difference between the Ending Balance and the Cleared Balance, then try to locate the error or use QuickBooks Locate Discrepancies feature from the Begin Reconciliation window. (If you are not finished and plan to return to this bank reconciliation later, click Leave.)
14. When the Select Reconciliation Report window appears, select type of Reconciliation Report: **Detail**

15 Click **Display.** If a Reconciliation Report windows appears stating that the report displays current data, select OK.

16 Export to **Excel or print** the Reconciliation Detail report

17 **Highlight** the items on the bank reconciliation report that are marked as cleared for the November bank reconciliation

18 **Close** the Reconciliation Detail report window

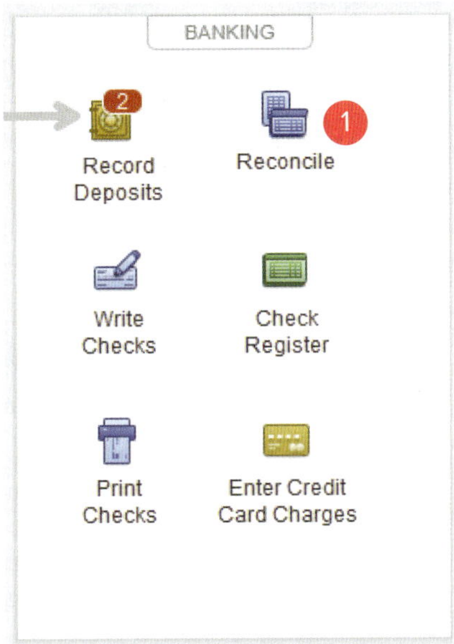

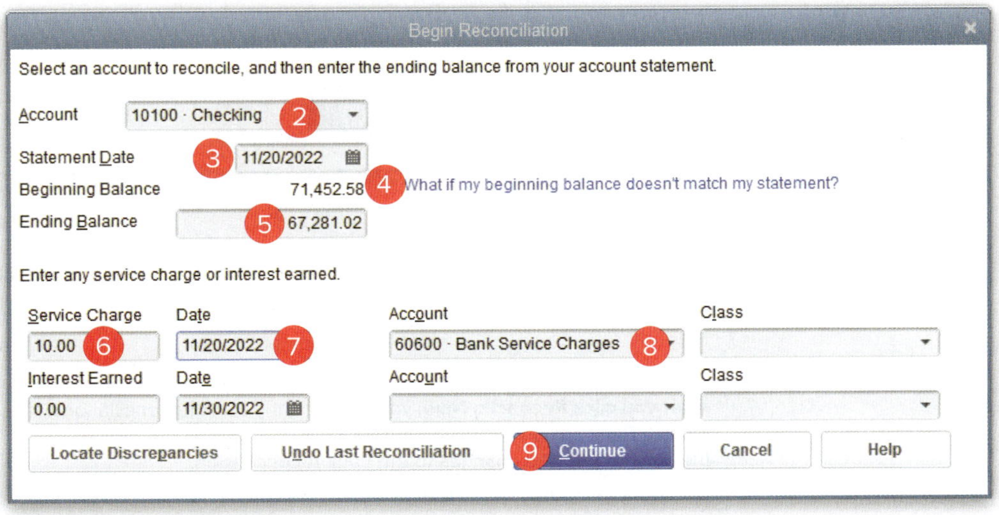

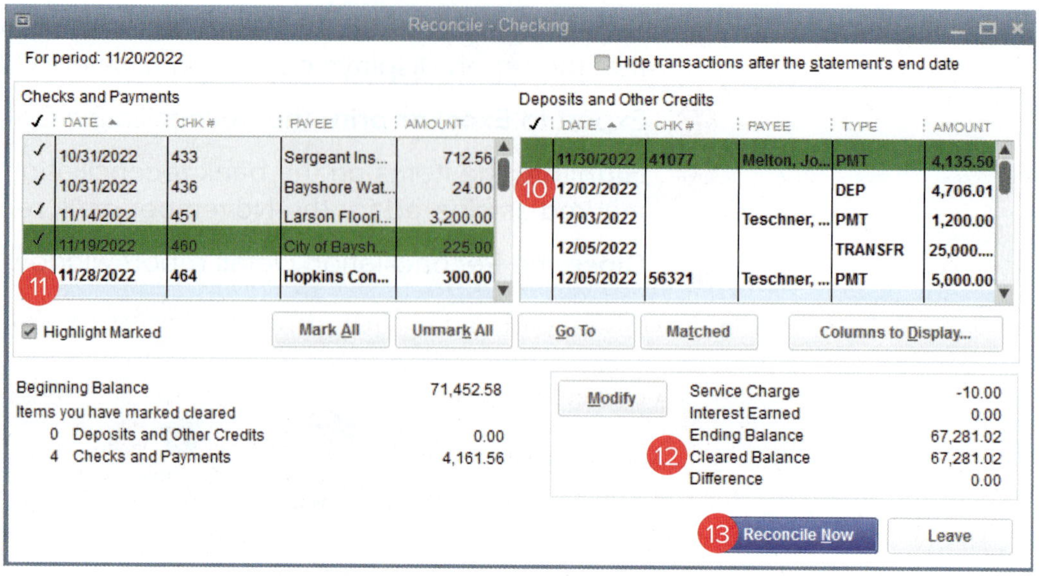

You have now completed the November bank reconciliation for Rock Castle Construction.

After you click Reconcile Now, you can view the Bank Reconciliation by selecting Reports Menu > Banking > Previous Reconciliation.

If you need to make changes to the bank reconciliation:

1. To return to the reconciliation screen to make changes, from the Begin Reconciliation window, click Locate Discrepancies.
2. Another way to change the status of a cleared item: Display the Check Register, then click the Cleared Status column until the appropriate status (cleared or uncleared) appears.

Section 4.10

ONLINE BANKING

QuickBooks offers an online banking feature so that you can conduct banking transactions online using the Internet. View online banking features through the Banking Menu.

The steps for using online banking with QuickBooks are:

1. Set up account for a participating financial institution
2. Enter transactions in QuickBooks and flag online payments
3. Download transactions into the QuickBooks bank feeds center
4. Match or add downloaded transactions into QuickBooks

You can access QuickBooks online banking features from the Banking Menu shown next.

1 Select **Banking** from the Menu Bar

2 Select **Bank Feeds**

3 Select **Bank Feeds Center**

4 In the Bank Feeds window, select the Bank Account: **ANYTIME Financial Account ending in ***1235**

5 Select: **Transactions List**

6 In the section, Tell QuickBooks how to handle these bank transactions, check the transaction for **Anton Teschner.** In the Action column, select **Approve.**

7 **Close** the Transactions List window and the Bank Feeds window

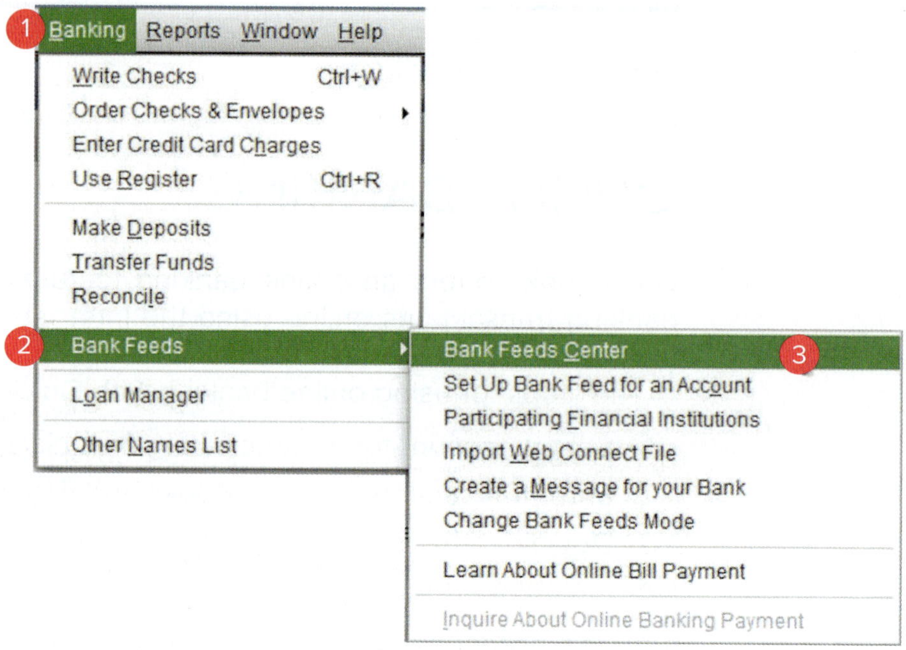
1
Banking
Reports
Window
Help
Write Checks Ctrl+W
Order Checks & Envelopes
Enter Credit Card Charges
Use Register Ctrl+R
Make Deposits
Transfer Funds
Reconcile
2
Bank Feeds
Loan Manager
Other Names List
Bank Feeds Center
3
Set Up Bank Feed for an Account
Participating Financial Institutions
Import Web Connect File
Create a Message for your Bank
Change Bank Feeds Mode
Learn About Online Bill Payment
Inquire About Online Banking Payment

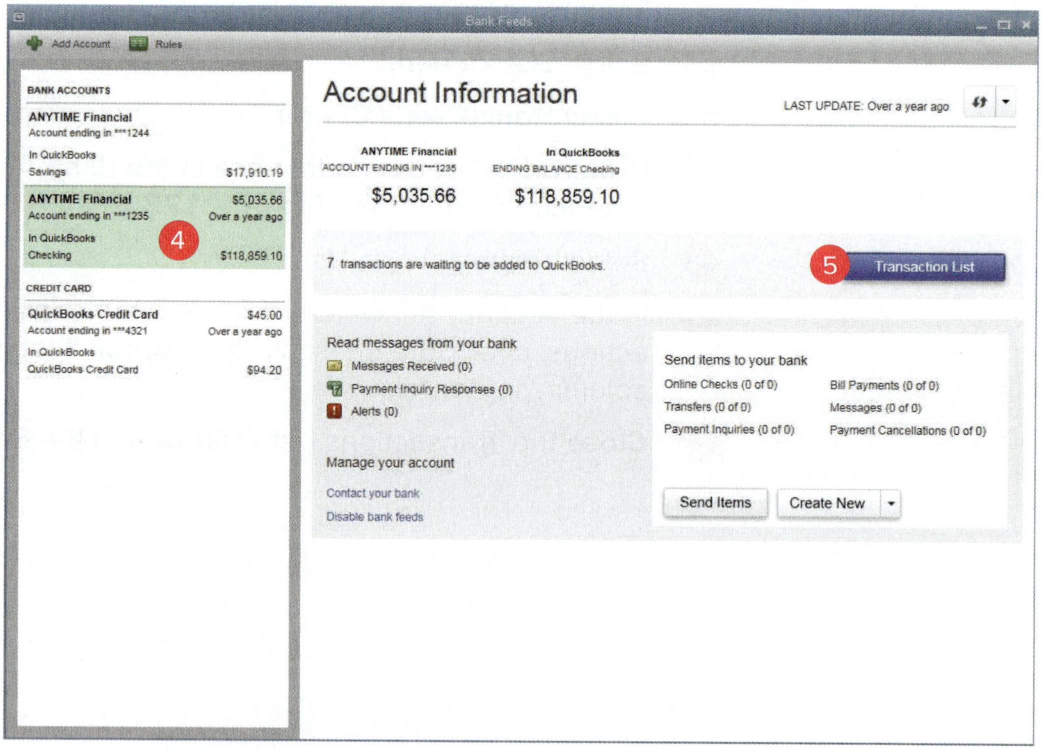
Add Account
Rules
BANK ACCOUNTS
ANYTIME Financial
Account ending in ***1244
In QuickBooks
Savings $17,910.19
ANYTIME Financial $5,035.66
Account ending in ***1235 Over a year ago
In QuickBooks
Checking $118,859.10
4
CREDIT CARD
QuickBooks Credit Card $45.00
Account ending in ***4321 Over a year ago
In QuickBooks
QuickBooks Credit Card $94.20
Account Information
LAST UPDATE: Over a year ago
ANYTIME Financial
ACCOUNT ENDING IN ***1235
$5,035.66
In QuickBooks
ENDING BALANCE Checking
$118,859.10
7 transactions are waiting to be added to QuickBooks.
5
Transaction List
Read messages from your bank
Messages Received (0)
Payment Inquiry Responses (0)
Alerts (0)
Manage your account
Contact your bank
Disable bank feeds
Send items to your bank
Online Checks (0 of 0)
Transfers (0 of 0)
Payment Inquiries (0 of 0)
Bill Payments (0 of 0)
Messages (0 of 0)
Payment Cancellations (0 of 0)
Send Items
Create New

Section 4.11

ENTER CREDIT CARD CHARGES

QuickBooks offers businesses the ability to enter credit card charges into QuickBooks and then to download credit card charges to update and match QuickBooks records.

C4.11.1 Credit Card Charge Journal Entry. To enter a credit card charge for a $50.00 trackpad purchased from Kershaw Computer Services:

1. From the Banking section of the Home Page, click the **Enter Credit Card Charges** icon
2. From the Enter Credit Card Charges window, select **Purchase/ Charge**
3. Select Purchased From: **Kershaw Computer Services**
4. Enter Date: **12/15/2022**
5. Enter Amount: **50.00**
6. Enter Memo: **Trackpad**
7. Select the **Expenses** tab
8. In the Account field, enter account number: **63000 - Office Supplies**
9. The Amount field should automatically display the amount of 50.00 dollars
10. Click the **Save** icon
11. Select the **Reports** tab
12. Select the **Transaction Journal** icon. Notice that this entry debits (increases) the balance of the expense account, Office Supplies, and credits (increases) the liability account, QuickBooks Credit Card account.
13. Export the Transaction Journal report to **Excel** or **print** the report
14. **Close** the Transaction Journal window and the Enter Credit Card Charges window

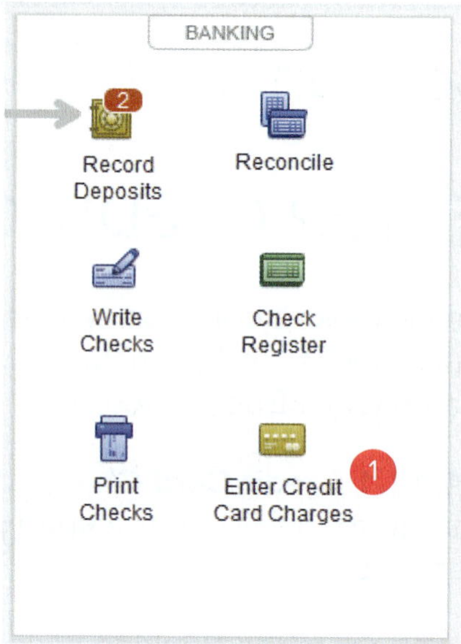
BANKING
Record Deposits
Reconcile
Write Checks
Check Register
Print Checks
Enter Credit Card Charges

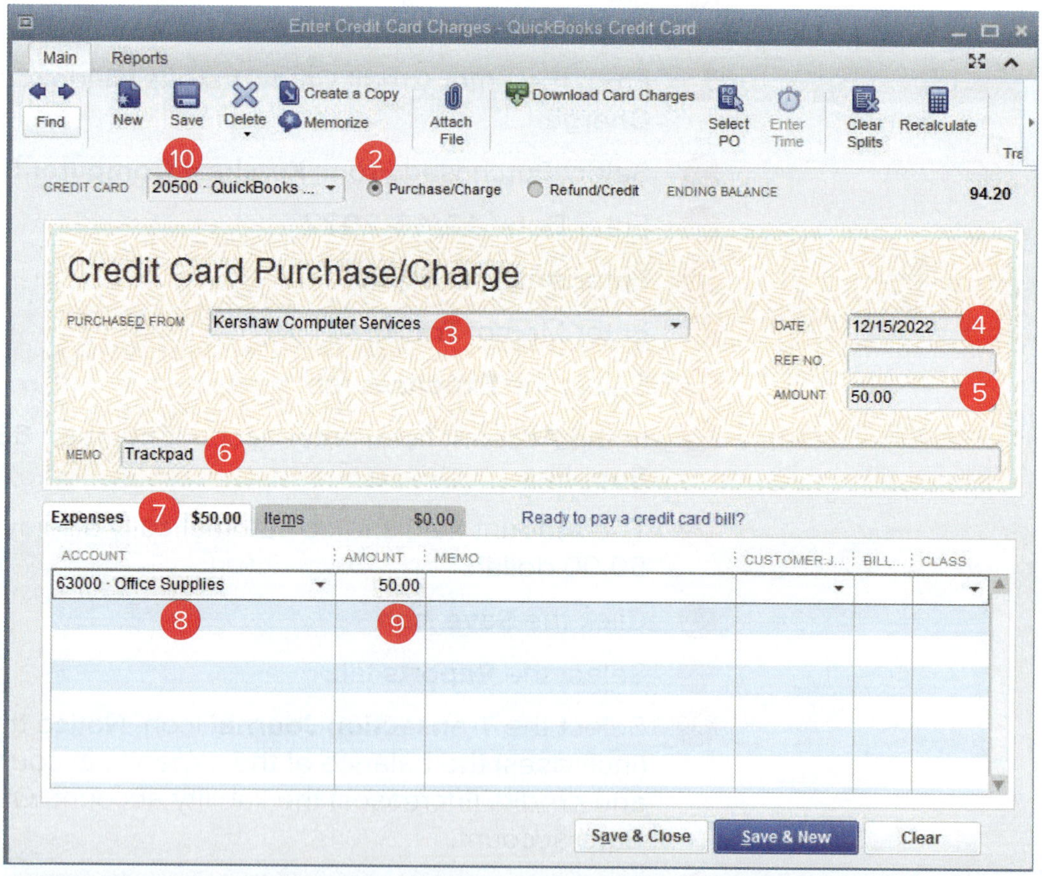
Enter Credit Card Charges - QuickBooks Credit Card
Main
Reports
Find
New
Save
Delete
Create a Copy
Memorize
Attach File
Download Card Charges
Select PO
Enter Time
Clear Splits
Recalculate
CREDIT CARD
20500 · QuickBooks ...
Purchase/Charge
Refund/Credit
ENDING BALANCE
94.20
Credit Card Purchase/Charge
PURCHASED FROM
Kershaw Computer Services
DATE
12/15/2022
REF NO.
AMOUNT
50.00
MEMO
Trackpad
Expenses
$50.00
Items
$0.00
Ready to pay a credit card bill?
ACCOUNT
AMOUNT
MEMO
CUSTOMER:J...
BILL...
CLASS
63000 · Office Supplies
50.00
Save & Close
Save & New
Clear

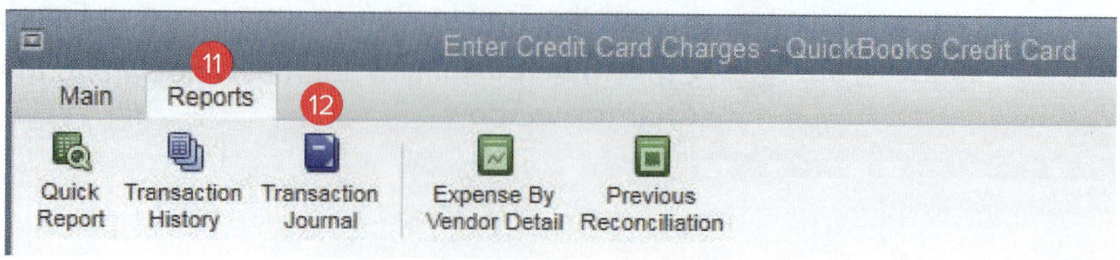
Enter Credit Card Charges - QuickBooks Credit Card
Main
Reports
Quick Report
Transaction History
Transaction Journal
Expense By Vendor Detail
Previous Reconciliation

Section 4.12

BACK UP QUICKBOOKS FILES

BACK UP QBB

Save a backup of your Chapter 4 file using the file name: **YourName Chapter 4 Backup.QBB.** For further instructions on how to back up your file, *see Appendix B: Back Up & Restore QuickBooks Files.*

QBW WORKFLOW

If you will be using the same computer to complete Chapter 4 QuickBooks exercises, just as in a business workflow, you can continue to use the same QBW file.

If you are using the QBW approach, leave your .QBW file open and proceed directly to Exercise 4.1.

QBB RESTORE

If you will be switching computers and are ending your computer session now, close your QBW file and exit QuickBooks. When you restart, you will restore your backup file to complete Exercise 4.1.

Section 4.13

ACCOUNTING ESSENTIALS

Debits and Credits

Accounting Essentials summarize important foundational accounting knowledge that may be useful when using QuickBooks

Why are understanding debits and credits important to understanding QuickBooks?

- For every transaction entered in QuickBooks, there is a corresponding entry using debits and credits. Even if we use QuickBooks online forms, such as invoices and bills, debit and credit entries are the core of the accounting system. Behind the scenes, the information we enter in online forms is converted to debit and credit entries. Understanding these debit and credit entries becomes crucial to understanding the accounting system, tracking errors, and making corrections.

Why can debits and credits be so confusing?

- Sometimes when working with debits and credits, it may seem confusing because sometimes a debit is an increase to an account and sometimes a debit is a decrease. Sometimes a credit is an increase to an account and sometimes a credit is a decrease. So we cannot assume a debit is always an increase, for example.

How do we know whether a debit or credit is an increase or decrease to an account?

- Whether a debit or credit increases or decreases an account depends upon the type of account. So we must know the account type before we know if the debit or credit is an increase or a decrease.
- Five different types of accounts are listed below along with the normal balance of the account and whether debit or credit increases the account balance.

Account Type	Debit/Credit	Effect on Balance
Assets	Debit	Increase
Liabilities	Credit	Increase
Equity	Credit	Increase
Revenues (Income)	Credit	Increase
Expenses	Debit	Increase

- For example, the deposit we recorded in this chapter using the QuickBooks deposit form resulted in a journal entry with debits and credits that we could view in the Journal. Notice that in that entry, the debit to Rock Castle Construction Checking account increased the balance. The credit to the Capital Stock account for $72,000 increased the Capital Stock account balance.

Account	Account Type	Debit/ Credit	Effect on Balance	Amount
Checking	Asset	Debit	Increase	$72,000
Capital Stock	Equity	Credit	Increase	$72,000

www.my-quickbooks.com

Go to **www.My-QuickBooks.com** to view additional QuickBooks resources including:

- **Excel Report Templates** to organize QuickBooks reports exported to Excel
- ***Computer Accounting with QuickBooks*** **updates,** sometimes required when there is a software update that affects the text
- **QuickBooks Video links**
- **QuickBooks Help and Support links**
- **Other QuickBooks Resources** to make learning QuickBooks easier and more effective
- **QuickBooks Issue Resolution** offers a guided approach to trouble-shooting QuickBooks

Troubleshooting QuickBooks and Correcting Errors are crucial QuickBooks skill to acquire. See www.My-QuickBooks.com > QB Issue Resolution for Troubleshooting QuickBooks tips. See Chapter 17, Quick Review Guide, for tips on Correcting Errors.

BACKSTORY

As you glance up from your work, you notice Mr. Castle charging past your cubicle with more documents in hand. He tosses a hefty stack of papers into your creaking inbox. *"Here is another deposit to record. Also, Washuta called to say they did not receive the check we sent them. You will need to void that check—I believe it was check no. 470. I have already called the bank and stopped payment. Also, here are more bills to pay."*

EXERCISE 4.1: Make Deposits

E4.1.1 QuickBooks File

If you will be using the same computer and the same Chapter 4.QBW file:

1. If your Chapter 4.QBW file is not already open, open it by selecting **File > Open Previous Company.** Select your **Chapter 4.QBW file.** If a QuickBooks Information window appears with a message about the sample company file, click **OK.**
2. Add **YourName Exercise 4.1** to the company name by selecting **Company menu > My Company.**

If you are not using the same computer that you used for Chapter 4, you will need to restore your Chapter 4 Backup.QBB file using the instructions in Appendix B: Back Up & Restore QuickBooks Files. After restoring, add YourName Exercise 4.1 to the company name.

E4.1.2 Make Deposits

Rock Castle invests another $5,000 investing in Rock Castle Construction.

1. Record the deposit for Mr. Castle's $5,000 check (No. 557). Record the deposit in Account 30100 Capital Stock with a deposit date of 12/18/2022. Use Memo: Investment.
2. Select the **Save** icon at the top of the Make Deposit window
3. Select the **Journal** icon to display the journal entry to QuickBooks created behind the screen for the deposit
4. Export to **Excel** or **print** the Transaction Journal
5. **Close** the Transaction Journal and the Make Deposits windows

E4.1.3 Deposit Detail Report

The Deposit Detail report lists all deposited and undeposited funds, including the amount of each payment included in the deposit and the customer who made the payment. The Deposit Detail report can prove useful when tracking customer payments that have been bundled into a single bank deposit.

1. From the Navigation Bar select **Reports** > **Banking** > **Deposit Detail**
2. Select Dates: **12/15/2022** To **12/18/2022**
3. Select **Run**
4. Export to **Excel** or **print** the Deposit Detail report
5. **Highlight** in the Deposit Detail report the deposit just recorded

E4.1.4 Back Up Exercise 4.1

Save a backup of your Exercise file using the file name: YourName Exercise 4.1 Backup.QBB. See *Appendix B: Back Up & Restore QuickBooks Files* for instructions.

EXERCISE 4.2: Write Checks

E4.2.1 QuickBooks File

If you will be using the same computer and the same QBW file:

1. Select your **QBW file.**
2. Add **YourName Exercise 4.2** to the company name by selecting **Company menu** > **My Company.**

If you are not using the same computer that you used for Chapter 4 and Exercise 4.1, you will need to restore your latest prior Backup.QBB file using the instructions in Appendix B: Back Up & Restore QuickBooks files. After restoring, add YourName Exercise 4.2 to the company name.

E4.2.2 Write Checks

1. Use the Write Checks window to record the following check.

Date	**12/18/2022**
Vendor	**Davis Business Associates**
Expense Account	**64230 Equipment Repairs**
Amount	**$270.00**
Check No.	**Select: Print Later**

2. Select the **Save** icon
3. Select the **Reports** tab
4. Select the **Transaction Journal** icon
5. Export the Transaction Journal report to **Excel** or **print** the report
6. **Close** the Transaction Journal and the Write Checks windows

E4.2.3 Check Detail Report

1. From the Report Center, select **Banking** > **Check Detail**
2. Select Dates From: **12/15/2022** To: **12/18/2022**
3. Export to **Excel** or **print** the Check Detail report
4. **Highlight** the transaction you entered in this exercise

E4.2.4 Back Up Exercise 4.2

Save a backup of your Exercise file using the file name: YourName Exercise 4.2 Backup.QBB. See *Appendix B: Back Up & Restore QuickBooks Files* for instructions.

EXERCISE 4.3: Void Checks

Since Washuta did not receive Check No. 470 and Mr. Castle stopped payment on the check, you need to void Check No. 470.

E4.3.1 QuickBooks File

If you will be using the same computer and the same QBW file:

1. Select your **QBW file.**
2. Add **YourName Exercise 4.3** to the company name by selecting **Company menu > My Company.**

> **If you are not using the same computer that you used for Chapter 4, Exercise 4.1 and Exercise 4.2,** you will need to restore your latest prior Backup.QBB file using the instructions in Appendix B: Back Up & Restore QuickBooks files. After restoring, add YourName Exercise 4.3 to the company name.

E4.3.2 Find Check

Find Check No. 470 made out to Washuta & Son Painting in the QuickBooks Check Register by completing the following steps.

1. View the **Check Register.** (Click Check Register icon in the Banking section of the Home page.)

2. Next, search the Check Register for Check No. 470 using the Go To feature. Click the **Go to** button in the upper left corner of the Check Register window.
3. In the Go To window:
    - Select Which Field: **Number/Ref**
    - Enter Search For: **470**
4. Click the **Next** button. If asked if you want to search from the beginning, click **Yes.**
5. Check No. 470 on 11/28/2022 to Washuta & Son Painting should appear in the Check Register window
6. **Close** the Go To window
7. To view Check No. 470, double-click on the Check Register entry for Washuta & Son Painting to drill down to the check. Leave Check No. 470 open on your screen.

E4.3.3 Void Check

The next task is to void Check No. 470. There are two ways to remove a check amount from the Check Register:

- Delete the check: This removes all record of the transaction
- Void the check: QuickBooks changes the amount deducted in the Check Register to zero but the voided check still appears in the Check Register, thus leaving a record of the transaction. Should questions arise later about the transaction, a voided check provides a better record than a deleted check.

For Check No. 470 you want to maintain a record of the transaction, so you want to void the check rather than delete it.

Void Check No. 470 by completing the following steps:

1. With Check No. 470 displayed, select the **down arrow** under the Delete icon and select **Void.** The Payment amount should now be $0.00. (Another way to void the check is from the Check Register as follows. With your cursor over Check No 470, **right-click** and from the pop-up menu select **Void Bill Pmt - Check.** VOID should now appear next to Check No. 470 in the Check Register.)
2. Select **Save & Close**
3. When asked if you are sure you want to record the voided check, click **Yes**

E4.3.4 Check Register Report

Next, prepare the Check Register QuickReport to verify the voided check.

1. With your cursor on the voided check No 470, **right-click** and from the pop-up menu, select **QuickReport**
2. Export to **Excel** or **print** the Register QuickReport
3. **Highlight** Check No. 470 on the Check Register report and verify that Check No. 470 is void, showing a check amount of $0.00
4. **Close** the Check Register window

E4.3.5 Back Up Exercise 4.3

Save a backup of your Exercise file using the file name: YourName Exercise 4.3 Backup.QBB. See *Appendix B: Back Up & Restore QuickBooks Files* for instructions.

EXERCISE 4.4: Bank Reconciliation

BACKSTORY

When you arrive at work the next morning, Rock Castle Construction's December bank statement is on your desk with the following note from Mr. Castle attached.

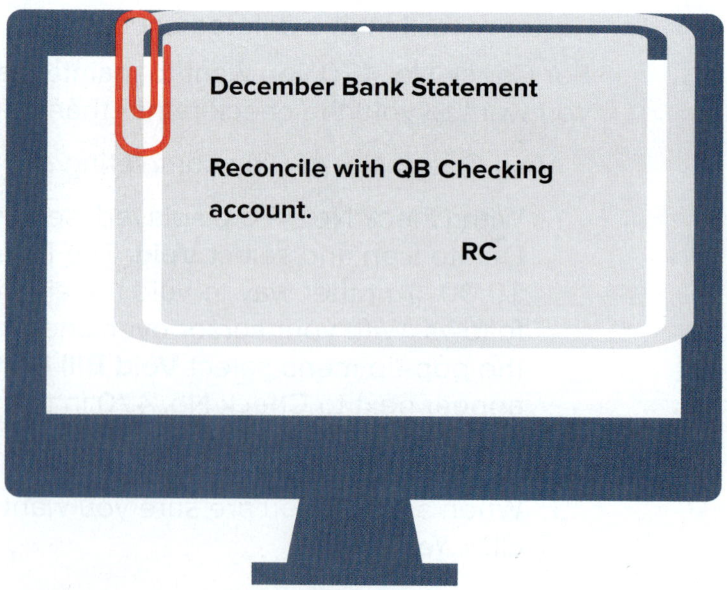

E4.4.1 QuickBooks File

If you will be using the same computer and the same QBW file:

1. Select your **QBW file.**
2. Add **YourName Exercise 4.4** to the company name by selecting **Company menu > My Company.**

> **If you are not using the same computer that you used for Chapter 4, Exercise 4.1, Exercise 4.2 and Exercise 4.3,** you will need to restore your latest prior Backup.QBB file using the instructions in Appendix B: Back Up & Restore QuickBooks files. After restoring, add YourName Exercise 4.4 to the company name.

E4.4.2 Print Previous Bank Reconciliation

Prepare the previous bank reconciliation as follows:

1. Click **Reports > Banking > Previous Reconciliation.** If necessary, select **Run.**
2. Select Type of Report: **Summary**
3. Select: **Transactions cleared plus any changes made to those transactions since the reconciliation**
4. Click **Display.** If a Reconciliation Report window appears, click **OK.**
5. Export to **Excel** or **print** the Reconciliation Summary report

E4.4.3 Reconcile Bank Statement

Reconcile a bank statement for Rock Castle Construction.

1. Reconcile Rock Castle's December bank statement that appears on the following page. If necessary, change the Statement Date and Service Charge Date to **12/20/2022.**

BANK STATEMENT

Rock Castle Construction		12-20-2022
1045 Main Street		Checking
Bayshore, CA 94326		
Previous Balance	11-20-2022	$67,281.02
+ Deposits	10	58,413.56
− Checks	12	15,996.28
− Service Charge		10.00
+ Interest Paid		0.00
Ending Balance	12-20-2022	$109,688.30

DEPOSITS

Date	Amount
11-30-2022	**4,135.50**
12-02-2022	**4,706.01**
12-03-2022	**1,200.00**
12-05-2022	**5,000.00**
12-05-2022	**25,000.00**
12-10-2022	**102.65**
12-10-2022	**1,000.00**
12-12-2022	**4,936.12**
12-14-2022	**4,700.00**
12-15-2022	**7,633.28**

CHECKS PAID		
Date	**No.**	**Amount**
11-28-2022	464	300.00
11-28-2022	465	500.00
11-28-2022	466	600.00
11-28-2022	467	800.00
11-28-2022	468	6,790.00
11-28-2022	469	2,000.00
11-30-2022	471	24.00
11-30-2022	472	656.23
11-30-2022	473	686.00
11-30-2022	474	218.00
11-30-2022	475	2,710.90
12-01-2022	476	711.15
Thank you for banking with us!		

2. In the Reconcile window (lower left corner) "Items you have marked cleared" should agree with the December bank statement:

   - Deposits and Other Credits $58,413.56
   - Checks and Payments $15,996.28
   - Ending Balance $109,688.30
   - Cleared Balance $109,688.30
   - Difference $ 0.00

3. If the difference between the Ending Balance and the Cleared Balance is zero, select **Reconcile Now.** (If the difference between the Ending Balance and the Cleared Balance is not zero, and you want to return to the bank reconciliation later, do NOT click Reconcile Now. Instead, click Leave.)

Another way to change the status of a cleared item:

1. Display the Check Register.
2. Click the Cleared Status column until the appropriate status (cleared or uncleared) appears.

After you click Reconcile Now, you can return to this Bank Reconciliation by selecting Reports menu > Banking > Previous Reconciliation.

E4.4.4 Print Bank Reconciliation Report

1. Export to **Excel** the bank reconciliation summary report
2. Export to **Excel** the bank reconciliation detail report
3 In the bank reconciliation detail report, **highlight** the checks and deposits cleared for the December bank statement

E4.4.5 Back Up Exercise 4.4

Save a backup of your Exercise file using the file name: YourName Exercise 4.4 Backup.QBB. See *Appendix B: Back Up & Restore QuickBooks Files* for instructions.

PROJECT 4.1

Larry's Landscaping

As an accounting consultant for Larry's Landscaping complete the following to enter transactions for the company.

QB SatNav

The objective of Project 4.1 is to facilitate your mastery of QuickBooks Desktop. As shown in the following QB SatNav, Project 4.1 focuses on QuickBooks Banking Transactions.

QB SatNav

1 QB SETTINGS

- Company Settings
- Chart of Accounts

2 QB TRANSACTIONS

> Money in *Money out >*

- **Banking**
- Customers & Sales
- Vendors & Expenses
- Employees & Payroll

3 QB REPORTS

- Reports

P4.1.1 QuickBooks File

1. Use either your QuickBooks Company file (QBW) or restore the backup file (QBB) that you completed for Project 3.1. (If you have issues with your QuickBooks file, contact your instructor.)
2. Update the Company Name to: **YourName Project 4.1 Larry's Landscaping**

P4.1.2 Deposits

Enter the following deposits for Larry's Landscaping.

1. Record the following deposits on the same deposit form.

Date	**12/17/2022**
Received From	**Gussman's Nursery**
Account	**4300 Other Income**
Memo	**Storage Rental Revenue**
Amount	**$324**
Cash/ Check No.	**Cash**

Date	**12/17/2022**
Received From<Add New, Other>	**Lynne's Space**
Account	**4300 Other Income**
Memo	**Storage Rental Revenue**
Amount	**$585**
Cash/ Check No.	**Check No. 2200**

2. Select the **Save** icon at the top of the Make Deposit window
3. Select the **Journal** icon to display the journal entry to QuickBooks created behind the screen for the deposit
4. Export to **Excel** or **print** the Transaction Journal
5. Record the following deposits on the same deposit form.

Date	**12/18/2022**
Received From	**Conner Garden Supply**
Account	**4300 Other Income**
Memo	**Storage Rental Revenue**
Amount	**$450**
Cash/ Check No.	**Cash**

Date	**12/18/2022**
Received From	**Bank of Anycity**
Account	**8000 Interest Income**
Memo	**Interest Revenue**
Amount	**$135**
Cash/ Check No.	**Check No. 11818**

6. Select the **Save** icon at the top of the Make Deposit window
7. Select the **Journal** icon to display the journal entry to QuickBooks created behind the screen for the deposit
8. Export to **Excel** or **print** the Transaction Journal
9. Export to **Excel** the Deposit Detail report for **December 17 through 18, 2022.** (Hint: Report Center > Banking.)

P4.1.3 Write Checks

Enter the banking transactions for Larry's Landscaping using the Write Checks window.

1. Write the following check for Larry's Landscaping.

Date	**12/17/2022**
To	**Computer Services by DJ**
Account	**7320 Computer Supplies**
Memo	**External Hard Disk**
Amount	**$126**
Check No.	**1465**

2. Select the **Save** icon
3. Select the **Reports** tab > **Transaction Journal** icon
4. Export the Transaction Journal report to **Excel** or **print** the report
5. Write the following check for Larry's Landscaping.

Date	**12/17/2022**
To	**Mike Scopellite**
Account	**7430 Professional Design Fees**
Memo	**Professional Design Consulting**
Amount	**$315**
Check No.	**1466**

6. Select the **Save** icon
7. Select the **Reports** tab > **Transaction Journal** icon
8. Export the Transaction Journal report to **Excel** or **print** the report

9. Write the following check for Larry's Landscaping.

Date	**12/18/2022**
To	**Sowers Office Equipment**
Account	**7300 Office Supplies**
Memo	**Special Order**
Amount	**$234**
Check No.	**1467**

10. Select the **Save** icon
11. Select the **Reports** tab > **Transaction Journal** icon
12. Export the Transaction Journal report to **Excel** or **print** the report
13. Write the following check for Larry's Landscaping.

Date	**12/18/2022**
To	**Nye Properties**
Account	**7500 Rent (Expense)**
Memo	**Rent**
Amount	**$810**
Check No.	**1468**

14. Select the **Save** icon
15. Select the **Reports** tab > **Transaction Journal** icon
16. Export the Transaction Journal report to **Excel** or **print** the report
17. Export to **Excel** the Check Detail report for **December 17 through 18, 2022.** (Hint: Report Center > Banking.)

P4.1.4 Bank Reconciliation

Reconcile a bank statement for Larry's Landscaping.

1. Reconcile the following bank statement.

BANK STATEMENT

Larry's Landscaping		11-30-2022
1045 Main Street		Checking
Bayshore, CA 94326		

Previous Balance	10-30-2022	$238,625.29
+ Deposits	2	5,775.80
− Checks	8	2,865.51
− Service Charge		25.00
+ Interest Paid		0.00
Ending Balance	11-30-2022	$241,510.58

DEPOSITS

Date	Amount
11-25-2022	**5,000.00**
11-30-2022	**775.80**

CHECKS PAID

Date	No.	Amount
10-22-2022	**1459**	**244.13**
10-28-2022	**1461**	**550.00**
11-22-2022	**1460**	**244.13**
11-28-2022	**1462**	**550.00**
11-29-2022	**1112**	**177.25**
11-30-2022	**1113**	**125.00**
11-30-2022	**1114**	**375.00**
11-30-2022	**1115**	**600.00**

Thank you for banking with us!

2. Export to **Excel** the bank reconciliation summary report
3. Export to **Excel** the bank reconciliation detail report
4. In the bank reconciliation detail report, **highlight** the checks and deposits cleared for the November bank statement

P4.1.5 Reports

1. Export to **Excel** the Journal report for December 17 through 18, 2022

P4.1.6 Back Up Project 4.1

Save a backup of your Project file using the file name: YourName Project 4.1 Backup.QBB. See *Appendix B: Back Up & Restore QuickBooks Files* for instructions.

Chapter 5

Customers and Sales

BACKSTORY

Just as you are finishing the last bank reconciliation and checking bank reconciliations off your smartphone reminders, Mr. Castle reappears. He always seems to know just when you are about to finish a task.

"While cash flow is crucial to our survival," he says, "*we also need to keep an eye on profits. We are in the business of selling products and services to our customers. We have to be certain that we charge customers enough to cover our costs and make a profit."*

Mr. Castle pulls out a pen and begins scribbling on a sheet of paper on your desk:

"We track the costs of each job we work on. A job is a project for a specific customer. For example, we are working on two jobs for Brian Cook: Job 1 is a second story addition and Job 2 is a kitchen remodeling job.

"In QuickBooks we use items to track the products and services we use on each project. On the 2nd story addition job we used four different items."

Pushing a stack of papers toward you, Mr. Castle says, *"Here are some customer transactions that need to be recorded in QuickBooks."*

Section 5.1

QuickBooks SatNav

QuickBooks SatNav is your satellite navigation for QuickBooks, assisting you in navigating QuickBooks

QuickBooks SatNav divides QuickBooks into three processes:

1. **QuickBooks Settings.** This includes Company Settings when setting up a new QuickBooks company and the Company Chart of Accounts.
2. **QuickBooks Transactions.** This includes recording transactions in QuickBooks. Transaction types can be categorized as Banking, Customers and Sales, Vendors and Expenses, and Employees and Payroll. In basic terms, recording transactions involves recording money in and money out.
3. **QuickBooks Reports.** QuickBooks reports are the output of the system, such as commonly used financial statements of Balance Sheet, Income Statement, and Statement of Cash Flows.

Chapter 5 focuses on customers and sales transactions as shown in the following QuickBooks SatNav.

QB SatNav

1 QB SETTINGS — CHAPTERS 1 2 11 12 13 14

- Company Settings
- Chart of Accounts

2 QB TRANSACTIONS — CHAPTERS 3 4 5 6 7 8 11 12 13 14

> Money in *Money out >*

- Banking
- **Customers & Sales**
- Vendors & Expenses
- Employees & Payroll

3 QB REPORTS — CHAPTERS 9 10 11 12 13 14

- Reports

Section 5.2

START QUICKBOOKS AND OPEN QUICKBOOKS COMPANY

START QUICKBOOKS

To start QuickBooks software, click the **QuickBooks** icon on your desktop. If a QuickBooks icon does not appear on your desktop, from Microsoft® Windows® click **Start** button > **Programs** > **QuickBooks** > **QuickBooks Premier Accountant Edition.**

RESTORE QBB STARTER FILE

Restore the QBB Starter file for this chapter as follows.

1. Select **File** > **Restore**
2. Using the directions in *Appendix B: Back Up & Restore QuickBooks Files,* restore the **CHAPTER 5 STARTER.QBB**
3. After restoring, add **YourName Chapter 5** to the company name by selecting **Company Menu** > **My Company**

Section 5.3

CUSTOMER NAVIGATION

The QuickBooks Home Page contains a Customers section that displays icons used for Customers functions. If necessary click the **Home** icon in the Navigation Bar to display the Home Page.

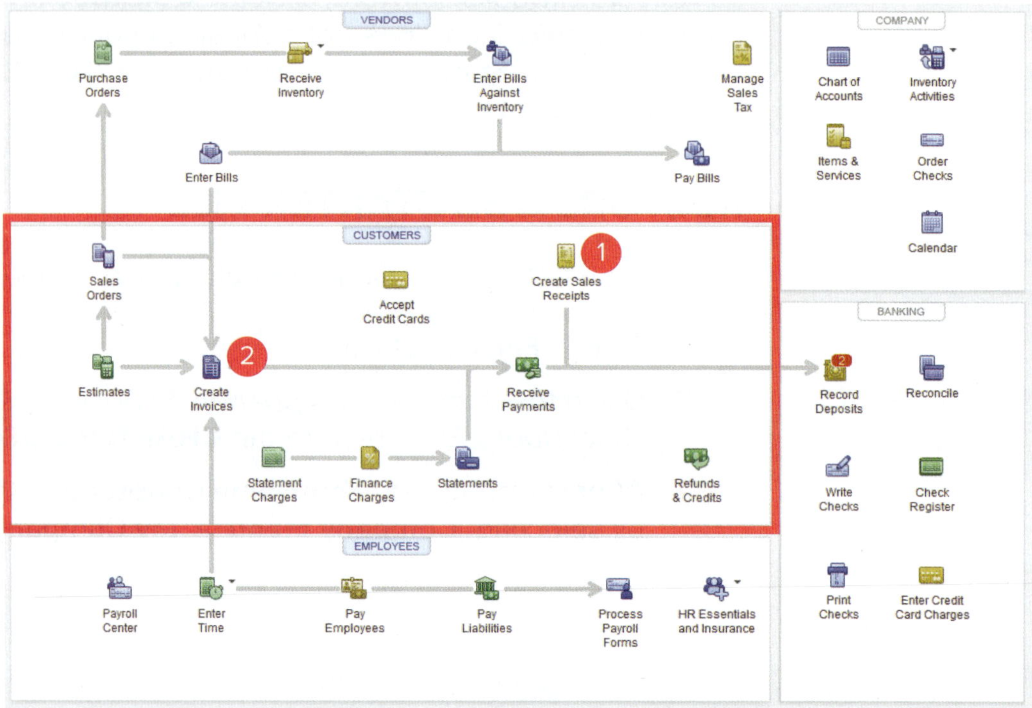

The Customers section of the Home Page is a flowchart of customer transactions.

Types of sales transactions that we can enter using QuickBooks include:

- **Invoices.** A sales transaction is recorded on an invoice when the product or service is provided to the customer, and the customer promises to pay later. These customer promises are called accounts receivable — amounts that we expect to receive in the future.
- **Receive Payments.** The Receive Payment onscreen form is used to record the transaction when the customer pays its account with cash, check, credit card, or online payment.

- **Estimates.** The Estimate onscreen form is used to record estimated costs of products and services to be provided to a customer in the future.
- **Refunds & Credits.** A Credit Memo onscreen form is used when we need to record a credit, or reduction, in the amount the customer is charged, such as when we issue a customer a refund.
- **Sales Receipts.** A Sales Receipt is used to record a sales transaction when the customer pays at the time of sale when the product or service is provided to the customer.

As the flowchart indicates, Rock Castle Construction can record a customer sale in two different ways:

1. **Create Sales Receipts.** The customer pays when Rock Castle Construction provides the good or service to the customer. The customer pays with cash, check, or credit card at the time of sale. The sale is recorded on a sales receipt.
2. **Create Invoices/Receive Payments.** The sale is recorded on an invoice when the good or service is provided to the customer. The customer promises to pay later. These customer promises are called accounts receivable — amounts that Rock Castle Construction expects to receive in the future. The customer may pay its account with cash, check, credit card, or online payment.

The first step in working with customer transactions is to enter customer information in the Customer List.

Section 5.4

CUSTOMER LIST

The Customer List contains customer information such as address, telephone number, and credit terms. Once customer information is entered in the Customer List, QuickBooks automatically transfers the customer information to the appropriate forms, such as sales invoices and sales returns. This feature enables you to enter customer information only once instead of entering the customer information each time a form is prepared.

The Customer List in QuickBooks also tracks projects (jobs) for each customer. For example, Rock Castle Construction is working on two projects for Brian Cook:

- Job 1: 2nd Story Addition
- Job 2: Kitchen

VIEW CUSTOMER LIST

To view the Customer List for Rock Castle Construction:

1. Click **Customers** in the Navigation Bar
2. The following Customer Center window appears, listing customers and jobs. Notice the two jobs listed for Brian Cook:
   - 2nd story addition
   - Kitchen
3. The Customers & Jobs List displays:
   - Customer name
   - Job name
   - Balance for each job
4. To view additional information about a customer, click the customer or job name. The Customer/Job Information window displays:
   - Customer address and contact information
   - Transaction information for the customer
   - Estimate information (if an estimate for the job was prepared)
   - Notes about the job

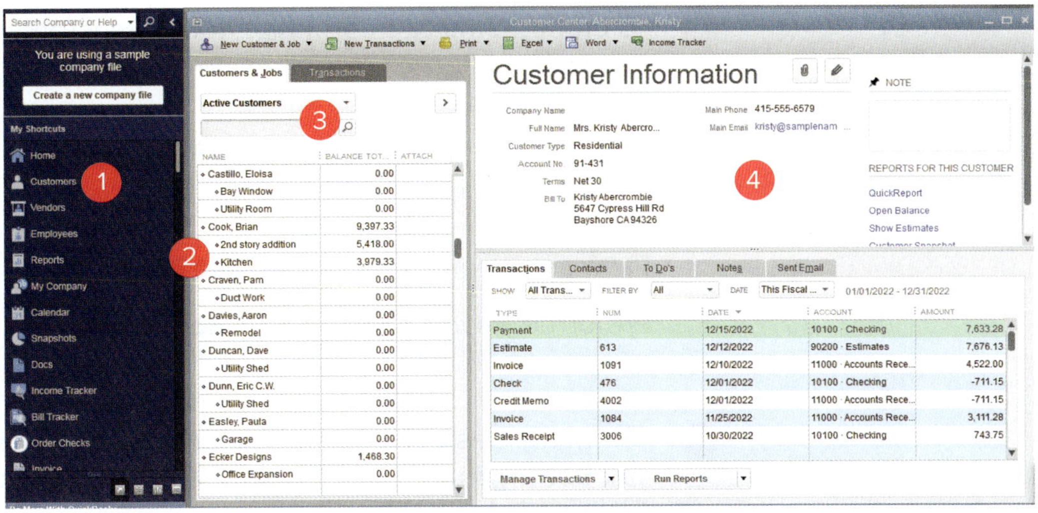

ADD NEW CUSTOMER

Rock Castle Construction needs to add a new customer, TJ Ryan, to the Customer List.

To add a new customer to the Customer List:

1. Click the **New Customer & Job** button at the top of the Customer Center
2. Click **New Customer** on the drop-down menu
3. When a blank New Customer window appears, select the **Address** Info tab. Enter the following information in the New Customer | Address Info window.

Customer Name	**Ryan, TJ**
Mr./Ms./. . .	**Mr.**
First Name	**TJ**
Last Name	**Ryan**
Main Phone	**415-555-1234**
Mobile	**415-555-5678**
Address Details Bill To / Ship To	**55 Scotch Drive** **Bayshore, CA 94326**

4. To enter payment information for the customer, click the **Payment Settings** tab. Enter the following information in the Payment Settings fields:

Account No.	**7890**
Credit Limit	**50,000**
Payment Terms	**Net 30**
Preferred Payment	**Check**

5. To enter sales tax information for the customer, click the **Sales Tax Settings** tab. Enter the following information in the Sales Tax Settings fields:

Tax Code	**Tax**
Tax Item	**San Tomas**

6. Click the **Additional Info** tab to display another customer information window. Enter the following information in the Additional Info field.

Customer Type	**Residential**

7. Click **OK** to add the new customer to Rock Castle Construction's Customer List

8. To sort the Customer List, with your cursor over the Customer List, **right-click** to display the pop-up menu > select: **Re-sort List.** If asked if you want to return this list to its original order, select **OK.**

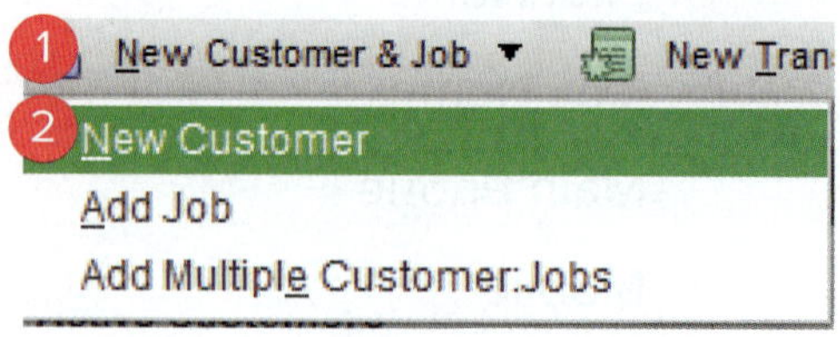

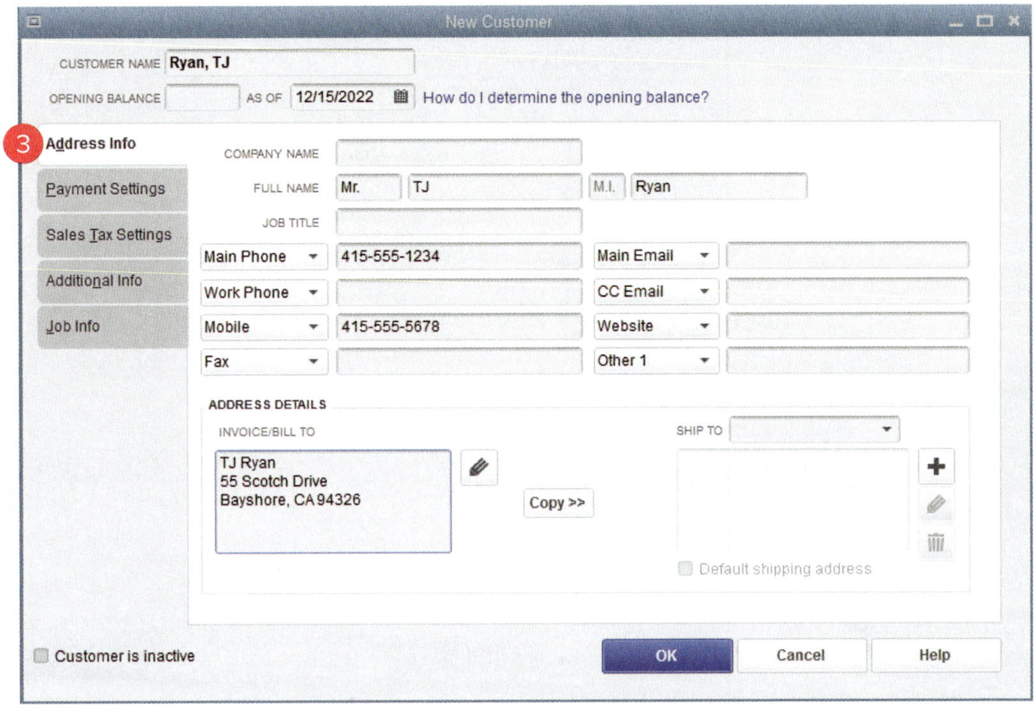
New Customer
CUSTOMER NAME Ryan, TJ
OPENING BALANCE AS OF 12/15/2022 How do I determine the opening balance?
3 Address Info
Payment Settings
Sales Tax Settings
Additional Info
Job Info
COMPANY NAME
FULL NAME Mr. TJ M.I. Ryan
JOB TITLE
Main Phone 415-555-1234
Work Phone
Mobile 415-555-5678
Fax
Main Email
CC Email
Website
Other 1
ADDRESS DETAILS
INVOICE/BILL TO
TJ Ryan
55 Scotch Drive
Bayshore, CA 94326
Copy >>
SHIP TO
Default shipping address
Customer is inactive
OK
Cancel
Help

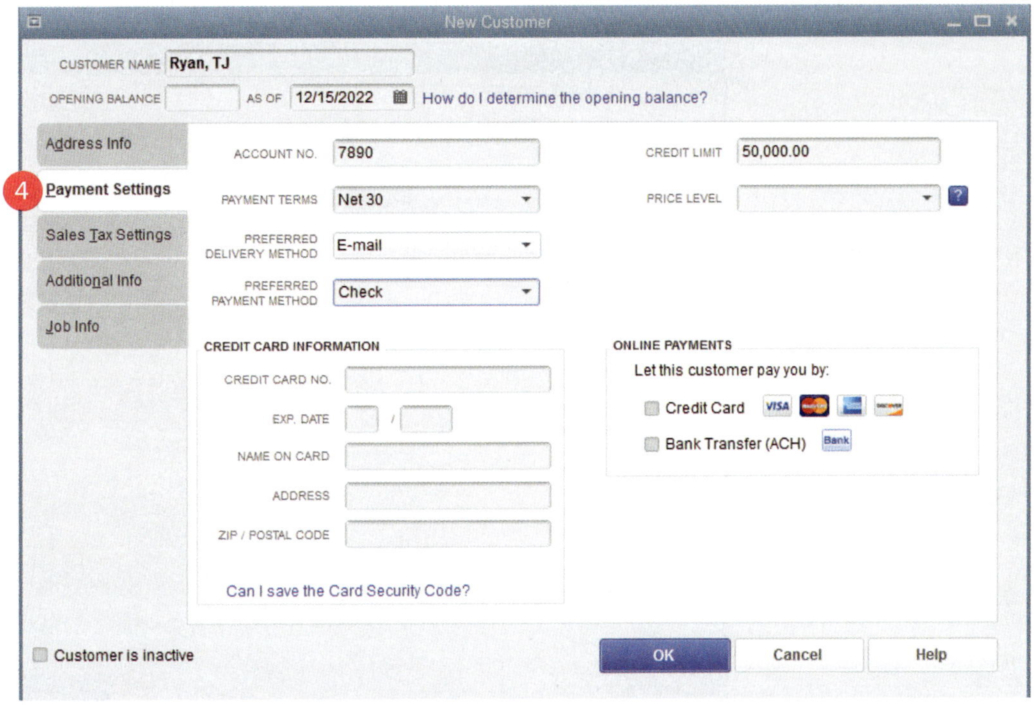
New Customer
CUSTOMER NAME Ryan, TJ
OPENING BALANCE AS OF 12/15/2022 How do I determine the opening balance?
Address Info
4 Payment Settings
Sales Tax Settings
Additional Info
Job Info
ACCOUNT NO. 7890
PAYMENT TERMS Net 30
PREFERRED DELIVERY METHOD E-mail
PREFERRED PAYMENT METHOD Check
CREDIT LIMIT 50,000.00
PRICE LEVEL
CREDIT CARD INFORMATION
CREDIT CARD NO.
EXP. DATE
NAME ON CARD
ADDRESS
ZIP / POSTAL CODE
Can I save the Card Security Code?
ONLINE PAYMENTS
Let this customer pay you by:
Credit Card
Bank Transfer (ACH)
Customer is inactive
OK
Cancel
Help

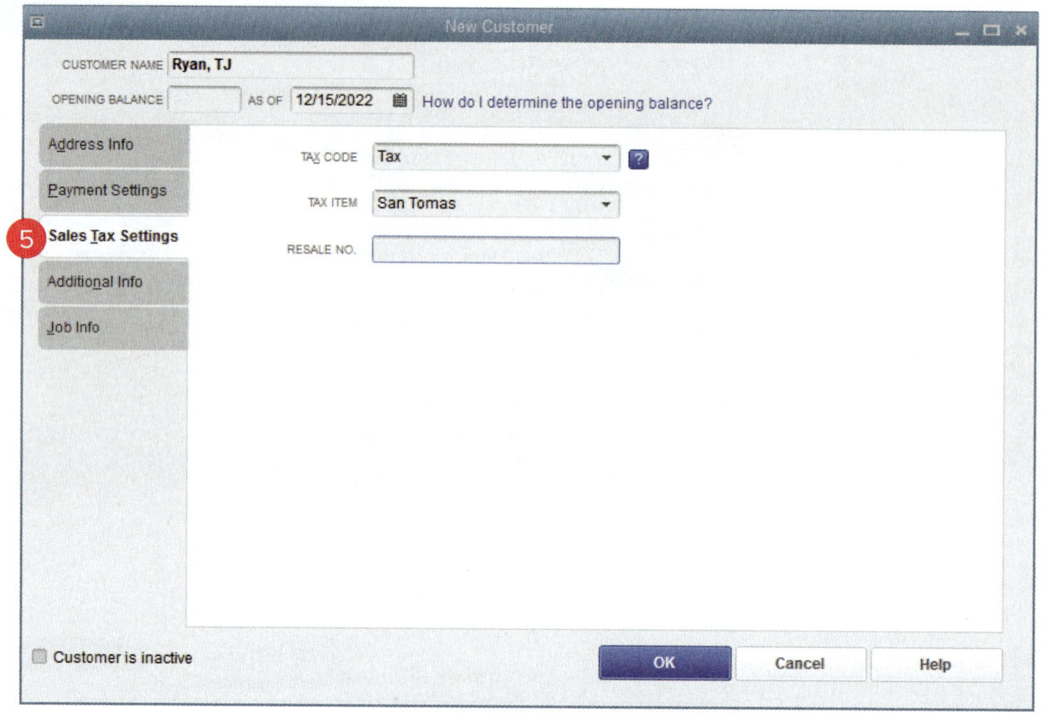
New Customer
CUSTOMER NAME Ryan, TJ
OPENING BALANCE
AS OF 12/15/2022
How do I determine the opening balance?
Address Info
Payment Settings
5 Sales Tax Settings
Additional Info
Job Info
TAX CODE Tax
TAX ITEM San Tomas
RESALE NO.
Customer is inactive
OK
Cancel
Help

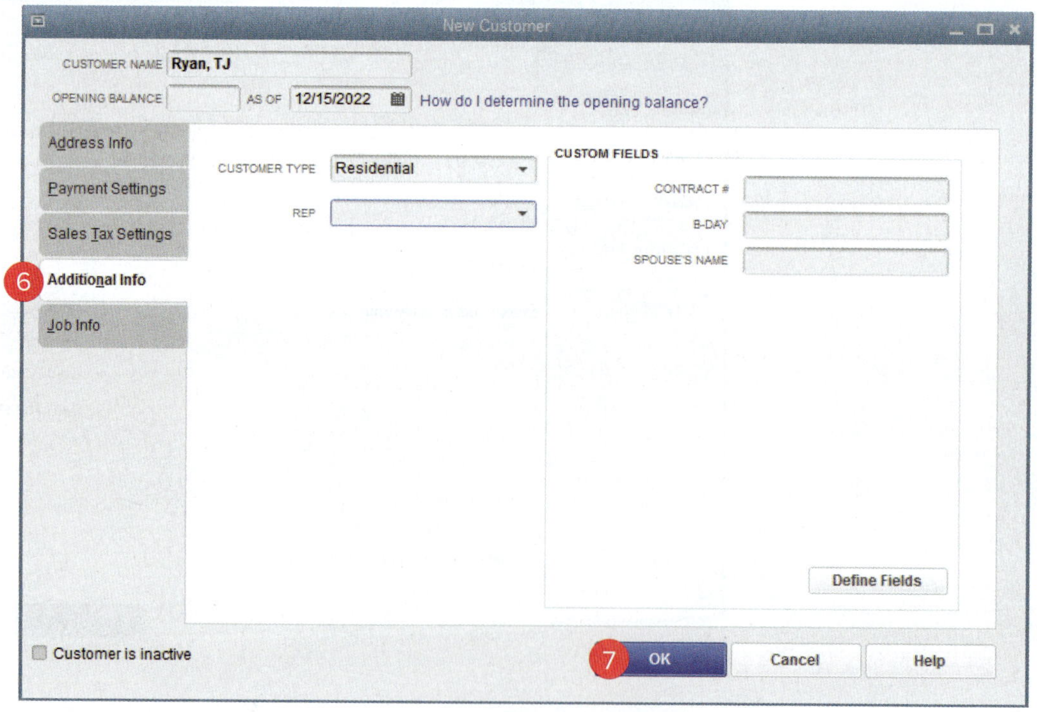
New Customer
CUSTOMER NAME Ryan, TJ
OPENING BALANCE
AS OF 12/15/2022
How do I determine the opening balance?
Address Info
Payment Settings
Sales Tax Settings
6 Additional Info
Job Info
CUSTOMER TYPE Residential
REP
CUSTOM FIELDS
CONTRACT #
B-DAY
SPOUSE'S NAME
Define Fields
Customer is inactive
7 OK
Cancel
Help

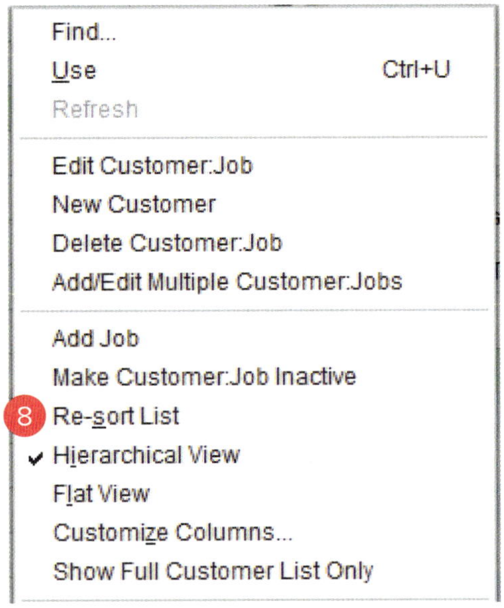

EDIT CUSTOMER INFORMATION

Enter the email address for TJ Ryan by editing the customer information as follows:

1. Select **TJ Ryan** in the Customers & Jobs window
2. Click the **Edit Customer** icon in the Customer Information window. Or **Right - click** > **Edit Customer: Job.**
3. When the Edit Customer window appears, enter or revise the customer or job information as needed. In this instance, click the **Address Info** tab. Then enter the Main Email: tjryan@www.com.
4. Click **OK** to record the new information and close the Edit Customer window

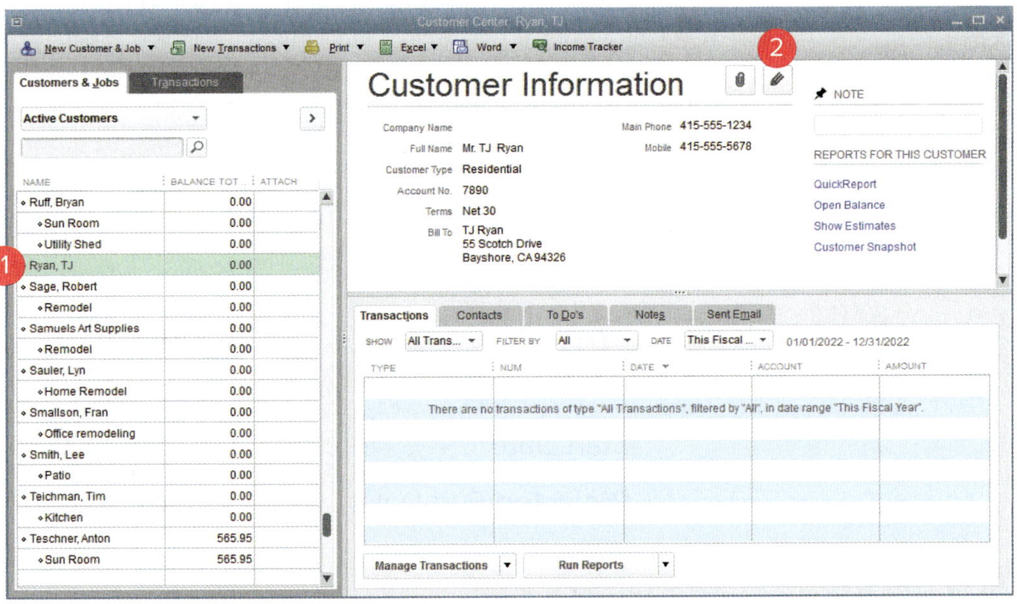

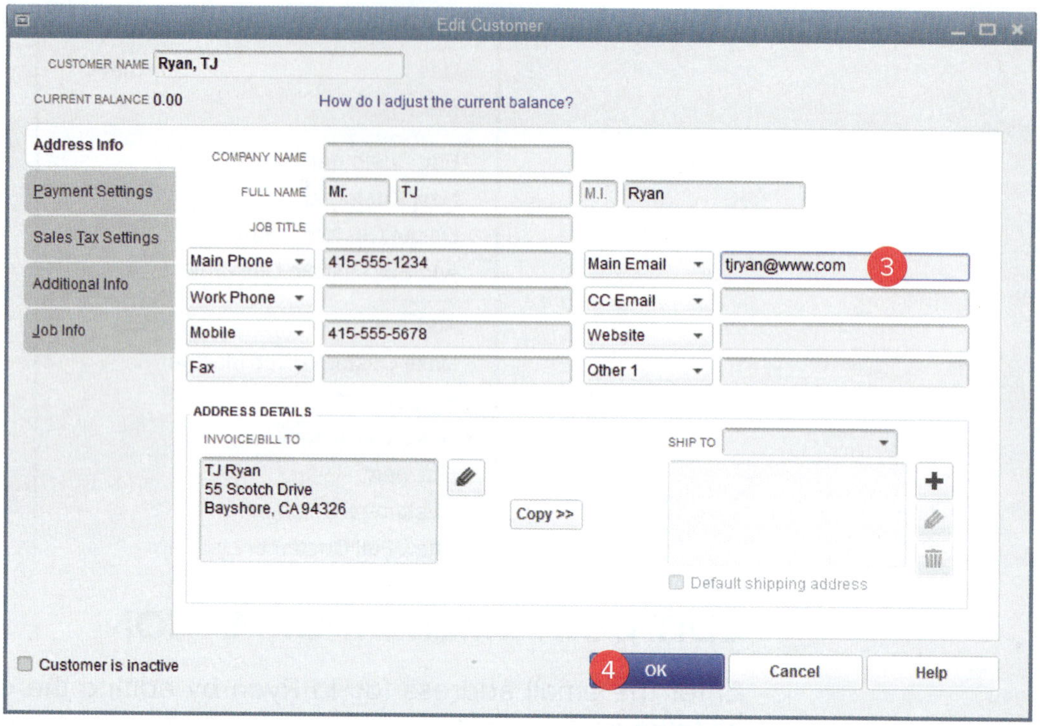

ADD A JOB

To add a Screen Porch job for TJ Ryan, complete the following steps:

1. Click on the customer, **TJ Ryan,** in the Customers & Jobs window
2. Click the **New Customer & Job** button at the top of the Customer Center window
3. Select **Add Job** from the drop-down menu. (Or right-click > Add Job.)
4. In the New Job window, enter the Job Name: **Screen Porch**
5. Enter the Opening Balance: **0.00**
6. Click the **Job Info** tab
7. Enter the following information in the Job Info fields:

Job Description	**Screen Porch**
Job Type	**Remodel**
Job Status	**Pending**
Start Date	**02/01/2023**
Projected End Date	**03/15/2023**

8 Click **OK** to close the New Job window

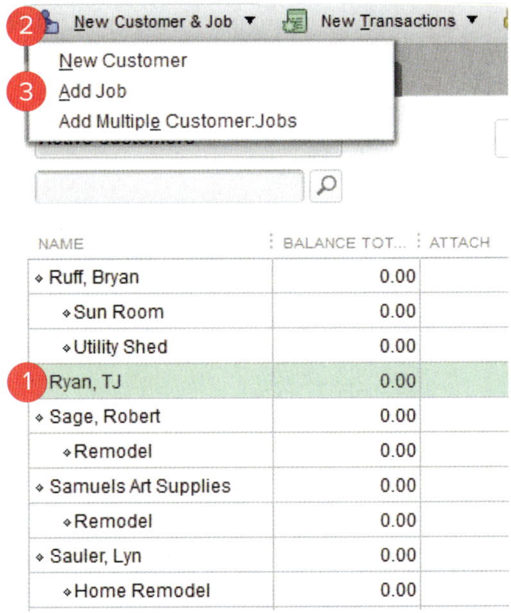

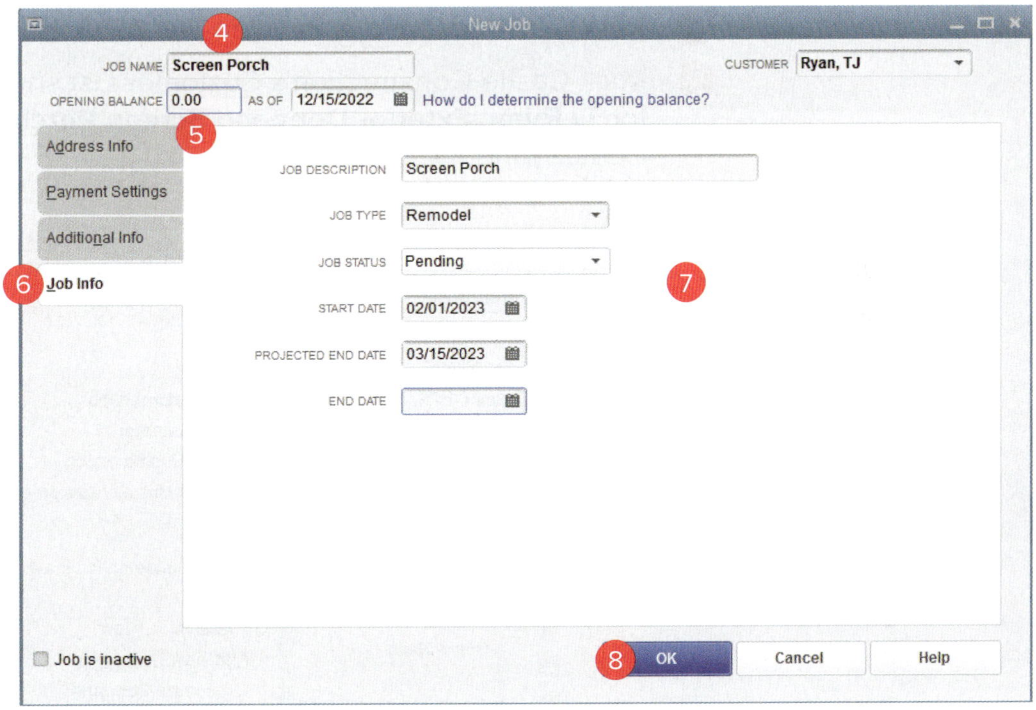

TJ Ryan tells Rock Castle Construction that he will hire them to do the screen porch job on one condition—he needs Rock Castle Construction as soon as possible to replace a damaged exterior door that will not close. Rock Castle sends a workman out to begin work on replacing the door right away.

To add the Exterior Door job:

1. Click on the customer, **TJ Ryan,** in the Customers & Jobs window
2. **Right - click > Add Job**
3. In the Job Name field at the top of the New Job window, enter: **Exterior Door**
4. Enter Opening Balance: **0.00**
5. Click the **Job Info** tab, then enter the following information

Job Description	**Replace Exterior Door**
Job Type	**Repairs**
Job Status	**Awarded**
Start Date	**12/15/2022**
Projected End Date	**12/18/2022**

6. Click **OK** to record the new job and close the New Job window
7. Rock Castle Construction's Customer List should now list two jobs for **TJ Ryan: Exterior Door** and **Screen Porch. Close** the Customer Center window.

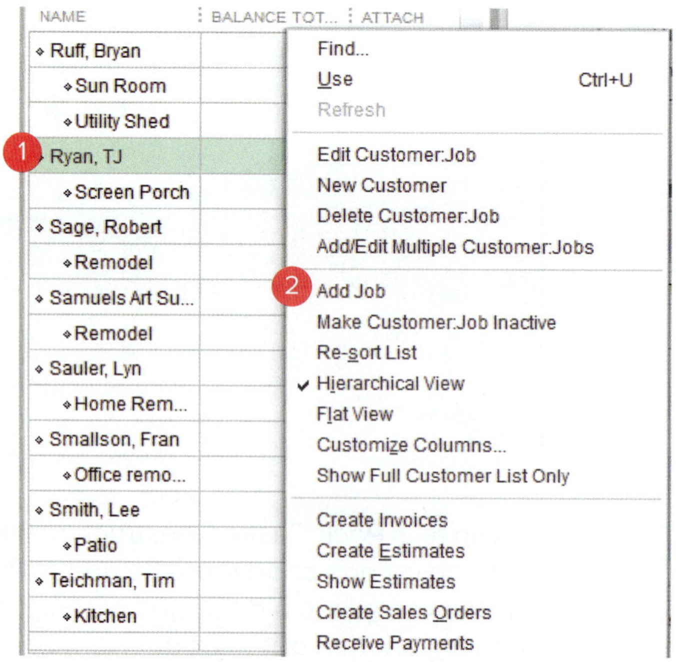

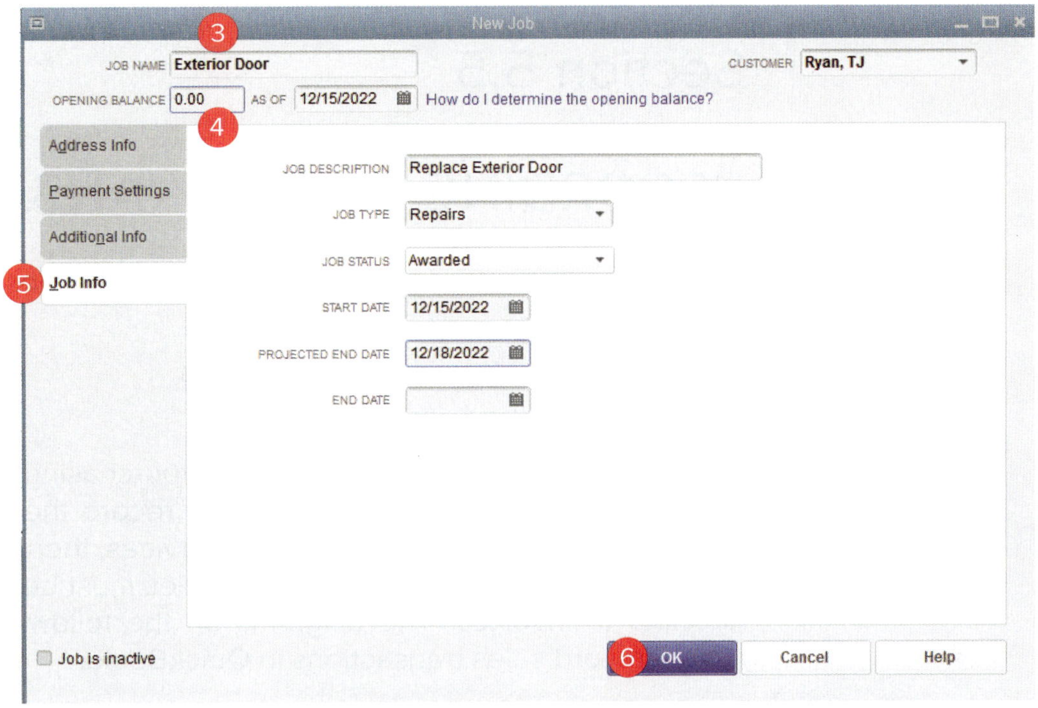

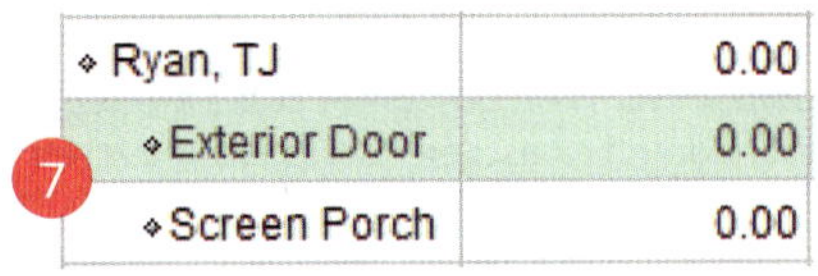

PRINT CUSTOMER LIST

C5.4.1 Customer List. To print the Customer List:

1. From Customer Center, select **Excel** > **Export Customer List**
2. Select **Replace an existing worksheet**
3. Export the Customer List to **Excel**

Section 5.5

RECORDING SALES TRANSACTIONS

Two main ways to record customers and sales transactions using QuickBooks are:

- Customer Sales using Sales Receipts
- Customer Sales using Invoices

If the customer pays on the spot when purchasing a product or service, then the Sales Receipt can be used to record the sale. If the customer pays later after receiving products or services, then an Invoice is used.

When using QuickBooks, customer sales must be recorded using Sales Receipts or Invoices. The diagrams on the following pages summarize how to record sales transactions in QuickBooks.

> **Bank deposits other than customer sales** are recorded using the Bank Deposit onscreen form. Bank deposits not related to customer sales was covered in the previous chapter.

Section 5.6

CUSTOMER SALES RECEIPTS

If the customer payment is *received at the same time* the product or service is provided, we record the customer sale using the Sales Receipt form.

The customer payment may consist of cash, check, or credit card.

When using Sales Receipts to record customer sales:

1. **Create Sales Receipts.** Create a sales receipt record the customer sale for product given and customer payment received in form of cash, check or credit card.
2. **Make Deposit.** Create a Bank Deposit to move customer payment from Undeposited Funds account to the Checking account.

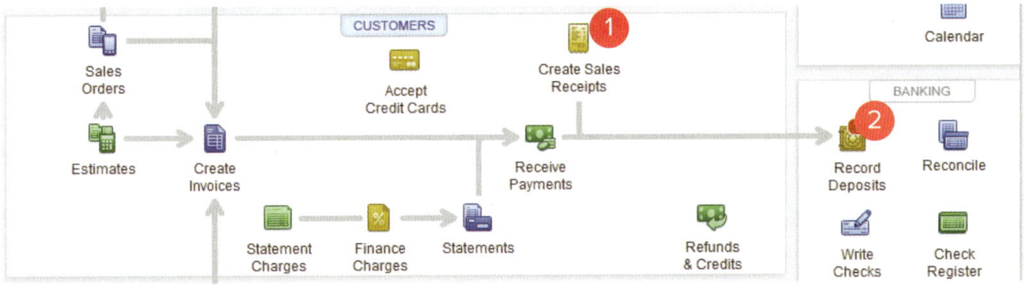

CREATE SALES RECEIPT

One of Rock Castle Construction's customers, Ernesto Natiello, wants to purchase an extra brass hinge for doors that Rock Castle Construction installed. Ernesto pays $20 in cash for the extra hinge.

To create a Sales Receipt for the customer sale:

1. From the Customers section of the Home Page, click **Create Sales Receipts** to display the Enter Sales Receipts window. (If asked if you would like to complete the Payment Interview, select No.)
2. In the Enter Sales Receipts window, select Customer: **Natiello, Ernesto**
3. Select Date: **12/15/2022**

4. Select Payment Method: **Cash.** Other types of payment include Check, Credit Card, Debit Card, or Check. If Payment Method is Check, enter the customer check no. in **Check No.** field.
5. Select item from the Item drop-down menu or Add New Item. In this case, select **Brass Hinges.**
6. Select Quantity: **1**
7. Enter Rate: **20.00**
8. Select Tax: **Tax**
9. Select Tax: **San Tomas**
10. Select **Print Later** checkbox
11. Select Customer Message: **Thank you for your business.**
12. Select **Save.** Leave the Enter Sales Receipts window open on your screen.

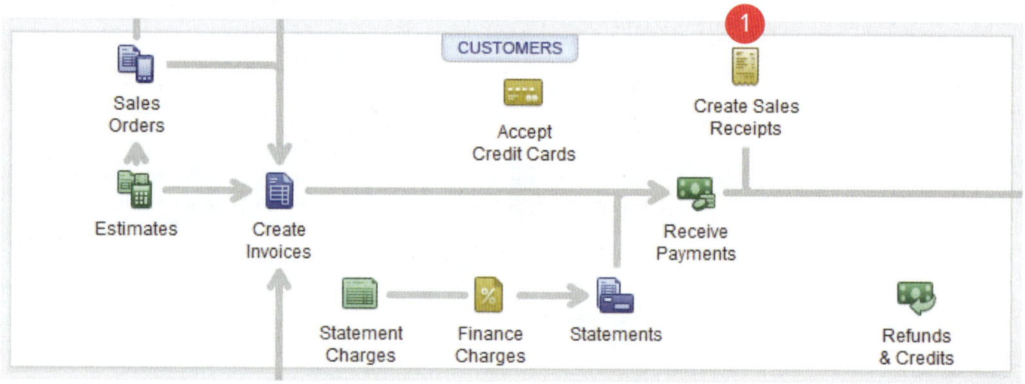

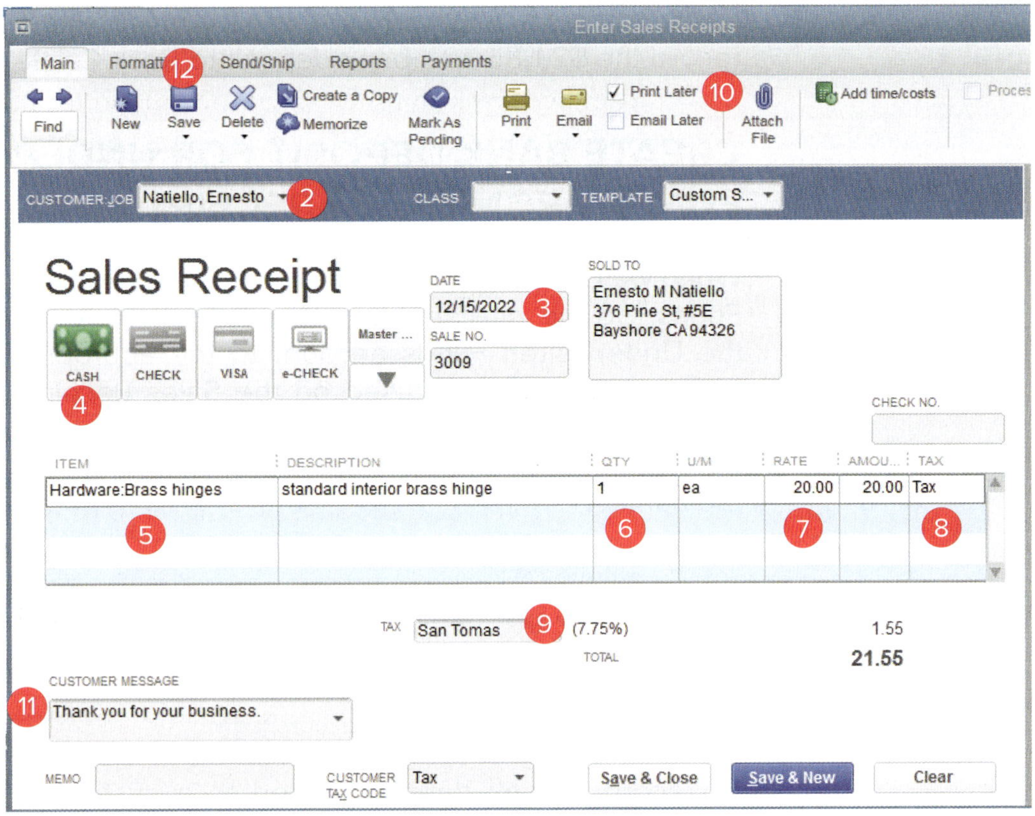

C5.6.1 Sales Receipt Journal Entry. To view the journal entry that QuickBooks created behind the screen for the sales receipt entered and saved using the Enter Sales Receipt onscreen form above, complete the following steps.

1. From the Enter Sales Receipts onscreen form, select the **Reports** tab
2. Select the **Transaction Journal** icon
3. Export the Transaction Journal report to **Excel** or **print** the report
4. **Close** the Transaction Journal window
5. **Close** the Enter Sales Receipts window

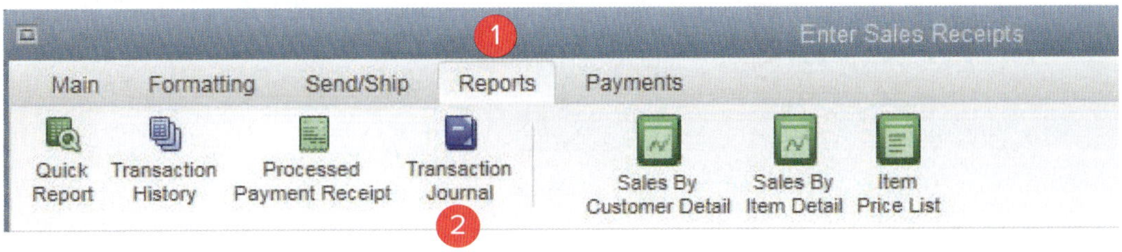

QuickBooks records the $21.55 as undeposited funds. Next, we will record the $21.55 as a bank deposit to Rock Castle's Checking account.

CREATE BANK DEPOSIT FOR UNDEPOSITED FUNDS FROM SALES RECEIPT

When we recorded the Sales Receipt, QuickBooks recorded Undeposited Funds. So we must create a Bank Deposit to transfer the funds from the Undeposited Funds account to the appropriate Checking account. Undeposited Funds is used on the Sales Receipt so that the customer payment will be bundled with other customer payments when deposited. Then our totals will correspond to the bank deposit total shown by the bank.

> **When we create a Sales Receipt** we *must* create a bank deposit to transfer the funds from the Undeposited Funds account to the appropriate bank account. Otherwise, the funds will remain in the Undeposited Funds account instead of appearing in our Checking account.

To record a bank deposit related to a customer sale when the Sales Receipt onscreen form was used:

1. Click the **Record Deposits** icon in the Banking section of the Home Page to display the Payments to Deposit window. The Payments to Deposit window lists undeposited funds that have been received but not yet deposited in the bank.
2. Select the payments to transfer from the undeposited funds account to the Checking account. In this case select **Natiello, Ernesto** for the amount of **$21.55.**
3. Click **OK** to display the following Make Deposits window
4. Select Deposit To: **10100 Checking**
5. Select Date: **12/15/2022**
6. Verify the Amount field displays **$21.55**
7. Select **Save**

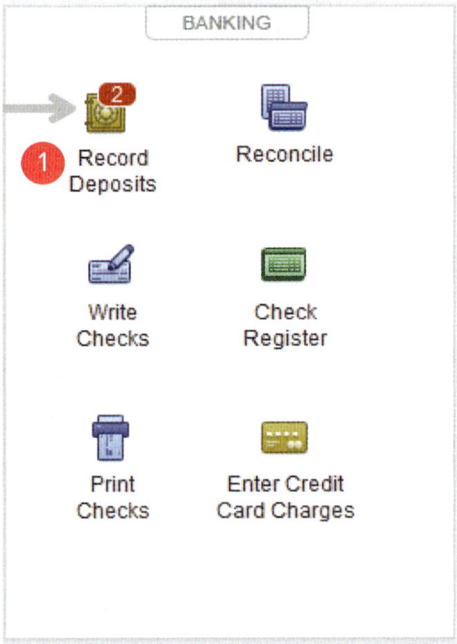
BANKING
2
1
Record Deposits
Reconcile
Write Checks
Check Register
Print Checks
Enter Credit Card Charges

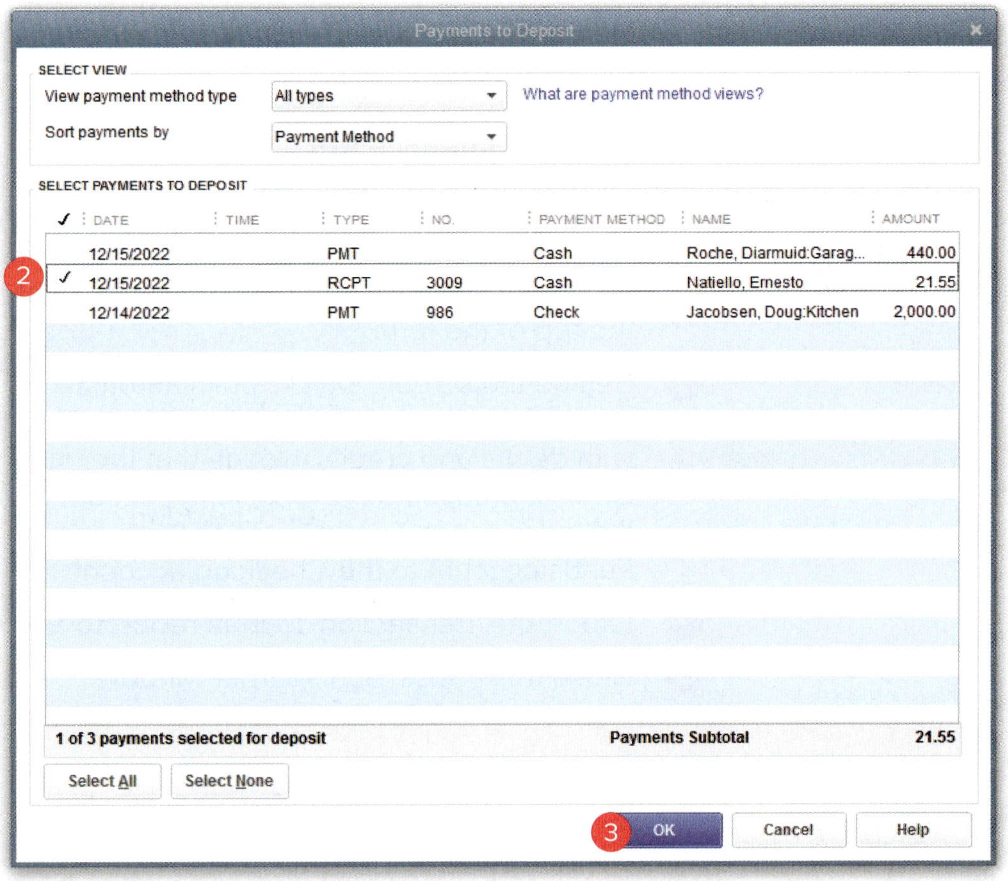
Payments to Deposit
SELECT VIEW
View payment method type
All types
What are payment method views?
Sort payments by
Payment Method
SELECT PAYMENTS TO DEPOSIT
✓ DATE TIME TYPE NO. PAYMENT METHOD NAME AMOUNT
12/15/2022 PMT Cash Roche, Diarmuid:Garag... 440.00
2
✓ 12/15/2022 RCPT 3009 Cash Natiello, Ernesto 21.55
12/14/2022 PMT 986 Check Jacobsen, Doug:Kitchen 2,000.00
1 of 3 payments selected for deposit
Payments Subtotal 21.55
Select All
Select None
3
OK
Cancel
Help

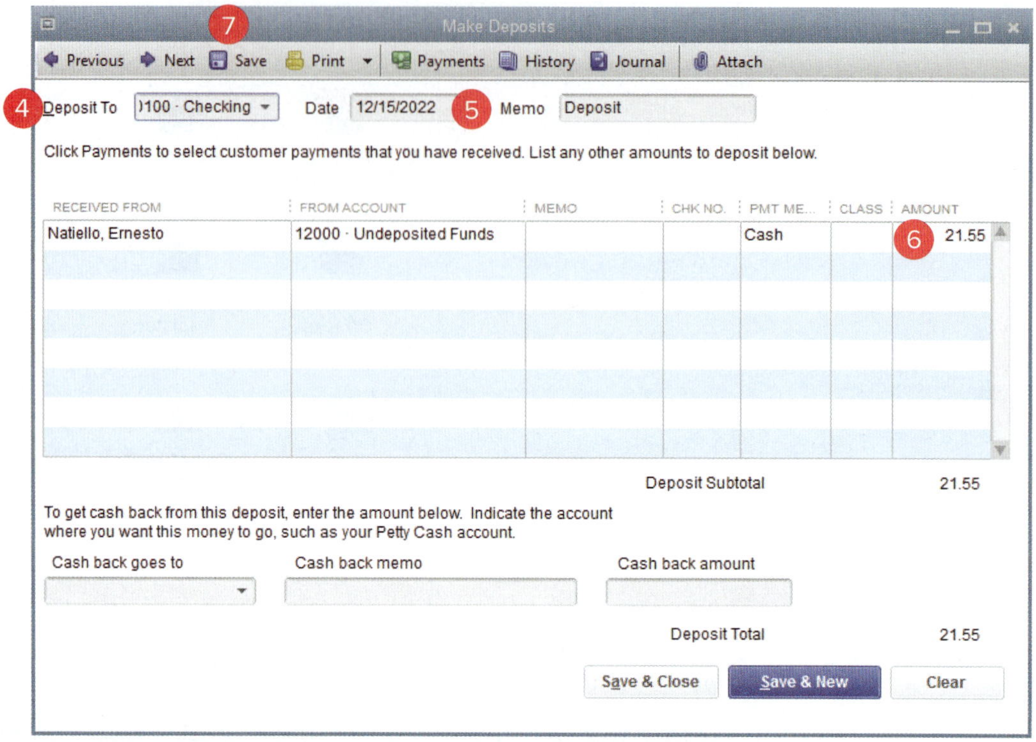

C5.6.2 Deposit Journal Entry. To view the journal entry that QuickBooks created behind the screen for the deposit entered and saved using the Record Deposit onscreen form above, complete the following steps.

1. From the Make Deposits onscreen form, select the **Journal** icon at the top of the form
2. Behind the screen, QuickBooks automatically converted the information in the Make Deposits onscreen form into a journal entry with debits and credits. Notice that the journal entry displays a Debit (increase) to the Checking account and a Credit (decrease) to Undeposited Funds to move the funds from the Undeposited Funds account to the Checking account.
3. Export the Transaction Journal report to **Excel** or **print** the report
4. **Close** the Transaction Journal window

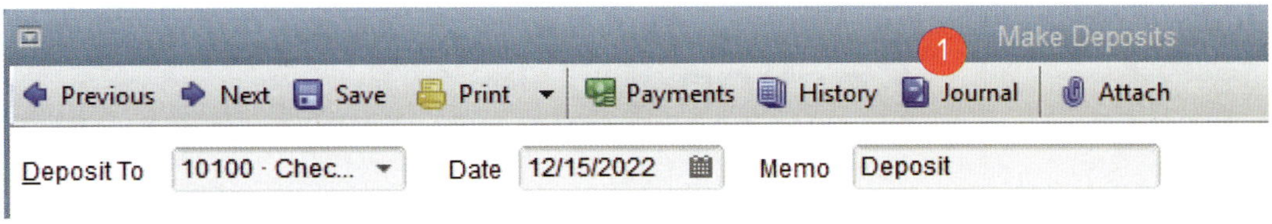
Make Deposits
1
Previous
Next
Save
Print
Payments
History
Journal
Attach
Deposit To
10100 · Chec...
Date
12/15/2022
Memo
Deposit

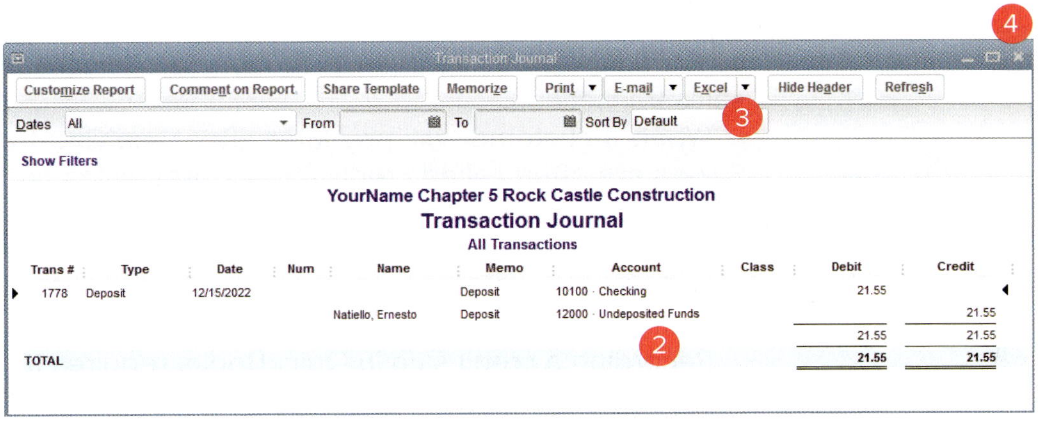
Transaction Journal
4
Customize Report
Comment on Report
Share Template
Memorize
Print
E-mail
Excel
Hide Header
Refresh
Dates
All
From
To
Sort By
Default
3
Show Filters
YourName Chapter 5 Rock Castle Construction
Transaction Journal
All Transactions
Trans # Type Date Num Name Memo Account Class Debit Credit
1778 Deposit 12/15/2022 Deposit 10100 · Checking 21.55
Natiello, Ernesto Deposit 12000 · Undeposited Funds 21.55
21.55 21.55
2
TOTAL 21.55 21.55

Section 5.7

CUSTOMER INVOICES

If products or services are given to the customer and the customer will pay later, then we use an Invoice instead of a Sales Receipt to record the sales transaction.

When a customer will pay later after receiving the product or service, theses are often called credit sales. Credit sales occur when Rock Castle Construction provides goods and services to customers and in exchange receives a promise that the customers will pay later. This promise to pay is called an *account receivable* because Rock Castle expects to *receive* the account balance in the future.

Recording a credit sale in QuickBooks requires three steps:

1. **Create Invoices.** Create an invoice to bill the customer for the product or service provided. QuickBooks records accounts receivable and the sales amount.
2. **Receive Payments.** Receive payment from the customer. QuickBooks reduces accounts receivable and increases undeposited funds.
3. **Record Deposits.** Deposit the customer's payment in the bank.

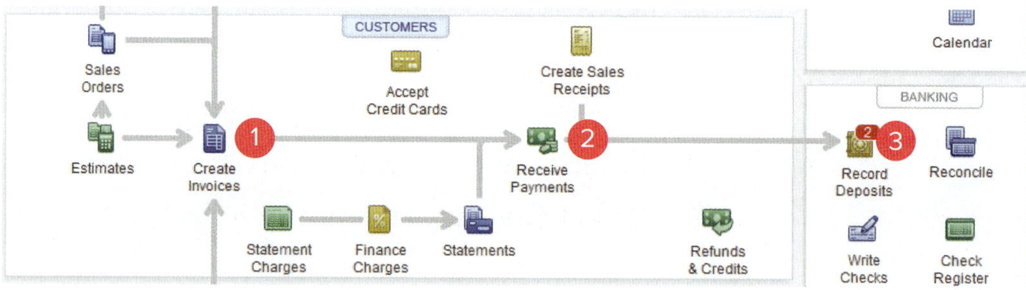

CREATE INVOICE

An invoice is used to record sales on credit when the customer will pay later. An invoice is a bill that contains detailed information about the items (products and services) provided to a customer.

If QuickBooks' time-tracking feature (tracking time worked on each job) is not used, then time worked on a job is entered directly on the invoice. In this chapter, assume that time tracking is not used and that time worked on a job is entered on the invoice form. For more information about time tracking, see Chapter 8.

Next, you will create an invoice for Rock Castle Construction. Rock Castle sent a workman to the Ryan residence immediately after receiving the phone call from TJ Ryan requesting an exterior door replacement as soon as possible. The workman spent one hour at the site the first day.

In this instance, Rock Castle Construction was not asked to provide an estimate before starting the work. Charges for products and labor used on the Ryan door replacement job will be recorded on an invoice.

When using an Invoice to record customer sales:

1. In the Customers section of the Home Page, click the **Create Invoices** icon to display the Create Invoices window
2. From the Create Invoices window, select the Template: **Rock Castle Invoice**
3. Enter the Customer:Job by selecting **Ryan, TJ: Exterior Door** from the drop-down Customer: Job List. (Make certain to select the customer name and the correct job: Exterior Door. To add new customers from the Create Invoices window: Select Add New from the Customer drop-down list.)
4. Select Date: **12/15/2022**
5. Enter charges for the service provided the customer. Enter Item: **Repairs.** Press **Tab.** Description should automatically display: Repair work.
6. Enter Quantity: **1** (hour).
7. The Rate should automatically display **$35.00.** The Amount should automatically display **$35.00.**
8. From the drop-down list, select Tax: **Non-Taxable Sales**
9. Select **Save** and leave the Create Invoices window open

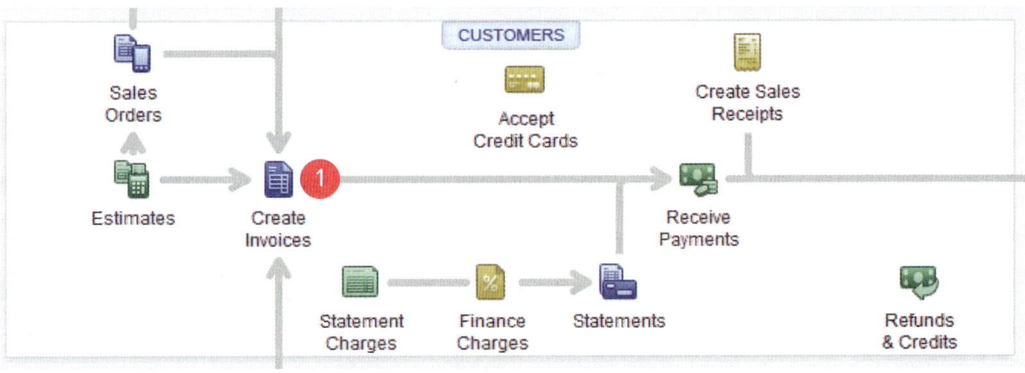

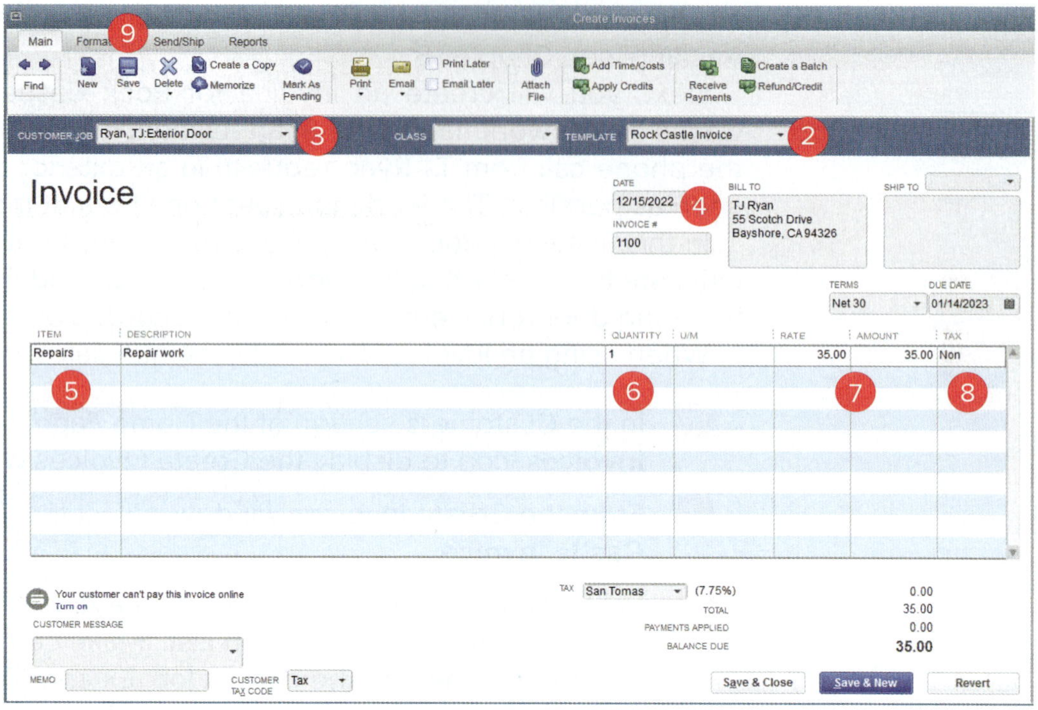

A Pending Invoice can used if the invoice is left open and additional charges will be added later. To mark an invoice as pending, right-click on the invoice and select Mark as Pending from the pop-up menu.

A Progress Invoice is used if the customer is billed as the work progresses rather than when the work is fully completed.

To print envelopes for invoices and shipping labels, click the down arrow by the Print icon on the Invoice.

C5.7.1 Invoice Journal Entry. To view the journal entry that QuickBooks created behind the screen for the invoice entered and saved using the Create Invoices onscreen form, complete the following steps.

1. From the Create Invoices onscreen form, select the **Reports** tab
2. Select the **Transaction Journal** icon
3. Export the Transaction Journal report to **Excel** or **print** the report

4. Notice that the journal entry records an increase (debit) to Accounts Receivable for $35.00, the net amount of the invoice
5. **Close** the Transaction Journal window

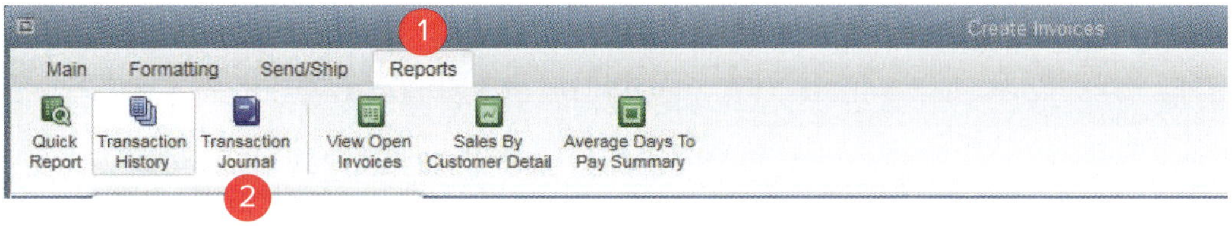

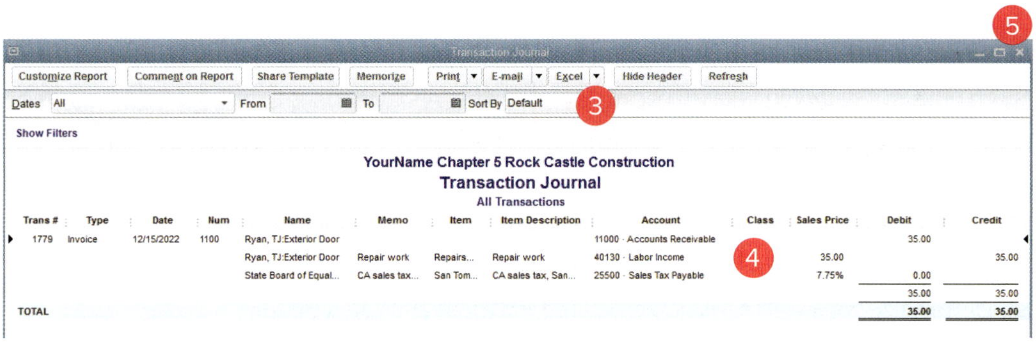

Trans #	Type	Date	Num	Name	Memo	Item	Item Description	Account	Class	Sales Price	Debit	Credit
1779	Invoice	12/15/2022	1100	Ryan, TJ:Exterior Door				11000 · Accounts Receivable			35.00	
				Ryan, TJ:Exterior Door	Repair work	Repairs...	Repair work	40130 · Labor Income		35.00		35.00
				State Board of Equal...	CA sales tax...	San Tom...	CA sales tax, San...	25500 · Sales Tax Payable		7.75%	0.00	
											35.00	35.00
TOTAL											35.00	35.00

Later in the day on December 15, 2022, one of the Rock Castle Construction crews located an exterior door and finished installing the new door at the Ryan residence. To record the additional products and services used:

1. Display **Invoice No. 1100.** If it is not already displayed on your screen, display the invoice for the Exterior Door job again:
   - Click the **Create Invoices** icon
   - When the Create Invoices window appears, click **Find**
   - Enter Invoice No.: **1100**
   - Click **Find**
2. Enter the following items as new line items on Invoice No. 1100 for the Ryan Exterior Door job:

Exterior wood door	1 @ $120	Taxable Sales
Repair work	4 hours	Non-Taxable Sales

3. If we wanted to email the invoice to the customer, we would select the Email icon
4. Select **Save** and leave the Invoice displayed. If you receive a message stating you have changed the transaction and asking if you want to record your changes, select **Yes.**

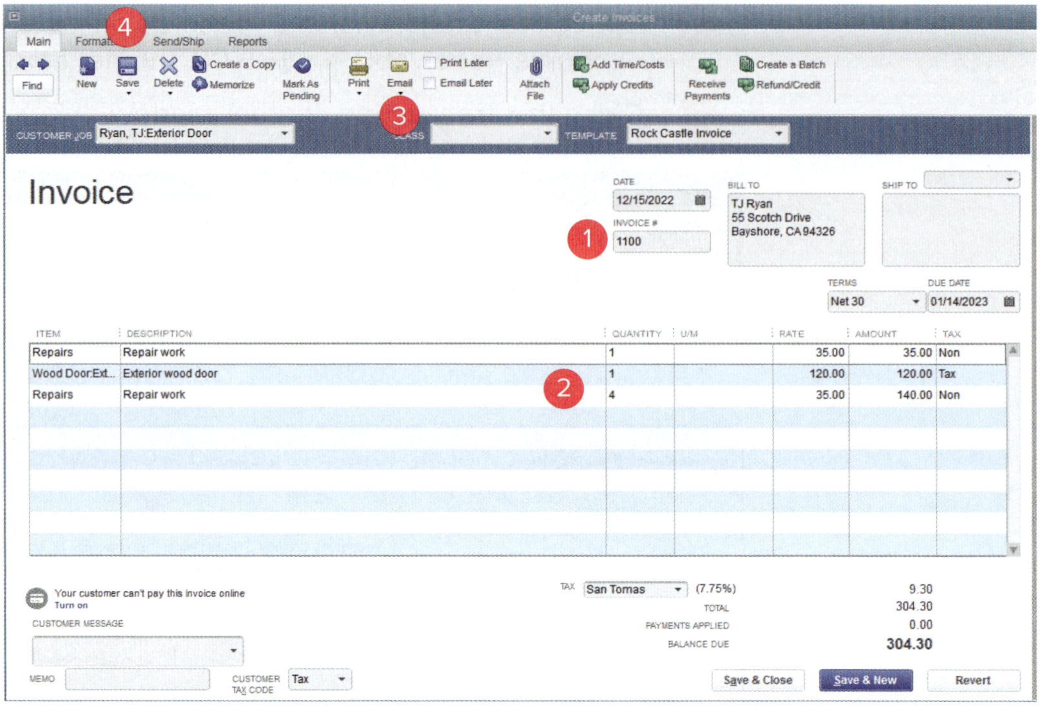

C5.7.2 Invoice Journal Entry. To view the journal entry that QuickBooks created behind the screen for the updated invoice, complete the following steps.

1. From the Create Invoices onscreen form, select the **Reports** tab
2. Select the **Transaction Journal** icon
3. Export the Transaction Journal report to **Excel** or **print** the report
4. Notice that the journal entry records an increase (debit) to Accounts Receivable for $304.30, the net amount of the invoice
5. **Close** the Transaction Journal window

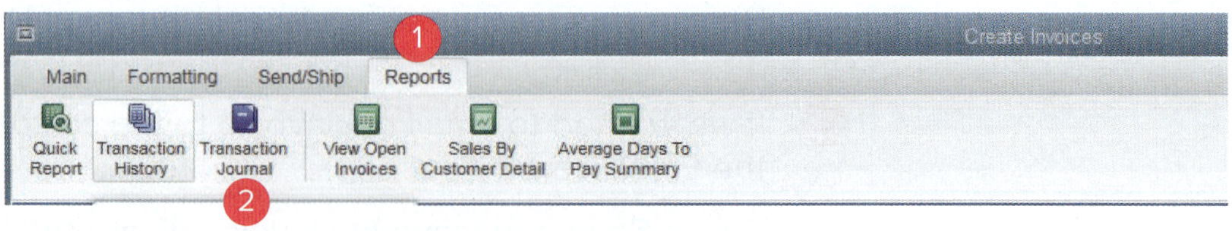

QuickBooks will record the sale and record an account receivable for the amount to be received from the customer in the future.

The Invoice Total is $304.30. Notice that the Exterior Door is a taxable item and QuickBooks automatically calculates and adds sales tax of $9.30 for the door.

CREATE RECEIVE PAYMENT

Recall that when recording credit sales in QuickBooks, you first create an invoice and then record the customer's payment. When a credit sale is recorded on an invoice, QuickBooks records (debits) an Account Receivable—an amount to be received from the customer in the future. When the customer's payment is received, the Account Receivable account is reduced (credited).

Customers may pay in the following ways:

1. **Credit card,** such as Visa, MasterCard, American Express, or Diners Club over the phone, in person, or by mail. Using QuickBooks' Merchant Account Service, you can obtain online authorization and then download payments directly into QuickBooks.
2. **Online** by credit card or bank account transfer.
3. **Customer check** delivered either in person or by mail.

To record a customer's payment received to pay an outstanding invoice, such as payment by check for the Exterior Door job:

1. Click the **Receive Payments** icon in the Customers section of the Home Page to display the Receive Payments window
2. Select Received From: **Ryan, TJ: Exterior Door.** Invoice No. 1100 for $304.30 should appear as an outstanding invoice.
3. Select Date: **12/17/2022**
4. Select Invoice Number **1100** when it appears. QuickBooks will automatically enter the selected invoice amount of $304.30 into the Amount field.
5. Select: Pmt. Method: **Check**
6. Enter Check No. **1005**
7. Notice that there is no Save icon on the Receive Payments window. Select **Save & New.**
8. Select the **Find** back arrow to display the customer payment just recorded

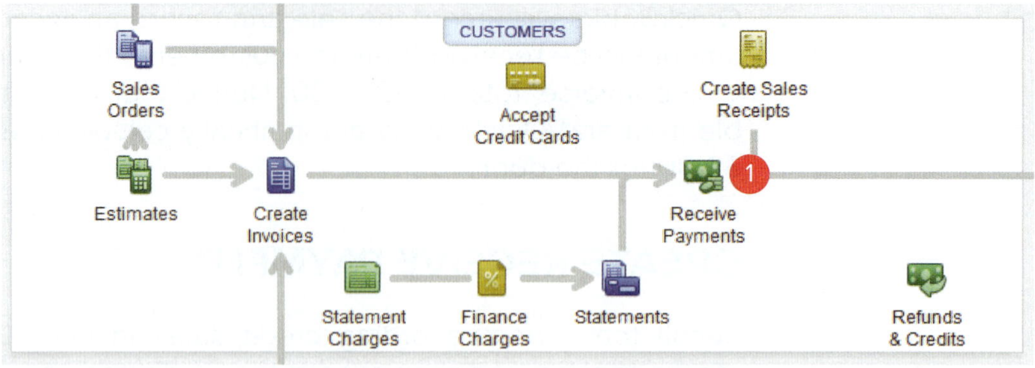

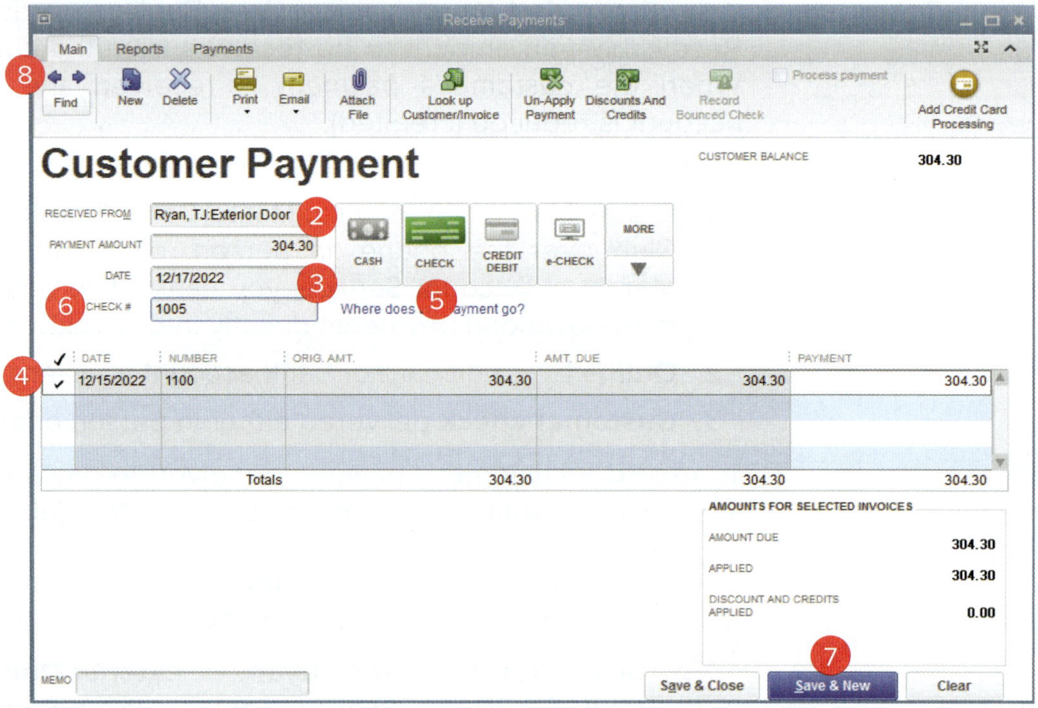

C5.7.3 Receive Payment Journal Entry. To view the journal entry that QuickBooks created behind the screen for the customer payment received, complete the following steps.

1. From the Receive Payments onscreen form, select the **Reports** tab
2. Select the **Transaction Journal** icon
3. Export the Transaction Journal report to **Excel** or **print** the report
4. Notice that when a customer's payment is recorded as received, QuickBooks increases (debits) the Undeposited Funds account and decreases (credits) the customer's account receivable.
5. **Close** the Transaction Journal and the Receive Payments windows

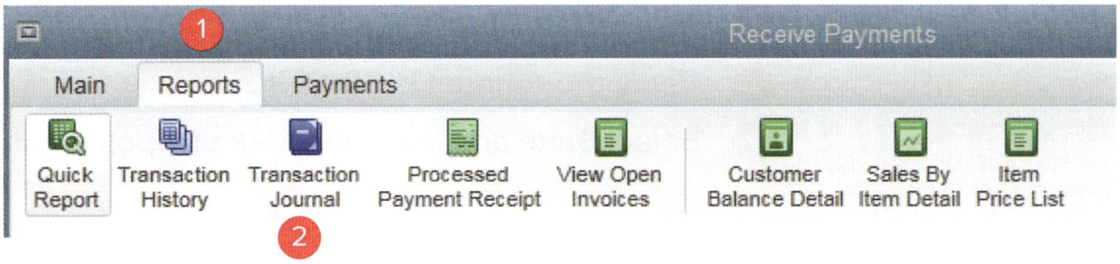

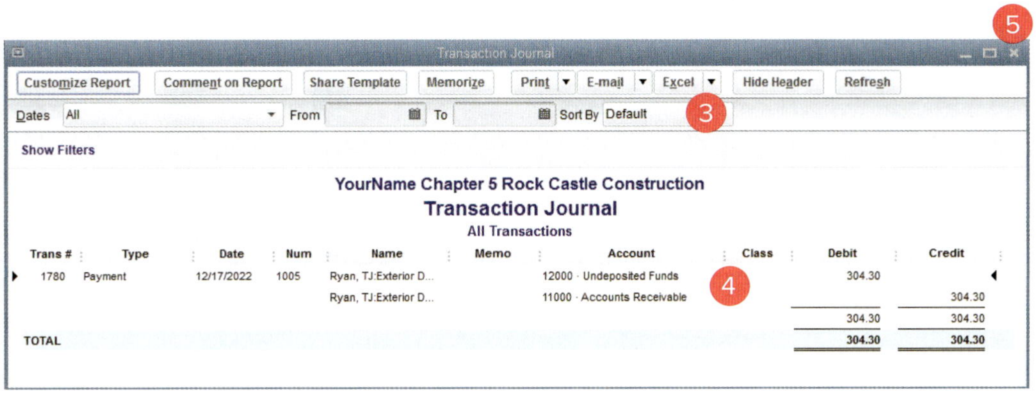

CREATE BANK DEPOSIT FOR UNDEPOSITED FUNDS FROM RECEIVE PAYMENT

By default customer payments received are recorded in the Undeposited Funds account, so we must create a bank deposit to transfer the funds from the Undeposited Funds account to the appropriate bank account. Otherwise, the funds will remain in the Undeposited Funds account and we will not be able to use the funds to pay bills, for example.

To record a bank deposit related to a customer payment recorded using the Receive Payment onscreen form:

1. Click the **Record Deposits** icon in the Banking section of the Home Page to display the Payments to Deposit window
2. The Payments to Deposit window lists undeposited funds that have been received but not yet deposited in the bank. From the Select Existing Payments section, select the the **TJ Ryan** payment of **$304.30** that was added to undeposited funds when we recorded the customer payment on **12/17/2022.**
3. Click **OK** to display the following Make Deposits window
4. Select Deposit To: **10100 Checking**

5 Select Date: **12/17/2022**

6 Verify the Amount is **$304.30**

7 Select **Save** and leave the Make Deposits window displayed

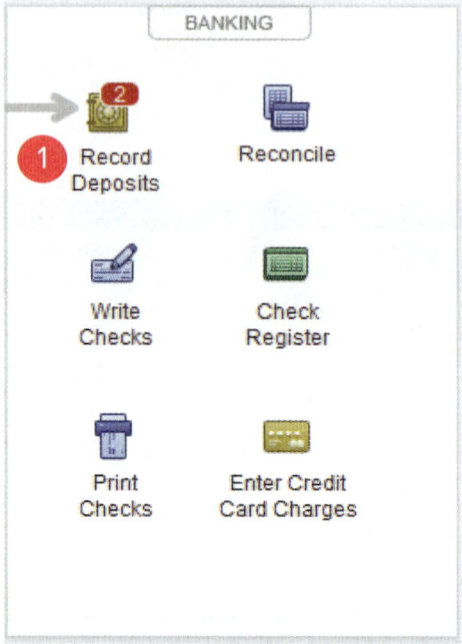

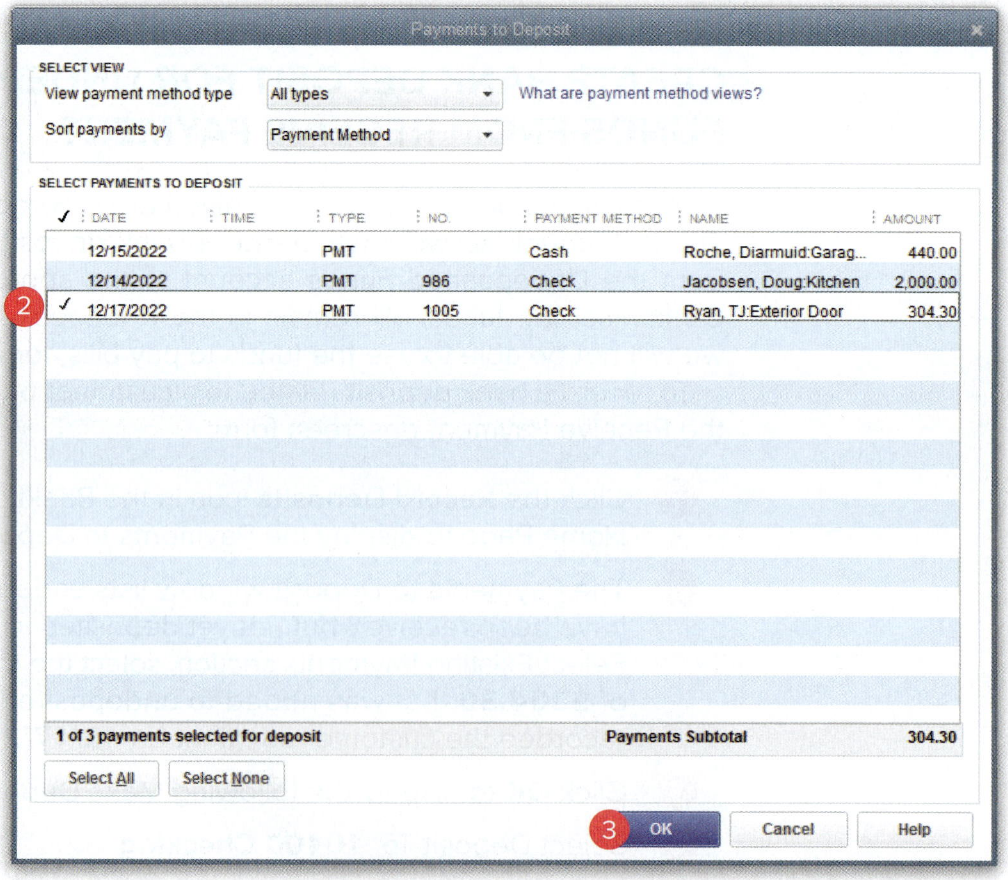

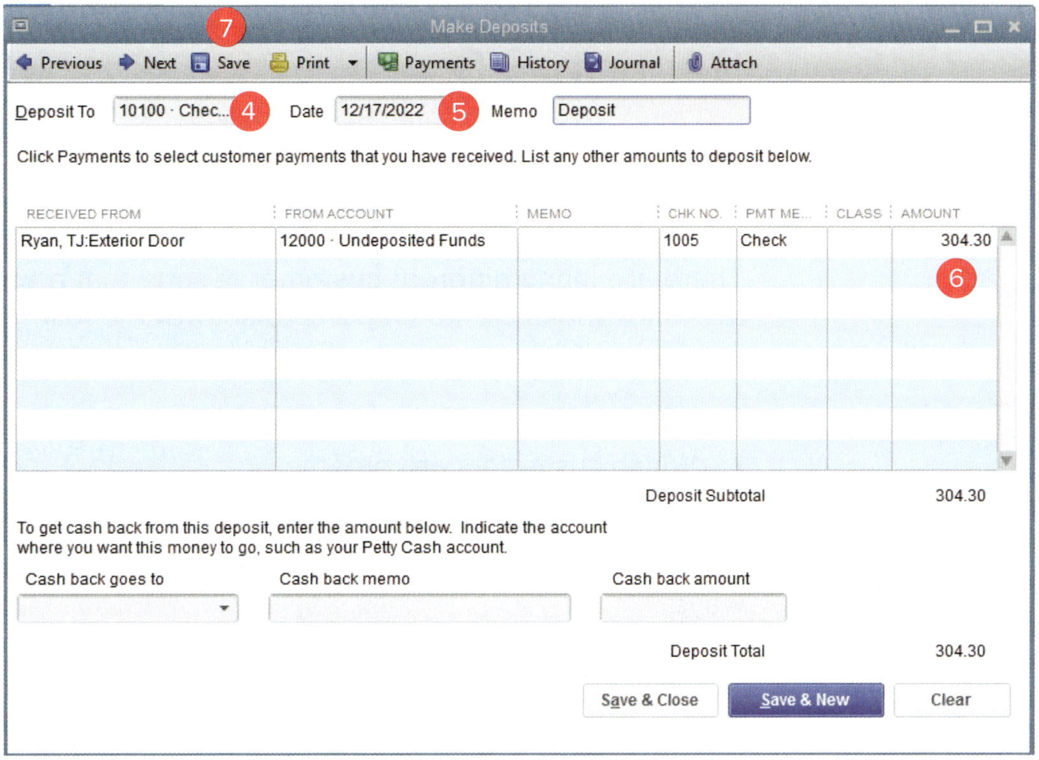

C5.7.4 Deposit Journal Entry. To view the journal entry that QuickBooks created behind the screen for the deposit entered and saved using the Record Deposit onscreen form, complete the following steps.

1. From the Make Deposits onscreen form, select the **Journal** icon at the top of the form
2. Export the Transaction Journal report to **Excel** or **print** the report
3. Notice that the journal entry displays a Debit (increase) to the Checking account and a Credit (decrease) to Undeposited Funds to move the funds from the Undeposited Funds account to the Checking account
4. **Close** the Transaction Journal window
5. On the Make Deposits window, select **Save & Close** to save the deposit

Section 5.8

CUSTOMER REPORTS

There are many different customer reports that a business may find useful. QuickBooks creates reports to answer the following questions:

- Which customers owe us money?
- Which customers have overdue balances?
- Which customers are profitable?
- Which jobs are profitable?

Customer reports can be accessed in QuickBooks in several different ways:

1. **Report Center.** Permits you to locate reports by type of report. (Click **Reports** icon, then click **Customers & Receivables.**)
2. **Reports Menu.** Reports listed on the Reports Menu are grouped by type of report. (From the **Reports** Menu, click **Customers & Receivables.**)
3. **Memorized Customer Reports.** Selected customer reports are memorized for convenience. (From the **Reports Menu,** select **Memorized Reports** > **Customers.**)

In this chapter, you will use the Report Center to access customer reports.

1. To display the Report Center, click **Reports** on the Navigation Bar
2. Select the **List View** icon
3. Select: **Customers & Receivables** to display customer reports that can be accessed in QuickBooks
4. Scroll down to view the three categories of Customers & Receivables reports:
    - Accounts Receivable Aging reports
    - Customer Balance reports
    - Lists reports

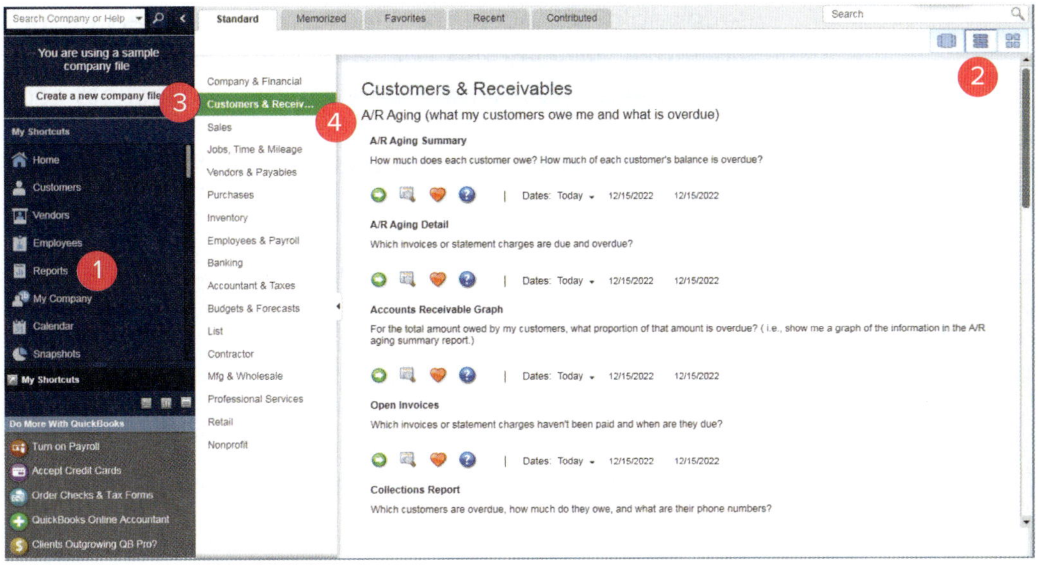

ACCOUNTS RECEIVABLE REPORTS: WHICH CUSTOMERS OWE US MONEY?

Accounts Receivable reports provide information about which customers owe your business money. When Rock Castle Construction makes a credit sale, the company provides goods and services to a customer in exchange for a promise that the customer will pay later. Sometimes the customer breaks the promise and does not pay. Therefore, a business should have a credit policy to ensure that credit is extended only to customers who are likely to keep their promise and pay their bills.

After credit has been extended, a business needs to track accounts receivable to determine if accounts are being collected in a timely manner. The following reports provide information useful in tracking accounts receivable.

1. Accounts Receivable Aging Summary (age of amounts due you by customers)
2. Accounts Receivable Aging Detail
3. Customers with Open Invoices (invoices not yet paid)
4. Collections Report (overdue customer accounts with contact information)

ACCOUNTS RECEIVABLE AGING SUMMARY REPORT

The Accounts Receivable Aging Summary report provides information about the age of customer accounts. This report lists the age of accounts receivable balances. In general, the older an account, the less likely the customer will pay the bill. Therefore, it is important to monitor the age of accounts receivable and take action to collect old accounts.

C5.8.1 A/R Aging Summary. To print the Accounts Receivable Aging Summary:

1. From the Report Center, select **Customers & Receivables**
2. Select **A/R Aging Summary**
3. Select Date: **Today**
4. Select **Run**
5. In the A/R Aging Summary window, select Sort By: **Total**
6. Sort in **Descending (Z to A)** order. If necessary, click and drag to adjust the column widths
7. Export the report to **Excel** or **print**
8. **Close** the A/R Aging Summary window

CUSTOMERS WITH OPEN INVOICES REPORT

Customers with open invoices are those who have an unbilled or unpaid balance. It is important to track the status of open accounts to determine:

- Are these amounts unbilled? The sooner the balances are billed, the sooner your company receives cash to pay your bills.
- Are these amounts billed but not yet due?
- Are these amounts billed and overdue? These accounts should be monitored closely with an action plan for collecting the accounts.

C5.8.2 Open Invoice Report. The Open Invoices report lists all customers with open balances and can be printed as follows:

1. From the Customers & Receivables section of the Report Center, click **Open Invoices**
2. Select Date: **Today**
3. Select **Run**
4. Export to **Excel** or **print** the Open Invoices report

5. Notice the Aging column in the report. This column indicates the age of overdue accounts.
6. **Close** the Open Invoices window

COLLECTIONS REPORT: CUSTOMERS WITH OVERDUE BALANCES

When reviewing the age of accounts receivable, a business should monitor overdue accounts closely and maintain ongoing collection efforts to collect its overdue accounts.

The Collections Report lists customers with overdue account balances. In addition, the Collections Report includes a contact phone number for convenience in contacting the customer.

C5.8.3 Collections Report. To print the Collections Report summarizing information for all customers with overdue balances:

1. From the Customers & Receivables section of the Report Center, select: **Collections Report**
2. Select Date: **Today**
3. Select **Run.** No customers have overdue balances so it appears that you are doing a good job collecting customer payments on accounts.
4. Export to **Excel** or **print** the Collections report
5. **Close** the Collections Report window

The Collections Report provides the information necessary to monitor and contact overdue accounts and should be prepared and reviewed on a regular basis.

PROFIT AND LOSS REPORTS: WHICH CUSTOMERS AND JOBS ARE PROFITABLE?

To improve profitability in the future, a business should evaluate which customers and jobs have been profitable in the past. This information permits a business to improve profitability by:

- Increasing business in profitable areas
- Improving performance in unprofitable areas
- Discontinuing unprofitable areas

The following QuickBooks reports provide information about customer and job profitability:

1. Income by Customer Summary
2. Income by Customer Detail
3. Job Profitability Summary
4. Job Profitability Detail

INCOME BY CUSTOMER SUMMARY REPORT

To determine which customers are generating the most profit for your business, it is necessary to look at both the sales for the customer and associated costs.

C5.8.4 Income by Customer Summary Report. To print the Income by Customer Summary Report:

1. From the Report Center, select **Company & Financial** > **Income by Customer Summary**
2. Select: **This Fiscal Year-to-date**
3. Select **Run**
4. In the Income by Customer Summary window, select Sort By: **Total**
5. Sort in **Descending (Z to A)** order. If necessary, click and drag to adjust the column widths.
6. Export to **Excel** or **print** the report
7. **Highlight** Rock Castle Construction's most profitable customer
8. **Close** the Income by Customer Summary window

QuickBooks offers other additional reports about customers that provide information useful to a business. These reports can be accessed from the Report Center.

Section 5.9

BACK UP QUICKBOOKS FILES

BACK UP QBB

Save a backup of your Chapter 5 file using the file name: **YourName Chapter 5 Backup.QBB.** For further instructions on how to back up your file, *see Appendix B: Back Up & Restore QuickBooks Files.*

QBW WORKFLOW

If you are using the Workflow approach, leave your .QBW file open and proceed directly to Exercise 5.1.

QBB RESTORE

If you are using the Restore approach and ending your computer session now, close your QBW file and exit QuickBooks. When you restart, you will restore your backup file to complete Exercise 5.1.

Section 5.10

ACCOUNTING ESSENTIALS

Customer Sales and Accounts Receivable

Accounting Essentials summarize important foundational accounting knowledge that may be useful when using QuickBooks

What are Accounts Receivable?

- Accounts Receivable are amounts that a customer owes our business. When our business makes a credit sale, our business provides goods and services to a customer in exchange for the customer's promise to pay later.
- When a credit sale is recorded on an invoice, QuickBooks Online records (debits) an Account Receivable—an amount to be received from the customer in the future. When the customer's payment is received, the Account Receivable account is reduced (credited).
- Sometimes the customer breaks the promise and does not pay. So a business should have a credit policy to ensure that credit is extended only to customers who are likely to keep their promise and pay their bills.
- After credit has been extended, a business needs to track accounts receivable to determine if accounts are being collected in a timely manner.

How can a business track accounts receivable to make certain customers are paying on time?

- Accounts Receivable Aging reports provide information about which customers owe our business money, how much the customer owes, and the age of the customer accounts receivable balances.
- In general, the older an account, the less likely the customer will pay the bill. So it is important to monitor the age of accounts receivable and take action to collect old accounts.

What happens if a customer does not pay the accounts receivable balance?

- When a customer does not pay the accounts receivable balance, then it is called a bad debt or uncollectible account.
- At the time a credit sale occurs, it is recorded as an increase to sales and an increase to accounts receivable.
- Occasionally a company is unable to collect a customer payment and must write off the customer's account as a bad debt or uncollectible account. When an account is uncollectible, the account receivable is written off or removed from the accounting records.
- There are two different methods that can be used to account for bad debts:

1. **Direct write-off method.** This method records bad debt expense when it becomes apparent that the customer is not going to pay the amount due. If the direct write-off method is used, the customer's uncollectible account receivable is removed and bad debt expense is recorded at the time a specific customer's account becomes uncollectible. The direct write-off method is used for tax purposes.
2. **Allowance method.** The allowance method estimates bad debt expense and establishes an allowance or reserve for uncollectible accounts. When using the allowance method, uncollectible accounts expense is estimated in advance of the write-off. The estimate can be calculated as a percentage of sales or as a percentage of accounts receivable. (For example, 2% of credit sales might be estimated to be uncollectible.) This method should be used if uncollectible accounts have a material effect on the company's financial statements used by investors and creditors.

- To record a bad debt, make a journal entry to remove the customer's account receivable (credit Accounts Receivable) and debit either Bad Debt Expense (direct write-off method) or the Allowance for Uncollectible Accounts (allowance method).

www.my-quickbooks.com

Go to www.My-QuickBooks.com to view additional QuickBooks resources including:

- **Excel Report Templates** to organize QuickBooks reports exported to Excel
- ***Computer Accounting with QuickBooks* updates,** sometimes required when there is a software update that affects the text

- **QuickBooks Video links**
- **QuickBooks Help and Support links**
- **Other QuickBooks Resources** to make learning QuickBooks easier and more effective
- **QuickBooks Issue Resolution** offers a guided approach to troubleshooting QuickBooks

> **Troubleshooting QuickBooks and Correcting Errors** are crucial QuickBooks skill to acquire. See www.My-QuickBooks.com > QB Issue Resolution for Troubleshooting QuickBooks tips. See Chapter 17, Quick Review Guide, for tips on Correcting Errors.

BACKSTORY

"I just finished the Cecilia job, Mr. Castle." A workman tosses a job ticket over your cubicle wall into your inbox as he walks past. *"Mrs. Cecilia's chihuahua, Pepe, really did a number on that door. No wonder she wanted it replaced before her party tonight. Looks better than ever now!"*

You hear Mr. Castle reply, *"We want to keep Mrs. Cecilia happy. She will be a good customer."*

EXERCISE 5.1: Customer and Job List

First, you will need to add Ms. Cecilia as a new customer and then add a new job.

E5.1.1 QuickBooks File

If you will be using the same computer and the same Chapter 5.QBW file:

1. If your Chapter 5.QBW file is not already open, open it by selecting **File > Open Previous Company.** Select your **Chapter 5.QBW file.** If a QuickBooks Information window appears with a message about the sample company file, click **OK.**
2. Add **YourName Exercise 5.1** to the company name by selecting **Company Menu > My Company.**

> **If you are not using the same computer that you used for Chapter 5,** you will need to restore your Chapter 5 If Backup.QBB file using the instructions in Appendix B: Back Up & Restore QuickBooks Files. After restoring, add YourName Exercise 5.1 to the company name.

E5.1.2 Add New Customer

1. Add the following customer to the Customer List.

Customer	**Cecilia, Maria**
Address Info:	
First Name	**Maria**
Last Name	**Cecilia**
Main Phone	**415-555-6565**
Address	**65 5th Avenue**
	Bayshore, CA 94326
Payment Settings:	
Account No.	**12736**
Payment Terms	**Net 30**
Preferred Payment Method	**VISA**
Credit LImit	**20,000**
Sales Tax Settings:	
Tax Code	**Tax**
Tax Item	**San Tomas**
Additional Info:	
Customer Type	**Residential**

2. **Close** the New Customer window

E5.1.3 Add New Job

Add a new job for Maria Cecilia.

1. Add the new Maria Cecilia job using the following information.

Job Name	**Door Replacement**
Job Description	**Interior Door Replacement**
Job Type	**Repairs**
Job Status	**Closed**
Start Date	**12/17/2022**
Projected End	**12/17/2022**
End Date	**12/17/2022**

E5.1.4 Customer List

1. **Sort** the Customer List. (Hint: Right-click > Re-sort List.)
2. Export to **Excel** or **print** the Customer List

E5.1.5 Back Up Exercise 5.1

Save a backup of your Exercise file using the file name: YourName Exercise 5.1 Backup.QBB. See *Appendix B: Back Up & Restore QuickBooks Files* for instructions.

EXERCISE 5.2: Invoice

E5.2.1 QuickBooks File

If you will be using the same computer and the same QBW file:

1. Select your **QBW file.**
2. Add **YourName Exercise 5.2** to the company name by selecting **Company Menu > My Company.**

> **If you are not using the same computer that you used for Chapter 5 and Exercise 5.1,** you will need to restore your prior Backup.QBB file using the instructions in Appendix B: Back Up & Restore QuickBooks Files. After restoring, add YourName Exercise 5.2 to the company name.

E5.2.2 Create Invoice

Create an invoice for Maria Cecilia. an interior door replacement using the following information:

1. Create an invoice for an interior door replacement using the following information:

Customer: Job	**Cecilia, Maria: Door Replacement**
Customer Template	**Rock Castle Invoice**
Date	**12/17/2022**
Invoice No.	**1101**
Items	• **1 Wood Door: Interior @ $72.00** • **1 Hardware: Standard Doorknob @ 30.00** • **Installation Labor: 3 hours @ $35.00**

2. Select the **Save** icon
3. Select the **Reports** tab
4. Select the **Transaction Journal** icon
5. Export the Transaction Journal report to **Excel** or **print** the report
6. **Close** the Transaction Journal and the Invoice windows

E5.2.3 Back Up Exercise 5.2

Save a backup of your Exercise file using the file name: YourName Exercise 5.2 Backup.QBB. See *Appendix B: Back Up & Restore QuickBooks Files* for instructions.

EXERCISE 5.3: Customer Credit

BACKSTORY

"It's time you learned how to record a credit to a customer's account." Mr. Castle groans, then rubbing his temples, he continues, *"Ms. Cecilia called earlier today to tell us she was very pleased with her new bathroom door. However, she ordered locking hardware for the door, and standard hardware with no lock was installed instead. Although she appreciates our prompt service, she would like a lock on her bathroom door. We sent a workman over to her house, and when the hardware was replaced, she paid the bill.*

"We need to record a credit to her account for the standard hardware and then record a charge for the locking hardware set. And we won't charge her for the labor to change the hardware."

E5.3.1 QuickBooks File

If you will be using the same computer and the same QBW file:

1. Select your **QBW file.**
2. Add **YourName Exercise 5.3** to the company name by selecting **Company Menu > My Company.**

> **If you are not using the same computer that you used for Chapter 5, Exercise 5.1 and Exercise 5.2,** you will need to restore your latest prior Backup.QBB file using the instructions in Appendix B: Back Up & Restore QuickBooks files. After restoring, add YourName Exercise 5.3 to the company name.

E5.3.2 Record Customer Credit

Record a credit to Mrs. Cecilia's account for the $30.00 she was previously charged for standard door hardware by completing the following steps:

1. Click the **Refunds and Credits** icon in the Customers section of the Home Page
2. Select Customer and Job: **Cecilia, Maria: Door Replacement**
3. Select Template: **Custom Credit Memo.** Credit No. 1102 should automatically appear
4. Select Date: **12/20/2022**
5. Select Item: **Hardware Standard Doorknobs**
6. Enter Quantity: **1**
7. Select the **Save** icon
8. When the Available Credit window appears, select **Apply to invoice.** (If an Apply Credit to Invoices window appears, select the credit of $32.33, then select Done.)
9. Select **Reports** tab > **Transaction Journal**
10. Export the Transaction Journal report to **Excel** or **print** the report
11. **Close** the Transaction Journal and the Create Credit Memos/ Refunds windows

E5.3.3 Create Invoice

1. Create a new invoice (Invoice No. 1103) for Maria Cecilia: Door Replacement on 12/20/2022 to record the charges for the interior door locking hardware
2. Select the **Save** icon

3. Select the **Reports** tab > **Transaction Journal**
4. Export the Transaction Journal report to **Excel** or **print** the report
5. **Close** the Transaction Journal and the Invoice windows

E5.3.4 Back Up Exercise 5.3

Save a backup of your Exercise file using the file name: YourName Exercise 5.3 Backup.QBB. See *Appendix B: Back Up & Restore QuickBooks Files* for instructions.

EXERCISE 5.4: Receive Customer Payments

E5.4.1 QuickBooks File

If you will be using the same computer and the same QBW file:

1. Select your **QBW file.**
2. Add **YourName Exercise 5.4** to the company name by selecting **Company Menu > My Company.**

> **If you are not using the same computer that you used for Chapter 5, Exercise 5.1, Exercise 5.2 and Exercise 5.3,** you will need to restore your latest prior Backup.QBB file using the instructions in Appendix B: Back Up & Restore QuickBooks files. After restoring, add YourName Exercise 5.4 to the company name.

E5.4.2 Receive Payment

"*Oops! Almost forgot to give you this,*" Rock Castle says as he drops a scrap of paper into your inbox. In Mr. Castle's handwriting, the paper contains the following: *On 12/15/2022 Maria Cecilia prepaid $223.53 for door replacement using her VISA credit card.*

Record the payment received from Maria Cecilia for the net amount due for the door replacement.

1. Record Mrs. Cecilia's payment for the door replacement by VISA credit card for $223.53 on 12/15/2022.

Card No.	**4444-5555-6666-7777**
Exp. Date	**07/2023**

2. Select **Save & New**
3. Select the **Find** back arrow to display the customer payment just recorded
4. From the Receive Payments onscreen form, select the **Reports** tab > **Transaction Journal**
5. Export the Transaction Journal report to **Excel** or **print** the report
6. **Close** the Transaction Journal and the Receive Payments windows

E5.4.3 Back Up Exercise 5.4

Save a backup of your Exercise file using the file name: YourName Exercise 5.4 Backup.QBB. See *Appendix B: Back Up & Restore QuickBooks Files* for instructions.

EXERCISE 5.5: Make Deposits

E5.5.1 QuickBooks File

If you will be using the same computer and the same QBW file:

1. Select your **QBW file.**
2. Add **YourName Exercise 5.5** to the company name by selecting **Company Menu > My Company.**

If you are not using the same computer that you used for prior Chapter 5 and Exercises, you will need to restore your latest prior Backup.QBB file using the instructions in Appendix B: Back Up & Restore QuickBooks files. After restoring, add YourName Exercise 5.5 to the company name.

E5.5.2 Make Deposit

1. On 12/20/2022, record the deposit from Maria Cecilia's payment for $223.53
2. Select the **Save** icon at the top of the Make Deposits window
3. Select the **Journal** icon to display the journal entry to QuickBooks created behind the screen for the deposit
4. Export to **Excel** or **print** the Transaction Journal
5. **Close** the Transaction Journal and the Make Deposits windows

E5.5.3 Deposit Detail Report

1. Export to **Excel** or **print** the Deposit Detail report for 12/20/2022

E5.5.4 Back Up Exercise 5.5

Save a backup of your Exercise file using the file name: YourName Exercise 5.5 Backup.QBB. See *Appendix B: Back Up & Restore QuickBooks Files* for instructions.

EXERCISE 5.6: Customer Reports

In this exercise, we create additional customer reports that a business might find useful.

E5.6.1 QuickBooks File

If you will be using the same computer and the same QBW file:

1. Select your **QBW file.**
2. Add **YourName Exercise 5.6** to the company name by selecting **Company Menu > My Company.**

> **If you are not using the same computer that you used for prior Chapter 5 and Exercises,** you will need to restore your latest prior Backup.QBB file using the instructions in Appendix B: Back Up & Restore QuickBooks files. After restoring, add YourName Exercise 5.6 to the company name.

E5.6.2 Average Days to Pay Summary

Prepare the Average Days to Pay Summary report for Rock Castle Construction as follows.

1. From the Report Center, select **Customers & Receivables**
2. Select **Average Days to Pay Summary** report
3. Select Dates: **All**
4. Export to **Excel** or **print** the Average Days to Pay Summary report
5. **Highlight** how many days on average it takes for a customer to pay Rock Castle Construction

E5.6.3 Transaction List by Customer

Prepare a Transaction List by Customer report as follows.

1. From the Report Center, select **Customers & Receivables**
2. Select **Transaction List by Customer** report
3. Select Dates **From: 12/15/2022 To: 12/20/2022**
4. Export to **Excel** or **print** the report

E5.6.4 Journal

Prepare the Journal as follows.

1. From the Report Center, select **Accountant and Taxes > Journal**
2. Select Dates **From: 12/17/2022 To: 12/20/2022**
3. Export to **Excel** or **print** the Journal

E5.6.5 Back Up Exercise 5.6

Save a backup of your Exercise file using the file name: YourName Exercise 5.6 Backup.QBB. See *Appendix B: Back Up & Restore QuickBooks Files* for instructions.

Would you like more information about correcting errors in QuickBooks? Go to www.My-QuickBooks.com, select QB Issue Resolution link.

PROJECT 5.1

Larry's Landscaping

As an accounting consultant for Larry's Landscaping complete the following to enter customer and sales transactions for the company.

QB SatNav

The objective of Project 5.1 is to facilitate your mastery of QuickBooks Desktop. As shown in the following QB SatNav, Project 5.1 focuses on QB Customers and Sales Transactions.

QB SatNav

1 QB SETTINGS

- Company Settings
- Chart of Accounts

2 QB TRANSACTIONS

> Money in *Money out >*

- Banking
- **Customers & Sales**
- Vendors & Expenses
- Employees & Payroll

3 QB REPORTS

- Reports

P5.1.1 QuickBooks File

1. Use either your QuickBooks Company file (QBW) or restore the backup file (QBB) that you completed for Project 4.1. (If you have issues with your QuickBooks file, contact your instructor.)
2. Update the Company Name to: **YourName Project 5.1 Larry's Landscaping**

P5.1.2 Sales Receipts

1. Enter the following sales receipt for Larry's Landscaping.

Template	**Sales Receipt - Retail**
Date	**12/20/2022**
Customer	**Dave Perry**
Item	**Fertilizer (Lawn & Garden)**
Quantity	**9**
Payment	**Check (No. 622)**

2. Select the **Save** icon
3. Select the **Reports** tab > **Transaction Journal**
4. Export the Transaction Journal report to **Excel** or **print** the report
5. Enter the following sales receipt for Larry's Landscaping.

Template	**Sales Receipt - Retail**
Date	**12/21/2022**
Customer	**Jean Paulney**
Item	**Rocks (Garden Rocks)**
Quantity	**7**
Payment	**Cash**

6. Select the **Save** icon
7. Select the **Reports** tab > **Transaction Journal**
8. Export the Transaction Journal report to **Excel** or **print** the report

P5.1.3 Invoices

1. Enter the following invoice for Larry's Landscaping.

Date	**12/21/2022**
Customer	**Anne Loomis**
Item	**Pest Control Service**
Quantity	**1**
Price Each	**$60.00**
Tax	**Non**

2. Select the **Save** icon
3. Select the **Reports** tab > **Transaction Journal**
4. Export the Transaction Journal report to **Excel** or **print** the report
5. Enter the following invoice for Larry's Landscaping.

Date	**12/20/2022**
Customer	**Russell Chiropractic**
Item	**Weekly Garden Service**
Quantity	**1**
Price Each	**$75.00**
Tax	**Non**

6. Select the **Save** icon
7. Select the **Reports** tab > **Transaction Journal**
8. Export the Transaction Journal report to **Excel** or **print** the report
9. Enter the following invoice for Larry's Landscaping.

Date	**12/20/2022**
Customer	**Gwen Price**
Item	**Tree Removal**
Quantity	**1**
Price Each	**$80.00**
Tax	**Non**

10. Select the **Save** icon
11. Select the **Reports** tab > **Transaction Journal**
12. Export the Transaction Journal report to **Excel** or **print** the report
13. **Close** the Transaction Journal and the Invoice windows

P5.1.4 Receive Payments

1. Record the following customer payments received by Larry's Landscaping.

Date	**12/19/2022**
Customer	**Susie Rummens**
Invoice No.	**No. 126**
Amount	**$135.00**
Payment Method	**Check (No. 321)**

Date	**12/20/2022**
Customer	**Bob Heldt**
Invoice No.	**No. 123**
Amount	**$1,825.92**
Payment Method	**Check (No. 823)**

Date	**12/21/2022**
Customer	**Mike Balak**
Invoice No.	**No. 116**
Amount	**$180**
Payment Method	**Check (No. 1281)**

P5.1.5 Make Deposits

1. Record the following deposits transferring funds from Undeposited Funds to the Checking account.

Deposit Date	**12/21/2022**
Customer	**Jean Paulney**
Amount	**$72.69**

Deposit Date	**12/21/2022**
Customer	**Susie Rummens**
Amount	**$135.00**

Deposit Date	**12/21/2022**
Customer	**Bob Heldt**
Amount	**$1,825.92**

Deposit Date	**12/21/2022**
Customer	**Dave Perry**
Amount	**$18.12**

Deposit Date	**12/21/2022**
Customer	**Mike Balak**
Amount	**$180.00**

2. Select the **Save** icon at the top of the Make Deposits window
3. Select the **Journal** icon to display the Transaction Journal
4. Export to **Excel** or **print** the Transaction Journal
5. **Close** the Transaction Journal and the Make Deposits windows

P5.1.6 Reports

1. Export to **Excel** the Journal report for **December 19 through 21, 2022**
2. Export to **Excel** the Open Invoices report for Larry's Landscaping for **December 21, 2022**
3. Export to **Excel** the Deposit Detail report for **December 19 through 21, 2022**

P5.1.7 Back Up Project 5.1

Save a backup of your Project file using the file name: YourName Project 5.1 Backup.QBB. See *Appendix B: Back Up & Restore QuickBooks Files* for instructions.

Chapter 6

Vendors and Expenses

BACKSTORY

Mr. Castle walks up to your desk with another stack of paperwork. At this point, you are wondering if he has file cabinets full of never-ending paper just waiting to bring it to you one stack at a time.

Setting the stack onto your desk, Mr. Castle jovially says, *"Now that you are almost caught up with customers and sales transactions, here are some vendor transactions for you. To make it a bit easier on you, I've been thinking we can work on inventory later. Let's just focus on getting caught up on vendors and expense transactions and save inventory transactions until later.*

"How does that sound to you? We don't want to overwhelm you. . . not just yet anyway," he laughs.

"Absolutely Mr Castle." You nod in agreement.

Section 6.1

QuickBooks SatNav

QuickBooks SatNav is your satellite navigation for QuickBooks, assisting you in navigating QuickBooks

QuickBooks SatNav divides QuickBooks into three processes:

1. **QuickBooks Settings.** This includes Company Settings when setting up a new QuickBooks company and the Company Chart of Accounts.
2. **QuickBooks Transactions.** This includes recording transactions in QuickBooks. Transaction types can be categorized as Banking, Customers and Sales, Vendors and Expenses, and Employees and Payroll. In basic terms, recording transactions involves recording money in and money out.
3. **QuickBooks Reports.** QuickBooks reports are the output of the system, such as commonly used financial statements of Balance Sheet, Income Statement, and Statement of Cash Flows.

Chapter 6 focuses on vendors and expense transactions as shown in the following QuickBooks SatNav.

QB SatNav

1 QB SETTINGS CHAPTERS 1 2 11 12 13 14

Company Settings
Chart of Accounts

2 QB TRANSACTIONS CHAPTERS 3 4 5 6 7 8 11 12 13 14

> Money in *Money out >*

Banking
Customers/Sales
Vendors/Expenses
Employees/Payroll

3 QB REPORTS CHAPTERS 9 10 11 12 13 14

Reports

Section 6.2

START QUICKBOOKS AND OPEN QUICKBOOKS COMPANY

START QUICKBOOKS

To start QuickBooks software, click the **QuickBooks** icon on your desktop. If a QuickBooks icon does not appear on your desktop, from Microsoft® Windows® click **Start** button > **Programs** > **QuickBooks QuickBooks Premier Accountant Edition.**

QuickBooks Accountant includes all the features of QuickBooks Pro plus features for client services. If you use QuickBooks Pro, your screens may appear slightly different than those appearing in this text.

RESTORE QBB STARTER FILE

Restore the QBB Starter file for this chapter as follows.

1. Select **File** > **Restore**
2. Using the directions in *Appendix B: Back Up & Restore QuickBooks Files,* restore the **CHAPTER 6 STARTER.QBB**
3. After restoring, add **YourName Chapter 6** to the company name by selecting **Company Menu** > **My Company**

Section 6.3

VENDOR NAVIGATION

The QuickBooks Home Page contains a Vendors section that displays icons used for vendor functions. If necessary click the **Home** icon in the Navigation Bar to display the Home Page.

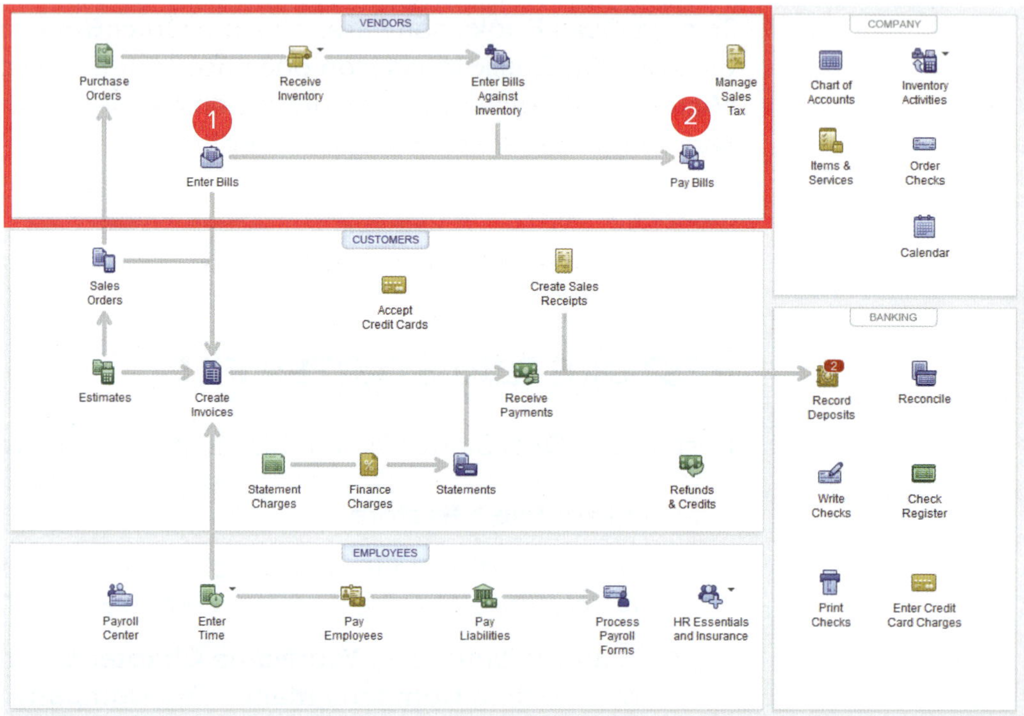

The Vendors section of the Home Page is a flowchart of vendor transactions. In this chapter we are going to focus on the following vendor transactions:

1. **Enter Bills.** Use the Enter Bills window to record bills for services received. Examples include rent, utilities expense, insurance expense, and accounting and professional services. QuickBooks will record an obligation (accounts payable liability) to pay the bill later.
2. **Pay Bills.** Use the Pay Bills window to select the bills that are due and you are ready to pay.

Section 6.4

VENDOR LIST

The first step in working with vendor transactions is to enter vendor information in the Vendor List.

The Vendor List contains information for each vendor, such as address, telephone number, and credit terms. Vendor information is entered in the Vendor List and then QuickBooks automatically transfers the vendor information to the appropriate forms, such as purchase orders and checks. This feature enables you to enter vendor information only once in QuickBooks instead of entering the vendor information each time a form is prepared.

QuickBooks considers a vendor to be any individual or organization that provides products or services to your company. QuickBooks considers all of the following to be vendors:

- Suppliers from whom you buy inventory or supplies
- Service companies that provide services to your company, such as cleaning services or landscaping services
- Financial institutions, such as banks, that provide financial services including checking accounts and loans
- Tax agencies such as the IRS. The IRS is considered a vendor because you pay taxes to the IRS
- Utility and telephone companies

VIEW VENDOR LIST

To view the Vendor List for Rock Castle Construction:

1. Click **Vendors** in the Navigation Bar
2. Click the **Vendors** tab. The following Vendor List appears listing vendors with whom Rock Castle Construction does business. The Vendor List also displays the balance currently owed each vendor.
3. To view additional information about a vendor, click the vendor's name, and Vendor Information will appear on the right side of the Vendor Center.

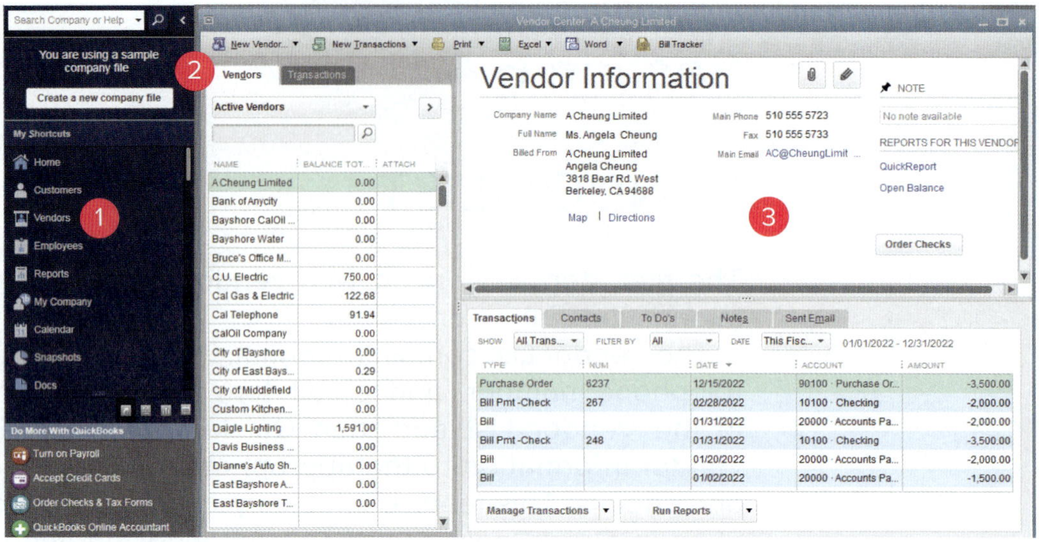

ADD NEW VENDOR

Rock Castle Construction needs to add a new vendor, Andre Window & Door, to the Vendor List.

To add a new vendor to the Vendor List:

1. Click the **New Vendor** button at the top of the Vendor Center
2. Click **New Vendor** on the drop-down menu
3. Select the **Address Info** tab in the New Vendor window. Enter the following information.

Vendor Name	**Andre Window & Door**
Company Name	**Andre Window & Door**
Full Name	**Andre LaFortune**
Main Phone	**415-555-1955**
Mobile	**415-555-1988**
Main Email	**andre@windowdoor.com**
Address	**28 Beach Street Bayshore, CA 94326**

4. Select the **Payment Settings** tab and enter the following information

Account No.	**58101**
Payment Terms	**Net 15**
Print on Check as	**Andre Window & Door**

5 Select the **Tax Settings** tab and enter the following information

Vendor Tax ID	**37-1958101**
Vendor Eligible for 1099	**Yes**

6 Select the **Additional Info** tab and enter the following information

Vendor Type	**Materials**

7 Click **OK** to add the new vendor to Rock Castle Construction's Vendor List and close the New Vendor window

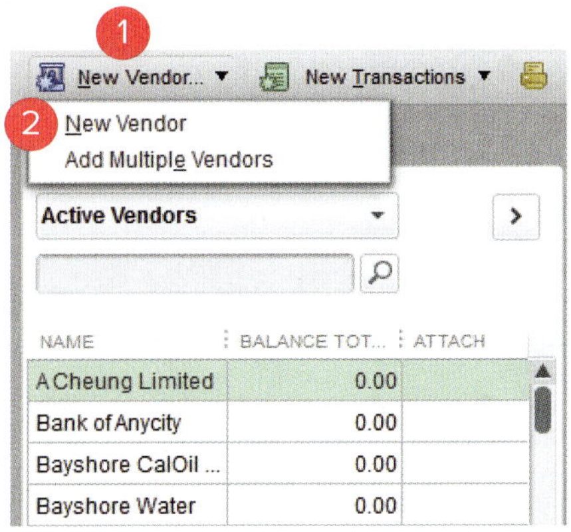

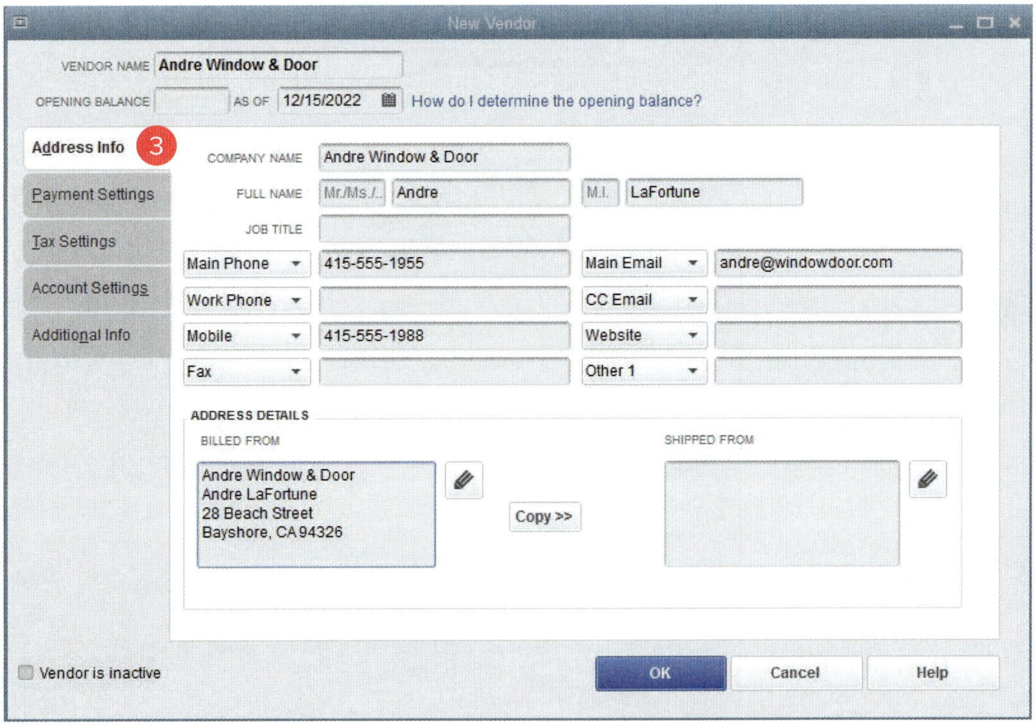

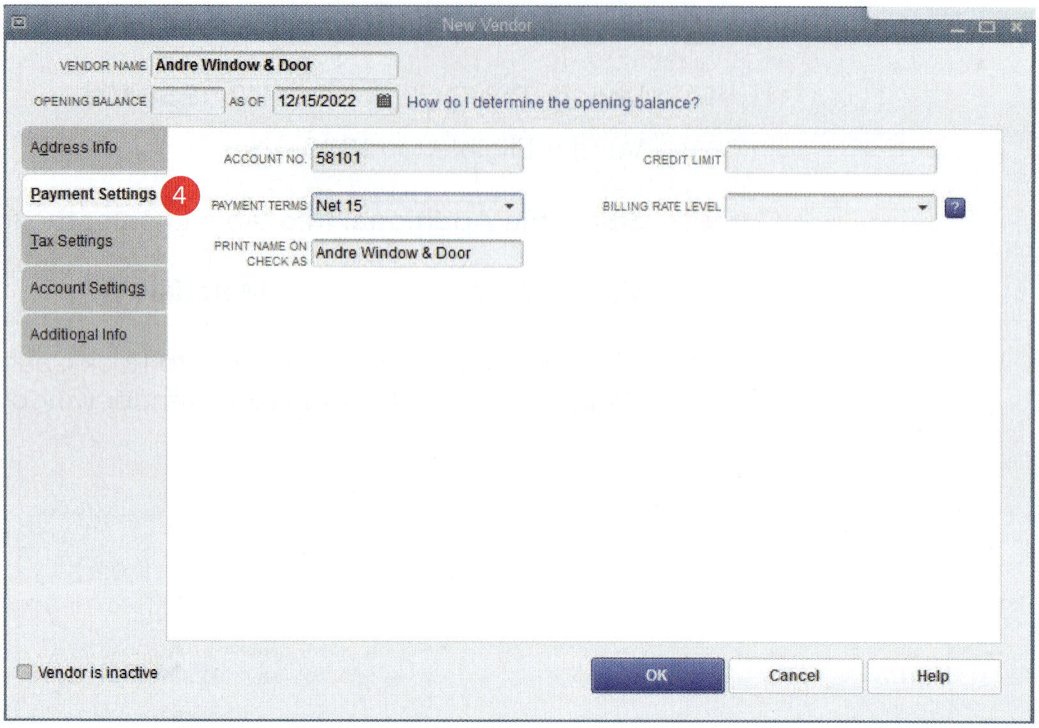
New Vendor
VENDOR NAME Andre Window & Door
OPENING BALANCE AS OF 12/15/2022 How do I determine the opening balance?
Address Info
Payment Settings
4
Tax Settings
Account Settings
Additional Info
ACCOUNT NO. 58101
CREDIT LIMIT
PAYMENT TERMS Net 15
BILLING RATE LEVEL
PRINT NAME ON CHECK AS Andre Window & Door
Vendor is inactive
OK
Cancel
Help

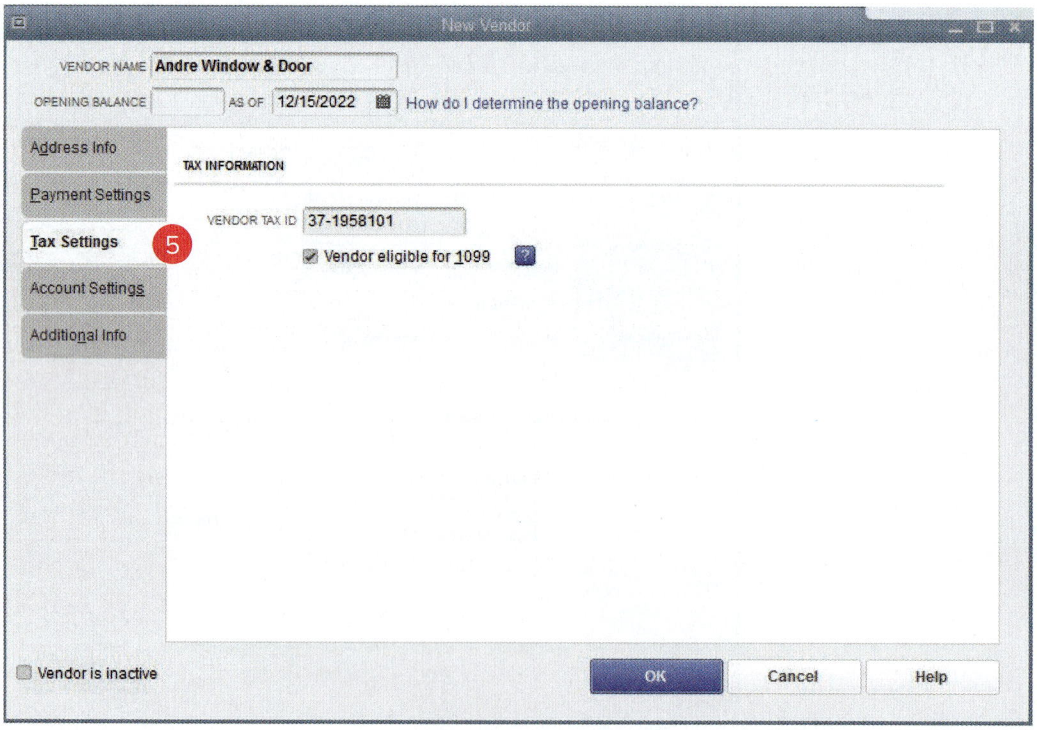
New Vendor
VENDOR NAME Andre Window & Door
OPENING BALANCE AS OF 12/15/2022 How do I determine the opening balance?
Address Info
Payment Settings
Tax Settings
5
Account Settings
Additional Info
TAX INFORMATION
VENDOR TAX ID 37-1958101
Vendor eligible for 1099
Vendor is inactive
OK
Cancel
Help

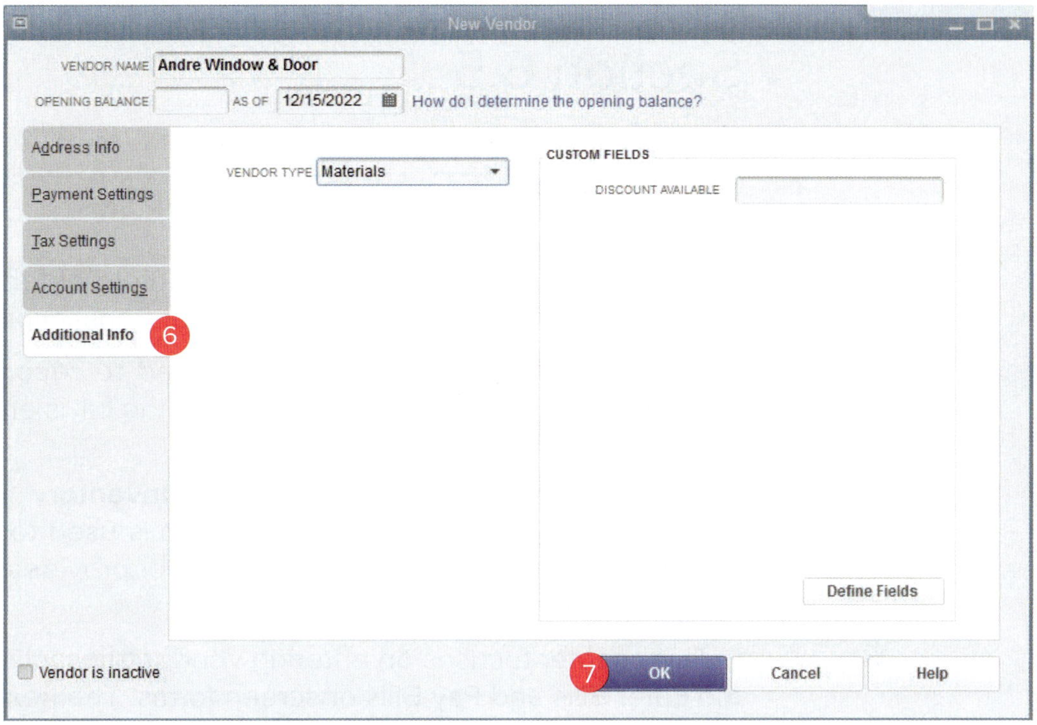

To edit vendor information later, simply click the vendor's name in the Vendor List window. The vendor information will appear on the right side of the Vendor Center. Click the Edit Vendor button, make the necessary changes in the Edit Vendor window that appears, and then click OK to close the Edit Vendor window.

The Vendor List can also be imported from Excel into QuickBooks.

EXPORT VENDOR LIST

C6.4.1 Vendor List. Export the Vendor List as follows:

1. From Vendor Center, select **Excel** > **Export Vendor List**
2. Select **Replace an existing worksheet**
3. Export the Vendor List to **Excel**

Section 6.5

VENDOR TRANSACTIONS

After creating a Vendor List, you are ready to enter vendor transactions. There are two basic ways to enter vendor transactions using QuickBooks.

1. **Enter Bills** > **Pay Bills.** This is used to record services, such as utilities or accounting services. After the bill is entered, it is paid when it is due.
2. **Enter Purchase Orders** > **Receive Inventory** > **Enter Bills Against Inventory** > **Pay Bills.** This approach is used to record the purchase of inventory items. The purchase order provides a record of the items ordered.

This chapter focuses on entering vendor transactions for services using the Enter Bills and Pay Bills onscreen forms. The next chapter covers how to record the purchase of inventory items using Purchase Orders.

Section 6.6

ENTER BILLS

To record services instead of inventory received, use the Enter Bills icon. Expenses that can be recorded using the Enter Bills window include utilities, insurance, and rent.

Recording bills for services, such as utilities, in QuickBooks requires two steps:

1. **Enter Bills.** Record bills received for services.
2. **Pay Bills.** Select bills to pay.

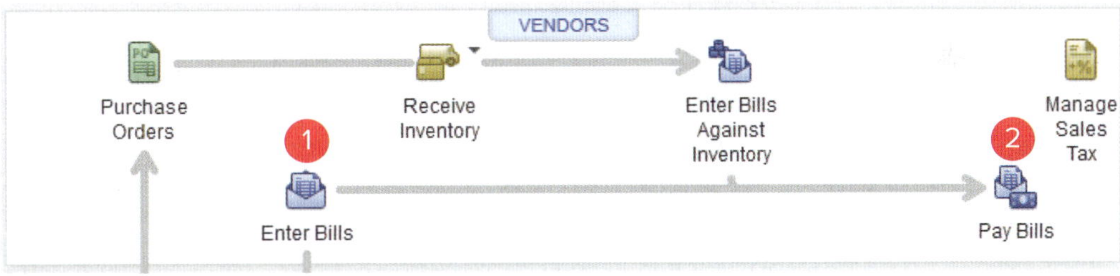

To enter bills for expenses:

1. Click the **Enter Bills** icon in the Vendors section of the Home Page
2. When the Enter Bills window appears, click the **Expenses** tab
3. Enter the following information for Rock Castle's water bill in the Enter Bills window

Vendor	**Bayshore Water**
Date	**12/24/2022**
Amount Due	**$54.00**
Terms	**Net 30**
Account	**65130: Water**

4. Select **Save** and leave the Enter Bills window open

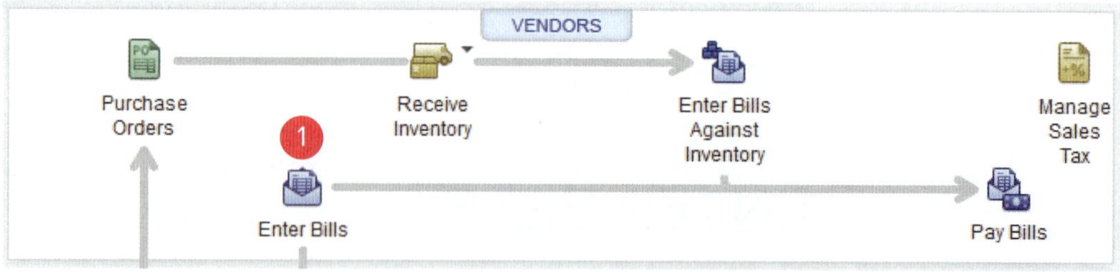
VENDORS
Purchase Orders
Receive Inventory
Enter Bills Against Inventory
Manage Sales Tax
1
Enter Bills
Pay Bills

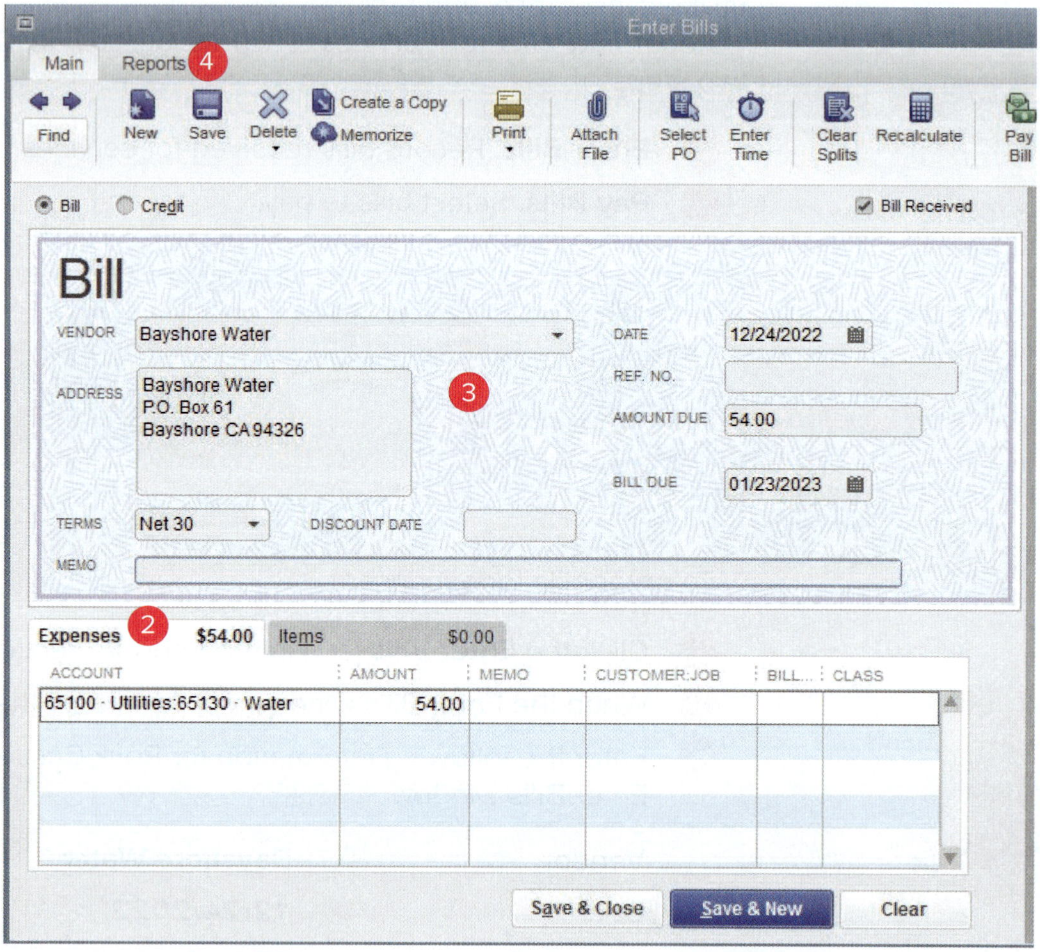
Enter Bills
Main
Reports
4
Find
New
Save
Delete
Create a Copy
Memorize
Print
Attach File
Select PO
Enter Time
Clear Splits
Recalculate
Pay Bill
Bill
Credit
Bill Received
Bill
VENDOR
Bayshore Water
DATE
12/24/2022
ADDRESS
Bayshore Water
P.O. Box 61
Bayshore CA 94326
3
REF. NO.
AMOUNT DUE
54.00
BILL DUE
01/23/2023
TERMS
Net 30
DISCOUNT DATE
MEMO
Expenses
2
$54.00
Items
$0.00
ACCOUNT
AMOUNT
MEMO
CUSTOMER:JOB
BILL...
CLASS
65100 · Utilities:65130 · Water
54.00
Save & Close
Save & New
Clear

C6.6.1 Bill Journal Entry. To view the journal entry that QuickBooks created behind the screen for the bill entered and saved using the Enter Bills onscreen form, complete the following steps.

1. From the Enter Bills onscreen form, select the **Reports** tab
2. Select the **Transaction Journal** icon
3. Export the Transaction Journal report to **Excel** or **print** the report. Notice that the entry shows a debit (increase) to Water Expense and a credit (increase) to Accounts Payable for the amount of the entered bill.
4. **Close** the Transaction Journal window
5. **Close** the Enter Bills window

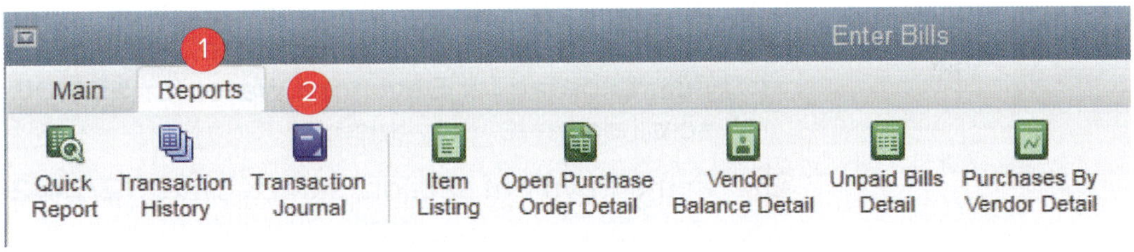

The next time you pay bills in QuickBooks, the water bill will appear on the list of bills to pay.

Section 6.7

PAY BILLS

After entering the bill, the next step is to pay the bill.

SELECT BILLS TO PAY

To select the bills to pay:

1. Click the **Pay Bills** icon in the Vendors section of the Home Page
2. Select Show bills: **Show all bills**
3. Select the bills you want to pay. Typically, you would select the bills that are due first. In this case, however, select bill that you just recorded for **Bayshore Water** for **$54.00.** If necessary, scroll down to view this bill.
4. In the Payment section, select: Date: **12/24/2022**
5. Select Method: **Check**
6. Select: **To be printed**
7. Select Account: **Checking**
8. Click **Pay Selected Bills**
9. When the Payment Summary window displays, if we wanted to print the checks, we would select Print Checks. In this case, select **Done.**

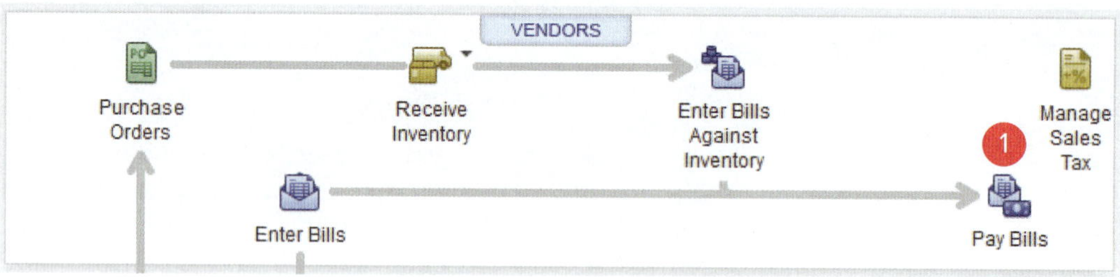

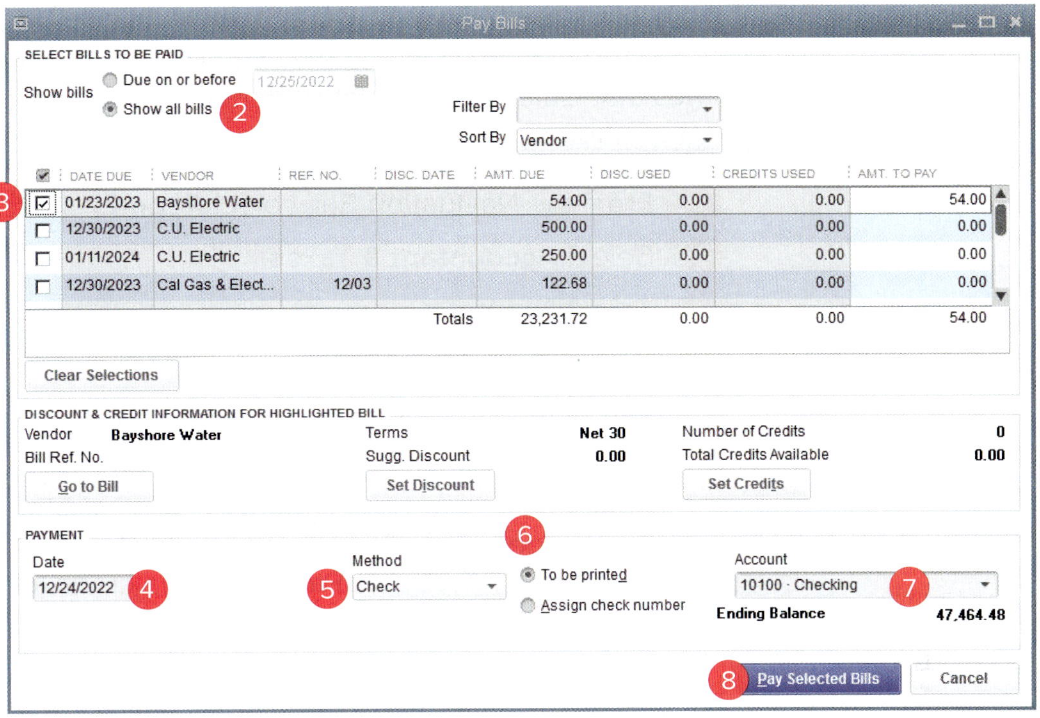

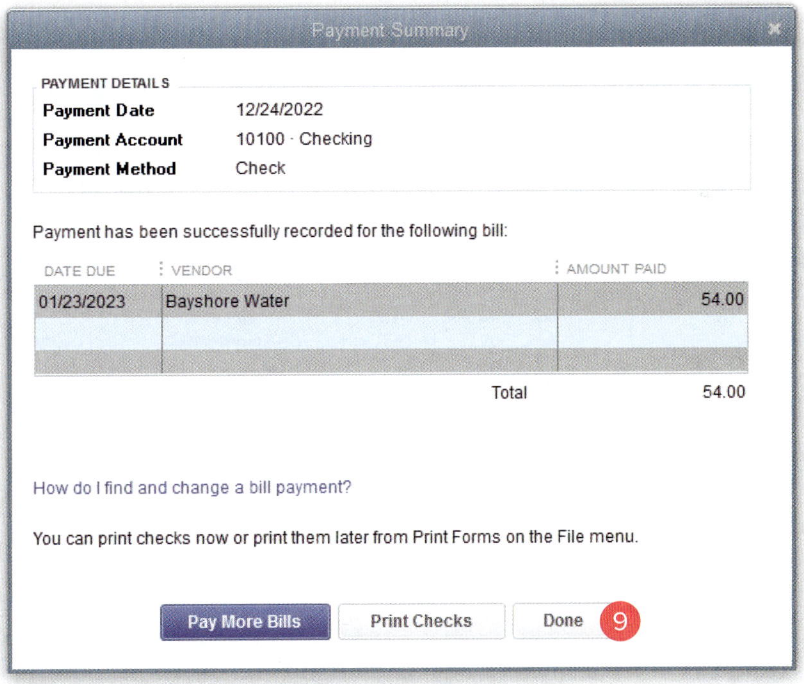

To pay by debit card, select Method: Check > Assign check number. Then use DC (for debit card) as the check number.

C6.7.1 Pay Bills Journal Entries. Another way to view the behind the screen journal entry is to use the Report Center. To view the journal entries that QuickBooks created behind the screen when bills were entered and selected for payment, complete the following steps.

1. From the Navigation Bar, select **Reports**
2. Select **Accountant & Taxes**
3. Select **Journal**
4. Select Date: **12/24/2022**
5. Export the Journal report to **Excel** or **print** the report
6. Notice that the first journal entry records the expense with a debit and records an account payable of $54.00 with a credit. The second journal entry records paying the bill with a debit (decreases) Accounts Payable and a credit (decreases) the Checking account for $54.00.
7. **Close** the Journal window

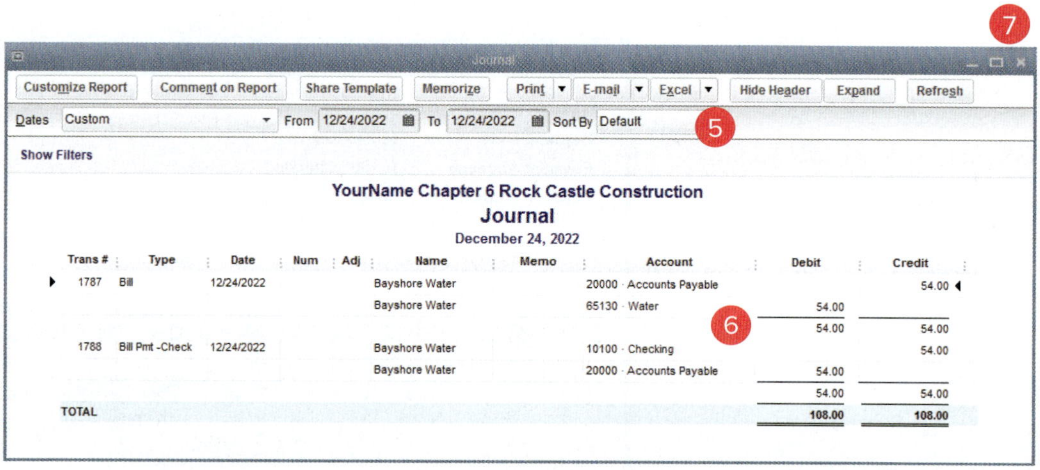

YourName Chapter 6 Rock Castle Construction
Journal
December 24, 2022

Trans #	Type	Date	Num	Adj	Name	Memo	Account	Debit	Credit
1787	Bill	12/24/2022			Bayshore Water		20000 · Accounts Payable		54.00
					Bayshore Water		65130 · Water	54.00	
								54.00	54.00
1788	Bill Pmt -Check	12/24/2022			Bayshore Water		10100 · Checking		54.00
					Bayshore Water		20000 · Accounts Payable	54.00	
								54.00	54.00
TOTAL								108.00	108.00

Section 6.8

VENDOR REPORTS

QuickBooks provides vendor reports to answer the following questions:

- How much do we owe? (Accounts Payable reports)
- How much have we purchased? (Purchase reports)
- How much inventory do we have? (Inventory reports)

QuickBooks offers several different ways to access vendor reports:

1. **Vendor Center.** Summarizes vendor information in one location (Access the Vendor Center by clicking the Vendors icon on the Navigation Bar.)
2. **Report Center.** Permits you to locate reports by type of report (Click the Reports icon on the Navigation Bar, then see Vendors & Payables, Purchases, and Inventory reports).
3. **Reports Menu.** Reports are grouped by type of report (See Vendors & Payables, Purchases, and Inventory reports).

ACCOUNTS PAYABLE REPORTS: HOW MUCH DO WE OWE?

Accounts payable consists of amounts that your company is obligated to pay in the future. Accounts Payable reports tell you how much you owe vendors and when amounts are due.

The following Accounts Payable reports provide information useful when tracking amounts owed vendors:

1. Accounts Payable Aging Summary
2. Accounts Payable Aging Detail
3. Unpaid Bills Detail

The Accounts Payable Aging Summary summarizes accounts payable balances by the age of the account. This report helps to track any past due bills as well as provides information about bills that will be due shortly.

Although you can access the vendor reports in several different ways, we will access this report from the Report Center.

C6.8.1 A/P Aging Summary. To prepare the A/P Aging Summary report:

1. Select **Reports** in the Navigation Bar
2. Select: **Vendors & Payables**
3. Select: **A/P Aging Summary**
4. Select Date: **12/24/2022**
5. Select **Run**
6. Export to **Excel** or **print** the report
7. **Highlight** the vendors and amounts of any past due accounts payable
8. **Close** the A/P Aging Summary window

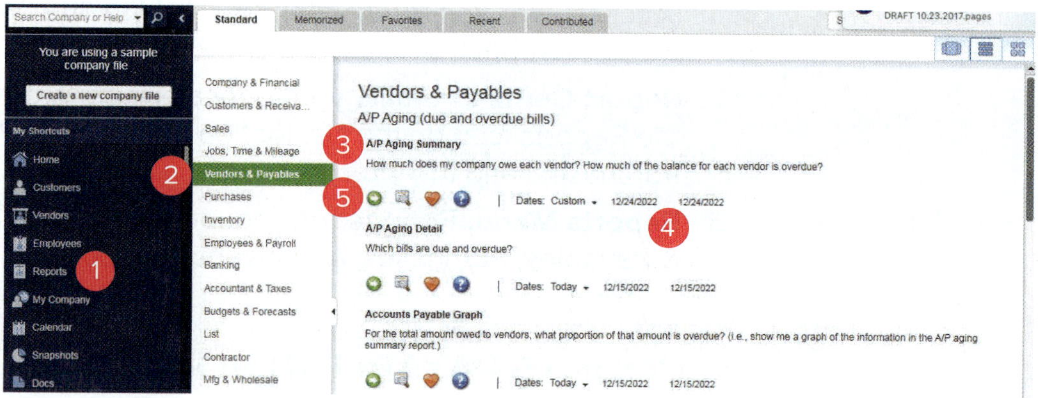

Section 6.9

BACK UP QUICKBOOKS FILES

BACK UP QBB

Save a backup of your Chapter 6 file using the file name: **YourName Chapter 6 Backup.QBB.** For further instructions on how to back up your file, *see Appendix B: Back Up & Restore QuickBooks Files.*

QBW WORKFLOW

If you are using the Workflow approach, leave your .QBW file open and proceed directly to Exercise 6.1.

QBB RESTORE

If you are using the Restore approach and ending your computer session now, close your QBW file and exit QuickBooks. When you restart, you will restore your backup file to complete Exercise 6.1.

Section 6.10

ACCOUNTING ESSENTIALS

Vendors Transactions, Accounts Payable, and 1099s

Accounting Essentials summarize important foundational accounting knowledge that may be useful when using QuickBooks

What are Accounts Payable?

- Accounts payable consists of amounts that our business is obligated to pay in the future. When our business makes purchases on credit, our business is promising to pay that amount in the future.
- When a purchase is made and recorded as a bill, accounts payable is increased by a credit. When the bill is paid, the accounts payable is decreased by a debit.

How can a business track accounts payables to make certain it is paying on time?

- Accounts Payable reports provide information to track amounts we owe vendors. An Accounts Payable Aging report summarizes accounts payable balances by the age of the account. This report helps us to track how much we owe vendors and when amounts are due, including the age of past due bills.

What is a 1099 and when does my company need to prepare 1099s?

- IRS Form 1099 must be completed for sole proprietorships and partnerships to which we paid $600 or more for services in a year. The vendor's Tax ID No. is required to complete the 1099. QuickBooks can assist in tracking amounts and preparing 1099s for appropriate vendors. To learn more about preparing 1099s, see www.irs.gov.

www.my-quickbooks.com

Go to **www.My-QuickBooks.com** to view additional QuickBooks resources including:

- **Excel Report Templates** to organize QuickBooks reports exported to Excel
- ***Computer Accounting with QuickBooks* updates,** sometimes required when there is a software update that affects the text
- **QuickBooks Video links**
- **QuickBooks Help and Support links**
- **Other QuickBooks Resources** to make learning QuickBooks easier and more effective
- **QuickBooks Issue Resolution** offers a guided approach to troubleshooting QuickBooks

Troubleshooting QuickBooks and Correcting Errors are crucial QuickBooks skill to acquire. See www.My-QuickBooks.com > QB Issue Resolution for Troubleshooting QuickBooks tips. See Chapter 17, Quick Review Guide, for tips on Correcting Errors.

EXERCISE 6.1: Enter Bills

BACKSTORY

When you arrive at work, you decide to sort through the papers stacked in the corner of your cubicle. You discover another unpaid utility bill amid the clutter.

E6.1.1 QuickBooks File

If you will be using the same computer and the same Chapter 6. QBW file:

1. If your Chapter 6.QBW file is not already open, open it by selecting **File > Open Previous Company.** Select your **Chapter 6.QBW file.** If a QuickBooks Information window appears with a message about the sample company file, click **OK.**

2. Add **YourName Exercise 6.1** to the company name by selecting **Company Menu > My Company.**

> **If you are not using the same computer that you used for Chapter 6,** you will need to restore your Chapter 6 Backup.QBB file using the instructions in Appendix B: Back Up & Restore QuickBooks Files. After restoring, add YourName Exercise 6.1 to the company name.

E6.1.2 Enter Bills

Use the Enter Bills icon in the Vendors section of the Home Page to enter the following bills.

1. Enter the following utility bill for Rock Castle Construction.

Vendor	**Cal Telephone**
Date	**12/26/2022**
Amount Due	**$63.00**
Account	**65120: Telephone**

2. Select the **Save** icon at the top of the Enter Bills window
3. Select the **Reports** tab
4. Select the **Transaction Journal** icon
5. Export the Transaction Journal report to **Excel** or **print** the report
6. **Close** the Transaction Journal and the Enter Bills windows

E6.1.3 Back Up Exercise 6.1

Save a backup of your Exercise file using the file name: YourName Exercise 6.1 Backup.QBB. See *Appendix B: Back Up & Restore QuickBooks Files* for instructions.

EXERCISE 6.2: Pay Bills

E6.2.1 QuickBooks File

If you will be using the same computer and the same QBW file:

1. Select your **QBW file.**
2. Add **YourName Exercise 6.2** to the company name by selecting **Company Menu > My Company.**

If you are not using the same computer that you used for Chapter 6 and Exercise 6.1, you will need to restore your latest prior Backup.QBB file using the instructions in Appendix B: Back Up & Restore QuickBooks files. After restoring, add YourName Exercise 6.2 to the company name.

E6.2.2 Pay Bills

1. On **12/26/2022,** pay by check the Cal Telephone bill that you entered. (Hint: Select Show all bills.)
2. From the Navigation Bar, select **Reports** > **Accountant & Taxes** > **Journal**
3. Select Date: **12/26/2022**
4. Export the Journal report to **Excel** or **print** the report
5. **Close** the Journal window

E6.2.3 Back Up Exercise 6.2

Save a backup of your Exercise file using the file name: YourName Exercise 6.2 Backup.QBB. See *Appendix B: Back Up & Restore QuickBooks Files* for instructions.

EXERCISE 6.3: Vendor Reports

E6.3.1 QuickBooks File

If you will be using the same computer and the same QBW file:

1. Select your **QBW file.**
2. Add **YourName Exercise 6.3** to the company name by selecting **Company Menu** > **My Company.**

If you are not using the same computer that you used for Chapter 6, Exercise 6.1 and Exercise 6.2, you will need to restore your latest prior Backup.QBB file using the instructions in Appendix B: Back Up & Restore QuickBooks files. After restoring, add YourName Exercise 6.3 to the company name.

E6.3.2 Check Detail Report

To review the transactions you entered, print a Check Detail report as follows.

1. From the Report Center, select **Banking** > **Check Detail**
2. Select Date **From: 12/24/2022 To: 12/26/2022**
3. Export to **Excel** or **print** the report
4. **Close** the Check Detail window

E6.3.3 Accounts Payable Aging Detail Report

The Accounts Payable Aging Summary summarizes accounts payable balances by the age of the account.

1. From the Report Center, select **Vendors & Payables** > **A/P Aging Detail**
2. Select Date **12/26/2022**
3. Select **Run**
4. Export to **Excel** or **print** the report
5. **Highlight** the vendors and amounts of any past due accounts payable
6. **Close** the A/P Aging Detail window

E6.3.4 Back Up Exercise 6.3

Save a backup of your Exercise file using the file name: YourName Exercise 6.3 Backup.QBB. See *Appendix B: Back Up & Restore QuickBooks Files* for instructions.

PROJECT 6.1

Larry's Landscaping

As an accounting consultant for Larry's Landscaping complete the following to enter vendors and expense transactions for the company.

QB SatNav

The objective of Project 6.1 is to facilitate your mastery of QuickBooks Desktop. As shown in the following QB SatNav, Project 6.1 focuses on QB Vendors and Expense Transactions.

QB SatNav

1 QB SETTINGS

- Company Settings
- Chart of Accounts

2 QB TRANSACTIONS

> Money in *Money out >*

- Banking
- Customers/Sales
- **Vendors/Expenses**
- Employees/Payroll

3 QB REPORTS

- Reports

P6.1.1 QuickBooks File

1. Use either your QuickBooks Company file (QBW) or restore the backup file (QBB) that you completed for Project 5.1. (If you have issues with your QuickBooks file, contact your instructor.)
2. Update the Company Name to: **YourName Project 6.1 Larry's Landscaping**

P6.1.2 Enter Bills

1. Use the Enter Bills icon to enter the following bill received by Larry's Landscaping.

Date	**12/23/2022**
Vendor	**Carole Design Media**
Account	**6000 Advertising Expense**
Terms	**Net 30**
Amount Due	**$198.00**

2. Select the **Save** icon
3. Select the **Reports** tab > **Transaction Journal**
4. Export the Transaction Journal report to **Excel** or **print** the report
5. Enter the following bill for Larry's Landscaping.

Date	**12/23/2022**
Vendor	**Brown Equipment Rental**
Account	**7120 Equipment Rental**
Terms	**Net 15**
Amount Due	**$540.00**

6. Select the **Save** icon
7. Select the **Reports** tab > **Transaction Journal**
8. Export the Transaction Journal report to **Excel** or **print** the report
9. Enter the following bill for Larry's Landscaping.

Date	**12/23/2022**
Vendor	**Campion Patrick, CPA**
Account	**7410 Accounting Expense**
Terms	**Net 30**
Amount Due	**$300.00**

10. Select the **Save** icon
11. Select the **Reports** tab > **Transaction Journal**
12. Export the Transaction Journal report to **Excel** or **print** the report

P6.1.3 Pay Bills

1. Pay the following bills for Larry's on 12/23/2022.

Vendor	**Brown Equipment Rental**
Amount Due	**$540.00**
Vendor	**Carole Design Media**
Amount Due	**$198.00**
Vendor	**Campion, Patrick CPA**
Amount Due	**$300.00**
Vendor	**Townley Insurance Agency**
Amount Due	**$427.62**
Vendor	**Great Statewide Bank**
Amount Due	**$699.12**

2. From the Navigation Bar, select **Reports** > **Accountant & Taxes** > **Journal**
3. Select Date: **12/23/2022**
4. Export the Journal report to **Excel** or **print** the report
5. **Close** the Journal window

P6.1.4 Reports

1. Export to **Excel** the Unpaid Bills Detail report for **December 23, 2022**
2. Export to **Excel** the Check Detail report for Larry's Landscaping for **December 23, 2022**
3. Export to **Excel** the Accounts Payable Aging Detail report as of **December 23, 2022**

P6.1.5 Back Up Project 6.1

Save a backup of your Project file using the file name: YourName Project 6.1 Backup.QBB. See *Appendix B: Back Up & Restore QuickBooks Files* for instructions.

Chapter 7

Inventory

Backstory

As you work your way through stacks of paper in your desk's inbox, you hear Mr. Castle's rapid footsteps coming in your direction. He whips around the corner of your cubicle with another stack of papers in hand.

In his usual rapid-fire delivery, Mr. Castle begins, *"This is the way we do business."* He quickly sketches the following:

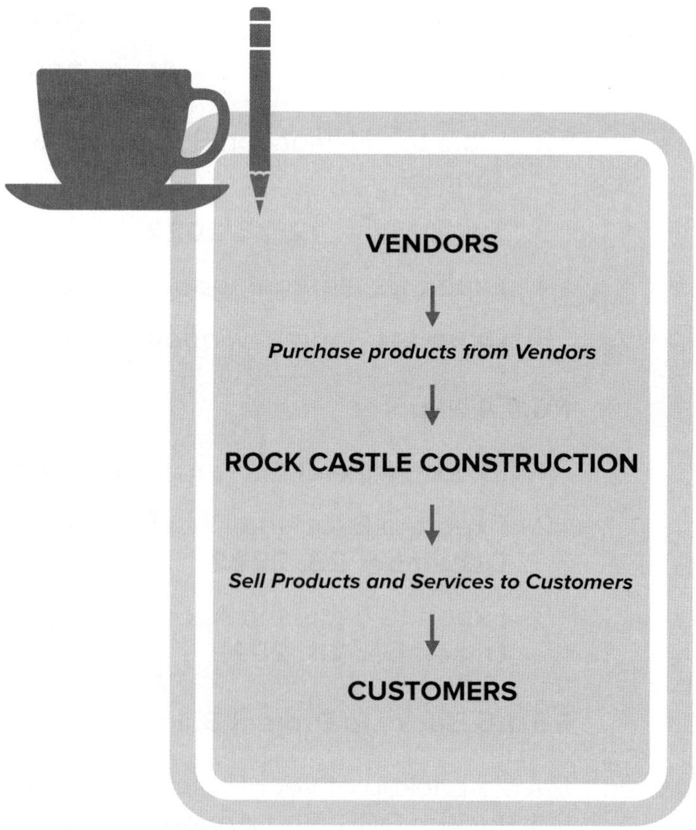

"We purchase products from our vendors and suppliers, and then we sell those products and provide services to our customers. We use QuickBooks to track the quantity and cost of items we purchase and sell."

Mr. Castle tosses the papers into your brand new inbox on your desk. *"Here are vendor and purchase transactions that need to be recorded."*

Mr. Castle races past, engaged in an intense conversation on his mobile phone.

Section 7.1

QuickBooks SatNav

QuickBooks SatNav is your satellite navigation for QuickBooks, assisting you in navigating QuickBooks

QuickBooks SatNav divides QuickBooks into three processes:

1. **QuickBooks Settings.** This includes Company Settings when setting up a new QuickBooks company and the Company Chart of Accounts.
2. **QuickBooks Transactions.** This includes recording transactions in QuickBooks. Transaction types can be categorized as Banking, Customers and Sales, Vendors and Expenses, and Employees and Payroll. In basic terms, recording transactions involves recording money in and money out.
3. **QuickBooks Reports.** QuickBooks reports are the output of the system, such as commonly used financial statements of Balance Sheet, Income Statement, and Statement of Cash Flows.

Chapter 7 focuses on inventory which is a type of vendor and expense transaction as shown in the following QuickBooks SatNav.

QB SatNav

1 QB SETTINGS — CHAPTERS 1 2 11 12 13 14

- Company Settings
- Chart of Accounts

2 QB TRANSACTIONS — CHAPTERS 3 4 5 6 7 8 11 12 13 14

> Money in *Money out >*

- Banking
- **Customers & Sales**
- **Vendors & Expenses**
- Employees & Payroll

3 QB REPORTS — CHAPTERS 9 10 11 12 13 14

- Reports

Section 7.2

START QUICKBOOKS AND OPEN QUICKBOOKS COMPANY

START QUICKBOOKS

To start QuickBooks software, click the **QuickBooks** icon on your desktop. If a QuickBooks icon does not appear on your desktop, from Microsoft® Windows® click **Start** button > **Programs** > **QuickBooks** > **QuickBooks Premier Accountant Edition.**

> **QuickBooks Accountant** includes all the features of QuickBooks Pro plus features for client services. If you use QuickBooks Pro, your screens may appear slightly different than those appearing in this text.

RESTORE QBB STARTER FILE

Restore the QBB Starter file for this chapter as follows.

1. Select **File** > **Restore**
2. Using the directions in *Appendix B: Back Up & Restore QuickBooks Files,* restore the **CHAPTER 7 STARTER.QBB**
3. After restoring, add **YourName Chapter 7** to the company name by selecting **Company Menu** > **My Company**

Section 7.3

VENDOR AND CUSTOMER TRANSACTIONS

If our company is a merchandising business that buys and resells goods, then we must maintain inventory records to account for the items we purchase from vendors and resell to customers.

The following diagram summarizes vendor and customer transactions.

VENDORS	1 → Purchase Products from Vendors	OUR COMPANY	2 → Sell Products to Customers	CUSTOMERS

We can use QuickBooks for inventory to record:

1. **Vendor transactions,** including placing product orders, receiving products, and paying bills
2. **Customer transactions,** including recording sale of product on invoices and receiving customer payments

The following table summarizes how to record Rock Castle Construction's business operations using QuickBooks.

	Activity	Type	Record Using...
1	Record vendor information	Vendor	**Vendor List**
2	Record inventory information: Set up inventory records to track the quantity and cost of items purchased	Vendor	**Item List**
3	Order goods: Use purchase orders (POs) to order goods from vendors	Vendor	**Purchase Orders**

	Activity	Type	Record Using...
4	Receive goods: Record goods received as inventory	Vendor	**Receive Items**
5	Receive bill: Record an obligation to pay a bill later (Account Payable)	Vendor	**Enter Bills**
6	Pay for goods: Pay bills for the goods received	Vendor	**Pay Bills**
7	Record customer information	Customer	**Customer List**
8	Sell goods and bill customers: Record customer's promise to pay later (Account Receivable)	Customer	**Invoice**
9	Receive customer payment: Record cash collected and reduce customer's Account Receivable	Customer	**Receive Payments**
10	Deposit customers' payments in bank account	Customer	**Deposit**

Section 7.4

VENDOR NAVIGATION

After opening the company file for Rock Castle Construction, click the **Home** icon in the Navigation Bar.

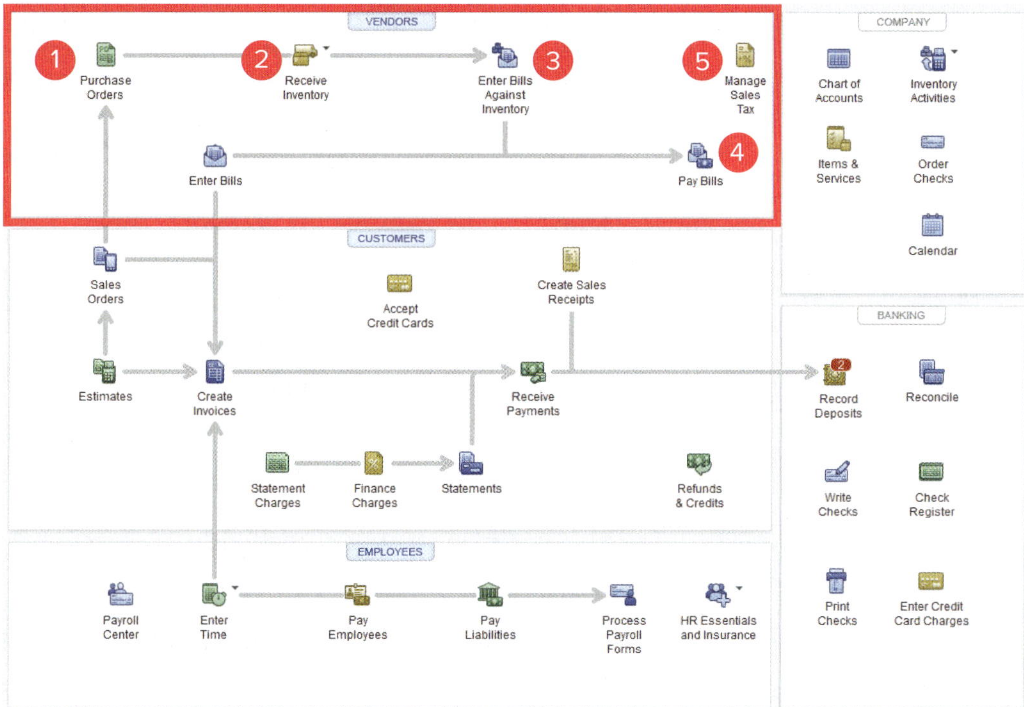

The Vendors section of the Home Page is a flowchart of vendor transactions. Chapter 6 covered how to enter bills for services, such as utilities or professional services. Chapter 7 covers how to use QuickBooks to record the purchase of products, instead of services.

As the flowchart indicates, vendor transactions for purchasing products can be recorded using QuickBooks as follows.

1. **Purchase Orders.** Use the Purchase Orders window to record an order to purchase goods.
2. **Receive Inventory.** Use the Receive Items window to record goods received.

3. **Enter Bills Against Inventory.** When the bill is received, use the Enter Bills Against Inventory window to record the bill. When the bill is entered, QuickBooks records accounts payable to reflect the obligation to pay the bill later.
4. **Pay Bills.** Use the Pay Bills window to select the bills that are due and you are ready to pay.
5. **Manage Sales Tax.** Sales taxes are charged on retail sales to customers. The sales tax collected from customers must be paid to the appropriate state agency.

The Vendor List contains vendor information that QuickBooks automatically transfers to the appropriate forms, such as purchase orders and bills. The Vendor List was covered in Chapter 6.

The Items and Services List, discussed next, is used to record information about products and services purchased from vendors.

Section 7.5

ITEMS & SERVICES LIST

QuickBooks defines an item as anything that your company buys, sells, or resells including products, shipping charges, and sales taxes. Items provide supporting detail for accounts.

QuickBooks classifies products and services purchased and sold into three different categories of items:

1. **Service Items.** Service items can be services that are purchased *or* sold. For example, service items include:
   - Services you buy from vendors, such as cleaning services
   - Services you sell to customers, such as installation labor
2. **Inventory Items.** Inventory items are products that a business purchases, holds as inventory, and then resells to customers. QuickBooks traces the quantity and cost of inventory items in stock.

   For consistency, the same inventory item is used when recording sales and purchases. QuickBooks has the capability to track both the cost and the sales price for inventory items. For example, in Chapter 5, we recorded the sale of an inventory item, an interior door. When the interior door was recorded on a sales invoice, QuickBooks automatically updated our inventory records by reducing the quantity of doors on hand. If we purchased an interior door, then we would record the door on the purchase order using the same inventory item number that we used on the invoice, except the purchase order uses the door cost while the invoice uses the door selling price.
3. **Non-inventory Items.** Non-inventory items are products that a business purchases, but QuickBooks does not track the quantity on hand for non-inventory items. Non-inventory items include:
   - Items purchased for a specific customer job, such as a custom countertop
   - Items purchased and used by your company instead of resold to customers, such as office supplies or carpentry tools
   - Items purchased and resold (if the quantity on hand does not need to be tracked)

The Items and Services List (Item List) summarizes information about items (inventory items, non-inventory items, and service items) that a company purchases or sells.

QuickBooks tracks inventory costs using the weighted-average method. QuickBooks does not use FIFO (First-in, First-out) or LIFO (Last-in, First- out) inventory costing. The average cost of an inventory item is displayed in the Edit Item window.

QuickBooks does not track the quantity of non-inventory items. If it is important for your business to know the quantity of an item on hand, record the item as an inventory item.

VIEW ITEM LIST

To view the Item List in QuickBooks:

1. Click the **Items & Services** icon in the Company section of the Home Page
2. The Item List window will appear
3. Notice the **Type** column in the Item List, displaying Service, Inventory and Non-inventory items

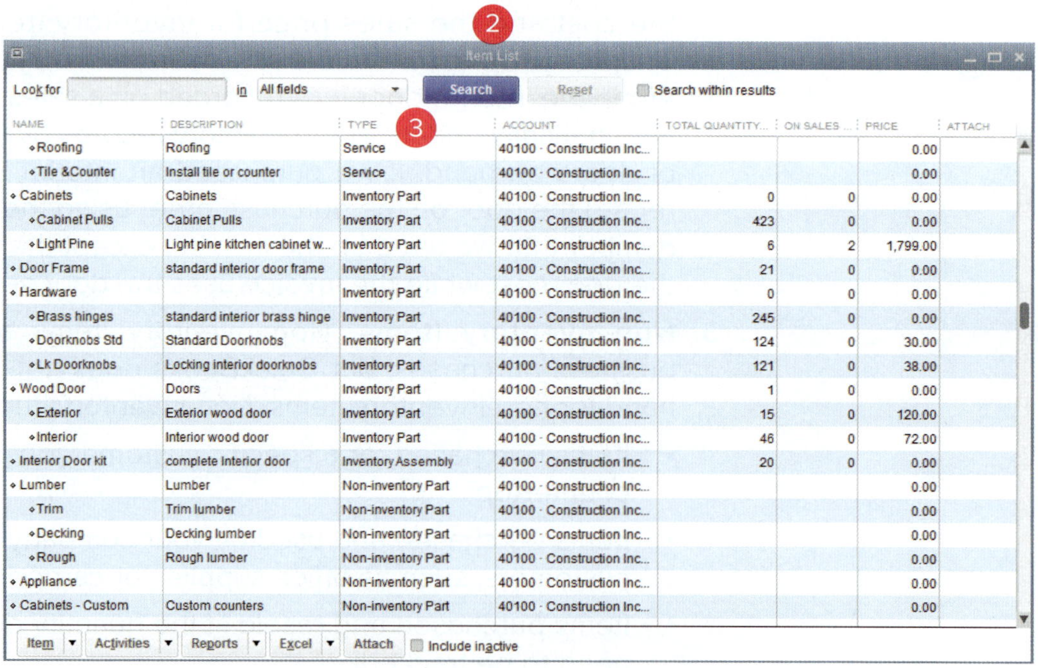

NAME	DESCRIPTION	TYPE	ACCOUNT	TOTAL QUANTITY...	ON SALES ...	PRICE	ATTACH
◦Roofing	Roofing	Service	40100 · Construction Inc...			0.00	
◦Tile &Counter	Install tile or counter	Service	40100 · Construction Inc...			0.00	
◦Cabinets	Cabinets	Inventory Part	40100 · Construction Inc...	0	0	0.00	
◦Cabinet Pulls	Cabinet Pulls	Inventory Part	40100 · Construction Inc...	423	0	0.00	
◦Light Pine	Light pine kitchen cabinet w...	Inventory Part	40100 · Construction Inc...	6	2	1,799.00	
◦Door Frame	standard interior door frame	Inventory Part	40100 · Construction Inc...	21	0	0.00	
◦Hardware		Inventory Part	40100 · Construction Inc...	0	0	0.00	
◦Brass hinges	standard interior brass hinge	Inventory Part	40100 · Construction Inc...	245	0	0.00	
◦Doorknobs Std	Standard Doorknobs	Inventory Part	40100 · Construction Inc...	124	0	30.00	
◦Lk Doorknobs	Locking interior doorknobs	Inventory Part	40100 · Construction Inc...	121	0	38.00	
◦Wood Door	Doors	Inventory Part	40100 · Construction Inc...	1	0	0.00	
◦Exterior	Exterior wood door	Inventory Part	40100 · Construction Inc...	15	0	120.00	
◦Interior	Interior wood door	Inventory Part	40100 · Construction Inc...	46	0	72.00	
◦Interior Door kit	complete Interior door	Inventory Assembly	40100 · Construction Inc...	20	0	0.00	
◦Lumber	Lumber	Non-inventory Part	40100 · Construction Inc...			0.00	
◦Trim	Trim lumber	Non-inventory Part	40100 · Construction Inc...			0.00	
◦Decking	Decking lumber	Non-inventory Part	40100 · Construction Inc...			0.00	
◦Rough	Rough lumber	Non-inventory Part	40100 · Construction Inc...			0.00	
◦Appliance		Non-inventory Part	40100 · Construction Inc...			0.00	
◦Cabinets - Custom	Custom counters	Non-inventory Part	40100 · Construction Inc...			0.00	

The Item List contains the following information:

- Item name
- Item description
- Item type (service, inventory, non-inventory, other charge, discount, sales tax item)
- Account used
- Quantity on hand
- Price of the item

ADD NEW ITEM

Rock Castle Construction needs to add two new items to the Item List: bifold doors and bifold door hardware. Because Rock Castle Construction wants to track the quantity of each item, both will be inventory items.

To add an inventory item to the Item List:

1. From the Item List window, **right-click** to display the following pop-up menu. Select **New.**
2. In the New Item window that appears, enter information about the bifold door inventory item. From the Type drop- down list, select **Inventory Part.** Then enter the following information in the New Item window.

Item Name/Number	**Bifold Doors**
Subitem of	**Wood Door**
Manufacturer's Part Number	**BD42**
Description on Purchase Transactions	**Bifold interior door**
Description on Sales Transactions	**Bifold interior door**
Cost	**45.00**
COGS Account	**50100 – Cost of Goods Sold**
Preferred Vendor	**Andre Window & Door**
Sales Price	**72.00**
Tax Code	**Tax**
Income Account	**40140 Materials Income**
Asset Account	**12100 – Inventory Asset**

Reorder Point (Min)	**2**
On Hand	**0**
Total Value	**0.00**
As of	**12/15/2022**

3. Click **Next** to record this inventory item and clear the fields to record another inventory item
4. Enter bifold door knobs as an **Inventory part** in the Item List using the following information:

Item Name/Number	**Bifold Knobs**
Subitem of	**Hardware**
Manufacturer's Part Number	**BK36**
Description on Purchase Transactions	**Bifold door hardware**
Description on Sales Transactions	**Bifold door hardware**
Cost	**6.00**
COGS Account	**50100 – Cost of Goods Sold**
Preferred Vendor	**Patton Hardware Supplies**
Sales Price	**13.00**
Tax Code	**Tax**
Income Account	**40140 Materials Income**
Asset Account	**12100 – Inventory Asset**
Reorder Point (Min)	**2**
On Hand	**0**
Total Value	**0.00**
As of	**12/15/2022**

5. Click **OK** to record the item and close the New Item window

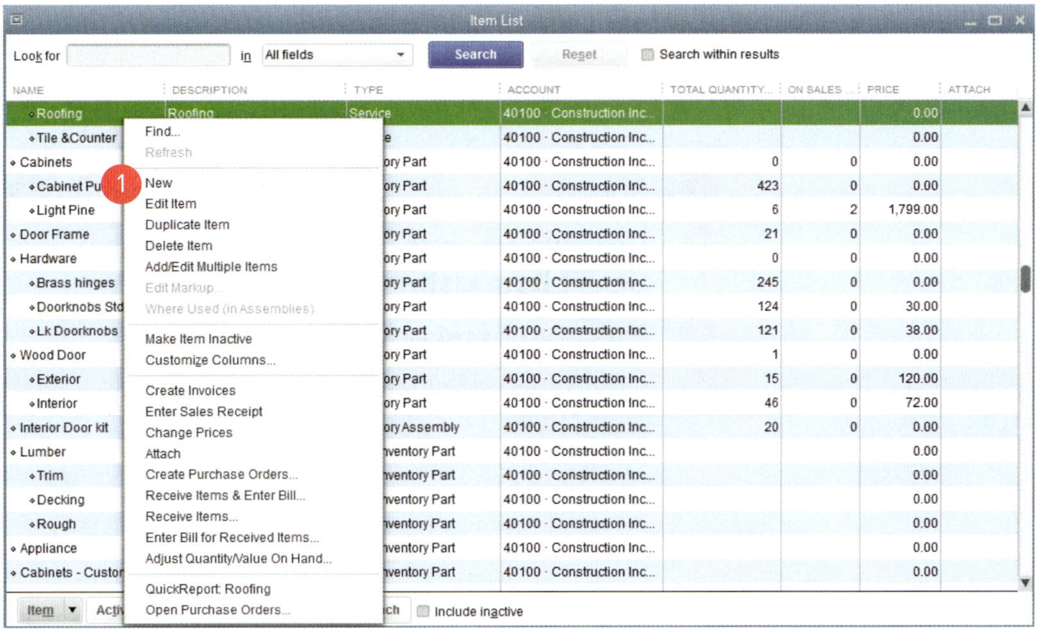
Item List
Look for
in All fields
Search
Reset
Search within results
NAME
DESCRIPTION
TYPE
ACCOUNT
TOTAL QUANTITY...
ON SALES ...
PRICE
ATTACH
Roofing Roofing Service 40100 · Construction Inc... 0.00
Tile &Counter 40100 · Construction Inc... 0.00
Cabinets 40100 · Construction Inc... 0 0 0.00
Cabinet Pu 40100 · Construction Inc... 423 0 0.00
Light Pine 40100 · Construction Inc... 6 2 1,799.00
Door Frame 40100 · Construction Inc... 21 0 0.00
Hardware 40100 · Construction Inc... 0 0 0.00
Brass hinges 40100 · Construction Inc... 245 0 0.00
Doorknobs Std 40100 · Construction Inc... 124 0 30.00
Lk Doorknobs 40100 · Construction Inc... 121 0 38.00
Wood Door 40100 · Construction Inc... 1 0 0.00
Exterior 40100 · Construction Inc... 15 0 120.00
Interior 40100 · Construction Inc... 46 0 72.00
Interior Door kit 40100 · Construction Inc... 20 0 0.00
Lumber 40100 · Construction Inc... 0.00
Trim 40100 · Construction Inc... 0.00
Decking 40100 · Construction Inc... 0.00
Rough 40100 · Construction Inc... 0.00
Appliance 40100 · Construction Inc... 0.00
Cabinets - Custo 40100 · Construction Inc... 0.00
Find...
Refresh
1
New
Edit Item
Duplicate Item
Delete Item
Add/Edit Multiple Items
Edit Markup...
Where Used (in Assemblies)
Make Item Inactive
Customize Columns...
Create Invoices
Enter Sales Receipt
Change Prices
Attach
Create Purchase Orders...
Receive Items & Enter Bill...
Receive Items...
Enter Bill for Received Items...
Adjust Quantity/Value On Hand...
QuickReport: Roofing
Open Purchase Orders...
Item
Include inactive

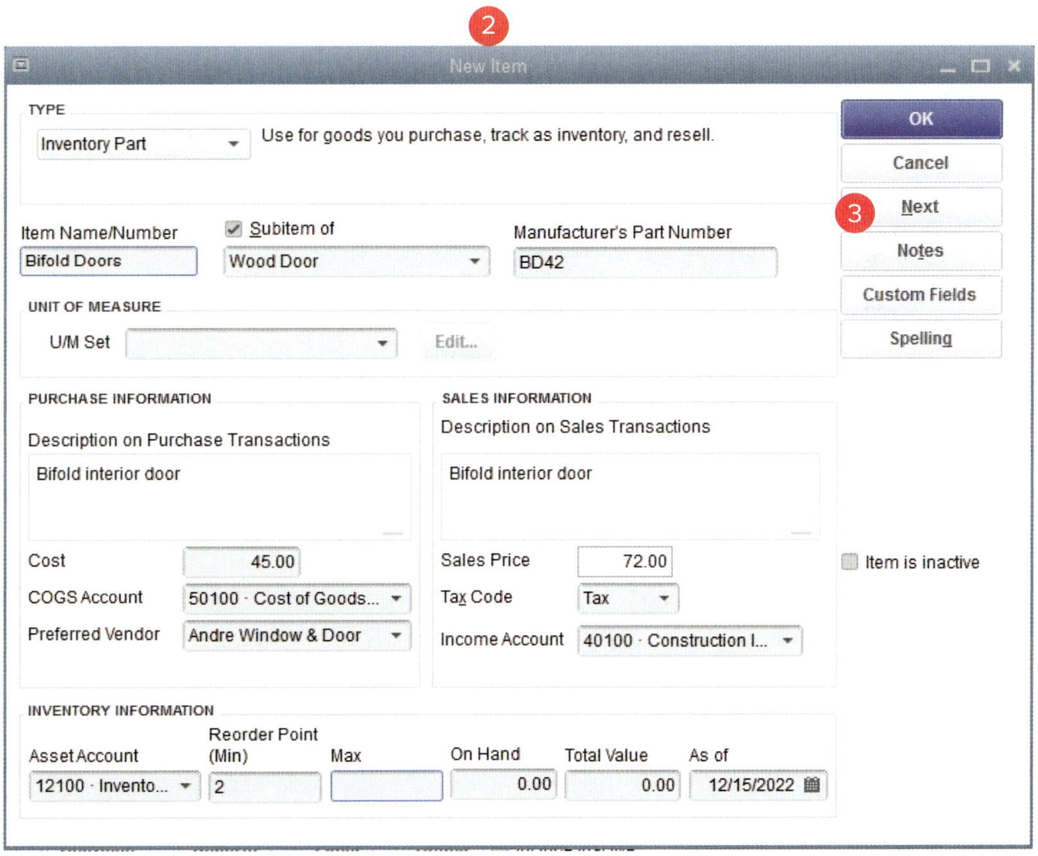
2
New Item
TYPE
Inventory Part
Use for goods you purchase, track as inventory, and resell.
OK
Cancel
3
Next
Notes
Custom Fields
Spelling
Item Name/Number
Bifold Doors
Subitem of
Wood Door
Manufacturer's Part Number
BD42
UNIT OF MEASURE
U/M Set
Edit...
PURCHASE INFORMATION
Description on Purchase Transactions
Bifold interior door
Cost 45.00
COGS Account 50100 · Cost of Goods...
Preferred Vendor Andre Window & Door
SALES INFORMATION
Description on Sales Transactions
Bifold interior door
Sales Price 72.00
Tax Code Tax
Income Account 40100 · Construction I...
Item is inactive
INVENTORY INFORMATION
Asset Account 12100 · Invento...
Reorder Point (Min) 2
Max
On Hand 0.00
Total Value 0.00
As of 12/15/2022

EXPORT ITEM LIST

C7.5.1 Item List. Prepare the Item List as follows:

1. Sort the Item List by selecting **Item** button > **Re - sort List**
2. Click the **Reports** button at the bottom of the Item List window. Select **Item Listing.**
3. Export to **Excel** or **print** the Item List
4. **Close** the Item List window

Section 7.6

VENDOR TRANSACTIONS

After creating a Vendor List and Item List, we are ready to enter vendor transactions. There are two basic ways to enter vendor transactions using QuickBooks.

1. **Enter Bills > Pay Bills.** This is used to record services, such as utilities or accounting services. After the bill is entered, it is paid when it is due.
2. **Enter Purchase Orders > Receive Inventory > Enter Bills Against Inventory > Pay Bills.** This approach is used to record the purchase of inventory items. The purchase order provides a record of the items ordered.

Chapter 6 focused on entering vendor transactions for services using the Enter Bills and Pay Bills onscreen forms. This chapter covers how to record the purchase of inventory items using Purchase Orders.

Display the Home Page to view the flowchart of vendor transactions. Recording the purchase of inventory using QuickBooks involves the following steps:

1. **Purchase Orders.** Create a purchase order to order items from vendors.
2. **Receive Inventory.** Record inventory items received.
3. **Enter Bills Against Inventory.** Record bill received and the obligation to pay the vendor later (accounts payable).
4. **Pay Bills.** Select bills to pay. Since the obligation is fulfilled, accounts payable is reduced.

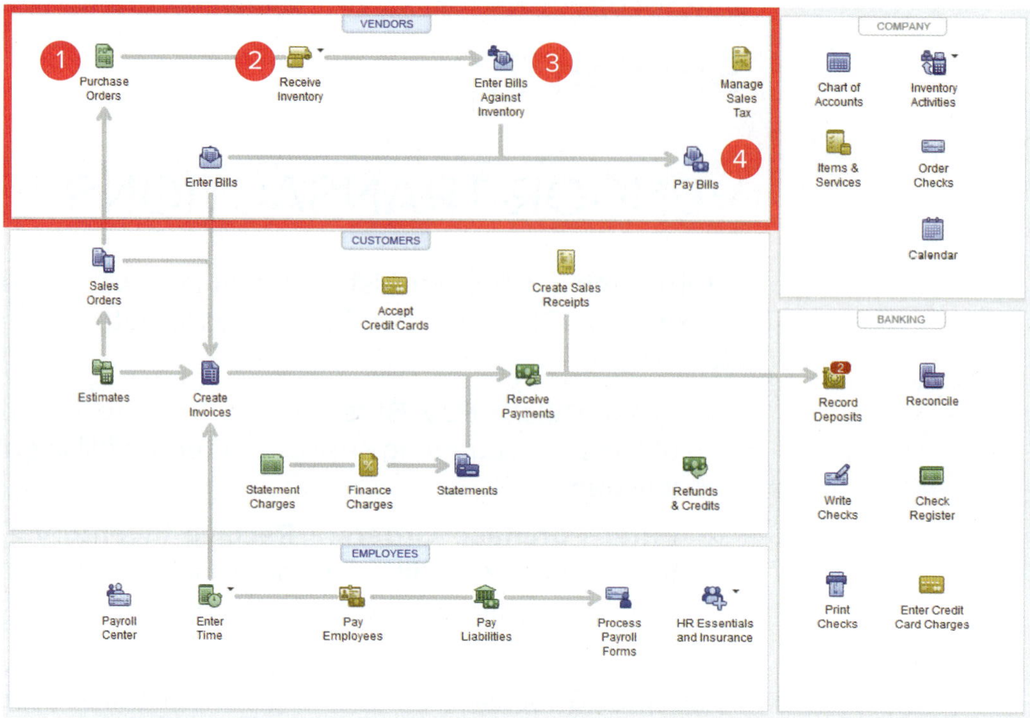
VENDORS
1
Purchase Orders
2
Receive Inventory
Enter Bills Against Inventory
3
Manage Sales Tax
Enter Bills
Pay Bills
4
CUSTOMERS
Sales Orders
Accept Credit Cards
Create Sales Receipts
Estimates
Create Invoices
Receive Payments
Statement Charges
Finance Charges
Statements
Refunds & Credits
EMPLOYEES
Payroll Center
Enter Time
Pay Employees
Pay Liabilities
Process Payroll Forms
HR Essentials and Insurance
COMPANY
Chart of Accounts
Inventory Activities
Items & Services
Order Checks
Calendar
BANKING
Record Deposits
Reconcile
Write Checks
Check Register
Print Checks
Enter Credit Card Charges

Section 7.7

CREATE PURCHASE ORDERS

A purchase order is a record of an order to purchase inventory from a vendor.

Rock Castle Construction wants to order 6 bifold interior doors and 6 sets of bifold door hardware to stock in inventory.

To create a purchase order:

1. Click the **Purchase Orders** icon in the Vendors section of the Home Page
2. From the drop-down Vendor List, select the vendor name: **Andre Window & Door**
3. Select Template: **Custom Purchase Order**
4. Enter the Purchase Order Date: **12/20/2022**
5. Select item ordered: **Wood Door: Bifold Doors.** ($45.00 now appears in the Rate column.)
6. Enter Quantity: **6.** ($270.00 should now appear in the Amount column.)
7. Select the **Save** icon. Leave the Create Purchase Orders window open on your screen.

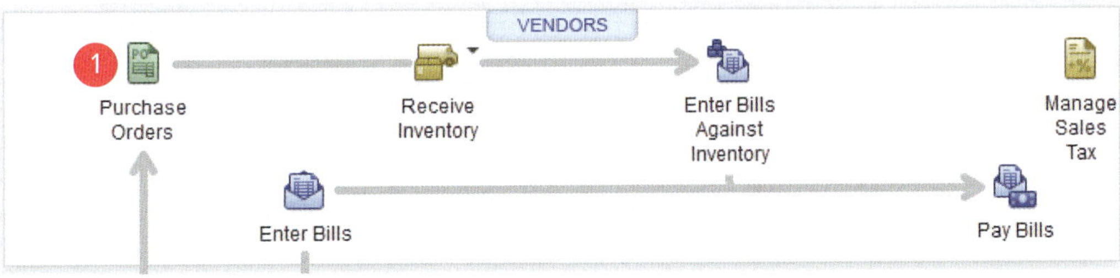

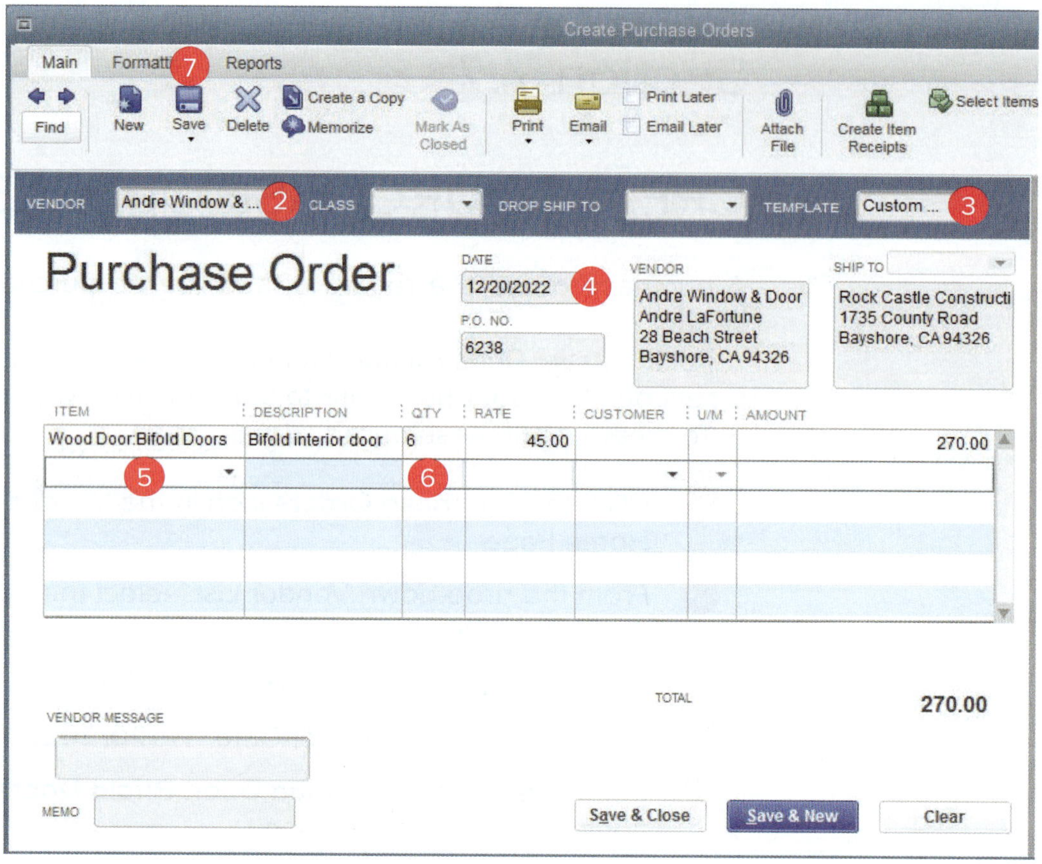

C7.7.1 Purchase Order Journal Entry. To display the journal entry that QuickBooks created behind the screen for this purchase order, complete the following steps.

1. From the Create Purchase Orders form, select the **Reports** tab
2. Select the **Transaction Journal** icon
3. Export the Transaction Journal report to **Excel** or **print** the report
4. **Close** the Transaction Journal window

To create a purchase order for bifold door hardware:

1. Click **Save & New** on the open Create Purchase Orders window
2. From the drop-down Vendor List, select the vendor name: **Patton Hardware Supplies**
3. Select Template: **Custom Purchase Order**
4. Enter the Purchase Order Date: **12/20/2022**

5. Select item ordered: **Hardware: Bifold Knobs**
6. Enter Quantity: **6**
7. Select the **Save** icon. Leave the Create Purchase Orders window open on your screen.

C7.7.2 Purchase Order Journal Entry. To display the journal entry that QuickBooks created behind the screen for this purchase order, complete the following steps.

1. From the Create Purchase Orders form, select the **Reports** tab
2. Select the **Transaction Journal** icon
3. Export the Transaction Journal report to **Excel** or **print** the report
4. **Close** the Transaction Journal window
5. Select **Save & Close** to close the Create Purchase Orders window

Section 7.8

RECEIVE INVENTORY

To record inventory items received on 12/22/2022 ordered from the vendor, Andre Window & Door, complete the following steps:

1. Click the **Receive Inventory** icon in the Vendors section of the Home Page
2. Select: **Receive Inventory without Bill**
3. In the Create Item Receipts window, select vendor: **Andre Window & Door**
4. If a purchase order for the item exists, QuickBooks will display the following Open POs Exist window. Click **Yes.**
5. When the following Open Purchase Orders window appears, select the purchase order for the items received
6. Click **OK**
7. The Create Item Receipts window will appear with a total of $270. If necessary, change the Date to: **12/22/2022.**
8. Although Rock Castle Construction ordered 6 bifold doors, only 5 were received. Change the quantity from 6 to **5.**
9. To record expenses associated with the items received, such as freight charges:
   - Click the **Expenses** tab in the Create Item Receipts window
   - To record $35.00 in freight charges on the bifold doors received, select Account: **54520 Freight & Delivery**
   - Enter Amount: **$35.00**
   - Click the **Recalculate** button

   The Total in the Create Item Receipts window is now $260.00.
10. Click the **Save** icon and leave the Create Item Receipts window open

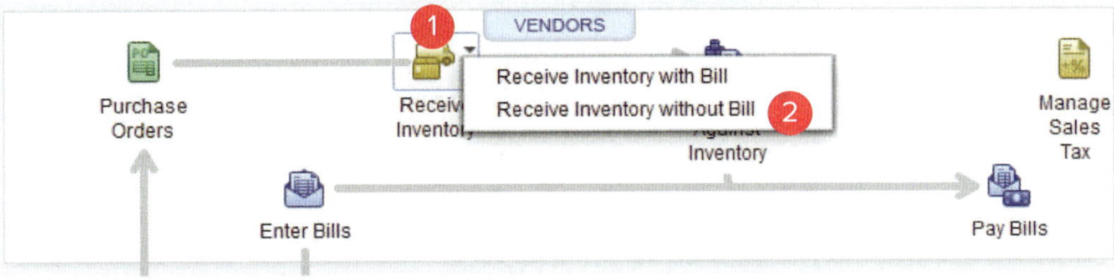
VENDORS
Purchase Orders
Receive Inventory
Receive Inventory with Bill
Receive Inventory without Bill
Inventory
Manage Sales Tax
Enter Bills
Pay Bills
1
2

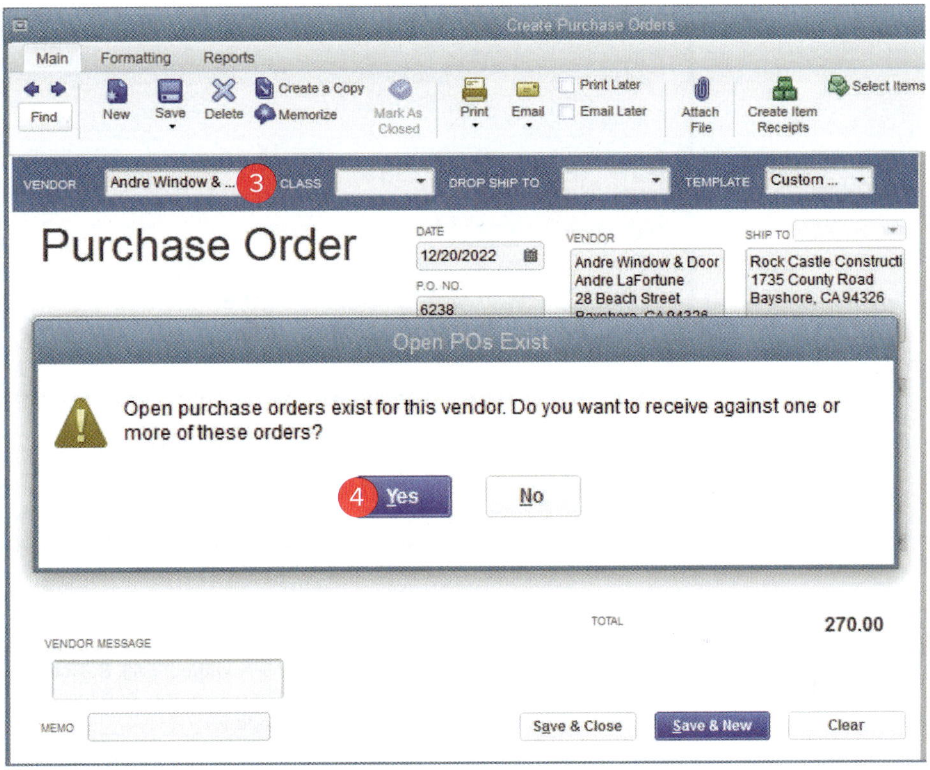
Create Purchase Orders
Main
Formatting
Reports
Find
New
Save
Delete
Create a Copy
Memorize
Mark As Closed
Print
Email
Print Later
Email Later
Attach File
Create Item Receipts
Select Items
VENDOR
Andre Window & ...
CLASS
DROP SHIP TO
TEMPLATE
Custom ...
Purchase Order
DATE
12/20/2022
P.O. NO.
6238
VENDOR
Andre Window & Door
Andre LaFortune
28 Beach Street
SHIP TO
Rock Castle Constructi
1735 County Road
Bayshore, CA 94326
Open POs Exist
Open purchase orders exist for this vendor. Do you want to receive against one or more of these orders?
Yes
No
TOTAL
270.00
VENDOR MESSAGE
MEMO
Save & Close
Save & New
Clear
3
4

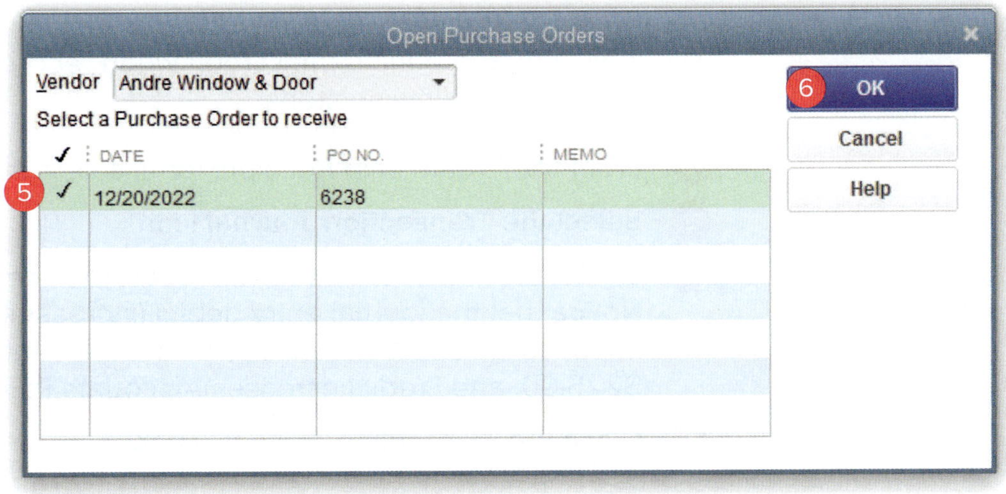
Open Purchase Orders
Vendor
Andre Window & Door
Select a Purchase Order to receive
DATE
PO NO.
MEMO
12/20/2022
6238
OK
Cancel
Help
5
6

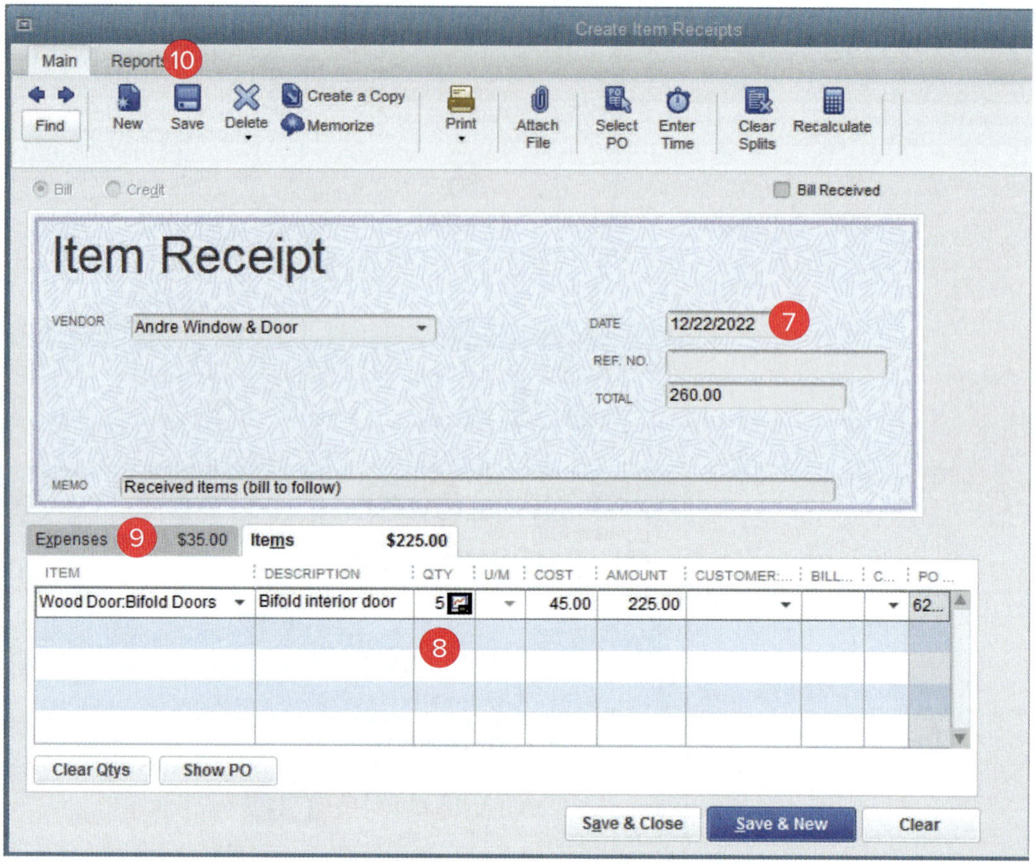

If we receive inventory and the bill at the same time, then we would select Receive Inventory > Receive Inventory with Bill (instead of Receive Inventory without Bill). Basically we are combining the two steps of Receiving Inventory and Entering Bills. When inventory and the bill are received at the same time, Bill Received is checked on the Item Receipt window.

C7.8.1 Receive Inventory Journal Entry. To display the journal entry that QuickBooks created behind the screen when recording receipt of inventory, complete the following steps.

1. From the Create Item Receipts form, select the **Reports** tab
2. Select the **Transaction Journal** icon
3. Export the Transaction Journal report to **Excel** or **print** the report. Notice that the journal entry debits (increases) Freight & Delivery Expense for $35.00, debits (increases) Inventory Asset for $225.00, and credit (increases) Accounts Payable by $260.00.
4. **Close** the Transaction Journal window

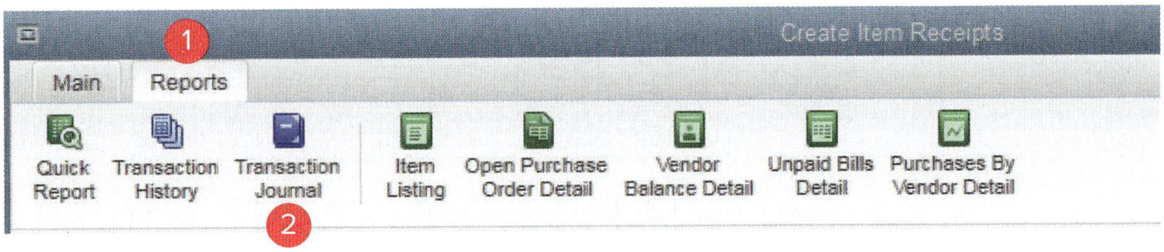

To record receipt of the bifold door hardware:

1. Click **Save & New** on the open Create Item Receipts window
2. From the drop-down Vendor List, select the vendor name: **Patton Hardware Supplies**
3. Select PO No.: **6239**
4. Enter Date: **12/22/2022**
5. Item ordered should appear in the Create Item Receipts window: **Hardware: Bifold Knobs**
6. Enter Quantity: **6**
7. Select the **Save** icon. Leave the Create Item Receipts window open on your screen.

C7.8.2 Receive Inventory Journal Entry. To display the journal entry that QuickBooks created behind the screen for receiving this inventory, complete the following steps.

1. From the Create Item Receipts form, select the **Reports** tab
2. Select the **Transaction Journal** icon
3. Export the Transaction Journal report to **Excel** or **print** the report
4. **Close** the Transaction Journal window
5. **Close** the Create Items Receipt window

Section 7.9

ENTER BILLS AGAINST INVENTORY

We may receive bills at three different times:

Receive Bill...	Record Using...
1 We receive a bill for services and no inventory items will be received, as for example, if the bill is for security services.	**Enter Bills**
2 We receive a bill at the same time we receive inventory items.	**Receive Inventory with Bill**
3 We receive inventory without a bill, and we receive the bill later.	**a. Receive Inventory without Bill** **b. Enter Bills Against Inventory**

In Chapter 6, we learned how to record bills for services (situation 1 above).

If we receive inventory and the bill at the same time (situation 2 above), then we would select Receive Inventory > Receive Inventory with Bill (instead of Receive Inventory without Bill). Basically we are combining the two steps of Receiving Inventory and Entering Bills.

In many cases, inventory is shipped to one location (for example, the Shipping and Receiving Department) and the bill sent to another location (the Accounting Department). So typically the situation where inventory and the bill are not received at the same time (situation 3 above) is a common occurrence.

Next, we will record the bill received for the bifold doors ordered and received from Andre Window & Door (situation 3 above).

To enter a bill received after inventory items are received:

1. Click the **Enter Bills Against Inventory** icon on the Vendors section of the Home Page
2. When the Select Item Receipt window appears, select Vendor: **Andre Window & Door.** If necessary, press **Tab.**

3. Select the **Item Receipt** that corresponds to the bill
4. Click **OK**
5. The Enter Bills window will appear. Notice that the Enter Bills window is the same as the Create Item Receipts window except:
    - Bill Received in the upper right corner is checked
    - The title of the form changes from Item Receipt to Bill
    - The window name changes from Create Item Receipts to Enter Bills
6. At this point, you can make any changes necessary, such as:
    - Change the date if the bill is received on a date different from the date the item was received. In this instance, the item and bill are both received on **12/22/2022.**
    - Terms should be **Net 15**
    - Ref. No.
    - Memo
    - Expenses, such as freight charges
7. The Amount Due of **$260.00** should agree with the amount shown on the vendor's bill
8. The Item displayed should be **Wood Door: Bifold Doors** with a quantity of **5,** the number received. A 3-way match typically occurs at this point before the bill is approved for payment: Compare (1) the PO, (2) The Item Receipt and (3) the Bill. In this case, (1) the PO displays a quantity of 6 bifold doors, (2) the Item Receipt shows that we only received 5 bifold doors, and (3) since we only want to pay for what we have received, the bill should be 5, not 6, bifold doors.
9. Click the **Save** icon. If asked if you want to record your changes, select **Yes.** Leave the Enter Bills window open.

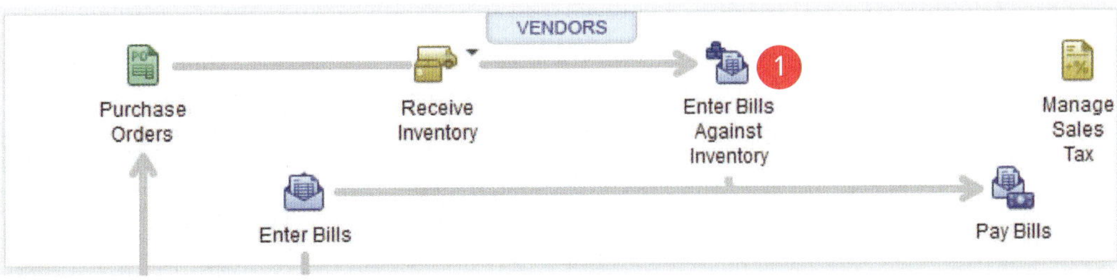

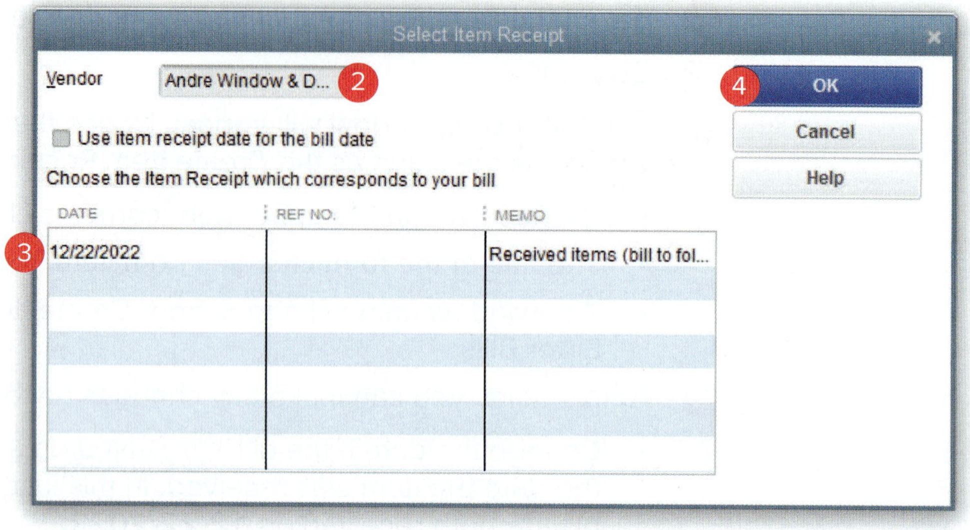
Select Item Receipt
Vendor
Andre Window & D...
2
4
OK
Cancel
Help
Use item receipt date for the bill date
Choose the Item Receipt which corresponds to your bill
DATE
REF NO.
MEMO
3
12/22/2022
Received items (bill to fol...

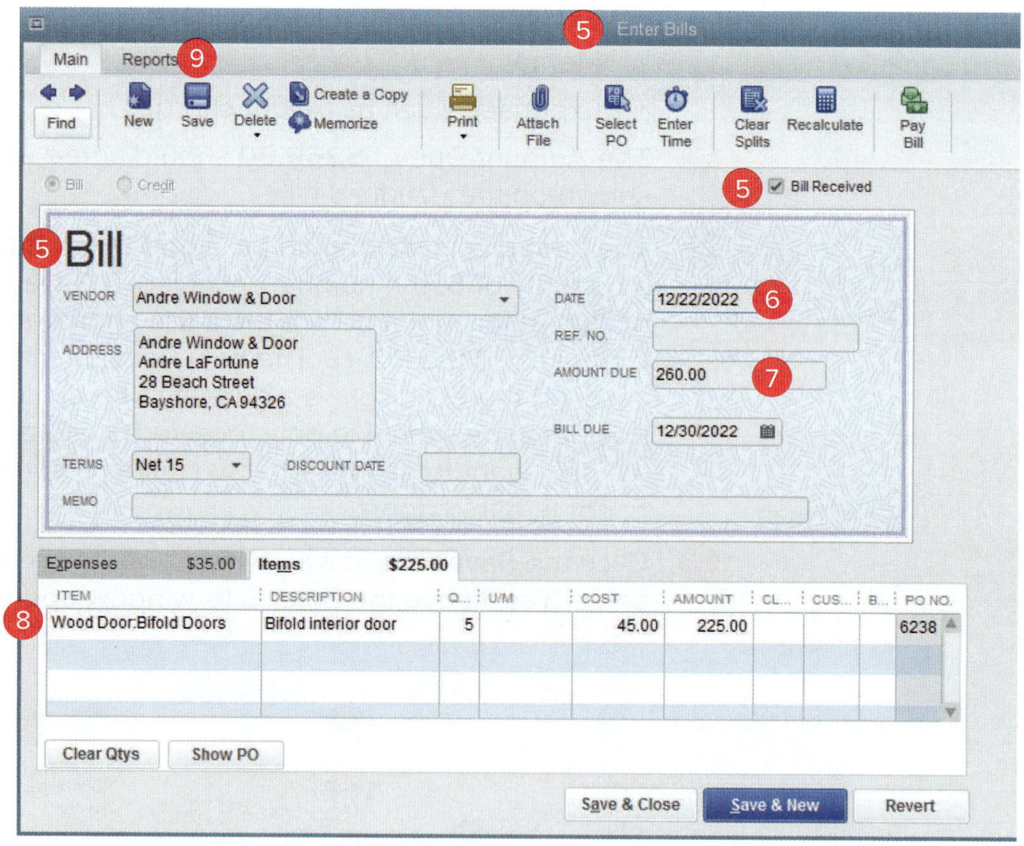
5
Enter Bills
Main
Reports
9
Find
New
Save
Delete
Create a Copy
Memorize
Print
Attach File
Select PO
Enter Time
Clear Splits
Recalculate
Pay Bill
Bill
Credit
5
Bill Received
5
Bill
VENDOR
Andre Window & Door
DATE
12/22/2022
6
ADDRESS
Andre Window & Door
Andre LaFortune
28 Beach Street
Bayshore, CA 94326
REF. NO.
AMOUNT DUE
260.00
7
BILL DUE
12/30/2022
TERMS
Net 15
DISCOUNT DATE
MEMO
Expenses $35.00
Items $225.00
ITEM
DESCRIPTION
Q...
U/M
COST
AMOUNT
CL...
CUS...
B...
PO NO.
8
Wood Door:Bifold Doors
Bifold interior door
5
45.00
225.00
6238
Clear Qtys
Show PO
Save & Close
Save & New
Revert

C7.9.1 Enter Bill Journal Entry. To display the journal entry that QuickBooks created behind the screen when recording the bill, complete the following steps.

1. From the Enter Bills form, select the **Reports** tab > **Transaction Journal**
2. Export the Transaction Journal report to **Excel** or **print** the report
3. **Close** the Transaction Journal window

To record receipt of the bifold door hardware:

1. Click the **Find arrows** in the upper left of the Enter Bills window to advance to the Item Receipt for the bifold door hardware purchased from Patton Hardware Supplies for $36.00
2. With the Create Item Receipts window displaying Patton Hardware Supplies for $36.00, to record the bill received for the bifold door hardware, check **Bill Received** in the upper right corner of the window. (Notice that the Item Receipt form title changes to Bill and the window name changed from Create Item Receipts to Enter Bills.)
3. Verify PO No.: **6239**
4. Verify Date: **12/22/2022**
5. Verify Item: **Hardware: Bifold Knobs**
6. Verify Quantity: **6**
7. Verify Terms: **Net 30**
8. Select the **Save** icon. Leave the Enter Bills window open on your screen.

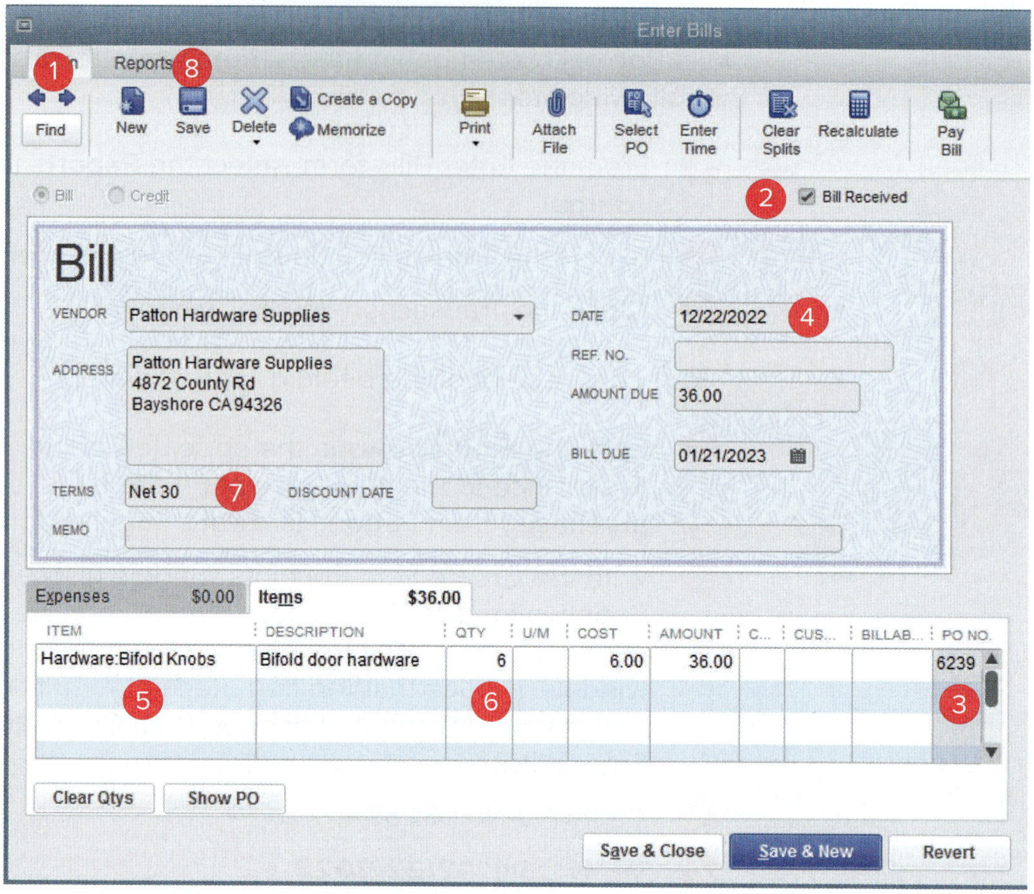

C7.9.2 Enter Bill Journal Entry. To display the journal entry that QuickBooks created behind the screen when recording the bill, complete the following steps.

1. From the Enter Bills form, select the **Reports** tab > **Transaction Journal**
2. Export the Transaction Journal report to **Excel** or **print** the report
3. **Close** the Transaction Journal window and the Enter Bills window

Notice that the journal entries for Item Receipts and Enter Bills are the same, except the Type column in the Journal changes from Item Receipt to Bill.

Section 7.10

PAY BILLS

After receiving the items and entering the bill, the next step is to pay the bill.

To select the bills to pay:

1. Click the **Pay Bills** icon in the Vendors section of the Home Page
2. Select Show bills: **Show all bills**
3. Select the bills you want to pay. Typically, you would select the bills that are due first. In this case, however, select the bill that you just recorded for:
   - **Andre Window and Door** for **$260.00**
   - **Patton Hardware Supplies** for **$36.00**

   If necessary, scroll down to view these two bills.
4. In the Payment section, select: Date: **12/23/2022**
5. Select Method: **Check**
6. Select: **To be printed**
7. Select Account: **Checking**
8. Select **Pay Selected Bills**
9. When the Payment Summary window displays, if we wanted to print the checks, we would select Print Checks. In this case, select **Done.**

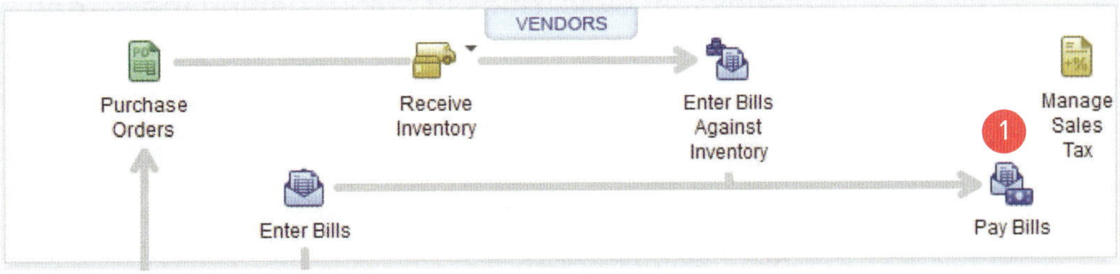

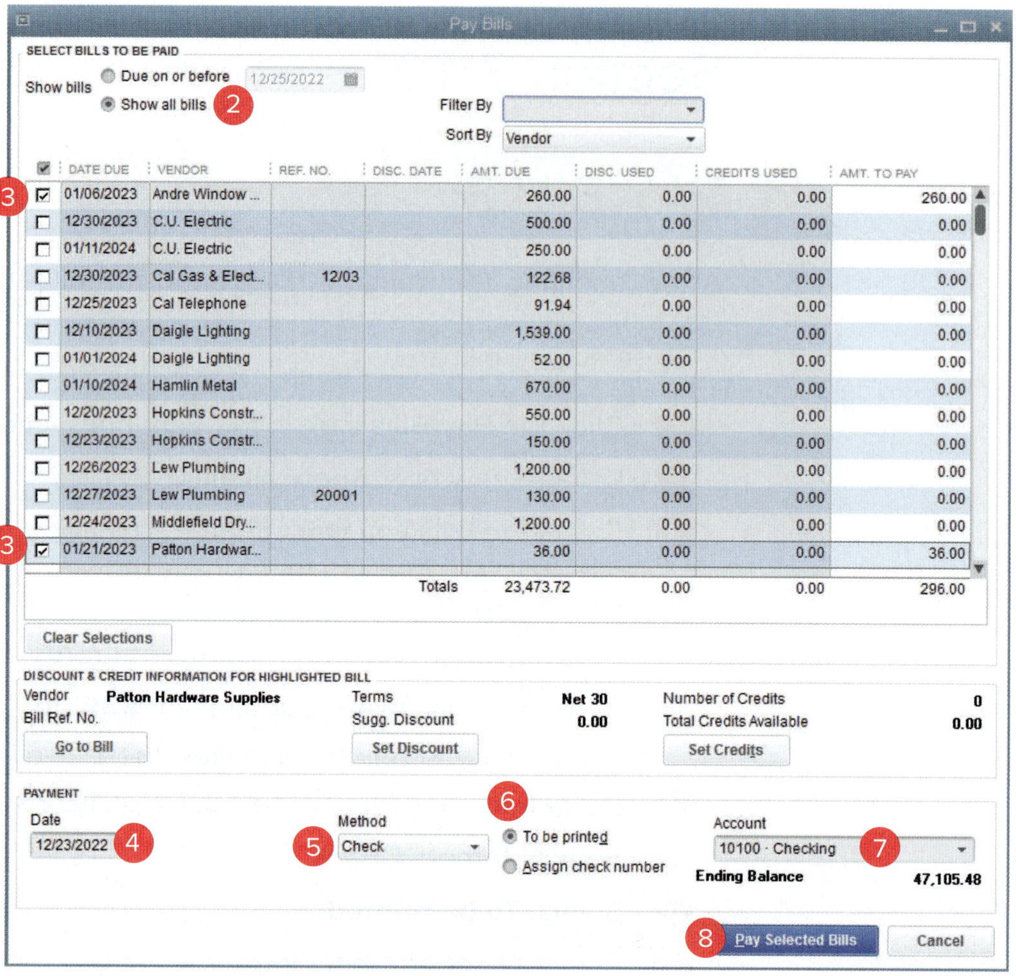

To pay by debit card, select Method: Check > Assign check number. Then use DC (for debit card) as the check number.

C7.10.1 Pay Bills Journal Entries. Another way to view the behind the screen journal entry is to use the Report Center. To view the journal entries that QuickBooks created behind the screen when bills were entered and selected for payment, complete the following steps.

1. From the Navigation Bar, select **Reports**
2. Select **Accountant & Taxes**
3. Select **Journal**
4. Select Date: **12/22/2022 To 12/23/2022**
5. Export the Journal report to **Excel** or **print** the report
6. **Close** the Journal window

Section 7.11

PAY SALES TAX

QuickBooks tracks the sales tax that you collect from customers and must remit to governmental agencies. When you set up a new company in QuickBooks, you identify which items and customers are subject to sales tax. In addition, you must specify the appropriate sales tax rate. Then whenever you prepare sales invoices, QuickBooks automatically calculates and adds sales tax to the invoices.

Rock Castle Construction is required to collect sales tax from customers on certain items sold. Rock Castle then must pay the sales tax collected to the appropriate governmental tax agency.

QuickBooks uses a two-step process to remit sales tax:

1. **Pay Sales Tax.** The Manage Sales Tax window lists the sales taxes owed and allows you to select the individual sales tax items you want to pay.
2. **Print Checks or E-Pay.** Print the check to pay the sales tax or if you are using a QuickBooks Payroll Service, your company may be able to e-pay the sales tax liability electronically.

To select the sales tax to pay:

1. Click the **Manage Sales Tax** icon in the Vendors section of the Home Page
2. When the Manage Sales Tax window appears, in the Pay Sales Tax section of the window, click the **Pay Sales Tax** button
3. When the following Pay Sales Tax window appears, select Pay From Account: **10100 Checking**
4. Select Check Date: **12/31/2022**
5. Show sales tax due through: **12/31/2022**
6. Check **To be printed**
7. Select: **Pay All Tax**
8. Click **OK**
9. Click **Close** to close the Manage Sales Tax window

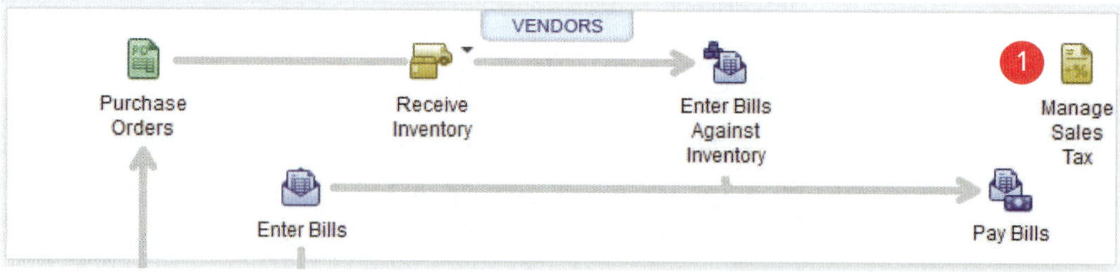
VENDORS
Purchase Orders
Receive Inventory
Enter Bills Against Inventory
1
Manage Sales Tax
Enter Bills
Pay Bills

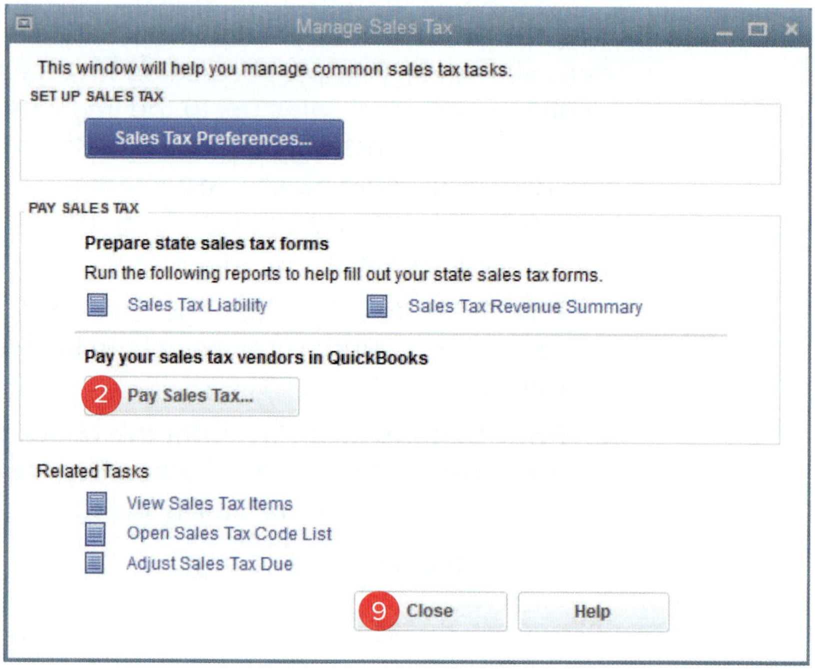
Manage Sales Tax
This window will help you manage common sales tax tasks.
SET UP SALES TAX
Sales Tax Preferences...
PAY SALES TAX
Prepare state sales tax forms
Run the following reports to help fill out your state sales tax forms.
Sales Tax Liability
Sales Tax Revenue Summary
Pay your sales tax vendors in QuickBooks
2
Pay Sales Tax...
Related Tasks
View Sales Tax Items
Open Sales Tax Code List
Adjust Sales Tax Due
9
Close
Help

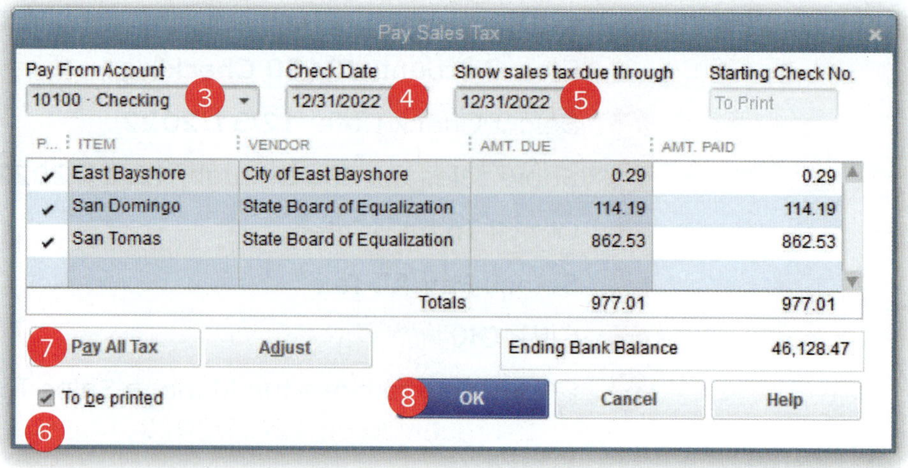
Pay Sales Tax
Pay From Account
10100 · Checking
3
Check Date
12/31/2022
4
Show sales tax due through
12/31/2022
5
Starting Check No.
To Print
P... ITEM VENDOR AMT. DUE AMT. PAID
East Bayshore City of East Bayshore 0.29 0.29
San Domingo State Board of Equalization 114.19 114.19
San Tomas State Board of Equalization 862.53 862.53
Totals 977.01 977.01
7
Pay All Tax
Adjust
Ending Bank Balance 46,128.47
To be printed
6
8
OK
Cancel
Help

Section 7.12

VENDOR REPORTS

QuickBooks provides vendor reports to answer the following questions:

- How much do we owe? (Accounts Payable reports)
- How much have we purchased? (Purchase reports)
- How much inventory do we have? (Inventory reports)

QuickBooks offers several different ways to access vendor reports:

1. **Vendor Center.** Summarizes vendor information in one location (Access the Vendor Center by clicking the Vendors icon on the Navigation Bar.)
2. **Report Center.** Permits you to locate reports by type of report (Click the Reports icon on the Navigation Bar, then see Vendors & Payables, Purchases, and Inventory reports).
3. **Reports Menu.** Reports are grouped by type of report (See Vendors & Payables, Purchases, and Inventory reports).

VENDOR CENTER

The Vendor Center summarizes vendor information in one convenient location. For convenience, some vendor reports can be created directly from the Vendor Center.

C7.12.1 Vendor Transaction Report. Display the Vendor Center as follows:

1. From the Navigation Bar, select **Vendors**
2. Select Vendor: **Andre Window & Door**
3. The Vendor Information section summarizes information about the vendor selected, including a list of the transactions for the specific vendor. In this case, you recorded three transactions for Andre Window & Door:
    - Purchase order on 12/20/2022
    - Bill received on 12/22/2022
    - Bill paid on 12/23/2022

4. Select **Bill Pymt – Check** on **12/23/2022** for **Andre Window & Door.** (Double-click on the Bill Pymt - Check to drill- down and view the check form to pay Andre Window & Door.)
5. With the cursor over the Vendor Transactions section of the window, **right-click** to display the pop-up menu. Select **View as a Report.**
6. Export to **Excel** or **print** the report of all transactions for Andre Window & Door for this fiscal year
7. **Close** the report window

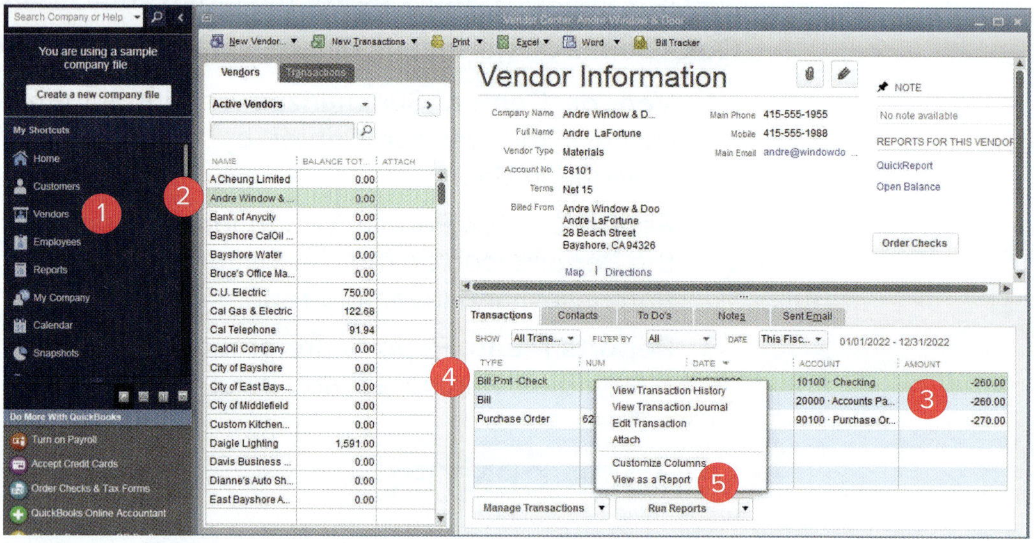

PURCHASE REPORTS: HOW MUCH HAVE WE PURCHASED?

Purchase reports provide information about purchases by item, by vendor, or by open purchase orders. Purchase reports include:

1. Open Purchase Orders (Outstanding Purchase Orders)
2. Purchases by Vendor Summary
3. Purchases by Item Summary

OPEN PURCHASE ORDERS REPORT

Open purchase orders are purchase orders for items ordered but not yet received. QuickBooks permits you to view all open purchase orders or just those for a specific vendor.

C7.12.2 Open Purchase Orders Report. To prepare the Open Purchase Orders report that lists all open purchase orders:

1. From the Report Center, select: **Purchases**
2. Select: **Open Purchase Orders**
3. Select Dates: **All.** Click **Run.**
4. Export to **Excel** or **print** the report
5. **Close** the Open Purchase Orders window

INVENTORY REPORTS: HOW MUCH INVENTORY DO WE HAVE?

Inventory reports list the amount and status of inventory. Inventory reports include:

1. Inventory Stock Status by Item
2. Physical Inventory Worksheet

INVENTORY STOCK STATUS BY ITEM

This report lists the quantity of inventory items on hand and on order. This information is useful for planning when and how many units to order.

C7.12.3 Inventory Stock Status Report. To print the Inventory Stock Status by Item report:

1. From the Report Center, select: **Inventory**
2. Select: **Inventory Stock Status by Item**
3. Enter Date: From: **12/22/2022** To: **12/22/2022.** Click **Run.**
4. Export to **Excel** or **print** the report
5. **Close** the Inventory Stock Status by Item window

PHYSICAL INVENTORY WORKSHEET

The Physical Inventory Worksheet is used when taking a physical count of inventory on hand. The worksheet lists the quantity of inventory items on hand and provides a blank column in which to enter the quantity counted during a physical inventory count. This worksheet permits you to compare your physical inventory count with your QuickBooks records.

C7.12.4 Physical Inventory Worksheet. To prepare the Physical Inventory Worksheet:

1. From the Report Center, select: **Inventory**
2. Select: **Physical Inventory Worksheet**
3. Enter Date: **12/31/2022.** Click **Run.**
4. Export to **Excel** or **print** the report
5. **Close** the Physical Inventory Worksheet window

QuickBooks offers other additional vendor reports that provide useful information to a business. These reports can also be accessed from the Reports Menu or from the Report Center.

Section 7.13

BACK UP QUICKBOOKS FILES

BACK UP QBB

Save a backup of your Chapter 7 file using the file name: **YourName Chapter 7 Backup.QBB.** For further instructions on how to back up your file, *see Appendix B: Back Up & Restore QuickBooks Files.*

QBW WORKFLOW

If you are using the Workflow approach, leave your .QBW file open and proceed directly to Exercise 7.1.

QBB RESTORE

If you are using the Restore approach and ending your computer session now, close your QBW file and exit QuickBooks. When you restart, you will restore your backup file to complete Exercise 7.1.

Section 7.14

ACCOUNTING ESSENTIALS

Inventory and Internal Control

Accounting Essentials summarize important foundational accounting knowledge that may be useful when using QuickBooks

How do we improve internal control over inventory?

- Internal control is a set of processes and procedures to safeguard assets and detect errors. Since inventory is one of the main targets of fraud and theft, we want to have a good system of internal control to safeguard inventory.
- One principle of internal control is periodically to compare and reconcile the actual asset with the accounting records to identify and track any discrepancies. So at least once a year, businesses typically reconcile:
    1. inventory on hand confirmed by a physical count of the asset on hand with
    2. inventory recorded in the accounting records

What is a 3-way match?

- Another principle of internal control is to use a 3-way match when ordering, receiving, and paying for inventory.
- Three-way match improves internal control by cross checking amounts across three different documents.
- Three-way match compares:
    1. What was *ordered?*
    2. What was *received?*
    3. What was *billed?*
- Basically, we want to compare what we *ordered* with what we *received,* and what we were *billed.* These three amounts should agree so that we are not paying for more than what we ordered or received.

www.my-quickbooks.com

Go to **www.My-QuickBooks.com** to view additional QuickBooks resources including:

- **Excel Report Templates** to organize QuickBooks reports exported to Excel
- ***Computer Accounting with QuickBooks* updates,** sometimes required when there is a software update that affects the text
- **QuickBooks Video links**
- **QuickBooks Help and Support links**
- **Other QuickBooks Resources** to make learning QuickBooks easier and more effective
- **QuickBooks Issue Resolution** offers a guided approach to troubleshooting QuickBooks

> **Troubleshooting QuickBooks and Correcting Errors** are crucial QuickBooks skill to acquire. See www.My-QuickBooks.com > QB Issue Resolution for Troubleshooting QuickBooks tips. See Chapter 17, Quick Review Guide, for tips on Correcting Errors.

EXERCISE 7.1: Vendor and Item Lists

BACKSTORY

Mr. Castle tosses you a document as he charges past your cubicle, shouting over his shoulder, *"That's info about our new supplier. From now on, Rock Castle will install closet shelving instead of waiting on unreliable subcontractors. We do a better job and we get it done on time!"*

E7.1.1 QuickBooks File

If you will be using the same computer and the same Chapter 7. QBW file:

1. If your Chapter 7.QBW file is not already open, open it by selecting **File > Open Previous Company.** Select your **Chapter 7.QBW file.** If

a QuickBooks Information window appears with a message about the sample company file, click **OK.**

2. Add **YourName Exercise 7.1** to the company name by selecting **Company Menu** > **My Company.**

> **If you are not using the same computer that you used for Chapter 7,** you will need to restore your Chapter 7 Backup.QBB file using the instructions in Appendix B: Back Up & Restore QuickBooks Files. After restoring, add YourName Exercise 7.1 to the company name.

E7.1.2 Add New Vendor

Add a new vendor to Rock Castle Construction's Vendor List.

1. Add the following vendor to the Vendor List.

Vendor	**Kelly's Closets**
Address Info:	
Company Name	**Kelly's Closets**
Address	**13 Rheims Road** **Bayshore, CA 94326**
Main Phone	**415-555-5813**
Payment Settings:	
Account No.	**58127**
Payment Terms	**Net 30**
Tax Settings:	
Vendor 1099	**No**
Additional Info:	
Vendor Type	**Materials**

2. From the Vendor Center, export to **Excel** the Vendor List

E7.1.3 Add New Inventory Items

Add the following inventory items to Rock Castle Construction's Item List.

1. Add the following items to the Item List.

Item Type	**Inventory Part**
Item Name	**Closet Materials**
Item Description	**Closet Materials**

COGS Account	**50100 – Cost of Goods Sold**
Income Account	**40140 – Materials Income**
Asset Account	**12100 – Inventory Asset**
Tax Code	**Tax**

2. Add the following three new inventory parts as **subitems** to Closet Materials. Use **Kelly's Closets** as the preferred vendor and the same accounts for Cost of Goods Sold, Materials Income and Inventory Asset.

Item Type	**Inventory Part**
Item Name	**6′ Closet Shelving**
Item Description	**6′ Closet Shelving**
Cost	**$22.00**
Sales Price	**$30.00**

Item Type	**Inventory Part**
Item Name	**12′ Closet Shelving**
Item Description	**12′ Closet Shelving**
Cost	**$36.00**
Sales Price	**$50.00**

Item Type	**Inventory Part**
Item Name	**Closet Install Kit**
Item Description	**Closet Installation Kit**
Cost	**$10.00**
Sales Price	**$16.00**

3. **Sort** the Item List by selecting **Item button** > **Re-sort List**
4. Export to **Excel** or **print** the Item List by selecting the **Reports button** > **Item Listing**

E7.1.4 Back Up Exercise 7.1

Save a backup of your Exercise file using the file name: YourName Exercise 7.1 Backup.QBB. See *Appendix B: Back Up & Restore QuickBooks Files* for instructions.

EXERCISE 7.2: Purchase Orders

E7.2.1 QuickBooks File

If you will be using the same computer and the same QBW file:

1. Select your **QBW file.**
2. Add **YourName Exercise 7.2** to the company name by selecting **Company Menu > My Company.**

> **If you are not using the same computer that you used for Chapter 7 and Exercise 7.1,** you will need to restore your latest prior Backup.QBB file using the instructions in Appendix B: Back Up & Restore QuickBooks files. After restoring, add YourName Exercise 7.2 to the company name.

E7.2.2 Create Purchase Order

Using the Purchase Orders icon in the Vendors section of the Home Page, record the following.

1. Create a purchase order to order **6** each of the new inventory items for **Kelly's Closets** from the prior exercise on **12/23/2022.**

12′ Closet Shelving	**6**
6′ Closet Shelving	**6**
Closet Install Kit	**6**

2. Select the **Save** icon at the top of the Create Purchase Orders window
3. Select the **Reports** tab
4. Select the **Transaction Journal** icon
5. Export the Transaction Journal report to **Excel** or **print** the report
6. **Close** the Transaction Journal and the Create Purchase Orders windows

E7.2.3 Back Up Exercise 7.2

Save a backup of your Exercise file using the file name: YourName Exercise 7.2 Backup.QBB. See *Appendix B: Back Up & Restore QuickBooks Files* for instructions.

EXERCISE 7.3: Receive Items

E7.3.1 QuickBooks File

If you will be using the same computer and the same QBW file:

1. Select your **QBW file.**
2. Add **YourName Exercise 7.3** to the company name by selecting **Company Menu** > **My Company.**

> **If you are not using the same computer that you used for Chapter 7, Exercise 7.1 and Exercise 7.2,** you will need to restore your latest prior Backup.QBB file using the instructions in Appendix B: Back Up & Restore QuickBooks files. After restoring, add YourName Exercise 7.3 to the company name.

E7.3.2 Receive Inventory

Using the Receive Inventory icon in the Vendors section of the Home Page, record inventory received.

1. On **12/24/2022,** record the receipt of the closet inventory items ordered on **12/23/2022.** There are no freight charges.
2. Select the **Save** icon at the top of the Create Item Receipts window
3. Select the **Reports** tab
4. Select the **Transaction Journal** icon
5. Export the Transaction Journal report to **Excel** or **print** the report
6. **Close** the Transaction Journal and the Create Item Receipts windows

E7.3.3 Back Up Exercise 7.3

Save a backup of your Exercise file using the file name: YourName Exercise 7.3 Backup.QBB. See *Appendix B: Back Up & Restore QuickBooks Files* for instructions.

EXERCISE 7.4: Enter Bills Against Inventory

E7.4.1 QuickBooks File

If you will be using the same computer and the same QBW file:

1. Select your **QBW file.**
2. Add **YourName Exercise 7.4** to the company name by selecting **Company Menu > My Company.**

> **If you are not using the same computer that you used for Chapter 7, Exercise 7.1 - 7.3,** you will need to restore your latest prior Backup.QBB file using the instructions in Appendix B: Back Up & Restore QuickBooks files. After restoring, add YourName Exercise 7.4 to the company name.

E7.4.2 Enter Bill Against Inventory

Using the Enter Bills Against Inventory icon in the Vendors section of the Home Page to record the following.

1. Record the receipt of the bill for the closet items on **12/27/2022**
2. Select the **Save** icon at the top of the Enter Bills window
3. Select the **Reports** tab
4. Select the **Transaction Journal** icon
5. Export the Transaction Journal report to **Excel** or **print** the report
6. **Close** the Transaction Journal and the Enter Bills windows

E7.4.3 Back Up Exercise 7.4

Save a backup of your Exercise file using the file name: YourName Exercise 7.4 Backup.QBB. See *Appendix B: Back Up & Restore QuickBooks Files* for instructions.

EXERCISE 7.5: Pay Bills

E7.5.1 QuickBooks File

If you will be using the same computer and the same QBW file:

1. Select your **QBW file.**
2. Add **YourName Exercise 7.5** to the company name by selecting **Company Menu > My Company.**

> **If you are not using the same computer that you used for Chapter 7, Exercise 7.1 - 7.4,** you will need to restore your latest prior Backup.QBB file using the instructions in Appendix B: Back Up & Restore QuickBooks files. After restoring, add YourName Exercise 7.5 to the company name.

E7.5.2 Pay Bills

Pay the following bills.

1. Pay the bill for the closet materials ordered from Kelly's Closets on **12/28/2022**
2. From the Navigation Bar, select **Reports** > **Accountant & Taxes** > **Journal**
3. Select Date: **12/28/2022**
4. Export the Journal report to **Excel** or **print** the report
5. **Close** the Journal window

E7.5.3 Back Up Exercise 7.5

Save a backup of your Exercise file using the file name: YourName Exercise 7.5 Backup.QBB. See *Appendix B: Back Up & Restore QuickBooks Files* for instructions.

EXERCISE 7.6: Reports

E7.6.1 QuickBooks File

If you will be using the same computer and the same QBW file:

1. Select your **QBW file.**
2. Add **YourName Exercise 7.6** to the company name by selecting **Company Menu** > **My Company.**

> **If you are not using the same computer that you used for Chapter 7, Exercise 7.1 - 7.5,** you will need to restore your latest prior Backup.QBB file using the instructions in Appendix B: Back Up & Restore QuickBooks files. After restoring, add YourName Exercise 7.6 to the company name.

E7.6.2 Open PO Report

1. Export to **Excel** or **print** the Open Purchase Orders report for Rock Castle Construction for **This Month: 12/01/2022 To 12/31/2022**

E7.6.3 Stock Status Report

Prepare the stock status report for Rock Castle Construction at December 31, 2022.

1. Export to **Excel** or **print** an Inventory Stock Status by Item report to check the status of the closet inventory items as of **12/31/2022**
2. **Highlight** the closet inventory items on the Inventory Stock Status printout
3. **Close** the report window

E7.6.4 Back Up Exercise 7.6

Save a backup of your Exercise file using the file name: YourName Exercise 7.6 Backup.QBB. See *Appendix B: Back Up & Restore QuickBooks Files* for instructions.

EXERCISE 7.7: Sales of Inventory

BACKSTORY

"I told you replacing Mrs. Ceclia's door hardware would pay off. She is going to become one of our best customers. Just wait and see." Mr. Castle appears to be in a much better mood today. *"Maria Cecilia just had us install new closet shelving in her huge walk-in closet. She said she wanted us to do it because we stand by our work."*

E7.7.1 QuickBooks File

If you will be using the same computer and the same QBW file:

1. Select your **QBW file.**
2. Add **YourName Exercise 7.7** to the company name by selecting **Company Menu > My Company.**

If you are not using the same computer that you used for Chapter 7, Exercise 7.1 - 7.6, you will need to restore your latest prior Backup.QBB file using the instructions in Appendix B: Back Up & Restore QuickBooks files. After restoring, add YourName Exercise 7.7 to the company name.

E7.7.2 Add Customer Job

Add the Closet Shelving job for Maria Cecilia to the Customer & Job List.

1. From the Customer Center, select **Cecilia, Maria** then **right-click** to display menu, and select **Add Job.**

Job Name	**Closet Shelving**
Job Description	**Replace Closet Shelving**
Job Type	**Repairs**
Job Status	**Closed**
Start Date	**12/27/2022**
Projected End Date	**12/27/2022**
End Date	**12/27/2022**

E7.7.3 Create Invoice

1. Create an invoice for the Cecilia closet shelving job using the following information.

Customer: Job	**Cecilia, Maria: Closet Shelving**
Custom Template	**Rock Castle Invoice**
Date	**12/27/2022**
Invoice No.	**1104**
Items and Quantities	• **(2) 12′ Closet Shelving** • **(2) 6′ Closet Shelving** • **(1) Closet Installation Kit** • **(3 hours) Installation Labor**

2. Select the **Save** icon
3. Select the **Reports** tab > **Transaction Journal**
4. Export the Transaction Journal report to **Excel** or **print** the report
5. **Close** the Transaction Journal and the Invoice windows

E7.7.4 Receive Customer Payment

1. Record Maria Cecilia payment for the Closet Shelving job (Check No. 625) for the full amount on **12/29/2022**
2. Select **Save & New**

3. Select the **Find** back arrow to display the customer payment just recorded
4. From the Receive Payments onscreen form, select the **Reports** tab > **Transaction Journal**
5. Export the Transaction Journal report to **Excel** or **print** the report
6. **Close** the Transaction Journal and the Receive Payments windows

E7.7.5 Make Deposit

1. Record the bank deposit for Maria Cecilia's payment on **12/29/2022**
2. Select the **Save** icon at the top of the Make Deposits window
3. Select the **Journal** icon to display the journal entry to QuickBooks created behind the screen for the deposit
4. Export to **Excel** or **print** the Transaction Journal
5. **Close** the Transaction Journal and the Make Deposits windows

E7.7.6 Back Up Exercise 7.7

Save a backup of your Exercise file using the file name: YourName Exercise 7.7 Backup.QBB. See *Appendix B: Back Up & Restore QuickBooks Files* for instructions.

PROJECT 7.1

Larry's Landscaping

As an accounting consultant for Larry's Landscaping complete the following to enter inventory transactions for the company.

QB SatNav

The objective of Project 7.1 is to facilitate your mastery of QuickBooks Desktop. As shown in the following QB SatNav, Project 7.1 focuses on QuickBooks transactions related to the purchase of inventory.

QB SatNav

1 QB SETTINGS

Company Settings
Chart of Accounts

2 QB TRANSACTIONS

> Money in   Money out >

Banking
Customers & Sales
Vendors & Expenses
Employees & Payroll

3 QB REPORTS

Reports

P7.1.1 QuickBooks File

1. Use either your QuickBooks Company file (QBW) or restore the backup file (QBB) that you completed for Project 6.1. (If you have issues with your QuickBooks file, contact your instructor.)
2. Update the Company Name to: **YourName Project 7.1 Larry's Landscaping**

P7.1.2 Enter Purchase Orders

1. Enter the following purchase order using the Purchase Orders icon.

Date	**12/22/2022**
Vendor	**Conner Garden Supplies**
Item	**1/2″ Vinyl Irrigation Line**
Quantity	**198**

2. Select the **Save** icon
3. Select the **Reports** tab > **Transaction Journal**
4. Export the Transaction Journal report to **Excel** or **print** the report
5. Enter the following purchase order for Larry's Landscaping.

Date	**12/23/2022**
Vendor	**Nolan Hardware and Supplies**
Item	**Plastic Sprinkler Piping**
Quantity	**100**

6. Select the **Save** icon
7. Select the **Reports** tab > **Transaction Journal**
8. Export the Transaction Journal report to **Excel** or **print** the report
9. Enter the following purchase order for Larry's Landscaping.

Date	**12/23/2022**
Vendor	**Willis Orchards**
Item	**Soil (2 cubic foot bag)**
Quantity	**54**

10. Select the **Save** icon
11. Select the **Reports** tab > **Transaction Journal**
12. Export the Transaction Journal report to **Excel** or **print** the report

P7.1.3 Enter Items Received

1. Record the following items received by Larry's Landscaping.

Date	**12/23/2022**
Vendor	**Nolan Hardware and Supplies**
PO No.	**7**
Item	**Sprinkler Head**
Quantity	**36**

2. Select the **Save** icon
3. Select the **Reports** tab > **Transaction Journal**
4. Export the Transaction Journal report to **Excel** or **print** the report

5. Enter the following item received for Larry's Landscaping.

Date	**12/23/2022**
Vendor	**Conner Garden Supplies**
PO No.	**12**
Item	**1/2″ Vinyl Irrigation Line**
Quantity	**198**

6. Select the **Save** icon
7. Select the **Reports** tab > **Transaction Journal**
8. Export the Transaction Journal report to **Excel** or **print** the report
9. Enter the following item received for Larry's Landscaping.

Date	**12/23/2022**
Vendor	**Gussman's Nursery**
PO No.	**11**
Item	**Lemon Tree, Citrus**
Quantity	**1**
Item	**Citrus Tree – Arizona Sweet**
Quantity	**1**

10. Select the **Save** icon
11. Select the **Reports** tab > **Transaction Journal**
12. Export the Transaction Journal report to **Excel** or **print** the report
13. Enter the following item received for Larry's Landscaping.

Date	**12/23/2022**
Vendor	**Nolan Hardware and Supplies**
PO No.	**13**
Item	**Plastic Sprinkler Piping**
Quantity	**100**

14. Select the **Save** icon
15. Select the **Reports** tab > **Transaction Journal**
16. Export the Transaction Journal report to **Excel** or **print** the report

P7.1.4 Enter Bills Against Inventory

1. Use the Enter Bills Against Inventory icon to enter the following bills received by Larry's Landscaping.

Date	**12/23/2022**
Vendor	**Gussman's Nursery**
PO No.	**11**
Terms	**Net 15**
Amount Due	**$92.00**

2. Select the **Save** icon
3. Select the **Reports** tab > **Transaction Journal**
4. Export the Transaction Journal report to **Excel** or **print** the report
5. Enter the following bill for Larry's Landscaping.

Date	**12/23/2022**
Vendor	**Conner Garden Supplies**
PO No.	**12**
Amount Due	**$23.76**

6. Select the **Save** icon
7. Select the **Reports** tab > **Transaction Journal**
8. Export the Transaction Journal report to **Excel** or **print** the report

P7.1.5 Pay Bills

1. Pay the following bills for Larry's on 12/23/2022.

Vendor	**Gussman's Nursery**
Amount Due	**$92.00**
Vendor	**Conner Garden Supplies**
Amount Due	**$23.76**
Vendor	**Conner Garden Supplies**
Amount Due	**$127.20**
Vendor	**Nolan Hardware and Supplies**
Amount Due	**$610.00**

2. From the Navigation Bar, select **Reports** > **Accountant & Taxes** > **Journal**
3. Select Date: **12/23/2022**
4. Export the Journal report to **Excel** or **print** the report
5. **Close** the Journal window

P7.1.6 Reports

Prepare the following reports for Larry's Landscaping.

1. Export to **Excel** the Open Purchase Orders report for Larry's Landscaping for This Fiscal Quarter, October 1 - December 31, 2022
2. Export to **Excel** the Check Detail report for Larry's Landscaping for December 22 and 23, 2022
3. Export to **Excel** the Accounts Payable Aging Detail report as of December 23, 2022

P7.1.7 Back Up Project 7.1

Save a backup of your Project file using the file name: YourName Project 7.1 Backup.QBB. See *Appendix B: Back Up & Restore QuickBooks Files* for instructions.

Chapter 8

Employees and Payroll

BACKSTORY

The next morning on your way to your cubicle, two employees ask you if their paychecks are ready yet. Apparently, Rock Castle employees expect their paychecks today?! Then your smartphone chimes repeatedly with incoming texts from the construction crews asking about their paychecks.

We need our paychecks 2day. We have bills 2 pay!

Understood.

Deciding that you do not want all the employees upset with you if paychecks are not ready on time, you take the initiative and ask Mr. Castle about the paychecks.

His reply: *"Oops! I was so busy I almost forgot about paychecks."* He hands you another stack of documents. *"Here—you will need these. I'm sure you won't have any trouble using QuickBooks to print the paychecks. And don't forget to pay yourself!"* he adds with a chuckle as he rushes out the door.

Section 8.1

QuickBooks SatNav

QuickBooks SatNav is your satellite navigation for QuickBooks, assisting you in navigating QuickBooks

QuickBooks SatNav divides QuickBooks into three processes:

1. **QuickBooks Settings.** This includes Company Settings when setting up a new QuickBooks company and the Company Chart of Accounts.
2. **QuickBooks Transactions.** This includes recording transactions in QuickBooks. Transaction types can be categorized as Banking, Customers and Sales, Vendors and Expenses, and Employees and Payroll. In basic terms, recording transactions involves recording money in and money out.
3. **QuickBooks Reports.** QuickBooks reports are the output of the system, such as commonly used financial statements of Balance Sheet, Income Statement, and Statement of Cash Flows.

Chapter 8 focuses on employee and payroll transactions as shown in the following QuickBooks SatNav.

QB SatNav

1 QB SETTINGS — CHAPTERS 1 2 11 12 13 14

- Company Settings
- Chart of Accounts

2 QB TRANSACTIONS — CHAPTERS 3 4 5 6 7 8 11 12 13 14

> Money in *Money out >*

- Banking
- Customers & Sales
- Vendors & Expenses
- **Employees & Payroll**

3 QB REPORTS — CHAPTERS 9 10 11 12 13 14

- Reports

Section 8.2

START QUICKBOOKS AND OPEN QUICKBOOKS COMPANY

START QUICKBOOKS

To start QuickBooks software, click the **QuickBooks** icon on your desktop. If a QuickBooks icon does not appear on your desktop, from Microsoft® Windows® click **Start** button > **Programs** > **QuickBooks** > **QuickBooks Premier Accountant Edition.**

> **QuickBooks Accountant** includes all the features of QuickBooks Pro plus features for client services. If you use QuickBooks Pro, your screens may appear slightly different than those appearing in this text.

RESTORE QBB STARTER FILE

Restore the QBB Starter file for this chapter as follows.

1. Select **File** > **Restore**
2. Using the directions in *Appendix B: Back Up & Restore QuickBooks Files,* restore the **CHAPTER 8 STARTER.QBB**
3. After restoring, add **YourName Chapter 8** to the company name by selecting **Company Menu** > **My Company**

Section 8.3

EMPLOYEE TRANSACTIONS

In Chapter 8 we will focus on recording employee and payroll transactions. Payroll involves preparing employee paychecks, withholding the appropriate amount in taxes, and paying the company's share of payroll taxes.

To assist in processing payroll, QuickBooks offers a time-tracking feature that permits us to track the amount of time worked. QuickBooks uses time tracked to:

1. Calculate employee paychecks
2. Transfer time to sales invoices to bill customers for work performed

Basically, there are two main aspects to using QuickBooks for Employee and Payroll purposes:

- Setting up payroll
- Processing payroll

PAYROLL SETUP

Payroll setup requires:

1. Turn on QuickBooks Payroll (Employees Menu, Payroll Setup)
2. Turn on Time Tracking preference (Edit Menu, Preferences, Time & Expenses)
3. Set up Employees List (Employees Menu, Employee List)

PAYROLL PROCESSING

Payroll processing consists of the following four main types of tasks:

1. **Enter Time.** QuickBooks permits us to track employee time worked to use in processing payroll and billing customers.
2. **Pay Employees.** Select employees to pay and create their paychecks.
3. **Pay Payroll Liabilities.** Pay payroll tax liabilities due governmental agencies such as the IRS. Payroll tax liabilities include federal income taxes withheld, state income taxes withheld, FICA (Social Security and Medicare), and unemployment taxes.
4. **Process Payroll Forms.** Process payroll forms including Forms 940, 941, W-2, and W-3 that must be submitted to governmental agencies.

Section 8.4

PAYROLL SETUP

Payroll setup in QuickBooks requires the following:

1. Turn on QuickBooks Payroll (Employees Menu, Payroll Setup)
2. Turn on Time Tracking preference (Edit Menu, Preferences, Time & Expenses)
3. Set up Employees List (Employees Menu, Employee List)

TURN ON QUICKBOOK PAYROLL

Payroll setup in QuickBooks is accessed from the Employees Menu.

1. Select **Employees**
2. Select **Payroll Setup**
3. The QuickBooks Payroll Setup window summarizes the steps to set up QuickBooks payroll and time tracking
4. Click **Finish Later**

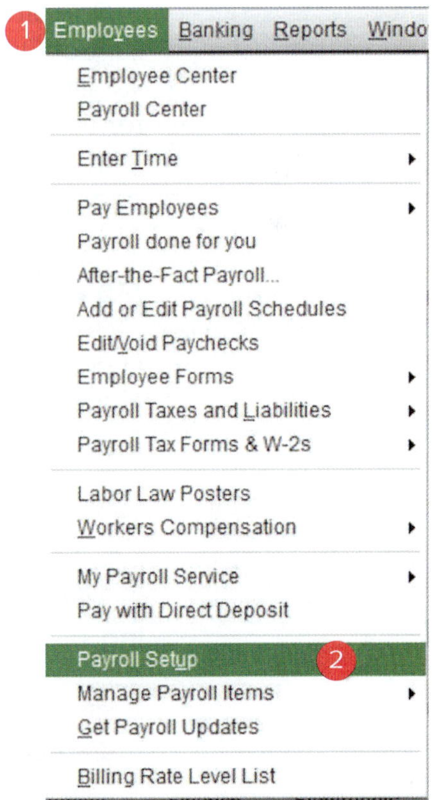

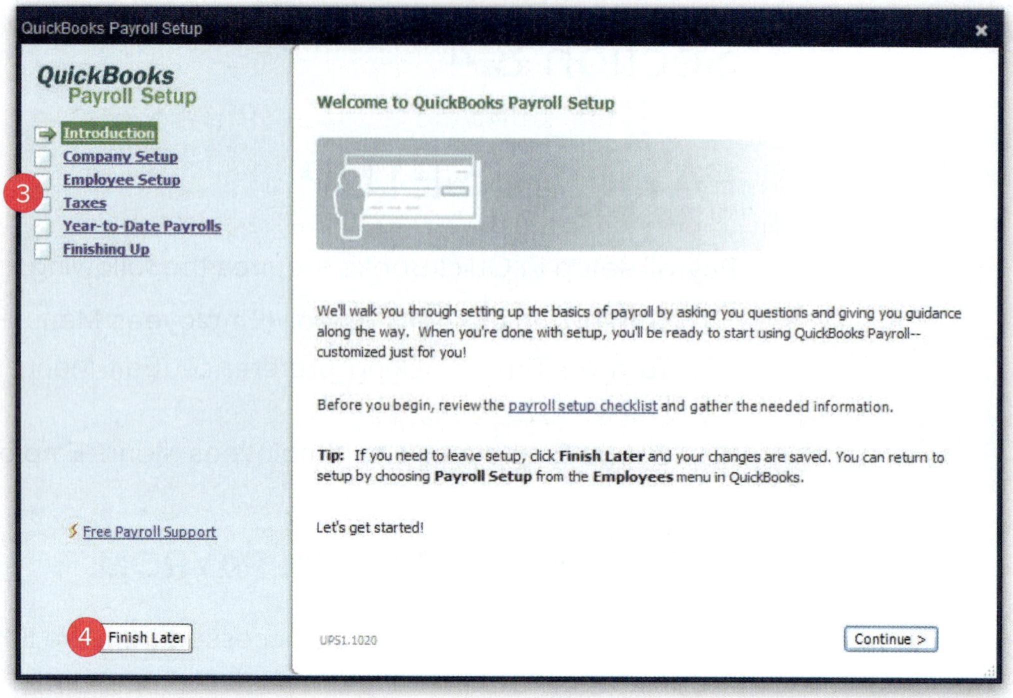

Payroll accounts for Rock Castle Construction have already been established. QuickBooks automatically creates a Chart of Accounts with payroll liability and payroll expense accounts. Payroll Items track supporting detail for the payroll accounts.

In this chapter, we will focus on customizing payroll using preferences and recording employee and payroll transactions.

PAYROLL AND TIME TRACKING PREFERENCES

Use QuickBooks Preferences to customize time tracking and payroll to suit your company's specific needs. There are two types of preferences that affect payroll:

1. Time-tracking preferences
2. Payroll and employees preferences

To turn on the QuickBooks time-tracking feature, complete the following steps:

1. Select **Edit Menu**
2. Select **Preferences**

3 When the Preferences window appears, select **Time & Expenses** from the left scrollbar

4 Then select the **Company Preferences** tab

5 Select Do you track time? **Yes**

6 Select First Day of Work Week: **Monday**

7 Leave the Preferences window open

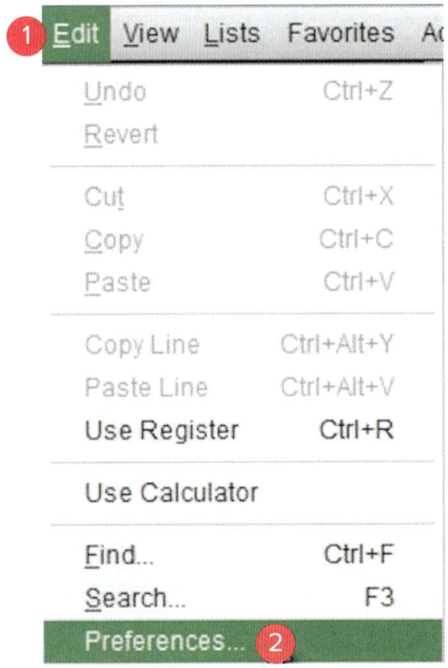

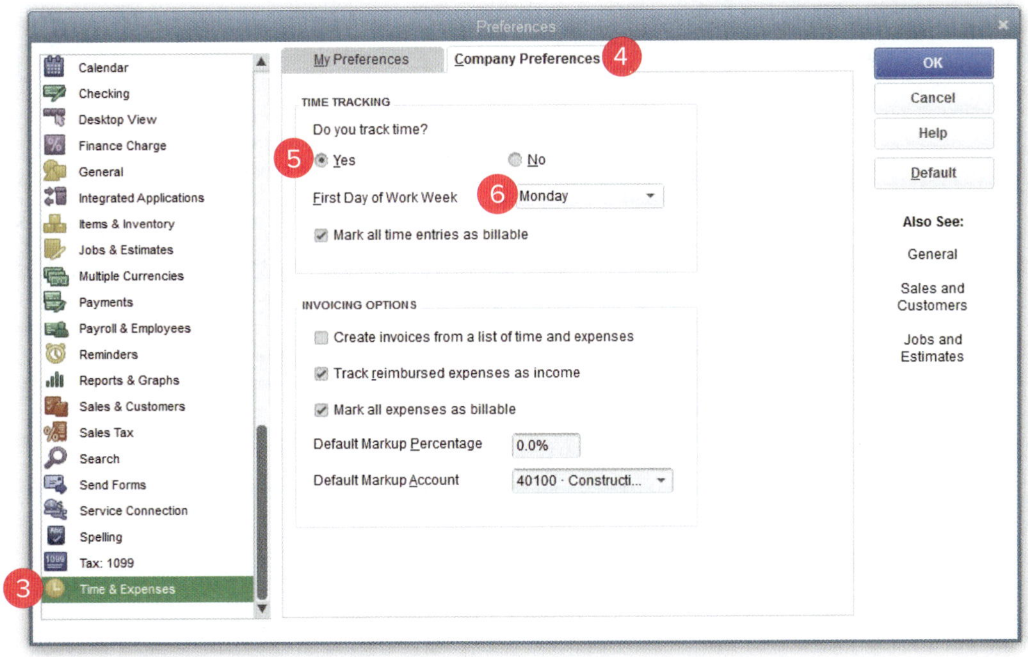

Next, select QuickBooks payroll and employees preferences for your company.

With the Preferences window open:

1. From the left scrollbar of the Preferences window, click on the **Payroll & Employees** icon
2. Select the **Company Preferences** tab
3. Select QuickBooks Payroll Features: **Full payroll**
4. Select Display Employee List by: **Last Name**
5. Click the **Employee Defaults** button to select payroll defaults
6. Select the checkbox: **Use time data to create paychecks.** Now QuickBooks will automatically use tracked time to calculate payroll.
7. Click **OK** to close the Employee Defaults window
8. Click **OK** again to close the Preferences window
9. When the warning message appears, click **OK**

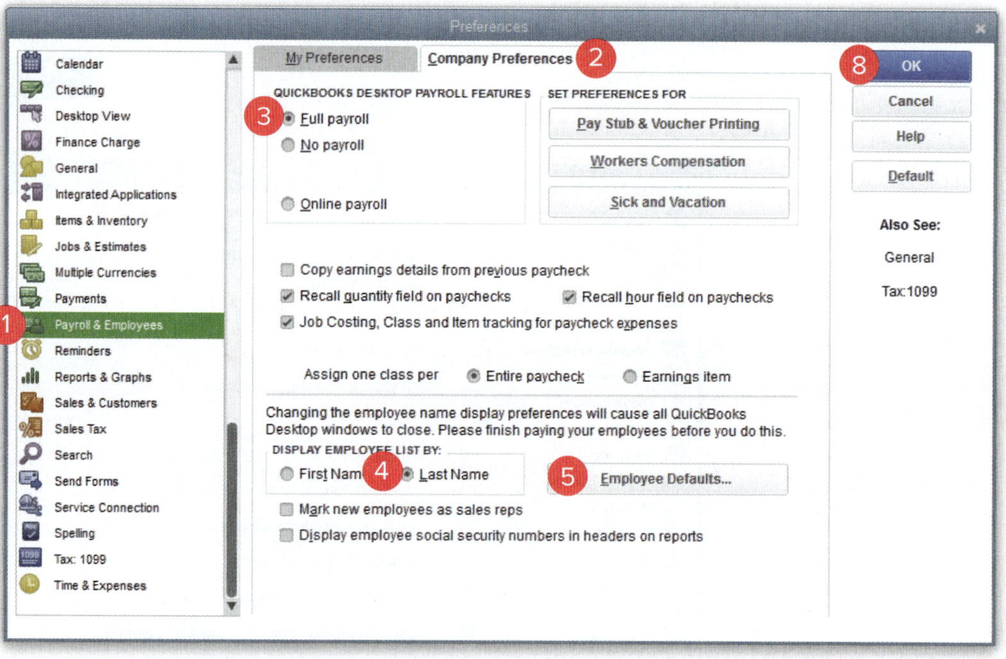

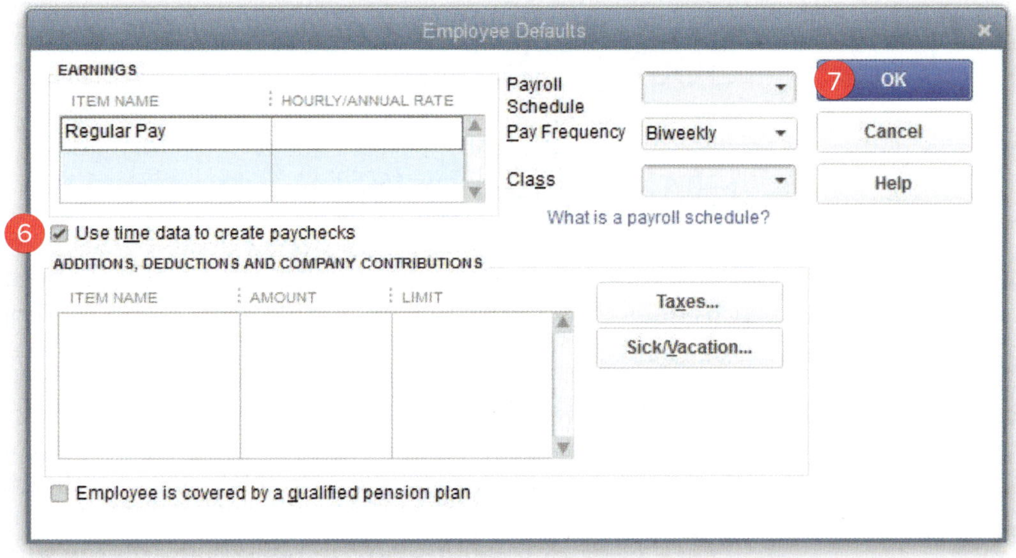

To save time, enter information common to most employees (such as a deduction for health insurance) as an employee default. QuickBooks then records the information for all employees. Later, you can customize the information as needed for a specific employee.

Now that the time-tracking and payroll preferences are set, we will edit and print the Employee List.

Section 8.5

EMPLOYEE LIST

The Employee List contains employee information such as address, telephone, salary or wage rate, and Social Security number.

VIEW EMPLOYEE LIST

To view the Employee List for Rock Castle Construction:

1. Click Employees on the Navigation Bar or click the **Employees** button on the Home Page to display the Employee Center
2. Click the **Employees** tab to display a list of employees
3. To view or edit employee information, **double-click the employee's name**

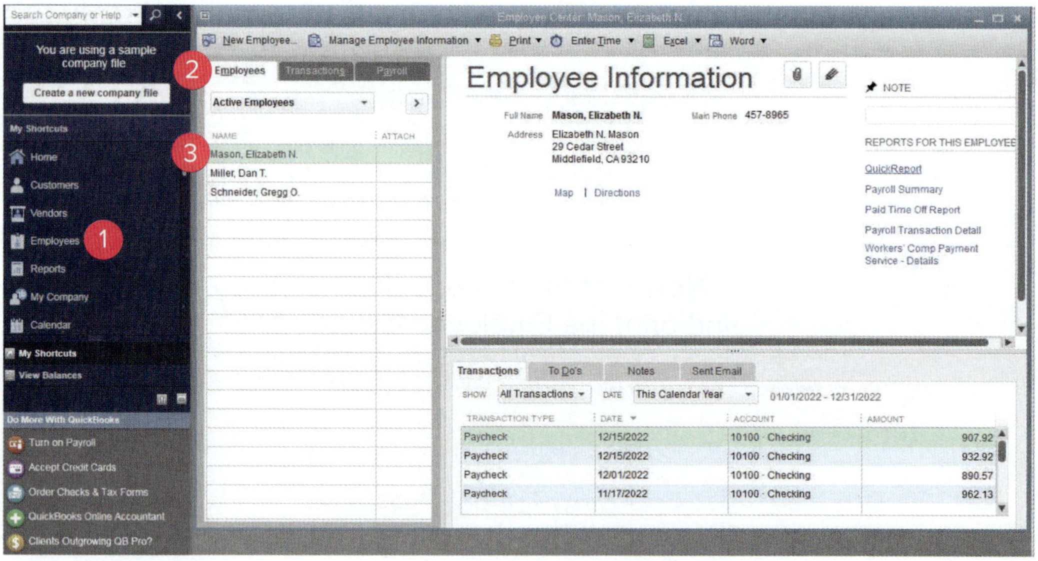

ADD NEW EMPLOYEE

To enter your name as a new employee in the Employee List:

1. Click the **New Employee** button in the Employee Center
2. When the blank New Employee window appears, select **Personal** tab. Enter the following information.

First Name	**[Enter your first name]**
Last Name	**[Enter your last name]**
Social Security No.	**333-22-4444**
Gender	**[Enter gender]**
Date of Birth	**[Enter a fictitious date of birth]**
Marital Status	**Married**
U.S. Citizen	**Yes**

3. Select the **Address & Contact** tab, then enter the following information.

Address	**555 Lakeview Lane**
	Bayshore, CA 94326
Main Email	**[Enter your email address]**

4. Select the **Additional Info** tab, then enter the following information.

Employee ID	**333-22-4444**
B-Day	**[Enter a fictitious birth date]**

5. Select the **Payroll Info** tab, then enter the following payroll information.

Earnings Name	**Regular Pay**
Hourly/Annual Rate	**10.00**
Use time data to create paychecks	**Yes**
Pay Frequency	**Biweekly**
Deductions	**Health Insurance**
Amount	**−25.00**
Limit	**−1200.00**

6. Select the Taxes button to view federal, state, and other tax information related to your employment, such as filing status and allowances.
7. Select the **Federal** tab and enter the following:
   - Filing Status: **Married**
   - Allowances for Federal: **1**
8. Select **State** tab > Allowances for State: **1**
9. Click **OK** to close the Taxes window
10. Click **OK** again to close the New Employee window and add your name to Rock Castle Construction's Employee List
11. When asked if you want to set up payroll information for sick leave and vacation, click **Leave As Is** to use the employee default information for these items
12. Leave the Employee Center window

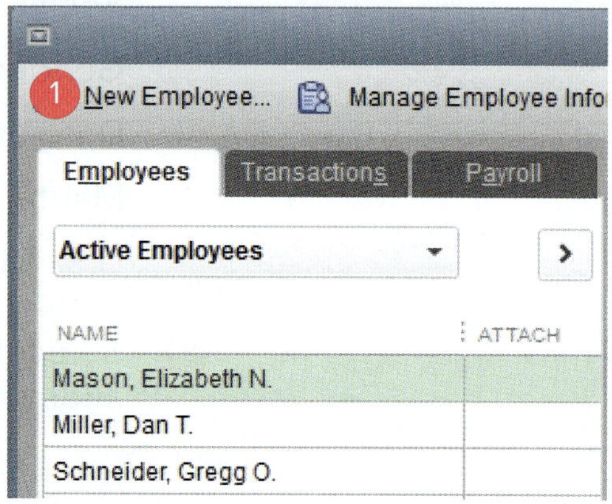

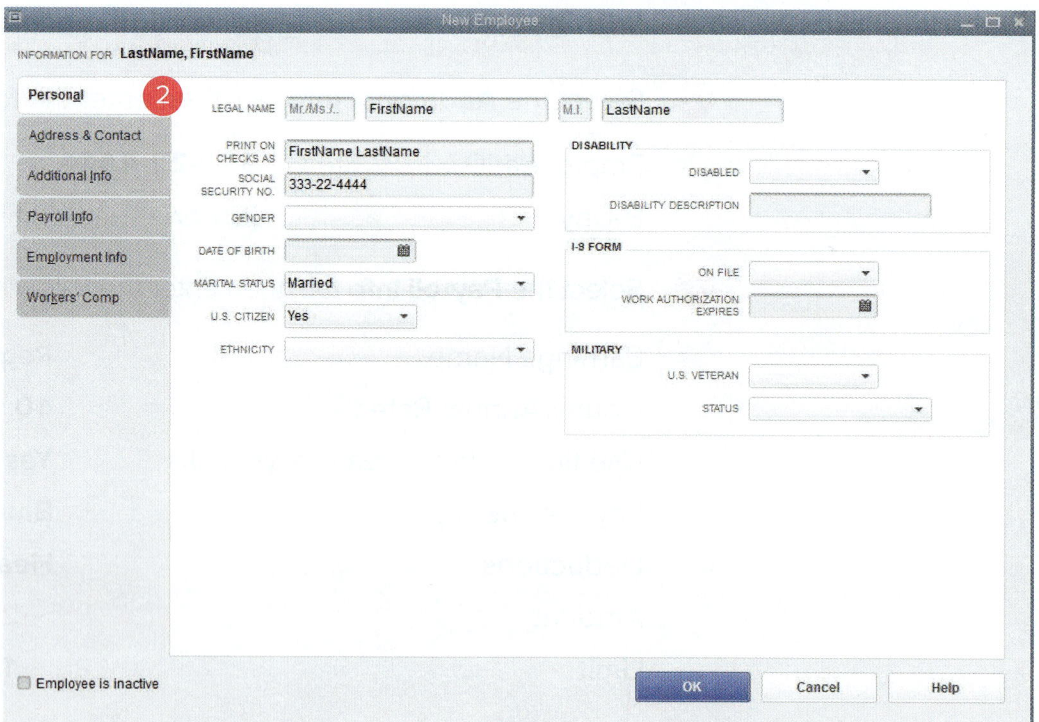

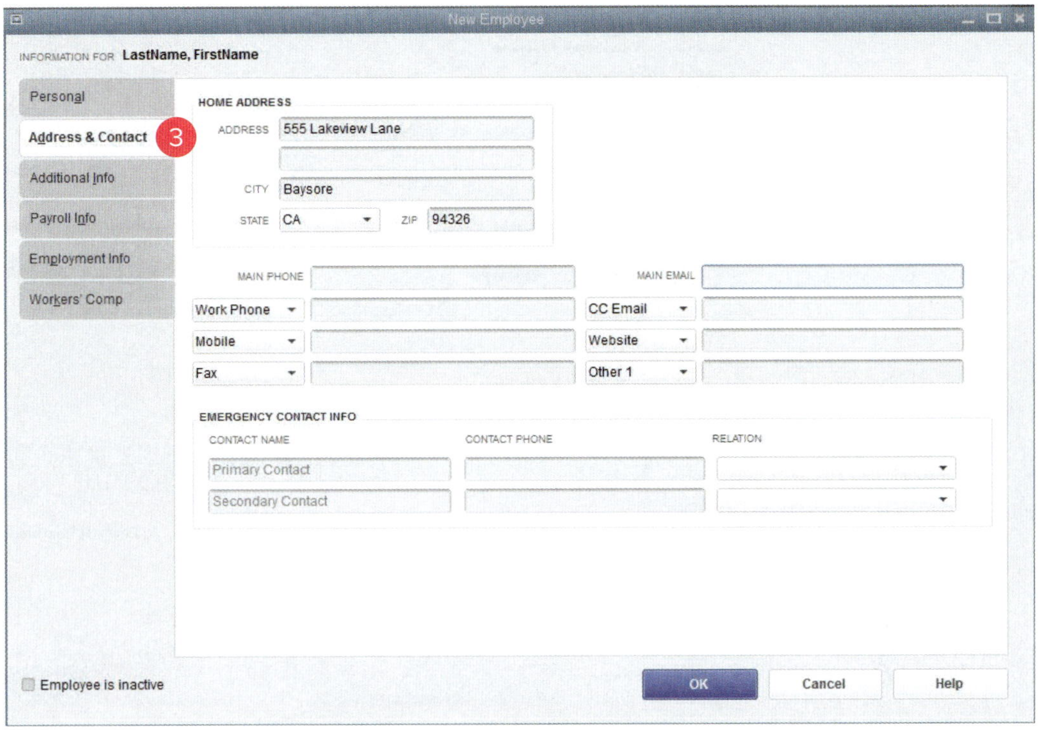
New Employee
INFORMATION FOR LastName, FirstName
Personal
Address & Contact
3
Additional Info
Payroll Info
Employment Info
Workers' Comp
HOME ADDRESS
ADDRESS 555 Lakeview Lane
CITY Baysore
STATE CA
ZIP 94326
MAIN PHONE
MAIN EMAIL
Work Phone
CC Email
Mobile
Website
Fax
Other 1
EMERGENCY CONTACT INFO
CONTACT NAME
CONTACT PHONE
RELATION
Primary Contact
Secondary Contact
Employee is inactive
OK
Cancel
Help

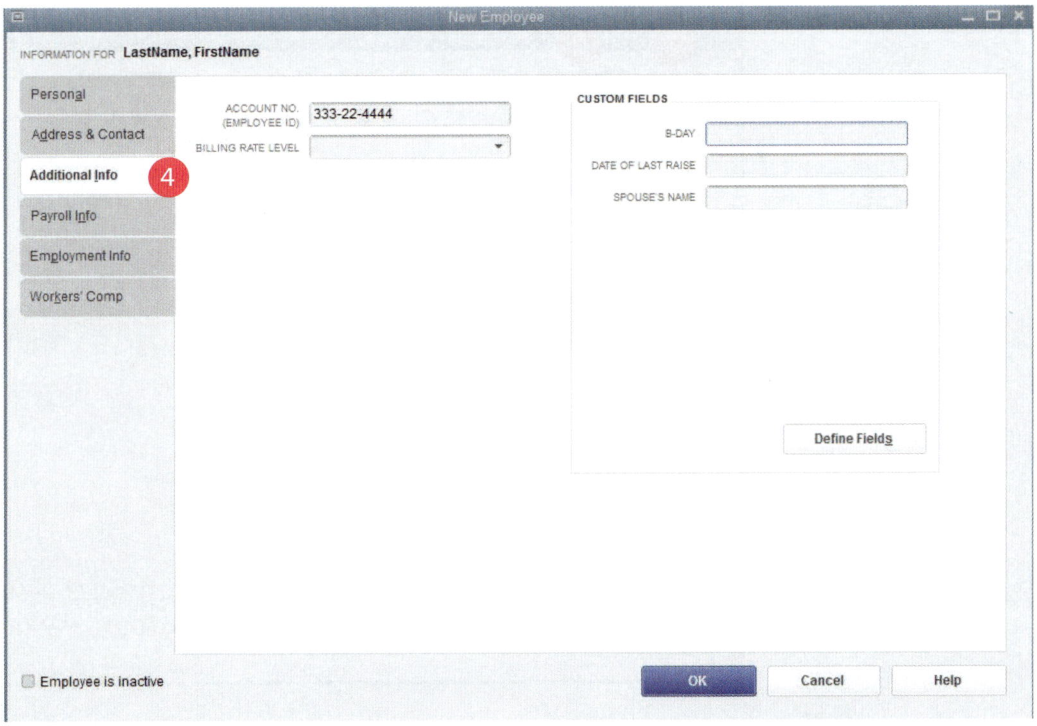
New Employee
INFORMATION FOR LastName, FirstName
Personal
Address & Contact
Additional Info
4
Payroll Info
Employment Info
Workers' Comp
ACCOUNT NO. (EMPLOYEE ID) 333-22-4444
BILLING RATE LEVEL
CUSTOM FIELDS
B-DAY
DATE OF LAST RAISE
SPOUSE'S NAME
Define Fields
Employee is inactive
OK
Cancel
Help

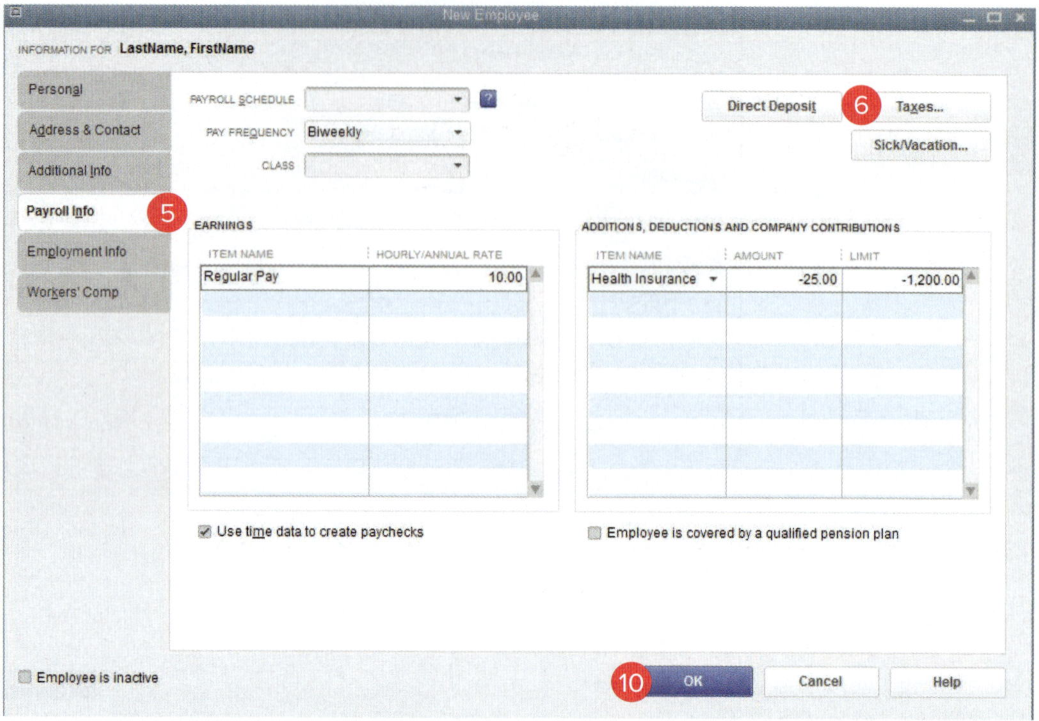
New Employee
INFORMATION FOR LastName, FirstName
Personal
Address & Contact
Additional Info
Payroll Info
Employment Info
Workers' Comp
PAYROLL SCHEDULE
PAY FREQUENCY Biweekly
CLASS
Direct Deposit
Taxes...
Sick/Vacation...
EARNINGS
ITEM NAME
HOURLY/ANNUAL RATE
Regular Pay 10.00
ADDITIONS, DEDUCTIONS AND COMPANY CONTRIBUTIONS
ITEM NAME
AMOUNT
LIMIT
Health Insurance -25.00 -1,200.00
Use time data to create paychecks
Employee is covered by a qualified pension plan
Employee is inactive
OK
Cancel
Help
5
6
10

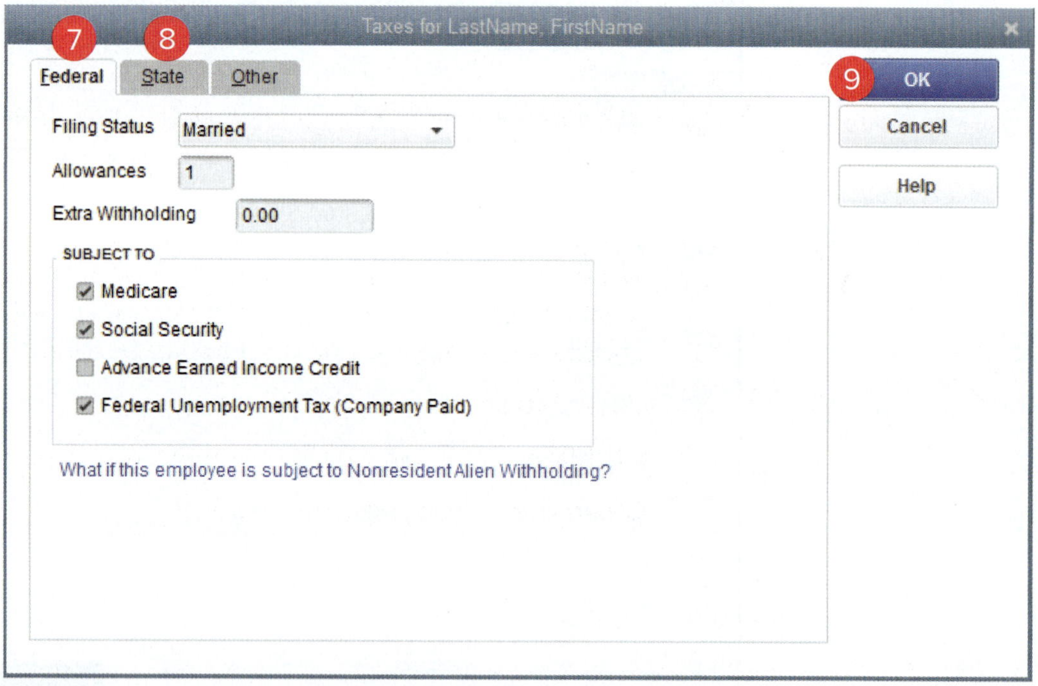
Taxes for LastName, FirstName
Federal
State
Other
Filing Status Married
Allowances 1
Extra Withholding 0.00
SUBJECT TO
Medicare
Social Security
Advance Earned Income Credit
Federal Unemployment Tax (Company Paid)
What if this employee is subject to Nonresident Alien Withholding?
OK
Cancel
Help
7
8
9

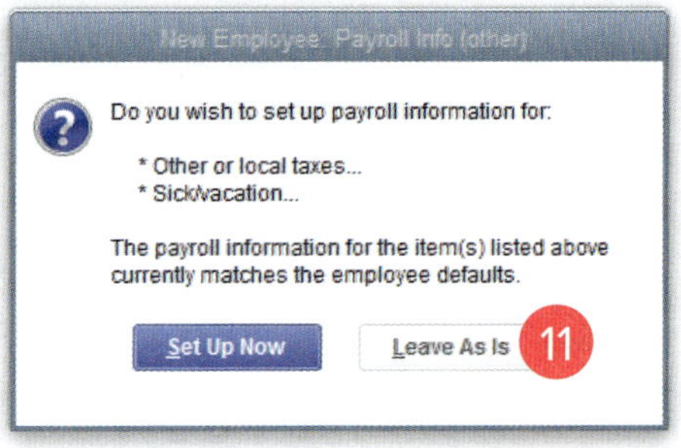

If you receive a message that you must update QuickBooks before you can use payroll, update QuickBooks, then proceed.

New employees complete Form W-4 to indicate filing status and allowances. To access hiring forms, such as Form W-4, from with QuickBooks, select Payroll Center from the Employee section of the Home Page > Hiring Forms.

EXPORT EMPLOYEE LIST

C8.5.1 Employee List. Export the Employee List as follows:

1. Click the **Name** bar to sort employee names in alphabetical order
2. At the top of the Employee Center, select **Excel**
3. Select **Export Employee List**
4. When the Export window appears, select **Replace an existing worksheet.** Browse and select your **CH8 REPORTS** Excel template. Select the appropriate worksheet.
5. Click **Export**
6. **Highlight** your name and information on the Employee List
7. **Close** the Employee Center window

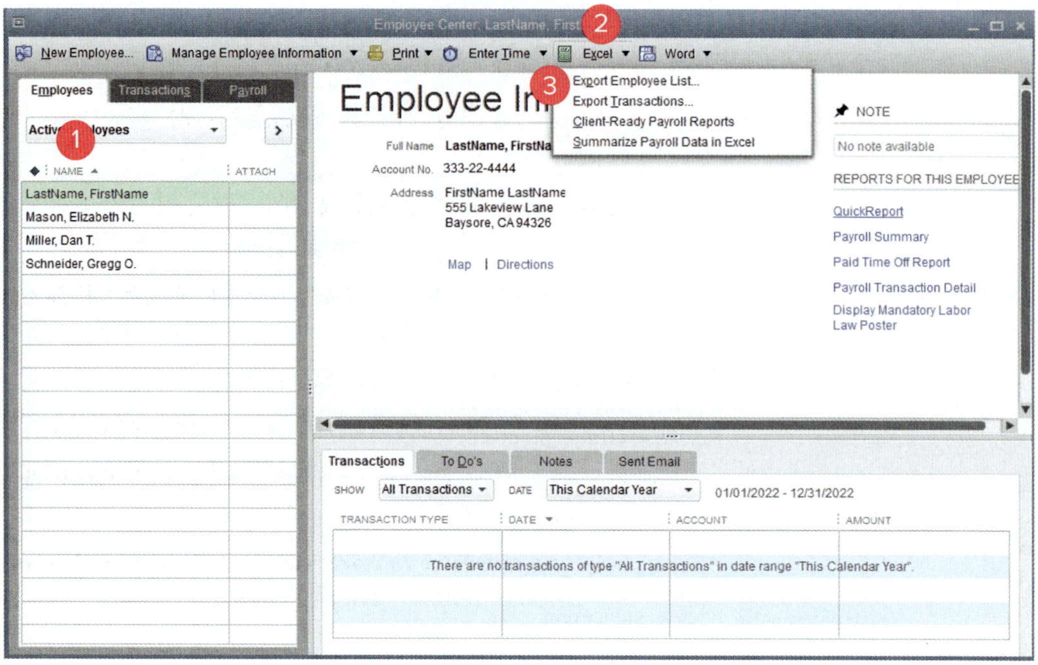
Employee Center: LastName, First
New Employee...
Manage Employee Information
Print
Enter Time
Excel
Word
Export Employee List...
Export Transactions...
Client-Ready Payroll Reports
Summarize Payroll Data in Excel
Employees
Transactions
Payroll
NAME
ATTACH
LastName, FirstName
Mason, Elizabeth N.
Miller, Dan T.
Schneider, Gregg O.
Full Name
Account No. 333-22-4444
Address
FirstName LastName
555 Lakeview Lane
Baysore, CA 94326
Map
Directions
NOTE
No note available
REPORTS FOR THIS EMPLOYEE
QuickReport
Payroll Summary
Paid Time Off Report
Payroll Transaction Detail
Display Mandatory Labor Law Poster
Transactions
To Do's
Notes
Sent Email
SHOW
All Transactions
DATE
This Calendar Year
01/01/2022 - 12/31/2022
TRANSACTION TYPE
DATE
ACCOUNT
AMOUNT
There are no transactions of type "All Transactions" in date range "This Calendar Year".
1
2
3

Section 8.6

EMPLOYEE NAVIGATION AND PAYROLL PROCESSING

If necessary, click the **Home** icon to view the Employees section of the Home Page.

To track time and process payroll in QuickBooks, we will use the Employees section of the Home Page. The Employees section of the Home Page is a flowchart of payroll transactions. As the flowchart indicates, there are four main steps to processing payroll using QuickBooks:

1. **Enter Time.** QuickBooks permits you to track employee time worked to use in processing payroll and billing customers. Simply enter time worked by employees. If the time-tracking feature is turned off, this icon will not appear.
2. **Pay Employees.** Select employees to pay and create their paychecks.
3. **Pay Payroll Liabilities.** Pay payroll tax liabilities due governmental agencies such as the IRS. Payroll tax liabilities include federal income taxes withheld, state income taxes withheld, FICA (Social Security and Medicare), and unemployment taxes.
4. **Process Payroll Forms.** Process payroll forms including Forms 940, 941, W-2, and W-3 that must be submitted to governmental agencies.

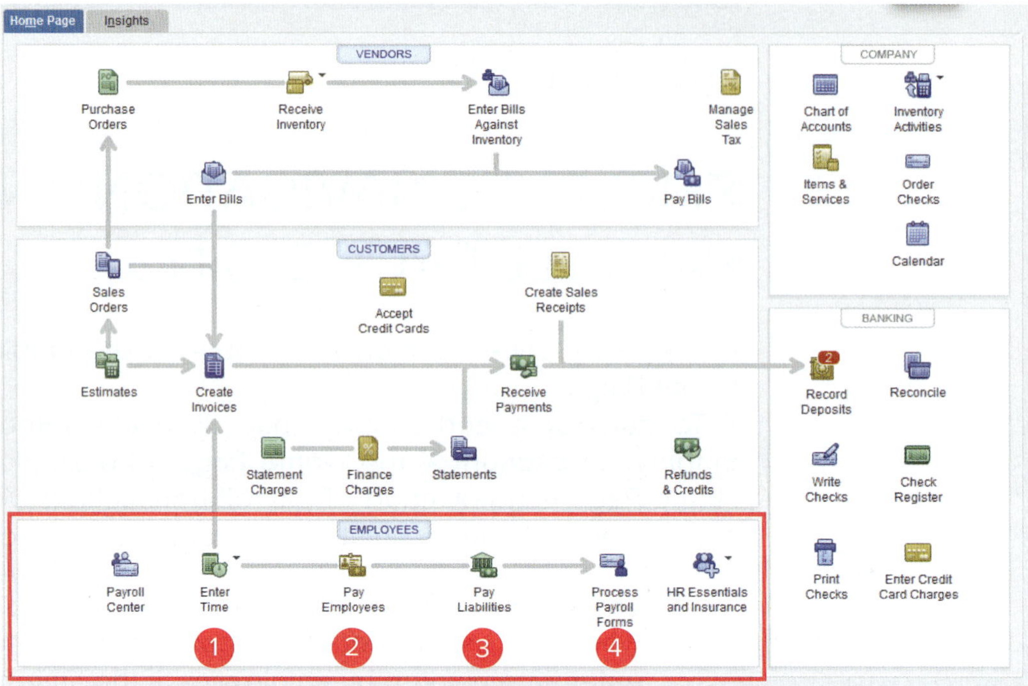

QuickBooks also has an Employee Center and a Payroll Center to help us manage employee and payroll information.

- **Employee Center.** The Employee Center can be accessed from the Navigation Bar and, as shown in the prior section of this chapter, contains the Employee List with employee information, such as address and Social Security number.
- **Payroll Center.** The Payroll Center is part of the Employee Center and is used to manage payroll and tax information, including information about wages, benefits, and withholding. The Payroll Center can be accessed by clicking the Payroll Center icon in the Employees section of the Home Page or by selecting the Payroll tab from the Employee Center.

Section 8.7

ENTER TIME

QuickBooks permits us to track time worked on various jobs.

Although this chapter focuses on time worked by employees, work can be performed by employees, subcontractors, or owners. The time-tracking feature can be used to track time worked by any of the three. How we record the payment, however, depends upon who performs the work: employee, subcontractor, or business owner.

Status	Pay Using QB Window. . .	Home Page
Employee	Pay Employees window	**Employees**
Subcontractor (Vendor)	Enter Bills window Pay Bills window	**Vendors**
Owner	Write Checks window	**Banking**

It is important that we determine the status of the individual performing the work. The status determines whether we record payments to the individual as an employee paycheck, vendor payment, or owner withdrawal.

> **Employees.** Employees complete Form W-4 when hired. Form W-2 summarizes annual wages and tax withholdings.

> **Independent Contractors.** No tax withholdings are necessary for independent contractors. Tax Form 1099-MISC summarizes payments.

> **Owner.** If a stockholder is also an employee, wages are recorded as payroll. If not wages, then payment to the stockholder is a dividend.

When employees use time tracking, the employee records the time worked on each job. The time data is then used to:

1. Prepare paychecks
2. Bill customers for time worked on specific jobs

QuickBooks Pro and QuickBooks Premier provide three different ways to track time.

1. **Time Single Activity.** Use the Stopwatch to time an activity and enter the time data. QuickBooks automatically records the time on the employee's weekly timesheet.
2. **Weekly Timesheet.** Use the weekly timesheet to enter time worked by each employee on various jobs during the week.
3. **Online Timesheets.** Enter billable hours from any Internet-connected computer. Download the timesheets into QuickBooks to process paychecks.

TIME SINGLE ACTIVITY

You will use the QuickBooks Stopwatch feature to time how long it takes you to complete payroll activities in this chapter.

To start the Stopwatch:

1. From the Employees section of the Home Page, select the **Enter Time** icon
2. Select **Time/Enter Single Activity**
3. When the Time/Enter Single Activity window appears, select Date: **12/15/2022.** You can use the Stopwatch to time activities for today's date only. However, for this activity, use the programmed date for the sample company: 12/15/2022.
4. Select Name: **Your LastName, FirstName**
5. If the work was for a particular job or customer, we would enter the job or customer name and the service item, then click Billable. In this case, your time is not billable to a particular customer's job, so **uncheck Billable.**
6. Select Payroll Item: **Regular Pay**
7. Enter Notes: **Process payroll**
8. Click the **Start** button to start the stopwatch
9. Leave the window open while you complete the following payroll activities

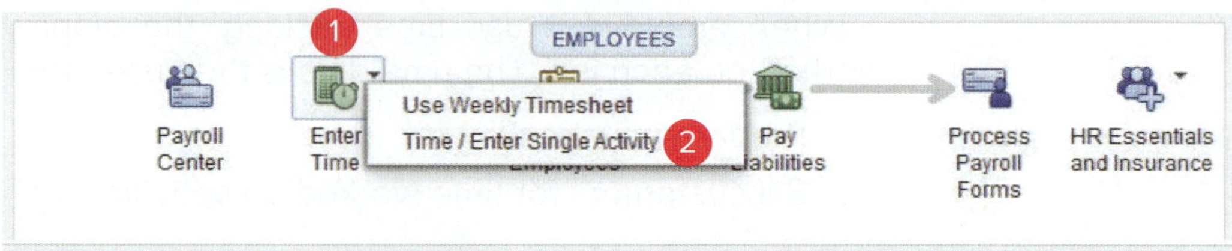

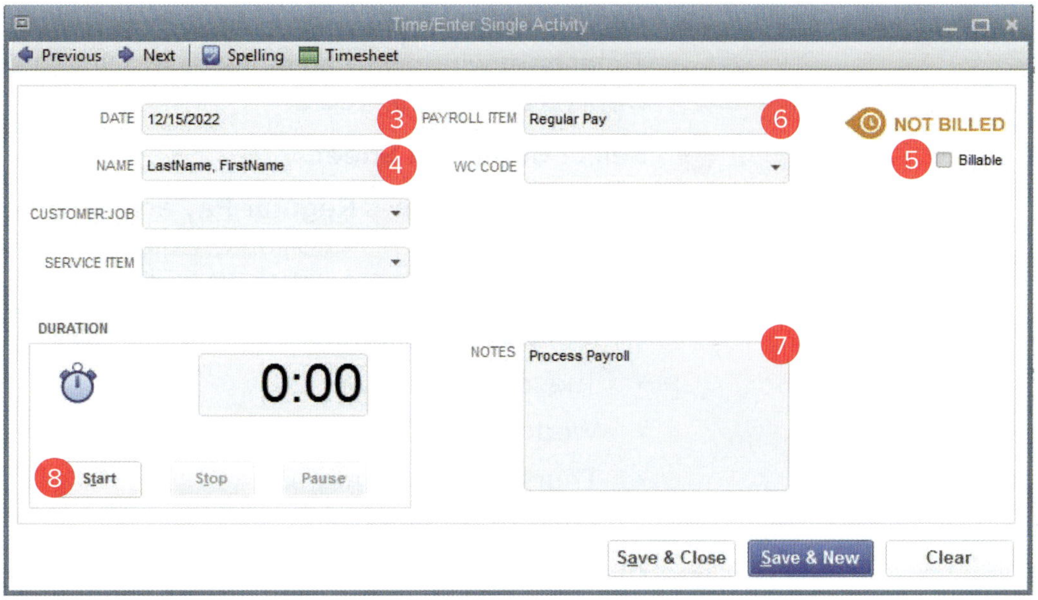

TIMESHEET

Rock Castle Construction pays employees biweekly. The last payday was December 15, 2022. The current pay period is December 16 through December 29, 2022 with payhecks due to be issued on on December 29, 2022.

Use the timesheet to enter the hours you worked for Rock Castle Construction during the last pay period.

To use QuickBooks timesheet feature:

1. In the Employees section of the Home Page, select **Enter Time**
2. Select **Use Weekly Timesheet**
3. Select Week Of: **Dec 12 to Dec 18, 2022**
4. Select Name: **LastName, First Name**
5. From the Payroll Item drop-down list, select **Regular Pay**
6. Because your time is not billable to a specific customer or job, **uncheck** the **Billable?** field in the last column to indicate these charges will not be transferred to an invoice.
7. Enter **6** hours for Friday, December 16

8 Click the **Next** button in the upper left corner of the Weekly Timesheet window to advance to the timesheet for the week of **Dec 19 to Dec 25, 2022**

9 Select **Copy Last Sheet.**

10 Verify Payroll Item is **Regular Pa**y and **Billable?** Is unchecked to mark your hours as nonbillable. Enter **6** hours for each of the following dates for a total of 30 hours for the week:

- Monday, December 19
- Tuesday, December 20
- Wednesday, December 21
- Thursday, December 22
- Friday, December 23

11 Click the **Next** button in the upper left corner of the Weekly Timesheet window to advance to the next timesheet

12 Select **Copy Last Sheet.** Verify Payroll Item is **Regular Pa**y and **Billable?** Is unchecked to mark your hours as nonbillable. Enter **6** hours for each of the following dates for a total of 24 hours for the week:

- Monday, December 26
- Tuesday, December 27
- Wednesday, December 28
- Thursday, December 29

13 Click **Save & New** to record your hours and display a new timesheet

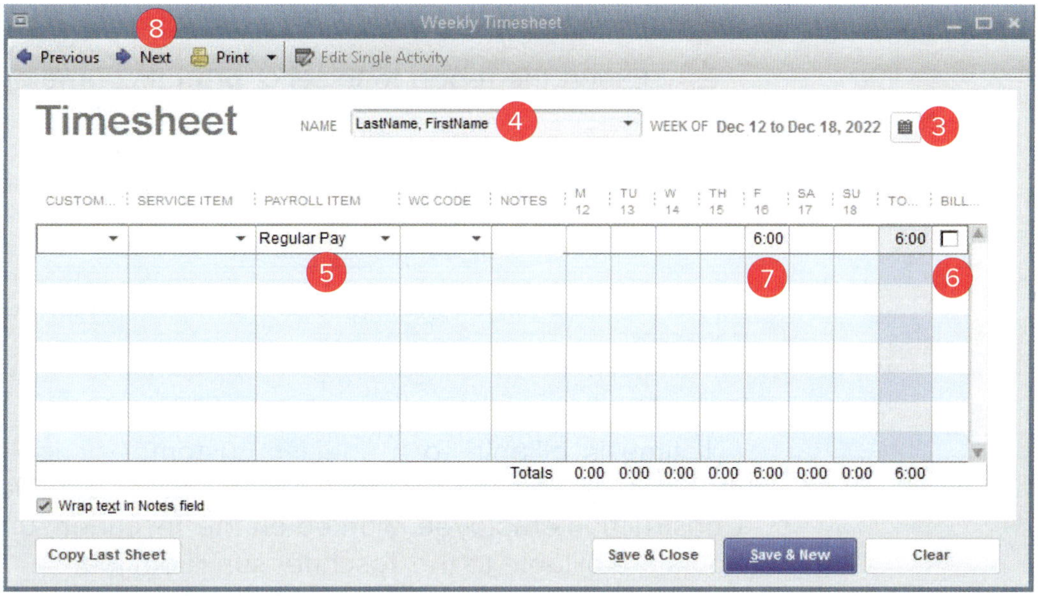

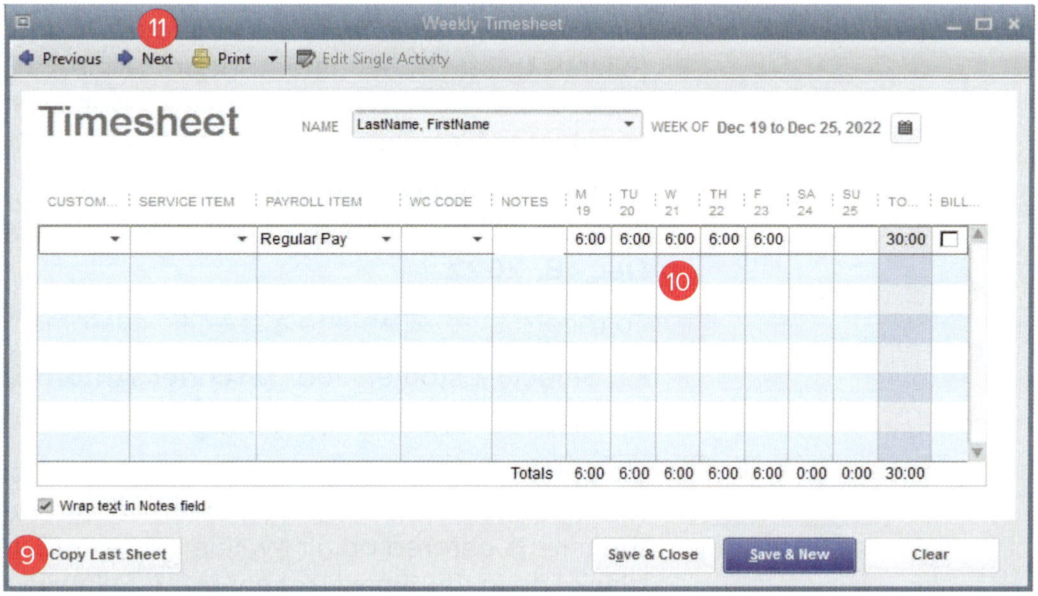

C8.7.1 Time by Name Report. To view the time that you worked, create a Time by Name report as follows.

1. From the Navigation Bar, select **Reports** > **Jobs, Time & Mileage** > **Time by Name**
2. Select Dates: **12/16/2022 To 12/29/2022**

3. Select **Run**
4. Export the report to **Excel** or **print** the Time by Name report

Use Copy Last Sheet if the timesheet does not change much from week to week.

If your time was billable to a specific customer or job, then select Customer: Job name and the Service Item.

If time is billable to a specific customer or job, this is indicated on the weekly timesheet. For example, Elizabeth Mason, a Rock Castle Construction employee, worked on the Teschner sun room; therefore, her hours are billable to the Teschner sun room job.

To enter billable hours on Elizabeth Mason's weekly timesheet:

1. On the new timesheet, select Employee Name: **Elizabeth N. Mason.** (Elizabeth Mason's name appears twice in the list, once as a vendor, and again as an employee. For the timesheet, be certain to select the employee, Elizabeth N. Mason.)
2. Click the **Previous** button in the upper left corner of the Weekly Timesheet window to change the timesheet dates to **Dec 12 to Dec 18, 2022**
3. To record time billable to a specific customer:
   - Select Customer: Job: **Teschner, Anton: Sun Room**
   - Select Service Item: **Framing**
4. Complete Elizabeth's weekly timesheet for framing the sunroom as follows. Notice that if the Customer: Job or Service Item changes, the time is entered on a new line in the timesheet. On the next blank line in the timesheet enter the following hours:

Friday, December 16	**8 hours**

5. Check: **Billable?**
6. Click the **Next** button in the upper left corner of the Weekly Timesheet window to advance to the timesheet for the week of **Dec 19 to Dec 25, 2022**

7 In the timesheet enter the following installation work that Elizabeth performed on the Teschner sun room.

- Select Customer: Job: **Teschner, Anton: Sun Room**
- Select Service Item: **Framing**
- Enter hours worked: **2 hours Monday, December 19**
- Check **Billable?**

8
- Select Customer: Job: **Teschner, Anton: Sun Room**
- Select Service Item: **Installation**
- Enter hours worked: **6 hours Monday, December 19**
- Check **Billable?**

9 Record **8** hours for each of the following dates that Elizabeth worked billable hours on installing the Teschner sun room:

- Tuesday, December 20
- Wednesday, December 21
- Thursday, December 22
- Friday, December 23

10 Click the **Next** button to record Elizabeth N. Mason's hours and display a new timesheet

11 Complete Elizabeth's weekly timesheet for framing the sunroom as follows. Notice that if the Customer: Job or Service Item changes, the time is entered on a new line in the timesheet.

Monday, December 26	**8 hours**
Tuesday, December 27	**8 hours**
Wednesday, December 28	**8 hours**
Thursday, December 29	**6 hours**

12 Click **Save & Close** to record the time sheet and close the Weekly Timesheet window

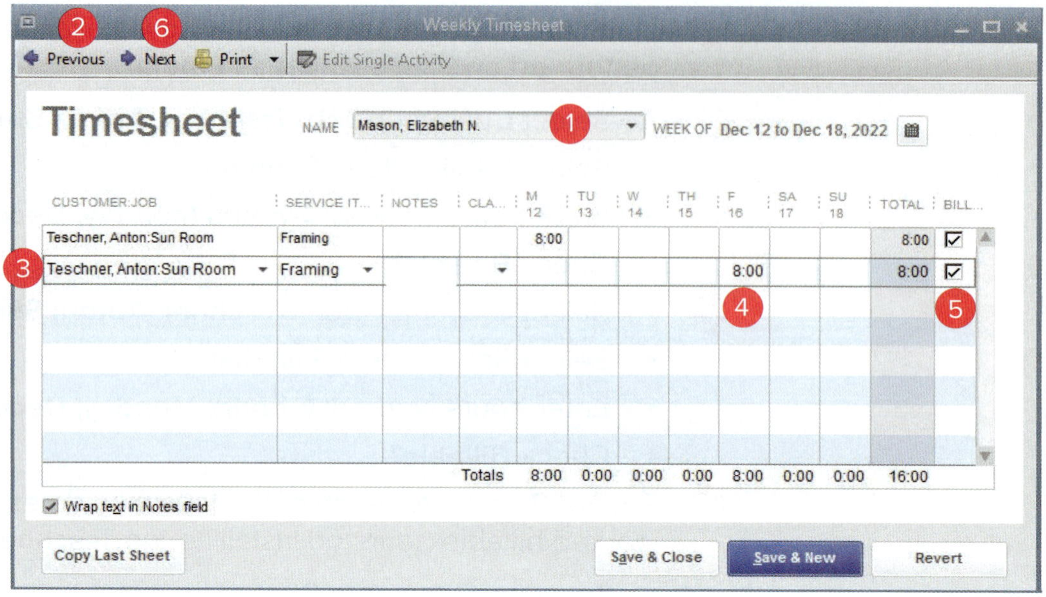
Weekly Timesheet
2
6
Previous
Next
Print
Edit Single Activity
Timesheet
NAME
Mason, Elizabeth N.
1
WEEK OF Dec 12 to Dec 18, 2022
CUSTOMER:JOB
SERVICE IT...
NOTES
CLA...
M 12
TU 13
W 14
TH 15
F 16
SA 17
SU 18
TOTAL
BILL...
Teschner, Anton:Sun Room
Framing
8:00
8:00
3
Teschner, Anton:Sun Room
Framing
8:00
8:00
4
5
Totals 8:00 0:00 0:00 0:00 8:00 0:00 0:00 16:00
Wrap text in Notes field
Copy Last Sheet
Save & Close
Save & New
Revert

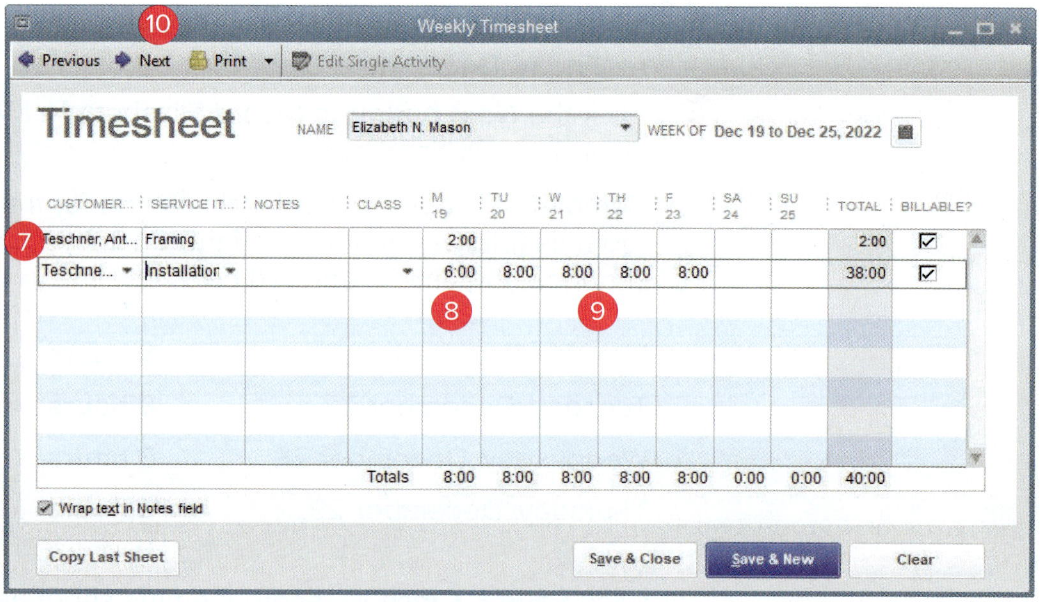
Weekly Timesheet
10
Previous
Next
Print
Edit Single Activity
Timesheet
NAME
Elizabeth N. Mason
WEEK OF Dec 19 to Dec 25, 2022
CUSTOMER...
SERVICE IT...
NOTES
CLASS
M 19
TU 20
W 21
TH 22
F 23
SA 24
SU 25
TOTAL
BILLABLE?
7
Teschner, Ant...
Framing
2:00
2:00
Teschne...
Installation
6:00 8:00 8:00 8:00 8:00
38:00
8
9
Totals 8:00 8:00 8:00 8:00 8:00 0:00 0:00 40:00
Wrap text in Notes field
Copy Last Sheet
Save & Close
Save & New
Clear

C8.7.2 Time by Name Report. To view the time that you and Elizabeth Mason worked, create a Time by Name report as follows.

1. From the Navigation Bar, select **Reports** > **Jobs, Time & Mileage** > **Time by Name**
2. Select Dates: **12/16/2022 To 12/29/2022**
3. Select **Run**
4. Export the report to **Excel** or **print** the Time by Name report

Later in the chapter, we will cover how to transfer tracked time to sales invoices.

Section 8.8

PAY EMPLOYEES

After entering time worked, the next step is to create employee paychecks. QuickBooks offers the following QuickBooks payroll services to streamline payroll calculations and processing:

- Basic Payroll
- Enhanced Payroll
- Full Service Payroll

QUICKBOOKS PAYROLL SERVICES

QuickBooks offers three levels of payroll services for the entrepreneur to use with QuickBooks software: QuickBooks Basic, Enhanced, or Full Service Payroll. When we subscribe to a payroll service, QuickBooks requires that we have an Internet connection. Then QuickBooks automatically calculates payroll tax deductions.

If using a QuickBooks payroll service for a business, turn on the payroll auto update feature of QuickBooks to ensure you have the latest tax tables. If you update payroll when using this text, your answers may not be the same as the check figures so ask your instructor if you should update payroll.

Features of the three levels of payroll services for entrepreneurs are summarized as follows.

QuickBooks Payroll Plan	Features
Basic Payroll	• Create paychecks using automatic calculation of payroll tax deductions • Tax forms are not automatically prepared. Entrepreneur must complete the tax forms or work with an accountant on payroll tax filings

QuickBooks Payroll Plan	Features
Enhanced Payroll	• Create paychecks using automatic calculation of payroll tax deductions • Generate payroll tax forms for filings automatically • File and pay taxes electronically
Full Service Payroll	• Entrepreneur enter hours and Intuit does the rest • Intuit runs and files payroll for entrepreneur • Intuit processes payroll taxes and filings

CREATE PAYCHECKS

The QuickBooks payroll service is active for the sample company file, Rock Castle Construction.

To create paychecks for Rock Castle Construction using the QuickBooks payroll service:

1. From the Employees section of the Home Page, click the **Pay Employees** icon to display the Employee Center: Payroll Center window
2. Notice that the following three tabs on the right side of the Payroll Center correspond to icons in the Employee section of the Home Page:
   - Pay Employees
   - Pay Liabilities
   - File Forms
3. In the Pay Employees section, select: **Start Unscheduled Payroll.** We can schedule payroll to run at regular times, such as every week. In that case, we would select Start Scheduled Payroll.
4. When the Enter Payroll Information window appears, notice there are three steps listed at the top of the window: **Enter Payroll Information -> Review & Create Paychecks -> Print & Distribute Paychecks**
5. Select Pay Period Ends: **12/29/2022.** This is the last day of this pay period. If the Pay Period Change window appears, click **No** to change the date without updating the hours worked.
6. Select Check Date: **12/29/2022**

7. Select Bank Account: **10100 Checking**
8. Select Employee: **Elizabeth N. Mason**
9. Click **Continue**
10. When the Review and Create Paychecks window appears, notice that the tax withholding amounts appear automatically because Rock Castle uses a payroll service. If we were calculating payroll taxes manually, we must enter the withholding amounts manually.
11. Select **Open Paycheck Detail**
12. Notice in the Preview Paycheck window that the QuickBooks payroll service automatically calculates payroll amounts
13. If direct deposit was used for employee paychecks, we would select Use Direct Deposit
14. Select **Save & Close** to close the Preview Paycheck window
15. Select **Finish Later**

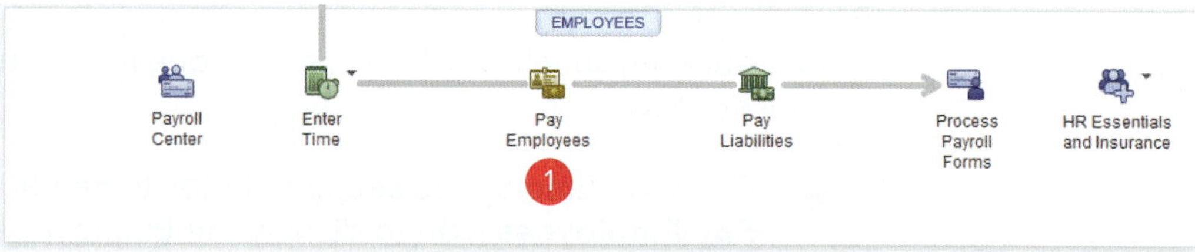

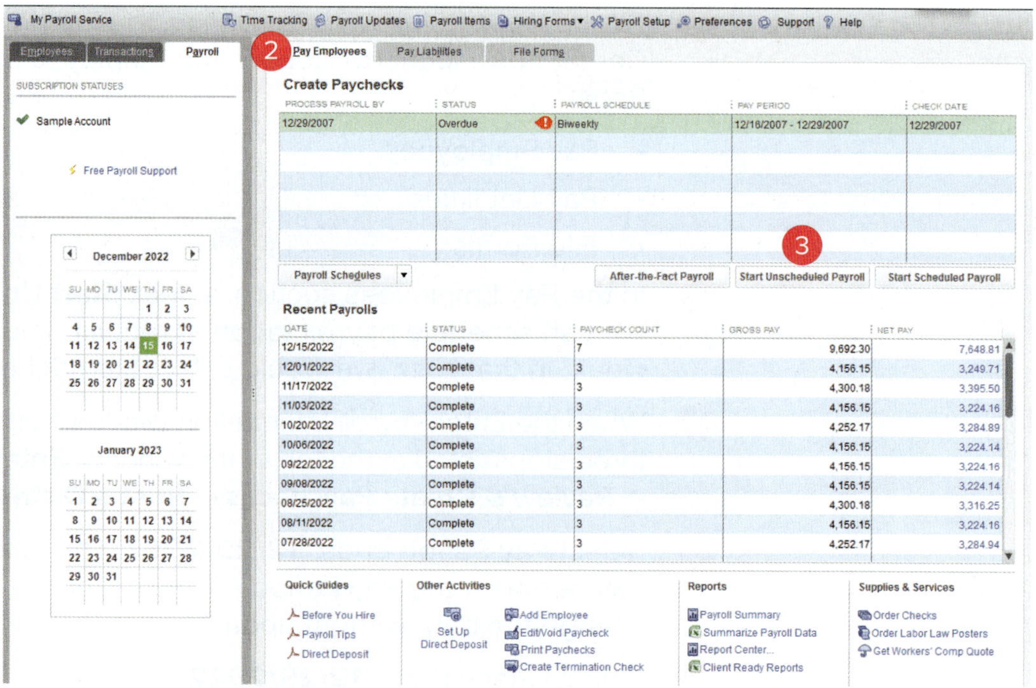

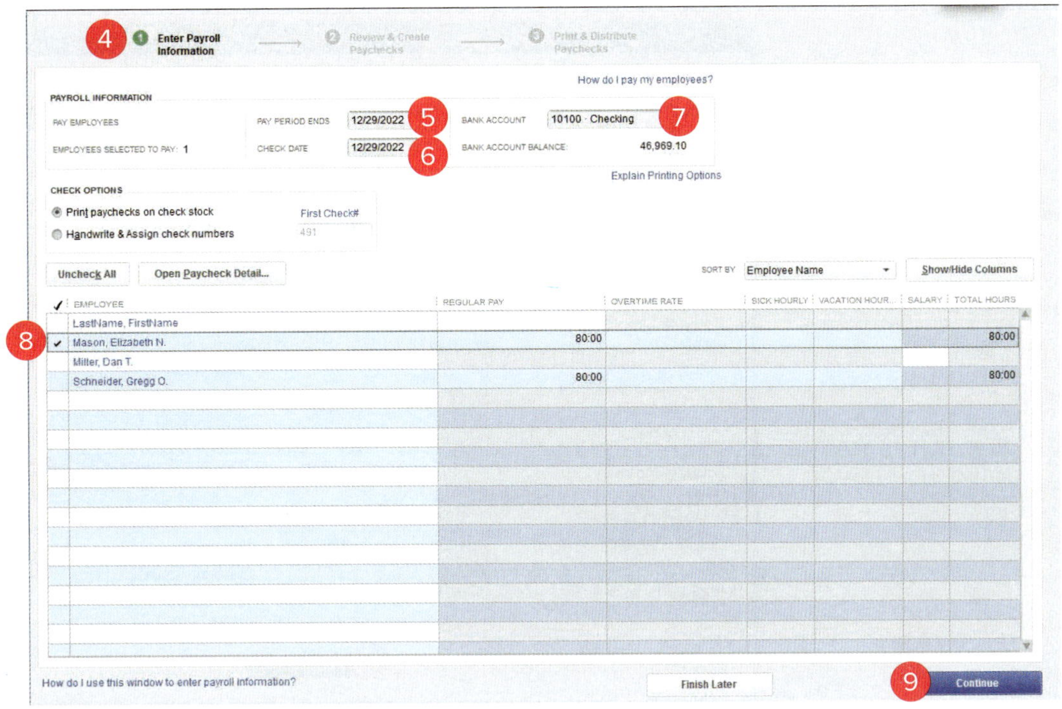
4
Enter Payroll Information
Review & Create Paychecks
Print & Distribute Paychecks
How do I pay my employees?
PAYROLL INFORMATION
PAY EMPLOYEES
EMPLOYEES SELECTED TO PAY: 1
PAY PERIOD ENDS 12/29/2022
5
CHECK DATE 12/29/2022
6
BANK ACCOUNT 10100 · Checking
7
BANK ACCOUNT BALANCE: 46,969.10
Explain Printing Options
CHECK OPTIONS
Print paychecks on check stock
Handwrite & Assign check numbers
First Check#
491
Uncheck All
Open Paycheck Detail...
SORT BY Employee Name
Show/Hide Columns
EMPLOYEE
REGULAR PAY
OVERTIME RATE
SICK HOURLY
VACATION HOUR...
SALARY
TOTAL HOURS
LastName, FirstName
8
Mason, Elizabeth N. 80:00 80:00
Miller, Dan T.
Schneider, Gregg O. 80:00 80:00
How do I use this window to enter payroll information?
Finish Later
9
Continue

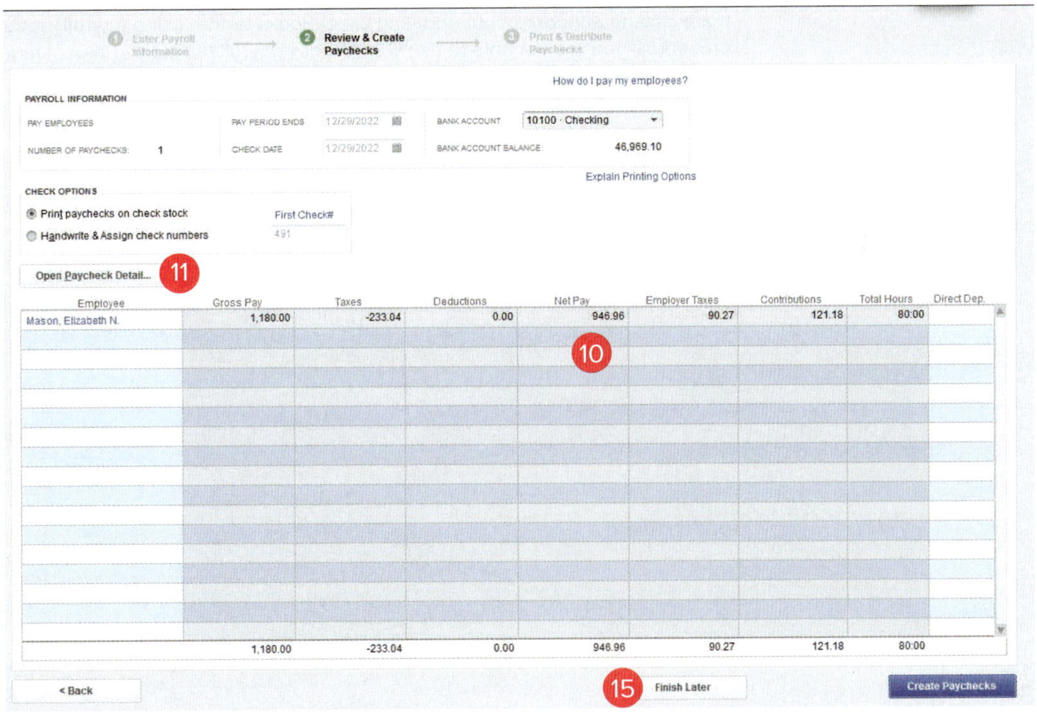
Enter Payroll Information
Review & Create Paychecks
Print & Distribute Paychecks
How do I pay my employees?
PAYROLL INFORMATION
PAY EMPLOYEES
NUMBER OF PAYCHECKS: 1
PAY PERIOD ENDS 12/29/2022
CHECK DATE 12/29/2022
BANK ACCOUNT 10100 · Checking
BANK ACCOUNT BALANCE: 46,969.10
Explain Printing Options
CHECK OPTIONS
Print paychecks on check stock
Handwrite & Assign check numbers
First Check#
491
Open Paycheck Detail...
11
Employee
Gross Pay
Taxes
Deductions
Net Pay
Employer Taxes
Contributions
Total Hours
Direct Dep.
Mason, Elizabeth N. 1,180.00 -233.04 0.00 946.96 90.27 121.18 80:00
10
1,180.00 -233.04 0.00 946.96 90.27 121.18 80:00
< Back
15
Finish Later
Create Paychecks

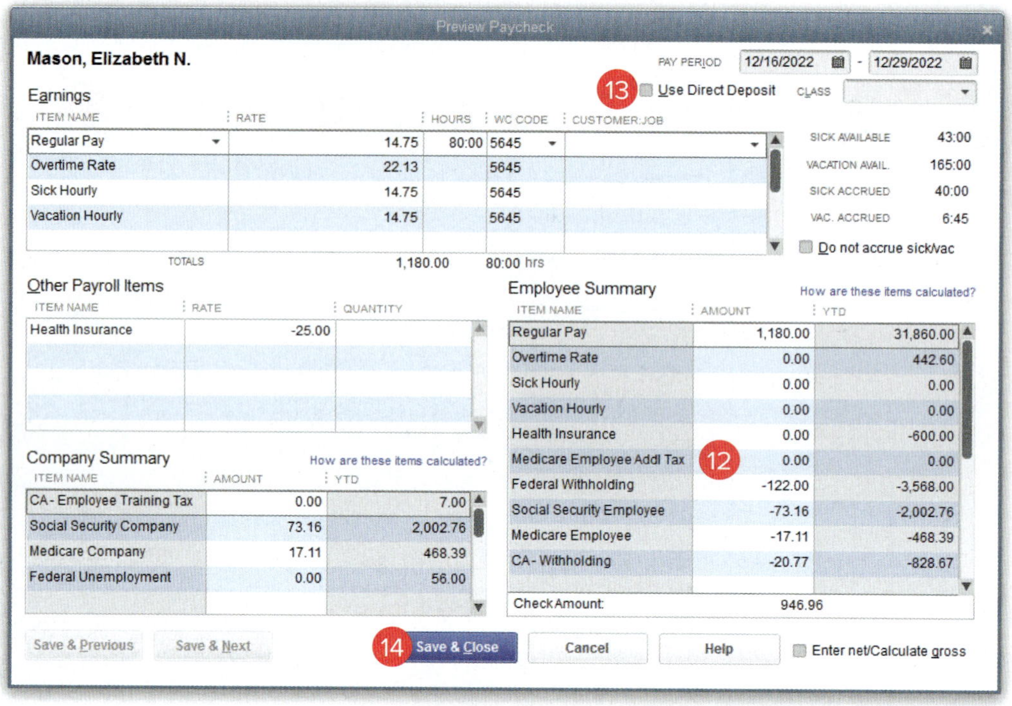

If a message appears about updating QuickBooks before using payroll, update QuickBooks and then proceed. If you are not able to use QuickBooks payroll tax tables, then manually enter amounts shown in the Create Paychecks window.

Section 8.9

PAY PAYROLL LIABILITIES

Payroll liabilities include amounts for:

- Federal income taxes withheld from employee paychecks
- State income taxes withheld from employee paychecks
- FICA (Social Security and Medicare, including both the employee and the employer portions)
- Unemployment taxes

Federal income taxes, state income taxes, and the employee portion of FICA are withheld from the employee, and the company has an obligation (liability) to remit these amounts to the appropriate tax agency. The employer share of FICA and unemployment taxes are payroll taxes the employer owes.

To pay the payroll tax liability:

1. If the Employee Center: Payroll Center window is already displayed, select the **Pay Liabilities** tab. (If the Employee Center: Payroll Center window is not already displayed, select the **Pay Liabilities** icon in the Employees section of the Home Page.)
2. In the Pay Taxes & Other Liabilities section of the Employee Center: Payroll Center window, you can view the upcoming scheduled payments for payroll liabilities. If any payments were due, you would select the payroll liabilities to pay, then click View/Pay. In the Due Date column, you can see that no payments are currently due for Rock Castle Construction.
3. Leave open the Employee Center: Payroll Center window

We will process payroll liability payments in the chapter exercises.

Section 8.10

FILE PAYROLL TAX FORMS

Notice that the third section of the Payroll Center is File Forms. Basically, payroll forms summarize the amount of payroll withholdings that have been collected and remitted. Payroll tax forms include:

- **Federal Form 940: Employer's Annual Federal Unemployment (FUTA) Tax Return.** This form summarizes the amount of unemployment tax paid and due by the employer.
- **Federal Form 941: Employer's Quarterly Federal Tax Return.** Filed with the IRS, this form summarizes the amount of federal income tax, Social Security, and Medicare withheld from employee paychecks for the quarter.
- **Federal Form 944: Employer's Annual Federal Tax Return.** Filed with the IRS, this form summarizes the amount of federal income tax, Social Security, and Medicare withheld from employee paychecks for the year. Form 944 is used by very small employers instead of filing Form 941 each quarter.
- **Form W-2: Wage and Tax Statement.** Before the end of January, an employer must provide W-2s to employees that summarize amounts paid for salaries, wages, and withholdings for the year.
- **Form W-3: Transmittal of Wage and Tax Statements.** Filed with the Social Security Administration, this form is a summary of all an employer's W-2 forms.

Close the Employee Center: Payroll Center window.
We will process payroll tax forms in the chapter exercises.

Section 8.11

TRANSFER TIME TO SALES INVOICES

Billable time can be transferred to a specific customer's invoice. This is shown in the Home Page by an arrow going from the Enter Time icon to the Create Invoices icon.

If we are using tracked time to bill customers, then the tasks are performed in the following order:

1. **Enter Time.** Time that is tracked by QuickBooks can be used to process payroll and bill customers. Enter time worked by employees, designating billable time to the specific customer and job.
2. **Transfer Time to Sales Invoices.** Record tracked time on an invoice for the appropriate customer and job.
3. **Pay Employees.** Select employees to pay and create their paychecks.
4. **Pay Payroll Liabilities.** Pay payroll tax liabilities due governmental agencies.
5. **Process Payroll Forms.** Process payroll forms that must be submitted to governmental agencies.

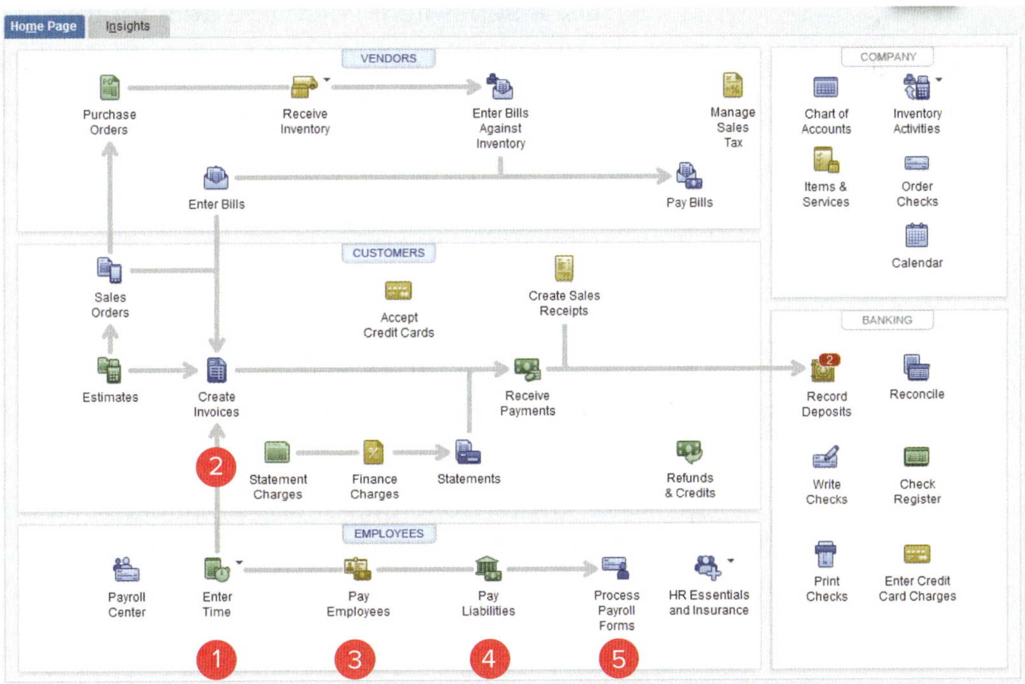

First, we must enter time worked, then open the Create Invoices window for the customer, and select the time billable to that customer. For the Teschner sun room job, we have already entered Elizabeth Mason's time.

To transfer billable time to the Teschner invoice:

1. Open the Create Invoices window by clicking the **Create Invoices** icon in the Customers section of the Home Page
2. From the Create Invoices window, select the customer job to be billed. In this instance, select Customer: Job: **Teschner, Anton: Sun Room**
3. If the following Billable Time/Costs window appears, select: **Select the outstanding billable time and costs to add to this invoice?**
4. Click **OK**
5. When the Choose Billable Time and Costs window appears, click the **Time** tab. Notice that items, expenses, and mileage can also be tracked and billed to specific customer jobs.
6. Click the **Select All** button to select all the billable times listed for the Teschner sun room job
7. We can transfer time to an invoice in three different ways:
    1. Combine all the selected times and costs into one entry on the invoice
    2. List a subtotal for each service item on the invoice
    3. List a separate invoice line item for each activity you check

    In this instance, we will list a separate invoice line item for each activity we check, so **uncheck Print selected time and costs as one invoice item** in the lower left corner of the Choose Billable Time and Costs window.
8. Click the **Options** button
9. Select **Enter a separate line on the invoice for each activity** on the Options for Transferring Billable Time window
10. Select **Transfer item descriptions**
11. Click **OK** to close the Options for Transferring Billable Time window
12. Click **OK** to close the Choose Billable Time and Costs window and add the labor cost to the Teschner invoice
13. Select Template: **Rock Castle Invoice**

14 Select Invoice Date: **12/27/2022**

15 Select **Save** and leave the Create Invoices window open

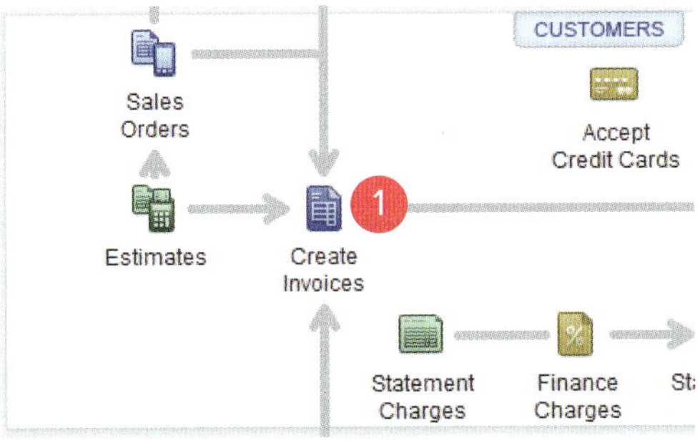

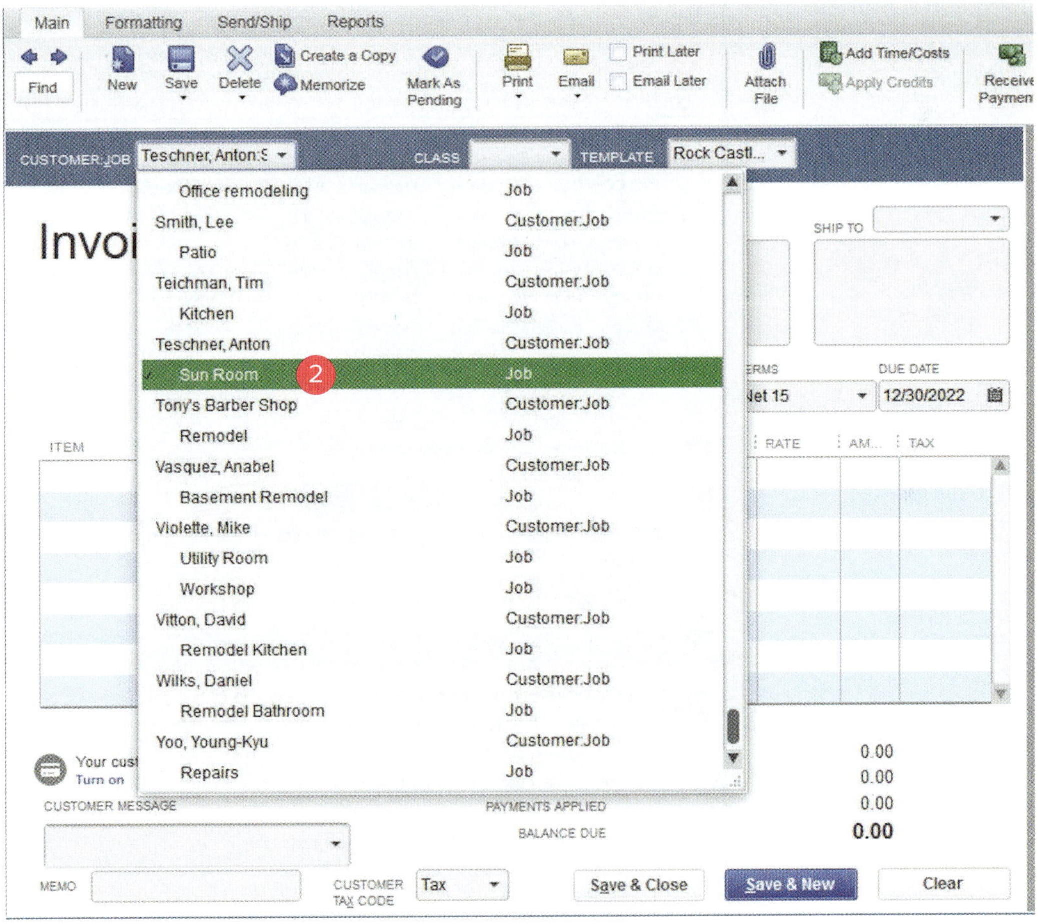

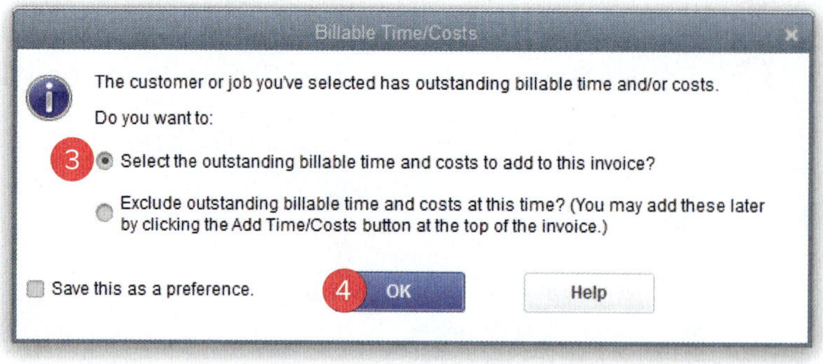
Billable Time/Costs
The customer or job you've selected has outstanding billable time and/or costs.
Do you want to:
3
Select the outstanding billable time and costs to add to this invoice?
Exclude outstanding billable time and costs at this time? (You may add these later by clicking the Add Time/Costs button at the top of the invoice.)
Save this as a preference.
4
OK
Help

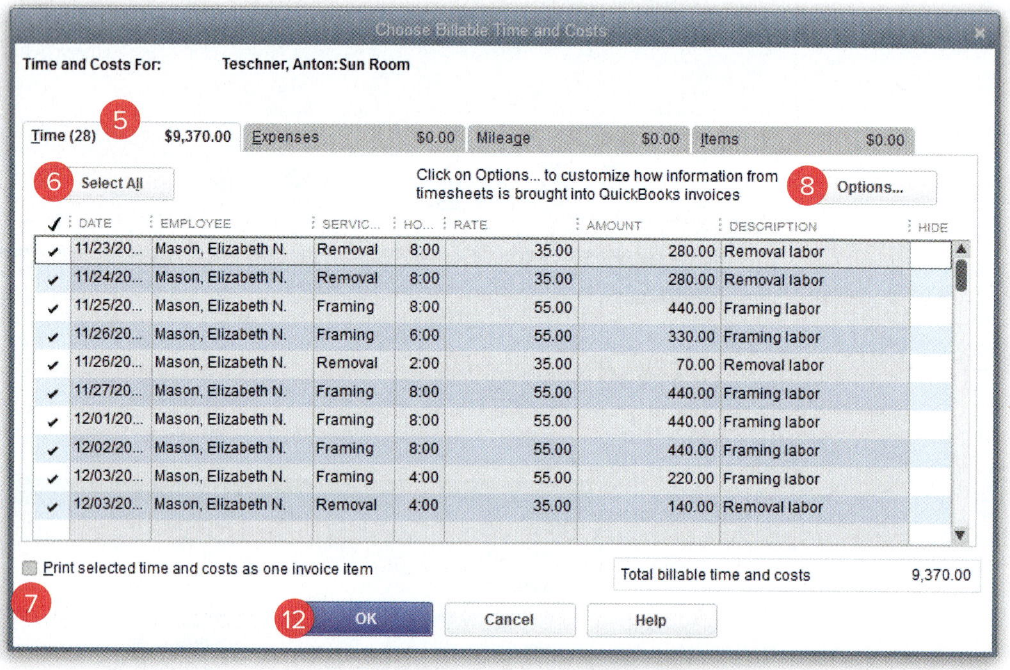
Choose Billable Time and Costs
Time and Costs For: Teschner, Anton:Sun Room
5
Time (28) $9,370.00
Expenses $0.00
Mileage $0.00
Items $0.00
6
Select All
Click on Options... to customize how information from timesheets is brought into QuickBooks invoices
8
Options...
DATE EMPLOYEE SERVIC... HO... RATE AMOUNT DESCRIPTION HIDE
11/23/20... Mason, Elizabeth N. Removal 8:00 35.00 280.00 Removal labor
11/24/20... Mason, Elizabeth N. Removal 8:00 35.00 280.00 Removal labor
11/25/20... Mason, Elizabeth N. Framing 8:00 55.00 440.00 Framing labor
11/26/20... Mason, Elizabeth N. Framing 6:00 55.00 330.00 Framing labor
11/26/20... Mason, Elizabeth N. Removal 2:00 35.00 70.00 Removal labor
11/27/20... Mason, Elizabeth N. Framing 8:00 55.00 440.00 Framing labor
12/01/20... Mason, Elizabeth N. Framing 8:00 55.00 440.00 Framing labor
12/02/20... Mason, Elizabeth N. Framing 8:00 55.00 440.00 Framing labor
12/03/20... Mason, Elizabeth N. Framing 4:00 55.00 220.00 Framing labor
12/03/20... Mason, Elizabeth N. Removal 4:00 35.00 140.00 Removal labor
Print selected time and costs as one invoice item
7
Total billable time and costs 9,370.00
12
OK
Cancel
Help

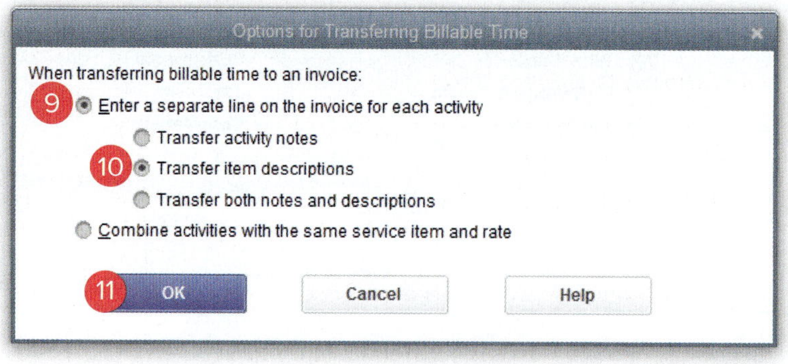
Options for Transferring Billable Time
When transferring billable time to an invoice:
9
Enter a separate line on the invoice for each activity
Transfer activity notes
10
Transfer item descriptions
Transfer both notes and descriptions
Combine activities with the same service item and rate
11
OK
Cancel
Help

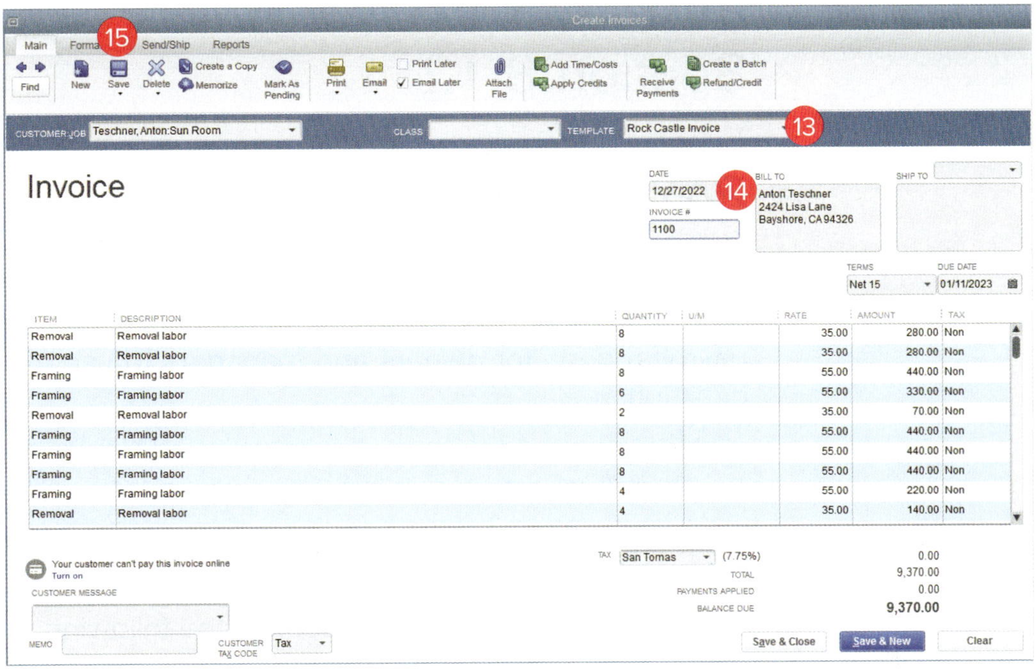

C8.11.1 Invoice Journal Entry. To view the journal entry that QuickBooks created behind the screen for the invoice entered and saved using the Create Invoices onscreen form, complete the following steps.

1. From the Create Invoices onscreen form, select the **Reports** tab
2. Select the **Transaction Journal** icon
3. Export the Transaction Journal report to **Excel** or **print** the report
4. **Close** the Transaction Journal window

If you had not entered the billable time when you opened the invoice, you can click the Add Time/Costs button to add billable time later.

Notice that items, expenses, and mileage can also be tracked and billed to specific customer jobs.

Stop the Stopwatch now by clicking the Stop button and then clicking Clear. Close the Stopwatch window.

Section 8.12

PAYROLL REPORTS

In addition to providing assistance with filing payroll tax forms with federal, state, and local governmental agencies, QuickBooks also provides payroll reports for owners and managers to use to answer the following questions:

- How much did we pay our employees and pay in payroll taxes? (Payroll reports)
- How much time did we spend classified by employee and job? (Project reports)

Payroll reports can be accessed in the following ways:

1. **Employee Center.** (Select Employees (Navigation Bar) > Reports for this Employee.)
2. **Report Center.** (Select Reports (Navigation Bar) > Employees & Payroll.)
3. **Reports Menu.** (Select Reports Menu > Employees & Payroll.)

PAYROLL REPORTS: HOW MUCH DID WE PAY FOR PAYROLL?

The payroll reports list the amounts paid to employees and the amounts paid in payroll taxes.

C8.12.1 Payroll Summary Report. To print the Payroll Summary report:

1. Select **Reports** in the Navigation Bar
2. In Grid view, select **Employees & Payroll**
3. Select **Payroll Summary**
4. Select Dates: **This Month** From: **12/01/2022** To: **12/31/2022**
5. Select **Run**
6. Export to **Excel** or **print** the report
7. **Close** the Payroll Summary Report window

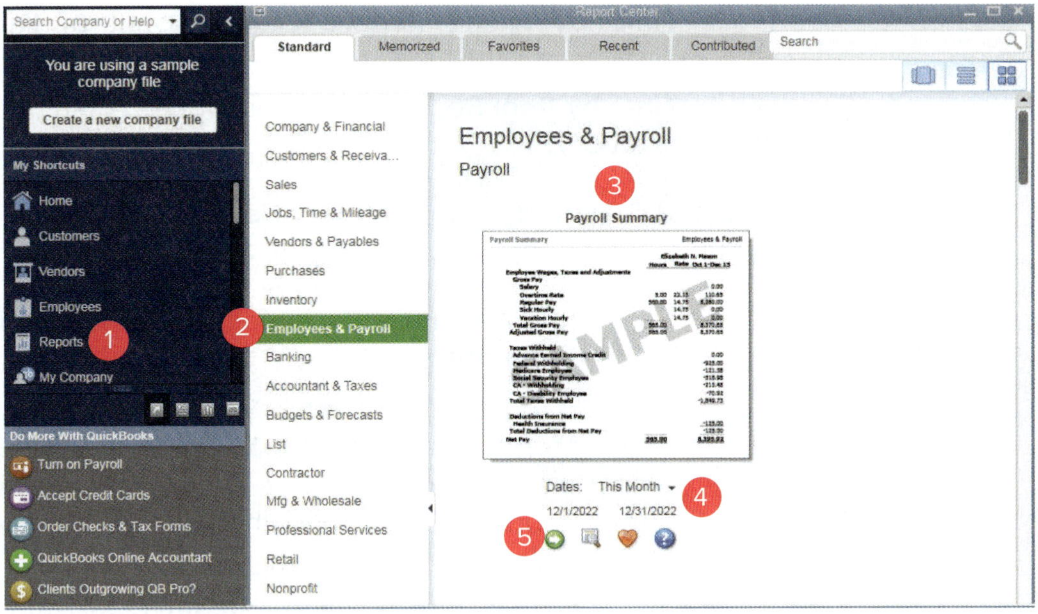

C8.12.2 Payroll Transaction Detail Report. The Payroll Transaction Detail report lists details about payroll transactions for the period and provides summary payroll totals. This report can be used if preparing payroll liability forms manually. To print the Payroll Transaction Detail report that provides detail about withholdings and deductions from employee paychecks:

1. Select **Reports** in the Navigation Bar
2. In Grid view, select **Employees & Payroll**
3. Select **Payroll Transaction Detail**
4. Select Dates: **This Month** From: **12/01/2022** To: **12/31/2022**
5. Select **Run**
6. Export to **Excel** or **print** the report
7. **Close** the Payroll Transaction Detail Report window

PROJECT REPORTS: HOW MUCH TIME DID WE USE?

Four different project reports are available in QuickBooks:

1. **Time by Job Summary Report.** Lists time spent on each job.
2. **Time by Job Detail Report.** Lists time by category spent on each job.

3. **Time by Name Report.** Lists amount of time worked by each employee.
4. **Time by Item Report.** Lists time worked on a particular job by service category.

C8.12.3 Time By Job Summary Report. To print the Time by Job Summary report:

1. From the Report Center, select: **Jobs, Time & Mileage > Time by Job Summary**
2. Export to **Excel** or **print** the Time by Job Summary report for **This Month** From: **12/01/2022** To: **12/31/2022.** (Note that the onscreen QuickBooks Time by Job Summary report indicates total hours is 358:00, but when exported to Excel total hours is 357:59.)
3. **Highlight** the job requiring the most time for December 2022

> **To create a report detailing time spent on a specific job:** 1. Report Center 2. Jobs, Time & Mileage 3. Time by Job Detail 4. Filter for Customer & Job

Section 8.13

BACK UP QUICKBOOKS FILES

BACK UP QBB

Save a backup of your Chapter 8 file [using the file name: **YourName Chapter 8 Backup.QBB.**

QBW WORKFLOW

If you are using the Workflow approach, leave your .QBW file open and proceed directly to Exercise 8.1.

QBB RESTORE

If you are using the Restore approach and ending your computer session now, close your QBW file and exit QuickBooks. When you restart, you will restore your backup file to complete Exercise 8.1.

Section 8.14

ACCOUNTING ESSENTIALS

Payroll Liabilities and Payroll Taxes

Accounting Essentials summarize important foundational accounting knowledge that may be useful when using QuickBooks

What are payroll liabilities?

- Payroll liabilities include two types of amounts:
  1. Amounts withheld from employee paychecks that must be paid to third parties
  2. Payroll tax expenses owed by the business
- Payroll liabilities include:
  - Federal income taxes withheld from employee paychecks
  - State income taxes withheld from employee paychecks
  - FICA (Social Security and Medicare, including both the
  - employee and the employer portions)
  - Unemployment taxes
- Federal income taxes, state income taxes, and the employee portion of FICA are withheld from the employee, and the company has an obligation (liability) to remit these amounts to the appropriate tax agency. The employer share of FICA and unemployment taxes are payroll taxes the employer owes.

Payroll Liabilities (Federal)	Withheld from Employee Pay	Payroll Tax Expense Owed by Business	Reported on Tax Form
Federal Income Taxes	X		941 Quarterly 944 Annual
FICA (SS + MEDICARE)	X	X	941 Quarterly 944 Annually
Federal Unemployment Tax		X	940 Annual

What are payroll tax forms?

- Basically, payroll forms summarize the amount of payroll withholdings that have been collected and remitted.
- Payroll tax forms include:
    - Federal Form 940: Employer's Annual Federal Unemployment (FUTA) Tax Return. This form summarizes the amount of unemployment tax paid and due by the employer.
    - Federal Form 941: Employer's Quarterly Federal Tax Return. Filed with the IRS, this form summarizes the amount of federal income tax, Social Security, and Medicare withheld from employee paychecks for the quarter.
    - Federal Form 944: Employer's Annual Federal Tax Return. Filed with the IRS, this form summarizes the amount of federal income tax, Social Security, and Medicare withheld from employee paychecks for the year. Form 944 is used by very small employers instead of filing Form 941 each quarter.
    - Form W-2: Wage and Tax Statement. Before the end of January, an employer must provide W-2s to employees that summarize amounts paid for salaries, wages, and withholdings for the year.
    - Form W-3: Transmittal of Wage and Tax Statements. Filed with the Social Security Administration, this form is a summary of all an employer's W-2 forms.

www.my-quickbooks.com

Go to **www.My-QuickBooks.com** to view additional QuickBooks resources including:

- **Excel Report Templates** to organize QuickBooks reports exported to Excel
- ***Computer Accounting with QuickBooks* updates,** sometimes required when there is a software update that affects the text
- **QuickBooks Video links**
- **QuickBooks Help and Support links**
- **Other QuickBooks Resources** to make learning QuickBooks easier and more effective
- **QuickBooks Issue Resolution** offers a guided approach to troubleshooting QuickBooks

> **Troubleshooting QuickBooks and Correcting Errors** are crucial QuickBooks skill to acquire. See www.My-QuickBooks.com > QB Issue Resolution for Troubleshooting QuickBooks tips. See Chapter 17, Quick Review Guide, for tips on Correcting Errors.

EXERCISE 8.1: Track Time and Print Paychecks

BACKSTORY

When sorting through the payroll documents that Mr. Castle gave you, you find the following unentered timesheets for Dan Miller and Gregg Schneider.

Timesheet

Dan Miller	Salary	Dec 16	Dec 19	Dec 20	Dec 21	Dec 22
Cook: 2nd Story	Installation	8				4
Pretell: 75 Sunset	Framing		8	8	7	4

Dan Miller	Salary	Dec 23	Dec 26	Dec 27	Dec 28	Dec 29
Pretell: 75 Sunset	Framing	8	8	8	8	3
Pretell: 75 Sunset	Installation					5

Timesheet

Gregg Schneider	Salary	Dec 16	Dec 19	Dec 20	Dec 21	Dec 22
Cook: 2nd Story	Installation	6	6		2	
Pretell: 75 Sunset	Framing		2	8	6	8

Gregg Schneider	Salary	Dec 23	Dec 26	Dec 27	Dec 28	Dec 29
Pretell: 75 Sunset	Framing	8	8	8	8	
Pretell: 75 Sunset	Installation					8

E8.1.1 QuickBooks File

If you will be using the same computer and the same Chapter 8.QBW file:

1. If your Chapter 8.QBW file is not already open, open it by selecting **File > Open Previous Company.** Select your **Chapter 8.QBW file.** If a QuickBooks Information window appears with a message about the sample company file, click **OK.**
2. Add **YourName Exercise 8.1** to the company name by selecting **Company Menu > My Company.**

> **If you are not using the same computer that you used for Chapter 8,** you will need to restore your Chapter 8 Backup.QBB file using the instructions in Appendix B: Back Up & Restore QuickBooks Files. After restoring, add YourName Exercise 8.1 to the company name.

E8.1.2 Enter Time

1. Enter the hours employee **Dan T. Miller** worked using QuickBooks weekly timesheet
2. Enter the hours employee **Gregg O. Schneider** worked using QuickBooks weekly timesheet

E8.1.3 Time by Name Report

1. From the Navigation Bar, select **Reports > Jobs, Time & Mileage > Time by Name**
2. Select Dates: **12/16/2022 To 12/29/2022**
3. Select **Run**
4. Export the report to **Excel** or **print** the Time by Name report

E8.1.4 Back Up Exercise 8.1

Save a backup of your Exercise file using the file name: YourName Exercise 8.1 Backup.QBB. See *Appendix B: Back Up & Restore QuickBooks Files* for instructions.

EXERCISE 8.2: Payroll Liabilities and Forms

BACKSTORY

"Payroll tax forms always give me a headache," Mr. Castle rubs his temples, muttering as he rushes past your cubicle. *"You can take care of those this year, can't you?"* he shouts over your cubicle wall.

You nod and reply confidently, *"Consider it done, Mr. Castle,"* to the back of his head as he rushes to his next appointment.

E8.2.1 QuickBooks File

If you will be using the same computer and the same QBW file:

1. Select your **QBW file.**
2. Add **YourName Exercise 8.2** to the company name by selecting **Company Menu** > **My Company.**

If you are not using the same computer that you used for Chapter 8 and Exercise 8.1, you will need to restore your latest prior Backup.QBB file using the instructions in Appendix B: Back Up & Restore QuickBooks files. After restoring, add YourName Exercise 8.2 to the company name.

E8.2.2 Pay Payroll Liabilities

To pay the payroll tax liability related to federal Forms 941/944:

1. Select the **Pay Liabilities** icon in the Employees section of the Home Page
2. In the Employee Center: Payroll Center window, select **Pay Liabilities** tab
3. In the Other Activities section, select **Create Custom Payments**
4. Select Dates: **12/01/2022 Through: 12/31/2022**
5. Select **OK**
6. In the Pay Liabilities window, select **To be printed**
7. Select Bank Account: **Checking**
8. Select Check Date: **12/15/2022**
9. Select: **Review liability check to enter expenses/penalties**

10. Select: **All Payroll Items except Health Insurance**
11. Select **Payroll Liabilities Report.** Export the report to **Excel.** Close the Payroll Liabilities report window.
12. Normally, we could select Create on the Pay Liabilities window to create the checks to pay the payroll liabilities. In this case, select **Cancel** on the Pay Liabilities window.
13. **Close** the Employee Center: Payroll Center window

E8.2.3 Payroll Transactions by Payee Report

1. From the Report Center, export to **Excel** or **print** the Payroll Transactions by Payee report for This Calendar Year **From: 01/01/2022 To: 12/31/2022**

E8.2.4 Back Up Exercise 8.2

Save a backup of your Exercise file using the file name: YourName Exercise 8.2 Backup.QBB. See *Appendix B: Back Up & Restore QuickBooks Files* for instructions.

EXERCISE 8.3: Transfer Time to Sales Invoices

BACKSTORY

"By the way, did I mention that I need a current sales invoice for the Jacobsen Kitchen job? Make sure all labor charges have been posted to the invoice," Mr. Castle shouts over the top of your cubicle as he rushes past.

E8.3.1 QuickBooks File

If you will be using the same computer and the same QBW file:

1. Select your **QBW file.**
2. Add **YourName Exercise 8.3** to the company name by selecting **Company Menu > My Company.**

If you are not using the same computer that you used for Chapter 8, Exercise 8.1 and Exercise 8.2, you will need to restore your latest prior Backup.QBB file using the instructions in Appendix B: Back Up & Restore QuickBooks files. After restoring, add YourName Exercise 8.3 to the company name.

E8.3.2 Transfer Time to Sales Invoice

Transfer time worked to the related Jacobsen Kitchen sales invoice as follows.

1. From the Customers section of the Home Page, click the **Create Invoices** icon
2. Transfer billable time and items to a sales invoice dated **12/22/2022** for the **Jacobsen Kitchen** job
3. From the Choose Billable Time and Costs window, click the **Time** tab, then click the **Select All** button to transfer employee time worked to the invoice. Select **Options button > Combine activities with the same service item and rate.**
4. **Save** the invoice
5. From the Create Invoices onscreen form, select the **Reports** tab
6. Select the **Transaction Journal** icon
7. Export the Transaction Journal report to **Excel** or **print** the report
8. **Close** the Transaction Journal window

E8.3.3 Time by Job Detail Report

The Time by Job Detail report provides information about time worked on each job. This report is useful for tracking that the time worked on a job is going as planned.

1. Export to **Excel** or **print** the Time by Job Detail report for 2022
2. **Highlight** any items on the report that are billable to specific jobs, yet still unbilled

E8.3.4 Back Up Exercise 8.3

Save a backup of your Exercise file using the file name: YourName Exercise 8.3 Backup.QBB. See *Appendix B: Back Up & Restore QuickBooks Files* for instructions.

PROJECT 8.1

Larry's Landscaping

As an accounting consultant for Larry's Landscaping complete the following to enter employees and payroll transactions for the company.

QB SatNav

The objective of Project 8.1 is to facilitate your mastery of QuickBooks Desktop. As shown in the following QB SatNav, Project 8.1 focuses on QuickBooks transactions related to employees and payroll.

QB SatNav

1 QB SETTINGS

- Company Settings
- Chart of Accounts

2 QB TRANSACTIONS

> Money in Money out >

- Banking
- Customers & Sales
- Vendors & Expenses
- **Employees & Payroll**

3 QB REPORTS

- Reports

P8.1.1 QuickBooks File

1. Use either your QuickBooks Company file (QBW) or restore the backup file (QBB) that you completed for Project 7.1. (If you have issues with your QuickBooks file, contact your instructor.)
2. Update the Company Name to: **YourName Project 8.1 Larry's Landscaping**

P8.1.2 Prepare Paychecks

1. Prepare and create (but do not print) the following paychecks for Larry's Landscaping. (Select the Pay Employees icon > Start Unscheduled Payroll.)

Pay Period Ends	**12/29/2022**
Check Date	**12/29/2022**
Employee	**Duncan Fisher**
Paycheck Amount	**$1,160.75**
Pay Period Ends	**12/29/2022**
Check Date	**12/29/2022**
Employee	**Jenny Miller**
Paycheck Amount	**$1,281.22**
Pay Period Ends	**12/29/2022**
Check Date	**12/29/2022**
Employee	**Shane Hamby**
Paycheck Amount	**$1,672.60**

(Note that paycheck amounts may vary slightly from amounts shown here due to QuickBooks Payroll Service updates for withholdings.)

P8.1.3 Reports

1. Export to **Excel** the Journal report for **December 29, 2022**
2. Export to **Excel** the Payroll Summary report for Larry's Landscaping for **December 16 - 29, 2022**

3. Export to **Excel** the Payroll Transaction Detail report for **December 16 - 29, 2022**
4. Export to **Excel** the Payroll Transactions by Payee report for **December 16 - 29, 2022**

P8.1.4 Back Up Project 8.1

Save a backup of your Project file using the file name: YourName Project 8.1 Backup.QBB. See *Appendix B: Back Up & Restore QuickBooks Files* for instructions.

Chapter 9

QuickBooks Adjustments

BACKSTORY

"Looks like we are going to need to bring our records up to date before preparing reports. So you are going to need to get up to speed on making adjusting entries, since no one else in the company knows how to make adjustments." Mr. Castle informs you early one morning.

"Ok, Mr. Castle, I'll take care of it," you reply with a smile. You had anticipated this was coming so you had started working on learning adjusting entries even before Mr. Castle mentioned it.

Section 9.1

QuickBooks SatNav

QuickBooks SatNav is your satellite navigation for QuickBooks, assisting you in navigating QuickBooks

QuickBooks SatNav divides QuickBooks into three processes:

1. **QuickBooks Settings.** This includes Company Settings when setting up a new QuickBooks company and the Company Chart of Accounts.
2. **QuickBooks Transactions.** This includes recording transactions in QuickBooks. Transaction types can be categorized as Banking, Customers and Sales, Vendors and Expenses, and Employees and Payroll. In basic terms, recording transactions involves recording money in and money out.
3. **QuickBooks Reports.** QuickBooks reports are the output of the system, such as commonly used financial statements of Balance Sheet, Income Statement, and Statement of Cash Flows.

Chapter 9 focuses on make adjustments necessary before preparing reports as shown in the following QuickBooks SatNav.

QB SatNav

1 QB SETTINGS CHAPTERS 1 2 11 12 13 14

- Company Settings
- Chart of Accounts

2 QB TRANSACTIONS CHAPTERS 3 4 5 6 7 8 11 12 13 14

> Money in Money out >

- Banking
- Customers & Sales
- Vendors & Expenses
- Employees & Payroll

3 QB REPORTS CHAPTERS 9 10 11 12 13 14

- Reports

Section 9.2

START QUICKBOOKS AND OPEN QUICKBOOKS COMPANY

START QUICKBOOKS

To start QuickBooks software, click the **QuickBooks** icon on your desktop. If a QuickBooks icon does not appear on your desktop, from Microsoft® Windows® click **Start** button > **Programs** > **QuickBooks** > **QuickBooks Premier Accountant Edition.**

> **QuickBooks Accountant** includes all the features of QuickBooks Pro plus features for client services. If you use QuickBooks Pro, your screens may appear slightly different than those appearing in this text.

RESTORE QBB STARTER FILE

Restore the QBB Starter file for this chapter as follows.

1. Select **File** > **Restore**
2. Using the directions in *Appendix B: Back Up & Restore QuickBooks Files,* restore the **CHAPTER 9 STARTER.QBB**
3. After restoring, add **YourName Chapter 9** to the company name by selecting **Company Menu** > **My Company**

> **! QuickBooks Desktop (QBDT)** Data Files are compressed backup files that can be restored and used. To use Starter Files, the compressed file must be restored following the instructions here. Since it is a compressed file, you cannot open and use the QuickBooks data files by simply clicking on the file. Instead you must follow the instructions here to unzip and restore the data file before using it.

Section 9.3

ACCOUNTING CYCLE

The accounting cycle is a series of accounting activities that a business performs each accounting period.

> **An accounting period** can be one month, one quarter, or one year.

The accounting cycle usually consists of the following steps.

- **Chart of Accounts.** The Chart of Accounts is a list of all accounts used to accumulate information about assets, liabilities, owners' equity, revenues, and expenses. Create a Chart of Accounts when the business is established and modify the Chart of Accounts as needed over time.
- **Transactions.** During the accounting period, record transactions with customers, vendors, employees, and owners.
- **Trial Balance.** A Trial Balance lists each account and the account balance at the end of the accounting period. Prepare a Trial Balance to verify that the accounting system is in balance—total debits should equal total credits. An unadjusted Trial Balance is a Trial Balance prepared before adjustments.
- **Adjustments.** At the end of the accounting period before preparing financial statements, make any adjustments necessary to bring the accounts up to date. Adjustments are entered in the Journal using debits and credits.
- **Adjusted Trial Balance.** Prepare an Adjusted Trial Balance (a Trial Balance after adjustments) to verify that the accounting system still balances. If additional account detail is required, print the general ledger (the collection of all the accounts listing the transactions that affected the accounts).
- **Financial Statements.** Prepare financial statements for external users (Profit & Loss, Balance Sheet, and Statement of Cash Flows). Prepare income tax summary reports and management reports.

Section 9.4

TRIAL BALANCE

The Trial Balance is a listing of all of a company's accounts and the ending account balances. The purpose of the Trial Balance is to verify account balances and that the accounting system balances. On a Trial Balance, all debit ending account balances are listed in the debit column and credit ending balances are listed in the credit column. If the accounting system balances, total debits equal total credits.

A Trial Balance is often prepared both before adjustments (Trial Balance) and after adjustments (Adjusted Trial Balance).

C9.4.1 Trial Balance. To view and print the Trial Balance for Rock Castle Construction:

1. Select **Reports** in the Navigation Bar
2. Select **Accountant & Taxes**
3. Select **Trial Balance**
4. Select Date Range: **This Fiscal Quarter** From: **10/01/2022** To: **12/31/2022**
5. Select **Run**
6. Export to **Excel** or **print** the report
7. **Close** the Trial Balance

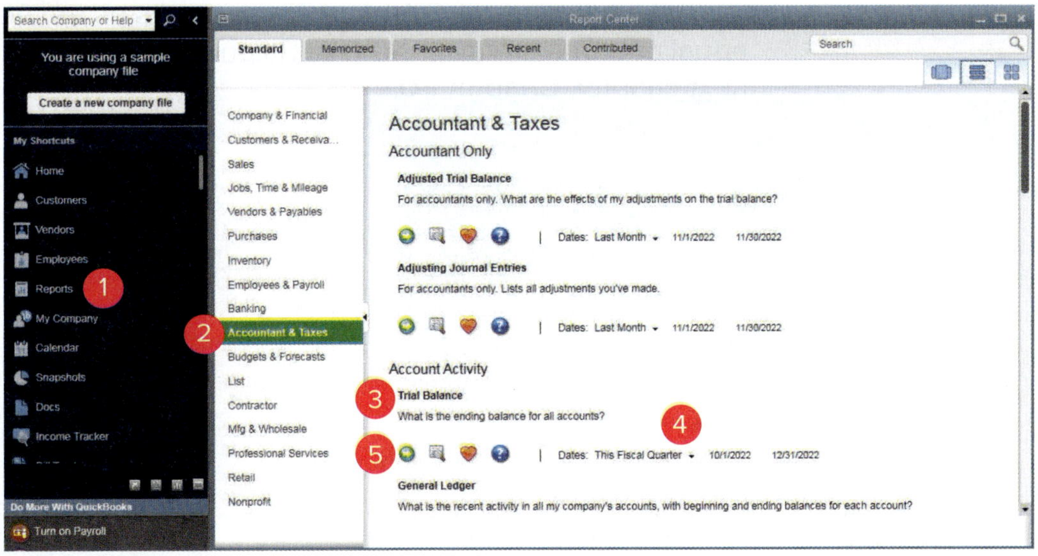

Section 9.5

ADJUSTING ENTRIES

WHY DO WE MAKE ADJUSTING ENTRIES?

Adjusting entries record adjustments necessary to bring the accounts up to date at the end of an accounting period. We want to make adjusting entries before preparing financial reports so the accounts reflected on the reports are up to date.

HOW DO WE MAKE ADJUSTING ENTRIES?

Adjustments are also called Adjusting Entries because the way we enter adjustments is by making entries in the Journal. Adjusting entries are entered in the onscreen QuickBooks Journal using debits and credits.

Some companies use QuickBooks to maintain their financial system throughout the year and then have an accountant prepare the adjusting entries at year end to enter into QuickBooks.

WHEN DO WE MAKE ADJUSTING ENTRIES?

Adjusting entries are dated the last day of the accounting period. Typically, we prepare adjusting entries after we prepare a Trial Balance to verify that our accounts are in balance. The Trial Balance lists all accounts with their debit and credit balances. This permits us to see that our total debits equal our total credits. The Trial Balance is discussed in more detail in the next chapter, Chapter 10.

Section 9.6

USING QUICKBOOKS TO MAKE ADJUSTING ENTRIES

USING THE JOURNAL TO RECORD ADJUSTING ENTRIES

We can use the QuickBooks onscreen Journal to enter adjusting entries. To make adjusting entries:

1. Select the **Accountant Menu**
2. Select **Make General Journal Entries**
3. When the Make General Journal Entries window appears, select Date: **12/31/2022**
4. Enter **Entry No: ADJ2022.1**
5. **Check** the **Adjusting Entry** box
6. On Line 1 select Account to Debit: **60900 Depreciation Expense**
7. Enter the Debit Amount: **50,000.00**
8. On Line 2 select Account to Credit: **17000 Accumulated Depreciation**
9. Enter the Credit Amount if the amount does not appear automatically: **50,000.00**
10. Select the **Save** icon and leave the Make General Journal Entries window open

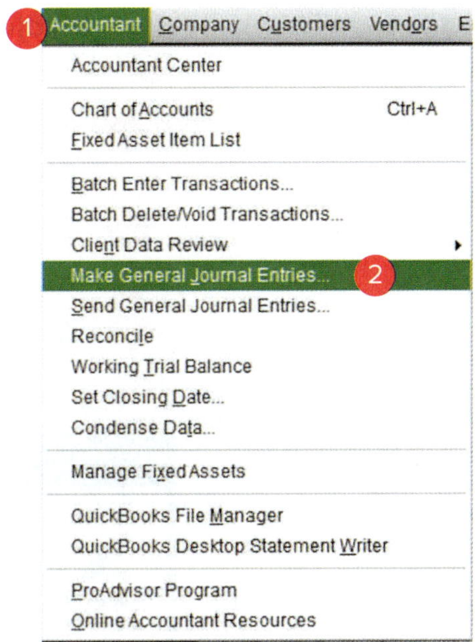

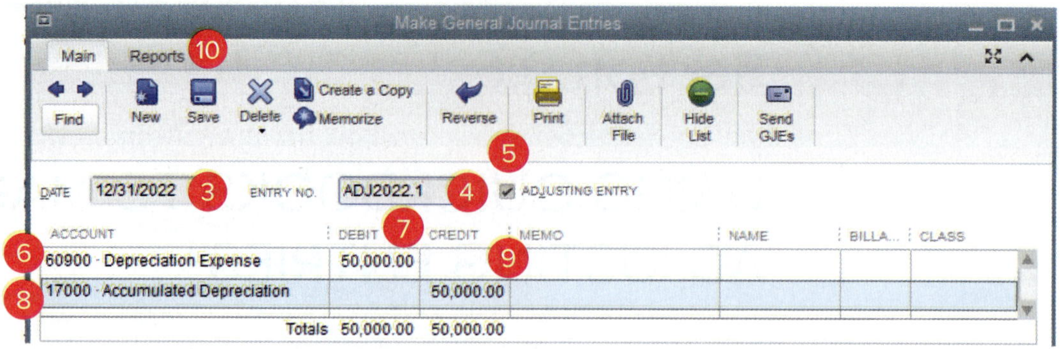

When making journal entries, including adjusting entries, accountants generally list Debits before Credits. Note that QuickBooks may not always list Debits before Credits in journal entries.

VIEW ADJUSTING JOURNAL ENTRIES

To view journal entries we recorded, display the Journal report. The Journal report also contains journal entries for all transactions recorded using onscreen forms, such as sales invoices. QuickBooks automatically converts transactions recorded in onscreen forms into journal entries with debits and credits.

If we are using QuickBooks Accountant Edition, we can view only the adjusting entries as follows by selecting the Adjusting Journal Entries report from the Report Center.

Another way to view the adjusting journal entries is from the Make General Journal Entires window as follows.

C9.6.1 Adjusting Journal Entries. To view the Adjusting Journal Entries report for the adjusting entry for depreciation that we just entered:

1. From the open Make General Journal Entries window, select the **Reports** tab
2. Select **Transaction Journal**
3. Export to **Excel** or print the **Journal**
4. **Close** the Journal window

MEMORIZE ADJUSTING ENTRIES

We can save our adjusting entries as memorized transactions. This saves us time. We will still need to update the amount of the adjustment, if needed.

To save an adjusting entry as a memorized transaction from the journal screen:

1. From the open Make General Journal Entries window, select **Main > Memorize** to save the adjusting entry as a memorized transaction that can be reused
2. Enter Template Name: **Adjusting Entry Depreciation.** (Since the Memorized Transactions are listed alphabetically, we want to name the Template so it automatically sorts in a way that is easy for us to find it.)
3. Select: **Add to my Reminders List** so we will be reminded to use the Memorized Transaction Template to make the adjusting entry.
4. Select How Often: **Annually**
5. Enter Next Date: **12/31/2023**
6. Select **OK**

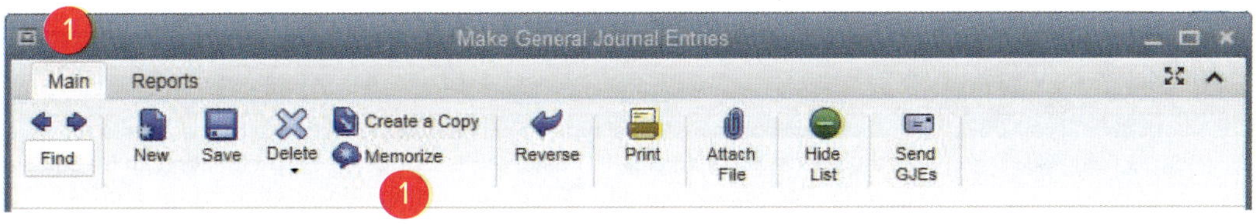

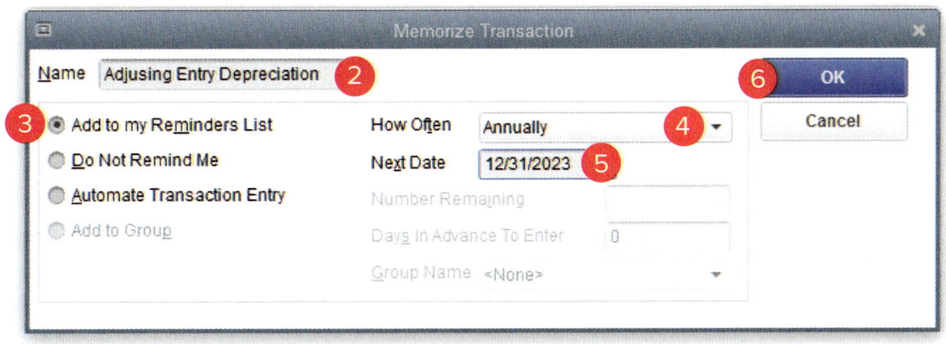

To use the memorized transaction, select Lists Menu > Memorized Transaction List.

Section 9.7

TYPES OF ADJUSTING ENTRIES

If we use the accrual basis of accounting to calculate profits, the following four types of adjusting entries may be necessary.

1. **Prepaid items.** Items that are prepaid, such as prepaid insurance or prepaid rent.
2. **Unearned items.** Items that a customer has paid us for, but we have not provided the product or service.
3. **Accrued expenses.** Expenses that are incurred but not yet paid or recorded.
4. **Accrued revenues.** Revenues that have been earned but not yet collected or recorded.

The accrual basis of accounting attempts to match expenses with the revenue (income) they generate. The cash basis records revenues (income) when cash is received and records expenses when cash is paid. The accrual basis attempts to record revenue (income) in the accounting period when it is earned (the product or service is provided) regardless of when the cash is received. The accrual basis attempts to record expenses in the accounting period it is incurred regardless of when the cash is paid.

Depreciation is a special type of prepaid item involving fixed assets, such as equipment. Depreciation is the allocation of an asset's cost over its useful life. Depreciation can be calculated in a number of different ways. For more information about calculating depreciation for tax purposes, go to www.irs.gov.

Section 9.8

PREPAID ITEMS: RELATED EXPENSE AND ASSET ACCOUNTS

Prepaid items are items that are paid in advance, such as prepaid insurance or prepaid rent. An adjustment may be needed to record the amount of the prepaid item that has not expired at the end of the accounting period. For example, an adjustment may be needed to record the amount of insurance that has not expired as Prepaid Insurance (an asset with future benefit) and the amount of insurance that has expired as Insurance Expense.

Adjusting entries for prepaid items typically affect an Expense account and an Asset account. Examples or related Expense and Asset accounts used for prepaid item adjusting entries are as follows.

Prepaid Items	Expense Account	Asset Account
Prepaid Insurance	Insurance Expense	Prepaid Insurance
Prepaid Rent	Rent Expense	Prepaid Rent
Office Supplies	Office Supplies Expense	Office Supplies

Basically we want to make certain that the amounts in the related Expense account (such as Insurance Expense) and Asset account (Prepaid Insurance) are appropriate.

The adjusting entry is a Journal entry recording the amount that needs to be transferred between the two accounts, an Expense account and an Asset account, to show the appropriate balance in each account.

Whether a debit or credit increases or decreases an account depends upon the type of account.

Account Type	Debit	Credit
Asset	Increase	Decrease
Liabilities	Decrease	Increase
Equity	Decrease	Increase
Revenues (Income)	Decrease	Increase
Expenses	Increase	Decrease

For example, if we need to make an adjusting entry to increase Insurance Expense and decrease Prepaid Insurance for $1,000, we would determine whether to debit or credit the accounts as follows:

Account	Account Type	Increase or Decrease?	Debit or Credit?	Amount
Insurance Expense	Expense	Increase	Debit	$1,000
Prepaid Insurance	Asset	Decrease	Credit	$1,000

An example of an adjusting entry for a prepaid item using the QuickBooks Journal follows.

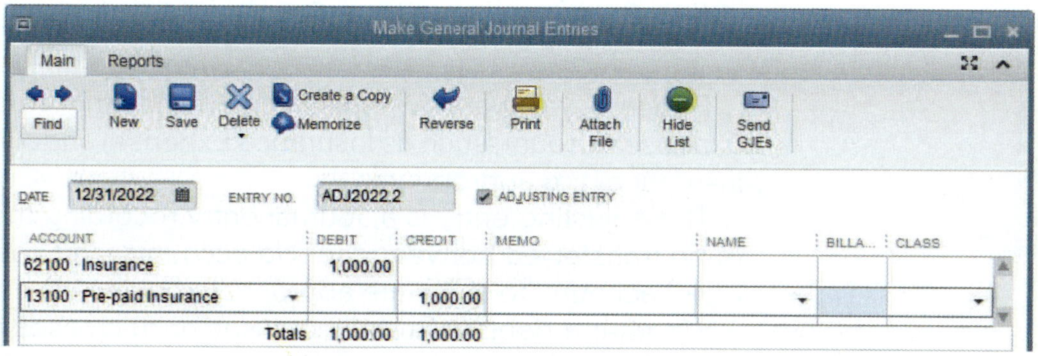

Section 9.9

UNEARNED ITEMS: RELATED REVENUE AND LIABILITY ACCOUNTS

Unearned items consist of revenue that we have not earned. If a customer pays in advance of receiving a service, such as when a customer makes a deposit, our business has an obligation (liability) to either provide the service in the future or return the customer's money. An adjustment may be necessary to bring the revenue account and unearned revenue (liability) account up to date.

Unearned Items	Revenue Account	Liability Account
Unearned Rent Revenue	Rent Revenue	Unearned Revenue
App Subscription	App Subscription Revenue	Unearned App Subscription Revenue

The adjusting entry is a Journal entry recording the amount that needs to be transferred between the two accounts, a Revenue account and a Liability account, to show the appropriate balance in each account.

For example, if we need to make an adjusting entry to increase Rent Revenue and decrease Unearned Revenue for $2,000, we would determine whether to debit or credit the accounts as follows:

Account	Account Type	Increase or Decrease?	Debit or Credit?	Amount
Rent Revenue	Revenue	Increase	Credit	$2,000
Unearned Revenue	Liablity	Decrease	Debit	$2,000

An example of an adjusting entry for unearned revenue using the QuickBooks Journal follows.

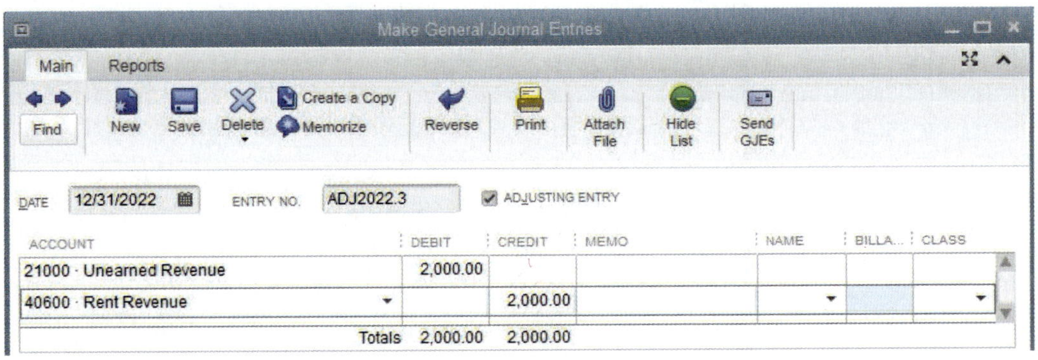

Section 9.10

ACCRUED EXPENSES: RELATED EXPENSE AND LIABILITY ACCOUNTS

Accrued expenses are expenses that are incurred but not yet paid or recorded. Examples of accrued expenses include accrued interest expense (interest expense that has been incurred but not yet paid).

Accrued Expenses	Expense Account	Liability Account
Accrued Interest Incurred	Interest Expense	Interest Payable
Accrued Taxes Payable	Tax Expense	Taxes Payable

The adjusting entry is a Journal entry recording the amount that needs to be transferred between the two accounts, an Expense account and a Liability account, to show the appropriate balance in each account.

If we need to make an adjusting entry to increase Interest Expense and increase Interest Payable for $3,000, we would determine whether to debit or credit the accounts as follows:

Account	Account Type	Increase or Decrease?	Debit or Credit?	Amount
Interest Expense	Expense	Increase	Debit	$3,000
Interest Payable	Liablity	Increase	Credit	$3,000

An example of an adjusting entry for accrued interest expense using the QuickBooks Journal follows.

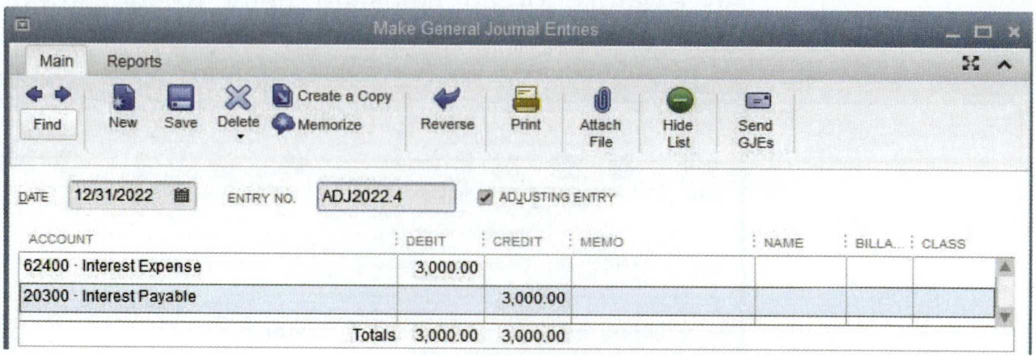

Section 9.11

ACCRUED REVENUES: RELATED REVENUE AND ASSET ACCOUNTS

Accrued revenues are revenues that have been earned but not yet collected or recorded. Examples of accrued revenues include interest revenue that has been earned but not yet collected or recorded.

Accrued Revenues	Revenue Account	Asset Account
Accrued Interest Earned	Interest Revenue	Interest Receivable
Accrued Rent Revenue	Rent Revenue	Rent Receivable

The adjusting entry is a Journal entry recording the amount that needs to be transferred between the two accounts, a Revenue account and an Asset account, to show the appropriate balance in each account.

If we need to make an adjusting entry to increase Interest Revenue and increase Interest Receivable for $4,000, we would determine whether to debit or credit the accounts as follows:

Account	Account Type	Increase or Decrease?	Debit or Credit?	Amount
Interest Revenue	Revenue	Increase	Credit	$4,000
Interest Receivable	Asset	Increase	Debit	$4,000

An example of an adjusting entry for accrued interest revenue using the QuickBooks Journal follows.

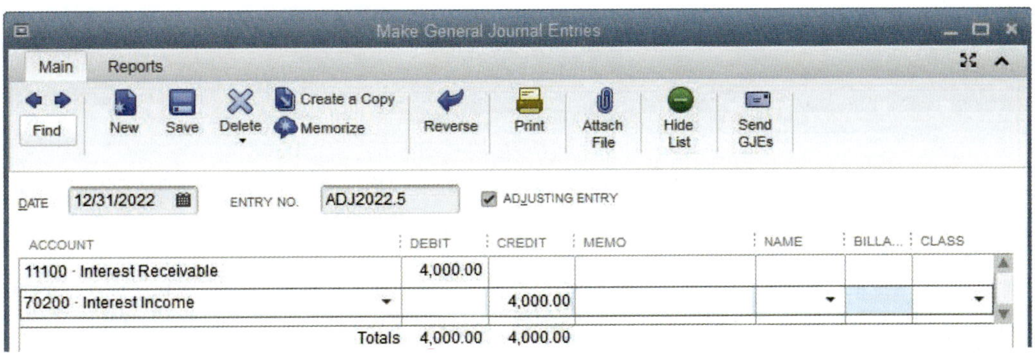

Section 9.12

BACK UP QUICKBOOKS FILES

BACK UP QBB

Save a backup of your Chapter 9 file using the file name: **YourName Chapter 9 Backup.QBB.**

QBW WORKFLOW

If you will be using the same computer to complete Chapter 9 QuickBooks exercises, just as in a business workflow, you can continue to use the same QBW file.

If you are using the QBW approach, leave your .QBW file open and proceed directly to Exercise 9.1.

QBB RESTORE

If you will be switching computers and are ending your computer session now, close your QBW file and exit QuickBooks. When you restart, you will restore your backup file to complete Exercise 9.1.

Section 9.13

ACCOUNTING ESSENTIALS

Accounting Adjustments and Corrections

Accounting Essentials summarize important foundational accounting knowledge that may be useful when using QuickBooks

Why are adjusting entries necessary?

- When the accrual basis of accounting is used, adjusting entries are often necessary to bring the accounts up to date at the end of the accounting period. The accrual basis records revenue (income) when it is earned (when products and services are provided to customers) regardless of when the cash is received from customers. So at year-end there may be revenue that has not been recorded that has been earned, such as interest revenue. The accrual basis records expenses when they are incurred (the benefits have expired) regardless of when the cash is paid. So again, at year-end there may be expenses that have been incurred, but not recorded, such as interest expense.
- The accrual basis is often viewed as a better measure of profit than the cash basis. The cash basis records revenue (income) when the cash is received and records expenses when the cash is paid.

In double-entry accounting, how do we know whether to use a debit or credit for adjusting entries?

- Whether a debit or credit increases or decreases an account depends upon the type of account.

Account Type	Debit	Credit
Assets	Increase	Decrease
Liabilities	Decrease	Increase
Equity	Decrease	Increase
Revenues (Income)	Decrease	Increase
Expenses	Increase	Decrease

What are corrections?

- Corrections, or correcting entries, fix mistakes in the accounting system. Adjusting entries, on the other hand, are not mistakes, but updates that are required to bring accounts to their correct balance as of a certain date.

How do we make a correction using journal entries?

- For example, assume the Cash account should have been debited for $200.00 and the Professional Fees Revenue account credited for $200.00. However, the following incorrect entry was made for $2,000.00 instead of $200.00.

Incorrect Entry	Account	Amount
Debit	Cash	$2,000.00
Credit	Professional Fees Revenue	$2,000.00

- Often the easiest way for us to correct an error is to make two correcting entries in the Journal:

  1. **Eliminate the effect of the incorrect entry by making the opposite journal entry with Correcting Entry 1:**

Correcting Entry 1	Account	Amount
Debit	Professional Fees Revenue	$2,000.00
Credit	Cash	$2,000.00

  2. **After eliminating the effect of the incorrect entry, make the following Correcting Entry 2 that should have been made initially:**

Correcting Entry 2	Account	Amount
Debit	Cash	$200.00
Credit	Professional Fees Revenue	$200.00

How do we correct errors on saved documents, such as invoices or purchase orders?

- Once a document has been saved, we can use one of three approaches to correct the error:
  1. **Display** the document, correct the error, then save the document again.
  2. **Void** the erroneous document, then create a new document. Voiding keeps a record of the document, but changes the amounts to zero.

3. **Delete** the erroneous document, then create a new document. Deleting the document erases the document from our system.

- Typically, options 1 or 2 are preferable because we have a better audit trail showing changes.

www.my-quickbooks.com

Go to www.My-QuickBooks.com to view additional QuickBooks resources including:

- **Excel Report Templates** to organize QuickBooks reports exported to Excel
- ***Computer Accounting with QuickBooks* updates,** sometimes required when there is a software update that affects the text
- **QuickBooks Video links**
- **QuickBooks Help and Support links**
- **Other QuickBooks Resources** to make learning QuickBooks easier and more effective
- **QuickBooks Issue Resolution** offers a guided approach to troubleshooting QuickBooks

Troubleshooting QuickBooks and Correcting Errors are crucial QuickBooks skill to acquire. See www.My-QuickBooks.com > QB Issue Resolution for Troubleshooting QuickBooks tips. See Chapter 17, Quick Review Guide, for tips on Correcting Errors.

EXERCISE 9.1: Adjusting Entry Prepaid Insurance

At December 31 Rock Castle Construction needs to make an adjusting journal entry to record $148.83 of Liability Insurance that has expired during the month of December. Use Entry No. ADJ2022.2. Use the following accounts to make the adjusting entry:

13100	Prepaid Insurance
62120	Liability Insurance Expense

E9.1.1 QuickBooks File

If you will be using the same computer and the same Chapter 9.QBW file:

1. If your Chapter 9.QBW file is not already open, open it by selecting **File > Open Previous Company.** Select your **Chapter 9.QBW**

file. If a QuickBooks Information window appears with a message about the sample company file, click **OK.**

2. Add **YourName Exercise 9.1** to the company name by selecting **Company Menu > My Company.**

> **If you are not using the same computer that you used for Chapter 9,** you will need to restore your Chapter 9 Backup.QBB file using the instructions in Appendix B: Back Up & Restore QuickBooks Files. After restoring, add YourName Exercise 9.1 to the company name.

E9.1.2 Prepaid Insurance Adjustment

Complete the following table.

Account	Account Type	Increase or Decrease?	Debit or Credit?	Amount
Insurance Expense	Expense	______1______	______2______	$______3______
Prepaid Insurance	Asset	______4______	______5______	$______6______

1. ______
2. ______
3. ______
4. ______
5. ______
6. ______

E9.1.3 Plan Adjusting Journal Entry

Complete the following.

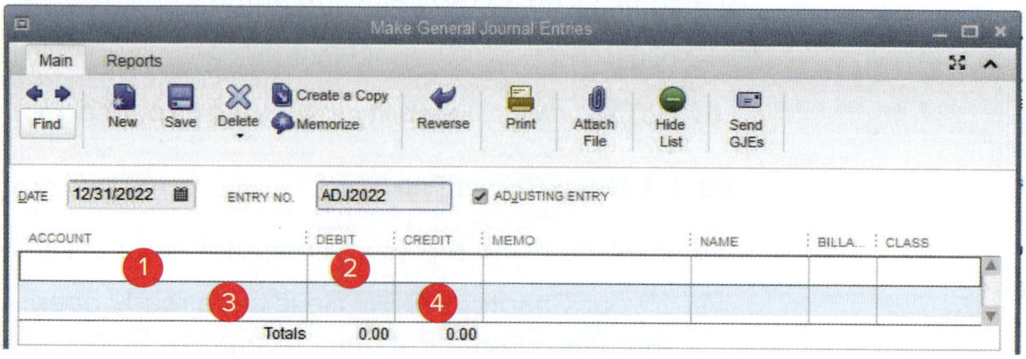

1. ______
2. ______
3. ______
4. ______

E9.1.4 Enter Adjusting Journal Entry

Next, enter the adjusting journal entry into the QuickBooks Journal.

1. Select **Accountant Menu** > **Make General Journal Entries**
2. Enter the adjusting journal entry using the information you prepared in the prior activity
3. From the open Make General Journal Entries window, select the **Reports tab** > **Transaction Journal**
4. Export to **Excel** or print the **Journal**

E9.1.5 Back Up Exercise 9.1

Save a backup of your Exercise file using the file name: YourName Exercise 9.1 Backup.QBB. See *Appendix B: Back Up & Restore QuickBooks Files* for instructions.

EXERCISE 9.2: Adjusting Entry Unearned Revenue

On December 1, 2022 Rock Castle Construction received $3,000 for unused storage space it leased to a subcontractor. The entire amount was recorded in the Checking account and as unearned rental revenue. The $3,000 payment was for three months of rent, beginning December 1, 2022. So an adjusting entry is needed to bring accounts up to date at December 31 and record the amount of rent revenue that has been earned as of December 31.

Use Entry No. ADJ2022.3. Use the following accounts to make the adjusting entry:

21000	Unearned Revenue
40600	Rent Revenue

E9.2.1 QuickBooks File

If you will be using the same computer and the same QBW file:

1. Select your **QBW file.**
2. Add **YourName Exercise 9.2** to the company name by selecting **Company Menu > My Company.**

> **If you are not using the same computer that you used for Chapter 9 and Exercise 9.1,** you will need to restore your latest prior Backup. QBB file using the instructions in Appendix B: Back Up & Restore QuickBooks files. After restoring, add YourName Exercise 9.2 to the company name.

E9.2.2 Unearned Revenue Adjustment

Complete the following table.

Account	Account Type	Increase or Decrease?	Debit or Credit?	Amount
Rent Revenue	Income	______1______	______2______	$______3______
Unearned Revenue	Liability	______4______	______5______	$______6______

1. ______
2. ______
3. ______
4. ______
5. ______
6. ______

E9.2.3 Plan Adjusting Journal Entry

Complete the following.

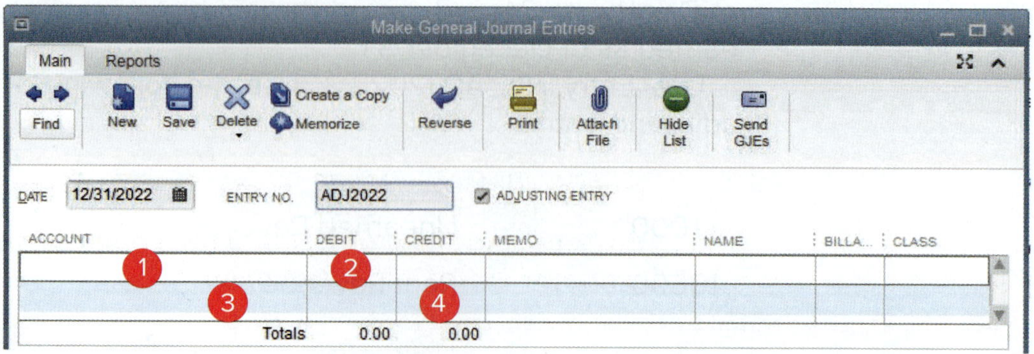

1. ______
2. ______
3. ______
4. ______

E9.2.4 Enter Adjusting Journal Entry

Next, enter the adjusting journal entry into the QuickBooks Journal.

1. Select **Accountant Menu** > **Make General Journal Entries**
2. Enter the adjusting journal entry using the information you prepared in the prior activity
3. From the open Make General Journal Entries window, select the **Reports tab** > **Transaction Journal**
4. Export to **Excel** or print the **Journal**

E9.2.5 Back Up Exercise 9.2

Save a backup of your Exercise file using the file name: YourName Exercise 9.2 Backup.QBB. See *Appendix B: Back Up & Restore QuickBooks Files* for instructions.

EXERCISE 9.3: Adjusting Entry Accrued Expenses

Interest incurred but not yet paid by Rock Castle Construction as of December 31, 2022, was $3,000 in total. Use Entry No. ADJ2022.4. Use the following accounts to make the adjusting entry:

20300	Interest Payable
62420	Loan Interest Expense

E9.3.1 QuickBooks File

If you will be using the same computer and the same QBW file:

1. Select your **QBW file.**
2. Add **YourName Exercise 9.3** to the company name by selecting **Company Menu** > **My Company.**

> **If you are not using the same computer that you used for Chapter 9, and Exercise 9.1 - 9.2,** you will need to restore your latest prior Backup.QBB file using the instructions in Appendix B: Back Up & Restore QuickBooks files. After restoring, add YourName Exercise 9.3 to the company name.

E9.3.2 Accrued Expense Adjustment

Complete the following table.

Account	Account Type	Increase or Decrease?	Debit or Credit?	Amount
Interest Expense	Expense	______1______	______2______	$______3______
Interest Payable	Liability	______4______	______5______	$______6______

1. ______
2. ______
3. ______
4. ______
5. ______
6. ______

E9.3.3 Plan Adjusting Journal Entry

Complete the following.

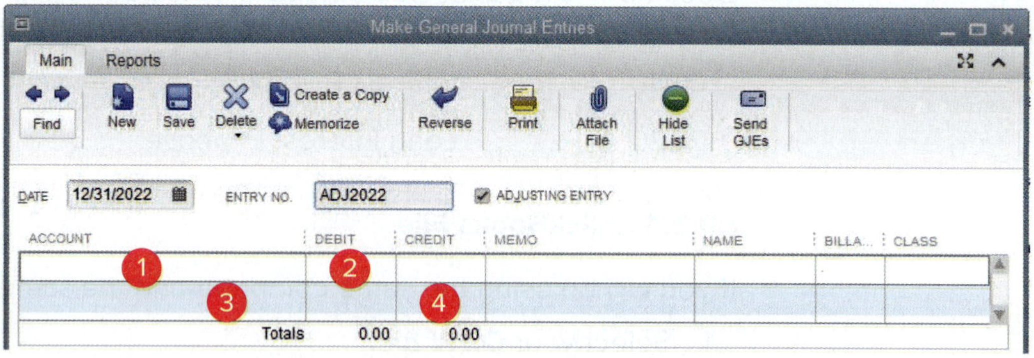

1. ______
2. ______
3. ______
4. ______

E9.3.4 Enter Adjusting Journal Entry

Next, enter the adjusting journal entry into the QuickBooks Journal.

1. Select **Accountant Menu** > **Make General Journal Entries**
2. Enter the adjusting journal entry using the information you prepared in the prior activity
3. From the open Make General Journal Entries window, select the **Reports tab** > **Transaction Journal**
4. Export to **Excel** or print the **Journal**

E9.3.5 Back Up Exercise 9.3

Save a backup of your Exercise file using the file name: YourName Exercise 9.3 Backup.QBB. See *Appendix B: Back Up & Restore QuickBooks Files* for instructions.

EXERCISE 9.4: Adjusting Entry Accrued Revenue

Rock Castle Construction has earned interest of $400 as of December 31, 2022. This interest has been earned, but not recorded or received. Interest of $400 needs to be recorded as an accrued revenue and Interest Receivable, an asset, recorded for the amount that Rock Castle Construction will receive in the future.

An adjusting entry is needed to bring accounts up to date at December 31. Use Entry No. ADJ2022.5. Use the following accounts to make the adjusting entry:

11100	Interest Receivable
70200	Interest Income

E9.4.1 QuickBooks File

If you will be using the same computer and the same QBW file:

1. Select your **QBW file.**
2. Add **YourName Exercise 9.4** to the company name by selecting **Company Menu > My Company.**

> **If you are not using the same computer that you used for Chapter 9, Exercise 9.1 - 9.3,** you will need to restore your latest prior Backup.QBB file using the instructions in Appendix B: Back Up & Restore QuickBooks files. After restoring, add YourName Exercise 9.4 to the company name.

E9.4.2 Accrued Revenue Adjustment

Complete the following table.

Account	Account Type	Increase or Decrease?	Debit or Credit?	Amount
Interest Revenue	Income	_____1_____	_____2_____	$_____3_____
Interest Receivable	Asset	_____4_____	_____5_____	$_____6_____

1. ______
2. ______
3. ______
4. ______
5. ______
6. ______

E9.4.3 Plan Adjusting Journal Entry

Complete the following.

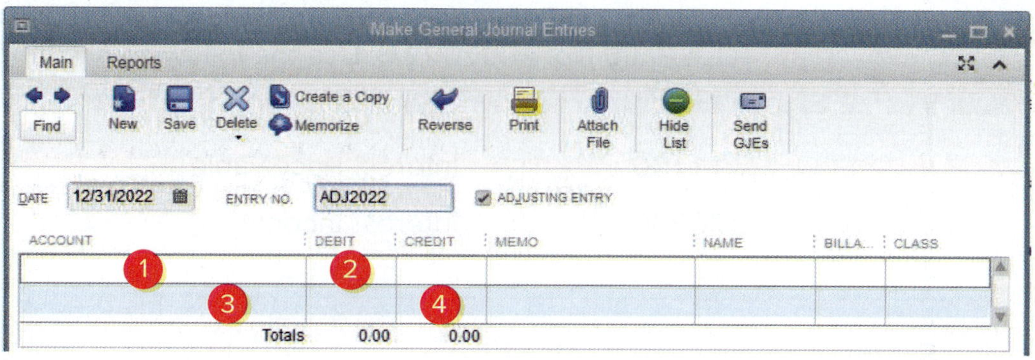

1. ______
2. ______
3. ______
4. ______

E9.4.4 Enter Adjusting Journal Entry

Next, enter the adjusting journal entry into the QuickBooks Journal.

1. Select **Accountant Menu** > **Make General Journal Entries**
2. Enter the adjusting journal entry using the information you prepared in the prior activity
3. From the open Make General Journal Entries window, select the **Reports tab** > **Transaction Journal**
4. Export to **Excel** or print the **Journal**

E9.4.5 Back Up Exercise 9.4

Save a backup of your Exercise file using the file name: YourName Exercise 9.4 Backup.QBB. See *Appendix B: Back Up & Restore QuickBooks Files* for instructions.

EXERCISE 9.5: Adjusted Trial Balance

Using the QuickBooks Company, Rock Castle Construction, complete the following.

Prepare an adjusted trial balance at December 31, 2022

E9.5.1 QuickBooks File

If you will be using the same computer and the same QBW file:

1. Select your **QBW file.**
2. Add **YourName Exercise 9.5** to the company name by selecting **Company Menu** > **My Company.**

If you are not using the same computer that you used for Chapter 9, Exercise 9.1 - 9.4, you will need to restore your latest prior Backup.QBB file using the instructions in Appendix B: Back Up & Restore QuickBooks files. After restoring, add YourName Exercise 9.5 to the company name.

E9.5.2 Adjusted Trial Balance

1. From the Report Center, select **Accountant & Taxes > Adjusted Trial Balance**
2. Select Date: **This Month 12/01/2022 To 12/31/2022.** Select **Run.**
3. Export to **Excel** or **print** the Adjusted Trial Balance
4. **Highlight** the adjustments and any adjusted trial balance account balances that changed as a result of adjustments

E9.5.3 Back Up Exercise 9.5

Save a backup of your Exercise file using the file name: YourName Exercise 9.5 Backup.QBB. See *Appendix B: Back Up & Restore QuickBooks Files* for instructions.

EXERCISE 9.6: Debits and Credits

Enter either Increase or Decrease in the following table to complete it.

- **Increase**
- **Decrease**

Account Type	Debit	Credit
Assets	______	______
Liabilities	______	______
Equity	______	______
Revenues (Income)	______	______
Expenses	______	______

PROJECT 9.1

Larry's Landscaping

As an accounting consultant for Larry's Landscaping complete the following to record adjustments to bring accounts up for the company.

QB SatNav

The objective of Project 9.1 is to facilitate your mastery of QuickBooks Desktop. Project 9.1 focuses on adjustments that is required as part of the report preparation process.

QB SatNav

1 QB SETTINGS

- Company Settings
- Chart of Accounts

2 QB TRANSACTIONS

> Money in *Money out >*

- Banking
- Customers & Sales
- Vendors & Expenses
- Employees & Payroll

3 QB REPORTS

- **Reports**

P9.1.1 QuickBooks File

1. Use either your QuickBooks Company file (QBW) or retore the backup file (QBB) that you completed for Project 8.1. (If you have issues with your QuickBooks file, contact your instructor.)
2. Update the Company Name to: **YourName Project 9.1 Larry's Landscaping**

P9.1.2 Trial Balance

1. Export to **Excel** the Trial Balance report for Larry's Landscaping for **This Fiscal Quarter, October 1 to December 31, 2022**

P9.1.3 Adjusting Entries

1. Enter the following adjusting entries for Larry's Landscaping.

Date	**12/31/2022**
Entry Number	**A108**
Account to Debit	**6700 Depreciation (Expense)**
Account to Credit	**1520 Accumulated Depreciation – Truck**
Amount	**$432.00**

Date	**12/31/2022**
Entry Number	**A109**
Account to Debit	**6900 Insurance (Expense)**
Account to Credit	**Prepaid Insurance**
Amount	**$180.00**

2. Export to **Excel** the Adjusting Journal Entries report for **December 31, 2022.** (Select: Report Center > Accountant & Taxes > Adjusting Journal Entries.)

P9.1.4 Reports

1. Export to **Excel** the Adjusted Trial Balance for Larry's Landscaping at **December 31, 2022**
2. **Highlight** the adjustments and any adjusted trial balance account balances that changed as a result of adjustments

P9.1.5 Back Up Project 9.1

Save a backup of your Project file using the file name: YourName Project 9.1 Backup.QBB. See *Appendix B: Back Up & Restore QuickBooks Files* for instructions.

Chapter 10

QuickBooks Reports

BACKSTORY

"I need an income tax summary report ASAP—" Mr. Castle barks as he races past your cubicle. In a few seconds he charges past your cubicle again. *"Don't forget to adjust the accounts first. You'll need to use those confounded debits and credits!*

"Also, I need a P&L, balance sheet, and cash flow statement for my meeting with the bankers this afternoon. Throw in a graph or two if it'll make us look good."

Smiling, you push the Send button on your smartphone to send Mr. Castle the links to the financials. Then you send him a text message.

Done

What's Next?

Section 10.1

QuickBooks SatNav

QuickBooks SatNav is your satellite navigation for QuickBooks, assisting you in navigating QuickBooks

QuickBooks SatNav divides QuickBooks into three processes:

1. **QuickBooks Settings.** This includes Company Settings when setting up a new QuickBooks company and the Company Chart of Accounts.
2. **QuickBooks Transactions.** This includes recording transactions in QuickBooks. Transaction types can be categorized as Banking, Customers and Sales, Vendors and Expenses, and Employees and Payroll. In basic terms, recording transactions involves recording money in and money out.
3. **QuickBooks Reports.** QuickBooks reports are the output of the system, such as commonly used financial statements of Balance Sheet, Income Statement, and Statement of Cash Flows.

Chapter 10 focuses on preparing reports as shown in the following QuickBooks SatNav.

QB SatNav

1 QB SETTINGS

CHAPTERS 1 2 11 12 13 14

Company Settings
Chart of Accounts

2 QB TRANSACTIONS

CHAPTERS 3 4 5 6 7 8 11 12 13 14

> Money in *Money out >*

Banking
Customers & Sales
Vendors & Expenses
Employees & Payroll

3 QB REPORTS

CHAPTERS 9 10 11 12 13 14

Reports

Section 10.2

START QUICKBOOKS AND OPEN QUICKBOOKS COMPANY

START QUICKBOOKS

To start QuickBooks software, click the **QuickBooks** icon on your desktop. If a QuickBooks icon does not appear on your desktop, from Microsoft® Windows® click **Start** button > **Programs** > **QuickBooks** > **QuickBooks Premier Accountant Edition.**

> **QuickBooks Accountant** includes all the features of QuickBooks Pro plus features for client services. If you use QuickBooks Pro, your screens may appear slightly different than those appearing in this text.

RESTORE QBB STARTER FILE

Restore the QBB Starter file for this chapter as follows.

1. Select **File** > **Restore**
2. Using the directions in *Appendix B: Back Up & Restore QuickBooks Files,* restore the **CHAPTER 10 STARTER.QBB**
3. After restoring, add **YourName Chapter 10** to the company name by selecting **Company Menu** > **My Company**

> **! QuickBooks Desktop (QBDT)** Data Files are compressed backup files that can be restored and used. To use Starter Files, the compressed file must be restored following the instructions here. Since it is a compressed file, you cannot open and use the QuickBooks data files by simply clicking on the file. Instead you must follow the instructions here to unzip and restore the data file before using it.

Section 10.3

FINANCIAL REPORTS: RESULTS OF THE ACCOUNTING CYCLE

As mentioned in the prior chapter, the accounting cycle is a series of accounting activities that a business performs each accounting period.

> **An accounting period** can be one month, one quarter, or one year.

The accounting cycle usually consists of the following steps.

- **Chart of Accounts.** The Chart of Accounts is a list of all accounts used to accumulate information about assets, liabilities, owners' equity, revenues, and expenses. Create a Chart of Accounts when the business is established and modify the Chart of Accounts as needed over time. (The Chart of Accounts was discussed in Chapters 1 and 2 of this text.)
- **Transactions.** During the accounting period, record transactions with customers, vendors, employees, and owners. (Transactions were explored in Chapters 3, 4, 5, 6, 7, and 8 of this text.)
- **Trial Balance.** A Trial Balance lists each account and the account balance at the end of the accounting period. Prepare a Trial Balance to verify that the accounting system is in balance—total debits should equal total credits. An unadjusted Trial Balance is a Trial Balance prepared before adjustments.
- **Adjustments.** At the end of the accounting period before preparing financial statements, make any adjustments necessary to bring the accounts up to date. Adjustments are entered in the Journal using debits and credits. (Adjustments were covered in Chapter 9 of this text.)
- **Adjusted Trial Balance.** Prepare an Adjusted Trial Balance (a Trial Balance after adjustments) to verify that the accounting system still balances. If additional account detail is required, print the general ledger (the collection of all the accounts listing the transactions that affected the accounts).
- **Financial Statements.** Prepare financial statements for external users (Profit & Loss, Balance Sheet, and Statement of Cash Flows). Prepare income tax summary reports and management reports.

Section 10.4

TRIAL BALANCE

The Trial Balance is a listing of all of a company's accounts and the ending account balances. A Trial Balance is often prepared before making adjustments to verify account balances and that the accounting system balances. Preparing a Trial Balance was covered in Chapter 9.

Section 10.5

ADJUSTING ENTRIES

The QuickBooks Journal is used to record adjustments. Adjustments are often necessary to bring the accounts up to date at the end of the accounting period.

If we use the accrual basis of accounting to calculate profits, the following four types of adjusting entries may be necessary.

1. **Prepaid items.** Items that are prepaid, such as prepaid insurance or prepaid rent.
2. **Unearned items.** Items that a customer has paid us for, but we have not provided the product or service.
3. **Accrued expenses.** Expenses that are incurred but not yet paid or recorded.
4. **Accrued revenues.** Revenues that have been earned but not yet collected or recorded.

To make adjusting entries using the Journal:

1. Select the **Accountant Menu**
2. Select **Make General Journal Entries**
3. From the Make General Journal Entries window, select Date: **12/31/2022**
4. Enter Entry No: **ADJ2022.1**
5. **Check** the **Adjusting Entry** box
6. Select Account to Debit: **60900 Depreciation Expense**
7. Enter Debit amount: **50,000.00**
8. Select Account to Credit: **17000 Accumulated Depreciation**

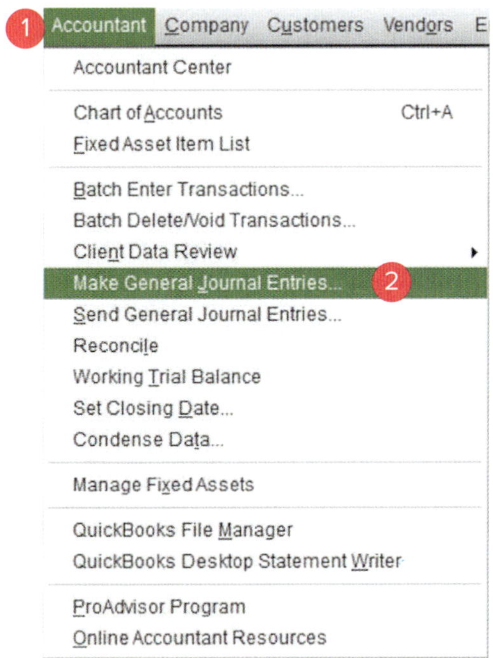

9. If it does not appear automatically, enter Credit amount: **50,000.00.**

10. Normally we would select Save & New or Save & Close, but in this case, **Cancel** without saving instead

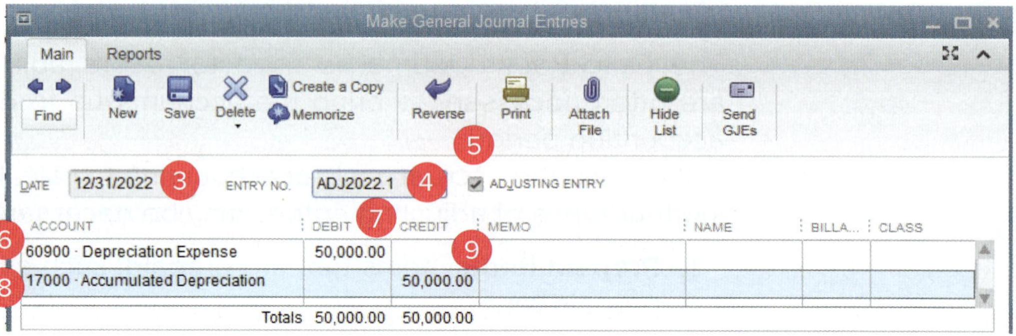

For more detailed information about adjusting entries, see Chapter 9.

Section 10.6

ADJUSTED TRIAL BALANCE

The Adjusted Trial Balance is prepared to verify that the accounting system still balances after adjusting entries are made, and that the adjustments have been made appropriately.

C10.6.1 Adjusted Trial Balance. Since adjusting entries were already entered in Chapter 9, print an Adjusted Trial Balance as follows:

1. From the Report Center, select **Accountant & Taxes** > **Adjusted Trial Balance**
2. Select Date: **12/31/2022.** Select **Run.**
3. Notice the Unadjusted (Trial) Balance columns containing account balances *before* adjusting entries
4. Notice the Adjustments columns containing the amounts for adjusting entries at December 31, 2022
5. Notice the Adjusted (Trial) Balance columns containing account balances *after* adjusting entries
6. Export to **Excel** or **print** the Adjusted Trial Balance
7. Leave the Adjusted Trial Balance report open on your screen

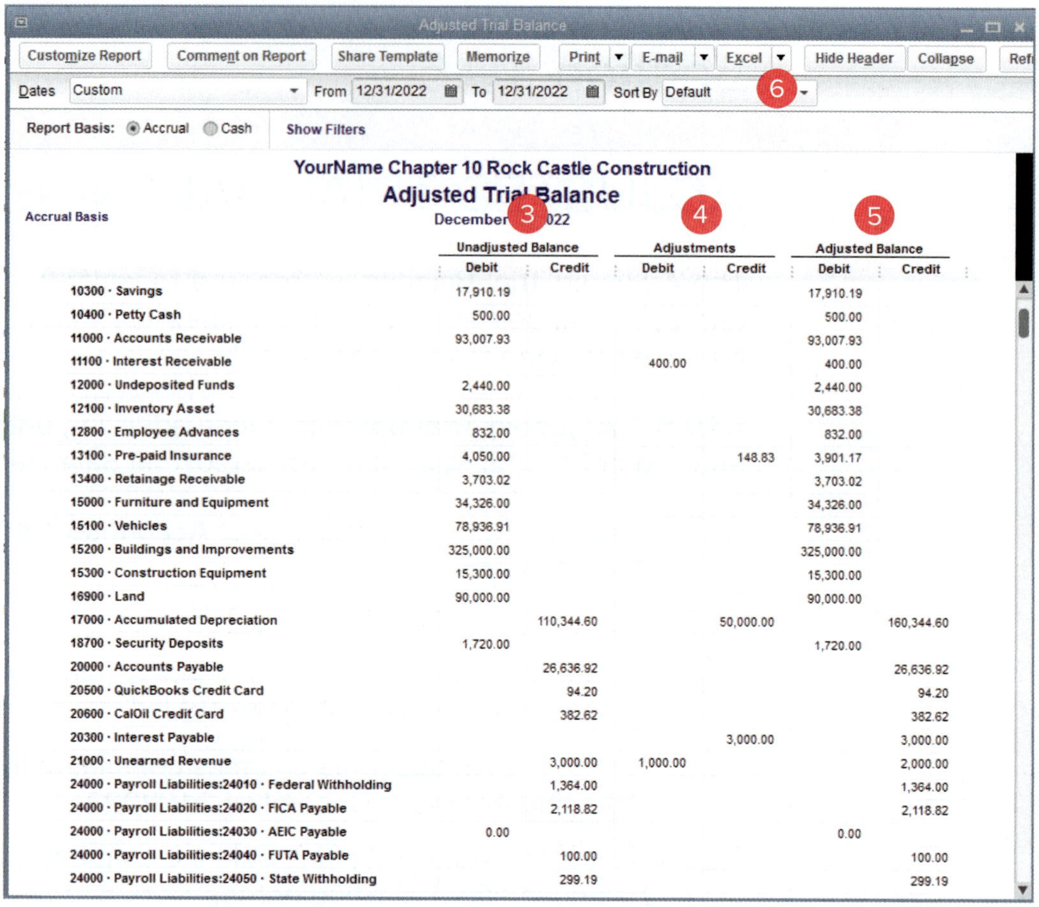

YourName Chapter 10 Rock Castle Construction
Adjusted Trial Balance
Accrual Basis — December 31, 2022

	Unadjusted Balance		Adjustments		Adjusted Balance	
	Debit	Credit	Debit	Credit	Debit	Credit
10300 · Savings	17,910.19				17,910.19	
10400 · Petty Cash	500.00				500.00	
11000 · Accounts Receivable	93,007.93				93,007.93	
11100 · Interest Receivable			400.00		400.00	
12000 · Undeposited Funds	2,440.00				2,440.00	
12100 · Inventory Asset	30,683.38				30,683.38	
12800 · Employee Advances	832.00				832.00	
13100 · Pre-paid Insurance	4,050.00			148.83	3,901.17	
13400 · Retainage Receivable	3,703.02				3,703.02	
15000 · Furniture and Equipment	34,326.00				34,326.00	
15100 · Vehicles	78,936.91				78,936.91	
15200 · Buildings and Improvements	325,000.00				325,000.00	
15300 · Construction Equipment	15,300.00				15,300.00	
16900 · Land	90,000.00				90,000.00	
17000 · Accumulated Depreciation		110,344.60		50,000.00		160,344.60
18700 · Security Deposits	1,720.00				1,720.00	
20000 · Accounts Payable		26,636.92				26,636.92
20500 · QuickBooks Credit Card		94.20				94.20
20600 · CalOil Credit Card		382.62				382.62
20300 · Interest Payable				3,000.00		3,000.00
21000 · Unearned Revenue		3,000.00	1,000.00			2,000.00
24000 · Payroll Liabilities:24010 · Federal Withholding		1,364.00				1,364.00
24000 · Payroll Liabilities:24020 · FICA Payable		2,118.82				2,118.82
24000 · Payroll Liabilities:24030 · AEIC Payable	0.00				0.00	
24000 · Payroll Liabilities:24040 · FUTA Payable		100.00				100.00
24000 · Payroll Liabilities:24050 · State Withholding		299.19				299.19

Section 10.7

MEMORIZED REPORTS

When we prepare reports, we can create memorized reports for future use. To memorize a report, first create the report and then use the memorize feature of QuickBooks.

For example, Rock Castle Construction could save time in the future by memorizing reports, such as the Adjusted Trial Balance.

CREATE A MEMORIZED REPORT

To create a memorized Adjusted Trial Balance report for Rock Castle Construction:

1. To memorize the Adjusted Trial Balance open on your screen from the prior activity, select the **Memorize** button
2. In the Name Field enter **Rock Castle Construction Adjusted Trial Balance**
3. Select Save in Memorized Report Group: **Accountant**
4. Click **OK**
5. **Close** the Adjusted Trial Balance window

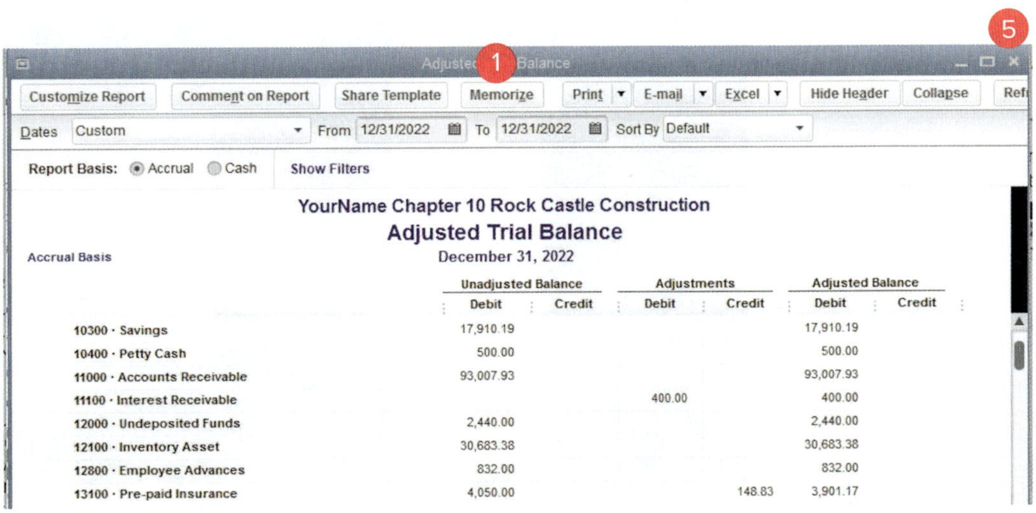

USE A MEMORIZED REPORT

To use a memorized report:

1. Select the **Memorized** tab at the top of the Report Center window
2. Select **Accountant** on the left of the Report Center window
3. When the Memorized List window appears, double-click on **Rock Castle Construction Adjusted Trial Balance** to display the Adjusted Trial Balance
4. At this point, we would make any changes as needed, such as the date. In this case, select **Cancel** since we have already exported the Adjusted Trial Balance.

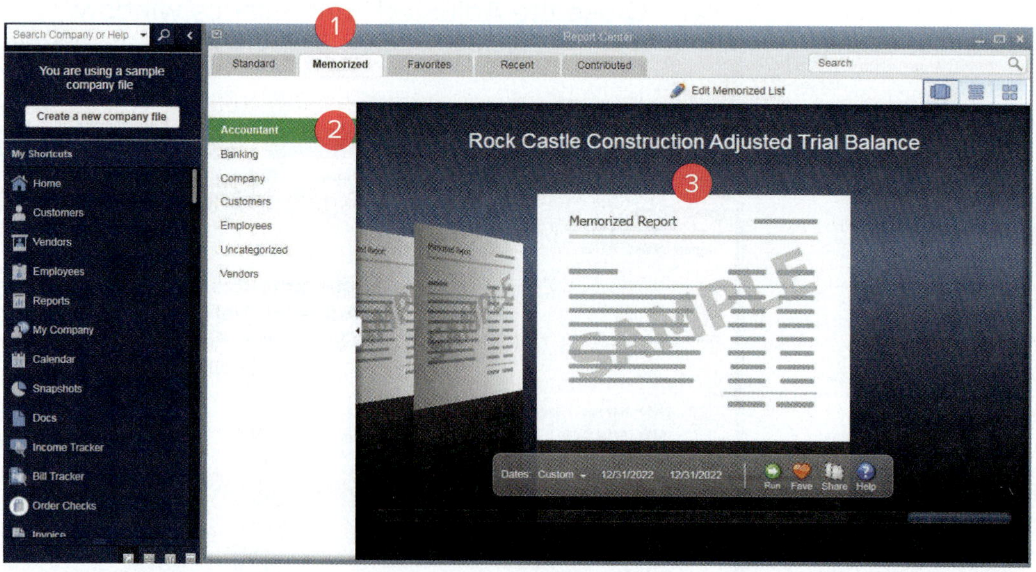

Section 10.8

FINANCIAL STATEMENTS

Financial statements are standardized financial reports given to bankers and investors. The three main financial statements are the Profit & Loss, Balance Sheet, and Statement of Cash Flows.

PROFIT AND LOSS

The Profit and Loss Statement lists sales (sometimes called revenues) and expenses for a specified accounting period. Profit, or net income, can be measured two different ways:

1. **Cash basis.** A sale is recorded when cash is collected from the customer. Expenses are recorded when cash is paid.
2. **Accrual basis.** Sales are recorded when the good or service is provided regardless of when the cash is collected from the customer. Expenses are recorded when the cost is incurred or expires, even if the expense has not been paid.

QuickBooks permits you to prepare the Profit and Loss Statement using either the accrual or the cash basis. QuickBooks also permits you to prepare Profit and Loss Statements monthly, quarterly, or annually.

C10.8.1 Profit and Loss Statement. To prepare a Profit and Loss Statement for Rock Castle Construction using the accrual basis:

1. From the Report Center, select **Company & Financial** > **Profit & Loss Standard**
2. Select Date: **This Fiscal Year.** Select **Run.**
3. Click the **Customize Report** button. Click the **Display** tab, and then select Report Basis: **Accrual.** Click **OK.**
4. Export to **Excel** or **print** the Profit and Loss Statement
5. **Close** the Profit & Loss window

BALANCE SHEET

The Balance Sheet presents a company's financial position on a particular date. The Balance Sheet can be prepared at the end of a month, quarter, or year. The Balance Sheet lists:

1. **Assets.** What a company owns. On the Balance Sheet, assets are recorded at their historical cost, the amount you paid for the asset when you purchased it. Note that historical cost can be different from the market value of the asset, which is the amount the asset is worth now.
2. **Liabilities.** What a company owes. Liabilities are obligations that include amounts owed vendors (accounts payable) and bank loans (notes payable).
3. **Owners' equity.** The residual that is left after liabilities are satisfied. Also called net worth, owners' equity is increased by owners' contributions and net income. Owners' equity is decreased by owners' withdrawals (or dividends) and net losses.

C10.8.2 Balance Sheet. To prepare a Balance Sheet for Rock Castle Construction at 12/31/2022:

1. From the Report Center, select **Company & Financial** > **Balance Sheet Standard**
2. Select Date: **This Fiscal Year.** Select **Run.**
3. Export to **Excel** or **print** the Balance Sheet
4. **Close** the Balance Sheet window
5. **Highlight** the second single largest asset listed on the Balance Sheet

STATEMENT OF CASH FLOWS

The Statement of Cash Flows summarizes cash inflows and cash outflows for a business over a period of time. Cash flows are grouped into three categories:

1. **Cash flows from operating activities.** Cash inflows and outflows related to the company's primary business, such as cash flows from sales and operating expenses.
2. **Cash flows from investing activities.** Cash inflows and outflows related to acquisition and disposal of long-term assets.

3. **Cash flows from financing activities.** Cash inflows and outflows to and from investors and creditors (except for interest payments). Examples include: loan principal repayments and investments by owners.

C10.8.3 Statement of Cash Flows. To print the Statement of Cash Flows for Rock Castle Construction:

1. From the Report Center, select **Company & Financial** > **Statement of Cash Flows**
2. Select Date: **This Fiscal Year.** Select **Run.**
3. Export to **Excel** or **print** the Statement of Cash Flows
4. **Close** the Statement of Cash Flows window
5. **Highlight** any items on the Statement of Cash Flows that you might classify differently than shown on the statement

Section 10.9

TAX REPORTS

QuickBooks provides two different approaches that you can use when preparing your tax return.

1. Create your QuickBooks income tax reports and then enter the tax information on your income tax return or into your tax software.
2. Export your QuickBooks accounting data to tax software, such as TurboTax software, and then use TurboTax to complete your income tax return.

Three different income tax reports are provided by QuickBooks:

1. **Income Tax Preparation report.** Lists the assigned tax line for each account.
2. **Income Tax Summary report.** Summarizes income and expenses that should be listed on a business income tax return.
3. **Income Tax Detail report.** Provides more detailed information about the income or expense amount appearing on each tax line of the Income Tax Summary report.

INCOME TAX PREPARATION REPORT

Before printing the Income Tax Summary report, check your QuickBooks accounts to see that the correct Tax Line is selected for each account.

C10.9.1 Income Tax Preparation Report. An easy way to check the Tax Line specified for each account is to print the Income Tax Preparation report as follows.

1. From the Report Center, select **Accountant & Taxes** > **Income Tax Preparation**
2. Select Date: **This Tax Year.** Select **Run.**
3. Export to **Excel** or **print** the income Tax Preparation report
4. **Close** the Income Tax Preparation window

To determine if the correct tax line has been entered for each account, compare the tax lines listed on the Income Tax Preparation report with the business income tax return.

For example, if we wanted to change the Tax Line for the Postage account from Unassigned to the appropriate Tax Line:

1. From the Home Page, select **Chart of Accounts**
2. From the Chart of Accounts window, right-click on the account: **63100 Postage**
3. Select **Edit Account**
4. When the Edit Account window appears, change the Tax-Line Mapping from Unassigned to: **Other Deductions: Postage & delivery**
5. To save the changes, click **Save and Close**
6. **Close** the Chart of Accounts window

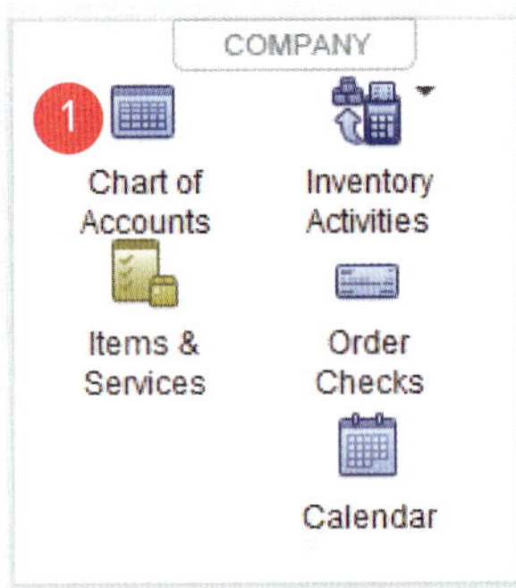

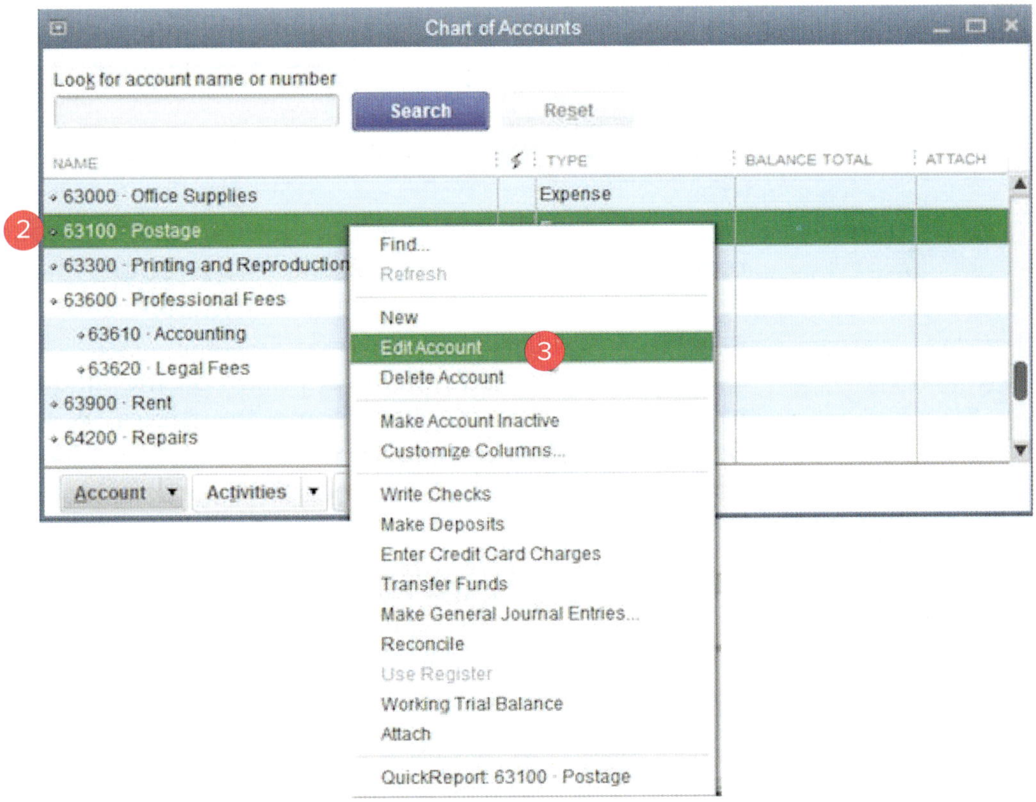

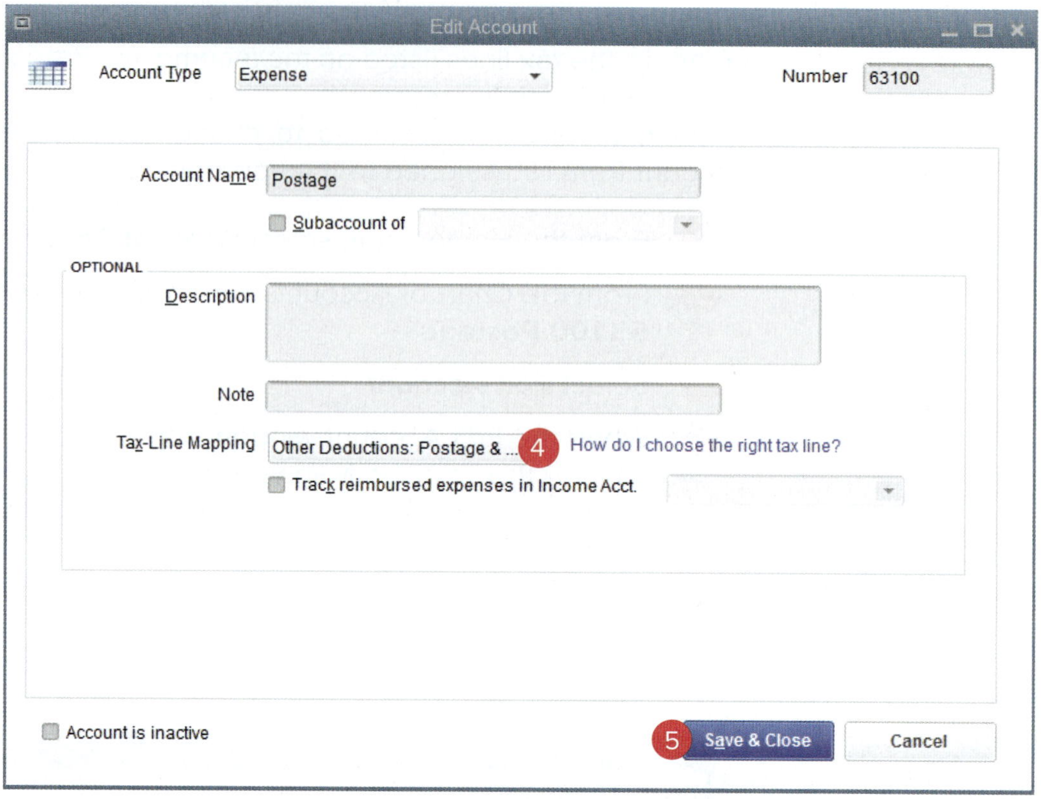

INCOME TAX SUMMARY REPORT

After we confirm that the Tax Line for each account is correct, we are ready to print an Income Tax Summary report. The Income Tax Summary report lists sales and expenses that should appear on the business federal tax return filed with the IRS.

A business can use the information on the Income Tax Summary report to manually complete its income tax return. A sole proprietorship files Schedule C (attached to the owner's personal 1040 tax return). A corporation files Form 1120. A subchapter S corporation files Form 1120S.

INCOME TAX DETAIL REPORT

If you want to view detail for the line items shown on the Income Tax Summary report, we could display the Income Tax Detail report.

Section 10.10

MANAGEMENT REPORTS

Reports used by management do not have to follow a specified set of rules such as the Internal Revenue Code. Instead, management reports are prepared as needed to provide management with information for making operating and business decisions.

Management reports include:

- Cash flow forecast
- Accounts receivable aging (See Chapter 5)
- Accounts payable aging (See Chapter 6)
- Inventory reports (See Chapter 7)
- Budgets (See Chapter 15)

CASH FLOW FORECAST

QuickBooks permits you to forecast cash flows. This enables you to project whether you will have enough cash to pay bills when they are due. If it appears that you will need additional cash, then you can arrange for a loan or line of credit to pay your bills. The Cash Flow Forecast report lists projected cash inflows and cash outflows.

C10.10.1 Cash Flow Forecast. To prepare a Cash Flow Forecast report for Rock Castle Construction:

1. From the Report Center, select: **Company & Financial** > **Cash Flow Forecast**
2. Select Date: **Next 4 Weeks.** Click **Run.**
3. Export to **Excel** or **print** the Cash Flow Forecast report
4. **Close** the Cash Flow Forecast window

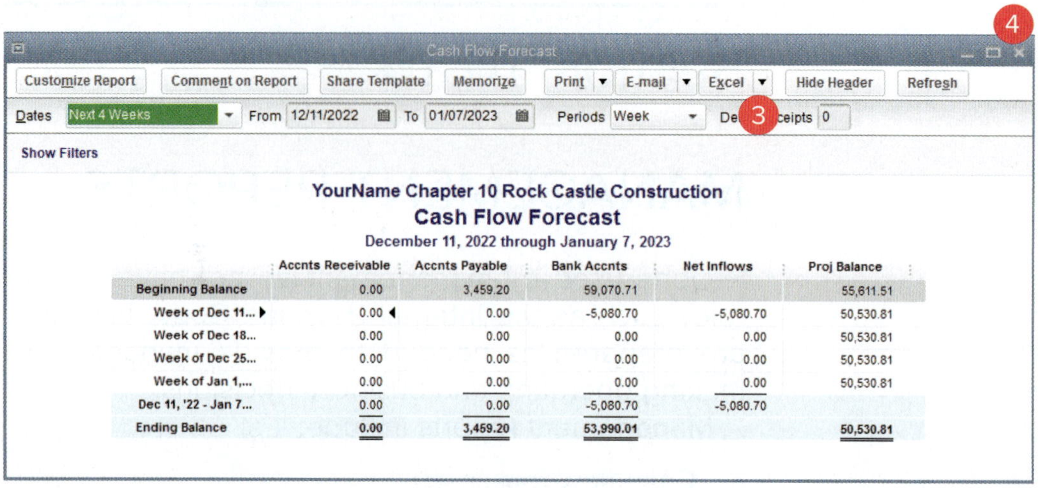

We can also email reports. For example, a client might email QuickBooks reports to the accountant for review. To email a QuickBooks report, select the Email button at the top of the Reports window.

Section 10.11

FINANCIAL INSIGHTS

The accounting cycle addresses the logistics of making certain the accounting system balances with the Trial Balance, making necessary adjustments to bring accounts up to date, and preparing financial reports. However, entrepreneurs often need more than this from financial software. They are often looking for financial insights as to how they can improve their business. QuickBooks now offers an Insights digital dashboard to assist entrepreneurs in this endeavor.

To use QuickBooks Insights:

1. From the Home Page, select: **Insights**
2. Select the **arrow** to the right of the screen to advance to the next insight
3. Notice in the yearly comparison how Rock Castle's income has increased in 2022
4. Select the **right** arrow again to advance to the next insight
5. This insight shows the top customers by sales, listing Brian Cook as the top customer. Although sales by customers are important, profitability by customer might be even more important for business success.

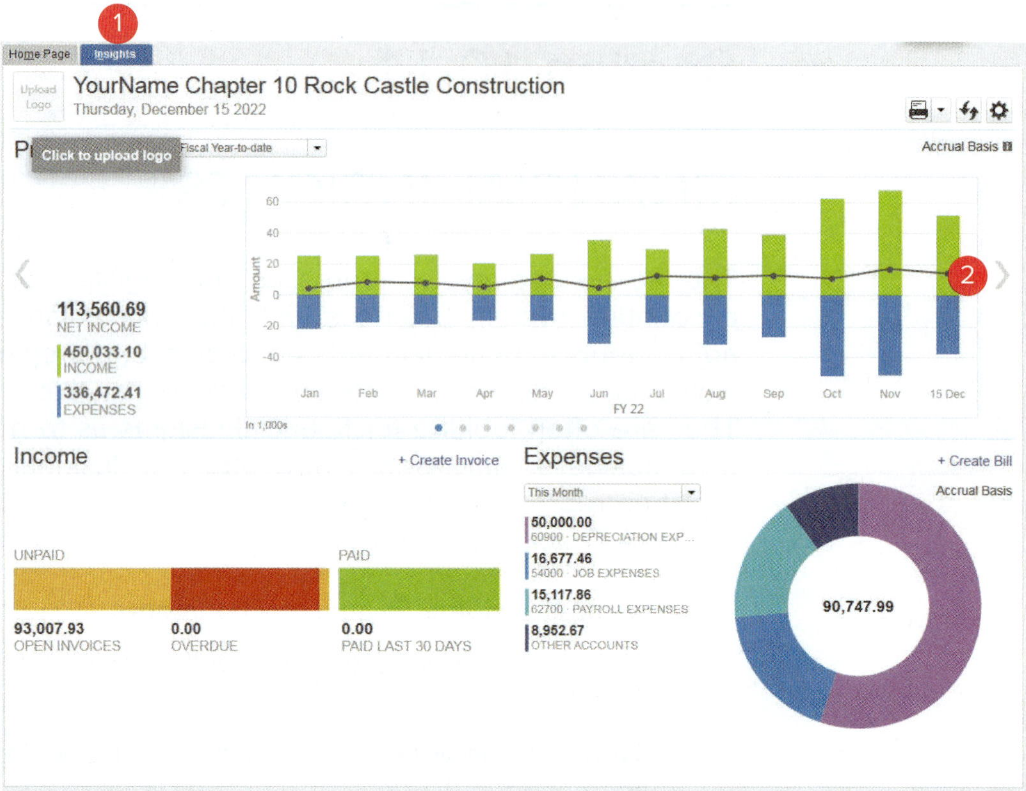
1
Home Page
Insights
YourName Chapter 10 Rock Castle Construction
Thursday, December 15 2022
Click to upload logo
Fiscal Year-to-date
Accrual Basis
113,560.69
NET INCOME
450,033.10
INCOME
336,472.41
EXPENSES
2
FY 22
In 1,000s
Income
+ Create Invoice
UNPAID
PAID
93,007.93
OPEN INVOICES
0.00
OVERDUE
0.00
PAID LAST 30 DAYS
Expenses
+ Create Bill
This Month
Accrual Basis
50,000.00
60900 · DEPRECIATION EXP...
16,677.46
54000 · JOB EXPENSES
15,117.86
62700 · PAYROLL EXPENSES
8,952.67
OTHER ACCOUNTS
90,747.99

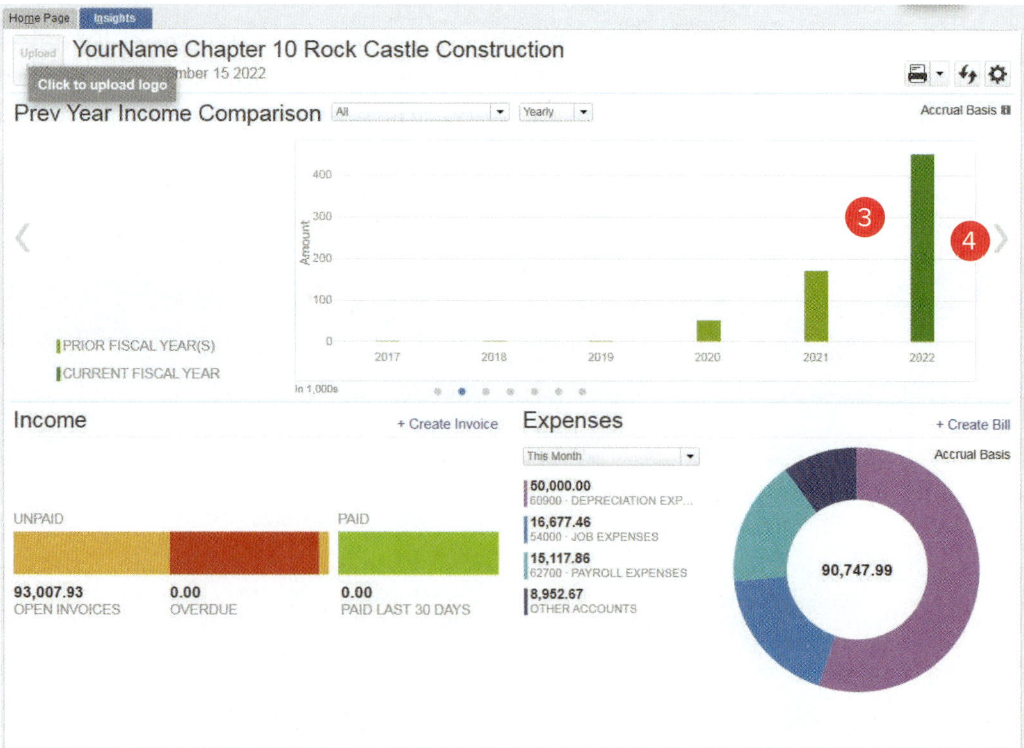
Home Page
Insights
YourName Chapter 10 Rock Castle Construction
Click to upload logo
Prev Year Income Comparison
All
Yearly
Accrual Basis
3
4
PRIOR FISCAL YEAR(S)
CURRENT FISCAL YEAR
In 1,000s
Income
+ Create Invoice
UNPAID
PAID
93,007.93
OPEN INVOICES
0.00
OVERDUE
0.00
PAID LAST 30 DAYS
Expenses
+ Create Bill
This Month
Accrual Basis
50,000.00
60900 · DEPRECIATION EXP...
16,677.46
54000 · JOB EXPENSES
15,117.86
62700 · PAYROLL EXPENSES
8,952.67
OTHER ACCOUNTS
90,747.99

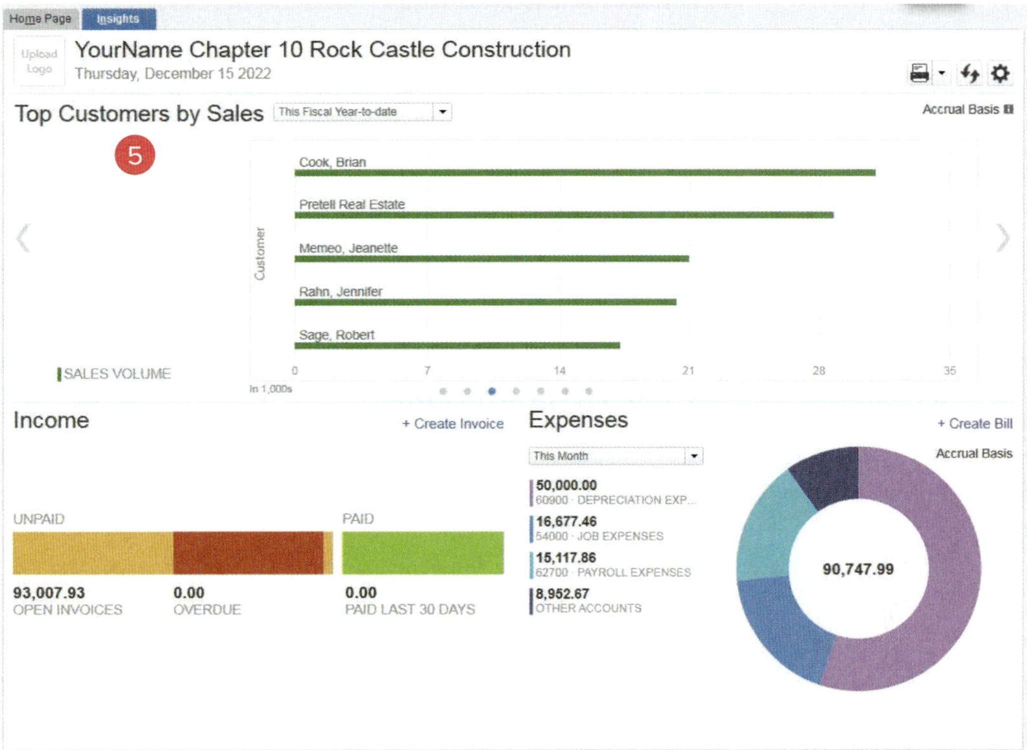
Home Page
Insights
YourName Chapter 10 Rock Castle Construction
Thursday, December 15 2022
Top Customers by Sales
This Fiscal Year-to-date
Accrual Basis
5
Cook, Brian
Pretell Real Estate
Memeo, Jeanette
Rahn, Jennifer
Sage, Robert
Customer
SALES VOLUME
0
7
14
21
28
35
In 1,000s
Income
+ Create Invoice
UNPAID
PAID
93,007.93
OPEN INVOICES
0.00
OVERDUE
0.00
PAID LAST 30 DAYS
Expenses
+ Create Bill
This Month
Accrual Basis
50,000.00
60900 · DEPRECIATION EXP...
16,677.46
54000 · JOB EXPENSES
15,117.86
62700 · PAYROLL EXPENSES
8,952.67
OTHER ACCOUNTS
90,747.99

Section 10.12

BACK UP QUICKBOOKS FILES

BACK UP QBB

Save a backup of your Chapter 10 file using the file name: **YourName Chapter 10 Backup.QBB.**

QBW WORKFLOW

If you will be using the same computer to complete Chapter 10 QuickBooks exercises, just as in a business workflow, you can continue to use the same QBW file.

If you are using the QBW approach, leave your .QBW file open and proceed directly to Exercise 10.1.

QBB RESTORE

If you will be switching computers and are ending your computer session now, close your QBW file and exit QuickBooks. When you restart, you will restore your backup file to complete Exercise 10.1.

Section 10.13

ACCOUNTING ESSENTIALS

Financial Reports

Accounting Essentials summarize important foundational accounting knowledge that may be useful when using QuickBooks

What is the objective of financial reporting?

The objective of financial reporting is to provide information to external users for decision making.

What are three types of financial reports a business prepares?

1. **Financial statements.** Financial statements are reports used by investors, owners, and creditors to make decisions. A banker might use the financial statements to decide whether to make a loan to a company. A prospective investor might use the financial statements to decide whether to invest in a company.

   The three financial statements most frequently used by external users are:

   - **Profit and Loss** (also referred to as the P & L or Income Statement) lists income and expenses, summarizing the income a company has earned and the expenses incurred to earn the income.
   - **Balance Sheet** lists assets, liabilities, and owners' equity, summarizing what a company *owns* and *owes* on a particular date.
   - **Statement of Cash Flows** lists cash flows from operating, investing, and financing activities of a business.

2. **Tax forms.** The objective of the tax form is to provide information to federal and state tax authorities. When preparing tax returns, a company uses different rules from those used to prepare financial statements. When preparing a federal tax return, use the Internal Revenue Code.

   Tax forms include the following:

   - Federal income tax return
   - State tax return

- Federal Payroll Forms 940, 941/944, W-2, W-3
- Federal Form 1099

3. **Management reports.** Management reports are used by internal users (managers) to make decisions regarding company operations. These reports are created to satisfy a manager's information needs.

   Examples of reports that managers use include:

   - Cash budget that projects amounts of cash that will be collected and spent in the future. (Note a Statement of Cash Flows focuses on cash inflows and outflows in the *past.* A Cash Budget focuses on expected cash flows in the *future.)*
   - Accounts receivable aging report that lists the age and balance of customer accounts receivable so accounts are collected in a timely manner.

www.my-quickbooks.com

Go to **www.My-QuickBooks.com** to view additional QuickBooks resources including:

- **Excel Report Templates** to organize QuickBooks reports exported to Excel
- ***Computer Accounting with QuickBooks*** **updates,** sometimes required when there is a software update that affects the text
- **QuickBooks Video links**
- **QuickBooks Help and Support links**
- **Other QuickBooks Resources** to make learning QuickBooks easier and more effective
- **QuickBooks Issue Resolution** offers a guided approach to trouble-shooting QuickBooks

Troubleshooting QuickBooks and Correcting Errors are crucial QuickBooks skill to acquire. See www.My-QuickBooks.com > QB Issue Resolution for Troubleshooting QuickBooks tips. See Chapter 17, Quick Review Guide, for tips on Correcting Errors.

EXERCISE 10.1: Profit and Loss, Vertical Analysis

BACKSTORY

You vaguely recall from your college accounting course that performing financial statement analysis can reveal additional useful information. Since Mr. Castle asked for whatever additional information he might need, you decide to print a vertical analysis of the Profit and Loss Statement using QuickBooks.

E10.1.1 QuickBooks File

If you will be using the same computer and the same Chapter 10.QBW file:

1. If your Chapter 10.QBW file is not already open, open it by selecting **File** > **Open Previous Company.** Select your **Chapter 10.QBW file.** If a QuickBooks Information window appears with a message about the sample company file, click **OK.**
2. Add **YourName Exercise 10.1** to the company name by selecting **Company Menu** > **My Company.**

> **If you are not using the same computer that you used for Chapter 10,** you will need to restore your Chapter 10 Backup. QBB file using the instructions in Appendix B: Back Up & Restore QuickBooks Files. After restoring, add YourName Exercise 10.1 to the company name.

E10.1.2 Profit and Loss, Vertical Analysis

Prepare a customized Profit and Loss Statement that shows each item on the statement as a percentage of sales (income):

1. From the Report Center, select **Company & Financial** > **Profit & Loss Standard**
2. Select Dates: **This Fiscal Year.** Click **Run.**
3. To customize the report, click the **Customize Report** button
4. When the Modify Report window appears, select **Display** tab
5. Select: **% of Income**
6. Click **OK**

7. Export to **Excel** or **print** the report
8. **Highlight** the single largest expense as a percentage of income
9. **Highlight** the profit margin (net income as a percentage of sales)
10. Memorize the Profit & Loss Vertical Analysis report. Save in the Memorized Report Group: **Accountant.**

E10.1.3 Back Up Exercise 10.1

Save a backup of your Exercise file using the file name: YourName Exercise 10.1 Backup.QBB. See *Appendix B: Back Up & Restore QuickBooks Files* for instructions.

EXERCISE 10.2: Balance Sheet, Vertical Analysis

BACKSTORY

Also, you decide to prepare a customized Balance Sheet that displays each account on the Balance Sheet as a percentage of total assets. This vertical analysis indicates the proportion of total assets that each asset represents. For example, inventory might be 30 percent of total assets. Vertical analysis also helps to assess the percentage of assets financed by debt versus owners' equity.

E10.2.1 QuickBooks File

If you will be using the same computer and the same QBW file:

1. Select your **QBW file.**
2. Add **YourName Exercise 10.2** to the company name by selecting **Company Menu** > **My Company.**

> **If you are not using the same computer that you used for Chapter 10 and Exercise 10.1,** you will need to restore your latest prior Backup.QBB file using the instructions in Appendix B: Back Up & Restore QuickBooks files. After restoring, add YourName Exercise 10.2 to the company name.

E10.2.2 Balance Sheet, Vertical Analysis

Prepare a customized Balance Sheet that shows each account as a percentage of total assets.

1. From the Report Center, select: **Company & Financial** > **Balance Sheet Standard**
2. Select Dates: **This Fiscal Year.** Click **Run.**
3. Click the **Customize Report** button and select: **% of Column**
4. Export to **Excel** or **print** the customized Balance Sheet
5. **Highlight** the asset that represents the largest percentage of total assets
6. **Highlight** the percentage of assets financed with debt. (Hint: What is the percentage of total liabilities?)

E10.2.3 Back Up Exercise 10.2

Save a backup of your Exercise file using the file name: YourName Exercise 10.2 Backup.QBB. See *Appendix B: Back Up & Restore QuickBooks Files* for instructions.

EXERCISE 10.3: Analysis

BACKSTORY

"Last year, the bank told us we had money in the bank, but QuickBooks told us we were broke and had no money in our Checking account to pay bills." Mr. Castle casts you a look as he rushes past your cubicle—a look that warns you to be ready to answer a QuickBooks question.

"We had to hire an accountant last year to find the missing cash in QuickBooks." Rock Castle now pauses as you anticipated the upcoming question. *"Will we need to hire an accountant this year to find the missing cash or can you show me the money?"*

Rapidly, you reply, *"Mr. Castle, this year we know where all our cash is."* When you look up to show him some QuickBooks reports, Mr. Castle is already back in his office on the phone.

E10.3.1 QuickBooks File

If you will be using the same computer and the same QBW file:

1. Select your **QBW file.**
2. Add **YourName Exercise 10.3** to the company name by selecting **Company Menu** > **My Company.**

> **If you are not using the same computer that you used for Chapter 10, Exercise 10.1 and Exercise 10.2,** you will need to restore your latest prior Backup.QBB file using the instructions in Appendix B: Back Up & Restore QuickBooks files. After restoring, add YourName Exercise 10.3 to the company name.

E10.3.2 General Ledger: Show Me the Money

To show Mr. Castle the money, complete the following steps.

1. Display a General Ledger report (**Report Center** > **Accountant & Taxes** > **General Ledger**) for Rock Castle Construction for December 15 to December 31, 2022
2. To display all accounts in use with a balance, select **Customize Report button** > **Display tab** > **Advanced** > **In Use** > **Report Date** > **OK**
3. To filter for all asset accounts, select **Customize Report button** > **Accounting (Filter)** > **All assets** > **Include split detail? No** > **OK**
4. Export to **Excel** or **print** the General Ledger report using the filter
5. **Highlight** the account on your General Ledger report where you think the accountant found the missing cash last year

E10.3.3 Ratios

In addition to the QuickBooks reports you will be providing Mr. Castle, you decide that preparing ratio analysis for him will provide additional insight into Rock Castle Construction operations.

Using your QuickBooks reports from this chapter and exercises, calculate the following ratios.

1. The Current Ratio is used as a measure of how well current assets cover the current liabilities that will be due within the next year. If an enterprise has $2 in current assets for each $1 in current liabilities, the current ratio is stated as 2:1.

   Calculate the Current Ratio (Current Assets/Current Liabilities) for Rock Castle Construction. ______:______

2. The debt ratio focuses on the percentage of company assets financed with debt as opposed to equity. For example, a debt ratio of 40% indicates that 40 percent of the enterprise's assets are financed with debt. Too high a debt ratio can indicate increased risk of default on the debt.

   Calculate the Debt Ratio (Total Liabilities/Total Assets) for Rock Castle Construction. ______%

3. The profit margin shows the percentage of each sales dollar that is left in profit. For example, a profit margin of 10% indicates that on average, 10 cents of each dollar of sales is profit. Profit margin varies greatly by industry with some industries, such as discount stores, having low profit margins.

   Calculate the Profit Margin (Net Income or Net Profit/Total Sales) for Rock Castle Construction for this fiscal quarter. ______%

4. Prepare a brief email to Rock Castle summarizing the results of your ratio analysis and outlining your conclusions, comments, or recommendations based on your analysis.

E10.3.4 Back Up Exercise 10.3

Save a backup of your Exercise file using the file name: YourName Exercise 10.3 Backup.QBB. See *Appendix B: Back Up & Restore QuickBooks Files* for instructions.

EXERCISE 10.4: Income Tax Preparation Report

BACKSTORY

In order to cross check the change to the Tax Line for 63100 Postage account that you completed in this chapter, you decide to run another Income Tax Preparation report.

E10.4.1 QuickBooks File

If you will be using the same computer and the same QBW file:

1. Select your **QBW file.**
2. Add **YourName Exercise 10.4** to the company name by selecting **Company Menu** > **My Company.**

If you are not using the same computer that you used for Chapter 10 and Exercise 10.1 - 10.3 you will need to restore your latest prior Backup.QBB file using the instructions in Appendix B: Back Up & Restore QuickBooks files. After restoring, add YourName Exercise 10.4 to the company name.

E10.4.2 Income Tax Preparation Report

Prepare an Income Tax Preparation report for Rock Castle Construction at December 31, 2022.

1. From the Report Center, select: **Accountant & Taxes** > **Income Tax Preparation**
2. Select Dates: **This Tax Year.** Click **Run.**
3. Export to **Excel** or **print** the report
4. Verify and **highlight** the changed tax line item for account: **63100 Postage**
5. **Close** the Income Tax Preparation report

E10.4.3 Back Up Exercise

Save a backup of your Exercise file using the file name: YourName Exercise 10.4 Backup.QBB. See *Appendix B: Back Up & Restore QuickBooks Files* for instructions.

PROJECT 10.1

Larry's Landscaping

As an accounting consultant for Larry's Landscaping complete the following to create QuickBooks reports.

QB SatNav

The objective of Project 10.1 is to facilitate your mastery of QuickBooks Desktop. Project 10.1 focuses on QuickBooks Reports.

QB SatNav

1 QB SETTINGS

Company Settings
Chart of Accounts

2 QB TRANSACTIONS

> Money in *Money out >*

Banking
Customers & Sales
Vendors & Expenses
Employees & Payroll

3 QB REPORTS

Reports

P10.1.1 QuickBooks File

1. Use either your QuickBooks Company file (QBW) or restore the backup file (QBB) that you completed for Project 9.1. (If you have issues with your QuickBooks file, contact your instructor.)
2. Update the Company Name to: **YourName Project 10.1 Larry's Landscaping**

P10.1.2 Profit and Loss

1. Export to **Excel** the Profit and Loss Standard report for **January 1 to December 31, 2022**
2. On the Profit and Loss report, **highlight** the item that generates the most income (revenue) for Larry's Landscaping

3. Export to **Excel** the Profit and Loss Standard report for **January 1 to December 31, 2022** with a vertical analysis showing each item as a percentage of income
4. **Highlight** the single largest expense as a percentage of income
5. **Highlight** the profit margin (net income as a percentage of sales)

P10.1.3 Balance Sheet

1. Export to **Excel** the Balance Sheet Standard report as of **December 31, 2022**
2. Export to **Excel** the Balance Sheet Standard report with a vertical analysis showing each account as a percentage of total assets as of **December 31, 2022**
3. On the vertical analysis Balance Sheet, **highlight** the asset that represents the largest percentage of total assets
4. **Highlight** the percentage of assets financed with debt. (Hint: What is the percentage of total liabilities?)

P10.1.4 Statement of Cash Flows

1. Export to **Excel** the Statement of Cash Flows report for **January 1 to December 31, 2022**

P10.1.5 Accounts Receivable Aging

1. Export to **Excel** the Accounts Receivable (A/R) Aging Summary at **December 31, 2022**

P10.1.6 Accounts Payable Aging

1. Export to **Excel** the Accounts Payable (A/P) Aging Summary at **December 31, 2022**

P10.1.7 Back Up Project 10.1

Save a backup of your Project file using the file name: YourName Project 10.1 Backup.QBB. See *Appendix B: Back Up & Restore QuickBooks Files* for instructions.

Chapter 11

QuickBooks Service Company

BACKSTORY

Lately, you've considered starting your own business and becoming an entrepreneur. You have been looking for a business opportunity that would use your talents to make money.

While working at Rock Castle Construction, you have overheard conversations that some of the customers have been dissatisfied with the quality of the paint jobs. In addition, you believe there is a demand for custom painting. You know that Rock Castle Construction lost more than one job because it could not find a subcontractor to do custom painting.

One morning when you arrive at work, you hear Mr. Castle's voice booming throughout the office. "That's the second time this month!" he roars into the telephone. *"How are we supposed to finish our jobs on time when the painting subcontractor doesn't show up?!"* Mr. Castle slams down the phone.

That morning you begin to seriously consider the advantages and disadvantages of starting your own painting service business. Perhaps you could pick up some work from Rock Castle Construction. You could do interior and exterior painting for homes and businesses including custom-painted murals while continuing to work part-time for Rock Castle Construction maintaining its accounting records. Now that you have learned QuickBooks, you can quickly enter transactions and create the reports Mr. Castle needs, leaving you time to operate your own painting service business.

When you return from lunch, you notice Maria Cecilia in Mr. Castle's office. Then you overhear Mr. Castle telling her, *"We would like to help you, Mrs. Cecilia, but we don't have anyone who can do a custom-painted landscape on your dining room wall. If I hear of anyone who does that type of work, I will call you."*

You watch as the two of them shake hands and Mrs. Cecilia walks out the front door. Sensing a window of opportunity, you turn to Mr. Castle and ask, *"Would you mind if I help out Mrs. Cecilia with the mural?"*

Mr. Castle nods his approval. *"If it keeps one of our customers happy, then I'm happy."*

You swiftly pursue Mrs. Cecilia into the parking lot.

"Mrs. Cecilia—"

She stops and turns to look at you. *"Mrs. Cecilia—I understand that you are looking for someone to paint a landscape mural in your home. I would like to bid on the job."*

With a sparkle in her eye, Mrs. Cecilia asks, *"How soon can you start?"*

"As soon as I get off work this afternoon!" you reply as the two of you shake hands. *"Would you like a bid on the job?"*

Without hesitation, Mrs. Cecilia replies, *"I trust you will be fair to your first customer."*

When you reenter the office building, Mr. Castle is waiting for you. Finally, Mr. Castle speaks, handing you a note. *"Congratulations. Here is a customer you should call — who would like a marble faux painting in his home's foyer."*

"Thanks, Mr. Castle. I'll do that right away," you reply as you head toward your cubicle.

Walking back to your cubicle, you quickly make start-up decisions:

1. To use the sole proprietorship form of business.
2. To name your business Paint Palette.
3. To use environmentally friendly paints and European painting techniques (faux and murals) for competitive advantage.
4. To invest in a computer so that you can use QuickBooks to maintain the accounting records for your business.

Now you will have two sources of income:

- Wages from Rock Castle Construction reported on your W-2 and attached to your 1040 tax return.
- Income from your painting business reported on a Schedule C attached to your 1040 tax return.

So you decide to treat yourself to a reward—a new smartphone—and use social media marketing to reach new customers for your new business endeavor.

Preferring to use your savings rather than take out a bank loan, you invest $6,000 of your savings to launch Paint Palette. Then you prepare the following list of items your business will need.

My Business Needs....

Computer & printer	**$1,500**
Paint equipment (ladder, drop clothes, etc)	**500**
Paint supplies (paint brushes, rollers, etc)	**300**
Van lease	**200/mo**

Section 11.1

QB SatNav

The objective of this chapter is to facilitate your mastery of QuickBooks Desktop. We will cover setting up a new QuickBooks service company, customize the QuickBooks Chart of Accounts, enter QuickBooks transactions, and create reports. This chapter provides the opportunity to integrate knowledge of QuickBooks Desktop through all three phases of the QB SatNav.

As shown in the following QB SatNav, Chapter 11 QuickBooks Service Company covers all three processes: QB Settings, QB Transactions, and QB Reports.

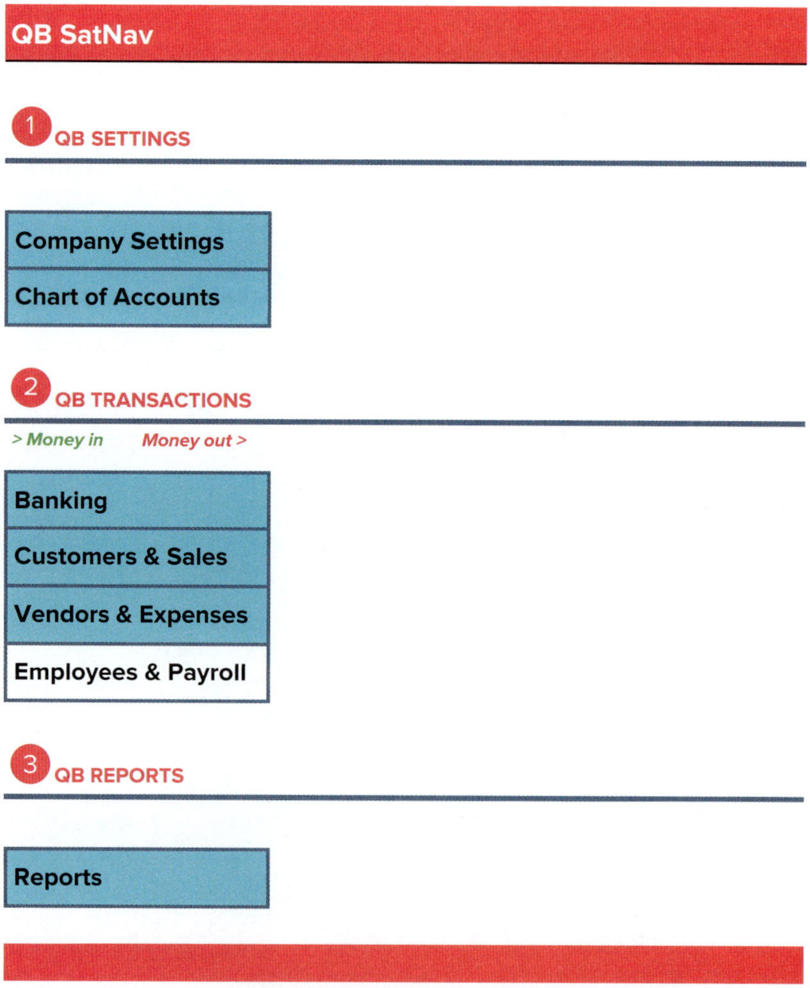

Section 11.2

NEW QUICKBOOKS SERVICE COMPANY

In this chapter, you will set up a new service company in QuickBooks by completing the following steps:

- **EasyStep Interview.** Use the EasyStep Interview to enter information and preferences for the new company. Based on the information entered, QuickBooks automatically creates a Chart of Accounts.
- **Create Lists.**
  - **Customer List.** In the Customer List, enter information about customers to whom you sell products and services.
  - **Vendor List.** In the Vendor List, enter information about vendors from whom you buy products, supplies, and services.
  - **Item List.** In the Item List, enter information about (1) products and services you sell to customers and (2) products and services you buy from vendors.
- **Customize the Chart of Accounts.** Modify the Chart of Accounts to customize it for your business.
- **Record Transactions.** Enter business transactions in QuickBooks using onscreen forms and the onscreen Journal.
- **Reports.** After preparing adjusting entries, print financial reports.

If you hired employees, you would also enter information into the Employee List. In this case, Paint Palette has no employees.

Download the Excel Report Template for Chapter 11 at www.My-QuickBooks.com, QB2018 link.

Section 11.3

CREATE NEW COMPANY

START QUICKBOOKS

To start QuickBooks software, click the **QuickBooks** icon on your desktop. If a QuickBooks icon does not appear on your desktop, from Microsoft® Windows® click **Start** button > **Programs** > **QuickBooks** > **QuickBooks Premier Accountant Edition.**

EASYSTEP INTERVIEW

To create a new company data file in QuickBooks, use the EasyStep Interview. The EasyStep Interview asks you a series of questions about your business. Then QuickBooks uses the information to customize QuickBooks to fit your business needs.

Four options for how to set up a new company are:

- Express Start: Recommended for new QuickBooks users, this option will ask you a few basic questions and do the rest for you.
- Detailed Start: This option lets you control the setup and fine-tune the company file to meet your specific needs.
- Create: This choice permits you to create quickly a new company file by copying the preferences and key lists from an existing company.
- Other Options: This option lets you convert data from Quicken or other accounting software to create a new QuickBooks company file.

Create a new QuickBooks company using the EasyStep Interview as follows:

1. Select **Create a new company**
2. When the QuickBooks Setup window appears, select **Detailed Start**
3. When the EasyStep Interview Enter Your Company Information window appears, enter Company Name: **YourName Paint Palette.** Press the **Tab** key, and QuickBooks will automatically enter the company name in the Legal name field. Since the company will

do business under its legal name, the Company name and Legal name fields are the same.

4 Enter the company information.

Tax ID	**333-22-4444**
Address	**333 Universe Boulevard**
City	**Bayshore**
State	**CA**
Zip	**94326**
Phone	**800-555-1358**
Email	<**Enter your email address**>

5 Select **Next**

6 In the Select Your Industry window, select **General Service-based Business**

7 Select **Next**

8 When the How Is Your Company Organized? window appears, select **Sole Proprietorship.**

How your business entity is organized (Sole Proprietorship, Partnership, Limited Liability Partnership (LLP), Limited Liability Company (LLC), C Corporation, S Corporation, or Non-Profit) determines which tax form and tax lines you use.

9 Select **Next**

10 Select the first month of your fiscal year: **January**

11 Select **Next**

12 In the Set Up Your Administrator Password window:

- Enter your administrator **password**
- Retype the **password**

13 Select **Next.** When the Create Your Company File window appears, click **Next** to choose a file name and location to save your company file.

14 When the Filename for New Company window appears, select Save in: **Desktop**

15 Enter File name: **YourName Chapter 11**

16 Click **Save**

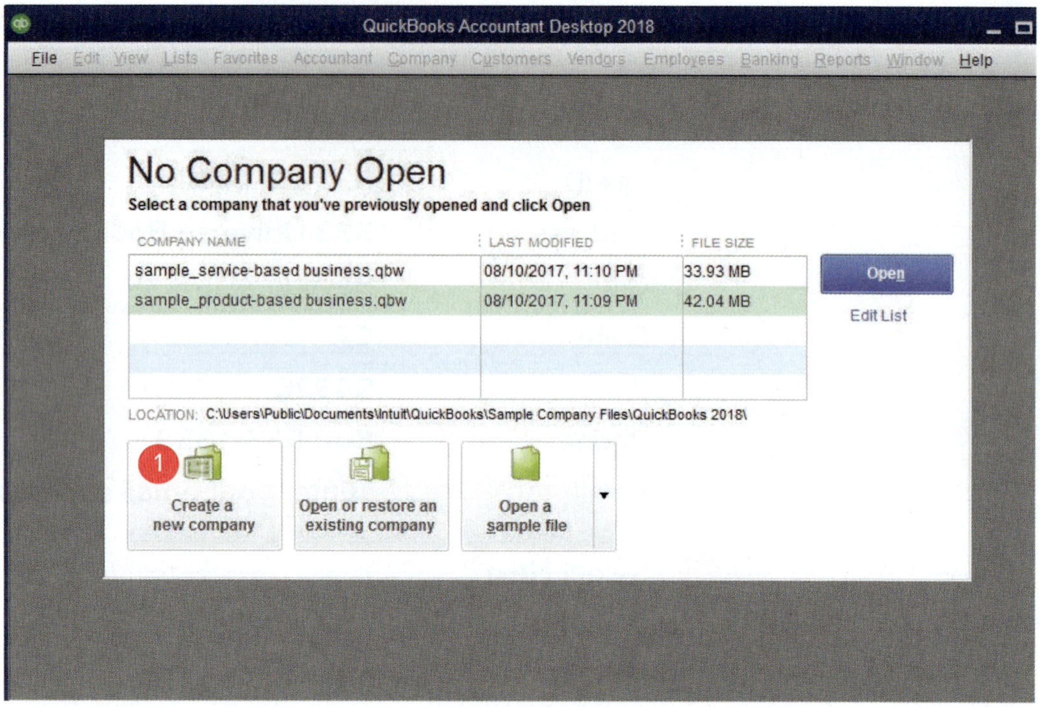
QuickBooks Accountant Desktop 2018
File Edit View Lists Favorites Accountant Company Customers Vendors Employees Banking Reports Window Help
No Company Open
Select a company that you've previously opened and click Open
COMPANY NAME
LAST MODIFIED
FILE SIZE
sample_service-based business.qbw
08/10/2017, 11:10 PM
33.93 MB
sample_product-based business.qbw
08/10/2017, 11:09 PM
42.04 MB
Open
Edit List
LOCATION: C:\Users\Public\Documents\Intuit\QuickBooks\Sample Company Files\QuickBooks 2018\
1
Create a new company
Open or restore an existing company
Open a sample file

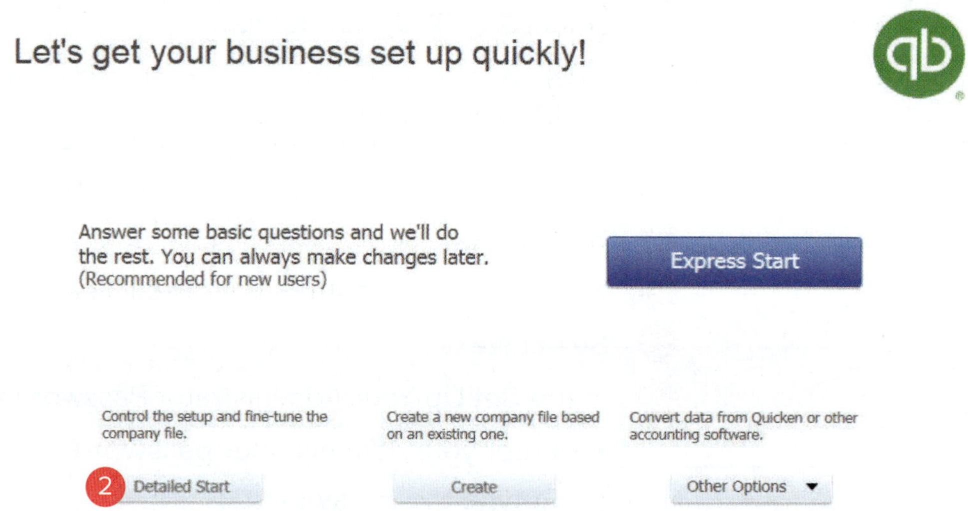
Let's get your business set up quickly!
Answer some basic questions and we'll do the rest. You can always make changes later. (Recommended for new users)
Express Start
Control the setup and fine-tune the company file.
Create a new company file based on an existing one.
Convert data from Quicken or other accounting software.
2
Detailed Start
Create
Other Options

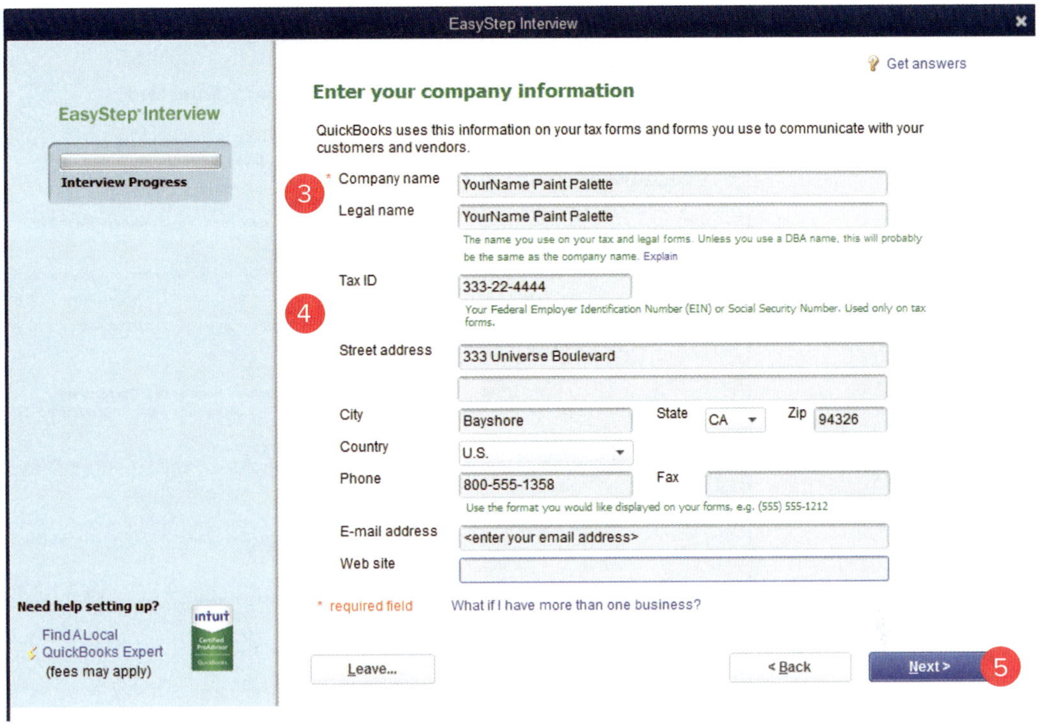
EasyStep Interview
Get answers
Enter your company information
QuickBooks uses this information on your tax forms and forms you use to communicate with your customers and vendors.
3
* Company name
YourName Paint Palette
Legal name
YourName Paint Palette
The name you use on your tax and legal forms. Unless you use a DBA name, this will probably be the same as the company name. Explain
Tax ID
333-22-4444
4
Your Federal Employer Identification Number (EIN) or Social Security Number. Used only on tax forms.
Street address
333 Universe Boulevard
City
Bayshore
State
CA
Zip
94326
Country
U.S.
Phone
800-555-1358
Fax
Use the format you would like displayed on your forms, e.g. (555) 555-1212
E-mail address
<enter your email address>
Web site
* required field
What if I have more than one business?
EasyStep Interview
Interview Progress
Need help setting up?
Find A Local QuickBooks Expert
(fees may apply)
intuit
Leave...
< Back
Next >
5

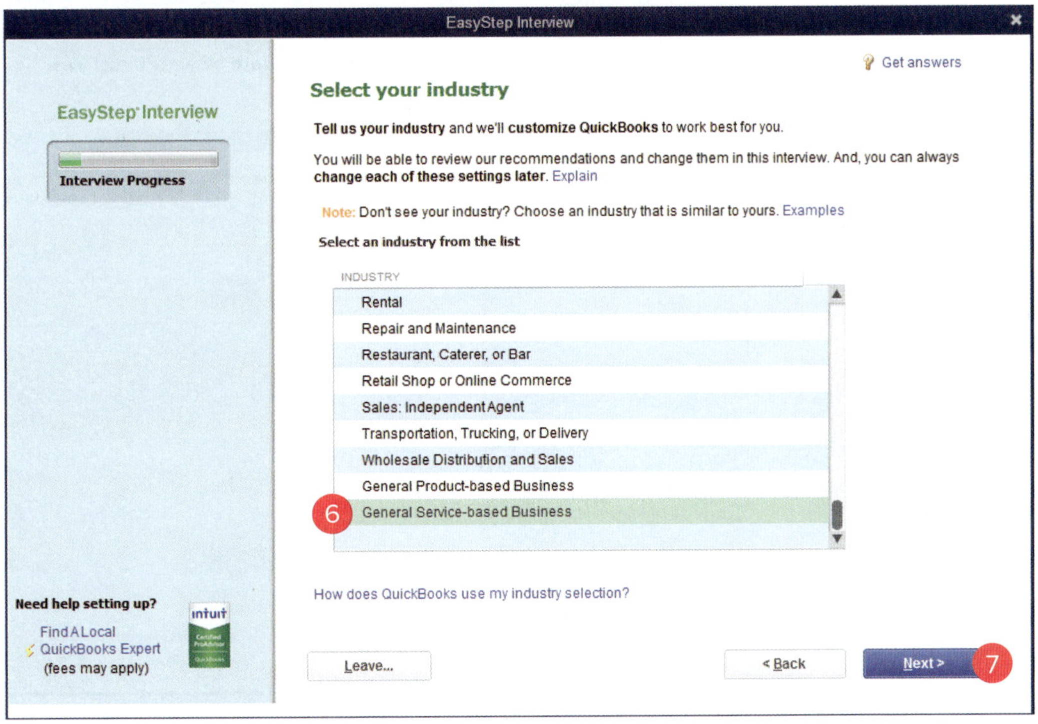
EasyStep Interview
Get answers
Select your industry
Tell us your industry and we'll customize QuickBooks to work best for you.
You will be able to review our recommendations and change them in this interview. And, you can always change each of these settings later. Explain
Note: Don't see your industry? Choose an industry that is similar to yours. Examples
Select an industry from the list
INDUSTRY
Rental
Repair and Maintenance
Restaurant, Caterer, or Bar
Retail Shop or Online Commerce
Sales: Independent Agent
Transportation, Trucking, or Delivery
Wholesale Distribution and Sales
General Product-based Business
6
General Service-based Business
How does QuickBooks use my industry selection?
EasyStep Interview
Interview Progress
Need help setting up?
Find A Local QuickBooks Expert
(fees may apply)
intuit
Leave...
< Back
Next >
7

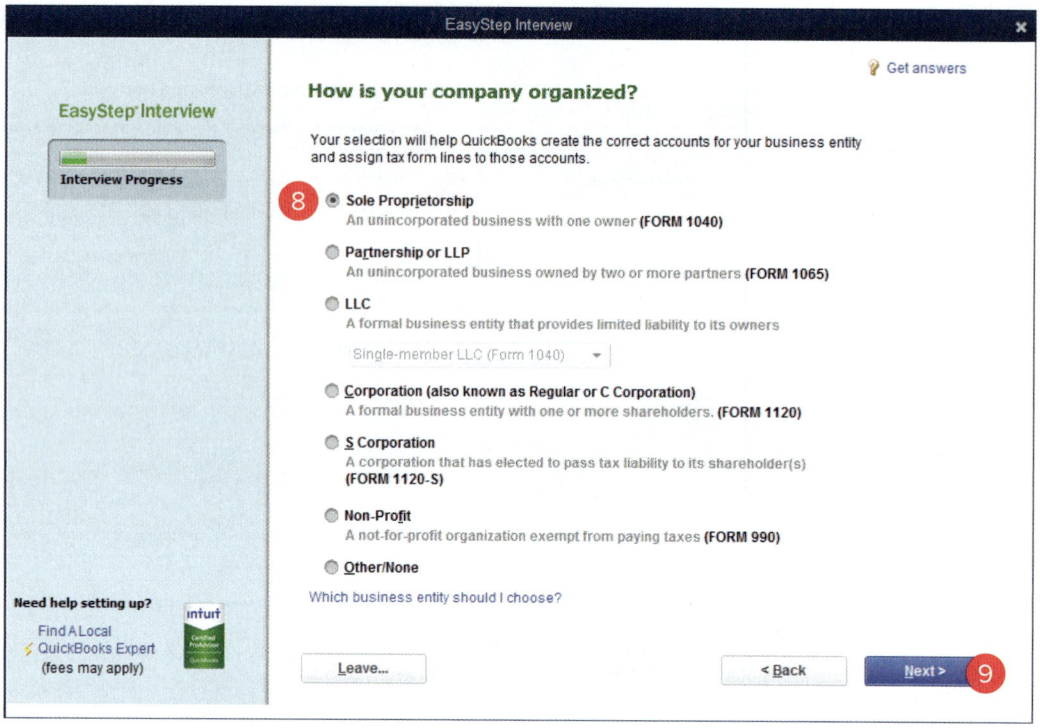
EasyStep Interview
EasyStep Interview
Interview Progress
Get answers
How is your company organized?
Your selection will help QuickBooks create the correct accounts for your business entity and assign tax form lines to those accounts.
8
Sole Proprietorship
An unincorporated business with one owner (FORM 1040)
Partnership or LLP
An unincorporated business owned by two or more partners (FORM 1065)
LLC
A formal business entity that provides limited liability to its owners
Single-member LLC (Form 1040)
Corporation (also known as Regular or C Corporation)
A formal business entity with one or more shareholders. (FORM 1120)
S Corporation
A corporation that has elected to pass tax liability to its shareholder(s) (FORM 1120-S)
Non-Profit
A not-for-profit organization exempt from paying taxes (FORM 990)
Other/None
Which business entity should I choose?
Need help setting up?
Find A Local QuickBooks Expert
(fees may apply)
intuit
Leave...
< Back
Next >
9

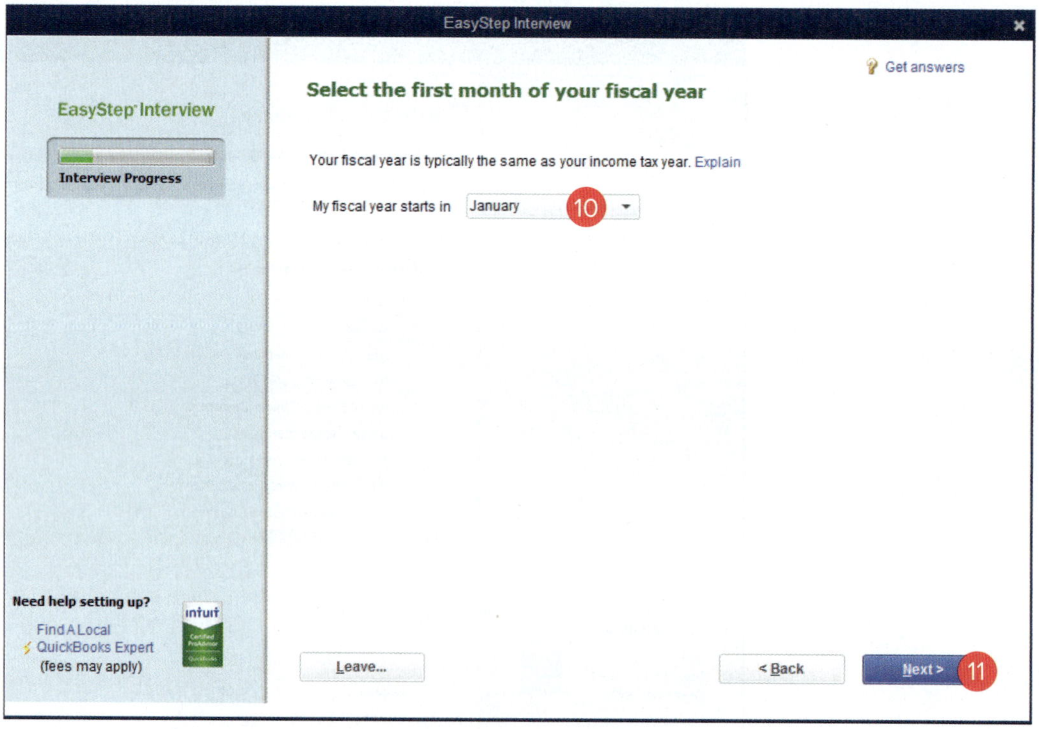
EasyStep Interview
EasyStep Interview
Interview Progress
Get answers
Select the first month of your fiscal year
Your fiscal year is typically the same as your income tax year. Explain
My fiscal year starts in
January
10
Need help setting up?
Find A Local QuickBooks Expert
(fees may apply)
intuit
Leave...
< Back
Next >
11

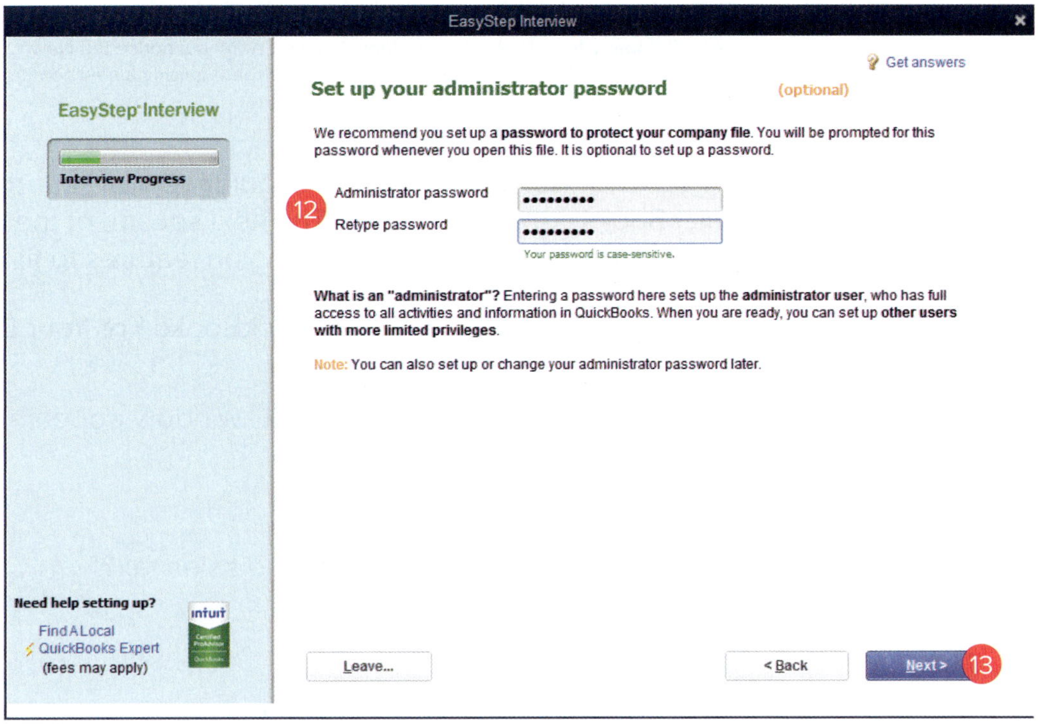
EasyStep Interview
Get answers
Set up your administrator password
(optional)
EasyStep Interview
Interview Progress
We recommend you set up a password to protect your company file. You will be prompted for this password whenever you open this file. It is optional to set up a password.
12
Administrator password
Retype password
Your password is case-sensitive.
What is an "administrator"? Entering a password here sets up the administrator user, who has full access to all activities and information in QuickBooks. When you are ready, you can set up other users with more limited privileges.
Note: You can also set up or change your administrator password later.
Need help setting up?
Find A Local QuickBooks Expert
(fees may apply)
Leave...
< Back
Next >
13

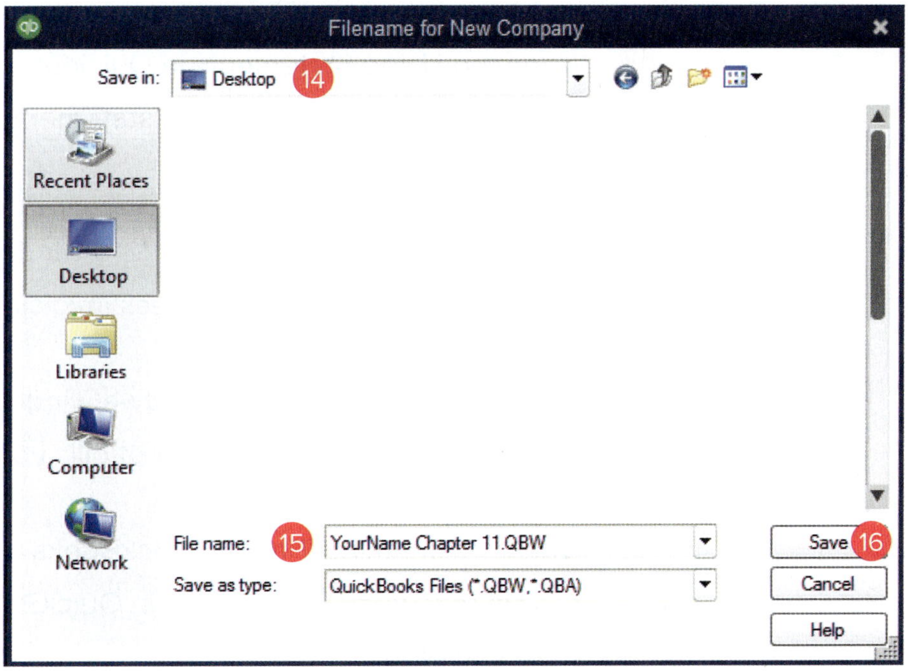
Filename for New Company
Save in:
Desktop
14
Recent Places
Desktop
Libraries
Computer
Network
File name:
15
YourName Chapter 11.QBW
Save as type:
QuickBooks Files (*.QBW,*.QBA)
Save
16
Cancel
Help

> **New Company from Existing Company.** On the File Menu, notice the New Company from Existing Company File option. This choice permits you to create quickly a new company file by copying the preferences and key lists from an existing company.

The My Shortcuts window should appear on the left side of your QuickBooks company screen. The next section of the EasyStep Interview is to customize QuickBooks by turning on features to fit your business needs.

1. When the Customizing QuickBooks For Your Business window appears, click **Next**
2. When the What Do You Sell? window appears:
   - Select **Services only**
   - Click **Next**
3. When asked "Do you charge sales tax?"
   - Select **No**
   - Click **Next**
4. When asked "Do you want to create estimates in QuickBooks?"
   - Select **Yes**
   - Click **Next**
5. When the Using Statements in QuickBooks window appears:
   - "Do you want to use billing statements in QuickBooks?" Select **Yes**
   - Click **Next**
6. When the Using Progress Invoicing window appears:
   - "Do you want to use progress invoicing?" Select **No**
   - Click **Next**
7. When the Managing Bills You Owe window appears:
   - "Do you want to keep track of bills you owe?" Select **Yes**
   - Click **Next**
8. When the Tracking Time in QuickBooks window appears:
   - "Do you want to track time in QuickBooks?" Select **Yes**
   - Click **Next**
9. When the Do You Have Employees? window appears:
   - Select **No**
   - Click **Next**

10 Read the Using Accounts in QuickBooks window. Click **Next.**

11 When the Select a Date to Start Tracking Your Finances window appears:

- Select **Use today's date or the first day of the quarter or month**
- Enter Date **01/01/2023**
- Click **Next**

12 When the Review Income and Expense Accounts window appears, click **Next**

13 When the Congratulations! window appears, click **Go to Setup**

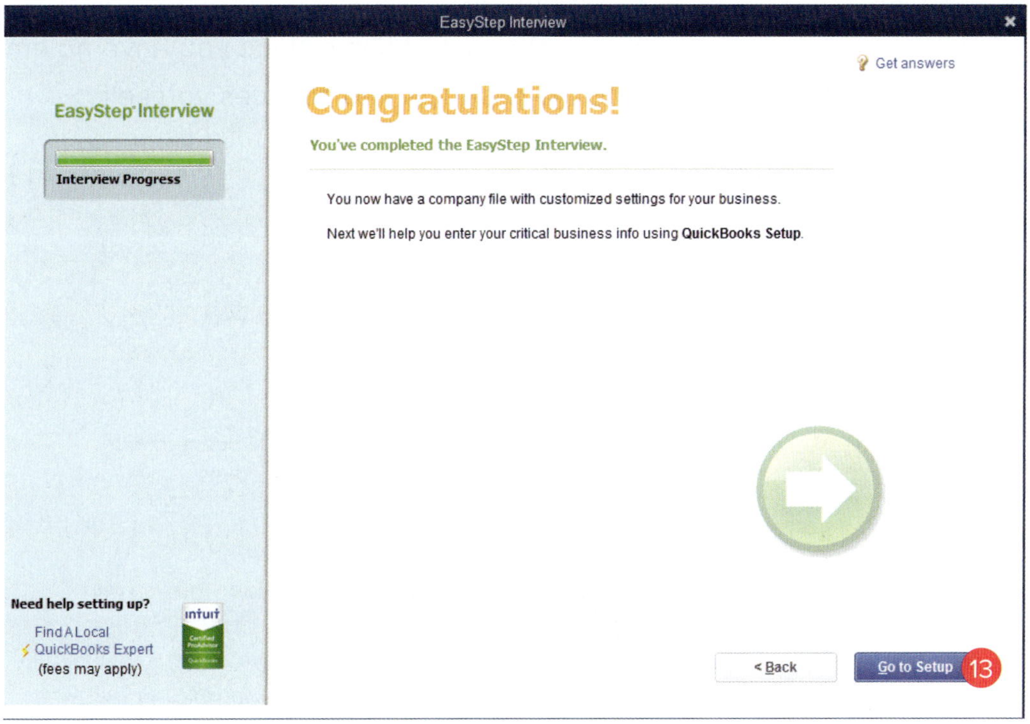

Section 11.4

QUICKBOOKS COMPANY SETUP

After the EasyStep Interview is finished, you can start using the QuickBooks company file or you can finish the company setup using the following QuickBooks Setup window.

As shown in the QuickBooks Setup window, you can:

1. Add the people you do business with:
   - Customer List
   - Vendor List
   - Employee List (Omit since you have no employees.)
2. Add the products and services you sell
   - Item List
3. Add your bank accounts

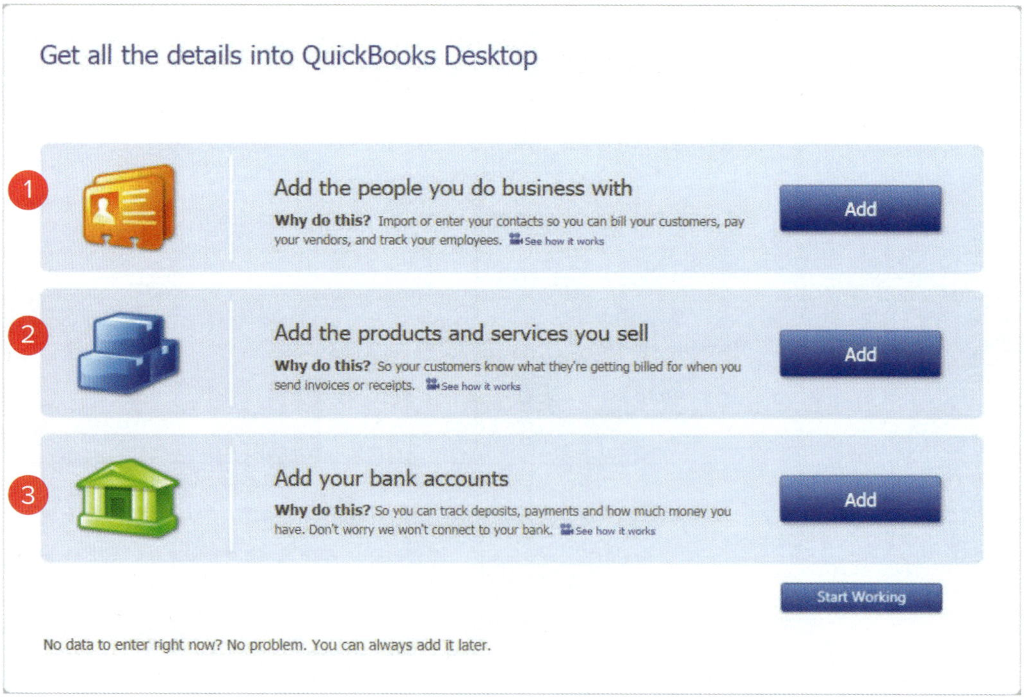

After completing these steps, you can customize your QuickBooks company file by completing the following:

1. Complete the company information
2. Customize preferences
3. Customize your Chart of Accounts

Section 11.5

ADD THE PEOPLE YOU DO BUSINESS WITH

As you know from Chapter 5, the Customer List contains information about the customers to whom you sell services. In addition, the Customer List also contains information about jobs or projects for each customer. Currently, Paint Palette has two customers:

1. Maria Cecilia, who wants a custom landscape mural painted on her dining room wall
2. TJ Ryan, who wants marble faux painting in his home's foyer

As you know from Chapter 6, the Vendor List contains information about vendors from whom you buy products and services. Paint Palette needs to add Brewer Paint Supplies as a vendor.

To add customers, vendors, and employees to your QuickBooks company file:

1. In the Add the People You Do Business With section of the QuickBooks Setup window, click the **Add** button
2. You have several options for how to add information about people you do business with as shown in the following Add the People You Do Business With window. Select **Paste from Excel or enter manually.**
3. Select **Continue**
4. When the Select Who to Add window appears, enter the following information about your first customer, Maria Cecilia.

Name	**Cecilia, Maria**
First Name	**Maria**
Last Name	**Cecilia**
Email	**mariacecilia@www.com**
Phone	**415-555-6565**
Address	**65 5th Avenue**
City, State, Zip	**Bayshore, CA 94326**
Contact Name	**Maria Cecilia**

5. Select **Customer** radio button for Maria Cecilia
6. Move to the next line and enter the following information about Brewer Paint Supplies

Name	**Brewer Paint Supplies**
Company Name	**Brewer Paint Supplies**
Email	**brewerpaint@www.com**
Phone	**415-555-6372**
Address	**18 Spring Street**
City, State, Zip	**Bayshore, CA 94326**
Contact Name	**Mark Brewer**

7. Select **Vendor** radio button for Brewer Paint Supplies
8. Click **Continue**
9. If you had opening balances, you could enter those now. Instead, click **Continue**

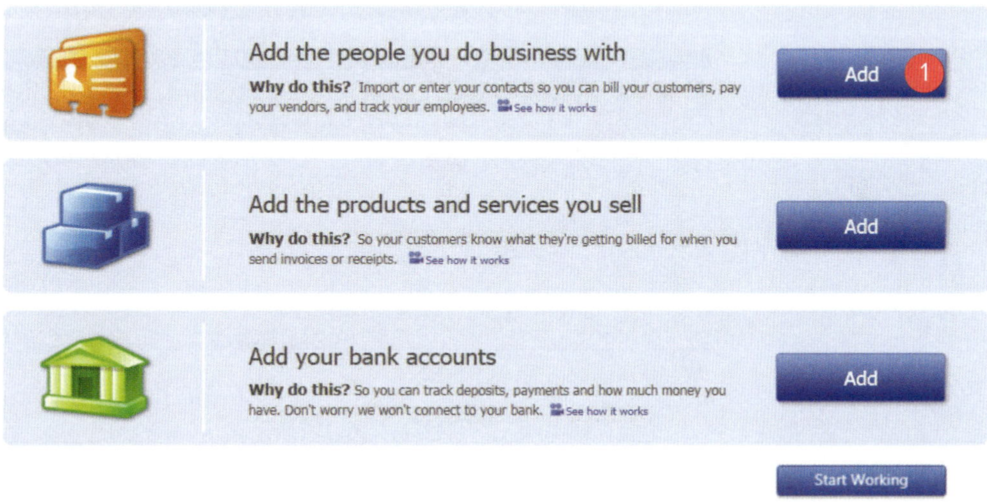

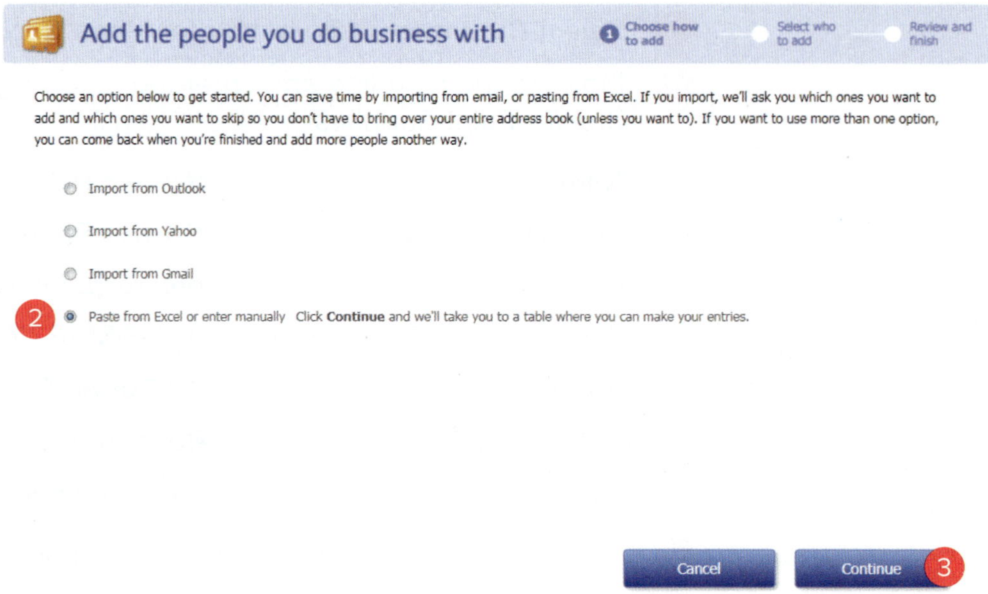
Add the people you do business with
1 Choose how to add
Select who to add
Review and finish
Choose an option below to get started. You can save time by importing from email, or pasting from Excel. If you import, we'll ask you which ones you want to add and which ones you want to skip so you don't have to bring over your entire address book (unless you want to). If you want to use more than one option, you can come back when you're finished and add more people another way.
Import from Outlook
Import from Yahoo
Import from Gmail
2
Paste from Excel or enter manually Click **Continue** and we'll take you to a table where you can make your entries.
Cancel
Continue
3

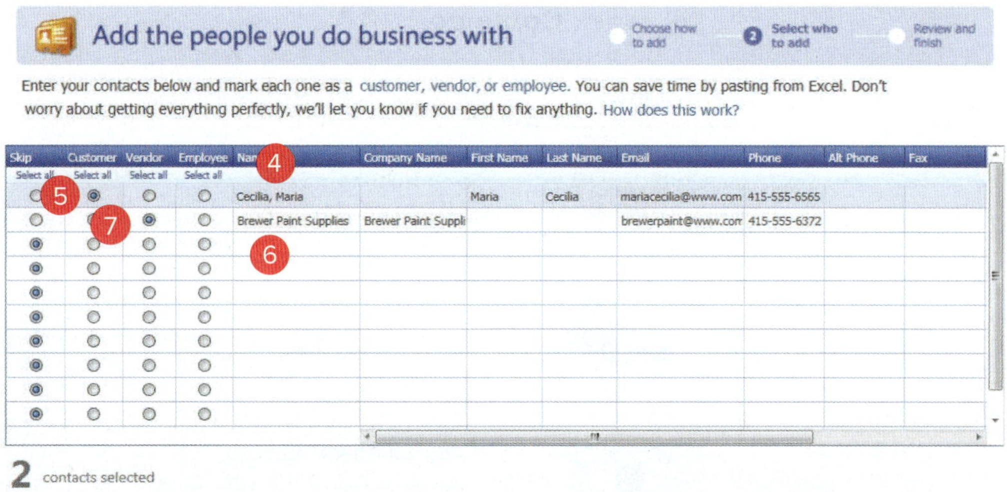
Add the people you do business with
Choose how to add
2 Select who to add
Review and finish
Enter your contacts below and mark each one as a customer, vendor, or employee. You can save time by pasting from Excel. Don't worry about getting everything perfectly, we'll let you know if you need to fix anything. How does this work?
Skip Customer Vendor Employee Name Company Name First Name Last Name Email Phone Alt Phone Fax
Select all Select all Select all Select all
4
5
Cecilia, Maria Maria Cecilia mariacecilia@www.com 415-555-6565
7
Brewer Paint Supplies Brewer Paint Suppli brewerpaint@www.com 415-555-6372
6
2 contacts selected
Cancel
Continue
8

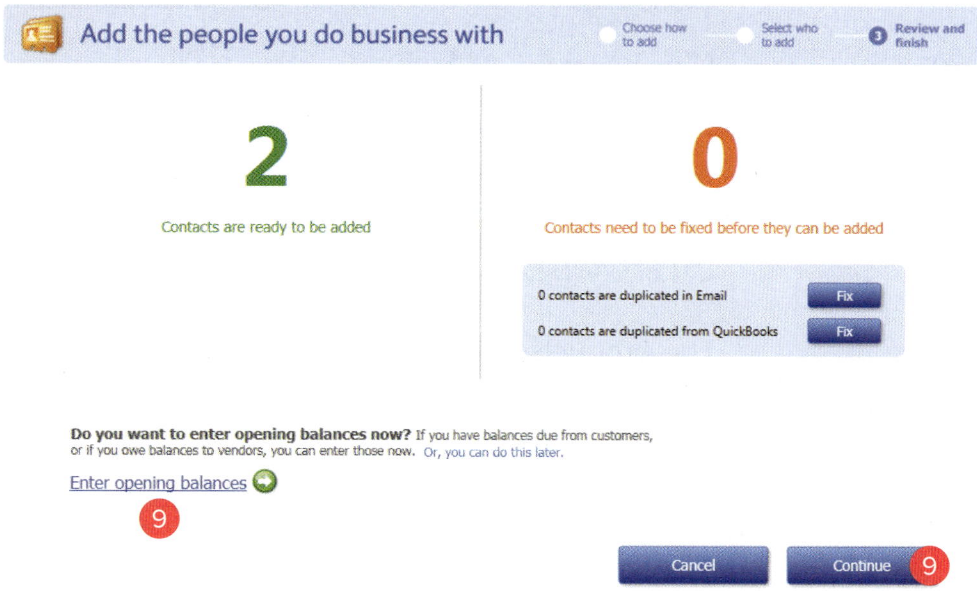
Add the people you do business with
Choose how to add
Select who to add
Review and finish
2
Contacts are ready to be added
0
Contacts need to be fixed before they can be added
0 contacts are duplicated in Email
Fix
0 contacts are duplicated from QuickBooks
Fix
Do you want to enter opening balances now? If you have balances due from customers, or if you owe balances to vendors, you can enter those now. Or, you can do this later.
Enter opening balances
9
Cancel
Continue
9

Section 11.6

ADD THE PRODUCTS AND SERVICES YOU SELL

The products and services you sell are entered into an Item List. As you know from Chapter 7, the Item List contains information about service items, inventory items, and non-inventory items. Paint Palette plans to sell four different service items to customers:

1. Labor: mural painting
2. Labor: faux painting
3. Labor: interior painting
4. Labor: exterior painting

To add a service item to the Item List for Paint Palette:

1. In the Add the Products and Services You Sell section of the QuickBooks Setup window, select the **Add** button
2. Select Item type **Service**
3. Select **Continue**
4. Enter the following information about the new service item:

Name	**Labor**
Description	**Painting labor**
Price	**0.00**

5. Click **Continue**
6. Click **Continue** again to return to the QuickBooks Setup window

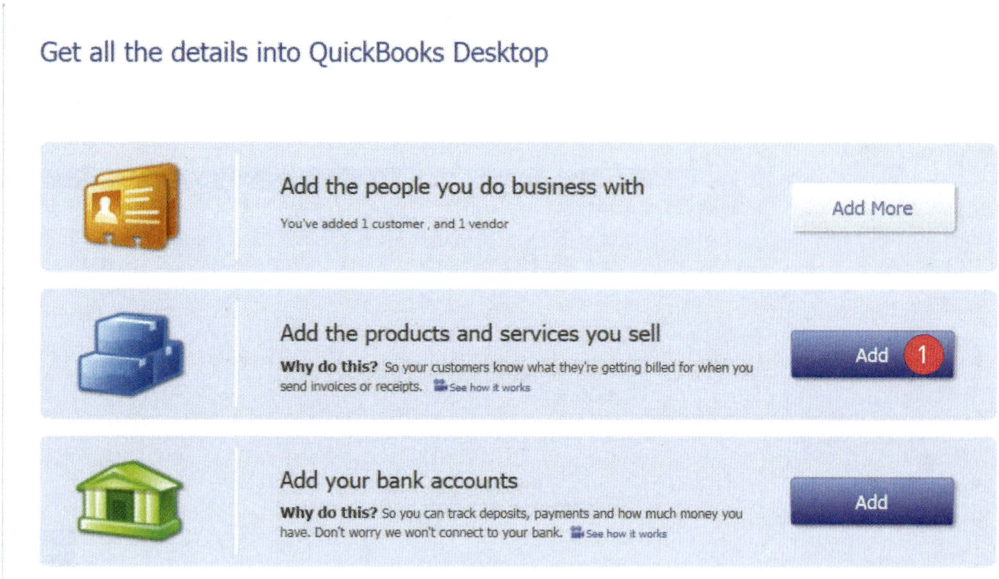
Get all the details into QuickBooks Desktop
Add the people you do business with
You've added 1 customer , and 1 vendor
Add More
Add the products and services you sell
Why do this? So your customers know what they're getting billed for when you send invoices or receipts. See how it works
Add
1
Add your bank accounts
Why do this? So you can track deposits, payments and how much money you have. Don't worry we won't connect to your bank. See how it works
Add

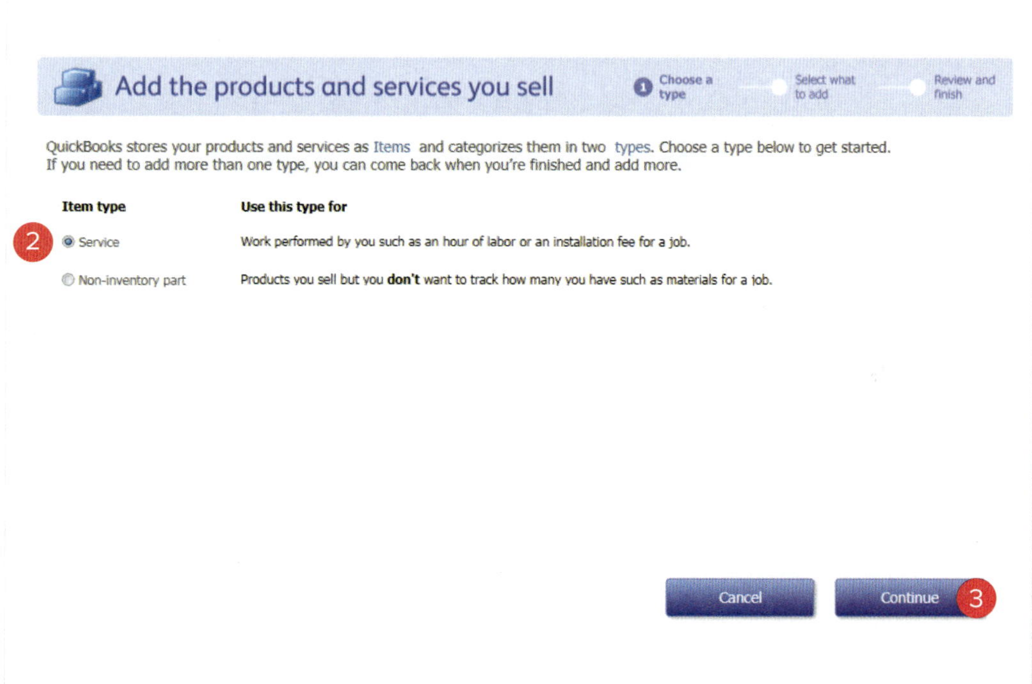
Add the products and services you sell
Choose a type
Select what to add
Review and finish
QuickBooks stores your products and services as Items and categorizes them in two types. Choose a type below to get started.
If you need to add more than one type, you can come back when you're finished and add more.
Item type
Use this type for
2
Service
Work performed by you such as an hour of labor or an installation fee for a job.
Non-inventory part
Products you sell but you don't want to track how many you have such as materials for a job.
Cancel
Continue
3

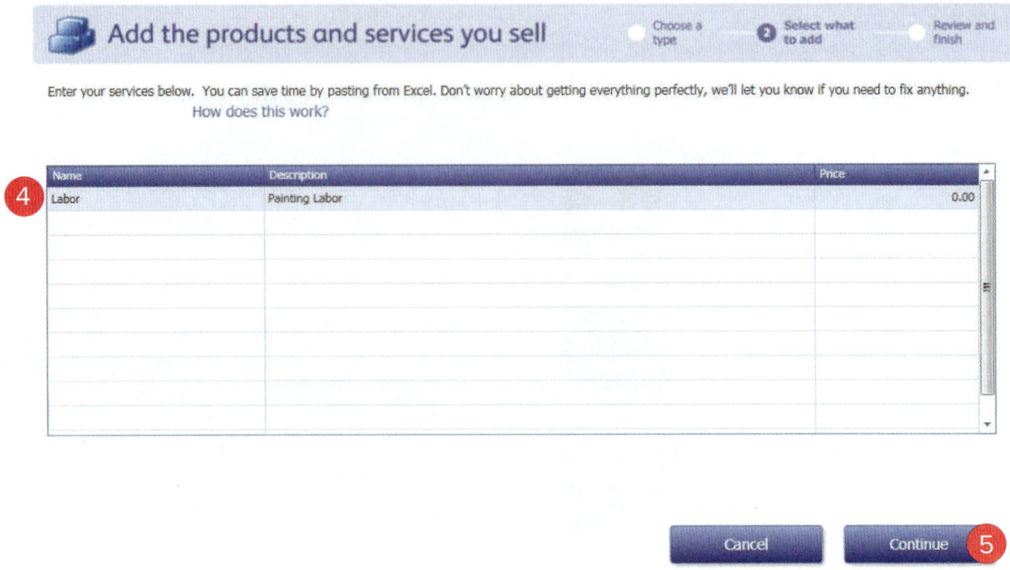
Add the products and services you sell
Choose a type
2 Select what to add
Review and finish
Enter your services below. You can save time by pasting from Excel. Don't worry about getting everything perfectly, we'll let you know if you need to fix anything.
How does this work?
Name
Description
Price
4
Labor
Painting Labor
0.00
Cancel
Continue
5

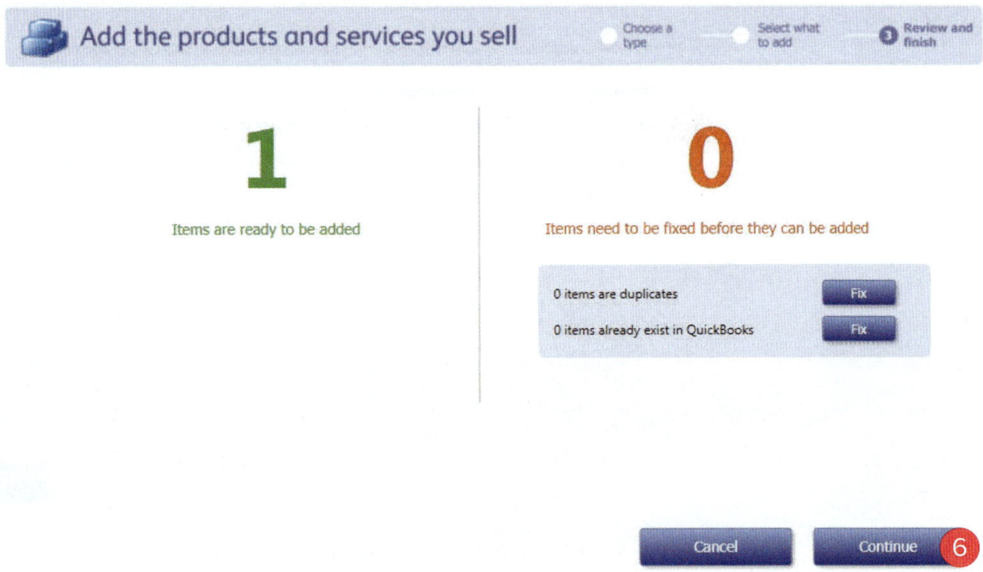
Add the products and services you sell
Choose a type
Select what to add
3 Review and finish
1
Items are ready to be added
0
Items need to be fixed before they can be added
0 items are duplicates
Fix
0 items already exist in QuickBooks
Fix
Cancel
Continue
6

Section 11.7

ADD YOUR BANK ACCOUNTS

Bank accounts in QuickBooks are used to track your company's deposits, payments, and current bank balances. A QuickBooks company file can have more than one bank account. For example, some companies use one bank account for payroll and another bank account for all other banking items.

To add a bank account for Paint Palette:

1. In the Add Your Bank Accounts section of the QuickBooks Setup window, click the **Add** button
2. Enter the following information about Paint Palette's bank account

Account Name	**Checking**
Account Number	**123456789**
Opening Balance	**0.00**
Opening Balance Date	**01/01/2023**

3. Select **Continue**
4. When asked if you want to order checks designed for QuickBooks, select **No Thanks**
5. Click **Continue** to return to the QuickBooks Setup window
6. Select **Start Working** at the bottom of the QuickBooks Setup window
7. When the New Feature Tour window appears, explore the new features, then select **Next** until reaching the final new feature
8. **Close** the New Feature Tour window

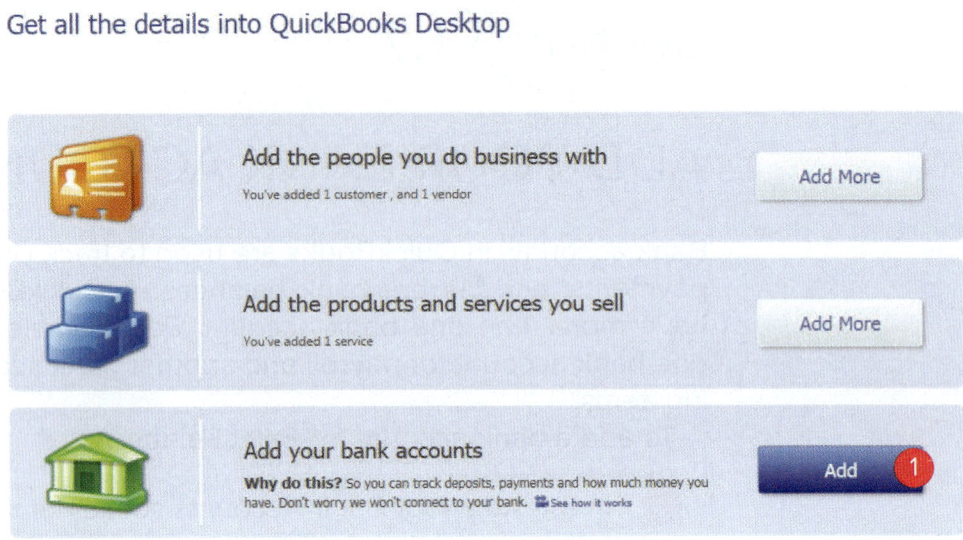
Get all the details into QuickBooks Desktop
Add the people you do business with
You've added 1 customer , and 1 vendor
Add More
Add the products and services you sell
You've added 1 service
Add More
Add your bank accounts
Why do this? So you can track deposits, payments and how much money you have. Don't worry we won't connect to your bank. See how it works
Add
1

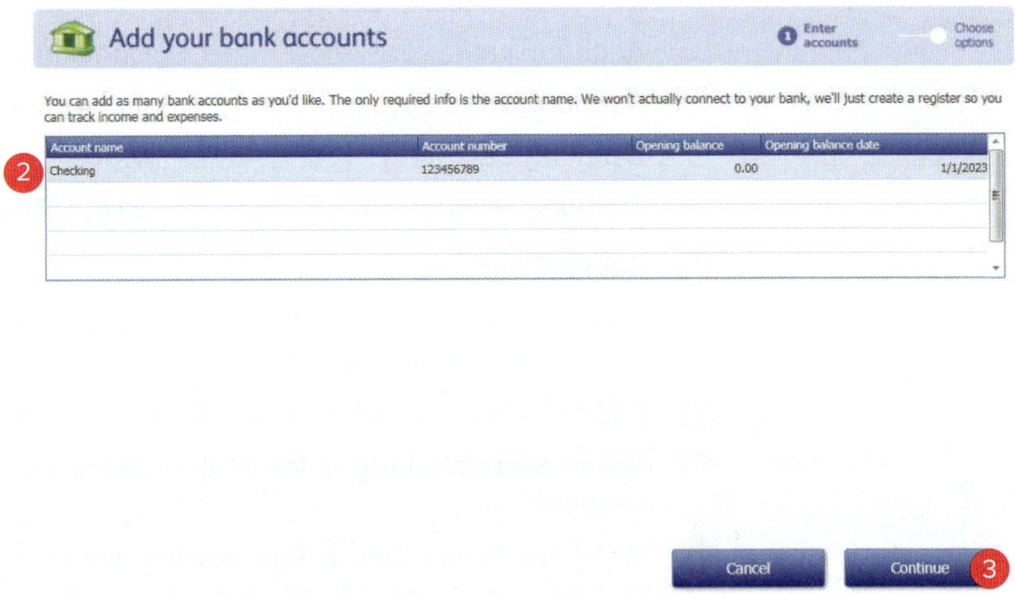
Add your bank accounts
Enter accounts
Choose options
You can add as many bank accounts as you'd like. The only required info is the account name. We won't actually connect to your bank, we'll just create a register so you can track income and expenses.
Account name
Account number
Opening balance
Opening balance date
2
Checking
123456789
0.00
1/1/2023
Cancel
Continue
3

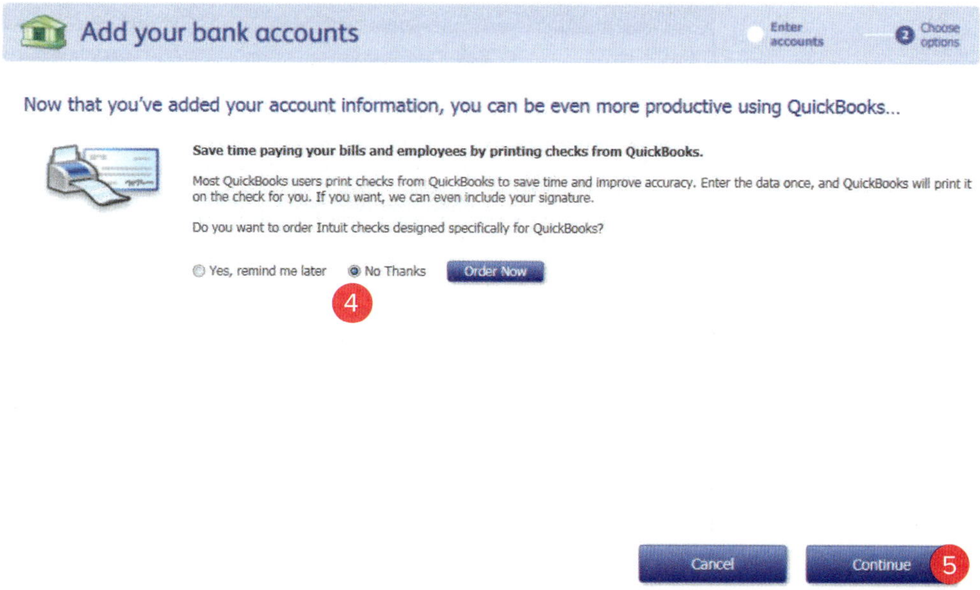
Add your bank accounts
Enter accounts
2 Choose options
Now that you've added your account information, you can be even more productive using QuickBooks...
Save time paying your bills and employees by printing checks from QuickBooks.
Most QuickBooks users print checks from QuickBooks to save time and improve accuracy. Enter the data once, and QuickBooks will print it on the check for you. If you want, we can even include your signature.
Do you want to order Intuit checks designed specifically for QuickBooks?
Yes, remind me later
No Thanks
Order Now
4
Cancel
Continue
5

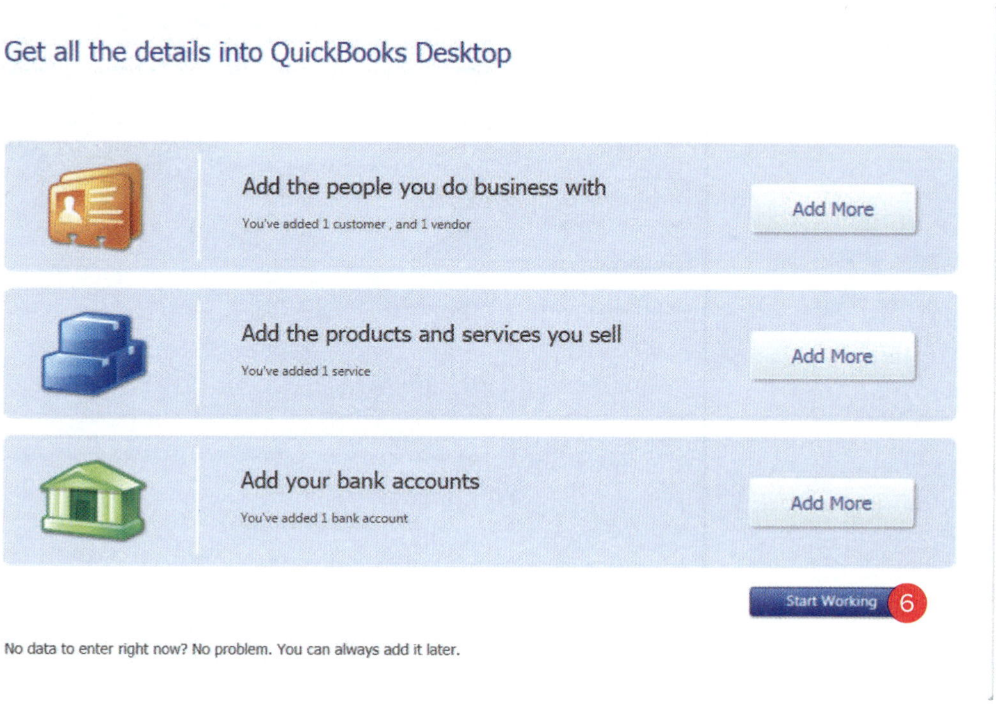
Get all the details into QuickBooks Desktop
Add the people you do business with
You've added 1 customer , and 1 vendor
Add More
Add the products and services you sell
You've added 1 service
Add More
Add your bank accounts
You've added 1 bank account
Add More
Start Working
6
No data to enter right now? No problem. You can always add it later.

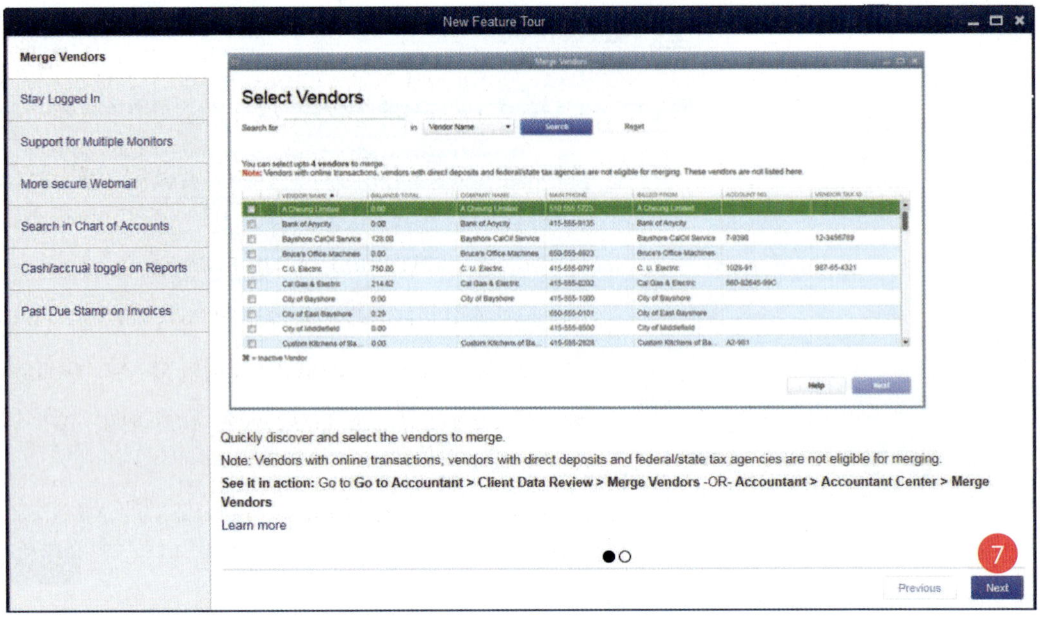
New Feature Tour
Merge Vendors
Stay Logged In
Support for Multiple Monitors
More secure Webmail
Search in Chart of Accounts
Cash/accrual toggle on Reports
Past Due Stamp on Invoices
Select Vendors
Quickly discover and select the vendors to merge.
Note: Vendors with online transactions, vendors with direct deposits and federal/state tax agencies are not eligible for merging.
See it in action: Go to Go to Accountant > Client Data Review > Merge Vendors -OR- Accountant > Accountant Center > Merge Vendors
Learn more
7
Previous
Next

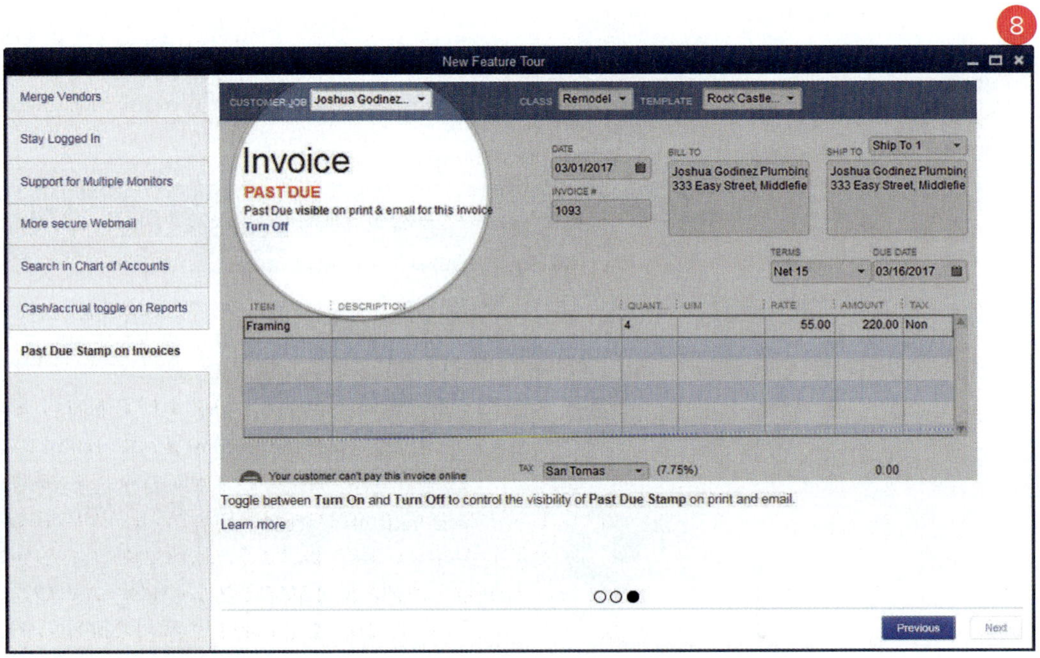
8
New Feature Tour
Merge Vendors
Stay Logged In
Support for Multiple Monitors
More secure Webmail
Search in Chart of Accounts
Cash/accrual toggle on Reports
Past Due Stamp on Invoices
CUSTOMER:JOB Joshua Godinez...
CLASS Remodel
TEMPLATE Rock Castle...
Invoice
PAST DUE
Past Due visible on print & email for this invoice
Turn Off
DATE 03/01/2017
INVOICE # 1093
BILL TO Joshua Godinez Plumbing 333 Easy Street, Middlefie
SHIP TO Ship To 1 Joshua Godinez Plumbing 333 Easy Street, Middlefie
TERMS Net 15
DUE DATE 03/16/2017
ITEM DESCRIPTION QUANT... U/M RATE AMOUNT TAX
Framing 4 55.00 220.00 Non
Your customer can't pay this invoice online
TAX San Tomas (7.75%) 0.00
Toggle between Turn On and Turn Off to control the visibility of Past Due Stamp on print and email.
Learn more
Previous
Next

Section 11.8

CUSTOMER, VENDOR, AND ITEM LISTS

CUSTOMER LIST

C11.8.1 Customer List. Before printing the Customer List, let's add a new job for Maria Cecilia.

1. To add a new job, first display the Customer Center by selecting **Customers** on the Navigation Bar
2. Select Maria Cecilia in the Customers & Jobs List, then **right-click** to display the pop-up menu. Select **Add Job.**
3. Enter the following information into the New Job window:

Job Name	**Dining Room**
Opening Balance	**0.00**
As of	**01/01/2023**
Job Description	**Dining Room Landscape Mural**
Job Type <Add New>	**Mural**
Job Status	**Awarded**
Start Date	**01/03/2023**

4. Click **OK** to save
5. To export to Excel or print the Customer List, click the **Excel** button at the top of the Customer Center
6. Click **Export Customer List**
7. Select **Replace an existing worksheet**
8. **Browse** for **YourName CH11 REPORTS** Excel file
9. Select worksheet: **C11.8.1 CUS**
10. Select **Advanced**
11. Uncheck **Space between columns**

12. Check **Row height**
13. Uncheck **Include QuickBooks Export Guide worksheet with helpful advice**
14. Select **On printed report and screen**
15. Click **OK**
16. Select **Export**
17. If an Export Report Alert window appears asking if you want to continue, select **Do not display this message in the future** > **Yes**
18. **Close** the Customer Center

VENDOR LIST

C11.8.2 Vendor List. To export the Vendor List for Paint Palette:

1. Display the Vendor Center by selecting **Vendors** on the Navigation Bar
2. Select the **Excel** button at the top of the Vendor Center
3. Select **Export Vendor List**
4. Export to **Excel** the Vendor List
5. **Close** the Vendor Center

ITEM LIST

C11.8.3 Item List. To export the Item List for Paint Palette:

1. Display the Report Center by selecting **Reports** on the Navigation Bar
2. Select **List**
3. Select **Item Listing**
4. Select Date **01/01/2023**
5. Select **Run**

6 With the Item Listing report displayed on your screen, export to **Excel.**

! When exporting to Excel, remember to select Advanced Excel Options:

- Uncheck **Space between columns**
- Uncheck **Include QuickBooks Export Guide worksheet with helpful advice**
- Select **On printed report and screen**

7 **Close** the Item Listing window and the Report Center window

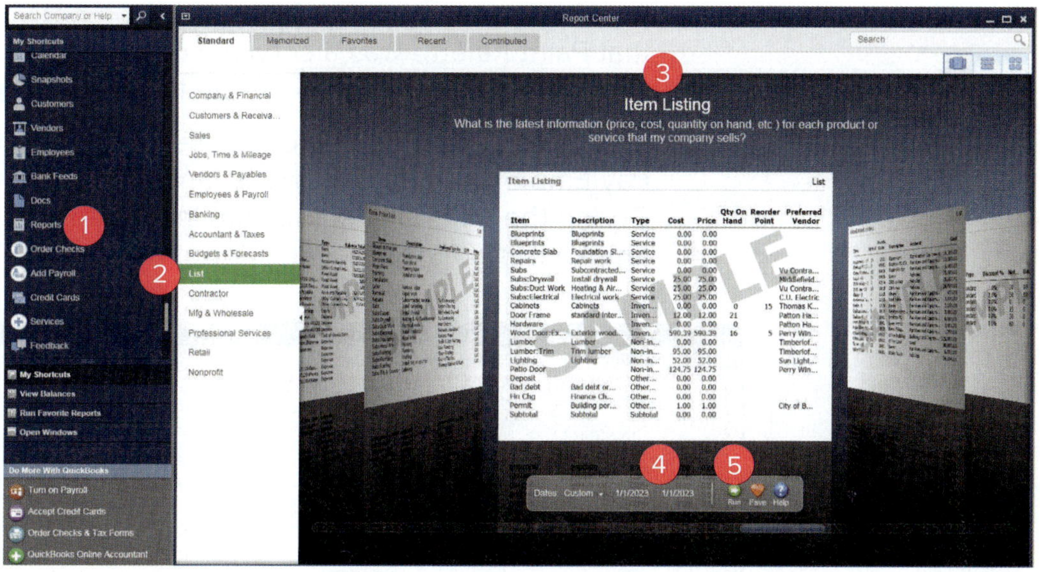

Section 11.9

CUSTOMIZE QUICKBOOKS

Notice that the Home Page for Paint Palette differs from the Home Page for Rock Castle Construction in the following ways:

1. The Vendors section of the Home Page for Paint Palette does not include Purchase Orders, Receive Inventory, and Enter Bills Against Inventory icons. During the company setup, you indicated that Paint Palette was a service company. Since you will not be selling a product, you will not be tracking inventory for resale.
2. Also notice that the Employees section does not include the Pay Employees, Pay Liabilities, and Process Payroll Forms icons. During the company setup, you indicated that there were no employees so these icons are not needed for Paint Palette.

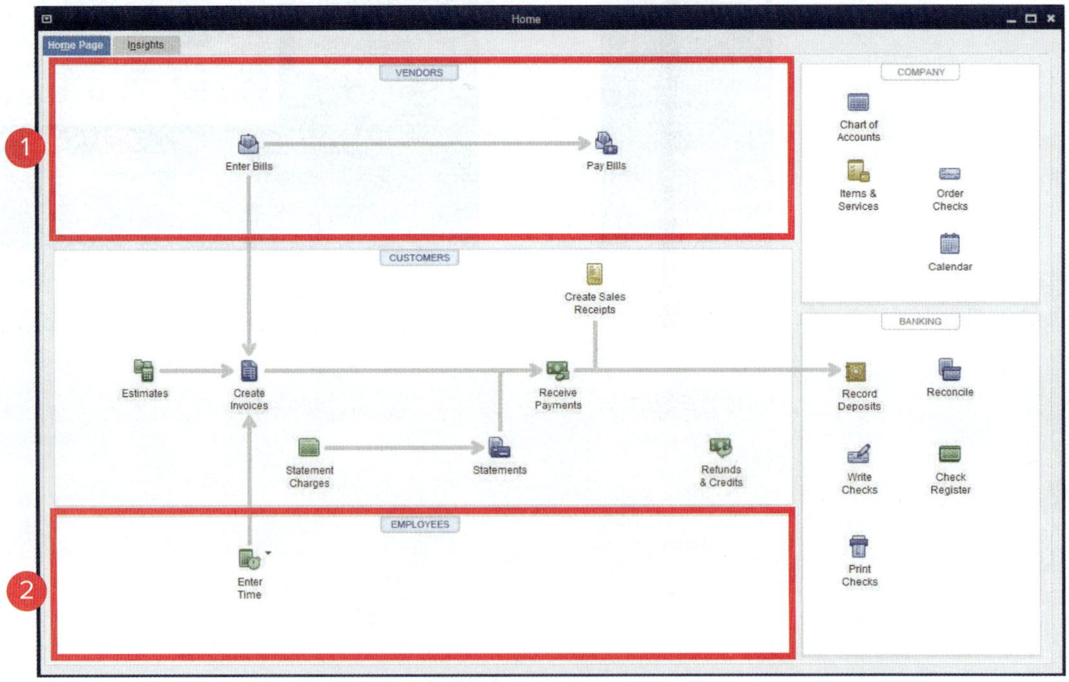

Next, we will customize QuickBooks for Paint Palette by entering company information and customizing preferences.

ENTER COMPANY INFORMATION

To enter additional company information:

1. Select **My Company** on the Navigation Bar
2. Select **Edit**
3. Update the Company Name: **YourName Chapter 11 Paint Palette**
4. Click **OK**
5. Verify Income Tax Form: **Form 1040 (Sole Proprietor)**
6. **Close** the My Company window

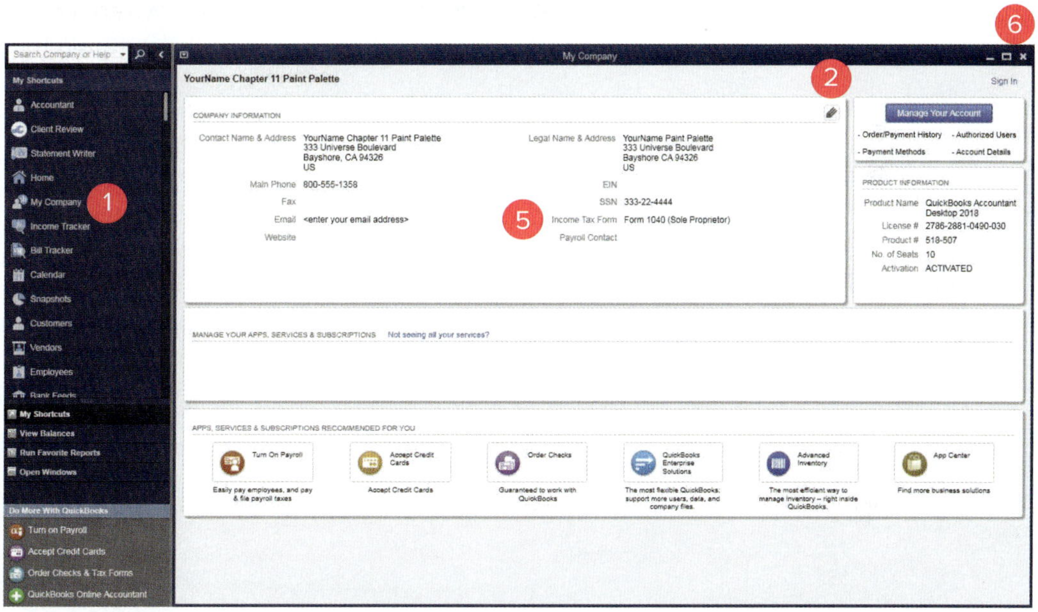

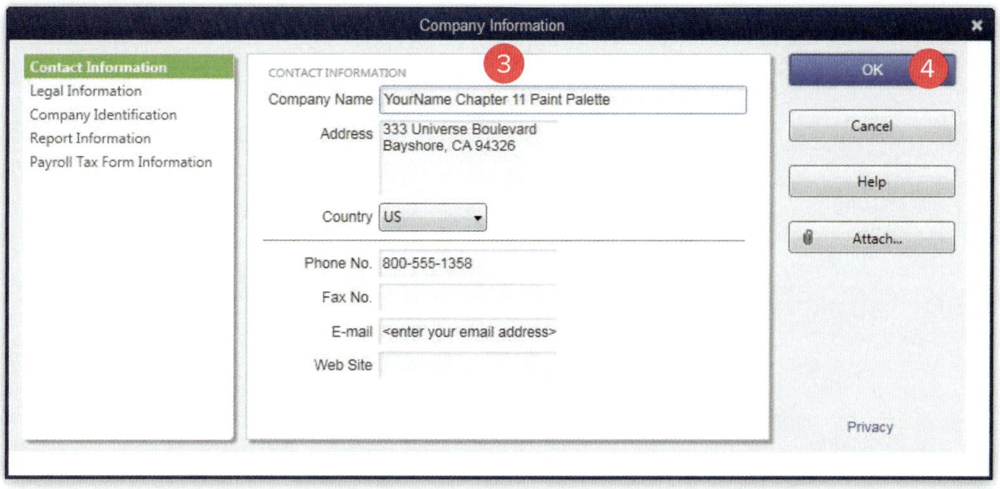

CUSTOMIZE QUICKBOOKS PREFERENCES

To customize your QuickBooks preferences:

1. Select **Edit Menu** > **Preferences** > **General** > **My Preferences**
2. Select Default Date to Use for New Transactions: **Use the last entered date as default**
3. Select **Desktop View** > **My Preferences** > **Show Home Page when opening a company file**
4. To customize the appearance of your QuickBooks, select **Company File Color Scheme**
5. Click **OK** to close the Preferences window

Section 11.10

CUSTOMIZE CHART OF ACCOUNTS

The Chart of Accounts is a list of all the accounts Paint Palette will use when maintaining its accounting records. The Chart of Accounts is like a table of contents for accounting records.

In the EasyStep Interview, when you selected General Service-based Business as the type of industry, QuickBooks automatically created a Chart of Accounts for Paint Palette. Then QuickBooks permits you to customize the Chart of Accounts to fit your accounting needs.

DISPLAY CHART OF ACCOUNTS

To display the following Chart of Accounts window:

1. Click **Chart of Accounts** icon in the Company section of the Home Page
2. Notice that the Chart of Accounts does not list the account numbers

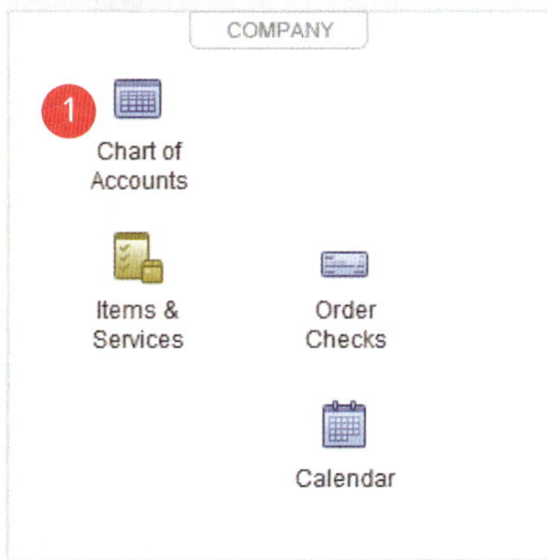

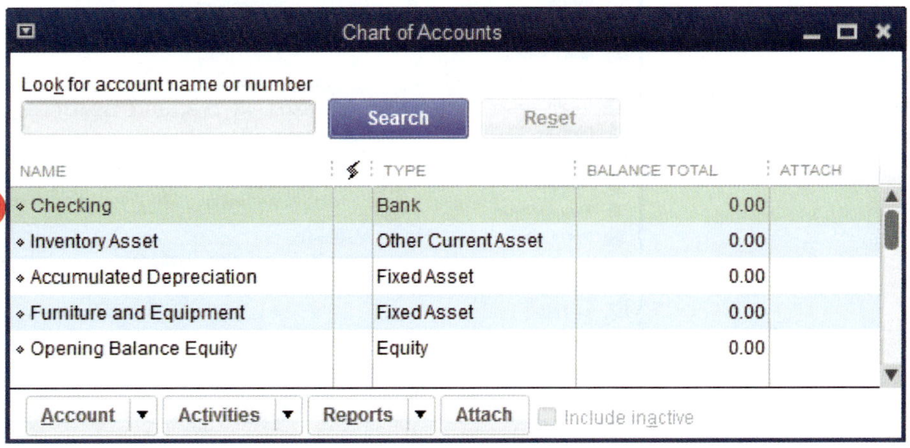

DISPLAY ACCOUNT NUMBERS

Display account numbers in the Chart of Accounts by completing the following steps:

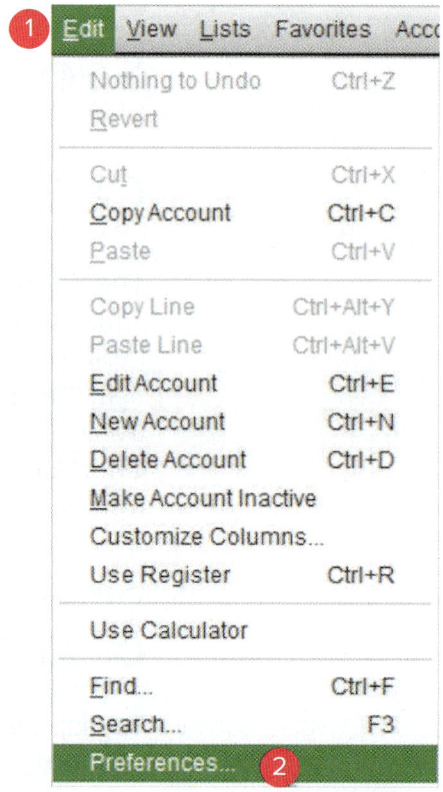

1. Select **Edit Menu**
2. Select **Preferences**
3. When the Preferences window appears, select the **Accounting** icon on the left scrollbar
4. Select the **Company Preferences** tab
5. Select **Use account numbers**
6. Uncheck **Warn if transactions are 30 day(s) in the future**
7. Click **OK** to close the Preferences window

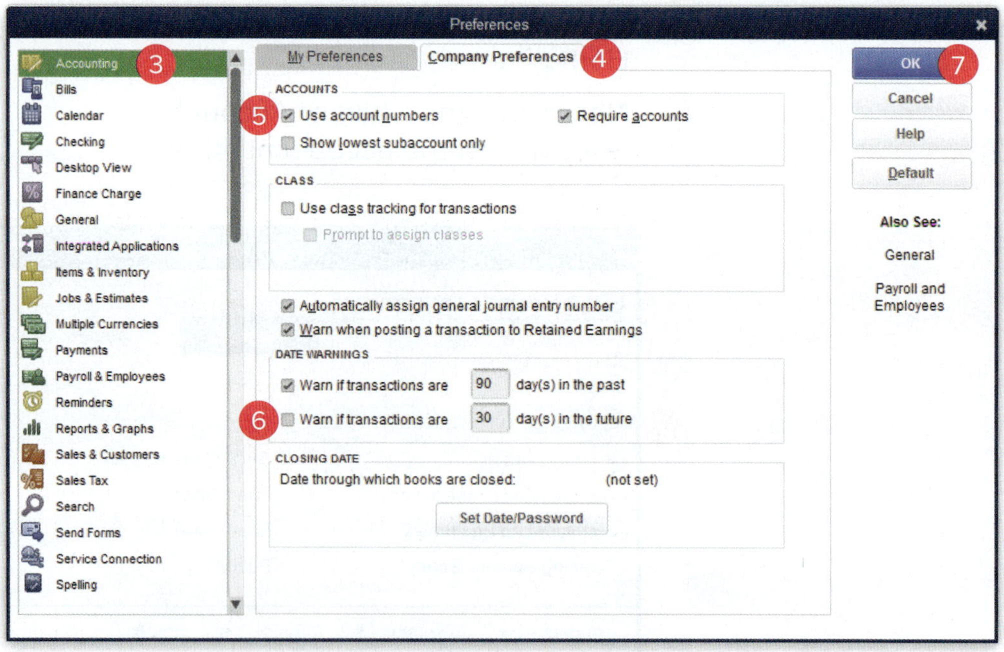

Your Chart of Accounts should now display account numbers.

ADD NEW ACCOUNTS

Paint Palette will be purchasing a new computer. To account for the computer, you will need to add the following three accounts to the Chart of Accounts:

Account	**Computer**
Subaccount	**Computer Cost**
Subaccount	**Accumulated Depreciation Computer**

The Computer Cost subaccount contains the original cost of the computer. The Accumulated Depreciation subaccount for the computer accumulates all depreciation recorded for the computer over its useful life. The parent account, Computer, will show the net book value of the computer (cost minus accumulated depreciation).

> **Fixed Asset Item List.** If your business has a large number of fixed asset accounts, you can use the Fixed Asset Item List to track fixed asset information.

To add new accounts to the Chart of Accounts for Paint Palette:

1. From the Chart of Accounts window, **right-click** to display the pop-up menu. Then select **New**.
2. From the Add New Account: Choose Account Type window, select **Fixed Asset (major purchases)**
3. Click **Continue**
4. When the Add New Account window appears, select Account Type: **Fixed Asset**
5. Enter Account Number: **14100**
6. Enter Account Name: **Computer**
7. Enter Description: **Computer**
8. Select Tax Line: <**Unassigned**>
9. Click **Save & New** to enter another account

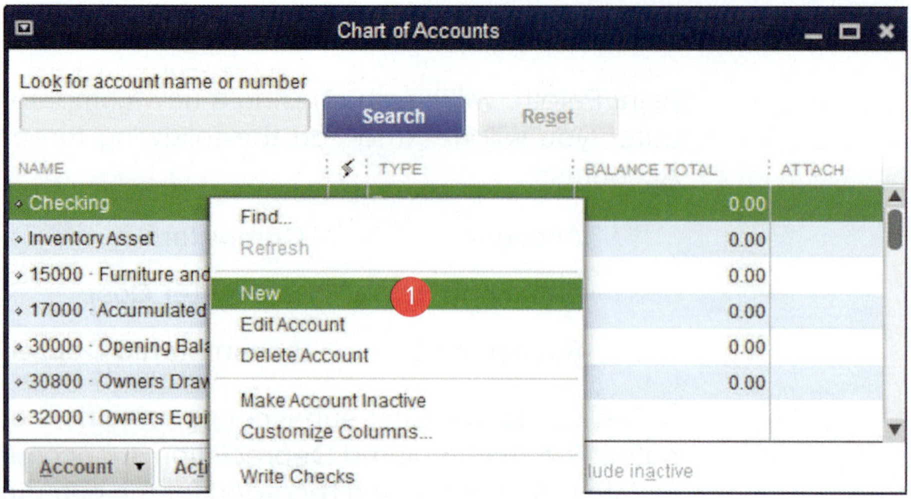
Chart of Accounts
Look for account name or number
Search
Reset
NAME
TYPE
BALANCE TOTAL
ATTACH
Checking
Inventory Asset
15000 · Furniture and
17000 · Accumulated
30000 · Opening Bal
30800 · Owners Draw
32000 · Owners Equi
0.00
0.00
0.00
0.00
0.00
0.00
Find...
Refresh
New
1
Edit Account
Delete Account
Make Account Inactive
Customize Columns...
Write Checks
Account
lude inactive

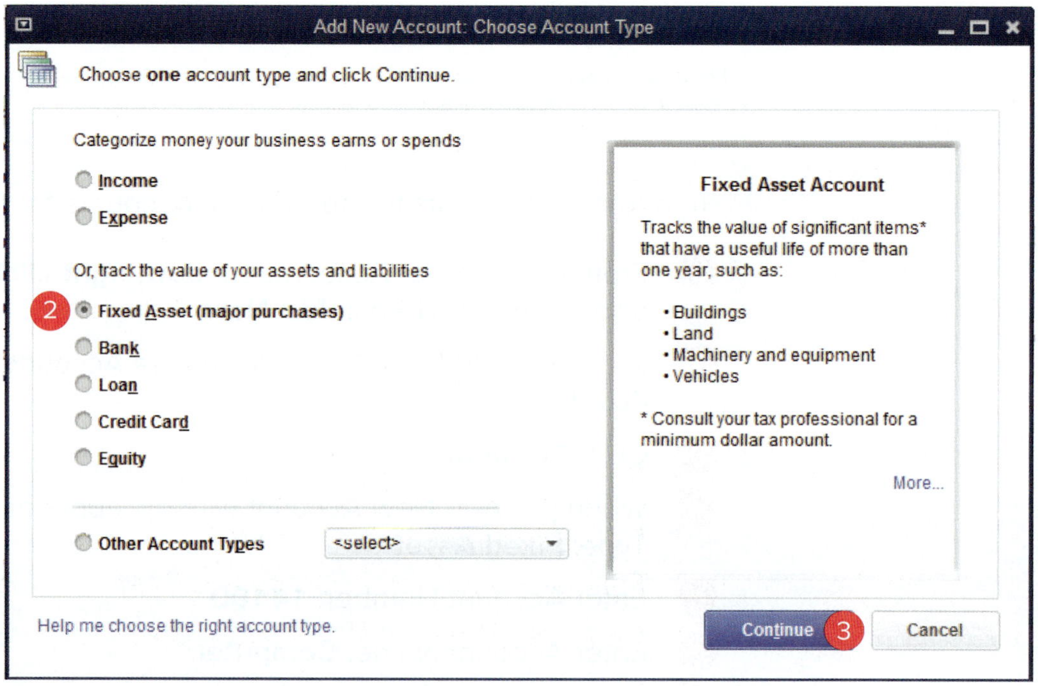
Add New Account: Choose Account Type
Choose **one** account type and click Continue.
Categorize money your business earns or spends
Income
Expense
Or, track the value of your assets and liabilities
2
Fixed Asset (major purchases)
Bank
Loan
Credit Card
Equity
Other Account Types
<select>
Fixed Asset Account
Tracks the value of significant items* that have a useful life of more than one year, such as:
• Buildings
• Land
• Machinery and equipment
• Vehicles
* Consult your tax professional for a minimum dollar amount.
More...
Help me choose the right account type.
Continue
3
Cancel

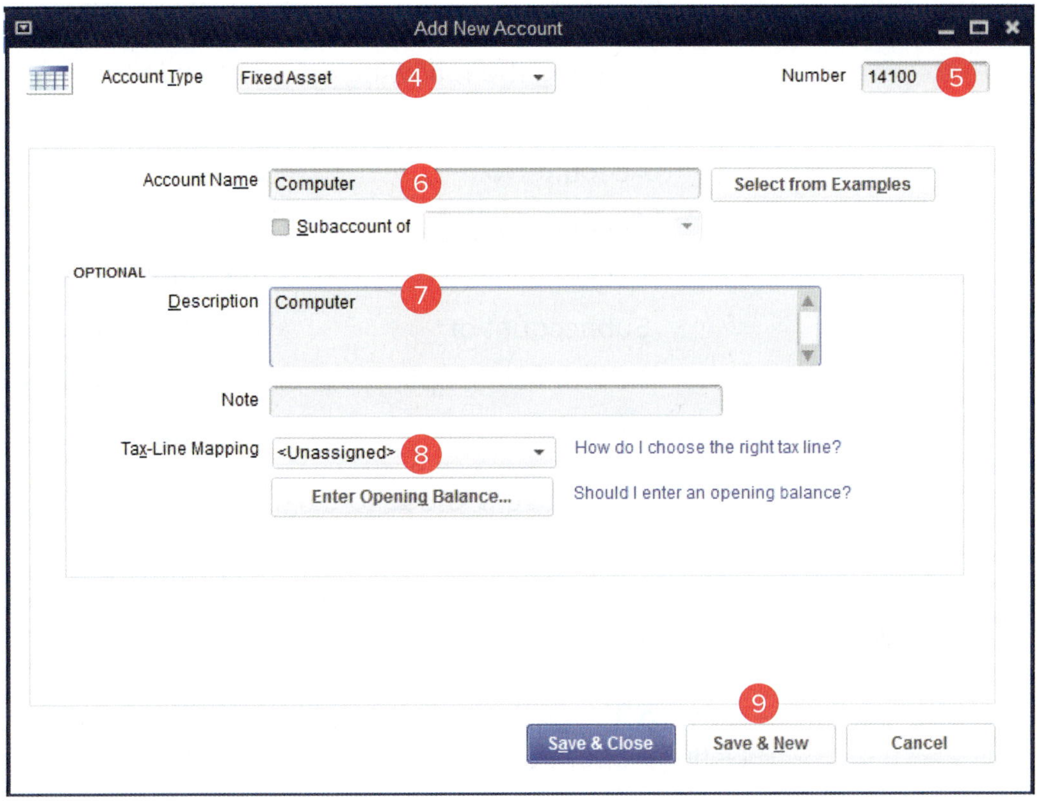

ADD NEW SUBACCOUNTS

When a blank Add New Account window appears, add a Computer Cost subaccount as follows:

1. Select Account Type: **Fixed Asset**
2. Enter Account Number: **14200**
3. Enter Account Name: **Computer Cost**
4. Check Subaccount of: **14100 – Computer**
5. Enter Description: **Computer Cost**
6. Select Tax Line: <**Unassigned**>
7. Click **Save & New** to add another subaccount

8. Add the Accumulated Depreciation Computer subaccount by entering the following information in the Add New Account window:

Account No.	**14300**
Account Type	**Fixed Asset**
Account Name	**Accumulated Depr Computer**
Subaccount of	**14100 Computer**
Account Description	**Accumulated Depreciation Computer**
Tax Line	**Unassigned**

9. Click **Save & Close** to close the Add New Account window

CREATE CHART OF ACCOUNTS (ACCOUNT LISTING) REPORT

C11.10.1 Chart of Accounts. To create the Chart of Accounts (Account Listing) report, complete the following steps:

1. From the Report Center select **List (or Accountant & Taxes)** > **Account Listing**
2. Select Date: **01/01/2023.** Select **Run.**
3. Export to **Excel** or **print** the Chart of Accounts
4. **Close** the Account Listing and Report Center windows
5. **Close** the Chart of Accounts window

Section 11.11

TRANSACTIONS

Next we will enter business transactions for Paint Palette's first year of operations. These include transactions with the owner, customers, and vendors.

RECORD OWNER'S INVESTMENT

To launch your new business, you invest $9,000 in Paint Palette. In order to keep business records and your personal records separate, you open a business Checking account at the local bank for Paint Palette. You then deposit your personal check for $9,000 in the business Checking account.

In Chapters 3 and 4 you recorded deposits using the Record Deposits icon in the Banking section of the Home Page. You can also record deposits directly in the Check Register. QuickBooks then transfers the information to the Make Deposits window.

C11.11.1 Deposit Journal Entry. To record the deposit to Paint Palette's Checking account using the Make Deposits window, complete the following steps:

1. Click the **Record Deposits** icon in the Banking section of the Home Page
2. In the Make Deposits window, select Deposit To: **Checking**
3. Select Date: **01/01/2023**
4. On the Received From drop-down list, select <**Add New**>. Select **Other,** then click **OK.** Enter Name: YourName. Click **OK.**
5. Account: **30000: Opening Balance Equity.** Press the **Tab** key.
6. Memo: **Invested $9,000 in business**
7. Check No.: **1001**
8. Payment Method: **Check**
9. Amount: **9000.00**
10. Select the **Save** icon at the top of the Make Deposits window
11. Select the **Journal** icon at the top of the Make Deposits window
12. Export the Transaction Journal to **Excel** or **print** the report
13. **Close** the Transaction Journal window and the Make Deposits window

Section 11.12

VENDOR AND EXPENSE TRANSACTIONS

Vendor and expense transactions can be either purchases made with a check or credit card or credit purchases on account that will be paid later.

RECORD VENDOR AND EXPENSE TRANSACTIONS USING THE WRITE CHECKS WINDOW

Paint Palette purchased a computer for $1,500. Because Paint Palette paid by check at the purchase, you can use the Write Checks window to record the purchase.

C11.12.1 Check Journal Entry. To record the computer purchase using the Write Checks window:

1. Click the **Write Checks** icon in the Banking section of the Home Page
2. In the following Write Checks window, select Bank Account: **Checking**
3. Select Date: **01/01/2023**
4. Pay to the Order of <Add New Vendor>: **Cornell Technologies**
5. Amount: **1500.00**
6. Account: **14200 Computer Cost**
7. Check: **Print Later**
8. Select the **Save** icon at the top of the Write Checks window
9. Select the **Reports tab** > **Transaction Journal**
10. Export the Transaction Journal report to **Excel** or **print** the report
11. **Close** the Transaction Journal and Write Checks windows

RECORD CREDIT VENDOR AND EXPENSE TRANSACTIONS USING THE ENTER BILLS WINDOW

When items are purchased on credit, a two-step process is used to record the purchase in QuickBooks.

	Action	Record Using. . .	Result
1	**Enter bill when received**	Enter Bills window	QuickBooks records an expense (or asset) and records an obligation to pay the bill later (accounts payable).
2	**Pay bill when due**	Pay Bills window	QuickBooks reduces accounts payable when the bill is paid. Bills can be paid using a check, credit card, or debit card.

C11.12.2 Bill Journal Entry. Next, we will enter bills for items Paint Palette purchased on credit. The first bill is for paint and supplies that Paint Palette purchased for the Cecilia job.

1. Click the **Enter Bills** icon in the Vendors section of the Home Page
2. Select Date: **01/03/2023**
3. Select Vendor: **Brewer Paint Supplies**
4. Enter Amount Due: **360.00**
5. Select Terms: **Net 30**
6. Click the **Expenses** tab
7. Select Account <Add New>: **64800 Paint Supplies Expense**
8. Select Customer & Job: **Cecilia, Maria: Dining Room**
9. Verify that **Billable** is checked
10. Select the **Save** icon at the top of the Enter Bills window. If asked if you want to make the change in payment terms permanent, select **Yes.**
11. Select the **Reports tab** > **Transaction Journal**
12. Export the Transaction Journal report to **Excel** or **print** the report
13. From the Enter Bills window, select **Save & New**

Notice that QuickBooks records the bill as accounts payable, indicating that Paint Palette has an obligation to pay these amounts to vendors. QuickBooks increases liabilities (accounts payable) on the company's Balance Sheet.

RECORD A MEMORIZED TRANSACTION

Often a transaction is recurring, such as monthly rent or utility payments. QuickBooks' memorized transaction feature permits you to memorize or save recurring transactions.

Paint Palette leases a van for a monthly lease payment of $270. You will use a memorized transaction to reuse each month to record the lease payment.

C11.12.3 Bill Journal Entry. To create a memorized transaction, first, enter the transaction in QuickBooks. To enter the bill for the van lease payment for Paint Palette:

1. From the open Enter Bills window on your screen, enter the following information about the van lease bill.

Date	**01/04/2023**
Vendor <Add New>	**Joseph Leasing**
Amount Due	**270.00**
Terms	**Net 30**
Account	**67100 Rent Expense**
Memo	**Van lease**

2. Select **Memorize** icon at the top of the Enter Bills window
3. When the Memorize Transaction window appears, select **Add to my Reminders List**
4. Select How Often: **Monthly**
5. Enter Next Date: **02/01/2023**
6. Click **OK** to record the memorized transaction
7. Select the **Save** icon at the top of the Enter Bills window. If asked if you want to make the change in payment terms permanent, select **Yes.**

8. Select the **Reports tab** > **Transaction Journal**
9. Export the Transaction Journal report to **Excel** or **print** the report
10. Click **Save & Close** to close the Enter Bills window and record the van lease

To use a memorized transaction:

1. Select **Lists Menu** > **Memorized Transaction List**
2. When the Memorized Transaction List window appears, **double-click** the memorized transaction you want to use
3. QuickBooks displays the Enter Bills window with the memorized transaction data already entered. You can make any necessary changes on the form, such as changing the date. To record the bill in QuickBooks, you would click Save & Close.

   At this time, **close the Enter Bills window without saving.** Then **close** the Memorized Transaction List window. Later, you will use the memorized transaction in **Exercise 11.5** at the end of the chapter.

PAY BILLS

To pay bills already entered:

1. Click the **Pay Bills** icon in the Vendors section of the Home Page
2. When the Pay Bills window appears, select Show Bills: **Due on or before 02/04/2023,** then press the **Tab** key. (If a Warning window appears, click OK, and then select All Vendors from the Filter By drop-down list.)
3. Select to pay the **Brewer Paint Supplies bill for $360.00** and the **Joseph Leasing Bill for $270.00**
4. Select Payment Method: **Check**
5. Select **To be printed**
6. Select Payment Account: **Checking**
7. Enter Payment Date: **01/04/2023**
8. Click **Pay Selected Bills** to record the bills selected for payment
9. Select **Done** to close the Payment Summary window

C11.12.4 Pay Bills Journal Entries. To view the journal entries that QuickBooks created behind the screen when bills were entered and selected for payment, complete the following steps.

1. From the Navigation Bar, select **Reports** > **Accountant & Taxes** > **Journal**
2. Select Dates: **01/03/2023 to 01/04/2023**
3. Select **Run**
4. Export the Journal report to **Excel** or **print** the report
5. **Close** the Journal window

ADDITIONAL VENDOR AND EXPENSE TRANSACTIONS

See **Exercise 11.5** for additional vendor and expense transactions for Paint Palette.

Section 11.13

CUSTOMER AND SALES TRANSACTIONS

When using QuickBooks, sales transactions are recorded using three steps.

	Action	Record Using. . .	Result
1	**Prepare invoice to record charges for services provided customer**	Create Invoices window	The invoice is used to bill the customer for services. QuickBooks records the services provided on credit as an account receivable (an amount to be received in the future).
2	**Receive customer payment**	Receive Payments window	QuickBooks reduces accounts receivable and increases undeposited funds.
3	**Record bank deposit**	Make Deposits window	QuickBooks transfers the amount from undeposited funds to the bank account.

CUSTOMIZE INVOICE

Create a Custom Invoice Template with a Service Date column. This permits Paint Palette to bill customers once a month for all services provided during the month, listing each service date separately on the invoice.

To create a Custom Invoice Template, complete the following steps:

1. Click the **Create Invoices** icon in the Customers section of the Home Page
2. Click the **Formatting** tab in the upper portion of the Create Invoices window
3. Select **Manage Templates**
4. In the Manage Templates window, select **Intuit Service Invoice**
5. Then click **Copy**

6. To change the invoice template name, select **Copy of: Intuit Service Invoice**
7. In the Template Name field, change the template name to: **Service Date Invoice**
8. Click **OK** to close the Manage Templates window
9. Verify the Selected Template is: **Service Date Invoice**
10. Click the **Additional Customization** button
11. To add a Service Date column to the custom template, when the Additional Customization window appears, click the **Columns** tab
12. Check **Screen** and **Print**
13. Enter Title for Service Date: **Date**
14. Renumber the Order so they appear as shown
15. Click the **Layout Designer** button and adjust the field sizes as needed
16. Click **OK** to close the Layout Designer window. Click **OK** again to close the Customization windows.
17. To view the custom invoice, if necessary from the Create Invoices window, select Template: **Service Date Invoice**
18. Notice that the first column of the invoice is now the **Date** column

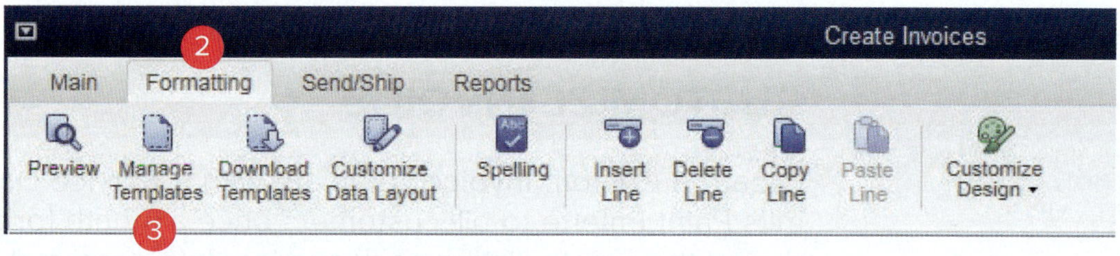

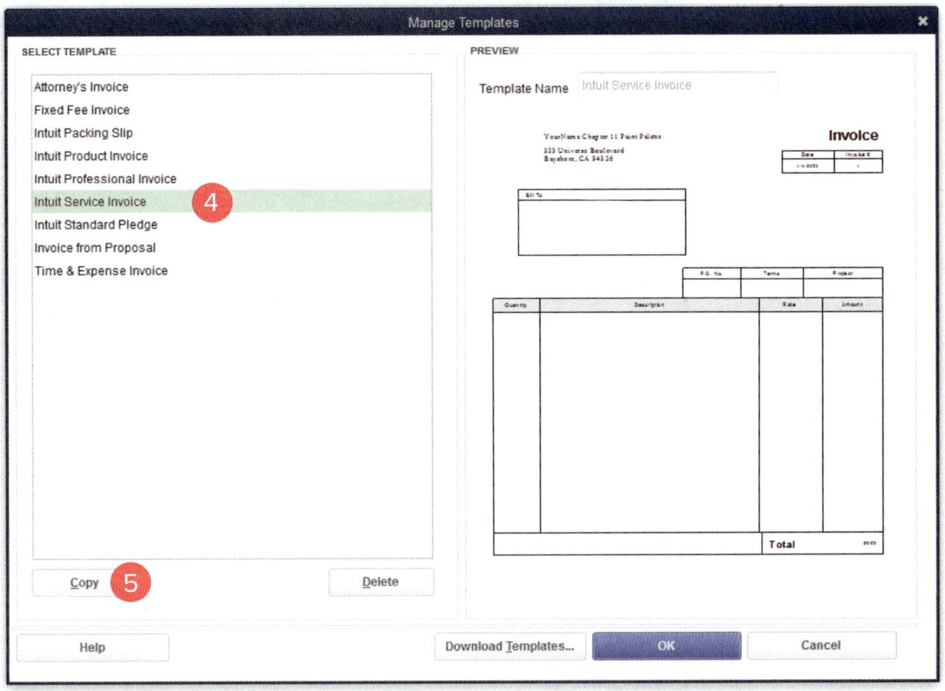
Manage Templates
SELECT TEMPLATE
Attorney's Invoice
Fixed Fee Invoice
Intuit Packing Slip
Intuit Product Invoice
Intuit Professional Invoice
Intuit Service Invoice
4
Intuit Standard Pledge
Invoice from Proposal
Time & Expense Invoice
Copy
5
Delete
PREVIEW
Template Name
Intuit Service Invoice
Invoice
Total
Help
Download Templates...
OK
Cancel

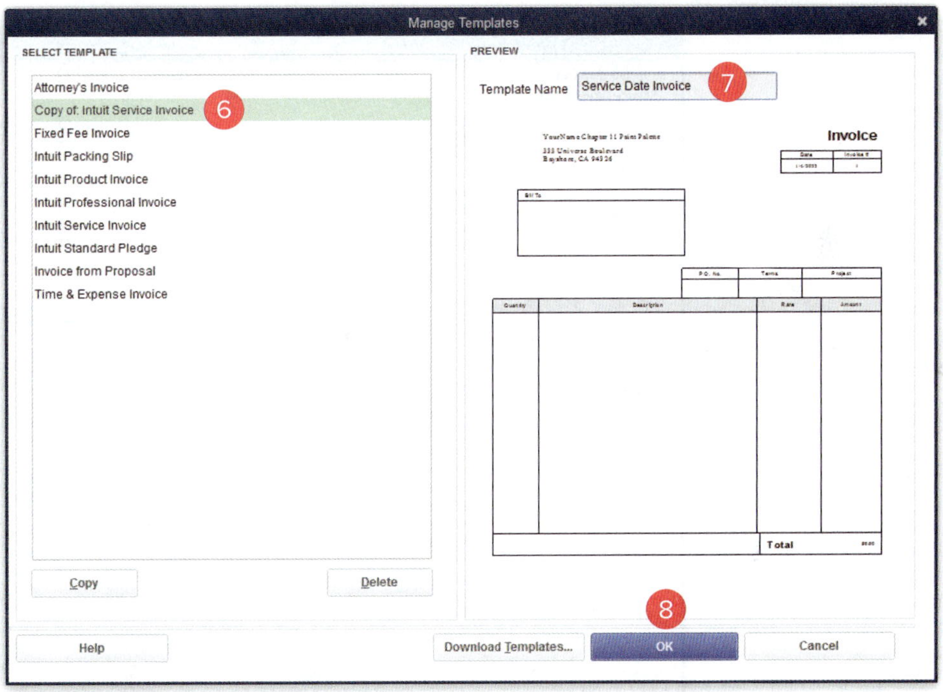
Manage Templates
SELECT TEMPLATE
Attorney's Invoice
Copy of: Intuit Service Invoice
6
Fixed Fee Invoice
Intuit Packing Slip
Intuit Product Invoice
Intuit Professional Invoice
Intuit Service Invoice
Intuit Standard Pledge
Invoice from Proposal
Time & Expense Invoice
Copy
Delete
PREVIEW
Template Name
Service Date Invoice
7
Invoice
Total
8
Help
Download Templates...
OK
Cancel

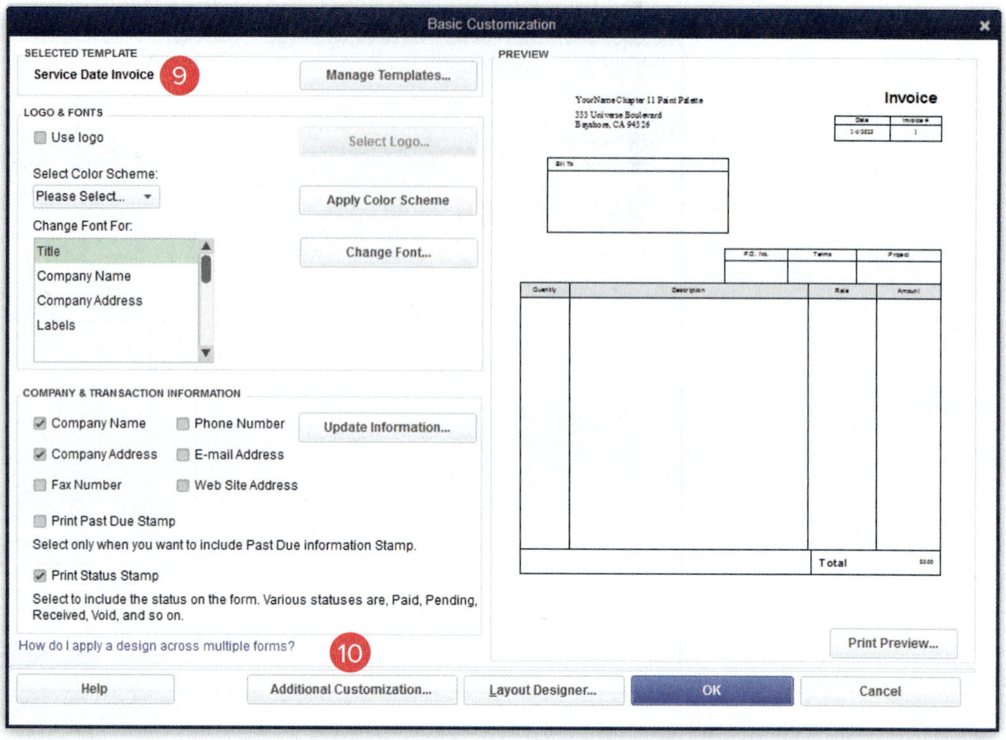
Basic Customization
SELECTED TEMPLATE
Service Date Invoice
9
Manage Templates...
LOGO & FONTS
Use logo
Select Logo...
Select Color Scheme:
Please Select...
Apply Color Scheme
Change Font For:
Title
Company Name
Company Address
Labels
Change Font...
COMPANY & TRANSACTION INFORMATION
Company Name
Phone Number
Update Information...
Company Address
E-mail Address
Fax Number
Web Site Address
Print Past Due Stamp
Select only when you want to include Past Due information Stamp.
Print Status Stamp
Select to include the status on the form. Various statuses are, Paid, Pending, Received, Void, and so on.
How do I apply a design across multiple forms?
10
PREVIEW
Invoice
Total
Print Preview...
Help
Additional Customization...
Layout Designer...
OK
Cancel

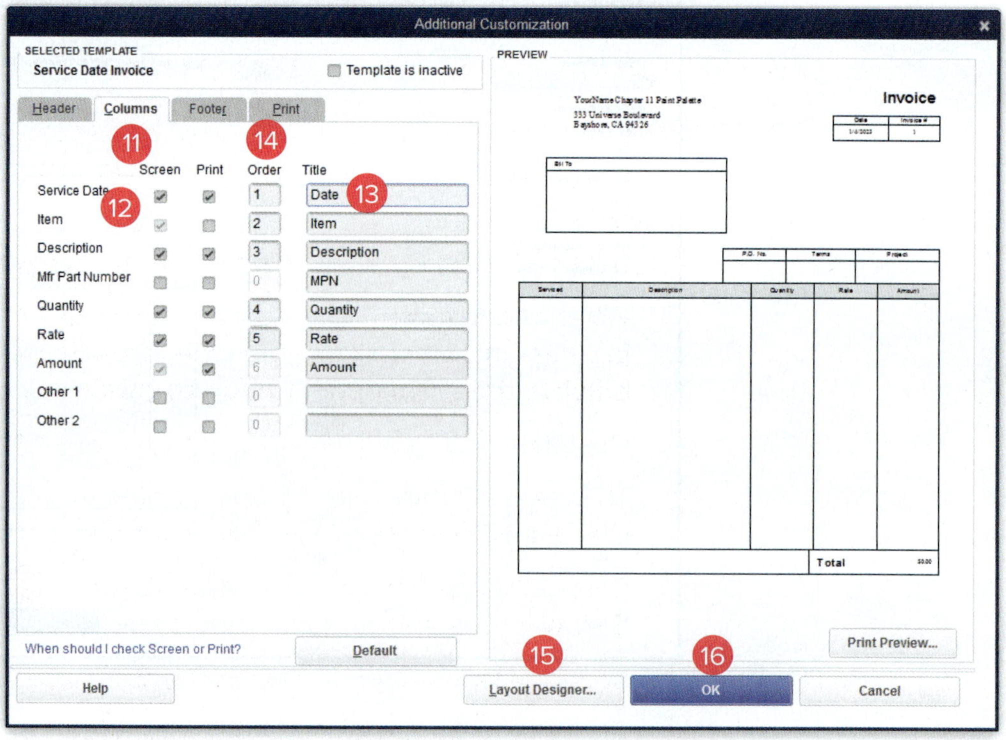
Additional Customization
SELECTED TEMPLATE
Service Date Invoice
Template is inactive
Header
Columns
Footer
Print
11
14
Screen
Print
Order
Title
Service Date
12
1
Date
13
Item
2
Item
Description
3
Description
Mfr Part Number
0
MPN
Quantity
4
Quantity
Rate
5
Rate
Amount
6
Amount
Other 1
0
Other 2
0
When should I check Screen or Print?
Default
PREVIEW
Invoice
Total
Print Preview...
15
16
Help
Layout Designer...
OK
Cancel

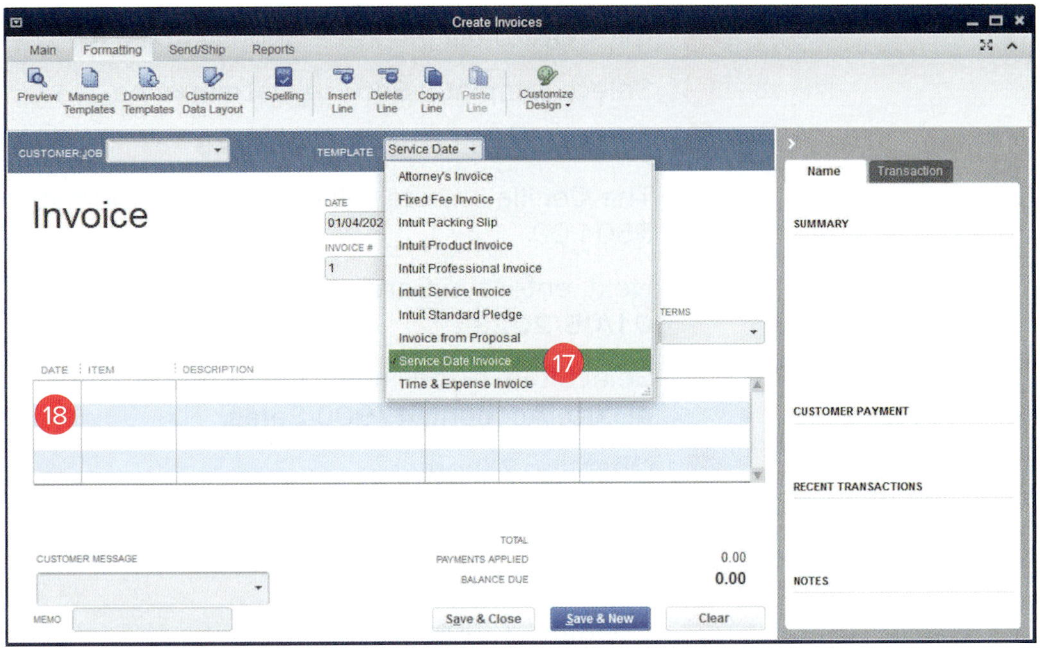

CREATE INVOICE

C11.13.1 Invoice Journal Entry. To create an invoice to record painting services provided by Paint Palette to Maria Cecilia during January:

1. If the Create Invoices window is not already open on your screen, select the **Create Invoices** icon in the Customers section of the Home Page
2. Select Customer & Job: **Cecilia, Maria: Dining Room**
3. When the Billable Time/Costs window appears to remind you the job has outstanding billable time, click **Select the outstanding billable time and costs to add to this invoice?**
4. Click **OK**
5. To select billable costs to apply to the Cecilia invoice, from the Choose Billable Time and Costs window select the **Expenses** tab
6. Enter Markup Amount or %: **40.0%.** (Be sure to enter %, otherwise $40 will be the markup.)
7. Select Markup Account: **47900 – Sales**
8. Check to select: **Brewer Paint Supplies**

9 Click **OK** to bill the Paint Supplies cost

10 Select Template: **Service Date Invoice**

11 Enter Invoice Date: **01/10/2023**

12 The Cecilia invoice will list Total Reimbursable Expenses of $504.00

13 Next, enter the Service Date in the Create Invoices window: **01/05/2023**

14 Select Item <Add New>: **Labor Mural.** Subitem of: **Labor.** Rate: **40.00.** Account: **47900 Sales.**

15 Quantity: **7** (hours)

16 Enter Date (column): **01/06/2023**

17 Select Item: **Labor Mural**

18 Quantity: **7** (hours)

19 Select **Print Later**

20 Select the **Save** icon

21 Select the **Reports tab** > **Transaction Journal**

22 Export to **Excel** or **print** the Transaction Journal

23 **Close** the Transaction Journal and Create Invoices windows

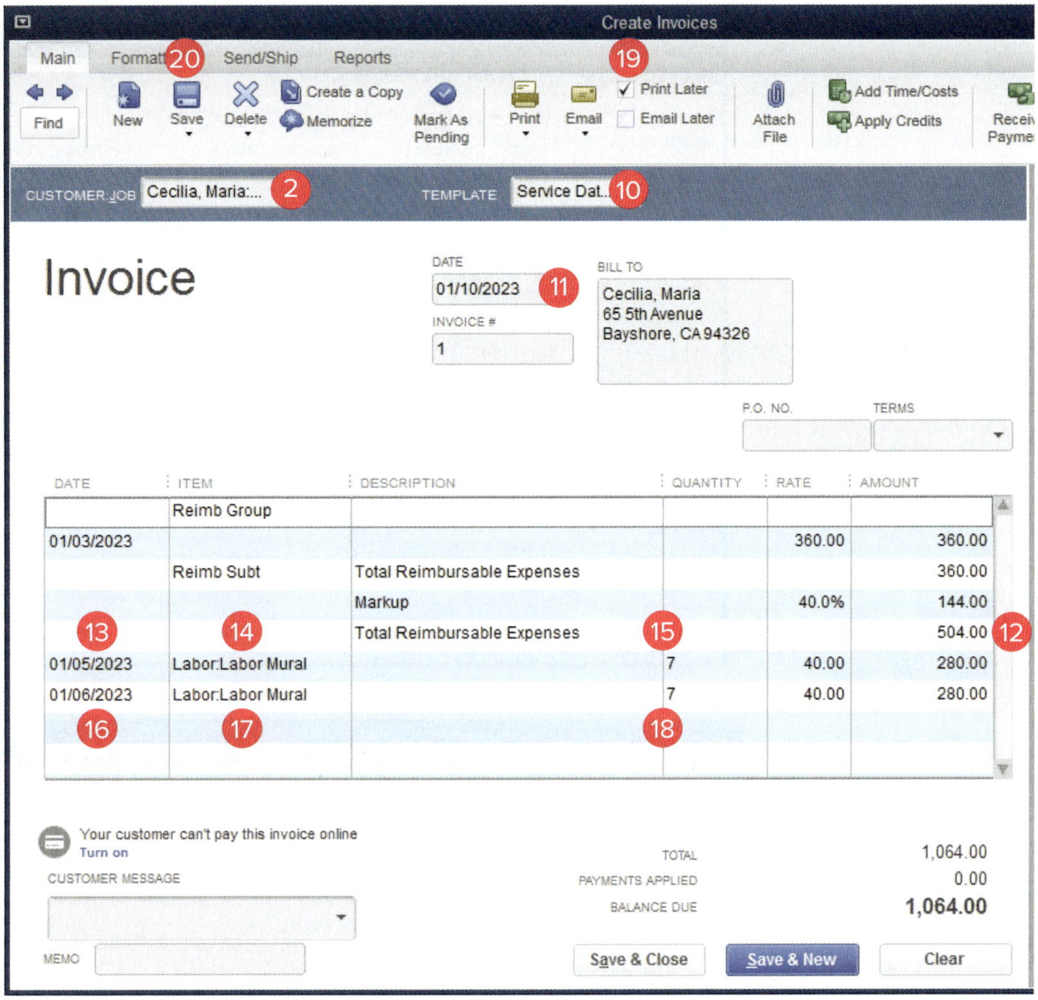
Create Invoices
Main
Formatting
Send/Ship
Reports
Find
New
Save
Delete
Create a Copy
Memorize
Mark As Pending
Print
Email
Print Later
Email Later
Attach File
Add Time/Costs
Apply Credits
CUSTOMER:JOB Cecilia, Maria:...
TEMPLATE Service Dat...
Invoice
DATE 01/10/2023
INVOICE # 1
BILL TO
Cecilia, Maria
65 5th Avenue
Bayshore, CA 94326
P.O. NO.
TERMS
DATE ITEM DESCRIPTION QUANTITY RATE AMOUNT
Reimb Group
01/03/2023 360.00 360.00
Reimb Subt Total Reimbursable Expenses 360.00
Markup 40.0% 144.00
Total Reimbursable Expenses 504.00
01/05/2023 Labor:Labor Mural 7 40.00 280.00
01/06/2023 Labor:Labor Mural 7 40.00 280.00
Your customer can't pay this invoice online
Turn on
CUSTOMER MESSAGE
MEMO
TOTAL 1,064.00
PAYMENTS APPLIED 0.00
BALANCE DUE 1,064.00
Save & Close
Save & New
Clear
2
10
11
12
13
14
15
16
17
18
19
20

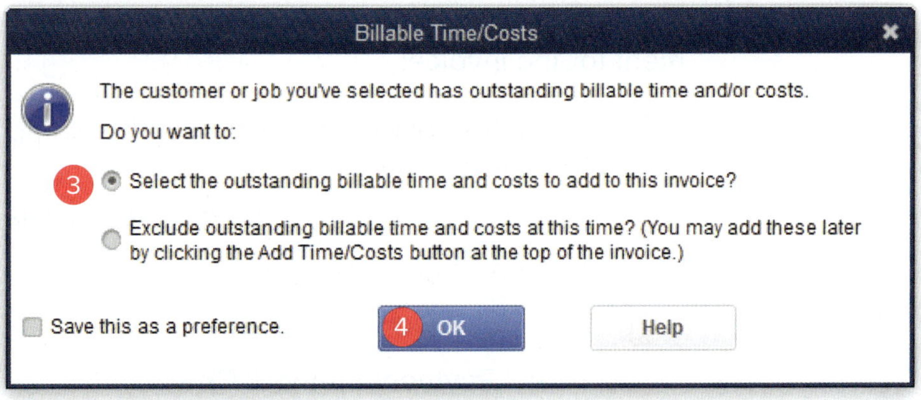
Billable Time/Costs
The customer or job you've selected has outstanding billable time and/or costs.
Do you want to:
Select the outstanding billable time and costs to add to this invoice?
Exclude outstanding billable time and costs at this time? (You may add these later by clicking the Add Time/Costs button at the top of the invoice.)
Save this as a preference.
OK
Help
3
4

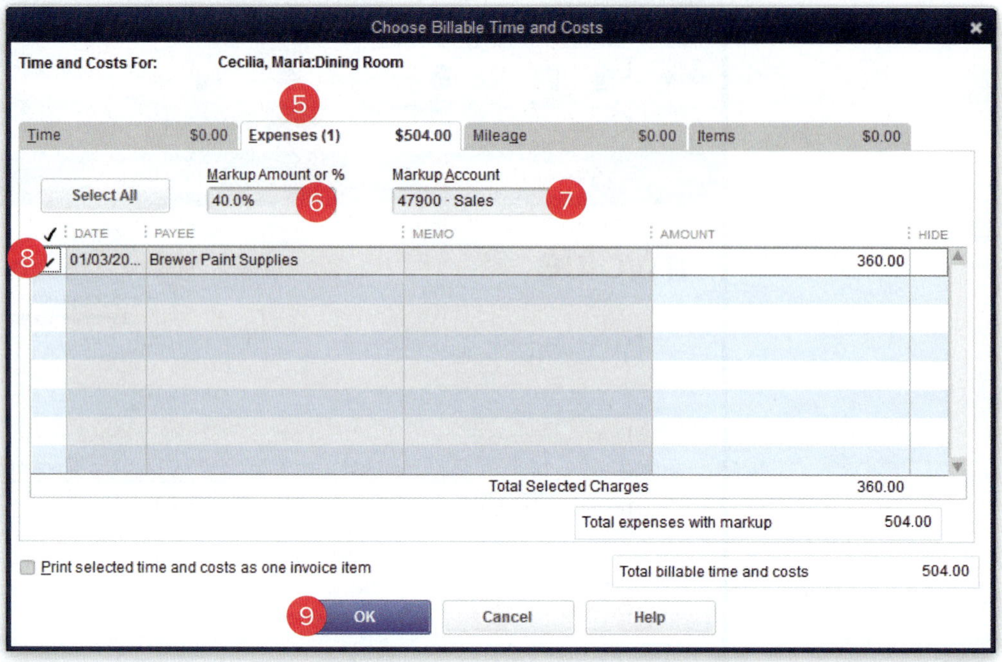

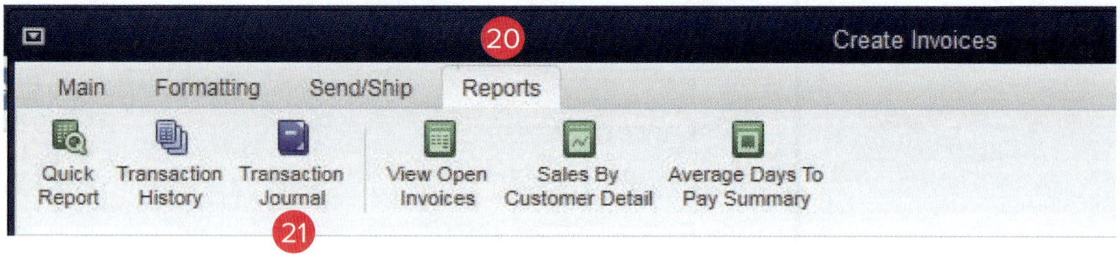

RECEIVE PAYMENT

C11.13.2 Receive Payment Journal Entry. To record Maria Cecilia's payment for the invoice:

1. From the Customers section of the Home Page, click the **Receive Payments** icon
2. Select Received From: **Cecilia, Maria: Dining Room**
3. Enter Amount: **1064.00**
4. Select Date: **01/11/2023**
5. Select Payment Method: **Check**
6. Enter Check No. **555**
7. Select **Save & New**
8. Select the **Find back arrow** to display the customer payment just recorded

9. Select **Reports tab** > **Transaction Journal**
10. Export the Transaction Journal report to **Excel** or **print** the report
11. **Close** the Transaction Journal and the Receive Payments windows

If a message appears regarding payment methods, select No.

Verify that QuickBooks has selected the outstanding invoice.

When a customer makes a payment, the customer's account receivable is reduced by the amount of the payment. In this case, Maria Cecilia's account receivable is reduced by $1,064.00.

MAKE DEPOSIT

C11.13.3 Deposit Journal Entry. To record the deposit of the customer's payment in the bank:

1. From the Banking section of the Home Page, click the **Record Deposits** icon
2. When the Payments to Deposit window appears, select the **payment from Maria Cecilia** for deposit
3. Click **OK** and the Make Deposits window appears
4. Select Deposit To: **Checking**
5. Select Date: **01/11/2023**
6. Verify the Amount is **$1064.00**
7. Select the **Save** icon at the top of the Make Deposits window
8. Select the **Journal** icon
9. Export the Transaction Journal report to **Excel** or **print** the report
10. **Close** the Transaction Journal and the Make Deposits windows

ADDITIONAL CUSTOMER AND SALES TRANSACTIONS

See **Exercise 11.6** for additional sales transactions for Paint Palette.

Section 11.14

ADJUSTING ENTRIES

At the end of Paint Palette's accounting period, December 31, 2023, it is necessary to record adjustments to bring the company's accounts up to date as of year-end.

As discussed in Chapters 9 and 10, the process of making adjustments typically includes the following.

- **Trial Balance.** A Trial Balance lists each account and the account balance at the end of the accounting period. Prepare a Trial Balance to verify that the accounting system is in balance—total debits should equal total credits. An unadjusted Trial Balance is a Trial Balance prepared before adjustments.
- **Adjustments.** At the end of the accounting period before preparing financial statements, make any adjustments necessary to bring the accounts up to date. Adjustments are entered in the Journal using debits and credits. (Adjustments were covered in Chapter 9 of this text.)
- **Adjusted Trial Balance.** Prepare an Adjusted Trial Balance (a Trial Balance after adjustments) to verify that the accounting system still balances. If additional account detail is required, print the general ledger (the collection of all the accounts listing the transactions that affected the accounts).

The following adjustments are necessary for Paint Palette at December 31, 2023:

1. Record depreciation expense for the computer for the year.
2. Record depreciation expense for the painting equipment for the year.
3. Record the amount of paint supplies that are still on hand at year-end. Unused paint supplies should be recorded as assets because they have future benefit.

See **Exercise 11.7** for additional information about making adjusting entries for Paint Palette.

Section 11.15

REPORTS

The next step in the accounting cycle is to print financial reports. Usually, a company prints the following financial reports for the year:

- Profit & Loss (also known as the P & L or Income Statement)
- Balance Sheet
- Statement of Cash Flows

The Profit & Loss, the Balance Sheet, and the Statement of Cash Flows are financial statements typically given to external users, such as bankers and investors.

To print the financial statements, from the Report Center, select: Company & Financial.

We will print financial statements for Paint Palette for the year 2023 in **Exercise 11.8.**

Section 11.16

CLOSE THE ACCOUNTING PERIOD

When using a manual accounting system, closing entries are made in the General Journal to close the temporary accounts (revenues, expenses, and withdrawals or dividends). Closing entries are used in order to start the new year with a zero balance in the temporary accounts.

QuickBooks automatically closes temporary accounts to start each new year with $-0- balances in all temporary accounts (revenues, expenses, and dividends).

To prevent changes to prior periods, QuickBooks permits you to restrict access to the accounting records for past periods that have been closed. See **Exercise 11.9** for instructions on closing the accounting period in QuickBooks.

Section 11.17

BACKUP QUICKBOOKS FILES

BACK UP QBB

Save a backup of your Chapter 11 file using the file name: **YourName Chapter 11 Backup.QBB.** For further instructions on how to back up your file, *see Appendix B: Back Up & Restore QuickBooks Files.*

QBW WORKFLOW

If you will be using the same computer to complete Chapter 11 QuickBooks exercises, just as in a business workflow, you can continue to use the same QBW file.

If you are using the QBW approach, leave your .QBW file open and proceed directly to Exercise 11.1.

QBB RESTORE

If you will be switching computers and are ending your computer session now, close your QBW file and exit QuickBooks. When you restart, you will restore your backup file to complete Exercise 11.1.

www.my-quickbooks.com

Go to **www.My-QuickBooks.com** to view additional QuickBooks resources including:

- **Excel Report Templates** to organize QuickBooks reports exported to Excel
- ***Computer Accounting with QuickBooks* updates,** sometimes required when there is a software update that affects the text
- **QuickBooks Video links**
- **QuickBooks Help and Support links**

- **Other QuickBooks Resources** to make learning QuickBooks easier and more effective
- **QuickBooks Issue Resolution** offers a guided approach to trouble-shooting QuickBooks

> **Troubleshooting QuickBooks and Correcting Errors** are crucial QuickBooks skill to acquire. See www.My-QuickBooks.com > QB Issue Resolution for Troubleshooting QuickBooks tips. See Chapter 17, Quick Review Guide, for tips on Correcting Errors.

EXERCISE 11.1: Chart of Accounts

In this exercise, you will add new accounts and subaccounts to Paint Palette's Chart of Accounts.

E11.1.1 QuickBooks File

If you will be using the same computer and the same Chapter 11.QBW file:

1. If your Chapter 11.QBW file is not already open, open it by selecting **File > Open Previous Company.** Select your **Chapter 11.QBW file.** If a QuickBooks Information window appears with a message about the sample company file, click **OK.**
2. Add **YourName Exercise 11.1** to the company name by selecting **Company Menu > My Company.**

> **If you are not using the same computer that you used for Chapter 11,** you will need to restore your Chapter 11 Backup.QBB file using the instructions in Appendix B: Back Up & Restore QuickBooks Files. After restoring, add YourName Exercise 11.1 to the company name.

E11.1.2 Add Accounts

1. Add the following new accounts and subaccounts to the Chart of Accounts for Paint Palette. Click **Save & New** after entering each account.

Account Name	**Paint Supplies**
Account No.	**13000**
Account Type	**Other Current Asset**

Account Description	**Paint Supplies on Hand**
Tax Line	**Unassigned**
Account Name	**Equipment**
Account No.	**14400**
Account Type	**Fixed Asset**
Account Description	**Equipment**
Tax Line	**Unassigned**
Account Name	**Equipment Cost**
Account No.	**14500**
Account Type	**Fixed Asset**
Account Description	**Equipment Cost**
Tax Line	**Unassigned**
Account Name	**Accumulated Depr Equipment**
Account No.	**14600**
Account Type	**Fixed Asset**
Account Description	**Accumulated Depreciation Equipment**
Tax Line	**Unassigned**

2. Edit the following account to appear as follows for Paint Palette Chart of Accounts.

Account Name	**Depreciation Expense**
Account No.	**62400**
Account Type	**Expense**
Account Description	**Depreciation of equipment, buildings, and improvements**
Tax Line	**Schedule C: Other business expenses**
Account Name	**Paint Supplies Expense**
Account No.	**64800**
Account Type	**Expense**
Account Description	**Paint Supplies Expense**
Tax Line	**Schedule C: Supplies (not from COGS)**

3. Export to **Excel** or **print** the Chart of Accounts (Select Report Center > List > Account Listing > January 11, 2023.)

E11.1.3 Back Up Exercise 11.1

Save a backup of your Exercise file using the file name: YourName Exercise 11.1 Backup.QBB. See *Appendix B: Back Up & Restore QuickBooks Files* for instructions.

EXERCISE 11.2: Customer List

In this exercise, you will add to Paint Palette's Customers List.

E11.2.1 QuickBooks File

If you will be using the same computer and the same QBW file:

1. Select your **QBW file.**
2. Add **YourName Exercise 11.2** to the company name by selecting **Company Menu > My Company.**

> **If you are not using the same computer that you used for Chapter 11 and Exercise 11.1,** you will need to restore your latest prior Backup.QBB file using the instructions in Appendix B: Back Up & Restore QuickBooks files. After restoring, add YourName Exercise 11.2 to the company name.

E11.2.2 Add Customers

1. Add TJ Ryan to Paint Palette's Customer List.

Customer	**Ryan, TJ**
Opening Balance	**0.00**
As of	**01/01/2023**
Address Info:	
First Name	**TJ**
Last Name	**Ryan**
Main Phone	**415-555-1234**

Mobile	**415-555-5678**
Address	**55 Scotch Drive**
	Bayshore, CA 94326
Payment Settings:	
Account No.	**1002**
Payment Terms	**Net 30**
Preferred Payment Method	**Check**
Additional Info:	
Customer Type	**Referral**

2. Click **OK** to close the New Customer window

E11.2.3 Add Job

1. To add a new job, select: **TJ Ryan**
2. **Right-click** to display pop-up menu. Select **Add Job.**
3. After entering the following job information, **close** the New Job window.

Job Info:	
Job Name	**Foyer**
Opening Balance	**0.00**
As of	**01/01/2023**
Job Description	**Foyer Marbled Faux Painting**
Job Type <Add New>	**Faux Painting**
Job Status	**Pending**

4. From the Customer Center, export the Customer List to **Excel.** (Print from Excel if your instructor requires printouts.)
5. **Close** the Customer Center

E11.2.4 Back Up Exercise 11.2

Save a backup of your Exercise file using the file name: YourName Exercise 11.2 Backup.QBB. See *Appendix B: Back Up & Restore QuickBooks Files* for instructions.

EXERCISE 11.3: Vendor List

In this exercise, you will add to Paint Palette's Vendors List.

E11.3.1 QuickBooks File

If you will be using the same computer and the same QBW file:

1. Select your **QBW file.**
2. Add **YourName Exercise 11.3** to the company name by selecting **Company Menu** > **My Company.**

> **If you are not using the same computer that you used for Chapter 11, Exercise 11.1, and Exercise 11.2,** you will need to restore your latest prior Backup.QBB file using the instructions in Appendix B: Back Up & Restore QuickBooks files. After restoring, add YourName Exercise 11.3 to the company name.

E11.3.2 Add Vendors

1. Edit the following vendor for the Paint Palette Vendor List.

Vendor	**Cornell Technologies**
Address Info:	
Company Name	**Cornell Technologies**
First Name	**Bill**
Last Name	**Cornell**
Main Phone	**415-555-8181**
Address	**108 Austin Avenue**
	Bayshore, CA 94326
Payment Settings:	
Account No.	**2002**
Payment Terms	**Net 30**
Credit Limit	**18000.00**
Tax Settings:	
Vendor Tax ID	**37-4356781**
Additional Info:	
Vendor Type	**Supplies**

2. Edit the following vendor for the Paint Palette Vendor List.

Vendor	**Joseph Leasing**
Address Info:	
Company Name	**Joseph Leasing**
First Name	**Joseph**
Last Name	**Asher**
Main Phone	**415-555-0412**
Address	**13 Appleton Drive**
	Bayshore, CA 94326
Payment Settings:	
Account No.	**2003**
Payment Terms	**Net 30**
Tax Settings:	
Vendor Tax ID	**37-1726354**
Additional Info:	
Vendor Type <Add New>	**Leasing**

3. From the Vendor Center, export the Vendor List to **Excel**
4. **Close** the Vendor Center

E11.3.3 Back Up Exercise 11.3

Save a backup of your Exercise file using the file name: YourName Exercise 11.3 Backup.QBB. See *Appendix B: Back Up & Restore QuickBooks Files* for instructions.

EXERCISE 11.4: Item List

In this exercise, you will add to Paint Palette's Item List.

E11.4.1 QuickBooks File

If you will be using the same computer and the same QBW file:

1. Select your **QBW file.**
2. Add **YourName Exercise 11.4** to the company name by selecting **Company Menu > My Company.**

> **If you are not using the same computer that you used for Chapter 11, and Exercises 11.1 – 11.3,** you will need to restore your latest prior Backup.QBB file using the instructions in Appendix B: Back Up & Restore QuickBooks files. After restoring, add YourName Exercise 11.4 to the company name.

E11.4.2 Add Items

1. Add the following items to Paint Palette's Item List. Click **Next** after entering each item.

Item Type	**Service**
Item Name	**Labor Faux**
Subitem of	**Labor**
Description	**Labor Faux Painting**
Rate	**36.00**
Account	**47900 - Sales**
Item Type	**Service**
Item Name	**Labor Interior**
Subitem of	**Labor**
Description	**Labor Interior Painting**
Rate	**20.00**
Account	**47900 – Sales**
Item Type	**Service**
Item Name	**Labor Exterior**
Subitem of	**Labor**
Description	**Labor Exterior Painting**
Rate	**30.00**
Account	**47900 – Sales**

2. Export the Item List to **Excel.** (From the Item List window, select Reports button > Item Listing.)

E11.4.3 Back Up Exercise 11.4

Save a backup of your Exercise file using the file name: YourName Exercise 11.4 Backup.QBB. See *Appendix B: Back Up & Restore QuickBooks Files* for instructions.

EXERCISE 11.5: Vendors and Expense Transactions

In this exercise, you will enter vendor and expense transactions for Paint Palette.

E11.5.1 QuickBooks File

If you will be using the same computer and the same QBW file:

1. Select your **QBW file.**
2. Add **YourName Exercise 11.5** to the company name by selecting **Company Menu** > **My Company.**

> **If you are not using the same computer that you used for Chapter 11 and Exercises 11.1 – 11.4,** you will need to restore your latest prior Backup.QBB file using the instructions in Appendix B: Back Up & Restore QuickBooks files. After restoring, add YourName Exercise 11.5 to the company name.

E11.5.2 Record Vendor and Expense Transactions

Paint Palette entered into the following vendor and expense transactions during 2023.

1. Record the vendor and expense transactions for Paint Palette. (Select View > Open Window List to streamline transaction entry.)

Date	**Transaction**
01/04/2023	Paint Palette made a credit purchase of $500 from Brewer Paint Supplies of painting equipment including ladders and drop cloths. The painting equipment is recorded as an asset because it will benefit more than one accounting period and will be depreciated over the useful life of the equipment. Use Account 14500 Equipment Cost to record the $500 purchase of painting equipment.
02/01/2023	Use the memorized transaction to record the bill for the February van lease to be paid later
02/28/2023	Paid following bills: • $500 Brewer Paint Supplies bill • Van lease bill for February

Date	Transaction
03/01/2023	Received bill for van lease for March
03/30/2023	Paid van lease for March (Due: 03/31/2023)
04/01/2023	Received bill for van lease for April
04/04/2023	Purchased $50 of paint supplies on account from Brewer Paint Supplies. Record as Paint Supplies Expense.
04/30/2023	• Paid van lease for April (Due: 05/01/2023) • Paid for paint supplies purchased on April 4
05/01/2023	Received bill for van lease for May
05/30/2023	Paid van lease for May (Due: 05/31/2023)
06/01/2023	Received bill for van lease for June
06/30/2023	Paid van lease for June (Due: 07/01/2023)
07/01/2023	Purchased $100 of paint supplies on account from Brewer Paint Supplies. Record as Paint Supplies Expense.
07/01/2023	Received bill for van lease for July
07/30/2023	• Paid van lease for July (Due: 07/31/2023) • Paid for paint supplies purchased on July 1
08/01/2023	Received bill for van lease for August
08/30/2023	Paid van lease for August (Due: 08/31/2023)
09/01/2023	Received bill for van lease for September
09/02/2023	Purchased $75 of paint supplies on account from Brewer Paint Supplies. Record as Paint Supplies Expense.
09/30/2023	• Paid September van lease (Due: 10/01/2023) • Paid for paint supplies purchased on 09/02/2023
10/01/2023	Received bill for van lease for October
10/30/2023	Paid van lease for October (Due: 10/31/2023)
11/01/2023	Received bill for van lease for November

Date	Transaction
11/30/2023	Paid van lease for November (Due: 12/01/2023)
12/01/2023	Received bill for van lease for December
12/20/2023	Purchased $150 of paint supplies on account from Brewer Paint Supplies. Record as Paint Supplies Expense.
12/30/2023	Paid van lease for December (Due: 12/31/2023)

2. Export to **Excel** or **print** the Expenses by Vendor Detail report for 2023. (Report Center > Company & Financial > Expenses by Vendor Detail.)
3. Export to **Excel** or **print** the Check Detail report for 2023. (Report Center > Banking > Check Detail.)

E11.5.3 Back Up Exercise 11.5

Save a backup of your Exercise file using the file name: YourName Exercise 11.5 Backup.QBB. See *Appendix B: Back Up & Restore QuickBooks Files* for instructions.

EXERCISE 11.6: Customers and Sales Transactions

In this exercise, you will enter customers and sales transactions for Paint Palette.

E11.6.1 QuickBooks File

If you will be using the same computer and the same QBW file:

1. Select your **QBW file.**
2. Add **YourName Exercise 11.6** to the company name by selecting **Company Menu > My Company.**

If you are not using the same computer that you used for Chapter 11 and Exercises 11.1–11.5, you will need to restore your latest prior Backup.QBB file using the instructions in Appendix B: Back Up & Restore QuickBooks files. After restoring, add YourName Exercise 11.6 to the company name.

E11.6.2 Sales Transactions and Deposit Summaries

1. Using the Service Date Invoice Template, record the customer and sales transactions for Paint Palette during the year 2023. (Select View > Open Window List to streamline transaction entry.)

Invoice Date	**02/28/2023**
Customer	**Maria Cecilia**
Job	**Dining Room**
Service Date	**02/10/2023**
Item	**Labor: Mural**
Hours	**10**
Service Date	**02/11/2023**
Item	**Labor: Mural**
Hours	**9**
Service Date	**02/15/2023**
Item	**Labor: Mural**
Hours	**10**
Service Date	**02/18/2023**
Item	**Labor: Mural**
Hours	**10**
Service Date	**02/20/2023**
Item	**Labor: Mural**
Hours	**12**
Service Date	**02/22/2023**
Item	**Labor: Mural**
Hours	**10**
Payment Received & Deposited	**03/15/2023**
Check No.	**675**

Invoice Date	**03/31/2023**
Customer	**Maria Cecilia**
Job	**Dining Room**
Service Date	**03/05/2023**

Item	**Labor: Mural**
Hours	**8**
Service Date	**03/09/2023**
Item	**Labor: Mural**
Hours	**10**
Service Date	**03/13/2023**
Item	**Labor: Mural**
Hours	**11**
Service Date	**03/20/2023**
Item	**Labor: Mural**
Hours	**10**
Service Date	**03/29/2023**
Item	**Labor: Mural**
Hours	**10**
Payment Received & Deposited	**04/15/2023**
Check No.	**690**
Invoice Date	**04/30/2023**
Customer	**TJ Ryan**
Job	**Foyer**
Service Date	**04/10/2023**
Item	**Labor: Faux**
Hours	**6**
Service Date	**04/15/2023**
Item	**Labor: Faux**
Hours	**7**
Service Date	**04/25/2023**
Item	**Labor: Faux**
Hours	**8**
Service Date	**04/29/2023**
Item	**Labor: Faux**
Hours	**8**

Payment Received & Deposited	**05/15/2023**
Check No.	**432**
Invoice Date	**05/31/2023**
Customer	**TJ Ryan**
Job	**Foyer**
Service Date	**05/10/2023**
Item	**Labor: Faux**
Hours	**8**
Service Date	**05/18/2023**
Item	**Labor: Faux**
Hours	**9**
Service Date	**05/25/2023**
Item	**Labor: Faux**
Hours	**8**
Payment Received & Deposited	**06/15/2023**
Check No.	**455**
Invoice Date	**06/30/2023**
Customer	**Maria Cecilia**
Job <Add New Job>	**Vaulted Kitchen**
Service Date	**06/10/2023**
Item	**Labor: Mural**
Hours	**10**
Service Date	**06/18/2023**
Item	**Labor: Mural**
Hours	**10**
Service Date	**06/28/2023**
Item	**Labor: Mural**
Hours	**10**
Payment Received & Deposited	**07/15/2023**
Check No.	**733**

Invoice Date	**07/31/2023**
Customer	**Maria Cecilia**
Job	**Vaulted Kitchen**
Service Date	**07/09/2023**
Item	**Labor: Mural**
Hours	**7**
Service Date	**07/18/2023**
Item	**Labor: Mural**
Hours	**10**
Service Date	**07/27/2023**
Item	**Labor: Mural**
Hours	**10**
Payment Received & Deposited	**08/15/2023**
Check No.	**750**

Invoice Date	**08/31/2023**
Customer	**Maria Cecilia**
Job	**Vaulted Kitchen**
Service Date	**08/09/2023**
Item	**Labor: Mural**
Hours	**8**
Service Date	**08/18/2023**
Item	**Labor: Mural**
Hours	**9**
Service Date	**08/22/2023**
Item	**Labor: Mural**
Hours	**10**
Payment Received & Deposited	**09/15/2023**
Check No.	**782**

Invoice Date	**10/31/2023**
Customer	**TJ Ryan**
Job <Add New Job>	**Screen Porch**
Service Date	**10/11/2023**
Item	**Labor: Mural**
Hours	**7**
Service Date	**10/20/2023**
Item	**Labor: Mural**
Hours	**5**
Service Date	**10/22/2023**
Item	**Labor: Mural**
Hours	**6**
Payment Received & Deposited	**11/15/2023**
Check No.	**685**

Invoice Date	**11/30/2023**
Customer	**TJ Ryan**
Job	**Screen Porch**
Service Date	**11/11/2023**
Item	**Labor: Mural**
Hours	**11**
Service Date	**11/18/2023**
Item	**Labor: Mural**
Hours	**6**
Service Date	**11/27/2023**
Item	**Labor: Mural**
Hours	**9**
Payment Received & Deposited	**12/15/2023**
Check No.	**725**

2. Export to **Excel** or **print** the Income by Customer Detail report for 2023. (Report Center > Company & Financial > Income by Customer Detail.)
3. Export to **Excel** or **print** the Deposit Detail report for 2023. (Report Center > Banking > Deposit Detail.)

E11.6.3 Back Up Exercise 11.6

Save a backup of your Exercise file using the file name: YourName Exercise 11.6 Backup.QBB. See *Appendix B: Back Up & Restore QuickBooks Files* for instructions.

EXERCISE 11.7: Adjustments

In this exercise, you will first print a Trial Balance and then record adjusting entries for Paint Palette.

E11.7.1 QuickBooks File

If you will be using the same computer and the same QBW file:

1. Select your **QBW file.**
2. Add **YourName Exercise 11.7** to the company name by selecting **Company Menu > My Company.**

If you are not using the same computer that you used for Chapter 11 and Exercises 11.1 – 11.6, you will need to restore your latest prior Backup.QBB file using the instructions in Appendix B: Back Up & Restore QuickBooks files. After restoring, add YourName Exercise 11.7 to the company name.

E11.7.2 Trial Balance

The purpose of the Trial Balance is to determine whether the accounting system is in balance (debits equal credits).

Create a Trial Balance for Paint Palette at December 31, 2023.

1. From the Report Center select **Accountant & Taxes > Trial Balance**
2. Select Dates **From: 12/31/2023 To: 12/31/2023**
3. Export to **Excel** or **print** the Trial Balance for Paint Palette
4. **Close** the Trial Balance window

E11.7.3 Adjusting Entries

At the end of the accounting period, it is necessary to make adjusting entries to bring a company's accounts up to date as of year-end. Three adjusting entries are needed for Paint Palette as of December 31, 2023.

1. To enter adjusting entries, select **Accountant Menu** > **Make General Journal Entries**
2. Next, use the Make General Journal Entries window to record the adjusting entry (A1) for depreciation expense on the computer for Paint Palette at December 31, 2023. The $1,500 computer cost will be depreciated over a useful life of five years. (Depreciation expense is calculated as $1500/5 years = $300 per year.) Use Account 62400 and 14300 to record the adjusting entry.
3. Record an adjusting entry (A2) to record depreciation expense for the painting equipment for the year. The $500 painting equipment cost is depreciated using straight-line depreciation over five years with no salvage value. Use Account No. 62400 and 14600 to record the adjusting entry.
4. On December 31, 2023, you take an inventory of unused paint supplies on hand to learn that $100 of paint supplies are still on hand as of that date. Since the supplies were recorded as supplies expense when originally purchased, an adjusting entry is needed (A3). Use Account 13000 to record the $100 of unused paint supplies as an asset with future benefit.
5. Click **Save & Close** to save the adjusting journal entries
6. To create an Adjusting Journal Entries report on December 31, 2023, for Paint Palette, from the Report Center, select **Accountant & Taxes** > **Adjusting Journal Entries**
7. Select Dates: **12/31/2023 To 12/31/2023**
8. Export to **Excel** or **print** the Adjusting Journal Entries report
9. **Close** the Adjusting Journal Entries report

E11.7.4 Adjusted Trial Balance

An Adjusted Trial Balance is simply a Trial Balance printed after adjusting entries are recorded.

Create an Adjusted Trial Balance for Paint Palette at December 31, 2023 after adjusting entires are entered.

1. Export to **Excel** or **print** an Adjusted Trial Balance at December 31, 2023. (Report Center > Accountant & Taxes > Adjusted Trial Balance.)
2. On the Adjusted Trial Balance, **highlight** amounts affected by the adjusting entries

E11.7.5 Back Up Exercise 11.7

Save a backup of your Exercise file using the file name: YourName Exercise 11.7 Backup.QBB. See *Appendix B: Back Up & Restore QuickBooks Files* for instructions.

EXERCISE 11.8: Reports

In this exercise, you will print out financial statements for Paint Palette for the year 2023.

E11.8.1 QuickBooks File

If you will be using the same computer and the same QBW file:

1. Select your **QBW file.**
2. Add **YourName Exercise 11.8** to the company name by selecting **Company Menu** > **My Company.**

> **If you are not using the same computer that you used for Chapter 11 and Exercises 11.1 – 11.7**, you will need to restore your latest prior Backup.QBB file using the instructions in Appendix B: Back Up & Restore QuickBooks files. After restoring, add YourName Exercise 11.8 to the company name.

E11.8.2 Journal

The Journal lists all the transactions entered, whether using an onscreen form or the Journal, in a debit and credit format. The Journal is often a useful tool when tracking errors or discrepancies in the accounting system.

Create a Journal for Paint Palette for 2023.

1. From the Report Center select **Accountant & Taxes** > **Journal**
2. Select Dates **From: 01/01/2023 To: 12/31/2023**

3. Export to **Excel** or **print** the Journal for Paint Palette
4. **Close** the Journal window

E11.8.3 Financial Statements

Create the following financial statements for Paint Palette for the year 2023.

1. Export to **Excel** or **print** the Profit & Loss, Standard
2. Export to **Excel** or **print** the Balance Sheet, Standard
3. Export to **Excel** or **print** the Statement of Cash Flows

E11.8.4 Back Up Exercise 11.8

Save a backup of your Exercise file using the file name: YourName Exercise 11.8 Backup.QBB. See *Appendix B: Back Up & Restore QuickBooks Files* for instructions.

EXERCISE 11.9: Close the Accounting Period

Complete Exercise 11.9 only after you have completed Exercise 11.8.

To prevent changes to prior periods, QuickBooks permits you to restrict access to the accounting records for past periods that have been closed.

The QuickBooks Administrator can restrict user access to closed periods either at the time a new user is set up or later.

E11.9.1 QuickBooks File

If you will be using the same computer and the same QBW file:

1. Select your **QBW file.**
2. Add **YourName Exercise 11.9** to the company name by selecting **Company Menu > My Company.**

If you are not using the same computer that you used for Chapter 11 and Exercises 11.1 – 11.8, you will need to restore your latest prior Backup.QBB file using the instructions in Appendix B: Back Up & Restore QuickBooks files. After restoring, add YourName Exercise 11.9 to the company name.

E11.9.2 Close the Accounting Period

To enter the closing date in QuickBooks:

1. Select **Company Menu** > **Set Up Users and Passwords** > **Set Up Users**
2. If necessary, enter information for the QuickBooks Administrator, then click **OK**
3. When the following User List window appears, click the **Closing Date** button
4. Enter the closing date: **12/31/2023**
5. Click **OK** to close the Set Closing Date and Password window

E11.9.3 Back Up Exercise 11.9

Save a backup of your Exercise file using the file name: YourName Exercise 11.9 Backup.QBB. See *Appendix B: Back Up & Restore QuickBooks Files* for instructions.

PROJECT 11.1

Germain Consulting

BACKSTORY

Mason Germain founded a new business, Germain Consulting, a firm that provides consulting and design services to companies using social media for marketing purposes. The firm advises companies regarding how to use internet marketing and social media tools, such as Facebook® and Instagram®, to market and promote their companies, products, and brands. Social media tools are revolutionizing marketing to promote dating services, spas, grocery stores, and even emergency rooms. Germain Consulting is poised to provide the expertise to assist firms in capitalizing upon social media to gain a competitive advantage.

You plan to maintain the accounting records using QuickBooks software.

QB SatNav

The objective of Project 11.1 is to facilitate your mastery of QuickBooks Desktop. As shown in the following QB SatNav, Project 11.1 covers all three processes: QB Settings, QB Transactions, and QB Reports. This project provides you with the opportunity to integrate your knowledge of QuickBooks Desktop through all three phases of QB SatNav for a service company.

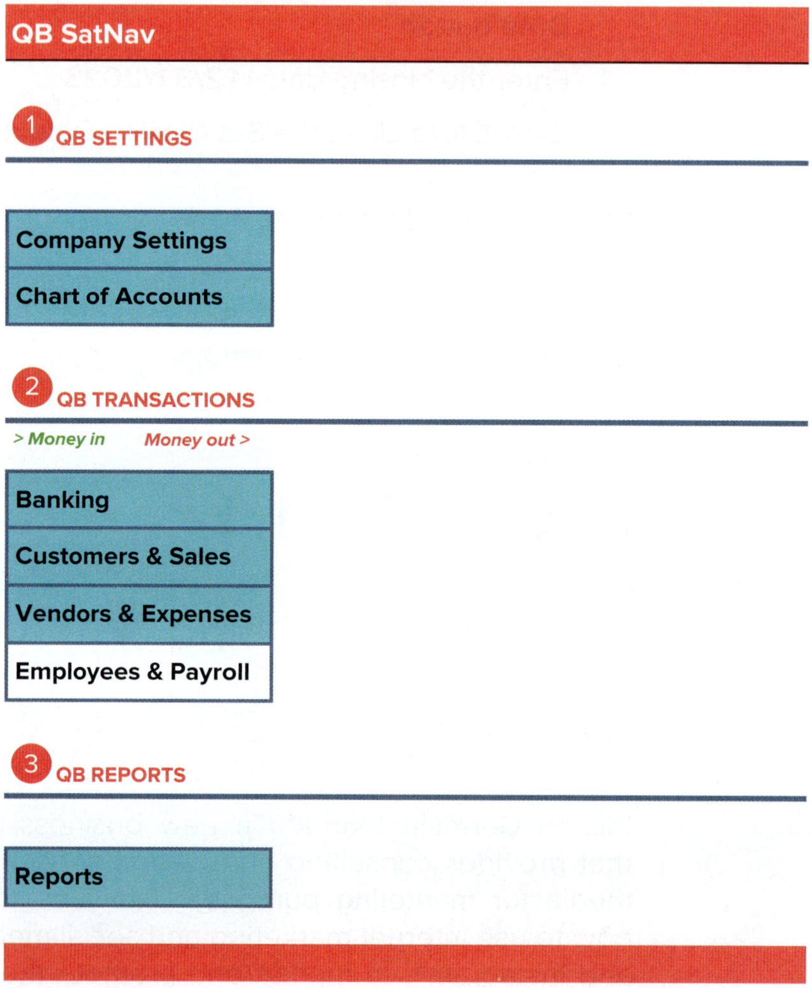

P11.1.1 New Company Setup

Create a new company in QuickBooks for Germain Consulting using the following information.

1. Use the EasyStep Interview to set up a new QuickBooks company.

Company name	**YourName Project 11.1 Germain Consulting**
Federal tax ID	**123-45-6789**
Address	**333 Paris Avenue**
City	**Bayshore**
State	**CA**
Zip	**94326**
Phone	**415-555-4320**
Email	<**Enter your email address**>
Industry	**General Service-based Business**
Type of organization	**Sole Proprietorship**
First month of fiscal year	**January**
File name	**YourName Project 11.1**
What do you sell?	**Services only**
Sales tax	**No**
Estimates	**Yes**
Billing statements	**No**
Progress invoicing	**No**
Track bills you owe	**Yes**
Track time	**Yes**
Employees	**No**
Start date	**01/01/2023**
Use recommended accounts	**Yes**
Bank account name	**Checking**
Bank account number	**2345678901**
Bank account balance	**0.00 as of 01/01/2023**

2. Click **Start Working** to exit QuickBooks Setup

P11.1.2 Add Customers

1. Add the following customers to the Customer List.

Customer	**Petit, Mimi**
Address Info:	
First Name	**Mimi**
Last Name	**Petit**
Main Phone	**415-555-2160**
Address	**220 Alsace Avenue**
	Bayshore, CA 94326
Payment Settings:	
Account No.	**12700**
Payment Terms	**Net 15**
Preferred Payment Method	**Check**
Customer Type	**From advertisement**
Customer	**Luminesse Link**
Address Info:	
First Name	**Luminesse**
Main Phone	**415-555-2222**
Address	**22 Beach Street**
	Bayshore, CA 94326
Payment Settings:	
Account No.	**13330**
Payment Terms	**Net 15**
Preferred Payment Method	**Check**
Customer Type	**Referral**
Customer	**Bichotte Supplies**
Address Info:	
First Name	**Bichotte**
Main Phone	**415-555-4567**
Address	**810 Francais Drive**
	Bayshore, CA 94326

Payment Settings:

Account No.	**19900**
Payment Terms	**Net 15**
Preferred Payment Method	**Check**
Customer Type	**Referral**

2. From the Customer Center, export to **Excel** the Customer List.

   ! When exporting to Excel, remember to select Advanced Excel Options:
   - Uncheck **Space between columns**
   - Check **Row height**
   - Uncheck **Include QuickBooks Export Guide worksheet with helpful advice**
   - Select **On printed report and screen**

P11.1.3 Add Vendors

1. Add the following vendors to the Vendor List.

Vendor	**Joseph Leasing**
Opening Balance	**$0.00 as of 01/01/2024**
Address Info:	
Company Name	**Joseph Leasing**
Full Name	**Joseph Asher**
Main Phone	**415-555-0412**
Address	**13 Appleton Drive**
	Bayshore, CA 94326
Payment Settings:	
Account No.	**2700**
Payment Terms	**Net 30**
Tax Settings:	
Vendor Tax ID	**37-1726354**
Additional Info:	
Vendor Type	**Service Providers**

Vendor	**Maria Cecilia Associates**
Opening Balance	**$0.00 as of 01/01/2024**
Address Info:	
Company Name	**Maria Cecilia Associates**
Full Name	**Maria Cecilia**
Main Phone	**415-555-6565**
Address	**65 5th Avenue**
	Bayshore, CA 94326
Payment Settings:	
Account No.	**4500**
Payment Terms	**Net 30**
Tax Settings:	
Vendor Tax ID	**37-3571656**
Vendor Type	**Suppliers**

2. From the Vendor Center, export to **Excel** the Vendor List

P11.1.4 Add Items

1. Add the following items to the Item List.

Item Type	**Service**
Item Name	**Internet Marketing**
Description	**Internet Marketing Consulting**
Rate	**$60.00**
Income Account	**Sales**
Item Type	**Service**
Item Name	**Social Media Marketing**
Description	**Social Media Marketing Consulting**
Rate	**$70.00**
Income Account	**Sales**

2. Export to **Excel** or **print** the Item List. (Use Report Center > List > Item Listing.)

! When exporting to Excel, remember to select Advanced Excel Options:

- Uncheck **Space between columns**
- Check **Row height**
- Uncheck **Include QuickBooks Export Guide worksheet with helpful advice**
- Select **On printed report and screen**

P11.1.5 Chart of Accounts

Complete the following for the Chart of Account.

1. Set Accounting preferences to display account numbers in the Chart of Accounts
2. From the Report Center, export to **Excel** the Chart of Accounts (Account Listing)

P11.1.6 Enter Transactions

Germain Consulting entered into the following transactions during January 2023.

1. Record the transactions for Germain Consulting. (Click View > Open Window List to streamline transaction entry.)

Date	Transaction
01/01/2023	Mason Germain invested $13,000 in the business (Check No. 432)
01/01/2023	Paid $700 for rent expense to Joseph Leasing. (Record with the two-step method using the Enter Bills and Pay Bills windows.)
01/02/2023	Purchased computer equipment for $2,400 on account from Maria Cecilia Associates (Account: Furniture & Equipment).
01/03/2023	Purchased copier/printer/fax machine for $900 on account from Maria Cecilia Associates (Account: Furniture & Equipment).
01/06/2023	Emailed invoice to Luminesse Link for 12 hours of Internet marketing consulting and 8 hours of social media marketing consulting. Use the Intuit Service Invoice template.

01/08/2023	Emailed invoice to Bichotte Supplies for 13 hours of Internet marketing consulting and 9 hours of social media marketing consulting
01/10/2023	Emailed invoice to Mimi Petit for 4 hours of Internet marketing consulting
01/15/2023	Emailed invoice to Bichotte Supplies for 18 hours of social media marketing consulting
01/20/2023	Paid $400 for office technology supplies from Maria Cecilia Associates. (Record as Office Supplies Expense using the Enter Bills and Pay Bills windows.)
01/20/2023	Received payment from Luminesse Link (Check No. 589) and recorded deposit
01/22/2023	Emailed invoice to Luminesse Link for 15 hours of Internet marketing consulting
01/22/2023	Received payment from Bichotte Supplies for $1410.00 (Check No. 935) and recorded deposit
01/23/2023	Received payment from Mimi Petit (Check No. 1245) and recorded deposit
01/24/2023	Paid $120 for office technology supplies from Maria Cecilia Associates. (Record as Office Supplies Expense using the Enter Bills and Pay Bills windows.)
01/27/2023	Emailed invoice to Mimi Petit for 3 hours of Internet marketing consulting and 8 hours of social media marketing consulting
01/28/2023	Received payment from Bichotte Supplies (Check No. 876) and recorded deposit
01/31/2023	Paid Maria Cecilia Associates bill for $2,400 computer

2. Export to **Excel** or **print** the Deposit Detail report for January 2023
3. Export to **Excel** or **print** the Check Detail report for January 2023
4. Export to **Excel** or **print** the Income by Customer Detail report for January 2023. (Report Center > Company & Financial > Income by Customer Detail.)

5. Export to **Excel** or **print** the Expenses by Vendor Detail report for January 2023. (Report Center > Company & Financial > Expenses by Vendor Detail.)

P11.1.7 Adjusting Entries

1. Export to **Excel** or **print** the Trial Balance report at January 31, 2023
2. Enter adjusting entries at January 31, 2023, using the following information.

   ADJ1: The $2,400 computer is depreciated over 24 months using straight-line depreciation and no salvage value. Use Account No. 62400 Depreciation Expense and Account No. 17000 Accumulated Depreciation.

   ADJ2: The $900 copier/printer/fax is depreciated over 36 months using straight-line depreciation and no salvage value. Use Account No. 62400 Depreciation Expense and Account No. 17000 Accumulated Depreciation.

   ADJ3: Office technology supplies on hand at January 31, 2023, totaled $50. Add a new current asset account, No. 13000, Office Supplies on Hand, to transfer $50 from the Office Supplies Expense account to Office Supplies on Hand account.
3. From the Report Center, export to **Excel** or **print** the Adjusting Journal Entries for January 31, 2023
4. Export to **Excel** or print the Adjusted Trial Balance report at January 31, 2023
5. On the Adjusted Trial Balance report, **highlight** the amounts affected by the adjusting entries

P11.1.8 Financial Reports

Create the following reports for Germain Consulting.

1. Export to **Excel** or **print** the Journal for the month of January 2023
2. Export to **Excel** or **print** the Profit & Loss, Standard for the month of January 2023
3. Export to **Excel** or **print** the Balance Sheet, Standard at January 31, 2023
4. Export to **Excel** or **print** the Statement of Cash Flows for the month of January 2023
5. Export to **Excel** or **print** the Cash Flow Forecast for the next month, 02/01/2023 to 02/28/2023

P11.1.9 Back Up Project 11.1

Save a backup of your Project file using the file name: YourName Project 11.1 Backup.QBB. See *Appendix B: Back Up & Restore QuickBooks Files* for instructions.

PROJECT 11.2

Raphael LLC

BACKSTORY

Raphael LLC, a start-up business, provides carpet, rugs and tile cleaning using the latest hi-tech cleaning equipment guaranteed to leave floors dazzling clean and clients smiling.

First, set up a new QuickBooks company file for Raphael LLC using the EasyStep Interview. Then create the Customer List, Vendor List, and the Item List for the new company. Then we will enter transactions for the new company and create reports.

QB SatNav

The objective of Project 11.2 is to facilitate your mastery of QuickBooks Desktop. As shown in the following QB SatNav, Project 11.2 covers all three processes: QB Settings, QB Transactions, and QB Reports. This project provides you with the opportunity to integrate your knowledge of QuickBooks Desktop through all three phases of QB SatNav for a service company.

QB SatNav

1 QB SETTINGS

- Company Settings
- Chart of Accounts

2 QB TRANSACTIONS

> Money in *Money out >*

- Banking
- Customers & Sales
- Vendors & Expenses
- Employees & Payroll

3 QB REPORTS

- Reports

P11.2.1 New Company Setup

Create a new company in QuickBooks for Raphael LLC using the following information.

1. Use the EasyStep Interview to set up a new QuickBooks company.

Company name	**YourName Project 11.2 Raphael LLC**
Federal tax ID	**130-13-3636**
Address	**1958 Rue Grand**
City	**Bayshore**
State	**CA**
Zip	**94326**
Main Phone	**415-555-1313**
Email	<**Enter your email address**>

Industry	**General Service-based Business**
Type of organization	**LLC Single-member LLC (Form 1040)**
First month of fiscal year	**January**
File name	**YourName Project 11.2**
What do you sell?	**Services only**
Sales tax	**No**
Estimates	**No**
Billing statements	**No**
Invoices	**Yes**
Progress invoicing	**No**
Track bills you owe	**Yes**
Track time	**Yes**
Employees	**No**
Start date	**01/01/2023**
Use recommended accounts	**Yes**
Bank account name	**Checking**
Bank account number	**1234567890**
Bank account balance	**0.00 as of 01/01/2023**

2. Click **Start Working** to exit QuickBooks Setup
3. Set preferences as follows:
   a. Accounting preferences to **display account numbers** in the Chart of Accounts
   b. Accounting preferences to **uncheck Warn if transactions are 30 day(s) in the future**
   c. Checking preferences to Open the Make Deposits form with **Checking** account

P11.2.2 Add Customer & Job

1. Add the following customer to the Customer List. (Use the Customer Center to add new customers.)

Customer	**Dent, Thomas**
Address Info:	
First Name	**Thomas**
Last Name	**Dent**
Main Phone	**415-555-4242**
Address	**36 Penny Lane**
	Bayshore, CA 94326
Payment Settings:	
Account No.	**1005**
Payment Terms	**Net 15**
Preferred Payment Method	**Check**
Additional Info:	
Customer Type	**From advertisement**

2. Click **OK** to close the New Customer window
3. To add a new job, select Thomas Dent in the Customer List, then **right-click** to display the pop-up menu. Select **Add Job.**
4. Enter the following job information.

Job Info:	
Job Name	**Rug cleaning**
Job Description	**Rug cleaning**
Job Type	**Residential**
Job Status	**Awarded**

5. From the Customer Center, export to **Excel** or **print** the Customer List.

   ! When exporting to Excel, remember to select Advanced Excel Options:

   - Uncheck **Space between columns**
   - Check **Row height**
   - Uncheck **Include QuickBooks Export Guide worksheet with helpful advice**
   - Select **On printed report and screen**

6. **Close** the Customer Center

P11.2.3 Add Vendors

1. Add the following vendors to the Vendor List.

Vendor	**Hart Cleaning Supplies**
Opening Balance	**$0.00 as of 01/01/2023**
Address Info:	
Company Name	**Hart Cleaning Supplies**
Full Name	**Martin Hart**
Main Phone	**415-555-7272**
Address	**72 Poisson Blvd**
	Bayshore, CA 94326
Payment Settings:	
Account No.	**2004**
Payment Terms	**Net 30**
Tax Settings:	
Vendor Tax ID	**37-6543219**
Additional Info:	
Vendor Type	**Supplies**

2. From the Vendor Center, export to **Excel** the Vendor List

P11.2.4 Add Items

1. Add the following items. Click **Next** after entering each item.

Item Type	**Service**
Item Name	**Rug Cleaning**
Description	**Rug Cleaning**
Account	**47900–Sales**
Item Type	**Service**
Item Name	**3x5 Rug Cleaning**
Subitem of	**Rug Cleaning**
Description	**3x5 Rug Cleaning**
Rate	**50.00**
Account	**47900–Sales**

Item Type	**Service**
Item Name	**5x7 Rug Cleaning**
Subitem of	**Rug Cleaning**
Description	**5x7 Rug Cleaning**
Rate	**70.00**
Account	**47900–Sales**

Item Type	**Service**
Item Name	**8x10 Rug Cleaning**
Subitem of	**Rug Cleaning**
Description	**8x10 Rug Cleaning**
Rate	**100.00**
Account	**47900–Sales**

2. Export to **Excel** or **print** the Item List as of January 1, 2023. (Use Report Center > List > Item Listing.)

   ! When exporting to Excel, remember to select Advanced Excel Options:

   - Uncheck **Space between columns**
   - Check **Row height**
   - Uncheck **Include QuickBooks Export Guide worksheet with helpful advice**
   - Select **On printed report and screen**

P11.2.5 Customize Chart of Accounts

Edit the Chart of Accounts and enter opening balances as follows.

1. Add the following information to the Chart of Accounts.

Account	**Cleaning Supplies**
Account No.	**13000**
Account Type	**Other Current Asset**
Account Description	**Cleaning Supplies**
Tax Line	**Unassigned**

Account	**Cleaning Equipment**
Account No.	**14400**

Account Type	**Fixed Asset**
Account Description	**Cleaning Equipment**
Tax Line	**Unassigned**

Account	**Cleaning Equipment Cost**
Account No.	**14500**
Account Type	**Fixed Asset**
Account Description	**Cleaning Equipment Cost**
Subaccount of	**14400 Cleaning Equipment**
Tax Line	**Unassigned**

Account	**Cleaning Equipment Acc Depr**
Account No.	**14600**
Account Type	**Fixed Asset**
Account Description	**Cleaning Equipment Accumulated Depreciation**
Subaccount of	**14400 Cleaning Equipment**
Tax Line	**Unassigned**

Account	**Accounts Payable**
Account No.	**21000**
Account Type	**Accounts Payable**
Account Description	**Accounts Payable**
Tax Line	**Unassigned**

Account	**Supplies Expense**
Account No.	**64800**
Account Type	**Expense**
Account Description	**Supplies Expense**
Tax Line	**Schedule C: Supplies (not from COGS)**

2. Export to **Excel** the Chart of Accounts (Account Listing) as of January 1, 2023. (Report Center > List > Account Listing.)

! When exporting to Excel, remember to select Advanced Excel Options:

- Uncheck **Space between columns**
- Check **Row height**
- Uncheck **Include QuickBooks Export Guide worksheet with helpful advice**
- Select **On printed report and screen**

P11.2.6 Enter Transactions

During January, Raphael LLC entered into the transactions listed below.

1. Record the following transactions. (To streamline transaction entry, select: View > Open Window List.)

Date	Transaction
01/01/2023	Raphael invested $8,000 cash in the business. (Use the Make Deposits window with Account No 30000 and Check No 501.)
01/02/2023	Purchased cleaning equipment for $800 from Hart Cleaning Supplies. (Use the Enter Bills and Pay Bills windows.)
01/05/2023	Purchased $200 of cleaning supplies on account from Hart Cleaning Supplies. (Use Enter Bills window to record Supplies Expense.)
01/09/2023	Using the Intuit Service Invoice Template, record cleaning rugs for Tom Dent on account: • (4) 3 × 5 • (6) 5 × 7 • (8) 8 × 10
01/20/2023	Paid Hart Cleaning Supplies bill
01/29/2023	Collected Tom Dent payment for cleaning services (Check No. 580) and deposited customer payment

2. Export to **Excel** the Deposit Detail report for January 2023
3. Export to **Excel** the Check Detail report for January 2023
4. Export to **Excel** or **print** the Income by Customer Detail report for January 2023. (Report Center > Company & Financial > Income by Customer Detail.)

5. Export to **Excel** or **print** the Expenses by Vendor Detail report for January 2023. (Report Center > Company & Financial > Expenses by Vendor Detail.)

P11.2.7 Adjusting Entries

1. Export to **Excel** the Trial Balance report at January 31, 2023
2. Make adjusting entires at January 31, 2023.

   ADJ1: Make an adjusting entry at January 31, 2023, to record one month of depreciation for the cleaning equipment. The cleaning equipment cost $800 and has a two-year (24-month) life and no salvage value resulting in depreciation expense of $33 per month.

   ADJ2: Make an adjusting entry to record cleaning supplies of $40 on hand at January 31, 2023.
3. From the Report Center, export to **Excel** the Adjusting Journal Entries for January 31, 2023
4. Export to **Excel** the Adjusted Trial Balance report at January 31, 2023
5. On the Adjusted Trial Balance report, **highlight** the amounts affected by the adjusting entries

P11.2.8 Financial Reports

Export to **Excel** or **print** the following reports for Raphael LLC for January 2023.

1. Export to **Excel** the Journal for the month of January 2023
2. Export to **Excel** the Profit & Loss, Standard for the month of January 2023
3. Export to **Excel** the Balance Sheet, Standard at January 31, 2023
4. Export to **Excel** the Statement of Cash Flows for the month of January 2023

P11.2.9 Back Up Project 11.2

Save a backup of your Project file using the file name: YourName Project 11.2 Backup.QBB. See *Appendix B: Back Up & Restore QuickBooks Files* for instructions.

Chapter 12

QuickBooks Service Company Case

BACKSTORY

Mookie The Beagle Spa™

Your friend and entrepreneur, CK Walker, previously founded a business Mookie The Beagle™ Concierge that provides pet care and pet healthcare services. With an accompanying app that streamlined and simplified pet care, Mookie The Beagle™ Concierge became a financial success.

One of CK's satisfied clients, TJ Ryan, encouraged CK to start a pet grooming business. TJ's Golden Labrador Retriever, Baxter, performs at agility dog shows, and TJ would like CK to do doggie massages and pet grooming for Baxter before and after shows.

After researching this business opportunity thoroughly, CK is now ready to add a related business endeavor, Mookie The Beagle Spa™. CK envisions the new business would provide mobile pet spa and grooming services. CK developed a smartphone Mookie The Beagle Spa app to schedule spa appointments, train pet parents about grooming maintenance between appointments, and more.

To maintain the financial records for Mookie The Beagle Concierge, CK Walker selected QuickBooks Online. For the new business venture, CK would like to try QuickBooks Desktop. Since he knew you were using QBDT at your Rock Castle Construction position, he approached you to inquire if you were willing to set up his new company in QuickBooks Desktop. CK could then compare and contrast QuickBooks Desktop and QuickBooks Online to see which he thinks is a better fit for his businesses going forward.

After goodnatured but heated negotiations, you and CK reach an agreement: you will assist CK with his QuickBooks Desktop needs, and he will assist you with marketing and promoting your painting business.

Download the Excel Report Template for Chapter 12 at www.My-QuickBooks.com, QB2018 link.

Section 12.1

QB SatNav

The objective of this chapter is to facilitate mastery of QuickBooks Desktop for a QuickBooks service company. We will cover setting up a new QuickBooks service company, customize the QuickBooks Chart of Accounts, enter QuickBooks transactions, and create reports. This chapter provides the opportunity to integrate knowledge of QuickBooks Desktop through all three phases of the QB SatNav.

As shown in the following QB SatNav, Chapter 12 QuickBooks Service Company Case covers all three processes: QB Settings, QB Transactions, and QB Reports.

QB SatNav

1 QB SETTINGS

- Company Settings
- Chart of Accounts

2 QB TRANSACTIONS

> Money in *Money out >*

- Banking
- Customers & Sales
- Vendors & Expenses
- Employees & Payroll

3 QB REPORTS

- Reports

Section 12.2

SET UP NEW QUICKBOOKS COMPANY AND CUSTOMIZE CHART OF ACCOUNTS

C12.2.1 Create New QuickBooks Company. Create a new company in QuickBooks for Mookie The Beagle™ Spa using the following information and the EasyStep Interview.

Company Name	**YourName Chapter 12 Mookie The Beagle Spa**
Tax ID	**123-45-6789**
Address	**432 Phoenician Way**
City	**Mountain View**
State	**CA**
ZIP	**94043**
Phone	**415-555-4320**
Email	**<Enter your email address>**
Industry	**General Service-based Business**
Type of organization	**Sole Proprietorship**
First month of fiscal year	**January**
File name	**YourName Chapter 12**
What do you sell?	**Services only**
Sales tax	**No**
Estimates	**No**
Billing statements	**No**
Invoices	**Yes**
Progress invoicing	**No**
Track bills you owe	**Yes**

Track time	**Yes**
Employees	**No**
Start date	**01/01/2023**
Use recommended accounts?	**Yes**
Bank account name	**Checking**
Bank account number	**9876543210**
Bank account balance	**0.00 as of 01/01/2023**

Select the tax form, Form 1040 (Sole Proprietorship), for Mookie The Beagle™ Spa.

1. Select **Company Menu**
2. Select **My Company**
3. Select Income Tax Form: **Form 1040 (Sole Proprietor)**

C12.2.2 Display Account Numbers. Display Account Numbers in the Chart of Accounts for Mookie The Beagle Spa.

1. Select **Edit Menu**
2. Select **Preferences**
3. Select **Accounting**
4. Select **Company Preferences**
5. Select **Use Account Numbers**

C12.2.3 Edit Chart of Accounts. Add the following accounts to the Chart of Accounts for Mookie The Beagle Spa.

Account No.	**14000**
Account Type	**Fixed Asset**
Account Name	**Pet Spa Equipment**
Account Description	**Pet Spa Equipment**
Tax Line	**Unassigned**

Account No.	**14100**
Account Type	**Fixed Asset**
Account Name	**Pet Spa Equipment Cost**
Subaccount of	**Pet Spa Equipment**
Account Description	**Pet Spa Equipment Cost**
Tax Line	**Unassigned**

Account No.	**14200**
Account Type	**Fixed Asset**
Account Name	**Pet Spa Equipment Acc Depr**
Subaccount of	**Pet Spa Equipment**
Account Description	**Pet Spa Equipment Accumulated Depreciation**
Tax Line	**Unassigned**

Account No.	**21000**
Account Type	**Credit Card**
Account Name	**VISA Credit Card**
Account Description	**VISA Credit Card**
Tax Line	**Unassigned**

Account No.	**64800**
Account Type	**Expense**
Account Name	**Supplies Expense**
Account Description	**Supplies Expense**
Tax Line	**Schedule C: Supplies (not from COGS)**

Account No.	**64810**
Account Type	**Expense**
Account Name	**Pet Spa Supplies Expense**
Subaccount of	**Supplies Expense**
Account Description	**Pet Spa Supplies Expense**
Tax Line	**Schedule C: Supplies (not from COGS)**

Account No.	**64820**
Account Type	**Expense**
Account Name	**Technology Supplies Expense**
Subaccount of	**Supplies Expense**
Account Description	**Pet Spa Supplies Expense**
Tax Line	**Schedule C: Supplies (not from COGS)**

Account No.	**67000**
Account Type	**Expense**
Account Name	**Lease Expense**
Account Description	**Lease Expense for vehicles and equipment**
Tax Line	**Schedule C: Rent/lease vehicles, equip.**

Edit the following accounts in the Chart of Accounts for Mookie The Beagle Spa to appear as follows.

Account No.	**62400**
Account Type	**Expense**
Account Name	**Depreciation Expense**
Account Description	**Depreciation on equipment, buildings, and improvements**
Tax Line <Change from Unassigned>	**Schedule C: Other business expenses**

Account No.	**67100**
Account Type	**Expense**
Account Name	**Rent Expense**
Account Description	**Rent paid for company offices or other structures used in the business**
Tax Line <Change from Schedule C: Rent/lease vehicles, equip.>	**Schedule C: Rent/lease other bus. prop.**

C12.2.4 Create Chart of Accounts Report. Generate a Chart of Accounts report for Mookie The Beagle Spa.

1. From the Report Center, select **List** > **Account Listing**
2. Export to **Excel** or **print** the Chart of Accounts (Account Listing) report for Mookie The Beagle Spa at 01/01/2023.

   ! When exporting to Excel, remember to select Advanced Excel Options:

   - Uncheck **Space between columns**
   - Check **Row height**
   - Uncheck **Include QuickBooks Export Guide worksheet with helpful advice**
   - Select **On printed report and screen**

Section 12.3

CUSTOMER LIST

C12.3.1 Using the following information, create a Customer List for Mookie The Beagle Spa. Note that Customer Type refers to how the customer learned about Mookie The Beagle Spa.

1. Using the following information, add a customer to Mookie The Beagle Spa Customer List.

Customer	**Cecilia, Maria**
Opening Balance	**0.00 as of 01/01/2023**
Address Info:	
First Name	**Maria**
Last Name	**Cecilia**
Mobile	**415-555-6565**
Address	**65 5th Avenue Bayshore, CA 94326**
Payment Settings:	
Account No.	**3001**
Payment Terms	**Net 30**
Preferred Payment Method	**Visa**
Additional Info:	
Customer Type <Add New>	**Direct Contact**

2. Add the following job for Maria Cecilia. (Add jobs by selecting the customer in the Customer List, right- click > Add Job.)

Job Info:	
Job Name	**Pepe**
Job Description	**Pepe Chihuahua**
Job Type <Add New>	**Small Pet**
Job Status	**Awarded**

3. Add another customer.

Customer	**Ryan, TJ**
Opening Balance	**0.00 as of 01/01/2023**
Address Info:	
First Name	**TJ**
Last Name	**Ryan**
Mobile	**415-555-4545**
Address	**55 Scotch Drive Bayshore, CA 94326**
Payment Settings:	
Account No.	**3002**
Payment Terms	**Net 30**
Preferred Payment Method	**Check**
Additional Info:	
Customer Type	**Referral**

4. Add the following job for TJ Ryan.

Job Info:	
Job Name	**Baxter**
Job Description	**Baxter Golden Retriever**
Job Type <Add New>	**Large Pet**
Job Status	**Awarded**

5. Add a new customer.

Customer	**Petit, Mimi**
Opening Balance	**0.00 as of 01/01/2023**
Address Info:	
First Name	**Mimi**
Last Name	**Petit**
Mobile	**415-555-2160**
Address	**220 Alsace Avenue Bayshore, CA 94326**

Payment Settings:

Account No.	**3003**
Payment Terms	**Net 30**
Preferred Payment Method	**Check**

Additional Info:

Customer Type <Add New>	**Internet**

6. Add the following job for Mimi Petit.

Job Info:

Job Name	**Bebe**
Job Description	**Bebe French Bulldog**
Job Type <Add New>	**Medium Pet**
Job Status	**Awarded**

7. Add a new customer.

Customer	**Martini, Graziella**
Opening Balance	**0.00 as of 01/01/2023**

Address Info:

First Name	**Graziella**
Last Name	**Martini**
Mobile	**415-555-1270**
Address	**13 Marco Drive Bayshore, CA 94326**

Payment Settings:

Account No.	**3004**
Payment Terms	**Net 30**
Preferred Payment Method	**Check**

Additional Info:

Customer Type <Add New>	**Social Media**

8. Add the following job for Graziella Martini.

   Job Info:

Job Name	**Mario**
Job Description	**Mario Italian Greyhound**
Job Type	**Small Pet**
Job Status	**Pending**

C12.3.2 From the Customer Center, export the Customer List to **Excel** or **print.**

Section 12.4

VENDOR LIST

C12.4.1 Using the following information, create a Vendor List for Mookie The Beagle Spa.

1. Add a new vendor.

Vendor	**Maria Cecilia Associates**
Opening Balance	**$0.00 as of 01/01/2023**
Address Info:	
Company Name	**Maria Cecilia Associates**
First Name	**Maria**
Main Phone	**415-555-7878**
Mobile	**415-555-6565**
Address	**65 5th Avenue** **Bayshore, CA 94326**
Payment Settings:	
Account No.	**4001**
Payment Terms	**Net 30**
Print on Check as	**Maria Cecilia Associates**
Tax Settings:	
Vendor Tax ID	**37-4356712**
Additional Info:	
Vendor Type	**Supplies**

2. Add new vendor.

Vendor	**Joseph Leasing**
Opening Balance	**$0.00 as of 01/01/2023**
Address Info:	
Company Name	**Joseph Leasing**

First Name	**Joseph**
Main Phone	**415-555-0412**
Address	**13 Appleton Drive** **Bayshore, CA 94326**
Payment Settings:	
Account No.	**4002**
Payment Terms	**Due on receipt**
Print on Check as	**Joseph Leasing**
Additional Info:	
Vendor Type <Add New>	**Leasing**

3. Add new vendor.

Vendor	**Bichotte Supplies**
Opening Balance	**$0 as of 01/01/2023**
Address Info:	
Company Name	**Bichotte Supplies**
First Name	**Bichotte**
Main Phone	**415-555-4567**
Address	**810 Francais Drive** **Bayshore, CA 94326**
Payment Settings:	
Account No.	**4003**
Payment Terms	**Net 30**
Print on Check as	**Bichotte Supplies**
Additional Info:	
Vendor Type	**Supplies**

4. Add new vendor.

Vendor	**Cathy PetCare Supplies**
Opening Balance	**$0 as of 01/01/2023**
Address Info:	
Company Name	**Cathy PetCare Supplies**

First Name	**Cathy**
Main Phone	**415-555-1010**
Address	**10 Chassure Street** **Bayshore, CA 94326**
Payment Settings:	
Account No.	**4004**
Payment Terms	**Net 30**
Print on Check as	**Cathy PetCare Supplies**
Additional Info:	
Vendor Type	**Suppliers**

C12.4.2 From the Vendor Center, export the Vendor List to **Excel** or **print.**

Section 12.5

ITEM LIST

C12.5.1 Enter the following items in the Item List for Mookie The Beagle Spa. Use the Income account: **47900 Sales.**

SUBITEM OF	NAME	TYPE	SALES DESCRIPTION	SALES PRICE
Shampoo	Shampoo Small	Service	Shampoo small dog	$30
Shampoo	Shampoo Medium	Service	Shampoo medium dog	$35
Shampoo	Shampoo Large	Service	Shampoo large dog	$40
Shampoo	Shampoo Extra Large	Service	Shampoo extra large dog	$45
Conditioner	Conditioner Small	Service	Conditioner small dog	$10
Conditioner	Conditioner Medium	Service	Conditioner medium dog	$10
Conditioner	Conditioner Large	Service	Conditioner large dog	$15
Conditioner	Conditioner Extra Large	Service	Conditioner extra large dog	$15
Blow Dry	Blow Dry Small	Service	Blow dry small dog	$15
Blow Dry	Blow Dry Medium	Service	Blow dry medium dog	$15
Blow Dry	Blow Dry Large	Service	Blow dry large dog	$20
Blow Dry	Blow Dry Extra Large	Service	Blow dry extra large dog	$20
Doggie Massage	Short Massage	Service	15 minutes	$15
Doggie Massage	Medium Massage	Service	30 minutes	$30
Doggie Massage	Extended Massage	Service	50 minutes	$50
Grooming	Trim Coat	Service	Trim doggie coat	$25
Grooming	Trim Nails	Service	Trim doggie nails and file	$10

C12.5.2 From the Report Center, export the Item List to **Excel** or **print.**

Section 12.6

CUSTOMIZE INVOICE TEMPLATE

Create a Custom Invoice Template with a Service Date column for Mookie The Beagle Spa. (See Chapter 11, Section 11.13, for step-by-step instructions on how to create a custom invoice with a Service Date column.) The Service Date column permits the company to bill clients once a month for all services provided during the month, listing each service date separately on the invoice.

Section 12.7

RECORD TRANSACTIONS

Mookie The Beagle Spa entered into the following transactions during the year.

C12.7.1 Record the following transactions for Mookie The Beagle Spa. Customers are billed monthly. To streamline transaction entry, use memorized transactions for recurring transactions as appropriate.

Date	Transaction
01/01/2023	CK Walker invested $7,200 in the business. (Use the Make Deposits window and Check No 5555.)
01/01/2023	Paid $360 for van lease expense to Joseph Leasing for use as Mookie's new mobile Pet Spa. (Record with the two-step method using the Enter Bills and Pay Bills windows. Use the Lease Expense account.)
01/02/2023	Purchased pet spa equipment for $1,100 on account from Cathy PetCare Supplies
01/03/2023	Purchased technology supplies for $180 on account from Maria Cecilia Associates. (Use the Technology Supplies Expense account.)
01/06/2023	Purchased office supplies for $90 with a VISA credit card from Bichotte Supplies. (Use the Enter Credit Card Charges window and Office Supplies Expense account.)
01/08/2023	Purchased $126 of pet spa supplies on account from Cathy PetCare to stock Mookie's new mobile Pet Spa. (Use the Pet Spa Supplies Expense account.)
01/10/2023	Purchased $80 of gasoline from FastFuel using VISA credit card. (Use the Enter Credit Card Charges window and the Automobile Expense account.)
01/20/2023	Paid by check Cathy PetCare Supplies bills of $1,226 for January purchases

Date	Transaction
01/30/2023	Emailed invoice to customer for the following work performed in January. **Use the Service Date Invoice Template to record all work performed for the same customer during the month on a single invoice, indicating the date of service in the Date column.** 01/13/2023 Maria Cecilia Job: Pepe Services: Shampoo Small Conditioner Small Blow Dry Small Trim Nails 01/20/2023 Maria Cecilia Job: Pepe Services: Medium Massage
02/01/2023	Paid $360 for van lease expense to Joseph Leasing
02/10/2023	Received payment from Maria Cecilia (VISA 5555 5555 5555 5555 Exp 01/2025) for January invoices. Recorded deposit.
02/20/2023	Purchased $50 of pet spa supplies from Cathy PetCare Supplies on account
02/22/2023	Paid VISA credit card bill for $170 (January purchases). (Use the Enter Bills window. Add VISA as a new vendor. Select Expense: Account 21000 Visa Credit Card. Then use Pay Bills window to pay the bill from the Checking account.)
02/28/2023	Emailed invoices to customers for the following work performed in February. **Use the Service Date Invoice Template to record all work performed for the same customer during the month on a single invoice, indicating the date of service in the Date column.** 02/02/2023 TJ Ryan Job: Baxter Services: Extended Massage Shampoo Large Conditioner Large Blow Dry Large Trim Nails 02/10/2023 TJ Ryan Job: Baxter Services: Extended Massage Shampoo Large Conditioner Large Blow Dry Large

Date	Transaction	
	02/13/2023	Maria Cecilia Job: Pepe Services: Shampoo Small Conditioner Small Blow Dry Small Trim Nails Medium Massage
	02/16/2023	Mimi Petit Job: Bebe Shampoo Medium Conditioner Medium Blow Dry Medium Trim Nails Extended Massage
	02/20/2023	TJ Ryan Job: Baxter Services: Extended Massage Shampoo Large Conditioner Large Blow Dry Large
	02/27/2023	TJ Ryan Job: Baxter Services: Extended Massage Shampoo Large Conditioner Large Blow Dry Large
	02/27/2023	Maria Cecilia Job: Pepe Services: Shampoo Small Conditioner Small Blow Dry Small Medium Massage
03/01/2023	Paid Maria Cecilia Associates for $180 of technology supplies	
03/01/2023	Paid $360 for van lease expense to Joseph Leasing	

Date	Transaction
03/10/2023	Received the following payments for prior month invoices. • Received payment from Maria Cecilia: Pepe (VISA) • Received payment from TJ Ryan: Baxter (Check No. 1234) • Received payment from Mimi Petit: Bebe (Check No. 178) • Recorded deposits
03/15/2023	Paid Cathy PetCare Supplies bill for $50
03/30/2023	Emailed invoices to customers for the following work performed in March. **Use the Service Date Invoice Template to record all work performed for the same customer during the month on a single invoice, indicating the date of service in the Date column.** 03/01/2023 TJ Ryan Job: Baxter Services: Extended Massage Shampoo Large Conditioner Large Blow Dry Large Trim Nails 03/08/2023 TJ Ryan Job: Baxter Services: Extended Massage Shampoo Large Conditioner Large Blow Dry Large 03/15/2023 Maria Cecilia Job: Pepe Services: Shampoo Small Conditioner Small Blow Dry Small Trim Nails Medium Massage 03/15/2023 TJ Ryan Job: Baxter Services: Extended Massage Shampoo Large Conditioner Large Blow Dry Large

Date	Transaction	
	03/22/2023	TJ Ryan Job: Baxter Services: Extended Massage Shampoo Large Conditioner Large Blow Dry Large
	03/16/2023	Mimi Petit Job: Bebe Shampoo Medium Conditioner Medium Blow Dry Medium Trim Nails Extended Massage
	03/27/2023	Maria Cecilia Job: Pepe Services: Shampoo Small Conditioner Small Blow Dry Small Medium Massage
	03/29/2023	TJ Ryan Job: Baxter Services: Extended Massage Shampoo Large Conditioner Large Blow Dry Large
	03/30/2023	Graziella Martini Job: Mario Shampoo Small Conditioner Small Blow Dry Small Extended Massage Trim Nails
04/01/2023	Paid $360 for van lease expense to Joseph Leasing	
04/10/2023	Received the following payments for prior month invoices. • Received payment from Maria Cecilia (VISA) • Received payment from TJ Ryan (Check No. 1342) • Received payment from Mimi Petit (Check No. 185) • Received payment from Graziella Martini (Check No. 572) • Recorded deposits	

Date	Transaction
04/20/2023	Purchased $63 of gasoline from FastFuel using VISA credit card
04/30/2023	Emailed invoices to customers for the following work performed in March. **Use the Service Date Invoice Template to record all work performed for the same customer during the month on a single invoice, indicating the date of service in the Date column.**
	04/01/2023 TJ Ryan Job: Baxter Services: Extended Massage Shampoo Large Conditioner Large Blow Dry Large Trim Nails
	04/08/2023 TJ Ryan Job: Baxter Services: Extended Massage Shampoo Large Conditioner Large Blow Dry Large
	04/15/2023 Maria Cecilia Job: Pepe Services: Shampoo Small Conditioner Small Blow Dry Small Trim Nails Medium Massage
	04/15/2023 TJ Ryan Job: Baxter Services: Extended Massage Shampoo Large Conditioner Large Blow Dry Large
	04/16/2023 Mimi Petit Job: Bebe Shampoo Medium Conditioner Medium Blow Dry Medium Trim Nails Extended Massage

Date	Transaction	
	04/22/2023	TJ Ryan Job: Baxter Services: Extended Massage Shampoo Large Conditioner Large Blow Dry Large
	04/27/2023	Maria Cecilia Job: Pepe Services: Shampoo Small Conditioner Small Blow Dry Small Medium Massage
	04/29/2023	TJ Ryan Job: Baxter Services: Extended Massage Shampoo Large Conditioner Large Blow Dry Large
	04/30/2023	Graziella Martini Job: Mario Shampoo Small Conditioner Small Blow Dry Small Extended Massage Trim Nails
05/01/2023	Paid $360 for van lease expense to Joseph Leasing	
05/10/2023	Received the following payments for prior month invoices. • Received payment from Maria Cecilia (VISA) • Received payment from TJ Ryan (Check No. 1363) • Received payment from Mimi Petit (Check No. 201) • Received payment from Graziella Martini (Check No. 577) • Recorded deposits	
05/22/2023	Paid VISA credit card bill for $63	
05/30/2023	Emailed invoices to customers for the following work performed in May.	

Date	Transaction	
	05/01/2023	TJ Ryan Job: Baxter Services: Extended Massage Shampoo Large Conditioner Large Blow Dry Large Trim Nails
	05/08/2023	TJ Ryan Job: Baxter Services: Extended Massage Shampoo Large Conditioner Large Blow Dry Large
	05/15/2023	Maria Cecilia Job: Pepe Services: Shampoo Small Conditioner Small Blow Dry Small Trim Nails Medium Massage
	05/15/2023	TJ Ryan Job: Baxter Services: Extended Massage Shampoo Large Conditioner Large Blow Dry Large
	05/16/2023	Mimi Petit Job: Bebe Shampoo Medium Conditioner Medium Blow Dry Medium Trim Nails Extended Massage
	05/22/2023	TJ Ryan Job: Baxter Services: Extended Massage Shampoo Large Conditioner Large Blow Dry Large

Date	Transaction	
	05/27/2023	Maria Cecilia Job: Pepe Services: Shampoo Small Conditioner Small Blow Dry Small Medium Massage
	05/29/2023	TJ Ryan Job: Baxter Services: Extended Massage Shampoo Large Conditioner Large Blow Dry Large
	05/30/2023	Graziella Martini Job: Mario Shampoo Small Conditioner Small Blow Dry Small Extended Massage Trim Nails
06/01/2023	Paid $360 for van lease expense to Joseph Leasing	
06/10/2023	Received the following payments for prior month invoices. • Received payment from Maria Cecilia (VISA) • Received payment from TJ Ryan (Check No. 1372) • Received payment from Mimi Petit (Check No. 210) • Received payment from Graziella Martini (Check No. 581) • Recorded deposits	
06/30/2023	Emailed invoices to customers for the following work performed in June.	
	06/01/2023	TJ Ryan Job: Baxter Services: Extended Massage Shampoo Large Conditioner Large Blow Dry Large Trim Nails

Date	Transaction	
	06/15/2023	Maria Cecilia Job: Pepe Services: Shampoo Small Conditioner Small Blow Dry Small Trim Nails Medium Massage
	06/16/2023	Mimi Petit Job: Bebe Shampoo Medium Conditioner Medium Blow Dry Medium Trim Nails Extended Massage
	06/16/2023	TJ Ryan Job: Baxter Services: Extended Massage Shampoo Large Conditioner Large Blow Dry Large
	06/27/2023	Maria Cecilia Job: Pepe Services: Shampoo Small Conditioner Small Blow Dry Small Medium Massage
	06/30/2023	Graziella Martini Job: Mario Shampoo Small Conditioner Small Blow Dry Small Extended Massage Trim Nails
07/01/2023	Paid $360 for van lease expense to Joseph Leasing	
07/10/2023	Received the following payments for prior month invoices. • Received payment from Maria Cecilia (VISA) • Received payment from TJ Ryan (Check No. 1381) • Received payment from Mimi Petit (Check No. 215) • Received payment from Graziella Martini (Check No. 589) • Recorded deposits	

Date	Transaction	
07/20/2023	Purchased $63 of gasoline from FastFuel using VISA credit card	
07/30/2023	Emailed invoices to customers for the following work performed in July.	
	07/01/2023	TJ Ryan Job: Baxter Services: Extended Massage Shampoo Large Conditioner Large Blow Dry Large Trim Nails
	07/08/2023	TJ Ryan Job: Baxter Services: Extended Massage Shampoo Large Conditioner Large Blow Dry Large
	07/15/2023	Maria Cecilia Job: Pepe Services: Shampoo Small Conditioner Small Blow Dry Small Trim Nails Medium Massage
	07/16/2023	Mimi Petit Job: Bebe Shampoo Medium Conditioner Medium Blow Dry Medium Trim Nails Extended Massage
	07/16/2023	TJ Ryan Job: Baxter Services: Extended Massage Shampoo Large Conditioner Large Blow Dry Large
	07/22/2023	TJ Ryan Job: Baxter Services: Extended Massage Shampoo Large Conditioner Large Blow Dry Large

Date	Transaction	
	07/27/2023	Maria Cecilia Job: Pepe Services: Shampoo Small Conditioner Small Blow Dry Small Medium Massage
	07/29/2023	TJ Ryan Job: Baxter Services: Extended Massage Shampoo Large Conditioner Large Blow Dry Large
	07/30/2023	Graziella Martini Job: Mario Shampoo Small Conditioner Small Blow Dry Small Extended Massage Trim Nails
08/01/2023	Paid $360 for van lease expense to Joseph Leasing	
08/10/2023	Received the following payments for prior month invoices. • Received payment from Maria Cecilia (VISA) • Received payment from TJ Ryan (Check No. 1390) • Received payment from Mimi Petit (Check No. 223) • Received payment from Graziella Martini (Check No. 595) • Recorded deposits	
08/22/2023	Paid VISA credit card bill for $63	
08/30/2023	Emailed invoices to customers for the following work performed in August.	
	08/01/2023	TJ Ryan Job: Baxter Services: Extended Massage Shampoo Large Conditioner Large Blow Dry Large Trim Nails

Date	Transaction	
	08/08/2023	TJ Ryan Job: Baxter Services: Extended Massage Shampoo Large Conditioner Large Blow Dry Large
	08/15/2023	Maria Cecilia Job: Pepe Services: Shampoo Small Conditioner Small Blow Dry Small Trim Nails Medium Massage
	08/16/2023	Mimi Petit Job: Bebe Shampoo Medium Conditioner Medium Blow Dry Medium Trim Nails Extended Massage
	08/16/2023	TJ Ryan Job: Baxter Services: Extended Massage Shampoo Large Conditioner Large Blow Dry Large
	08/22/2023	TJ Ryan Job: Baxter Services: Extended Massage Shampoo Large Conditioner Large Blow Dry Large
	08/27/2023	Maria Cecilia Job: Pepe Services: Shampoo Small Conditioner Small Blow Dry Small Medium Massage

Date	Transaction
	08/29/2023 TJ Ryan Job: Baxter Services: Extended Massage Shampoo Large Conditioner Large Blow Dry Large
	08/30/2023 Graziella Martini Job: Mario Shampoo Small Conditioner Small Blow Dry Small Extended Massage Trim Nails
09/01/2023	Paid $360 for van lease expense to Joseph Leasing
09/10/2023	Received the following payments for prior month invoices. • Received payment from Maria Cecilia (VISA) • Received payment from TJ Ryan (Check No. 1350) • Received payment from Mimi Petit (Check No. 234) • Received payment from Graziella Martini (Check No. 603) • Recorded deposits
09/20/2023	Purchased $45 of pet spa supplies from Cathy PetCare Supplies on account
09/30/2023	Emailed invoices to customers for the following work performed in September.
	09/01/2023 TJ Ryan Job: Baxter Services: Extended Massage Shampoo Large Conditioner Large Blow Dry Large Trim Nails
	09/08/2023 TJ Ryan Job: Baxter Services: Extended Massage Shampoo Large Conditioner Large Blow Dry Large

Date	Transaction	
	09/15/2023	Maria Cecilia Job: Pepe Services: Shampoo Small Conditioner Small Blow Dry Small Trim Nails Medium Massage
	09/16/2023	Mimi Petit Job: Bebe Shampoo Medium Conditioner Medium Blow Dry Medium Trim Nails Extended Massage
	09/16/2023	TJ Ryan Job: Baxter Services: Extended Massage Shampoo Large Conditioner Large Blow Dry Large
	09/22/2023	TJ Ryan Job: Baxter Services: Extended Massage Shampoo Large Conditioner Large Blow Dry Large
	09/27/2023	Maria Cecilia Job: Pepe Services: Shampoo Small Conditioner Small Blow Dry Small Medium Massage
	09/29/2023	TJ Ryan Job: Baxter Services: Extended Massage Shampoo Large Conditioner Large Blow Dry Large

Date	Transaction	
	09/30/2023	Graziella Martini Job: Mario Shampoo Small Conditioner Small Blow Dry Small Extended Massage Trim Nails
10/01/2023	Paid $360 for van lease expense to Joseph Leasing	
10/10/2023	Received the following payments for prior month invoices. • Received payment from Maria Cecilia (VISA) • Received payment from TJ Ryan (Check No. 1359) • Received payment from Mimi Petit (Check No. 243) • Received payment from Graziella Martini (Check No. 612) • Recorded deposits	
10/15/2023	Paid Cathy PetCare Supplies bill for $45	
10/30/2023	Emailed invoices to customers for the following work performed in October.	
	10/01/2023	TJ Ryan Job: Baxter Services: Extended Massage Shampoo Large Conditioner Large Blow Dry Large Trim Nails
	10/15/2023	Maria Cecilia Job: Pepe Services: Shampoo Small Conditioner Small Blow Dry Small Trim Nails Medium Massage
	10/16/2023	Mimi Petit Job: Bebe Shampoo Medium Conditioner Medium Blow Dry Medium Trim Nails Extended Massage

Date	Transaction
	10/22/2023 TJ Ryan Job: Baxter Services: Extended Massage Shampoo Large Conditioner Large Blow Dry Large
	10/27/2023 Maria Cecilia Job: Pepe Services: Shampoo Small Conditioner Small Blow Dry Small Medium Massage
	10/30/2023 Graziella Martini Job: Mario Shampoo Small Conditioner Small Blow Dry Small Extended Massage Trim Nails
11/01/2023	Paid $360 for van lease expense to Joseph Leasing
11/10/2023	Received the following payments for prior month invoices. • Received payment from Maria Cecilia (VISA) • Received payment from TJ Ryan (Check No. 1368) • Received payment from Mimi Petit (Check No. 252) • Received payment from Graziella Martini (Check No. 621) • Recorded deposits
11/30/2023	Emailed invoices to customers for the following work performed in November. 11/01/2023 TJ Ryan Job: Baxter Services: Extended Massage Shampoo Large Conditioner Large Blow Dry Large Trim Nails

Date	Transaction	
	11/08/2023	TJ Ryan Job: Baxter Services: Extended Massage Shampoo Large Conditioner Large Blow Dry Large
	11/15/2023	Maria Cecilia Job: Pepe Services: Shampoo Small Conditioner Small Blow Dry Small Trim Nails Medium Massage
	11/16/2023	Mimi Petit Job: Bebe Shampoo Medium Conditioner Medium Blow Dry Medium Trim Nails Extended Massage
	11/16/2023	TJ Ryan Job: Baxter Services: Extended Massage Shampoo Large Conditioner Large Blow Dry Large
	11/22/2023	TJ Ryan Job: Baxter Services: Extended Massage Shampoo Large Conditioner Large Blow Dry Large
	11/27/2023	Maria Cecilia Job: Pepe Services: Shampoo Small Conditioner Small Blow Dry Small Medium Massage

Date	Transaction	
	11/29/2023	TJ Ryan Job: Baxter Services: Extended Massage Shampoo Large Conditioner Large Blow Dry Large
	11/30/2023	Graziella Martini Job: Mario Shampoo Small Conditioner Small Blow Dry Small Extended Massage Trim Nails
12/01/2023	Paid $360 for van lease expense to Joseph Leasing	
12/10/2023	Received the following payments for prior month invoices. • Received payment from Maria Cecilia (VISA) • Received payment from TJ Ryan (Check No. 1377) • Received payment from Mimi Petit (Check No. 261) • Received payment from Graziella Martini (Check No. 630) • Recorded deposits	
12/20/2023	Purchased $54 of gasoline from FastFuel using VISA credit card	
12/30/2023	Emailed invoices to customers for the following work performed in December.	
	12/01/2023	TJ Ryan Job: Baxter Services: Extended Massage Shampoo Large Conditioner Large Blow Dry Large Trim Nails
	12/15/2023	Maria Cecilia Job: Pepe Services: Shampoo Small Conditioner Small Blow Dry Small Trim Nails Medium Massage

Date	Transaction	
	12/15/2023	Mimi Petit Job: Bebe Shampoo Medium Conditioner Medium Blow Dry Medium Trim Nails Extended Massage
	12/20/2023	TJ Ryan Job: Baxter Services: Extended Massage Shampoo Large Conditioner Large Blow Dry Large
	12/20/2023	Graziella Martini Job: Mario Shampoo Small Conditioner Small Blow Dry Small Extended Massage Trim Nails

C12.7.2 Export to **Excel** or **print** the Deposit Detail report for 2023.

C12.7.3 Export to **Excel** or **print** the Check Detail report for 2023.

C12.7.4 Export to **Excel** or **print** the Income by Customer Detail report for 2023.

C12.7.5 Export to **Excel** or **print** the Expenses by Vendor Detail report for 2023.

Section 12.8

ADJUSTING ENTRIES

Make adjusting entries for Mookie The Beagle Spa.

C12.8.1 Export to **Excel** or **print** the Trial Balance report for Mookie The Beagle Spa at December 31, 2023. Verify that Account 12000 Undeposited Funds has a $0.00 balance. **Highlight** the $0.00 balance in the Undeposited Funds account.

C12.8.2 Make adjusting entries for Mookie The Beagle Spa at December 31, 2023, using the following information.

1. **ADJ1:** A count of office supplies revealed $60 supplies on hand at December 31, 2023. (Add new account: 13100 Office Supplies on Hand, Other Current Asset.)
2. **ADJ2:** A count of pet spa supplies revealed $50 of supplies on hand at December 31, 2023 (Add new account: 13200 Pet Spa Supplies on Hand, Other Current Asset.)
3. **ADJ3:** The pet spa equipment cost $1,100 and has a five-year life and no salvage value.

C12.8.3 Export to **Excel** or **print** the Adjusting Journal Entries report on December 31, 2023.

C12.8.4 Export to **Excel** or **print** the Adjusted Trial Balance report for Mookie The Beagle Spa at December 31, 2023.

C12.8.5 On the Adjusted Trial Balance report, **highlight** the amounts affected by the adjusting entries.

Section 12.9

FINANCIAL REPORTS

Prepare financial reports for Mookie The Beagle Spa.

C12.9.1 Export to **Excel** or **print** the Profit and Loss by Job for the year 2023.

C12.9.2 Export to **Excel** or **print** the Profit and Loss, Standard for the year 2023.

C12.9.3 Export to **Excel** or **print** the Balance Sheet, Standard at December 31, 2023.

C12.9.4 Export to **Excel** or **print** the Statement of Cash Flows for the year of 2023.

C12.9.5 Export to **Excel** or **print** the Cash Flow Forecast for January 1, 2024 to January 31, 2024.

Section 12.10

BACK UP QUICKBOOKS FILES

Save a backup of your Chapter 12 file using the file name: **YourName Chapter 12 Backup.QBB.** For further instructions on how to back up your file, *see Appendix B: Back Up & Restore QuickBooks Files.*

Chapter 13

QuickBooks Merchandise Company

BACKSTORY

After only one year of operation, your painting service is growing as more customers learn of your custom murals. Customers take photos of whatever they want for their wall murals (sunsets, waterfalls, the beach, and so on) and then text the photos to your iPad. Then you display the photo on your iPad while you paint the mural on their walls or ceilings. It saves you time, you no longer have to guess what the customer wants, and customer satisfaction couldn't be better. You created a digital gallery of your completed murals for your website. As a promotion, you hold an annual contest for best photos for murals with an iPad as the winning prize.

You buy paint from a small boutique paint shop owned and operated by Sam Montroyal. He provides excellent customer service, delivers paint to a job when you run short, and custom mixes paint colors you use for your murals. To your dismay, you discover that Sam Montroyal is planning to close the store and retire, taking his first vacation since he opened the store 20 years ago. After your initial disappointment, however, you see a business opportunity.

If you owned the paint store, you could make a profit on the markup from paint sales made to your Paint Palette customers. In addition, you are certain you could land some large commercial customers for whom you have worked, such as Rock Castle Construction. With your connections, you could sell paint to other customers, including paint contractors and homeowners.

Convinced there is a profitable market for custom-mixed paint, you approach Sam Montroyal about purchasing his store. Sam agrees to sell the business to you for $11,000 cash. In addition, you agree to assume a $1,000 bank loan as part of the purchase agreement. You have some extra cash you can invest, and you decide to seek other investors to finance the remainder.

Joseph Asher of Joseph Leasing is a long-time customer of the paint store and owner of the store building. When he learns of your plans to buy the paint store, he eagerly offers to invest.

Joseph suggests that you investigate incorporating the new business to provide limited liability to the owners. You vaguely recall discussion of limited liability in your college accounting class and decide to email your college accounting professor, Pat Vollenger, for more information.

Professor Vollenger's email reply:

> **Subject: Limited Liability**
>
> Corporations provide investors with limited liability. The most the investor can lose is the amount invested in the corporation's stock. If you invest in a corproation, your personal assets are protected from claims against the paint store.
>
> For tax purposes, there are two different types of corporations:
>
> 1. S Corporation
> 2. C Corporation
>
> A C Corporation's earnings are subject to double taxation. The profits of the corporation are taxed (Form 1120) and then the dividends received by investors are taxed on their 1040s.
>
> If you meet the requirements to use an S Corporation, you can avoid this double taxation. An S Corporation files a Form 1020S and its earnings appear on your personal 1040 tax return, taxes at your personal income tax rate.
>
> Best wishes on your new business venture!

Joseph and you form an S Corporation. Joseph buys $6,000 of stock, and you buy $5,000 of stock. The stock proceeds are used to purchase the business from Sam Montroyal. Until you can hire a store manager, you will manage the store.

You prepare the following list of planned expenditures to launch the business:

Item	Estimated Cost
Color match computer equipment	$ 1,000
Supplies	$ 600
Store building & fixtures rent per month	$ 1,000

Paint Palette Store opens for business on January 1, 2024.

Section 13.1

QB SatNav

The objective of this chapter is to facilitate your mastery of QuickBooks Desktop. We will cover setting up a new QuickBooks merchandising company, customize the QuickBooks Chart of Accounts, enter QuickBooks transactions, and create reports. This chapter provides you with the opportunity to integrate your knowledge of QuickBooks Desktop through all three phases of the QB SatNav.

As shown in the following QB SatNav, Chapter 13 QuickBooks Merchandise Company covers all three processes: QB Settings, QB Transactions, and QB Reports.

QB SatNav

1 QB SETTINGS

- **Company Settings**
- **Chart of Accounts**

2 QB TRANSACTIONS

> Money in *Money out >*

- **Banking**
- **Customers & Sales**
- **Vendors & Expenses**
- **Employees & Payroll**

3 QB REPORTS

- **Reports**

Section 13.2

NEW QUICKBOOKS MERCHANDISING COMPANY

A company can sell customers either (1) a product or (2) a service. In Chapter 11, we maintained accounting records for a company that sells a service to customers. In this chapter, we will maintain an accounting system for a company that sells a product.

In Chapter 13, we will complete the following:

- **EasyStep Interview.** Use the EasyStep Interview to enter information and preferences for the new company. Based on the information entered, QuickBooks automatically creates a Chart of Accounts.
- **Create Lists.**
    - **Customer List.** In the Customer List, enter information about customers to whom you sell products and services.
    - **Vendor List.** In the Vendor List, enter information about vendors from whom you buy products, supplies, and services.
    - **Item List.** In the Item List, enter information about (1) products and services you sell to customers and (2) products and services you buy from vendors. Also we will create a sales tax item in the Item List.
- **Customize the Chart of Accounts.** Modify the Chart of Accounts to customize it for your business.
- **Record Transactions.** Enter business transactions in QuickBooks using onscreen forms and the onscreen Journal.
- **Create Reports.** After preparing adjusting entries, print financial reports.

If you hired employees, you would also enter information into the Employee List. In this case, there are no employees.

Download the Excel Report Template for Chapter 13 at www.My-QuickBooks.com, QB2018 link.

Section 13.3

CREATE NEW COMPANY

START QUICKBOOKS

To start QuickBooks software, click the **QuickBooks** icon on your desktop. If a QuickBooks icon does not appear on your desktop, from Microsoft® Windows® click **Start** button > **Programs** > **QuickBooks** > **QuickBooks Premier Accountant Edition.**

EASYSTEP INTERVIEW

To create a new company data file in QuickBooks, use the EasyStep Interview. The EasyStep Interview asks you a series of questions about your business. Then QuickBooks uses the information to customize QuickBooks to fit your business needs.

Create a new QuickBooks company using the EasyStep Interview as follows:

1. Select **Create a new company**
2. When the QuickBooks Setup window appears, select **Detailed Start**
3. When the EasyStep Interview Enter Your Company Information window appears, enter Company Name: **YourName Chapter 13 Paint Palette Store.** Press the **Tab** key, and QuickBooks will automatically enter the company name in the Legal name field. Since the company will do business under its legal name, the Company name and Legal name fields are the same.
4. Enter the company information.

Tax ID	**37-9875602**
Address	**864 Venus Boulevard**
City	**Bayshore**
State	**CA**
Zip	**94326**
Email	**<Enter your email address>**

5. Select **Next**
6. In the Select Your Industry window, select **Retail Shop or Online Commerce**
7. Select **Next**
8. When the How Is Your Company Organized? window appears, select **S Corporation**
9. Select **Next**
10. Select the first month of your fiscal year: **January**
11. Select **Next**
12. In the Set Up Your Administrator Password window:
    - Enter your administrator **password**
    - Retype the **password**
    - Click **Next**
13. When the Create Your Company File window appears, click **Next** to choose a file name and location to save your company file
14. When the Filename for New Company window appears, select Save in: **Desktop**
15. Enter File name: **YourName Chapter 13**
16. Click **Save**

The Navigation Bar and My Shortcuts window should appear on the left side of your QuickBooks company screen. The next section of the EasyStep Interview is to customize QuickBooks by turning on features to fit your business needs.

1. When the Customizing QuickBooks For Your Business window appears, click **Next**
2. What Do You Sell?
    - Select **Products only**
    - Click **Next**
3. How will you enter your sales in QuickBooks
    - Select **Record each sale individually**
    - Click **Next**
4. Do you charge sales tax?
    - Select **Yes**
    - Click **Next**

5. Do you want to create estimates in QuickBooks?
   - Select **No**
   - Click **Next**
6. Do you want to track sales orders before you invoice your customers?
   - Select **No**
   - Click **Next**
7. Do you want to use billing statements in QuickBooks?
   - Select **No**
   - Click **Next**
8. Do you want to use Invoices?
   - Select **Yes**
   - Click **Next**
9. Do you want to use progress invoicing?
   - Select **No**
   - Click **Next**
10. Do you want to keep track of bills you owe?
    - Select **Yes**
    - Click **Next**
11. Do you want to track inventory in QuickBooks?
    - Select **Yes**
    - Click **Next**
12. Do you want to track time in QuickBooks?
    - Select **Yes**
    - Click **Next**
13. Do You Have Employees?
    - Select **No**
    - Click **Next**
14. Read the Using Accounts in QuickBooks window. Click **Next.**
15. When the Select a Date to Start Tracking Your Finances window appears:
    - Select **Use today's date or the first day of the quarter or month**
    - Enter Date **01/01/2024**
    - Click **Next**

16. When the Review Income and Expense Accounts window appears, click **Next**
17. When the Congratulations! window appears, click **Go to Setup**

COMPLETE THE COMPANY SETUP

Use the following checklist to complete the company setup:

- Add bank account
- Customize QuickBooks preferences
- Add customers
- Add vendors
- Add products and services as items
- Customize Chart of Accounts
- Enter opening adjustments

Section 13.4

ADD BANK ACCOUNT

Bank accounts in QuickBooks are used to track your company's deposits, payments, and current bank balances. A QuickBooks company file can have more than one bank account. For example, some companies use one bank account for payroll and another bank account for all other banking items.

To add a bank account for Paint Palette Store:

1. In the Add Your Bank Accounts section of the QuickBooks Setup window, click the **Add** button
2. Enter the following information about Paint Palette's bank account

Account Name	**Checking**
Account Number	**4567891230**
Opening Balance	**0.00**
Opening Balance Date	**01/01/2024**

3. Select **Continue**
4. When asked if you want to order checks designed for QuickBooks, select **No Thanks**
5. Click **Continue** to return to the QuickBooks Setup window
6. Select **Start Working** at the bottom of the QuickBooks Setup window
7. If the New Feature Tour window appears, **close** the New Feature Tour window

In setting up QuickBooks for Paint Palette Store, the next step is to customize QuickBooks preferences.

Section 13.5

CUSTOMIZE QUICKBOOKS PREFERENCE

You will customize QuickBooks for Paint Palette Store by customizing QuickBooks preferences. To customize preferences:

1. Select **Edit Menu** > **Preferences** > **General** > **My Preferences**
2. Select Default Date to Use for New Transactions: **Use the last entered date as default**
3. Select **Accounting** > **Company Preferences.** Select the following Accounting preferences.
    - Select **Use account numbers**
    - Uncheck **Use class tracking for transactions**
    - Uncheck **Warn if transactions are 30 day(s) in the future**
4. Select **Checking** > **My Preferences.** Select default accounts to use.
    - Open the Write Checks form with **Checking** account
    - Open the Pay Bills form with **Checking** account
    - Open the Pay Sales Tax form with **Checking** account
    - Open the Make Deposits form with **Checking** account
5. Select **Desktop View** > **Company Preferences.** Verify the following preference settings. To change the settings for these preferences in the future, you would return to this screen.
    - Estimates (off)
    - Sales Tax (on)
    - Sales Orders (off)
    - Inventory (on)
    - Payroll (off)
    - Time Tracking (on)
6. Select **Sales Tax** > **Company Preferences.** Select Your Most Common Sales Tax Item: **State Tax.**
7. Click **OK** to save your customized preference settings

In setting up QuickBooks for Paint Palette Store, the next step is to enter information into lists for customers, vendors, and items.

Section 13.6

CUSTOMER, VENDOR, AND ITEM LISTS

CUSTOMER LIST

When using QuickBooks to account for a merchandising company that sells a product to customers, you must indicate whether the specific customer is charged sales tax.

Paint Palette Store will sell to:

1. Retail customers, such as homeowners who must pay sales tax
2. Wholesale customers, such as TJ Ryan Interiors, who resell the product and do not pay sales tax

Enter customer information in the Customer List.

1 Create a Customer List for Paint Palette Store using the following information.

Customer	**Cecilia, Maria**
Opening Balance	**0.00 as of 01/01/2024**
Address Info:	
First Name	**Maria**
Last Name	**Cecilia**
Mobile	**415-555-6565**
Address	**65 5th Avenue**
	Bayshore, CA 94326
Payment Settings:	
Account No.	**3001**
Payment Terms	**Net 30**
Sales Tax Settings:	
Tax Code	**Tax**
Tax Item	**State Tax**

Additional Info:

Customer Type **Residential**

Special Interest

- In the Custom Fields section, select **Define Fields** > enter **Label Special Interest** > select **Use for: Cust**
- In the Special Interest field you just created, enter **Provence**

Job Info:

Job Description **Custom Paint**

Job Type <Add New> **Custom Paint**

Job Status **Awarded**

2 **C13.6.1 Customer List.** From the Customer Center, export to **Excel** or **print** Paint Palette Store Customer List.

! When exporting to Excel, remember to select Advanced Excel Options:

- Uncheck **Space between columns**
- Check **Row height**
- Uncheck **Include QuickBooks Export Guide worksheet with helpful advice**
- Select **On printed report and screen**

VENDOR LIST

Next, enter vendor information in the Vendor List.

1 Create a Vendor List for Paint Palette Store using the following information.

Vendor **Brewer Paint Supplies**

Opening Balance **0.00 as of 01/01/2024**

Address Info:

Company Name **Brewer Paint Supplies**

Full Name **Mark Brewer**

Main Phone **415-555-3600**

Address **18 Spring Street**
Bayshore, CA 94326

Payment Settings:	
Account No.	**4001**
Payment Terms	**Net 30**
Print on Check as	**Brewer Paint Supplies**
Credit Limit	**15,000.00**
Tax Settings:	
Vendor Tax ID	**37-7832541**
Additional Info:	
Vendor Type	**Suppliers**

2 **C13.6.2 Vendor List.** From the Vendor Center, export to **Excel** or **print** Paint Palette Store Vendor List

ITEM LIST: INVENTORY

Each of the inventory items that Paint Palette Store sells is entered in the QuickBooks Item List. Paint Palette Store will stock and sell paint inventory to both retail and wholesale customers. The store will charge retail customers the full price and charge wholesale customers a discounted price. Because the sales price varies depending upon the type of customer, instead of entering the sales price in the Item List, you will enter the sales price on the invoice at the time of sale.

1 Create an Item List for Paint Palette Store inventory using the following information.

Item Type	**Inventory Part**
Item Name	**Paint Base**
Description	**Paint Base**
COGS Account	**50000 – Cost of Goods Sold**
Income Account	**46000 – Merchandise Sales**
Asset Account	**12100 – Inventory Asset**
Qty on Hand	**0.00 as of 01/01/2024**

Item Type	**Inventory Part**
Item Name	**IntBase 1 gal**
Subitem of	**Paint Base**
Description	**Interior Paint Base (1 gallon)**
Cost	**10.00**
COGS Account	**50000 – Cost of Goods Sold**
Tax Code	**Tax**
Income Account	**46000 – Merchandise Sales**
Asset Account	**12100 – Inventory Asset**
Qty on Hand	**0.00 as of 01/01/2024**

Item Type	**Inventory Part**
Item Name	**ExtBase 1 gal**
Subitem of	**Paint Base**
Description	**Exterior Paint Base (1 gallon)**
Cost	**10.00**
COGS Account	**50000 – Cost of Goods Sold**
Tax Code	**Tax**
Income Account	**46000 – Merchandise Sales**
Asset Account	**12100 – Inventory Asset**
Qty on Hand	**0.00 as of 01/01/2024**

Item Type	**Inventory Part**
Item Name	**Paint Color**
Description	**Paint Color**
COGS Account	**50000 – Cost of Goods Sold**
Income Account	**46000 – Merchandise Sales**
Asset Account	**12100 – Inventory Asset**
Qty on Hand	**0.00 as of 01/01/2024**

Item Type	**Inventory Part**
Item Name	**Stock Color**
Subitem of	**Paint Color**

Description	**Stock Paint Color**
Cost	**2.00**
COGS Account	**50000 – Cost of Goods Sold**
Tax Code	**Tax**
Income Account	**46000 – Merchandise Sales**
Asset Account	**12100 – Inventory Asset**
Qty on Hand	**0.00 as of 01/01/2024**

Item Type	**Inventory Part**
Item Name	**Custom Color**
Subitem of	**Paint Color**
Description	**Custom Paint Color**
Cost	**8.00**
COGS Account	**50000 – Cost of Goods Sold**
Tax Code	**Tax**
Income Account	**46000 – Merchandise Sales**
Asset Account	**12100 – Inventory Asset**
Qty on Hand	**0.00 as of 01/01/2024**

2 **C13.6.3 Item List.** Export to **Excel** or **print** the Item List as of January 1, 2024. (Use Report Center > List > Item Listing.)

! When exporting to Excel, remember to select Advanced Excel Options:

- Uncheck **Space between columns**
- Check **Row height**
- Uncheck **Include QuickBooks Export Guide worksheet with helpful advice**
- Select **On printed report and screen**

ITEM LIST: SALES TAX ITEM

A merchandiser selling products to consumers must charge sales tax. A sales tax item is created in the Item List with the rate and tax agency information.

To enter a sales tax item:

1. In the Item List window, **double-click** on **State Sales Tax**
2. When the Edit Item window appears, enter Tax Rate: **9.75%**
3. Enter Tax Agency: **California State Board of Equalization**
4. Click **OK**
5. If a Vendor Not Found window appears, select: **Quick Add.** If necessary, click **OK** again to close the Edit Item window.

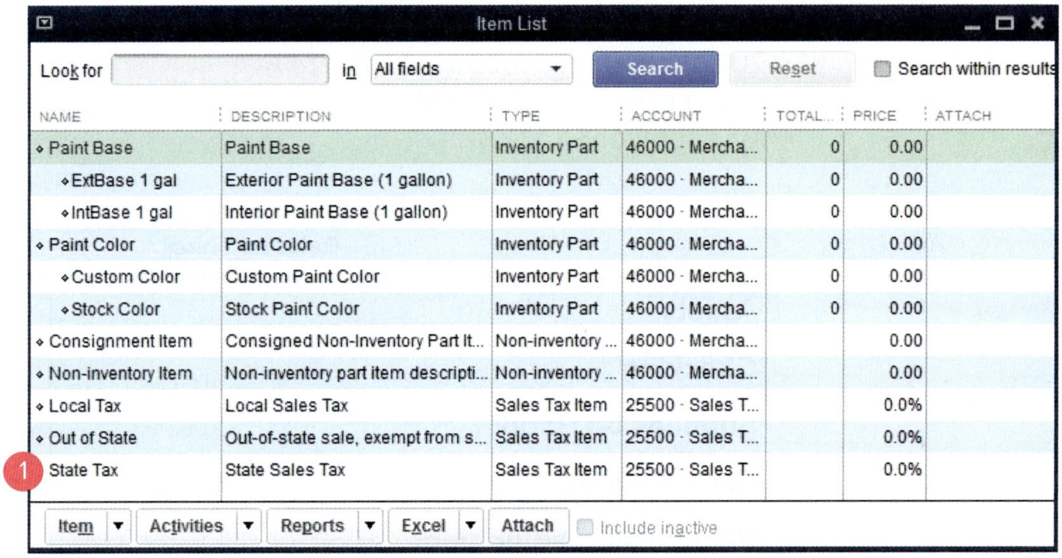

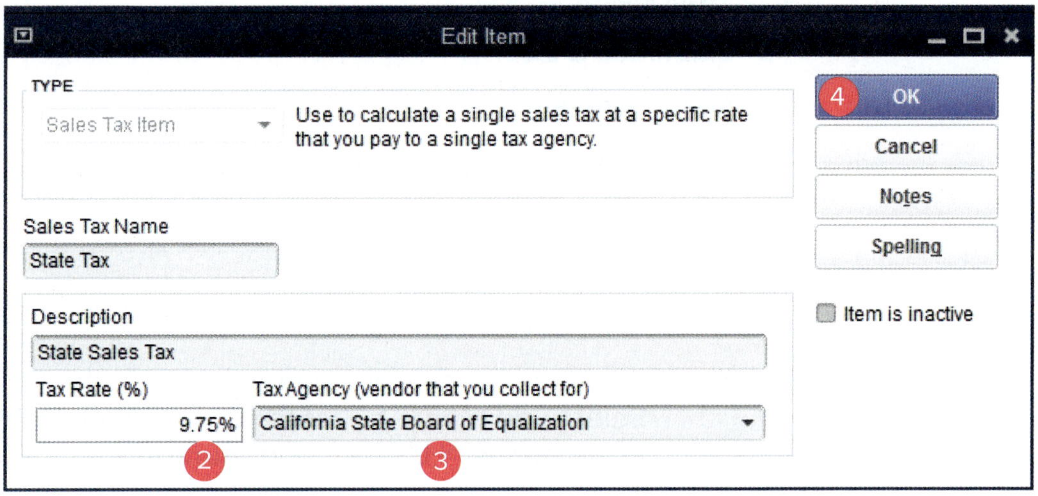

In setting up QuickBooks for Paint Palette Store, the next step is to customize the Chart of Accounts.

Section 13.7

CUSTOMIZE CHART OF ACCOUNTS

Based on your answers in the EasyStep Interview, QuickBooks automatically creates a Chart of Accounts for Paint Palette Store. You can customize the Chart of Accounts to suit your specific business needs.

Because you are purchasing an existing business, some accounts have opening balances. Opening balances for Paint Palette Store at January 1, 2024, appear as follows.

You purchased $5,000 in stock and Joseph purchased $6,000 in stock for a total of $11,000.

THE PAINT PALETTE STORE
Balance Sheet

Assets:	
Checking	$ 2,400
Supplies on Hand	$ 600
Store fixtures	$ 5,000
Paint mixing equipment	$ 4,000
Total Asset	$ 12,000
Liabilities & Equity:	
Notes payable	$ 1,000
Capital stock (opening balance equity)	$ 11,000
Total Liabilities & Equity	$ 12,000

Customize the Chart of Accounts and enter opening balances as follows:

1. If needed, display account numbers in the Chart of Accounts. Select **Edit Menu** > **Preferences** > **Accounting** > **Company Preferences** > **Use account numbers.**
2. Enter the opening balance for the company Checking account:
   - To open the Chart of Accounts, click the **Chart of Accounts** icon in the Company section of the Home Page

- Select **Checking** account
- **Right-click** to display the pop-up menu
- Select **Edit Account**
- When the Edit Account window for the Checking account appears, enter Account No.: **10100**
- Select **Enter Opening Balance**
- Enter Statement Ending Balance: **$2,400**
- Statement Ending Date: **01/01/2024**
- Click **OK**
- Click **Save & Close** to close the Edit Account window

3 Add the following accounts and opening balances to the Chart of Accounts. Abbreviate account titles as shown.

Account No.	**26000**
Account Type	**Other Current Liability**
Account Name	**Notes Payable**
Account Description	**Notes Payable**
Tax Line	**B/S-Liabs/Eq.: Other current liabilities**
Opening Balance	**$1,000 as of 01/01/2024**

Account No.	**12500**
Account Type	**Other Current Asset**
Account Name	**Supplies on Hand**
Account Description	**Supplies on Hand**
Tax Line	**B/S-Assets: Other current assets**
Opening Balance	**$600 as of 01/01/2024**

Account No.	**14000**
Account Type	**Fixed Asset**
Account Name	**Store Fixtures**
Account Description	**Store Fixtures**
Tax Line	**B/S-Assets: Buildings/oth. depr. assets**
Opening Balance	**$0 as of 01/01/2024**

Account No.	**14100**
Account Type	**Fixed Asset**
Account Name	**Store Fixtures Cost**
Subaccount of	**Store Fixtures**
Account Description	**Store Fixtures Cost**
Tax Line	**B/S-Assets: Buildings/oth. depr. assets**
Opening Balance	**$5,000 as of 01/01/2024**

Account No.	**14200**
Account Type	**Fixed Asset**
Account Name	**Store Fixtures Accumulated Depr**
Subaccount of	**Store Fixtures**
Account Description	**Store Fixtures Accumulated Depreciation**
Tax Line	**B/S-Assets: Buildings/oth. depr. assets**
Opening Balance	**$0 as of 01/01/2024**

Account No.	**14300**
Account Type	**Fixed Asset**
Account Name	**Paint Mixing Equipment**
Account Description	**Paint Mixing Equipment**
Tax Line	**B/S-Assets: Buildings/oth. depr. assets**
Opening Balance	**$0 as of 01/01/2024**

Account No.	**14400**
Account Type	**Fixed Asset**
Account Name	**Paint Mixing Equipment Cost**
Subaccount of	**Paint Mixing Equipment**
Account Description	**Paint Mixing Equipment Cost**
Tax Line	**B/S-Assets: Buildings/oth. depr. assets**
Opening Balance	**$4,000 as of 01/01/2024**

Account No.	**14500**
Account Type	**Fixed Asset**
Account Name	**Paint Mixing Equipment Acc Depr**
Subaccount of	**Paint Mixing Equipment**
Account Description	**Paint Mixing Equipment Accumulated Depreciation**
Tax Line	**B/S-Assets: Buildings/oth. depr. assets**
Opening Balance	**$0 as of 01/01/2024**

Account No.	**14600**
Account Type	**Fixed Asset**
Account Name	**Color Match Equipment**
Account Description	**Color Match Equipment**
Tax Line	**B/S-Assets: Buildings/oth. depr. assets**
Opening Balance	**$0 as of 01/01/2024**

Account No.	**14700**
Account Type	**Fixed Asset**
Account Name	**Color Match Equipment Cost**
Subaccount of	**Color Match Equipment**
Account Description	**Color Match Equipment Cost**
Tax Line	**B/S-Assets: Buildings/oth. depr. assets**
Opening Balance	**$0 as of 01/01/2024**

Account No.	**14800**
Account Type	**Fixed Asset**
Account Name	**Color Match Equipment Acc Depr**
Subaccount of	**Color Match Equipment**
Account Description	**Color Match Equipment Accumulated Depreciation**
Tax Line	**B/S-Assets: Buildings/oth. depr. assets**
Opening Balance	**$0 as of 01/01/2024**

4. From the Chart of Accounts window, edit the following accounts to update the tax lines:
   - 10100 Checking: **B/S-Assets: Cash**
   - 60200 Automobile Expense: **Other Deductions: Auto and truck**
   - 60400 Bank Service Charges: **Other Deductions: Bank charges**
   - 62400 Depreciation Expense: **Other Deductions: Other deductions**
   - 63300 Insurance Expense: **Other Deductions: Insurance**
   - 63500 Janitorial Expense: **Other Deductions: Janitorial & cleaning**
   - 64900 Office Supplies: **Other Deductions: Office expenses**
   - 66700 Professional Fees: **Other Deductions: Legal & professional fees**
   - 68100 Telephone Expense: **Other Deductions: Telephone**
   - 68600 Utilities: **Other Deductions: Utilities**
5. **Re-sort** the chart of accounts. (Select Account button > Re-sort List.)
6. **C13.7.1 Chart of Accounts.** From the Report Center, export to **Excel** or **print** the Chart of Accounts (Account Listing) report for Paint Palette Store.

Section 13.8

QUICKBOOKS OPENING ADJUSTMENTS

As discussed in Chapter 1, accounting systems use double-entry accounting where each entry must balance. In general, when an existing company with opening balances is set up in QuickBooks accounting software, as accounts receivable, accounts payable, and item balances are entered, QuickBooks offsets these entries with a balancing effect to other accounts.

For example, as customer accounts receivable opening balances are entered, QuickBooks offsets these to an Uncategorized Income account. As vendor accounts payable opening balances are entered, QuickBooks offsets these to an Uncategorized Expense account. As item opening balances are entered, QuickBooks offsets these to an Opening Balance Equity account. When opening balances are entered for all other accounts in the Chart of Accounts, QuickBooks offsets these to the Opening Balance Equity account.

For new start-up companies, the opening balances are zero. For existing companies that have opening balances, QuickBooks offsets these opening balances. Thus, when setting up existing companies in QuickBooks, the following opening adjustments must be recorded using journal entries.

1. When accounts receivable opening balances create Uncategorized Income, use an opening adjustment to transfer the Uncategorized Income to the Opening Balance Equity account.
2. When accounts payable opening balances create Uncategorized Expenses, use an opening adjustment to transfer the Uncategorized Expenses to the Opening Balance Equity account.
3. Opening balances for inventory items and all other accounts are offset by QuickBooks in the Opening Balance Equity account. At this point the balance in the Opening Balance Equity account consists of the transfers from Uncategorized Income and Uncategorized Expenses plus offsets from Inventory items and all other accounts. Use an opening adjustment to transfer the balance in the Opening Balance Equity account to the Capital Stock account.

Notice the description for the Opening Balance Equity account (No. 30000): Opening balances during setup post to this account. The balance of this account should be zero after completing your setup.

The following diagram summarizes the transfer of offsets used for opening balances in QuickBooks.

<table>
<tr><td>A/R Balances</td><td>></td><td>Uncategorized Income</td><td>></td><td rowspan="4">Opening Balance Equity</td><td rowspan="4">></td><td rowspan="4">Capital Stock</td></tr>
<tr><td>A/P Balances</td><td>></td><td>Uncategorized Expenses</td><td>></td></tr>
<tr><td>Item Balances</td><td colspan="3">></td></tr>
<tr><td>Other Balances</td><td colspan="3">></td></tr>
</table>

Next, prepare the opening adjustments for Paint Palette Store.

1. **C13.8.1 Trial Balance.** Export to **Excel** or **print** a Trial Balance report for Paint Palette Store dated 01/01/2024.
   - Compare your Trial Balance report to the check figures to verify your account balances are correct.
   - Note that QuickBooks records the offsetting amount to the opening account balances in an Opening Balance Equity account.
   - Since Paint Palette Store did not have any opening balances for customers or vendors, there is no Uncategorized Income or Uncategorized Expense accounts shown on the Trial Balance report.
   - Supplies on Hand have future benefit and are recorded in an asset account, No. 12500. Later, Supplies that have been used and the benefits expired will be recorded in the Supplies Expense account, No. 64800.
2. Transfer the Opening Balance Equity account balance to the Capital Stock account using a journal entry debiting the Opening Balance Equity account and crediting the Capital Stock account
3. Select **Save & Close** to close the Make General Journal Entries window
4. **C13.8.2 Adjusted Trial Balance.** Export to **Excel** or **print** the Adjusted Trial Balance (after the opening adjustment) on 01/01/2024. Verify that the Opening Balance Equity account balance was transferred to the Capital Stock account.
5. **C13.8.3 Balance Sheet Standard.** Export to **Excel** or **print** a Balance Sheet, Standard for Paint Palette Store dated 01/01/2024.

YourName Chapter 13 Paint Palette Store

Trial Balance

Accrual Basis

As of January 1, 2024

	Jan 1, 24	
	Debit	Credit
10100 · Checking	2,400.00	
12500 · Supplies on Hand	600.00	
14000 · Store Fixtures:14100 · Store Fixtures Cost	5,000.00	
14300 · Paint Mixing Equipment:14400 · Paint Mixing Equipment Cost	4,000.00	
26000 · Notes Payable		1,000.00
30000 · Opening Balance Equity		11,000.00
TOTAL	12,000.00	12,000.00

1

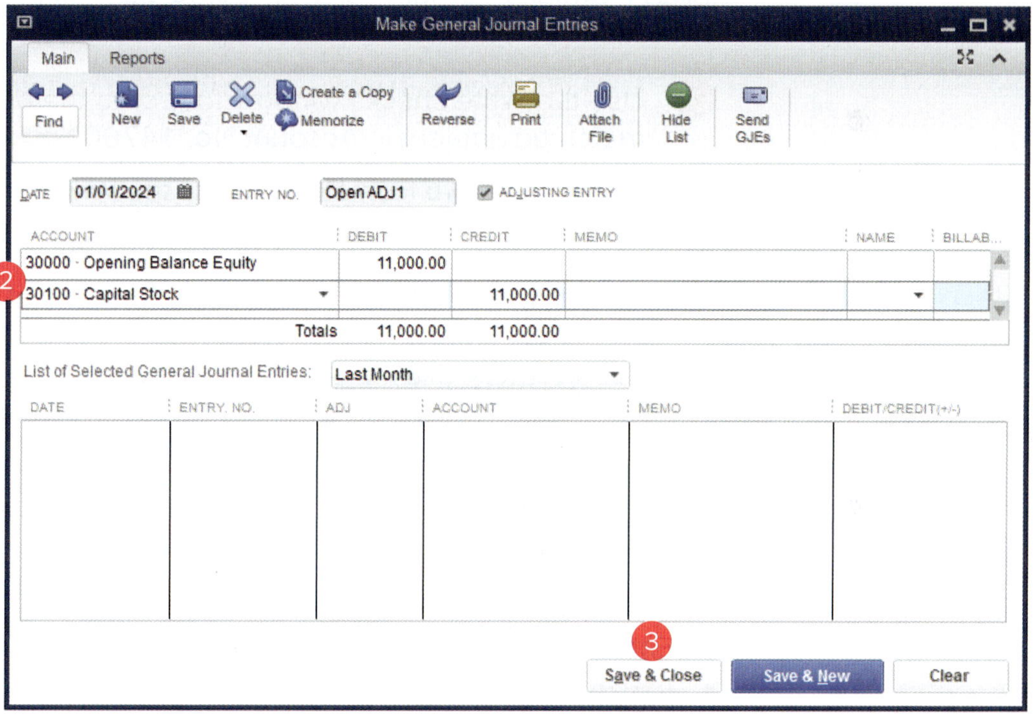

YourName Chapter 13 Paint Palette Store

Adjusted Trial Balance

Accrual Basis

January 1, 2024

	Unadjusted Balance		Adjustments		Adjusted Balance	
	Debit	Credit	Debit	Credit	Debit	Credit
10100 · Checking	2,400.00				2,400.00	
12500 · Supplies on Hand	600.00				600.00	
14000 · Store Fixtures:14100 · Store Fixtures Cost	5,000.00				5,000.00	
14300 · Paint Mixing Equipment:14400 · Paint Mixing Equipment C...	4,000.00				4,000.00	
26000 · Notes Payable		1,000.00				1,000.00
30000 · Opening Balance Equity		11,000.00	11,000.00		0.00	
30100 · Capital Stock				11,000.00		11,000.00
TOTAL	12,000.00	12,000.00	11,000.00	11,000.00	12,000.00	12,000.00

4

Section 13.9

VENDOR AND EXPENSE TRANSACTIONS

EQUIPMENT PURCHASES

On January 1, 2024, Paint Palette Store purchased computerized paint color matching equipment from Brewer Paint Supplies with a $1,000 check.

C13.9.1 Check Journal Entry. To record the paint color matching equipment purchase:

1. Use the Write checks window to record the purchase of the color match equipment in Account No. 14700
2. Select the **Save** icon at the top of the Write Checks window
3. Select the **Reports tab** > **Transaction Journal**
4. Export the Transaction Journal report to **Excel** or **print** the report

PURCHASING CYCLE

The purchasing cycle for a merchandising company consists of the following transactions:

1. Create a purchase order to order inventory.
2. Receive the inventory items ordered and update inventory.
3. Enter the bill in QuickBooks when the bill is received.
4. Pay the bill.

Next, you will record each of the above transactions in the purchasing cycle for Paint Palette Store.

CREATE A PURCHASE ORDER

The first step in the purchasing cycle is to create a purchase order which is sent to the vendor to order inventory. The purchase order provides a record of the type and quantity of item ordered.

Paint Palette Store needs to order 50 gallons of Interior Base Paint. To order the paint, Paint Palette Store must create a purchase order indicating the item and quantity desired.

C13.9.2 Purchase Order Journal Entry. To create a purchase order in QuickBooks:

1. Click the **Purchase Orders** icon in the Vendors section of the Home Page
2. Select Vendor: **Brewer Paint Supplies**
3. Select Template: **Custom Purchase Order**
4. Enter Date: **01/03/2024**
5. Enter the item ordered, by selecting Item: **Interior Paint Base (1 gallon)**
6. Enter Quantity: **50.** Automatically, $10 should appear in the Rate column and $500 appear in the Amount column.
7. Select: **Print Later**
8. Select the **Save** icon at the top of the Create Purchase Orders window
9. Select the **Reports tab** > **Transaction Journal**
10. Export the Transaction Journal report to **Excel** or **print** the report

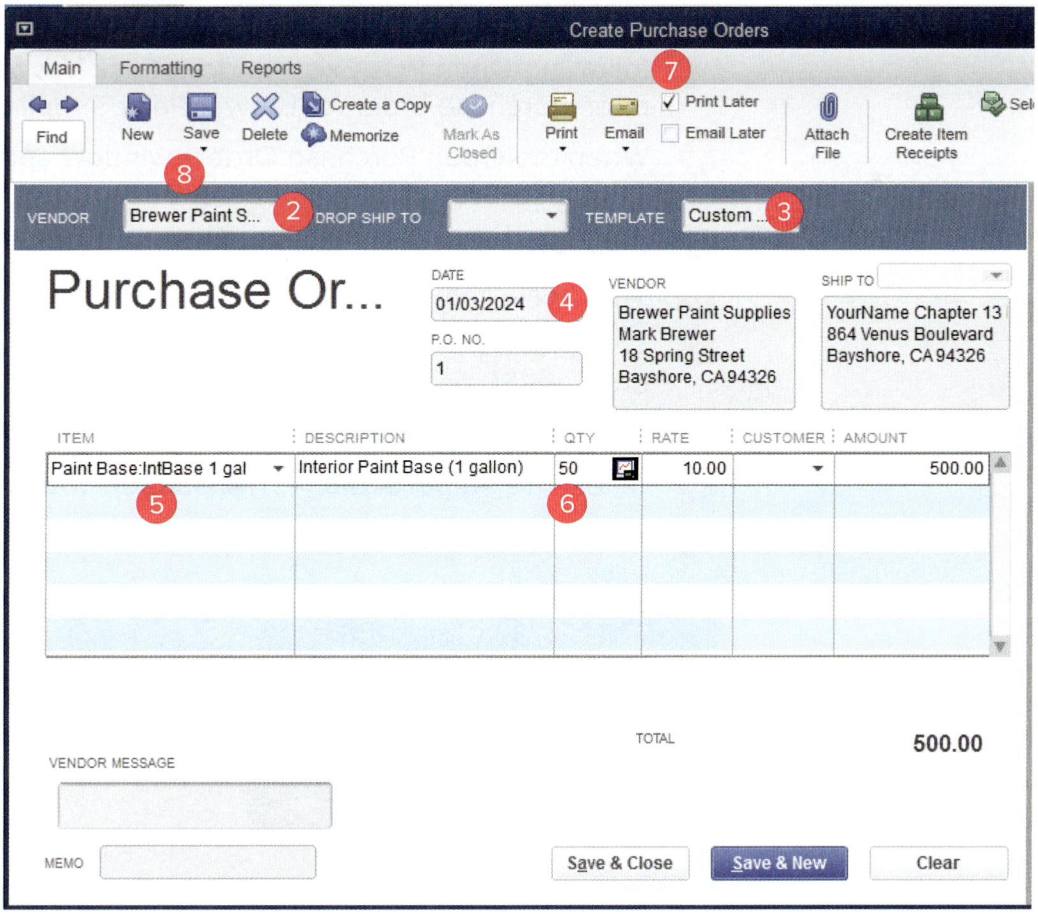

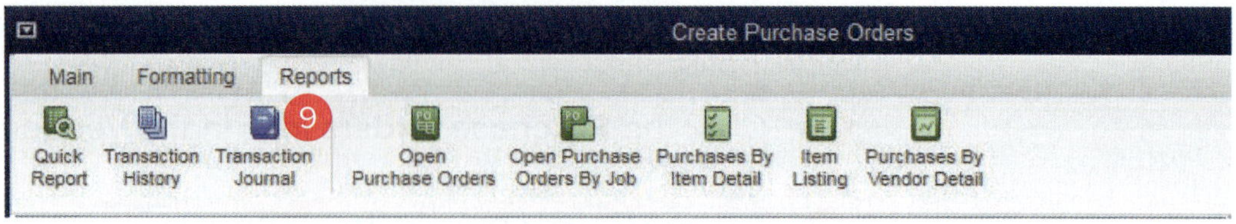

RECEIVE INVENTORY ITEMS

When the inventory items that have been ordered are received, record their receipt in QuickBooks. QuickBooks will then add the items received to the Inventory account.

On January 06, 2024, Paint Palette Store received 40 gallons of interior paint base from Brewer Paint Supplies.

C13.9.3 Receive Inventory Journal Entry. To record the inventory items received from Brewer Paint Supplies:

1. Click the **Receive Inventory** icon in the Vendors section of the Home Page. Select **Receive Inventory without Bill.**
2. When the Create Item Receipts window appears, select Vendor: **Brewer Paint Supplies**
3. If a purchase order for the vendor exists, QuickBooks displays the following Open POs Exist window. Click **Yes** to receive against an open purchase order for Brewer Paint Supplies.
4. When the Open Purchase Orders window appears, select **Purchase Order No. 1** dated **01/03/2024**
5. Click **OK**
6. The Create Item Receipts window will appear. Enter Date: **01/06/2024**
7. The quantity received (40 gallons) differs from the quantity ordered (50 gallons). Enter Quantity: **40.**
8. Click the **Save** icon and leave the Create Item Receipts window open
9. Select the **Reports tab** > **Transaction Journal**
10. Export the Transaction Journal report to **Excel** or **print** the report

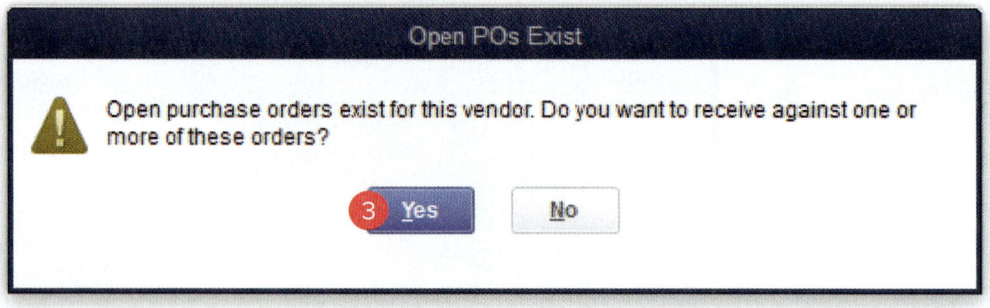

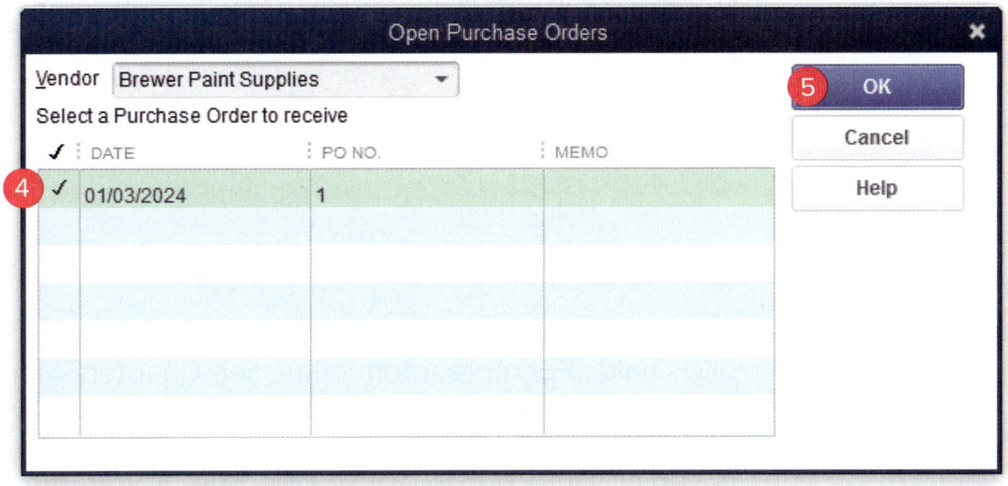
Open Purchase Orders
Vendor
Brewer Paint Supplies
Select a Purchase Order to receive
DATE
PO NO.
MEMO
01/03/2024
1
OK
Cancel
Help
4
5

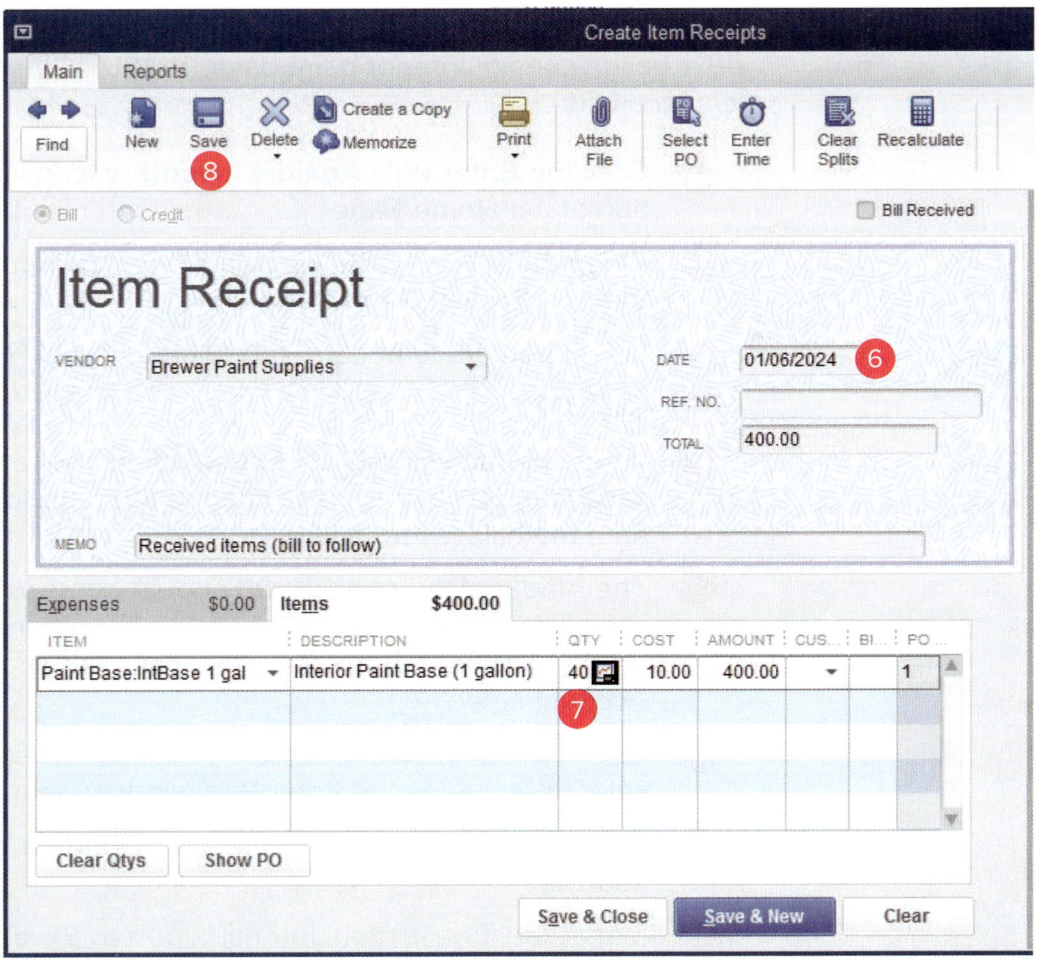
Create Item Receipts
Main
Reports
Find
New
Save
Delete
Create a Copy
Memorize
Print
Attach File
Select PO
Enter Time
Clear Splits
Recalculate
Bill
Credit
Bill Received
Item Receipt
VENDOR
Brewer Paint Supplies
DATE
01/06/2024
REF. NO.
TOTAL
400.00
MEMO
Received items (bill to follow)
Expenses
$0.00
Items
$400.00
ITEM
DESCRIPTION
QTY
COST
AMOUNT
CUS...
BI...
PO ...
Paint Base:IntBase 1 gal
Interior Paint Base (1 gallon)
40
10.00
400.00
1
Clear Qtys
Show PO
Save & Close
Save & New
Clear
6
7
8

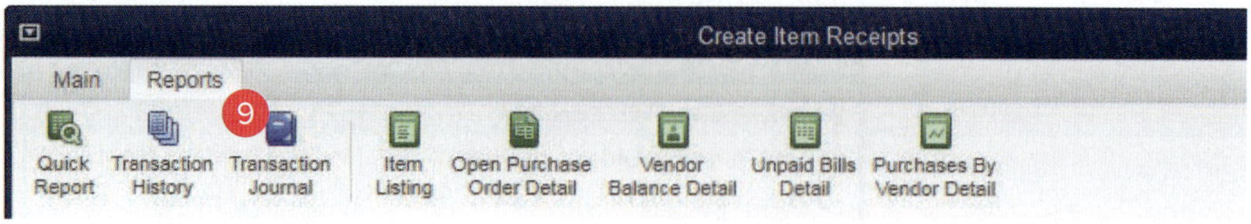

ENTER BILLS

Bills can be entered in QuickBooks when the bill is received or when the bill is paid. (For more information, see Chapters 6 and 7.)

Paint Palette Store will enter bills in QuickBooks when bills are received. At that time, QuickBooks records an obligation to pay the bill later (account payable). QuickBooks tracks bills due. If you use the reminder feature, QuickBooks will even remind you when it is time to pay bills.

C13.9.4 Enter Bill Journal Entry. Paint Palette Store previously received 40 1-gallon cans of interior paint base. To record the associated bill when it is received:

1. Click the **Enter Bills Against Inventory** icon in the Vendors section of the Home Page
2. When the following Select Item Receipt window appears, select Vendor: **Brewer Paint Supplies**
3. Select Item Receipt corresponding to the bill (**Date: 01/06/2024**)
4. Click **OK**
5. When the following Enter Bills window appears, make any necessary changes. In this case, change the date to **01/10/2024** (the date the bill was received).
6. The Amount Due of **$400.00** should agree with the amount shown on the vendor's bill received. (The Items tab should also display $400.00. Select the Expenses tab and verify there is no Account selected.)
7. Click the **Save** icon. If asked if you want to record your changes, select **Yes.** Leave the Enter Bills window open.
8. From the Enter Bills form, select the **Reports tab** > **Transaction Journal**
9. Export the Transaction Journal report to **Excel** or **print** the report

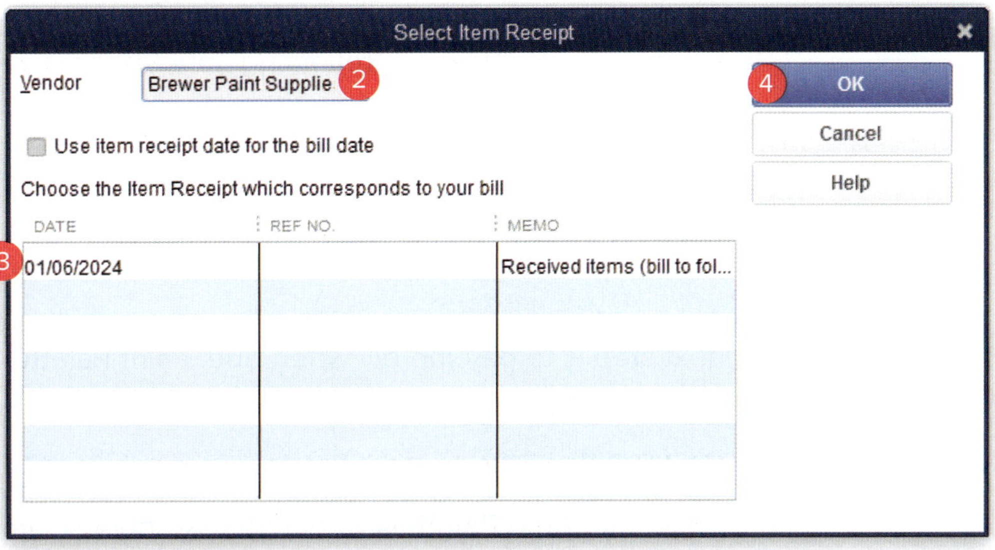
Select Item Receipt
Vendor
Brewer Paint Supplie
2
4
OK
Cancel
Help
Use item receipt date for the bill date
Choose the Item Receipt which corresponds to your bill
DATE
REF NO.
MEMO
3
01/06/2024
Received items (bill to fol...

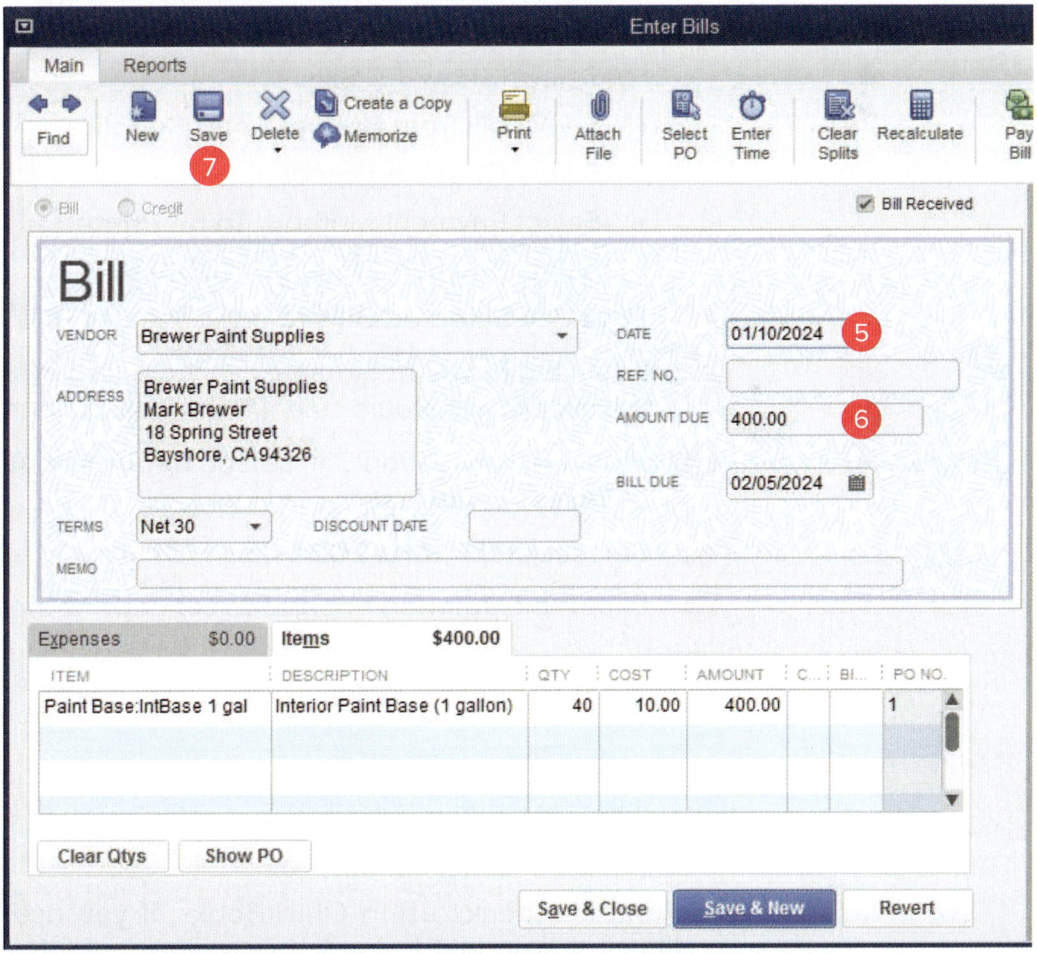
Enter Bills
Main
Reports
Find
New
Save
Delete
Create a Copy
Memorize
Print
Attach File
Select PO
Enter Time
Clear Splits
Recalculate
Pay Bill
7
Bill
Credit
Bill Received
Bill
VENDOR
Brewer Paint Supplies
DATE
01/10/2024
5
REF. NO.
ADDRESS
Brewer Paint Supplies
Mark Brewer
18 Spring Street
Bayshore, CA 94326
AMOUNT DUE
400.00
6
BILL DUE
02/05/2024
TERMS
Net 30
DISCOUNT DATE
MEMO
Expenses $0.00
Items $400.00
ITEM
DESCRIPTION
QTY
COST
AMOUNT
C...
BI...
PO NO.
Paint Base:IntBase 1 gal
Interior Paint Base (1 gallon)
40
10.00
400.00
1
Clear Qtys
Show PO
Save & Close
Save & New
Revert

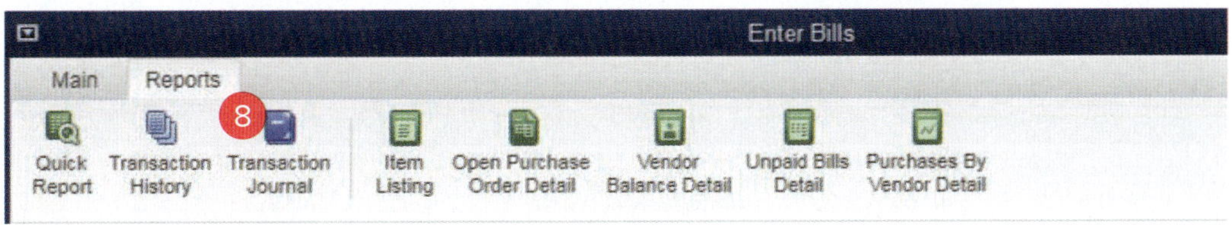
Enter Bills
Main
Reports
8
Quick Report
Transaction History
Transaction Journal
Item Listing
Open Purchase Order Detail
Vendor Balance Detail
Unpaid Bills Detail
Purchases By Vendor Detail

When you enter bills, QuickBooks automatically adds the amount of the bill to Accounts Payable, reflecting your obligation to pay the bills later.

> **If the items and the bill were received at the same time,** use the Receive Item with Bill window.

PAY BILLS

After receiving an inventory item and entering the bill in QuickBooks, the next step is to pay the bill when due. Paint Palette Store will pay the bills for paint and paint color that have been received and recorded.

C13.9.5 Pay Bills Journal Entries. To pay bills in QuickBooks:

1. Click the **Pay Bills** icon in the Vendors section of the Home Page
2. When the Pay Bills window appears:
    - Select: **Show All Bills**
    - Select bill from **Brewer Paint Supplies**
    - Select **Checking** account
    - Select Payment Method: **To be Printed**
    - Select Payment Date: **01/10/2024**
3. Click **Pay Selected Bills** to close the Pay Bills window
4. When the Payment Summary window displays, if we wanted to print the checks, we would select Print Checks. In this case, select **Done.**
5. From the Navigation Bar, select **Reports** > **Accountant** & **Taxes** > **Journal**
6. Select Date: **01/10/2024**
7. Export the Journal report to **Excel** or **print** the report

PRINT CHECKS

After selecting bills to pay, if checks are required, you can prepare checks in two different ways:

1. Write the checks manually, or
2. Print the checks using QuickBooks. If you use QuickBooks to print checks, preprinted check forms are inserted in the printer before printing.

Section 13.10

CUSTOMERS AND SALES TRANSACTIONS

SALES CYCLE

The sales cycle for a merchandising company consists of the following transactions:

1. Create an invoice to record the sale and bill the customer.
2. Receive the customer payments.
3. Deposit the customer payments in the bank.

Next, you will record each of these transactions in QuickBooks for Paint Palette Store.

CREATE INVOICES

When inventory is sold to a customer, the sale is recorded on an invoice in QuickBooks. The invoice lists the items sold, the quantity, and the price. In addition, if the product is sold to a retail customer, sales tax is automatically added to the invoice.

C13.10.1 Invoice Journal Entry. To create an invoice:

1. Click the **Create Invoices** icon in the Customers section of the Home Page
2. Using the Intuit Product Invoice Template, create an invoice for the following sales made by Paint Palette Store.

   Sale of 3 gallons of interior paint to Maria Cecilia

Date	**01/13/2024**
Customer	**Maria Cecilia**
Terms	**Net 30**
Quantity	**3 gallons**

Item Code	**Interior Paint Base (1 gallon)**
Price Each	**25.00**
Tax	**State Tax**

3. Select **Print Later**
4. Select the **Save** icon
5. Select the **Reports tab** > **Transaction Journal**
6. Export to **Excel** or **print** the Transaction Journal

RECEIVE PAYMENTS

When a credit sale is recorded, QuickBooks records an account receivable at the time the invoice is created. The account receivable is the amount that Paint Palette Store expects to receive from the customer later.

C13.10.2 Receive Payment Journal Entry. To record a payment received from a customer:

1. Click the **Receive Payments** icon in the Customers section of the Home Page
2. Record the following payments received by Paint Palette Store from a customer.

Date Received	**01/15/2024**
Customer	**Maria Ceclia**
Amount Received	**82.31**
Payment Method	**Check**
Check No.	**1001**

3. Select **Save & New**
4. Select the **Find back arrow** to display the customer payment just recorded
5. Select **Reports tab** > **Transaction Journal**
6. Export the Transaction Journal report to **Excel** or **print** the report

> **If a customer pays cash at the time of sale,** it can be recorded using the Sales Receipts window.

MAKE DEPOSITS

When the customer's payment is deposited in Paint Palette Store's Checking account, record the bank deposit in QuickBooks.

C13.10.3 Deposit Journal Entry. To record a bank deposit:

1. Click the **Record Deposits** icon in the Banking section of the Home Page
2. On January 16, 2024, record the deposit of customer payments received from **Maria Cecilia.** Select Deposit To: **Checking.**
3. Select the **Save** icon at the top of the Make Deposits window
4. Select the **Journal** icon
5. Export the Transaction Journal report to **Excel** or **print** the report

Section 13.11

ADJUSTING ENTRIES

Before preparing financial statements for Paint Palette Store for January, it is necessary to record adjustments to bring the company's accounts up to date.

> **Before making adjusting entries,** prepare a Trial Balance to see if the accounting system is in balance (debits equal credits).

The following adjustments are necessary for Paint Palette Store at January 31, 2024:

1. **ADJ1:** The store fixtures cost of $5,000 will be depreciated over a 10-year useful life with no salvage value. Depreciation expense is $42 per month. (See Exercise 13.6.)
2. **ADJ2:** The paint mixing equipment cost of $4,000 will be depreciated over a 5-year useful life with no salvage value. Depreciation expense is $67 per month. (See Exercise 13.6.)
3. **ADJ3:** The computer paint color match equipment cost of $1,000 will be depreciated over a four-year useful life with no salvage value. Depreciation expense is $21 per month. (See Exercise 13.6.)
4. **ADJ4:** A count of supplies on hand at the end of January totaled $400. The Supplies on Hand account balance before adjustment is $600, so Supplies on Hand (Account 12500) should be decreased by $200. An adjusting entry is required to transfer $200 from the Supplies on Hand account to the Supplies Expense account. So the adjusting entry will increase (debit) Supplies Expense (Account 64800) by $200, and decrease (credit) Supplies on Hand (Account 12500) by $200. (See Exercise 13.6.)
5. **ADJ5:** Interest on the notes payable balance is 1 percent per month. The adjusting entry to record interest expense for January 2024 and the liability for interest payable is $10. To record this adjustment, add Other Current Liability account: Account No. 21000 Interest Payable. (See Exercise 13.6.)

Next, use the Make General Journal Entries window to practice recording the adjusting entry for depreciation expense for Paint Palette Store at January 31, 2024. Depreciation expense is $42 per month.

1. Select **Accountant Menu > Make General Journal Entries.** If a message about numbering journal entries appears, click **OK.**
2. To record the entry for depreciation in the General Journal, select Date: **01/31/2024**
3. Entry No.: **ADJ1**
4. Select **Adjusting Entry**
5. Enter Account: **62400.** Press the **Tab** key to advance the cursor to the Debit column.
6. Enter **42.00**
7. Enter Account: **14200**
8. Enter Credit: **42.00**
9. Normally, we would select Save & Close, but in this case select **Clear.** Then **close** the Make General Journal Entries window. We will enter and save the adjusting entry in the exercises.

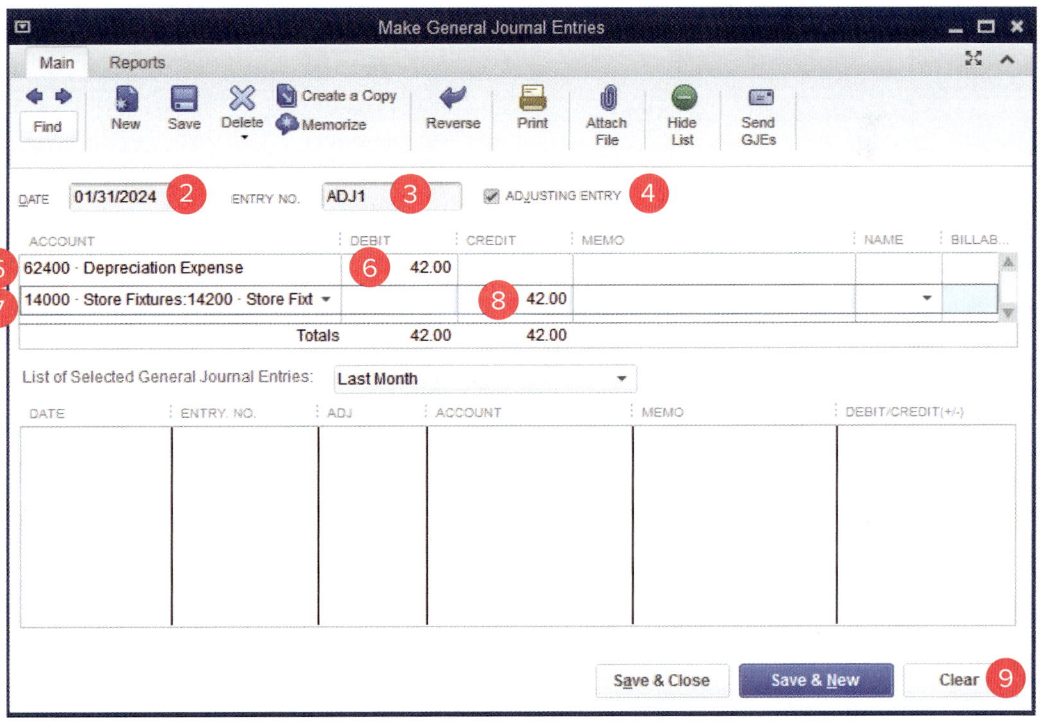

Section 13.12

FINANCIAL REPORTS

The next step in the accounting cycle is to print financial reports. Usually, a company prints the following financial reports for the year:

- Profit & Loss (also known as the P & L or Income Statement)
- Balance Sheet
- Statement of Cash Flows

The Profit & Loss, the Balance Sheet, and the Statement of Cash Flows are financial statements typically given to external users, such as bankers and investors.

To print the financial statements, from the Report Center, select: Company & Financial

We will print financial statements for Paint Palette Store in **Exercise 13.7.**

Section 13.13

BACK UP QUICKBOOKS FILES

BACK UP QBB

Save a backup of your Chapter 13 file using the file name: **YourName Chapter 13 Backup.QBB.** For further instructions on how to back up your file, *see Appendix B: Back Up & Restore QuickBooks Files.*

QBW WORKFLOW

If you will be using the same computer to complete Chapter 13 QuickBooks exercises, just as in a business workflow, you can continue to use the same QBW file.

If you are using the QBW approach, leave your .QBW file open and proceed directly to Exercise 13.1.

QBB RESTORE

If you will be switching computers and are ending your computer session now, close your QBW file and exit QuickBooks. When you restart, you will restore your backup file to complete Exercise 13.1.

www.my-quickbooks.com

Go to **www.My-QuickBooks.com** to view additional QuickBooks resources including:

- **Excel Report Templates** to organize QuickBooks reports exported to Excel
- ***Computer Accounting with QuickBooks* updates,** sometimes required when there is a software update that affects the text
- **QuickBooks Video links**
- **QuickBooks Help and Support links**
- **Other QuickBooks Resources** to make learning QuickBooks easier and more effective

- **QuickBooks Issue Resolution** offers a guided approach to troubleshooting QuickBooks

> **Troubleshooting QuickBooks and Correcting Errors** are crucial QuickBooks skill to acquire. See www.My-QuickBooks.com > QB Issue Resolution for Troubleshooting QuickBooks tips. See Chapter 17, Quick Review Guide, for tips on Correcting Errors.

EXERCISE 13.1: Chart of Accounts

In this exercise, you will add a new account to Paint Palette Store's Chart of Accounts.

E13.1.1 QuickBooks File

If you will be using the same computer and the same Chapter 13.QBW file:

1. If your Chapter 13.QBW file is not already open, open it by selecting **File** > **Open Previous Company.** Select your **Chapter 13.QBW file.** If a QuickBooks Information window appears with a message about the sample company file, click **OK.**
2. Add **YourName Exercise 13.1** to the company name by selecting **Company Menu** > **My Company.**

> **If you are not using the same computer that you used for Chapter 13,** you will need to restore your Chapter 13 Backup.QBB file using the instructions in Appendix B: Back Up & Restore QuickBooks Files. After restoring, add YourName Exercise 13.1 to the company name.

E13.1.2 Add Account

1. Add the following new account to the Chart of Accounts for Paint Palette Store.

Account Name	**Supplies Expense**
Account No.	**64800**
Account Type	**Expense**
Account Description	**Supplies Expense**
Tax Line	**Other Deductions: Supplies**

2. **Re-sort** the Chart of Accounts. (Select Account button > Re-sort List.)
3. Export to **Excel** or **print** the Chart of Accounts. (Select Report Center > List > Account Listing. Use Date: 01/01/2024.)

E13.1.3 Back Up Exercise 13.1

Save a backup of your Exercise file using the file name: YourName Exercise 13.1 Backup.QBB. See *Appendix B: Back Up & Restore QuickBooks Files* for instructions.

EXERCISE 13.2: Customer List

In this exercise, you will add to Paint Palette Store's Customer List.

E13.2.1 QuickBooks File

If you will be using the same computer and the same QBW file:

1. Select your **QBW file.**
2. Add **YourName Exercise 13.2** to the company name by selecting **Company Menu** > **My Company.**

> **If you are not using the same computer that you used for Chapter 13 and Exercise 13.1,** you will need to restore your latest prior Backup.QBB file using the instructions in Appendix B: Back Up & Restore QuickBooks files. After restoring, add YourName Exercise 13.2 to the company name.

E13.2.2 Add Customers

1. Add the following customers to Paint Palette Store's Customer List.

Customer	**TJ Ryan Interiors**
Address Info:	
Company Name	**TJ Ryan Interiors**
First Name	**TJ**
Main Phone	**415-555-4545**
Address	**55 Scotch Drive**
	Bayshore, CA 94326
Payment Settings:	
Account No.	**3005**
Payment Terms	**Net 30**
Sales Tax Settings:	
Tax Code	**Non**
Tax Item	**State Tax**
Additional Info:	
Customer Type	**Wholesale**

Special Interest	**Hi Tech**
Job Info:	
Job Description	**Custom & Stock Paint**
Job Type	**Commercial**
Job Status	**Awarded**
Customer	**Rock Castle Construction**
Address Info:	
Company Name	**Rock Castle Construction**
Mr./Ms./. . .	**Mr.**
First Name	**Rock**
Last Name	**Castle**
Main Phone	**415-555-7272**
Mobile	**415-555-5679**
Address	**1735 County Road**
	Bayshore, CA 94326
Payment Settings:	
Account No.	**3003**
Payment Terms	**Net 30**
Sales Tax Settings:	
Tax Code	**Non**
Tax Item	**State Tax**
Additional Info:	
Customer Type	**Wholesale**
Special Interest	**Various**
Job Info:	
Job Description	**Custom Paint**
Job Type	**Commercial**
Job Status	**Awarded**
Customer	**Graziella Italia Designs**
Address Info:	
Company Name	**Graziella Italia Designs**
First Name	**Graziella**
Main Phone	**415-555-1270**

Address	**13 Marco Drive**
	Bayshore, CA 94326
Payment Settings:	
Account No.	**3004**
Payment Terms	**Net 30**
Sales Tax Settings:	
Tax Code	**Non**
Tax Item	**State Tax**
Additional Info:	
Customer Type	**Wholesale**
Special Interest	**Italian**
Job Info:	
Job Description	**Custom & Stock Paint**
Job Type	**Commercial**
Job Status	**Awarded**

2. From the Customer Center, export to **Excel** or **print** Paint Palette Store Customer List

E13.2.3 Back Up Exercise 13.2

Save a backup of your Exercise file using the file name: YourName Exercise 13.2 Backup.QBB. See *Appendix B: Back Up & Restore QuickBooks Files* for instructions.

EXERCISE 13.3: Vendor List

In this exercise, you will add to Paint Palette Store's Vendors List.

E13.3.1 QuickBooks File

If you will be using the same computer and the same QBW file:

1. Select your **QBW file.**
2. Add **YourName Exercise 13.3** to the company name by selecting **Company Menu > My Company.**

> **If you are not using the same computer that you used for Chapter 13, Exercise 13.1, and Exercise 13.2,** you will need to restore your latest prior Backup.QBB file using the instructions in Appendix B: Back Up & Restore QuickBooks files. After restoring, add YourName Exercise 13.3 to the company name.

E13.3.2 Add Vendors

1. Add the following vendors to the Vendor List for Paint Palette Store.

Vendor	**Joseph Leasing**
Opening Balance	**0.00 as of 01/01/2024**
Address Info:	
Company Name	**Joseph Leasing**
First Name	**Joseph**
Main Phone	**415-555-0412**
Address	**13 Appleton Street**
	Bayshore, CA 94326
Payment Settings:	
Account No.	**4002**
Payment Terms	**Net 30**
Tax Settings:	
Vendor Tax ID	**37-1726354**
Additional Info:	
Vendor Type	**Leasing**

Vendor	**Crystalline Paints**
Opening Balance	**0.00 as of 01/01/2024**
Address Info:	
Company Name	**Crystalline Paints**
First Name	**Crystal**
Main Phone	**415-555-9999**
Address	**99 Beryl Avenue**
	Bayshore, CA 94326
Payment Settings:	
Account No.	**4003**
Payment Terms	**Net 30**
Tax Settings:	
Vendor Tax ID	**37-1726355**
Additional Info:	
Vendor Type	**Suppliers**

2. From the Vendor Center, export the Vendor List to **Excel**

E13.3.3 Back Up Exercise 13.3

Save a backup of your Exercise file using the file name: YourName Exercise 13.3 Backup.QBB. See *Appendix B: Back Up & Restore QuickBooks Files* for instructions.

EXERCISE 13.4: Vendors and Expenses Transactions

In this exercise, you will enter vendor and expense transactions for Paint Palette Store.

E13.4.1 QuickBooks File

If you will be using the same computer and the same QBW file:

1. Select your **QBW file.**
2. Add **YourName Exercise 13.4** to the company name by selecting **Company Menu > My Company.**

> **If you are not using the same computer that you used for Chapter 13, and Exercises 13.1 - 13.3,** you will need to restore your latest prior Backup.QBB file using the instructions in Appendix B: Back Up & Restore QuickBooks files. After restoring, add YourName Exercise 13.4 to the company name.

E13.4.2 Purchase Orders

Paint Palette Store entered into the following purchase orders for Paint Palette Store during January 2024.

1. Using the Purchase Order icon, enter the the following purchase orders.

Vendor	**Brewer Paint Supplies**
Date	**01/15/2024**
Item	**Exterior Paint Base (1 gallon)**
Quantity	**40**

Vendor	**Crystalline Paints**
Date	**01/18/2024**
Item	**Custom Color**
Quantity	**75 (cartons)**
Item	**Stock Color**

Quantity	**75 (cartons)**
Vendor	**Brewer Paint Supplies**
Date	**01/20/2024**
Item	**Interior Paint Base (1 gallon)**
Quantity	**60**

2. **Close** the Create Purchase Orders window
3. Export to **Excel** or p**rint** the Open Purchase Orders Detail report at January 20, 2024

E13.4.3 Receive Inventory Items

Paint Palette Store entered into the following vendor and expense transactions during January 2024.

1. Record the following inventory items received.

Vendor	**Brewer Paint Supplies**
Date	**01/16/2024**
PO No.	**2**
Item	**Exterior Paint Base (1 gallon)**
Quantity	**40**
Vendor	**Brewer Paint Supplies**
Date	**01/20/2024**
PO No.	**4**
Item	**Interior Paint Base (1 gallon)**
Quantity	**60**
Vendor	**Crystalline Paints**
Date	**01/21/2024**
PO No.	**3**
Item	**Custom Color**
Quantity	**75 (cartons)**
Item	**Stock Color**
Quantity	**75 (cartons)**

2. **Close** the Create Item Receipts window
3. Export to **Excel** or **print** the Item Listing from the Report Center as of January 21, 2024, showing the quantity on hand for each item in inventory. (Select Reports > List > Item Listing.)

E13.4.4 Enter Bills Against Inventory

Record the following bills received against inventory items for Paint Palette Store.

1. Using the Enter Bills Against Inventory icon, enter the following bills.

Vendor	**Brewer Paint Supplies**
Date Bill Received	**01/17/2024**
Terms	**Net 30**
PO No.	**2**
Item	**Exterior Paint Base (1 gallon)**
Quantity	**40**

2. Export to **Excel** the Transaction Journal for the above bill entered against inventory
3. Enter the following bill.

Vendor	**Crystalline Paints**
Date Bill Received	**01/22/2024**
Terms	**Net 30**
PO No.	**3**
Item	**Custom Color**
Quantity	**75 (cartons)**
Item	**Stock Color**
Quantity	**75 (cartons)**

4. Export to **Excel** the Transaction Journal for the above bill entered against inventory

E13.4.5 Enter Bill

Paint Palette Store received the following bill from Joseph Leasing for January rent.

1. Use the Enter Bills icon to enter the Joseph Leasing bill for January rent.

Vendor	**Joseph Leasing**
Date Bill Received	**01/12/2024**
Terms	**Net 30**
Amount Due	**$1,000.00**
Account	**67100 Rent Expense**

2. Record the bill for rent as a memorized transaction. With the Enter Bills window still open, click the **Memorize** icon.
3. Select the **Save** icon
4. From the Enter Bills form, select the **Reports tab** > **Transaction Journal**
5. Export the Transaction Journal report to **Excel** or **print** the report

E13.4.6 Pay Bills

After entering the purchase order, receiving the inventory item, and recording the bill, the next step is to pay the bill.

To pay bills for Paint Palette Store at January 31, 2024, complete the following.

1. Select the **Pay Bills** icon in the Vendors section of the Home Page
2. When the Pay Bills window appears:
   - Select: **Show All Bills**
   - Select bills from **Brewer Paint Supplies** and **Crystalline Paints**
   - Select **Checking** account
   - Select Payment Method: **To be Printed**
   - Select Payment Date: **01/31/2024**
3. Click **Pay Selected Bills** to close the Pay Bills window
4. Export to **Excel** or **print** the Check Detail Report for January 2024

E13.4.7 Back Up Exercise 13.4

Save a backup of your Exercise file using the file name: YourName Exercise 13.4 Backup.QBB. See *Appendix B: Back Up & Restore QuickBooks Files* for instructions.

EXERCISE 13.5: Customers and Sales Transactions

In this exercise, you will enter customer and sales transactions for Paint Palette Store.

E13.5.1 QuickBooks File

If you will be using the same computer and the same QBW file:

1. Select your **QBW file.**
2. Add **YourName Exercise 13.5** to the company name by selecting **Company Menu > My Company.**

If you are not using the same computer that you used for Chapter 13 and Exercises 13.1 - 13.4, you will need to restore your latest prior Backup.QBB file using the instructions in Appendix B: Back Up & Restore QuickBooks files. After restoring, add YourName Exercise 13.5 to the company name.

E13.5.2 Create Invoices

Create the following invoices for January for Paint Palette Store.

1. Sale of paint to TJ Ryan Interiors.

Date	**01/22/2024**
Customer	**TJ Ryan Interiors**
Terms	**Net 30**
Quantity	**30 gallons**
Item Code	**Interior Paint Base (1 gallon)**
Price Each	**20.00**
Quantity	**30**
Item Code	**Custom Color**
Price Each	**10.00**
Print Later	**Yes**
Tax	**Non**

2. Export to **Excel** the Transaction Journal for the above invoice
3. Sale of paint to Graziella Italia Designs.

Date	**01/25/2024**
Customer	**Graziella Italia Designs**

Terms	**Net 30**
Quantity	**50 gallons**
Item Code	**Interior Paint Base (1 gallon)**
Price Each	**20.00**
Quantity	**50**
Item Code	**Stock Color**
Price Each	**5.00**
Quantity	**20 gallons**
Item Code	**Exterior Paint Base (1 gallon)**
Price Each	**22.00**
Quantity	**20**
Item Code	**Custom Color**
Price Each	**10.00**
Print Later	**Yes**
Tax	**Non**

4. Export to **Excel** the Transaction Journal for the above invoice

E13.5.3 Receive Payments

When Paint Palette Store receives a customer payment, QuickBooks reduces the customer's account receivable by the amount of the payment.

1. Record the following customer payment received by Paint Palette Store.

Date Received	**01/31/2024**
Customer	**Graziella Italia Designs**
Amount Received	**1890.00**
Payment Method	**Check**
Check No.	**4567**

E13.5.4 Make Deposits

When a customer's payment is received QuickBooks records it in Undeposited Funds account. Next, make the deposit to transfer the funds from the Undeposited Funds account to the Checking account.

To make the deposit:

1. Click the **Record Deposits** icon in the Banking section of the Home Page

2. On January 31, 2024, record the deposit of customer payments received from Graziella Italia Designs. Select Deposit To: **Checking.**
3. Export to **Excel** or **print** the Transaction Journal report for this deposit
4. Export to **Excel** or **print** the Deposit Detail report for January 2024

E13.5.5 Back Up Exercise 13.5

Save a backup of your Exercise file using the file name: YourName Exercise 13.5 Backup.QBB. See *Appendix B: Back Up & Restore QuickBooks Files* for instructions.

EXERCISE 13.6: Adjustments

In this exercise, you will first print a Trial Balance and then record adjusting entries for Paint Palette Store.

E13.6.1 QuickBooks File

If you will be using the same computer and the same QBW file:

1. Select your **QBW file.**
2. Add **YourName Exercise 13.6** to the company name by selecting **Company Menu > My Company.**

> **If you are not using the same computer that you used for Chapter 13 and Exercises 13.1 - 13.5,** you will need to restore your latest prior Backup.QBB file using the instructions in Appendix B: Back Up & Restore QuickBooks files. After restoring, add YourName Exercise 13.6 to the company name.

E13.6.2 Trial Balance

The purpose of the Trial Balance is to determine whether the accounting system is in balance (debits equal credits).

Create a Trial Balance for Paint Palette Store at January 31, 2024.

1. From the Report Center select **Accountant & Taxes > Trial Balance**
2. Select Dates **From: 01/31/2024 To: 01/31/2024**
3. Export to **Excel** or **print** the Trial Balance for Paint Palette Store
4. **Close** the Trial Balance window

E13.6.3 Adjusting Entries

At the end of the accounting period, it is necessary to make adjusting entries to bring a company's accounts up to date as of year-end. The following adjusting entries are needed for Paint Palette Store at January 31, 2024.

1. To enter the following adjusting entries, select **Accountant Menu > Make General Journal Entries**
2. **ADJ1:** The store fixtures cost of $5,000 will be depreciated over a 10-year useful life with no salvage value. Depreciation expense is $42 per month.
3. **ADJ2:** The paint mixing equipment cost of $4,000 will be depreciated over a 5-year useful life with no salvage value. Depreciation expense is $67 per month.
4. **ADJ3:** The computer paint color match equipment cost of $1,000 will be depreciated over a four-year useful life with no salvage value. Depreciation expense is $21 per month.
5. **ADJ4:** A count of supplies on hand at the end of January totaled $400. The Supplies on Hand account balance before adjustment is $600, so Supplies on Hand (Account 12500) should be decreased by $200. An adjusting entry is required to transfer $200 from the Supplies on Hand account to the Supplies Expense account. So the adjusting entry will increase (debit) Supplies Expense (Account 64800) by $200, and decrease (credit) Supplies on Hand (Account 12500) by $200.
6. **ADJ5:** Interest on the notes payable balance is 1 percent per month. The adjusting entry to record interest expense for January 2024 and the liability for interest payable is $10. To record this adjustment, add Other Current Liability account: Account No. 21000 Interest Payable.
7. From the Report Center, export to **Excel** or **print** the adjusting journal entries for Paint Palette Store for January 31, 2024

E13.6.4 Adjusted Trial Balance

An Adjusted Trial Balance is simply a Trial Balance printed after adjusting entries are recorded.

Create an Adjusted Trial Balance for Paint Palette Store at January 31, 2024 after adjusting entries are entered.

1. Export to **Excel** or **print** an Adjusted Trial Balance at January 31, 2024 (Report Center > Accountant & Taxes > Adjusted Trial Balance)
2. On the Adjusted Trial Balance, **highlight** amounts affected by the adjusting entries

E13.6.5 Back Up Exercise 13.6

Save a backup of your Exercise file using the file name: YourName Exercise 13.6 Backup.QBB. See *Appendix B: Back Up & Restore QuickBooks Files* for instructions.

EXERCISE 13.7: Reports

In this exercise, you will prepare financial reports for Paint Palette Store for the January 2024.

E13.7.1 QuickBooks File

If you will be using the same computer and the same QBW file:

1. Select your **QBW file.**
2. Add **YourName Exercise 13.7** to the company name by selecting **Company Menu > My Company.**

> **If you are not using the same computer that you used for Chapter 13 and Exercises 13.1 - 13.6,** you will need to restore your latest prior Backup.QBB file using the instructions in Appendix B: Back Up & Restore QuickBooks files. After restoring, add YourName Exercise 13.7 to the company name.

E13.7.2 Journal

The Journal lists all the transactions entered, whether using an onscreen form or the Journal, in a debit and credit format. The Journal is often a useful tool when tracking errors or discrepancies in the accounting system.

Create a Journal for Paint Palette Store for January 2024.

1. From the Report Center select **Accountant & Taxes > Journal**
2. Select Dates **From: 01/01/2024 To: 01/31/2024**
3. Export to **Excel** or **print** the Journal for Paint Palette Store
4. **Close** the Journal window

E13.7.3 Financial Statements

Create the following financial statements for Paint Palette Store for the January 2024.

1. Export to **Excel** or **print** the Profit & Loss, Standard
2. Export to **Excel** or **print** the Balance Sheet, Standard
3. Export to **Excel** or **print** the Statement of Cash Flows

E13.7.4 Back Up Exercise 13.7

Save a backup of your Exercise file using the file name: YourName Exercise 13.7 Backup.QBB. See *Appendix B: Back Up & Restore QuickBooks Files* for instructions.

PROJECT 13.1

Ella's Knittery

BACKSTORY

Ella Juckem, owner of Ella's Knittery, has asked if you would be interested in maintaining the accounting records for her knitting and yarn shop. Ella, a business major at the local college, found that knitting was meditative and calming when she was stressed with her classes. So Ella decided to become an entrepreneur and open a knittery near her college campus. College students could drop by and connect with other students who enjoy knitting.

Ella would like to begin using QuickBooks software for her accounting records, converting from her current manual accounting system. After reaching agreement on your fee, Ella gives you the following information to enter into QuickBooks.

QB SatNav

The objective of Project 13.1 is to facilitate your mastery of QuickBooks Desktop. As shown in the following QB SatNav, Project 13.1 covers all three processes: QB Settings, QB Transactions, and QB Reports. This project provides you with the opportunity to integrate your knowledge of QuickBooks Desktop through all three phases of the QB SatNav.

QB SatNav

1 QB SETTINGS

- Company Settings
- Chart of Accounts

2 QB TRANSACTIONS

> Money in *Money out >*

- Banking
- Customers & Sales
- Vendors & Expenses
- Employees & Payroll

3 QB REPORTS

- Reports

P13.1.1 New Company Setup

Create a new company in QuickBooks for Ella's Knittery using the following information.

1. Use the EasyStep Interview to set up a new QuickBooks company.

Company name	**YourName Project 13.1 Ella's Knittery**
Federal tax ID	**37-1872613**
Address	**13 College Avenue**
City	**Bayshore**
State	**CA**
Zip	**94326**

Email	**<Enter your email address>**
Industry	**Retail Shop or Online Commerce**
Type of organization	**S Corporation**
First month of fiscal year	**January**
File name	**YourName Project 13.1**
What do you sell?	**Products only**
Enter sales	**Record each sale individually**
Sales tax	**Yes**
Estimates	**No**
Sales orders	**Yes**
Billing statements	**No**
Progress invoicing	**No**
Track bills you owe	**Yes**
Track inventory in QuickBooks	**Yes**
Track time	**Yes**
Employees	**No**
Start date	**01/01/2024**
Use recommended income and expense accounts	**Yes**
Bank account name	**Checking**
Bank account number	**3216549870**
Bank account balance	**0.00 as of 01/01/2024**

2. Click **Start Working** to exit QuickBooks Setup
3. **Display** account numbers in the Chart of Accounts

P13.1.2 Add Customer & Job

1. Add Marie Brewer to Ella's Knittery Customer List.

Customer	**Brewer, Marie**
Address Info:	
First Name	**Marie**

Last Name	**Brewer**
Main Phone	**415-555-3600**
Address	**18 Spring Street**
	Bayshore, CA 94326
Payment Settings:	
Account No.	**13000**
Payment Terms	**Net 15**
Preferred Payment Method	**Check**
Sales Tax Settings:	
Tax Code	**Tax**
Tax Item	**State Tax**

2. Next add Mimi Petit to Ella's Knittery Customer List.

Customer	**Petit, Mimi**
Address Info:	
First Name	**Mimi**
Last Name	**Petit**
Main Phone	**415-555-2160**
Address	**220 Alsace Avenue**
	Bayshore, CA 94326
Payment Settings:	
Account No.	**15000**
Payment Terms	**Net 15**
Preferred Payment Method	**Check**
Sales Tax Settings:	
Tax Code	**Tax**
Tax Item	**State Tax**

3. Click **OK**
4. From the Customer Center, export to **Excel** or **print** the Customer List.

! When exporting to Excel, remember to select Advanced Excel Options:

- Uncheck **Space between columns**
- Check **Row height**
- Uncheck **Include QuickBooks Export Guide worksheet with helpful advice**
- Select **On printed report and screen**

5. **Close** the Customer Center

P13.1.3 Add Vendors

1. Add the following vendors to the Vendor List for Ella's Knittery.

Vendor	**Joseph Leasing**
Opening Balance	**$0.00 as of 01/01/2024**
Address Info:	
Company Name	**Joseph Leasing**
Full Name	**Joseph Asher**
Main Phone	**415-555-0412**
Address	**13 Appleton Drive**
	Bayshore, CA 94326
Payment Settings:	
Account No.	**2700**
Payment Terms	**Net 30**
Tax Settings:	
Vendor Tax ID	**37-1726354**
Additional Info:	
Vendor Type	**Leasing**

Vendor	**Graziella Italia Designs**
Opening Balance	**$0.00 as of 01/01/2024**
Address Info:	
Company Name	**Graziella Italia Designs**
Full Name	**Graziella Martini**

Main Phone	**415-555-1270**
Address	**13 Marco Drive**
	Bayshore, CA 94326
Payment Settings:	
Account No.	**5400**
Payment Terms	**Net 30**
Tax Settings:	
Vendor Tax ID	**37-3571595**

Vendor	**Counte Threads**
Opening Balance	**$0.00 as of 01/01/2024**
Address Info:	
Company Name	**Counte Threads**
Full Name	**Suzanne Counte**
Main Phone	**415-555-1230**
Address	**720 San Luis Drive**
	Bayshore, CA 94326
Payment Settings:	
Account No.	**6300**
Payment Terms	**Net 30**
Tax Settings:	
Vendor Tax ID	**37-1599515**

Vendor	**Bichotte Supplies**
Opening Balance	**$0.00 as of 01/01/2024**
Address Info:	
Company Name	**Bichotte Supplies**
First Name	**Bichotte**
Main Phone	**415-555-4567**
Address	**810 Francais Drive**
	Bayshore, CA 94326

Payment Settings:	
Account No.	**8100**
Payment Terms	**Net 30**
Tax Settings:	
Vendor Tax ID	**37-1599517**

2. From the Vendor Center, export to **Excel** or **print** the Vendor List

P13.1.4 Add Items

1. Add the following items for Ella's Knittery.

Item Type	**Inventory Part**
Item Name	**Italian Yarn**
Description	**Italian Yarn 2 ply**
Income Account	**46000 – Merchandise Sales**

Item Type	**Inventory Part**
Item Name	**Italian Yarn Violet**
Subitem of	**Italian Yarn**
Description	**Italian Yarn Violet**
Sales Price	**36.00 (per skein)**
Income Account	**46000 – Merchandise Sales**

Item Type	**Inventory Part**
Item Name	**Italian Yarn Azure**
Subitem of	**Italian Yarn**
Description	**Italian Yarn Azure**
Sales Price	**27.00 (per skein)**
Income Account	**46000 – Merchandise Sales**

Item Type	**Inventory Part**
Item Name	**Alpaca Yarn**
Description	**Alpaca Yarn 3 ply**
Income Account	**46000 – Merchandise Sales**

Item Type	**Inventory Part**
Item Name	**Alpaca Yarn Creme**
Subitem of	**Alpaca Yarn**
Description	**Alpaca Yarn Creme**
Sales Price	**11.00 (per skein)**
Income Account	**46000 – Merchandise Sales**

Item Type	**Inventory Part**
Item Name	**Alpaca Yarn Earthen Tweed**
Subitem of	**Alpaca Yarn**
Description	**Alpaca Yarn Earthen Tweed**
Sales Price	**13.00 (per skein)**
Income Account	**46000 – Merchandise Sales**

Item Type	**Inventory Part**
Item Name	**Peruvian Wool**
Description	**Peruvian Wool Yarn 4 ply**
Income Account	**46000 – Merchandise Sales**

Item Type	**Inventory Part**
Item Name	**Peruvian Wool Yarn Charcoal**
Subitem of	**Peruvian Wool**
Description	**Peruvian Wool Yarn Charcoal**
Sales Price	**22.00 (per skein)**
Income Account	**46000 – Merchandise Sales**

Item Type	**Inventory Part**
Item Name	**Peruvian Wool Yarn Black**
Subitem of	**Peruvian Wool**
Description	**Peruvian Wool Yarn Black**
Sales Price	**26.00 (per skein)**
Income Account	**46000 – Merchandise Sales**

2. From the Item List, enter the 9.75% sales tax rate as follows: ***
   - **Double-click** on **State Tax** in the Item List
   - Enter Tax Rate: **9.75%**
   - Enter Tax Agency: **California State Board of Equalization**
   - Click **OK**
3. Export to **Excel** or **print** the Item List as of January 1, 2024. (Use Report Center > List > Item Listing.)

   ! When exporting to Excel, remember to select Advanced Excel Options:
   - Uncheck **Space between columns**
   - Check **Row height**
   - Uncheck **Include QuickBooks Export Guide worksheet with helpful advice**
   - Select **On printed report and screen**

P13.1.5 Customize Chart of Accounts

Edit the Chart of Accounts and enter opening balances as follows:

1. Enter the opening balance for the company Checking account:
   - To open the Chart of Accounts, click the **Chart of Accounts** icon in the Company section of the Home Page
   - Select **Checking** account. **Right-click** to display the pop-up menu.
   - Select **Edit Account**
   - When the Edit Account window for the Checking account appears, enter Account No.: **10100**
   - Enter Opening Balance: **$1,500** as of **01/01/2024**
   - Click **OK**
2. Enter the opening balance of **$2,500** for the Inventory Asset account
3. Add the following Notes Payable account and opening balance to the Chart of Accounts.

Account No.	**26000**
Account Type	**Other Current Liability**
Account Name	**Notes Payable**
Account Description	**Notes Payable**
Tax Line	**B/S-Liabs/Eq.: Other current liabilities**
Opening Balance	**$900 as of 01/01/2024**

4. From the Report Center, export to **Excel** or **print** the Chart of Accounts (Account Listing) report as of January 1, 2024, with opening balances for Ella's Knittery
5. Export to **Excel** or **print** a Trial Balance report for Ella's Knittery dated 01/01/2024. Verify your Trial Balance account balances are correct.
6. Transfer the Opening Balance Equity account balance to the Capital Stock account using a journal entry. Use Date: **01/01/2024** and Entry No.: **Open ADJ1.** Select **Save.** Export the opening balance adjusting entry to **Excel** by selecting the **Reports tab > Transaction Journal.**
7. Export to **Excel** or **print** the Adjusted Trial Balance (after opening adjustments) on 01/01/2024 to verify that the Opening Balance Equity account balance was transferred to the Capital Stock account

P13.1.6 Enter Transactions

Ella's Knittery entered into the following transactions during January 2024.

1. Record the transactions for Ella's Knittery.
   - Record all deposits to: **Checking.**
   - If necessary, change the Make Deposits default to **Checking.** (Select Edit Menu > Preferences > Checking > My Preferences > Open the Make Deposits form with 10100 Checking account.)
   - Use memorized transactions for recurring transactions.

Date	Transaction
01/01/2024	Ella's Knittery paid $1,200 store rent to Joseph Leasing. (Use Write Checks window, then create a memorized transaction.)
01/01/2024	Purchased $600 of office supplies on account from Bichotte Supplies. (Use Enter Bills window to record Office Supplies Expense.)
01/13/2024	Placed the following order with Counte Threads. • 20 skeins of Alpaca creme yarn at a cost of $8 each • 30 skeins of Alpaca earthen tweed yarn at a cost of $9.60 each (Click Yes if asked to update cost.)
01/15/2024	Received Alpaca yarn ordered on 01/13/2024

Date	Transaction
01/19/2024	Sold to Marie Brewer on account 10 skeins of Alpaca creme yarn and 12 skeins of Alpaca earthen tweed yarn. (Use Create Invoices window.)
01/19/2024	Received bill from Counte Threads for Alpaca yarn received on 01/15/2024
01/21/2024	Ordered the following yarn from Graziella Italia Designs on account. • 40 skeins of Italian Yarn Violet @ $13 each • 45 skeins of Italian Yarn Azure @ $12 each
01/23/2024	Received the Italian yarns ordered on 01/21/2024
01/25/2024	Sold 22 skeins of Italian Yarn Violet and 10 skeins of Italian Yarn Azure to Mimi Petit on account
01/25/2024	Paid Counte Threads for bill for Alpaca yarn
01/25/2024	Received and deposited to the Checking account the customer payment from Marie Brewer for sale of Alpaca yarn on 01/19/2024 (Check No. 1200)
01/27/2024	Paid $600 bill from Bichotte Supplies

2. Export to **Excel** or **print** the Deposit Detail report for January 2024
3. Export to **Excel** or **print** the Check Detail report for January 2024
4. Export to **Excel** or **print** the Transaction Detail by Account report for January 2024. (From the Report Center, select Accountant & Taxes > Transaction Detail by Account.)

P13.1.7 Adjusting Entries

1. Export to **Excel** or **print** the Trial Balance report for Ella's Knittery at January 31, 2024
2. Make adjusting entries for Ella's Knittery at January 31, 2024, using the following information.

   ADJ1: A count of supplies revealed $100 of supplies on hand. Since $600 of supplies were recorded as Office Supplies Expense when purchased and $100 still remain on hand unused, it is necessary to transfer $100 into an asset account, Office Supplies on Hand. Add a new account: 12500 Office Supplies on Hand as Account Type: Other Current Asset. Make the adjusting entry to transfer $100 from the Office Supplies Expense account to the Office Supplies on Hand account, an asset.

ADJ2: Make an adjusting entry to record Interest Expense and Interest Payable for $12.00. Add a new account: 21000 Interest Payable as Account Type: Other Current Liability.

3. From the Report Center, export to **Excel** or **print** the Adjusting Journal Entries for January 31, 2024
4. Export to **Excel** or print the Adjusted Trial Balance report for Ella's Knittery at January 31, 2024. **Highlight** the amounts affected by the adjusting entries.

P13.1.8 Financial Reports

Create the following reports for Ella's Knittery.

1. Export to **Excel** or **print** the Journal for the month of January 2024
2. Export to **Excel** or **print** the Profit & Loss, Standard for the month of January 2024
3. Export to **Excel** or **print** the Balance Sheet, Standard at January 31, 2024
4. Export to **Excel** or **print** the Statement of Cash Flows for the month of January 2024

P13.1.9 Back Up Project 13.1

Save a backup of your Project file using the file name: YourName Project 13.1 Backup.QBB. See *Appendix B: Back Up & Restore QuickBooks Files* for instructions.

PROJECT 13.2

Dragon Enterprises

BACKSTORY

Dragon Enterprises sells trendy smartphone accessories including earbuds, bluetooth earpieces, portable speakers, and cases. The company is converting from a manual accounting system to QuickBooks Desktop beginning January 2024.

QB SatNav

The objective of Project 13.2 is to facilitate your mastery of QuickBooks Desktop. As shown in the following QB SatNav, Project 13.2 covers all three processes: QB Settings, QB Transactions, and QB Reports. This project provides you with the opportunity to integrate your knowledge of QuickBooks Desktop through all three phases of the QB SatNav.

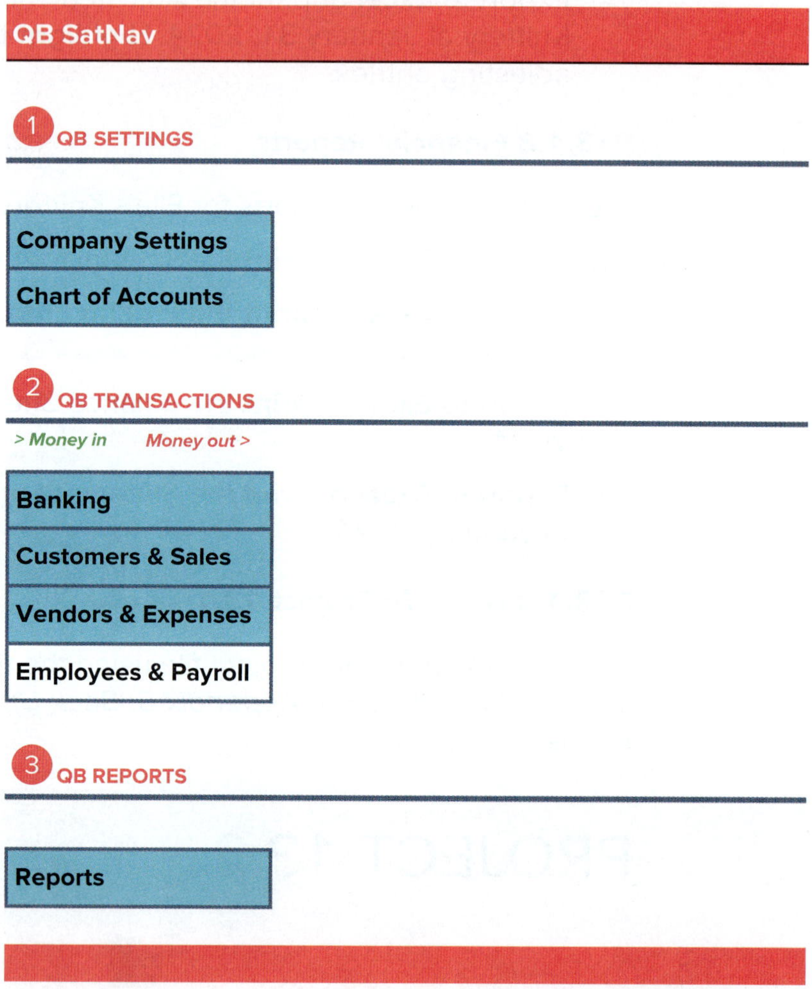

P13.2.1 New Company Setup

Create a new company in QuickBooks for Dragon Enterprises using the following information.

1. Use the EasyStep Interview to set up a new QuickBooks company.

Company name	**YourName Project 13.2 Dragon Enterprises**
Federal tax ID	**30-1957546**
Address	**63 Twin Lane**
City	**Bayshore**
State	**CA**
Zip	**94326**
Main Phone	**415-555-3334**
Email	**<Enter your email address>**
Industry	**Retail Shop or Online Commerce**
Type of organization	**S Corporation**
First month of fiscal year	**January**
File name	**YourName Project 13.2**
What do you sell?	**Products only**
Enter sales	**Record each sale individually**
Sales tax	**Yes**
Estimates	**No**
Sales orders	**Yes**
Billing statements	**No**
Invoices	**Yes**
Progress invoicing	**No**
Track bills you owe	**Yes**
Track inventory in QuickBooks	**Yes**
Track time	**Yes**
Employees	**No**
Start date	**01/01/2024**
Use recommended accounts	**Yes**
Bank account name	**Checking**
Bank account number	**7894561230**
Bank account balance	**0.00 as of 01/01/2024**

2. Click **Start Working** to exit QuickBooks Setup
3. Set preferences as follows:
   - Sales tax preferences to Your Most Common Sales Tax Item: **Out of State**
   - Accounting preferences to **Use account numbers** in the Chart of Accounts
   - Accounting preferences to **uncheck Warn if transactions are 30 day(s) in the future**
   - Checking preferences to Open the Make Deposits form with **10100 Checking** account

P13.2.2 Add Customers

1. Add the following customers to the Customer List for Dragon Enterprises.

Customer	**Petit, Mimi**
Address Info:	
First Name	**Mimi**
Last Name	**Petit**
Main Phone	**415-555-2160**
Address	**220 Alsace Avenue**
	Bayshore, CA 94326
Payment Settings:	
Account No.	**12700**
Payment Terms	**Net 15**
Preferred Payment Method	**Check**
Sales Tax Settings:	
Tax Code	**Tax**
Tax Item	**State Tax**
Customer Type	**Retail**
Customer	**Luminesse Link**
Company Name	**Luminesse Link**
Address Info:	

First Name	**Luminesse**
Main Phone	**415-555-2222**
Address	**22 Beach Street**
	Bayshore, CA 94326
Payment Settings:	
Account No.	**13330**
Payment Terms	**Net 15**
Preferred Payment Method	**Check**
Sales Tax Settings:	
Tax Code	**Non**
Customer Type	**Wholesale**

Customer	**Bichotte Supplies**
Company Name	**Bichotte Supplies**
Address Info:	
First Name	**Bichotte**
Main Phone	**415-555-4567**
Address	**810 Francais Drive**
	Bayshore, CA 94326
Payment Settings:	
Account No.	**19900**
Payment Terms	**Net 15**
Preferred Payment Method	**Check**
Sales Tax Settings:	
Tax Code	**Non**
Customer Type	**Wholesale**

2. From the Customer Center, export to **Excel** the Customer List.

   ! When exporting to Excel, remember to select Advanced Excel Options:
   - Uncheck **Space between columns**
   - Check **Row height**

- Uncheck **Include QuickBooks Export Guide worksheet with helpful advice**
- Select **On printed report and screen**

P13.2.3 Add Vendors

1. Add the following vendors to the Vendor List.

Vendor	**Joseph Leasing**
Opening Balance	**$0.00 as of 01/01/2024**
Address Info:	
Company Name	**Joseph Leasing**
Full Name	**Joseph Asher**
Main Phone	**415-555-0412**
Address	**13 Appleton Drive**
	Bayshore, CA 94326
Payment Settings:	
Account No.	**2700**
Payment Terms	**Due on receipt**
Tax Settings:	
Vendor Tax ID	**37-1726354**
Additional Info:	
Vendor Type	**Service Providers**

Vendor	**Maria Cecilia Associates**
Opening Balance	**$0.00 as of 01/01/2024**
Address Info:	
Company Name	**Maria Cecilia Associates**
Full Name	**Maria Cecilia**
Main Phone	**415-555-6565**
Address	**65 5th Avenue**
	Bayshore, CA 94326
Payment Settings:	
Account No.	**4500**

Payment Terms	**Net 30**
Tax Settings:	
Vendor Tax ID	**37-3571656**
Vendor Type	**Suppliers**

2. From the Vendor Center, export to **Excel** the Vendor List

P13.2.4 Add Items

1. Add the following items.

Item Type	**Inventory Part**
Item Name	**Bluetooth Earpiece**
Description	**Bluetooth Earpiece**
Cost	**7.00**
COGS Account	**50000 – Cost of Goods Sold**
Sales Price	**29.00**
Income Account	**46000 – Merchandise Sales**
Preferred Vendor	**Maria Cecilia Associates**
Asset Account	**12100 – Inventory Asset**
Tax	**Tax**
Qty on Hand	**0 as of 01/01/2024**

Item Type	**Inventory Part**
Item Name	**Smartphone Case**
Description	**Smartphone Case**
Cost	**10.00**
COGS Account	**50000 – Cost of Goods Sold**
Sales Price	**42.00**
Income Account	**46000 – Merchandise Sales**
Preferred Vendor	**Maria Cecilia Associates**
Asset Account	**12100 – Inventory Asset**
Tax	**Tax**
Qty on Hand	**0 as of 01/01/2024**

Item Type	**Inventory Part**
Item Name	**Portable Speaker**
Description	**Portable Speaker**
Cost	**30.00**
COGS Account	**50000 – Cost of Goods Sold**
Sales Price	**120.00**
Income Account	**46000 – Merchandise Sales**
Preferred Vendor	**Maria Cecilia Associates**
Asset Account	**12100 – Inventory Asset**
Tax	**Tax**
Qty on Hand	**0 as of 01/01/2024**

2. From the Item List, enter the 9.75% sales tax rate as follows:
   - **Double-click** on **State Tax** in the Item List
   - Enter Tax Rate: **9.75%**
   - Enter Tax Agency: **California State Board of Equalization**
   - Click O**K**
3. Export to **Excel** or **print** the Item List as of January 1, 2024. (Use Report Center > List > Item Listing.)

   ! When exporting to Excel, remember to select Advanced Excel Options:
   - Uncheck **Space between columns**
   - Check **Row height**
   - Uncheck **Include QuickBooks Export Guide worksheet with helpful advice**
   - Select **On printed report and screen**

P13.2.5 Customize Chart of Accounts

Edit the Chart of Accounts and enter opening balances as follows.

1. Add the following information to the Chart of Accounts with the opening balances as of 01/01/2024.

Account	**Checking**
Account No.	**10100**
Opening Balance	**$10,000**

Account	**Notes Payable**
Account No.	**26000**
Opening Balance	**$2,900**
Account Type	**Other Current Liability**
Account Description	**Notes Payable**
Tax Line	**B/S-Liabs/Eq: Other current liabilities**

Account	**Office Supplies on Hand**
Account No.	**12500**
Opening Balance	**$300**
Account Type	**Other Current Asset**
Account Description	**Office Supplies on Hand**
Tax Line	**B/S-Assets: Other current assets**

Account	**Store Fixtures**
Account No.	**14000**
Opening Balance	**$0**
Account Type	**Fixed Asset**
Account Description	**Store Fixtures**
Tax Line	**B/S-Assets: Buildings/oth depr assets**

Account	**Store Fixtures Cost**
Account No.	**14100**
Opening Balance	**$5,500**
Account Type	**Fixed Asset**
Subaccount of	**Store Fixtures**
Account Description	**Store Fixtures Cost**
Tax Line	**B/S-Assets: Buildings/oth depr assets**

Account	**Store Fixtures Acc Depr**
Account No.	**14200**
Opening Balance	**$0**
Account Type	**Fixed Asset**

Subaccount of	**Store Fixtures**
Account Description	**Store Fixtures Accumulated Depreciation**
Tax Line	**B/S-Assets: Buildings/oth depr assets**

2. Edit the following account to update the Tax Line as follows.

Account	**Office Supplies**
Account No.	**64900**
Account Type	**Expense**
Account Description	**Office Supplies Expense**
Tax Line	**Other Deductions: Supplies**

3. From the Report Center, export to **Excel** or **print** the Chart of Accounts (Account Listing) report as of January 1, 2024
4. Export to **Excel** or **print** a Trial Balance report dated 01/01/2024. Verify your Trial Balance account balances are correct.
5. Transfer the Opening Balance Equity account balance to the Capital Stock account using a journal entry. Use Entry No.: **Open ADJ1.** Select **Save.** Export the opening balance adjusting entry to **Excel** by selecting the **Reports tab** > **Transaction Journal.**
6. Export to **Excel** or **print** the Adjusted Trial Balance (after opening adjustments) to verify that the Opening Balance Equity account balance was transferred to the Capital Stock account.

P13.2.6 Enter Transactions

Dragon Enterprises entered into the following transactions during January 2024.

1. Record the following transactions.
   - Record all deposits to: **Checking.**
   - If necessary, change the Make Deposits default to **Checking.** (Select Edit Menu > Preferences > Checking > My Preferences > Open the Make Deposits form with 10100 Checking account.)

Date	Transaction
01/01/2024	Paid $300 for store rent to Joseph Leasing. (Use Write Checks window.)
01/02/2024	Ordered the following from Maria Cecilia Associates. • 300 Bluetooth earpieces • 210 smartphone cases • 60 portable speakers
01/04/2024	Received items ordered from Maria Cecilia Associates on 01/02/2024
01/05/2024	Sold the following to Luminesse Link on account. • 90 Bluetooth earpieces • 70 smartphone cases
01/06/2024	Received bill from Maria Cecilia Associates
01/08/2024	Sold the following to Bichotte Supplies on account. • 85 Bluetooth earpieces • 105 smartphone cases
01/11/2024	Sold the following to Mimi Petit on account. • 30 portable speakers • 15 Bluetooth earpieces
01/15/2024	Paid at time of purchase for $30 of office supplies from Carole Design Media. (Record using the Enter Bills and Pay Bills windows. Add new vendor: Carole Design Media. Use the Office Supplies on Hand account.)
01/20/2024	Received and deposited payment from Luminesse Link (Check No. 906)
01/22/2024	Received and deposited payment from Bichotte Supplies (Check No. 787)
01/24/2024	Sold the following to Luminesse Link on account. • 90 Bluetooth earpieces • 12 portable speakers

Date	Transaction
01/25/2024	Ordered 100 Bluetooth earpieces from Maria Cecilia Associates
01/26/2024	Received and deposited payment from Mimi Petit (Check No. 321)
01/27/2024	Received items ordered from Maria Cecilia Associates on 01/25/2024
01/28/2024	Received bill from Maria Cecilia Associates
01/29/2024	Sold the following to Bichotte Supplies on account. • 60 Bluetooth earpieces • 5 portable speakers
01/31/2024	Paid Maria Cecilia Associates bill due on 02/05/2024 (Check No. 503)

2. Export to **Excel** the Deposit Detail report for January 2024
3. Export to **Excel** the Check Detail report for January 2024
4. Export to **Excel** the Transaction Detail by Account report for January 2024. (From the Report Center, select Accountant & Taxes > Transaction Detail by Account.)

P13.2.7 Adjusting Entries

1. Export to **Excel** the Trial Balance report at January 31, 2024
2. Make adjusting entries at January 31, 2024, using the following information.

   ADJ1: A count of office supplies revealed $200 on hand. (Hint: Debit Account No. 64800: Office Supplies Expense for supplies used.)

   ADJ2: January depreciation expense for store fixtures was $90.

   ADJ3: Interest expense and interest payable on the Notes Payable equaled $43.00. Add Account No. 21000 Interest Payable (Other Current Liability).
3. From the Report Center, export to **Excel** the Adjusting Journal Entries for January 31, 2024
4. Export to **Excel** the Adjusted Trial Balance report at January 31, 2024. **Highlight** the amounts affected by the adjusting entries.

P13.2.8 Financial Reports

Create the following reports.

1. Export to **Excel** the Journal for the month of January 2024
2. Export to **Excel** the Profit & Loss, Standard for the month of January 2024
3. Export to **Excel** the Balance Sheet, Standard at January 31, 2024
4. Export to **Excel** the Statement of Cash Flows for the month of January 2024
5. Export to **Excel** the Customer Balance Detail report for January 1 - 31, 2024
6. Export to **Excel** the Vendor Balance Detail report for January 1 - 31, 2024

P13.2.9 Back Up Project 13.2

Save a backup of your Project file using the file name: YourName Project 13.2 Backup.QBB. See *Appendix B: Back Up & Restore QuickBooks Files* for instructions.

Chapter 14

QuickBooks Merchandise Company Case

BACKSTORY

Mookie The Beagle Spa™ Supplies

Your friend and entrepreneur, CK Walker, approaches you about a business opportunity. CK would like to buy an existing pet supply business and relaunch as Mookie The Beagle Spa™ Supplies. The company would offer Mookie The Beagle branded merchandise for pet grooming, and eventually pet apparel. To further differentiate product offerings, the MTB spa products would be formulated to omit toxic ingredients often found in pet supplies.

CK plans to keep operations lean by leasing storage space to stock merchandise for shipment to large retail customers and online consumers. This eliminates the need for an expensive brick and mortar storefront.

After negotiations, CK and you agree to invest $5,000 each in stock of the company. You also enter into an arrangement with CK to assist with QuickBooks Desktop for this newest business in exchange for spa services for Pugz, your pet pug puppy.

Download the Excel Report Template for Chapter 14 at www.My-QuickBooks.com, QB2018 link.

Section 14.1

QB SatNav

The objective of this chapter is to facilitate mastery of QuickBooks Desktop for a merchandising company. We will cover setting up a new QuickBooks merchandise company, customizing the QuickBooks Chart of Accounts, entering QuickBooks transactions, and creating reports. This chapter provides you with the opportunity to integrate your knowledge of QuickBooks Desktop through all three phases of QB SatNav for a merchandising company.

As shown in the following QB SatNav, Chapter 14 QuickBooks Service Company Case covers all three processes: QB Settings, QB Transactions, and QB Reports.

QB SatNav

1 QB SETTINGS

- **Company Settings**
- **Chart of Accounts**

2 QB TRANSACTIONS

> Money in *Money out >*

- **Banking**
- **Customers & Sales**
- **Vendors & Expenses**
- **Employees & Payroll**

3 QB REPORTS

- **Reports**

Section 14.2

SET UP NEW QUICKBOOKS COMPANY

C14.2.1 Create New QuickBooks Company. Create a new company in QuickBooks for Mookie The Beagle™ Spa Supplies using the following information and the EasyStep Interview.

Company Name	**YourName Chapter 14 Mookie The Beagle Spa Supplies**
Federal Tax ID	**37-7879146**
Address	**432 Phoenician Way**
City	**Mountain View**
State	**CA**
ZIP	**94043**
Email	**<Enter your own email address>**
Industry	**Retail Shop or Online Commerce**
Type of organization	**S Corporation**
First month of fiscal year	**January**
File name	**YourName Chapter 14**
What do you sell?	**Products only**
Enter sales	**Record each sale individually**
Sales tax	**Yes**
Estimates	**No**
Sales orders	**No**
Billing statements	**No**
Invoices	**Yes**
Progress invoicing	**No**
Track bills	**Yes**
Track inventory	**Yes**

Track time	**Yes**
Employees	**No**
Start date	**01/01/2024**
Use recommended accounts?	**Yes**
Bank account name	**Checking**
Bank account number	**4564564561**
Bank account balance	**0.00 as of 01/01/2024**

C14.2.2 Select Tax Return. Verify the tax form, 1120S (S Corporation), for Mookie The Beagle Spa™ Supplies.

1. Select **Company Menu**
2. Select **My Company**
3. Select Income Tax Form: **Form 1120S**

C14.2.3 Display Account Numbers in the Chart of Accounts for Mookie The Beagle Spa Supplies.

1. Select **Edit Menu**
2. Select **Preferences**
3. Select **Accounting**
4. Select **Company Preferences**
5. Select **Use Account Numbers**
6. Deselect **Warn if transactions are 30 day(s) in the future**

C14.2.4 Set preferences for Mookie The Beagle Spa Supplies.

1. Select **Edit Menu**
2. Select **Preferences**
3. Select **Checking**
4. Select **Open Make Deposits for with Checking**

Section 14.3

CUSTOMER LIST

C14.3.1 Using the following information, create a Customer List for Mookie The Beagle Spa Supplies.

Customer	**Maddy's Marvels**
Opening Balance	**$0.00 as of 01/01/2024**
Address Info:	
Company Name	**Maddy's Marvels**
First Name	**Maddy**
Mobile	**415-555-2727**
Address	**27 Aquarian Rue**
	Bayshore, CA 94326
Payment Settings:	
Account No.	**30001**
Payment Terms	**Net 30**
Sales Tax Settings:	
Tax Code	**Non**
Additional Info:	
Customer Type	**Wholesale**

Customer	**Cathy PetCare Supplies**
Opening Balance	**$0.00 as of 01/01/2024**
Address Info:	
Company Name	**Cathy PetCare Supplies**

First Name	**Cathy**
Main Phone	**415-555-1010**
Address	**10 Chassure Street**
	Bayshore, CA 94326
Payment Settings:	
Account No.	**30002**
Payment Terms	**Net 30**
Sales Tax Settings:	
Tax Code	**Non**
Additional Info:	
Customer Type	**Wholesale**

Customer	**Ryan, TJ**
Opening Balance	**$0.00 as of 01/01/2024**
Address Info:	
First Name	**TJ**
Last Name	**Ryan**
Mobile	**415-555-4545**
Address	**55 Scotch Drive**
	Bayshore, CA 94326
Payment Settings:	
Account No.	**30003**
Payment Terms	**Net 30**
Sales Tax Settings:	
Tax Code	**Tax**
Tax Item	**State Tax**
Additional Info:	
Customer Type <Add New>	**Online**

Customer	**Martini, Graziella**
Opening Balance	**$0.00 as of 01/01/2024**
Address Info:	
First Name	**Graziella**
Last Name	**Martini**
Main Phone	**415-555-1270**
Mobile	**415-555-7210**
Address	**13 Marco Drive**
	Bayshore, CA 94326
Payment Settings:	
Account No.	**30004**
Payment Terms	**Net 30**
Sales Tax Settings:	
Tax Code	**Tax**
Tax Item	**State Tax**
Additional Info:	
Customer Type	**Online**

C14.3.2 Export the Customer List to **Excel** or **print.**

! When exporting to Excel, remember to select Advanced Excel Options:

- Uncheck **Space between columns**
- Check **Row height**
- Uncheck **Include QuickBooks Export Guide worksheet with helpful advice**
- Select **On printed report and screen**

Section 14.4

VENDOR LIST

C14.4.1 Using the following information, create a Vendor List for Mookie The Beagle Spa Supplies.

1. Add a new vendor.

Vendor	**Maria Cecilia Associates**
Opening Balance	**$0 as of 01/01/2024**
Address Info:	
Company Name	**Maria Cecilia Associates**
First Name	**Maria**
Main Phone	**415-555-7878**
Mobile	**415-555-6565**
Address	**65 5th Avenue**
	Bayshore, CA 94326
Payment Settings:	
Account No.	**4001**
Payment Terms	**Net 30**
Print on Check as	**Maria Cecilia Associates**
Vendor Tax ID	**37-4356712**
Additional Info:	
Vendor Type	**Service Providers**

2. Add new vendor.

Vendor	**Joseph Leasing**
Opening Balance	**$0.00 as of 01/01/2024**
Address Info:	
Company Name	**Joseph Leasing**

First Name	**Joseph**
Main Phone	**415-555-0412**
Address	**13 Appleton Drive** **Bayshore, CA 94326**
Payment Settings:	
Account No.	**4002**
Payment Terms	**Net 30**
Print on Check as	**Joseph Leasing**
Vendor Tax ID	**37-1726354**
Additional Info:	
Vendor Type <Add New>	**Leasing**

3. Add new vendor.

Vendor	**Toronto LLC**
Opening Balance	**$0.00 as of 01/01/2024**
Address Info:	
Company Name	**Toronto LLC**
First Name	**Tor**
Main Phone	**415-555-5377**
Address	**416 Wellington Drive** **Bayshore, CA 94326**
Payment Settings:	
Account No.	**4003**
Payment Terms	**Net 30**
Print on Check as	**Toronto LLC**
Additional Info:	
Vendor Type	**Suppliers**

C14.4.2 Export the Vendor List to **Excel** or **print.**

Section 14.5

ITEM LIST

C14.5.1 Enter the following items in the Item List for Mookie The Beagle Spa Supplies. If necessary, display account numbers.

Use the following information when entering inventory items:

- Inventory asset account: **12100 Inventory Asset**
- Income account: **46000 Merchandise Sales**
- COGS Expense account: **50000 Cost of Goods Sold**
- Initial quantity on hand: **-0-**
- Tax Code: **Tax**

CATEGORY	ITEM NAME	TYPE	DESCRIPTION	COST	SALES PRICE
Pet Spa Product	MTB Organic Oatmeal Shampoo	Inventory	MookieTheBeagle Organic Oatmeal Shampoo	$ 5	$ 12
Pet Spa Product	MTB Organic Coconut Conditioner	Inventory	MookieTheBeagle Organic Coconut Oil Conditioner	$ 6	$ 13
Pet Spa Product	MTB Leave-in Detangler	Inventory	MookieTheBeagle Leave-in Detangler Spray	$ 4	$ 10
Pet Spa Product	MTB Cologne	Inventory	MookieTheBeagle Cologne Deodorizer	$ 6	$ 14
Pet Spa Tool	MTB Hair Dryer	Inventory	MookieTheBeagle Grooming Hair Dryer	$ 10	$ 22
Pet Spa Tool	MTB Grooming Brush	Inventory	MookieTheBeagle Grooming Bristle Brush	$ 4	$ 9
Pet Spa Tool	MTB Grooming Comb	Inventory	MookieTheBeagle Grooming Steel Comb	$ 3	$ 8

CATEGORY	ITEM NAME	TYPE	DESCRIPTION	COST	SALES PRICE
Pet Spa Tool	MTB Grooming Scissors	Inventory	MookieTheBeagle Grooming Scissors	$ 6	$ 12
Pet Spa Tool	MTB Doggie Toothbrush Set	Inventory	MookieTheBeagle Doggie Toothpaste and Toothbrush Set	$ 2	$ 10
Pet Spa Wipe	MTB Doggie Paw Wipes	Inventory	MookieTheBeagle Doggie Paw Wipes	$ 3	$ 8
Pet Spa Wipe	MTB Doggie Ear and Eye Wipes	Inventory	MookieTheBeagle Doggie Ear and Eye Wipes	$ 3	$ 8
Pet Spa Wipe	MTB Grooming Wipes	Inventory	MookieTheBeagle Grooming Wipes Multipurpose	$ 3	$ 8
Pet Spa Tool	MTB Massage Brush	Inventory	MookieTheBeagle Massage Brush	$ 8	$ 18

C14.5.2 From the Item List, enter the sales tax rate.

1. From the Item List, **double-click State Tax**
2. Enter Tax Rate: **9.5%**
3. Enter Tax Agency: **California State Board of Equalization**
4. Click **OK**

C14.5.3

1. Re-sort the Item List
2. From the Report Center, export the Item List to **Excel** or **print.**

   ! When exporting to Excel, remember to select Advanced Excel Options:

   - Uncheck **Space between columns**
   - Check **Row height**
   - Uncheck **Include QuickBooks Export Guide worksheet with helpful advice**
   - Select **On printed report and screen**

Section 14.6

CUSTOMIZE THE CHART OF ACCOUNTS

Customize the Chart of Accounts for Mookie The Beagle Spa Supplies.

C14.6.31 Enter the opening balance for the company Checking account in the Chart of Accounts for Mookie The Beagle Spa Supplies.

1. To open the Chart of Accounts, select the **Chart of Accounts** icon in the Company section of the Home Page
2. Select **Checking** account. **Right-click** to display the pop-up menu.
3. Select **Edit Account**
4. When the Edit Account window for the Checking account appears, enter Account No.: **10100**
5. Enter Opening Balance: **$2,000 as of 01/01/2024**

C14.6.2 Add the following accounts and opening balances to the Chart of Accounts for Mookie The Beagle Spa Supplies.

Account No.	**26000**
Account Type	**Long Term Liability**
Account Name	**Notes Payable**
Account Description	**Notes Payable**
Tax Line	**B/S-Liabs/Eq.:L-T Mortgage/note/bonds pay**
Opening Balance	**$2,000 as of 01/01/2024**

Account No.	**12500**
Account Type	**Other Current Asset**
Account Name	**Office Supplies on Hand**
Account Description	**Office Supplies on Hand**
Tax Line	**B/S-Assets:Other current assets**
Opening Balance	**$1,000 as of 01/01/2024**

C14.6.3 Using the Reports Center, export to **Excel** or **print** a Chart of Accounts (Account Listing) report for Mookie The Beagle Spa Supplies.

Section 14.7

RECORD OPENING ADJUSTMENTS

C14.7.1 Export to **Excel** or **print** a Trial Balance report for Mookie The Beagle Spa Supplies dated 01/01/2024.

C14.7.2 Prepare the following opening adjustment entry using the Journal.

1. Transfer the Opening Balance Equity account balance to the Capital Stock account**.** Use Entry No. **Open ADJ1.** Use Date: **01/01/2024.**
2. Select **Save**
3. Select the **Reports tab** > **Transaction Journal**
4. Export the opening balance adjusting entry to **Excel**

C14.7.3 Export to **Excel** or **print** an Adjusted Trial Balance report after opening adjustments for Mookie The Beagle Spa Supplies dated 01/01/2024. Verify that the Opening Balance Equity account balance was transferred to the Capital Stock account.

Section 14.8

RECORD TRANSACTIONS

Mookie The Beagle Spa Supplies entered into the following transactions during January 2024.

C14.8.1 Record the following transactions for Mookie The Beagle Spa. Customers are billed monthly. Use memorized transactions for recurring transactions.

Date	Transaction
01/01/2024	CK invested $5,000 cash in stock of Mookie The Beagle Spa Supplies. You invested $5,000 cash in the stock of the business. Deposit the funds into the company Checking account. (Use Make Deposits window.)
01/01/2024	Paid $300 rent to Joseph Leasing for storage space lease. (Use the Write Checks window, then create a memorized transaction.)
01/02/2024	Purchased technology services for $200 on account from Maria Cecilia Associates. (Use Enter Bills window to record Professional Fees Expense.)
01/03/2024	Ordered following inventory from Toronto LLC: • 200 MookieTheBeagle Organic Oatmeal Shampoo • 100 MookieTheBeagle Organic Coconut Oil Conditioner • 40 MookieTheBeagle Leave-in Detangler • 20 MookieTheBeagle Hair Dryer • 20 MookieTheBeagle Grooming Brush • 50 MookieTheBeagle Massage Brush
01/06/2024	Received items ordered from Toronto LLC

Date	Transaction
01/08/2024	Sold the following to Maddy's Marvels on account: • 100 MookieTheBeagle Organic Oatmeal Shampoo • 60 MookieTheBeagle Organic Coconut Oil Conditioner • 18 MookieTheBeagle Leave-in Detangler • 6 MookieTheBeagle Hair Dryer • 12 MookieTheBeagle Grooming Brush • 35 MookieTheBeagle Massage Brush
01/10/2024	Sold the following to Cathy PetCare Supplies on account: • 80 MookieTheBeagle Organic Oatmeal Shampoo • 32 MookieTheBeagle Organic Coconut Oil Conditioner • 15 MookieTheBeagle Leave-in Detangler • 6 MookieTheBeagle Hair Dryer • 4 MookieTheBeagle Grooming Brush • 10 MookieTheBeagle Massage Brush
01/12/2024	Received bill from Toronto LLC for inventory received on 1/06/2024
01/17/2024	Paid Toronto LLC bill for inventory purchased
01/18/2024	Sold the following online to TJ Ryan and received credit card payment at time of sale. (VISA 5555 5555 5555 5555 Exp: 05/2025) Include sales tax on this sale. (Use Create Invoices, Receive Payments and Make Deposits windows.) • 2 MookieTheBeagle Organic Oatmeal Shampoo • 1 MookieTheBeagle Organic Coconut Oil Conditioner • 1 MookieTheBeagle Grooming Brush • 1 MookieTheBeagle Hair Dryer • 2 MookieTheBeagle Massage Brush
01/21/2024	Ordered following inventory from Toronto LLC: • 20 MookieTheBeagle Doggie Toothpaste and Toothbrush Set • 100 MookieTheBeagle Doggie Paw Wipes • 100 MookieTheBeagle Doggie Ear and Eye Wipes • 100 MookieTheBeagle Grooming Wipes
01/22/2024	Received items ordered from Toronto LLC on 01/21/2024

Date	Transaction
01/23/2024	Sold the following online to Graziella Martini and received credit card payment at time of sale. (VISA 777 7777 7777 7777 Exp: 07/2027) Include sales tax on this sale. (Use Create Invoices, Receive Payments and Make Deposits windows.) • 2 MookieTheBeagle Grooming Wipes • 3 MookieTheBeagle Doggie Paw Wipes • 1 MookieTheBeagle Massage Brush • 1 MookieTheBeagle Doggie Toothpaste and Toothbrush Set
01/24/2024	Received and deposited payment from Cathy PetCare Supplies (Check No. 1313)
01/27/2024	Received and deposited payment from Maddy's Marvels (Check No. 2700)
01/28/2024	Sold the following to Maddy's Marvels on account: • 16 MookieTheBeagle Doggie Toothpaste and Toothbrush Set • 85 MookieTheBeagle Doggie Paw Wipes • 75 MookieTheBeagle Doggie Ear and Eye Wipes • 75 MookieTheBeagle Grooming Wipes
01/30/2024	Received bill from Toronto LLC for inventory received on 1/22/2024
01/31/2024	Paid $300 to Joseph Leasing for storage space lease for February rental

C14.8.2 Export to **Excel** or **print** the Deposit Detail report for January 2024.

C14.8.3 Export to **Excel** or **print** the Check Detail report for January 2024.

C14.8.4 Export to **Excel** or **print** the Transaction Detail by Account report for January 2024.

Section 14.9

ADJUSTING ENTRIES

Make adjustments at January 31, 2024 to bring accounts up to date before preparing financial reports for Mookie The Beagle Spa Supplies.

C14.9.1 Export to **Excel** or **print** the Trial Balance report for Mookie The Beagle Spa Supplies at January 31, 2024.

C14.9.2 Make adjusting entries for Mookie The Beagle Spa Supplies at January 31, 2024, using the following information.

1. **ADJ1:** Record February 2024 rent that was expensed as a prepaid asset. Add Account 13000 Prepaid Rent, Other Current Asset.
2. **ADJ2:** A count of office supplies on hand reveals that $400 of supplies are still on hand at January 31, 2024.
3. **ADJ3:** Interest expense and interest payable at January 31, 2024, on Notes Payable was $20. Add Account No. 21000, Interest Payable.

C14.9.3 Export to **Excel** or **print** the Adjusting Journal Entries report at January 31, 2024.

C14.9.4 Export to **Excel** or **print** the Adjusted Trial Balance report for Mookie The Beagle Spa Supplies at January 31, 2024. **Highlight** amounts affected by the adjusting entries.

Section 14.10

FINANCIAL REPORTS

Prepare financial reports for Mookie The Beagle Spa Supplies for January 2024.

C14.10.1 Export to **Excel** or **print** the Journal for the month of January 2024.

C14.10.2 Export to **Excel** or **print** the Profit and Loss, Standard for the month of January 2024.

C14.10.3 Export to **Excel** or **print** the Balance Sheet, Standard at January 31, 2024.

C14.10.4 Export to **Excel** or **print** the Statement of Cash Flows for the month of January 2024.

C14.10.5 Export to **Excel** or **print** the Accounts Receivable Aging Summary at January 31, 2024.

C14.10.6 Export to **Excel** or **print** the Accounts Payable Aging Summary at January 31, 2024.

Section 14.11

BACK UP QUICKBOOKS FILES

Save a backup of your Chapter 14 file using the file name: **YourName Chapter 14 Backup.QBB.** For further instructions on how to back up your file, *see Appendix B: Back Up & Restore QuickBooks Files.*

Chapter 15

Advanced QuickBooks Features for Accountants

BACKSTORY

During the month of January 2024 you continue to operate your painting service while still managing Paint Palette Store. You know that you need to budget for the coming year, providing you an opportunity to develop a business plan for the company.

In the new year, several commercial customers have approached you about custom painting for their offices and restaurants. Moreover, you continue to get referrals from your satisfied customers. The new customers want bids and estimates before they award contracts. Also, since some of these new jobs would require months to complete, you want to use progress billing (bill customers as the job progresses) in order to bring in a steady cash flow for your business.

Furthermore, you continue to provide QuickBooks consulting services for a variety of accounting clients. Therefore, to improve customer service for your QuickBooks clients, you continue to expand your knowledge and learn more about other advanced features of QuickBooks designed for the accounting professional.

Section 15.1

INTRODUCTION

This chapter covers some of the more advanced features of QuickBooks that are of interest to the accounting professional. These features include setting up budgets, progress billing, and the audit trail.

Section 15.2

START QUICKBOOKS AND OPEN QUICKBOOKS COMPANY

START QUICKBOOKS

To start QuickBooks software, click the **QuickBooks** icon on your desktop. If a QuickBooks icon does not appear on your desktop, from Microsoft® Windows® click **Start** button > **Programs** > **QuickBooks** > **QuickBooks Premier Accountant Edition.**

RESTORE QBB

Restore the backup (QBB) file for this chapter as follows.

1. Select **File** > **Restore**
2. Using the directions in *Appendix B: Back Up & Restore QuickBooks Files,* restore the **CHAPTER 15 STARTER.QBB** file. (If a password is requested, use KayQB2018.)
3. After restoring, add **YourName Chapter 15 Paint Palette** to the company name by selecting **Company Menu** > **My Company**

Section 15.3

BUDGETS

As Paint Palette enters its second year of operation, planning for future expansion is important to its continued success. You develop the following budget for 2024.

- January sales are expected to be $4,300. Sales are expected to increase by 5% each month thereafter.
- Paint supplies expense is budgeted at $30 per month.
- The van lease will increase to $280 per month. (Use Account No. 67100.)

To prepare budgets for Paint Palette using QuickBooks:

1. Select **Company Menu**
2. Select **Planning & Budgeting**
3. Select **Set Up Budgets**
4. In the Create New Budget window, select the year: **2024**
5. Select budget type: **Profit and Loss**
6. Select **Next**
7. Select **No additional criteria**
8. Select **Next**
9. Select **Create budget from scratch**
10. Click **Finish**

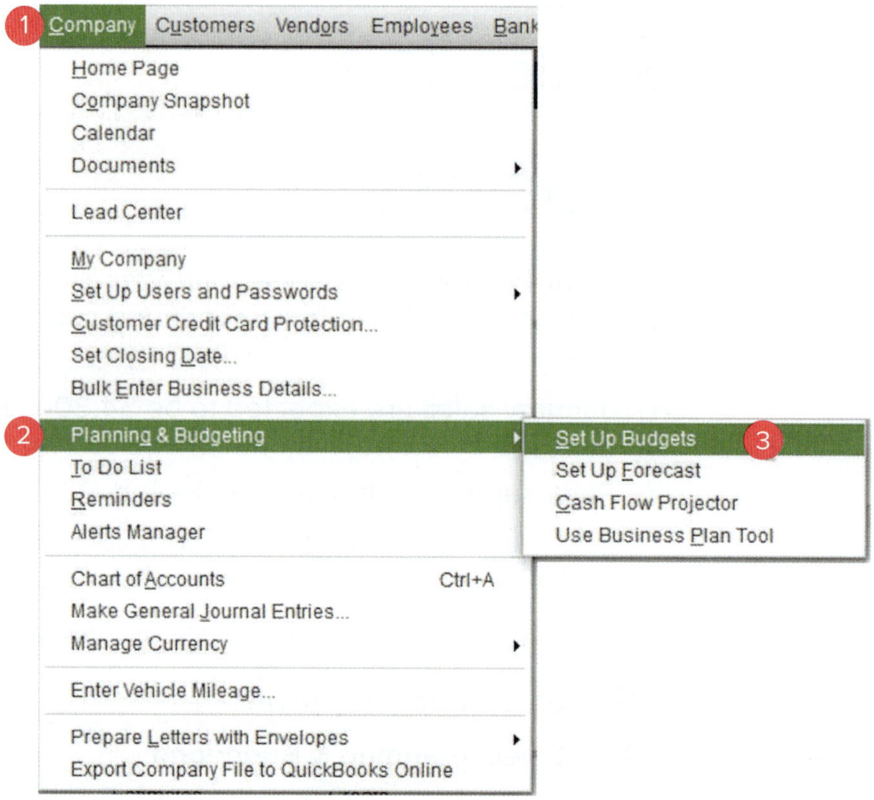
1
Company
Customers
Vendors
Employees
Bank
Home Page
Company Snapshot
Calendar
Documents
Lead Center
My Company
Set Up Users and Passwords
Customer Credit Card Protection...
Set Closing Date...
Bulk Enter Business Details...
2
Planning & Budgeting
To Do List
Reminders
Alerts Manager
Chart of Accounts
Ctrl+A
Make General Journal Entries...
Manage Currency
Enter Vehicle Mileage...
Prepare Letters with Envelopes
Export Company File to QuickBooks Online
Set Up Budgets
3
Set Up Forecast
Cash Flow Projector
Use Business Plan Tool

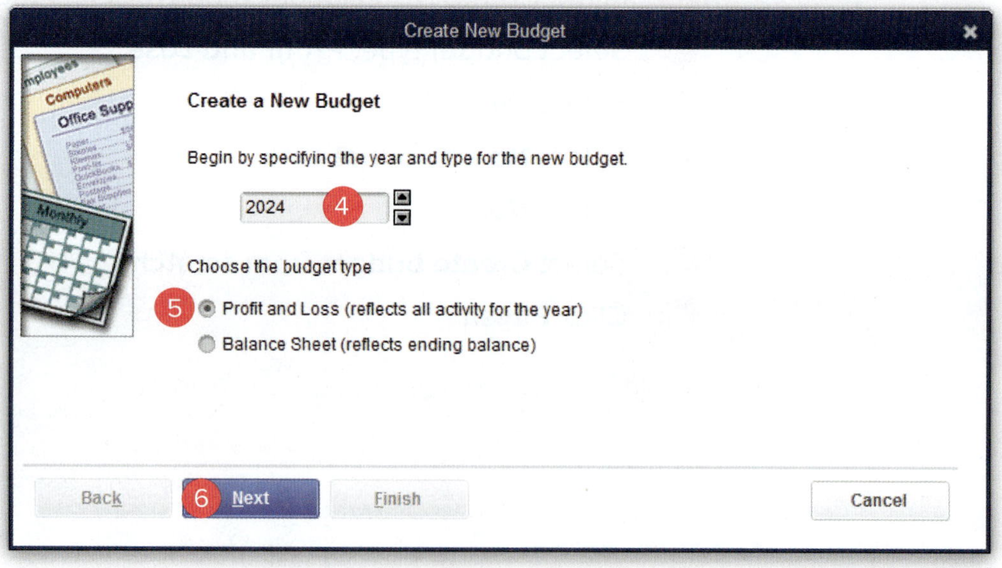
Create New Budget
Create a New Budget
Begin by specifying the year and type for the new budget.
2024
4
Choose the budget type
5
Profit and Loss (reflects all activity for the year)
Balance Sheet (reflects ending balance)
Back
6
Next
Finish
Cancel

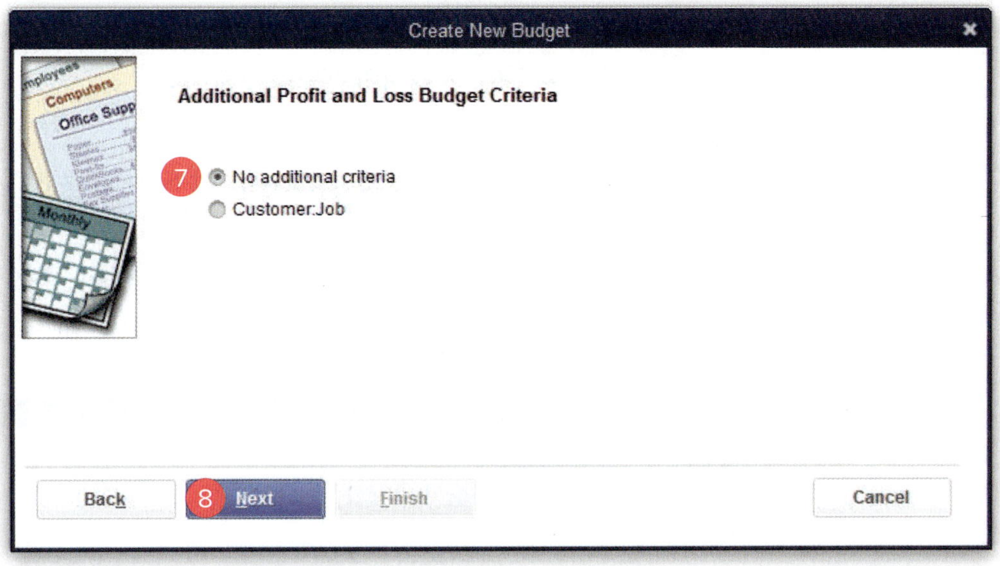

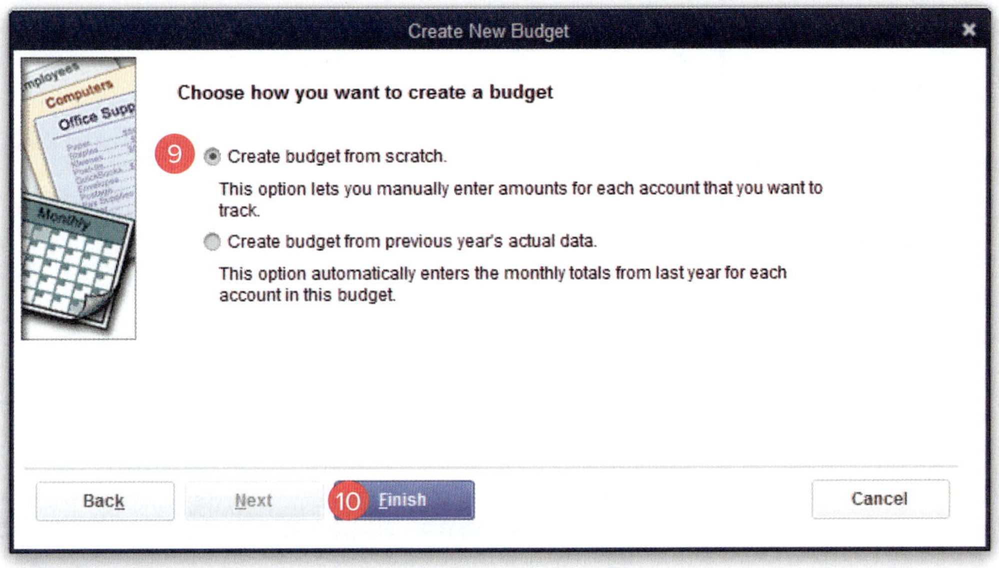

When the Set Up Budgets window appears:

1. Enter **4300.00** for 47900 Sales account in the Jan24 column
2. Click the **Copy Across** button
3. Click the **Adjust Row Amounts** button
4. When the following Adjust Row Amounts window appears, select Start at: **Currently selected month**
5. Select: **Increase each remaining monthly amount in this row by this dollar amount or percentage**

6. Enter **5.0%**
7. Check: **Enable compounding**
8. Click **OK**
9. Enter budget amounts for Paint Supplies Expense of **$30** per month
10. Enter Rent Expense for the van of **$280** per month
11. Click **OK** to close the Set Up Budgets window

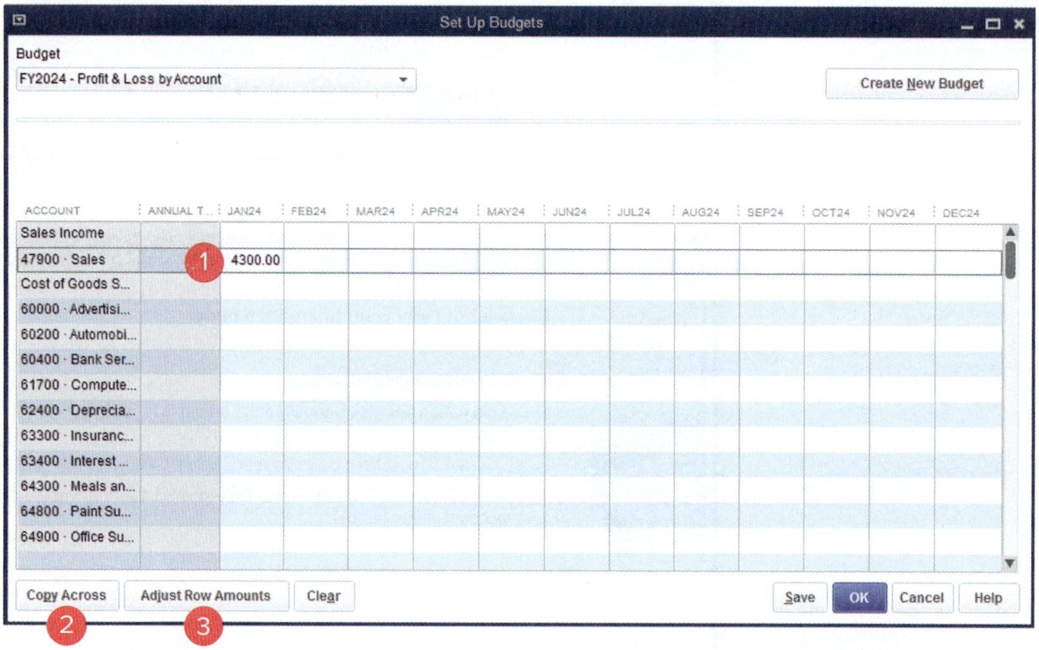

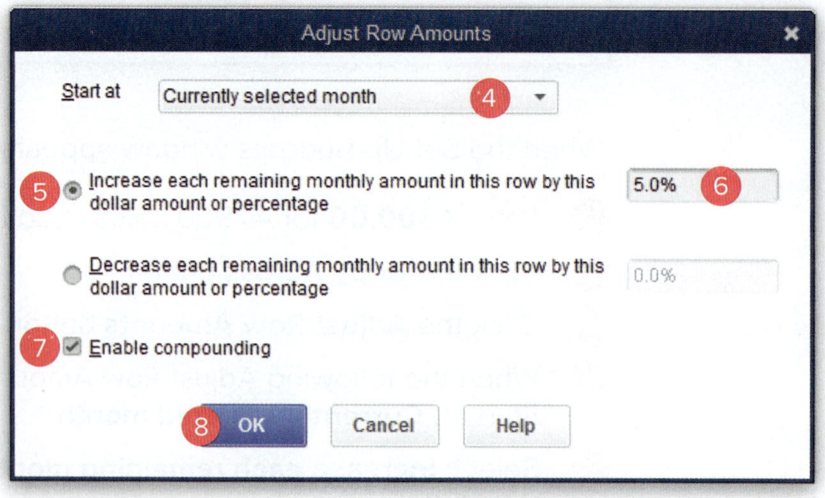

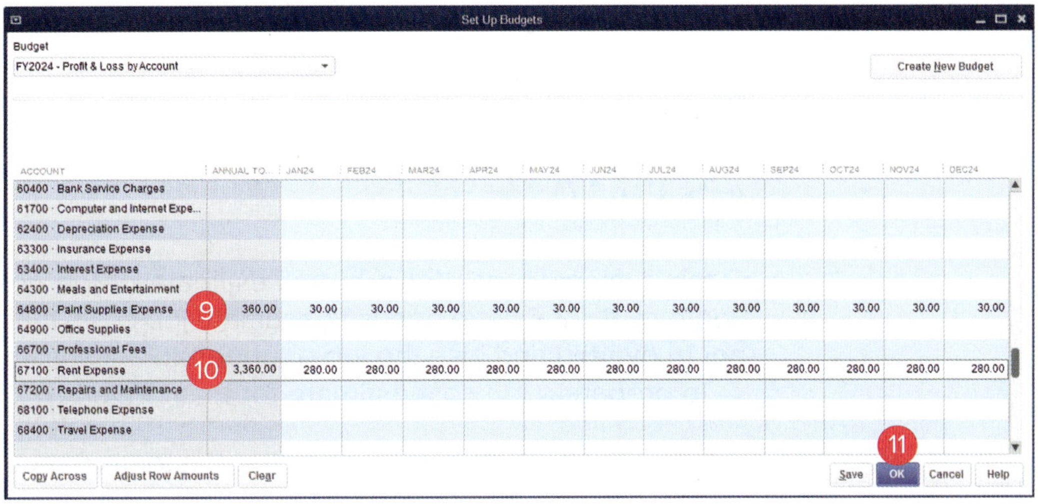

C15.3.1 Budget. Export to **Excel** or **print** the budget you created for Paint Palette:

1. From the Report Center select **Budgets & Forecasts** > **Budget Overview**
2. Select Dates: **01/01/2024 To: 12/31/2024.** Click **Run.**
3. Select: **FY2024 – Profit and Loss by Account** > **Next**
4. Select Report Layout: **Account by Month** > **Next** > **Finish**
5. Export to **Excel** or **print** the Budget Overview report.

   ! When exporting to Excel, remember to select Advanced Excel Options:

   - Uncheck **Space between columns**
   - Check **Row height**
   - Uncheck **Include QuickBooks Export Guide worksheet with helpful advice**
   - Select **On printed report and screen**
6. **Close** the Budget Overview window

Section 15.4

ESTIMATES

Often customers ask for a bid or estimate of job cost before awarding a contract. Paint Palette needs to estimate job costs that are accurate in order not to overbid and lose the job or underbid and lose money on the job.

To prepare a job cost estimate for Paint Palette:

1. Click the **Estimates** icon in the Customers section of the Home Page
2. In the Create Estimates window that appears, from the drop-down Customer List, select **<Add New>**
3. Enter Customer Name: **Karma Café**
4. Enter Company Name: **Karma Café**
5. Enter Address: **9 Passe Blvd, Bayshore, CA 94326**
6. Enter First Name: **Karma**
7. Click the Job Info tab, then enter Job Status: **Pending**
8. Click **OK** to close the New Customer window
9. To enter estimate information in the Create Estimates window, select Template: **Custom Estimate**
10. Select Date: **01/05/2024**
11. Enter Item: **Labor: Exterior Painting**
12. Enter Quantity **50**
13. Enter a second item: **Labor: Interior Painting**
14. Enter Quantity: **85**
15. Click **Save & Close** to close the Create Estimates window

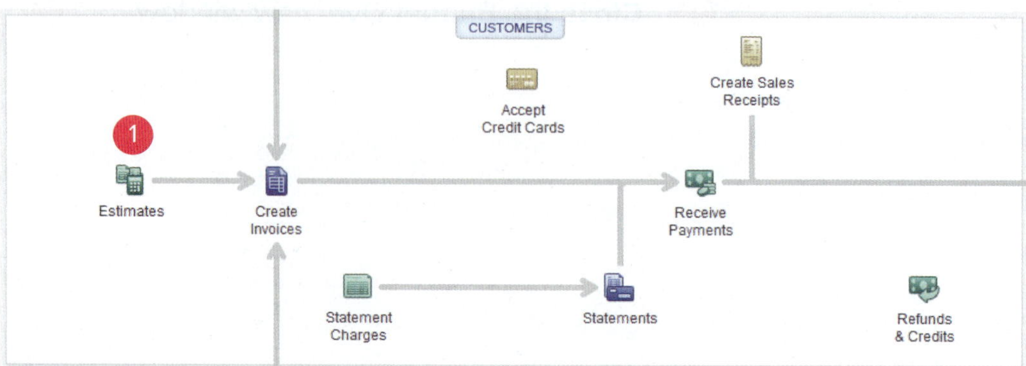

Section 15.5

PROGRESS BILLING

When undertaking a job that lasts a long period of time, a business often does not want to wait until the job is completed to receive payment for its work. The business often incurs expenses in performing the job that must be paid before the business receives payment from customers. This can create a cash flow problem. One solution to this problem is progress billing.

Progress billing permits a business to bill customers as the job progresses. Thus, the business receives partial payments from the customer before the project is completed.

After you give Karma Café your estimate of the paint job cost, Karma awards you the contract. The job will last about three weeks. However, instead of waiting three weeks to bill Karma, you bill Karma every week so that you will have cash to pay your bills.

To use progress billing in QuickBooks, first you must turn on the preference for progress invoicing.

To select the preference for progress invoicing:

1. Select **Edit Menu**
2. Select **Preferences**
3. Select **Jobs & Estimates**
4. Select **Company Preferences**
5. Select **Yes** to indicate you want to use Progress Invoicing
6. Check **Don't print items that have zero amount**
7. Click **OK** to save the Progress Invoicing preference and close the Preferences window. Click **OK** if a warning window appears.

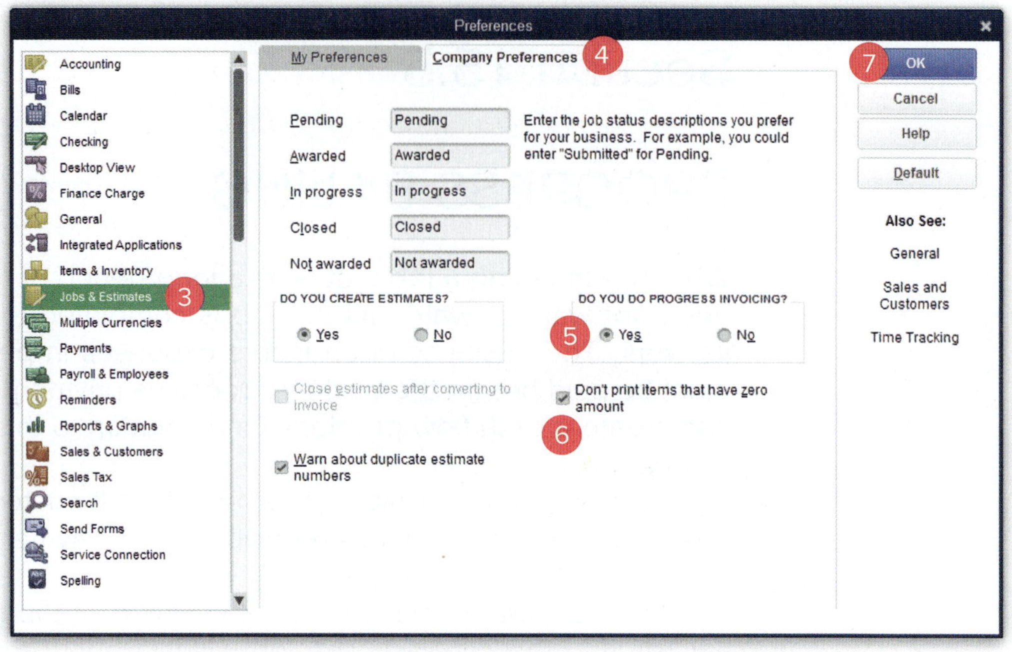

After selecting the Progress Invoicing preference, the Progress Invoice template is now available in the Create Invoices window.

C15.5.1 Progress Invoice. To create a progress invoice:

1. Click the **Create Invoices** icon in the Customers section of the Home Page
2. When the Create Invoices window appears, select Customer: **Karma Café**
3. Select the **Karma Café** estimate to invoice
4. Click **OK**
5. When the Create Progress Invoice Based On Estimate window appears, select: **Create invoice for the entire estimate (100%)**
6. Click **OK**
7. When the following Create Invoices window appears, the template should now be: **Progress Invoice**
8. Enter the number of hours actually worked on the Karma Café job
    - Enter Exterior Painting Labor Quantity: **20**
    - Enter Interior Painting Labor Quantity: **0**

9. Select the **Save** icon
10. Select the **Reports tab** at the top of the Create Invoices window
11. Select **Transaction Journal**
12. Export to **Excel** or **print** the Transaction Journal report
13. Click **Save & Close** to close the Create Invoices window. If a message appears, click **Yes** to record changes to the invoice.

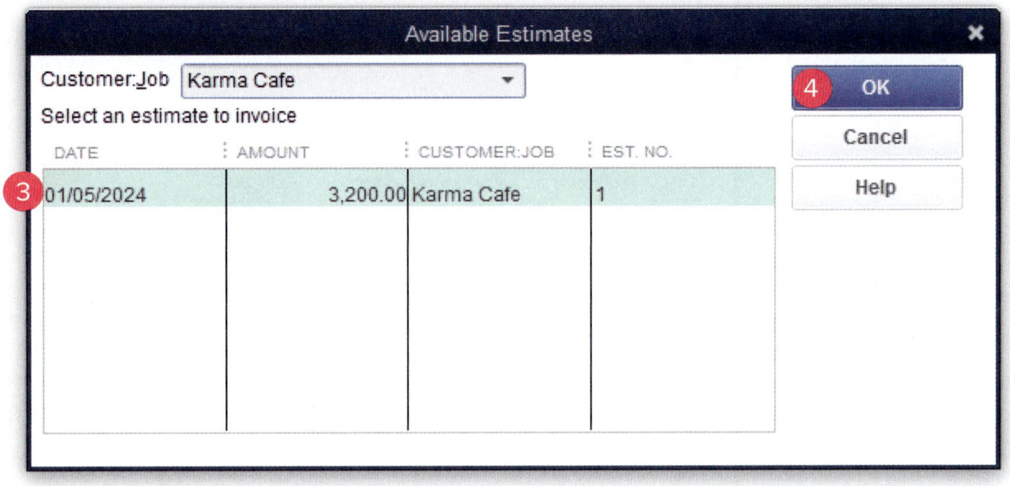

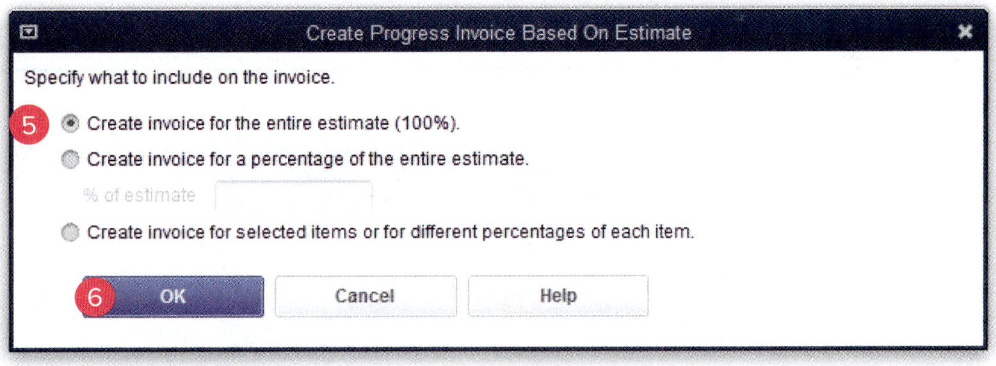

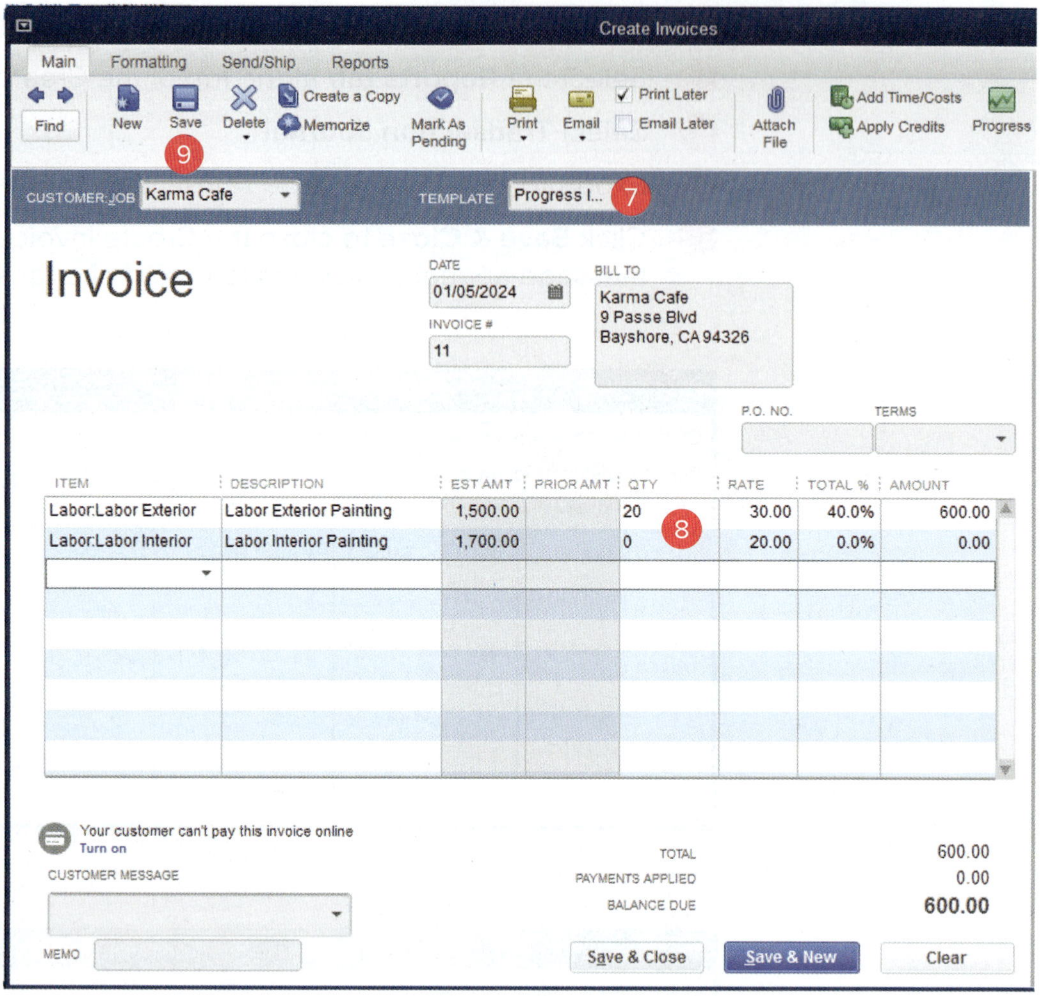
Create Invoices
Main
Formatting
Send/Ship
Reports
Find
New
Save
Delete
Create a Copy
Memorize
Mark As Pending
Print
Email
Print Later
Email Later
Attach File
Add Time/Costs
Apply Credits
Progress
9
CUSTOMER:JOB Karma Cafe
TEMPLATE Progress I...
7
Invoice
DATE 01/05/2024
INVOICE # 11
BILL TO Karma Cafe 9 Passe Blvd Bayshore, CA 94326
P.O. NO.
TERMS
ITEM DESCRIPTION EST AMT PRIOR AMT QTY RATE TOTAL % AMOUNT
Labor:Labor Exterior Labor Exterior Painting 1,500.00 20 30.00 40.0% 600.00
Labor:Labor Interior Labor Interior Painting 1,700.00 0 20.00 0.0% 0.00
8
Your customer can't pay this invoice online
Turn on
CUSTOMER MESSAGE
MEMO
TOTAL 600.00
PAYMENTS APPLIED 0.00
BALANCE DUE 600.00
Save & Close
Save & New
Clear

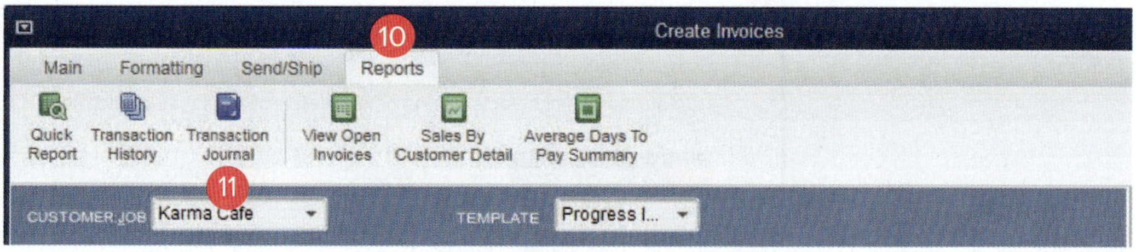
Create Invoices
10
Main
Formatting
Send/Ship
Reports
Quick Report
Transaction History
Transaction Journal
View Open Invoices
Sales By Customer Detail
Average Days To Pay Summary
11
CUSTOMER:JOB Karma Cafe
TEMPLATE Progress I...

C15.5.2 Progress Invoice. The following week you complete the exterior painting for Karma Café and work 17 hours on interior painting. Create another progress invoice for Karma Café by completing the following steps.

1. Display the Create Invoices window and select Customer: **Karma Café**
2. Select the **Karma Café** estimate to invoice, then click **OK**
3. When the Create Progress Invoice Based On Estimate window appears, select **Create invoice for selected items or for different percentages of each item**
4. Click **OK**
5. When the Specify Invoice Amounts for Items on Estimate window appears, Check: **Show Quantity and Rate**
6. Check: **Show Percentage**
7. Enter Exterior Painting Quantity: **30**
8. Enter Interior Painting Quantity: **17**
9. Click **OK** to record these amounts on the progress invoice
10. When the Create Invoices window appears, change the date of the progress invoice to: **01/12/2024**
11. Select the **Save** icon
12. Select the **Reports tab** > **Transaction Journal**
13. Export to **Excel** or **print** the Transaction Journal
14. Click **Save & Close** to close the Create Invoices window

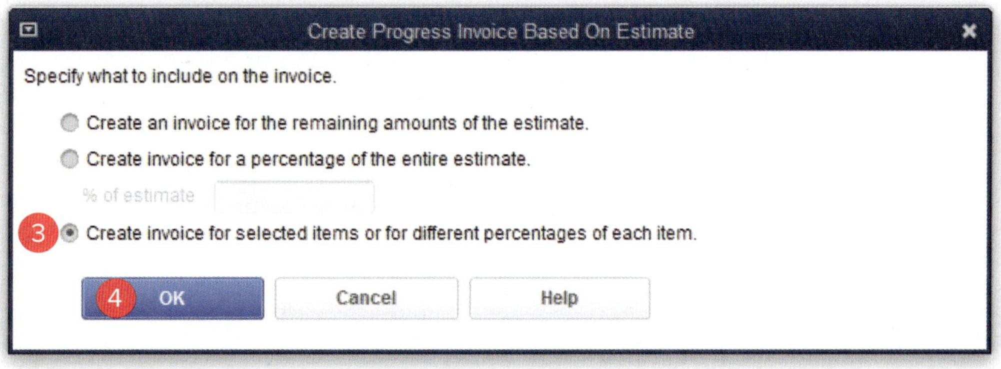

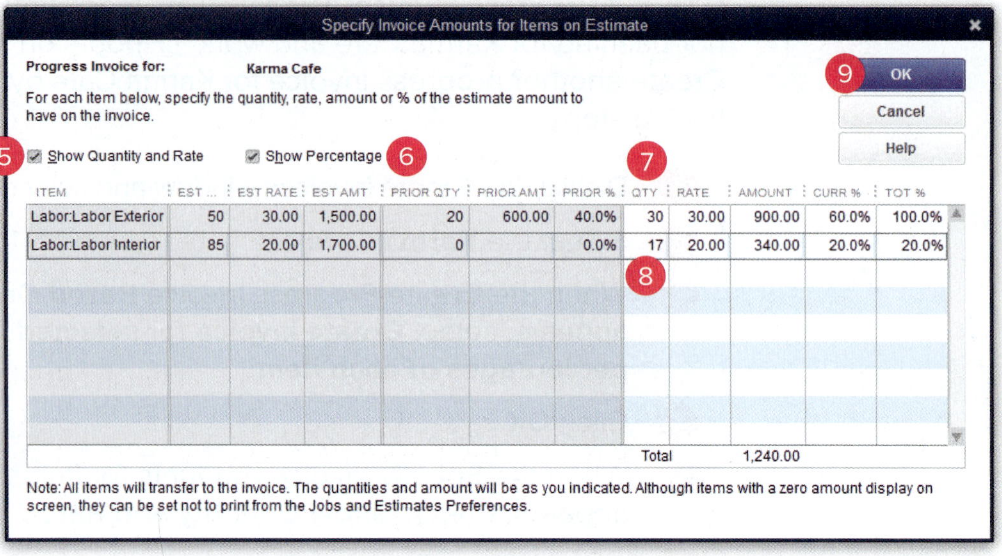

Customer payments received on progress invoices are recorded in the same manner as customer payments for standard invoices (see Chapter 5).

Section 15.6

CREDIT CARD SALES

As a convenience to your customers, you agree to accept credit cards as payment for services you provide. Karma Café would like to make its first payment using a VISA credit card.

In QuickBooks, you record credit card payments in the same manner that you record a payment by check; however, instead of selecting Check as the payment method, you select the type of credit card used.

C15.6.1 Deposit Journal Entry. To record a credit card sale using QuickBooks:

1. Click the **Receive Payments** icon in the Customers section of the Home Page
2. When the Receive Payments window appears, select Received From: **Karma Café.** QuickBooks will automatically display any unpaid invoices for Karma Café.
3. Select Invoice **11** for **600.00**
4. Enter Date: **01/30/2024**
5. Select Payment Method: **CREDIT DEBIT**
6. When the Enter Card Information window appears, select Payment: **Visa**
7. Enter Card Number: **19991999191999**
8. Enter Exp Date: **12/2024**
9. Select **Done**
10. To record the customer payment and close the Receive Payments window, click **Save & Close**
11. Since you are not using the Merchant Account Services, when the credit card payment is deposited at the bank on 01/30/2024,

record the deposit just as you would a check or cash deposit. Click the **Record Deposits** icon in the Banking section of the Home Page > From the Payments to Deposit window, select **Karma Café payment** for deposit > click **OK.**

12 From the Make Deposits window, select the **Save** icon

13 Select the **Journal** icon

14 Export to **Excel** or **print** the Deposit Journal report

15 **Close** the Journal report and the Make Deposits windows

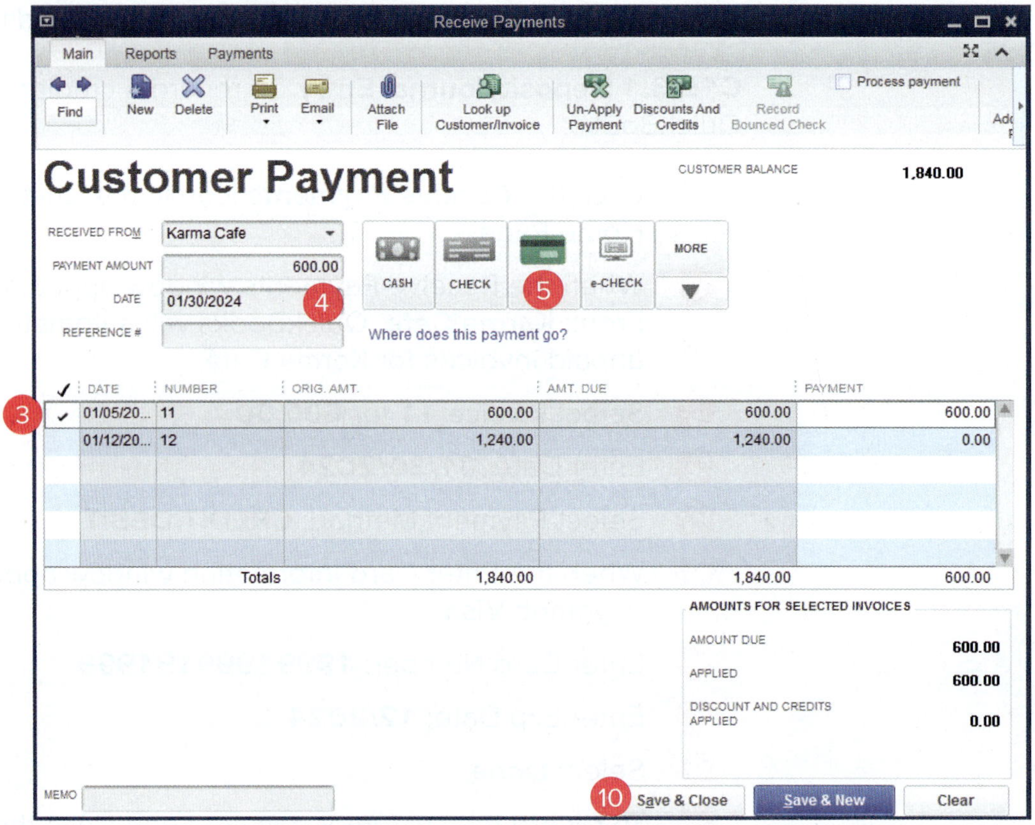

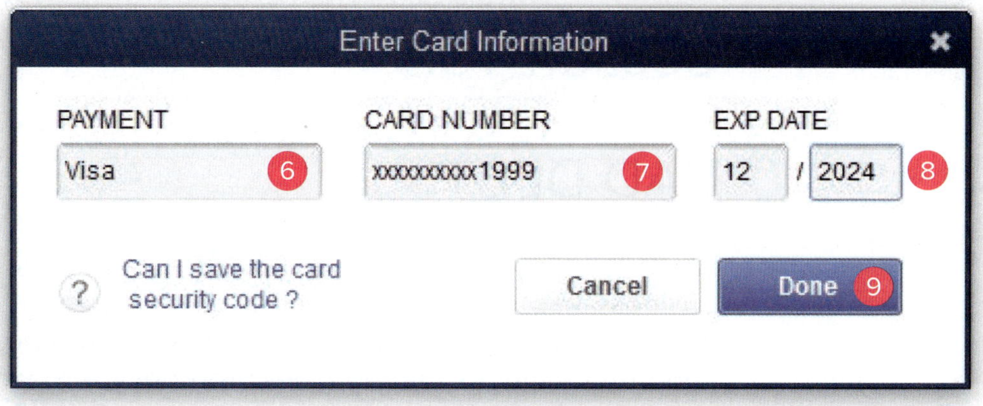

If the specific credit card is not listed on the Payment Method List, select Add New, then enter the name of the credit card.

Banks will accept bank credit card payments, such as Visa or Mastercard, the same as a cash or check deposit. You can record the credit card payment as a deposit to your checking account.

Section 15.7

BAD DEBTS

When Karma paid the bill for $600 for Karma Café, he tells you that his business has plummeted since a new restaurant opened next door. To your dismay, he tells you his café is closing and he will not be able to pay you the remainder that he owes. You decide to write off the Karma Café remaining $1,240 account balance as uncollectible.

Paint Palette uses the direct write-off method and records the uncollectible accounts expense when an account actually becomes uncollectible. To accomplish this, first we will create an account for tracking uncollectible accounts expense and then write off the customer's uncollectible account receivable.

To add a Bad Debt Expense account to the Chart of Accounts for Paint Palette, complete the following steps:

1. Click the **Chart of Accounts** icon in the Company section of the Home Page
2. Add the following account to the Chart of Accounts:

Account Type	**Expense**
Account No.	**67000**
Account Name	**Bad Debt Expense**
Tax Line	**Schedule C: Bad debts from sales/services**

Next, record the write-off of the uncollectible account receivable. There are three different methods to record a bad debt using QuickBooks:

1. Make a journal entry to remove the customer's account receivable (credit Accounts Receivable) and debit either Bad Debt Expense (direct write-off method) or the Allowance for Uncollectible Accounts (allowance method).
2. Use the Credit Memo window to record uncollectible accounts.
3. Use the Receive Payments window (Discounts And Credits icon) to record the write-off of the customer's uncollectible account. Use this method if you charged sales tax on the transaction written off.

To record the write-off of an uncollectible account receivable using the Receive Payments window (method 3 above), first change the preference for automatically calculating payments as follows:

1. Select **Edit Menu**
2. Select **Preferences**
3. Select **Payments**
4. Select **Company Preferences**
5. Uncheck **Automatically calculate payments**
6. Select **OK** to close the Preferences window

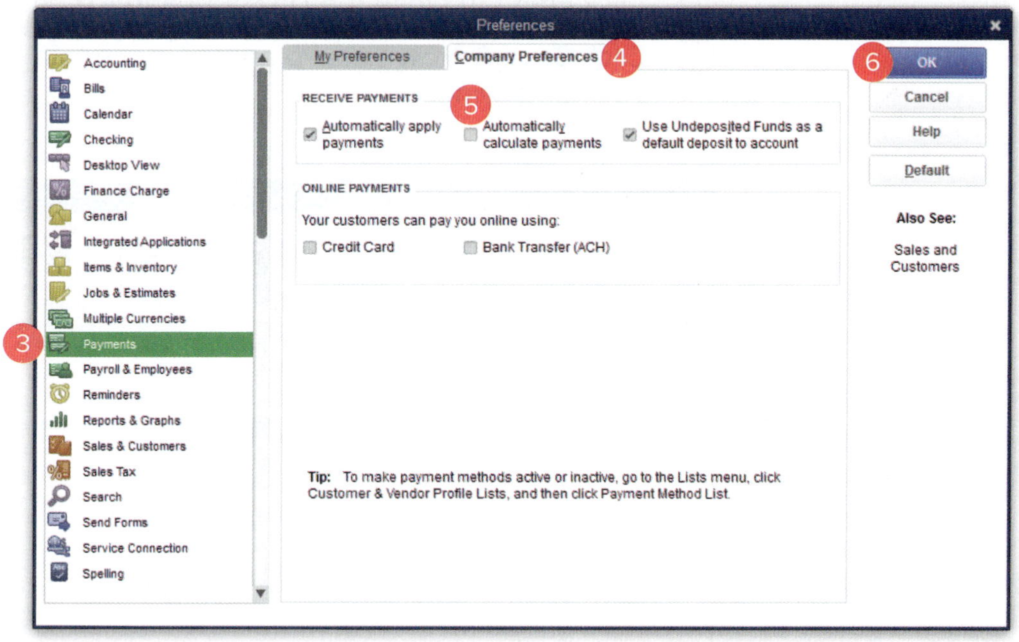

To record the write-off of an uncollectible account receivable using the Receive Payments window, complete the following steps:

1. Click the **Receive Payments** icon in the Customers section of the Home Page
2. When the Receive Payments window appears, select Received From: **Karma Café**
3. Leave the Payment Amount as **$0.00**
4. Enter Date: **01/30/2024**

5. Enter Memo: **Write off Uncollectible Account**
6. Select the outstanding invoice dated: **01/12/2024**
7. Because the Amount field is $0.00, a warning may appear. Click **OK.**
8. Highlight the invoice by clicking on its **Date** field
9. Click the **Discounts And Credits** icon in the Receive Payments window
10. When the Discount and Credits window appears, enter Amount of Discount: **1,240.00**
11. Select Discount Account: **67000 Bad Debt Expense**
12. Click **Done** to close the Discount and Credits window
13. Click **Save & New** to save and advance to a blank Receive Payments window

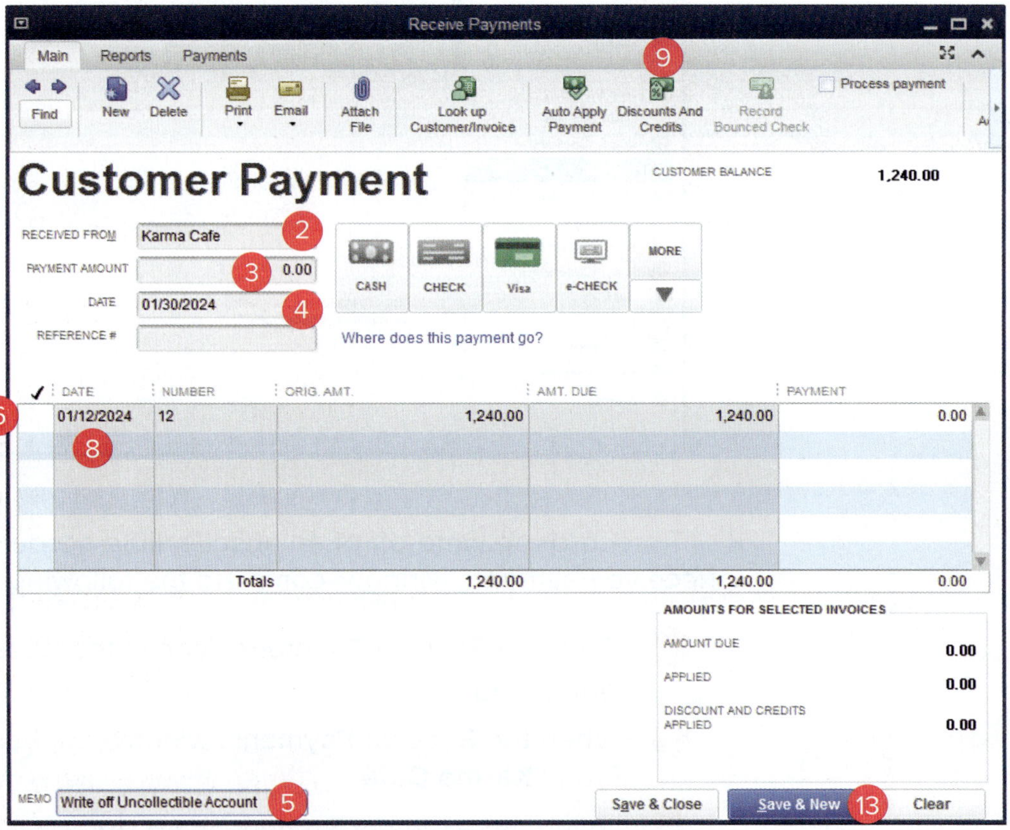

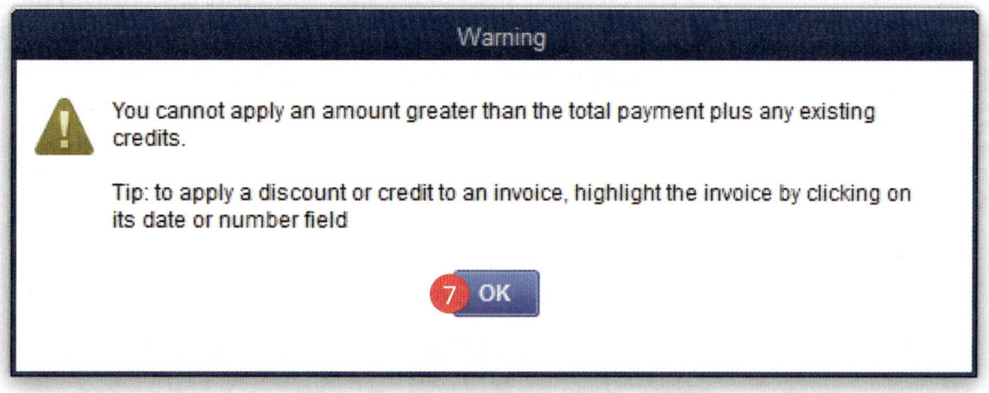
Warning
You cannot apply an amount greater than the total payment plus any existing credits.
Tip: to apply a discount or credit to an invoice, highlight the invoice by clicking on its date or number field
7
OK

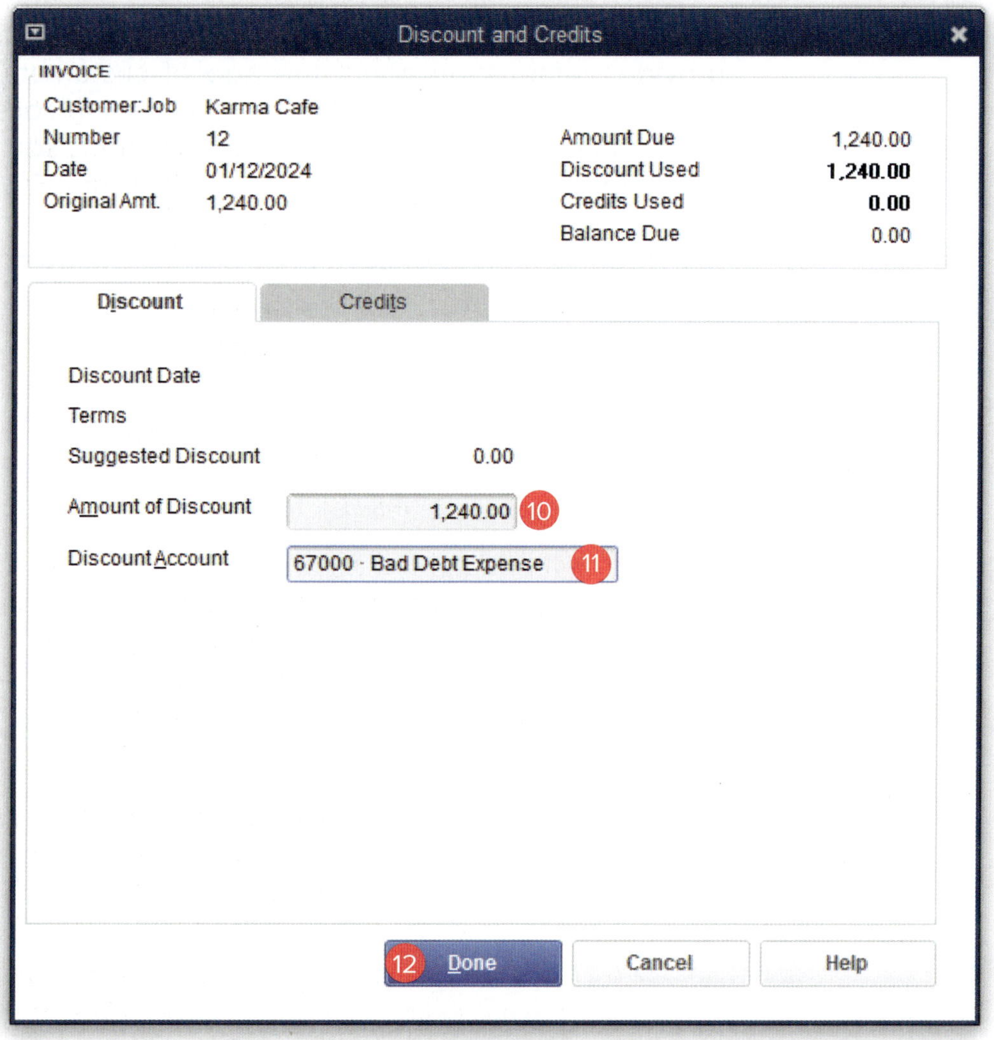
Discount and Credits
INVOICE
Customer:Job
Karma Cafe
Number
12
Date
01/12/2024
Original Amt.
1,240.00
Amount Due
1,240.00
Discount Used
1,240.00
Credits Used
0.00
Balance Due
0.00
Discount
Credits
Discount Date
Terms
Suggested Discount
0.00
Amount of Discount
1,240.00
10
Discount Account
67000 · Bad Debt Expense
11
12
Done
Cancel
Help

C15.7.1 Bad Debt Expense Journal Entry. To view the Journal entry that QuickBooks makes behind the screen when bad debt expense is recorded in this manner:

1. Select the **back Find arrow** until the Karma Cafe Receive Payment of $0.00 appears on the screen
2. Select the **Reports** tab
3. Select **Transaction Journal**
4. Export to **Excel** or **print** the Transaction Journal report
5. **Close** the Transaction Journal report and the Receive Payments windows

The Accounts Receivable Aging Summary report (discussed in Chapter 5) provides information about the age of customers' accounts receivable which can be useful for tracking and managing collections.

To reduce uncollectible customer accounts, some companies adopt a policy that requires customers to make a deposit or advance payment before beginning work on a project. In addition, companies often evaluate the creditworthiness of customers before extending credit.

Section 15.8

AUDIT TRAIL

The Audit Trail feature of QuickBooks permits you to track all changes (additions, modifications, and deletions) made to your QuickBooks records. When used appropriately, the Audit Trail feature improves internal control by tracking any unauthorized changes to accounting records. The owner (or manager) should periodically review the Audit Trail for discrepancies or unauthorized changes. The Audit Trail report is especially useful if you have more than one user for QuickBooks. This report permits you to determine which user made which changes.

> **Access to the Audit Trail** should be restricted to only the QuickBooks Administrator.

When you export the Audit Trail report to Excel, you can perform further analysis with the Auto Filter feature shown in the following example.

To illustrate how an accounting clerk, Ima M. Bezler, might attempt to embezzle funds, assume Ima pockets a customer's cash payment. If Ima just keeps the cash payment, the customer would receive another bill and possibly contact the company to complain, triggering an investigation into the customer's account activity. So Ima deletes any record of the customer's bill from QuickBooks.

> **Instead of deleting the bill, Ima might try to write off** the customer's account as uncollectible in order to ensure the customer does not receive another bill.

To test the Audit Trail feature, first record a customer invoice to Maria Cecilia for $120 using the Intuit Service Invoice template.

1. Select the **Create Invoices** icon
2. Select Template: **Service Date Invoice**
3. Select Invoice Date: **02/01/2024**
4. Select Customer Job: **Maria Cecilia Vaulted Kitchen**
5. Select Service Date: **02/01/2024**
6. Select Item: **Labor Mural**

7. Select Quantity: **3 hours**
8. Select **Save & Close** to close invoice

On 02/02/2024, Maria Cecilia pays her bill in cash. If Ima decides to keep the cash and delete the invoice (so that Maria Cecilia would not receive another bill), the Audit Trail maintains a record of the deleted invoice.

To delete the invoice:

1. Open the Cecilia invoice for $120 that you just created
2. Select **Edit Menu**
3. Select **Delete Invoice**
4. When asked if you are sure, select **OK**

The Audit Trail report will list the original transaction to record the $120 invoice and the change to delete the customer's $120 invoice.

To prepare the Audit Trail report:

1. From the Report Center, select **Accountant & Taxes**
2. Select **Audit Trail**
3. Select Dates: **All**
4. Select: **Run**

To create a filter to display **2024** transactions:

1. Select **Customize Report** > **Filters**
2. Remove Selected Filter: **Entered/Modified Today**
3. Choose Filter: **Date**
4. Select Date From: **01/01/2024 To: 12/31/2024**
5. Click **OK** to close the Modify Report window

C15.8.1. Audit Log. To export the Audit Trail to Excel:

1. Click the **Excel** button at the top of the Audit Trail window
2. Select: **Create New Worksheet**
3. Select **Replace an existing worksheet**
4. Select workbook: **YourLastName FirstName CH15 REPORTS.xls**

5 Select sheet: **C15.8.1 AUDIT**

6 Select the **Advanced** tab on the Send Report to Excel window

7 Uncheck: **Space between columns**

8 Check: **Auto Outline (allows collapsing/expanding)**

9 Check: **Auto Filtering (allows custom data filtering)**

10 Uncheck: **Include QuickBooks Export Guide worksheet with helpful advice**

11 Select Show report header: **On printed report and screen**

12 Select **OK** to close the Advanced Excel Options window

13 Select **Export**

14 **Highlight** the record of the deleted invoice dated 02/01/2024

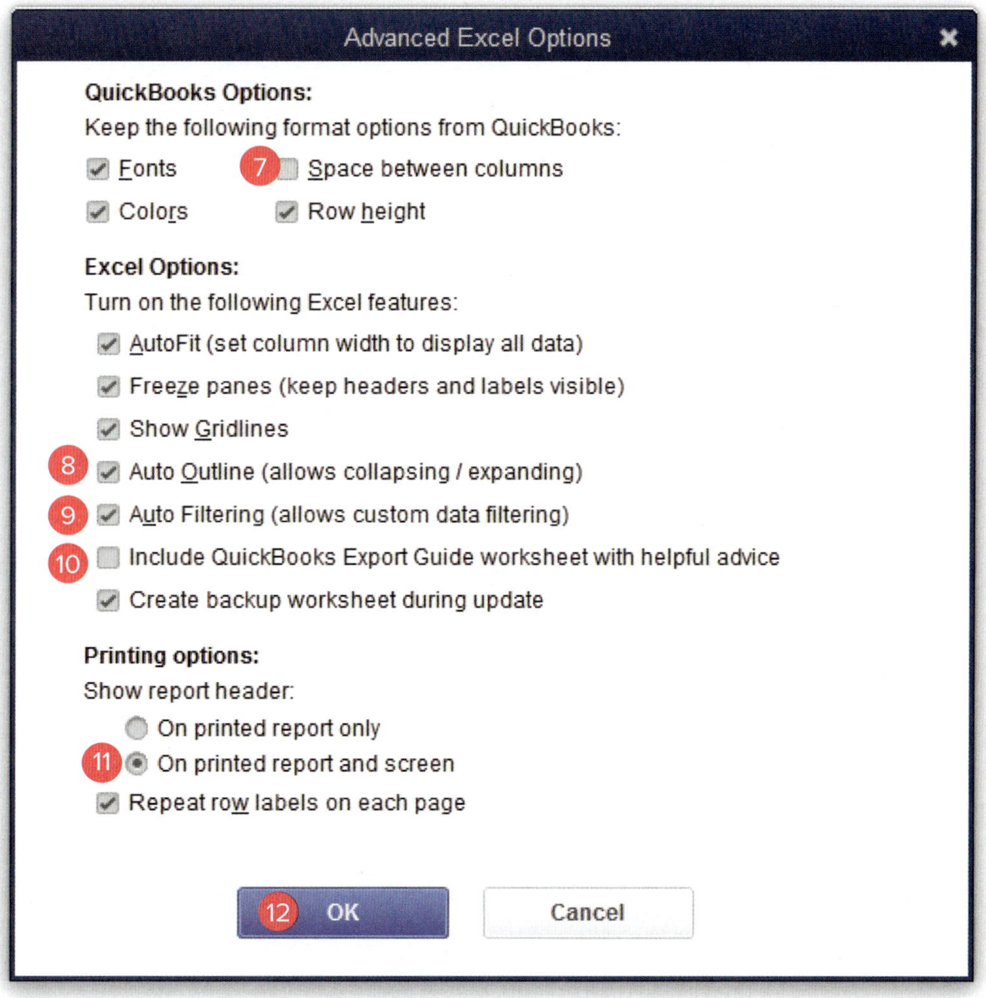

Notice in the Audit Trail report exported to Excel including the Auto Filter feature, each column heading becomes a drop-down list. This permits you to sort or select a filter of your choice from the drop-down lists. For example, you could use the Auto Filter to track all items recorded by a specific user (Last Modified by field).

To track deleted or changed items in the Audit Trail report, you can filter on the status of transactions to display Latest, Prior, or Deleted transactions (State field).

Note that the Audit Trail feature requires more storage for larger files because both original transactions and changed transactions are saved. So the Audit Trail feature may slow processing time.

Section 15.9

ACCOUNTANT'S COPY

If an accountant makes adjustments at year-end, QuickBooks can create a copy of the company data files for the accountant to use (Accountant's Copy). The accountant can make adjustments and changes to the Accountant's Copy. Then the Accountant's Copy is merged with the original company data. This permits the entrepreneur to continue using QuickBooks to record transactions at the same time the accountant reviews and makes changes to the records.

To create an Accountant's Copy of Paint Palette:

1. Select **File Menu**
2. Select **Send Company File**
3. Select **Accountant's Copy**
4. Select **Client Activities**
5. Select **Save File**
6. After reading the information on the Save Accountant's Copy window, select **Accountant's Copy**
7. Select **Next**
8. Select Dividing Date: **Custom 12/31/2024**
9. Normally you would select Next. In this case, select **Cancel.**

QuickBooks creates a copy of the QuickBooks company file for the accountant's temporary use. After the accountant has made necessary adjustments to the Accountant's Copy, the Accountant's Copy is then merged with the QuickBooks company data file, incorporating the accountant's changes into the company's records.

Section 15.10

ASK MY ACCOUNTANT

In the Chart of Accounts is an account entitled Ask My Accountant. Entrepreneurs using QuickBooks can use this account to record items when they are uncertain how to record specific items properly. The items can be recorded in this account and the accountant can review these items and record them properly before financial statements are prepared.

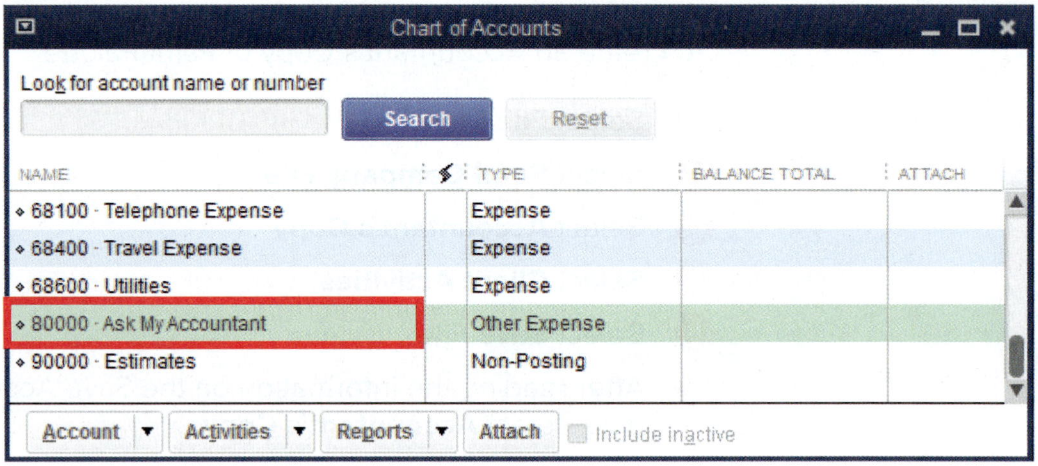

Section 15.11

BACK UP QUICKBOOKS FILES

BACK UP QBB

Save a backup of your Chapter 15 file using the file name: **YourName Chapter 15 Backup.QBB.**

QBW WORKFLOW

If you will be using the same computer to complete Chapter 15 QuickBooks exercises, just as in a business workflow, you can continue to use the same QBW file.

If you are using the QBW approach, leave your .QBW file open and proceed directly to Exercise 15.1.

QBB RESTORE

If you will be switching computers and are ending your computer session now, close your QBW file and exit QuickBooks. When you restart, you will restore your backup file to complete Exercise 15.1.

Section 15.12

ACCOUNTING ESSENTIALS

Bad Debts

Accounting Essentials summarize important foundational accounting knowledge that may be useful when using QuickBooks

What happens if a customer does not pay an accounts receivable balance?

- When a customer does not pay the accounts receivable balance, then it is called a bad debt or uncollectible account.
- At the time a credit sale occurs, it is recorded as an increase to sales and an increase to accounts receivable.
- Occasionally a company is unable to collect a customer payment and must write off the customer's account as a bad debt or uncollectible account. When an account is uncollectible, the account receivable is written off or removed from the accounting records.

What are two methods used to account for bad debts?

- There are two different methods that can be used to account for bad debts:
    1. **Direct write-off method.** This method records bad debt expense when it becomes apparent that the customer is not going to pay the amount due. If the direct write-off method is used, the customer's uncollectible account receivable is removed and bad debt expense is recorded at the time a specific customer's account becomes uncollectible. The direct write-off method is used for tax purposes.
    2. **Allowance method.** The allowance method estimates bad debt expense and establishes an allowance or reserve for uncollectible accounts. When using the allowance method, uncollectible accounts expense is estimated in advance of the write-off. The estimate can be calculated as a percentage of sales or as a percentage of accounts receivable. (For example, 2% of credit sales

might be estimated to be uncollectible.) This method should be used if uncollectible accounts have a material effect on the company's financial statements used by investors and creditors.

www.my-quickbooks.com

Go to **www.My-QuickBooks.com** to view additional QuickBooks resources including:

- **Excel Report Templates** to organize QuickBooks reports exported to Excel
- ***Computer Accounting with QuickBooks* updates,** sometimes required when there is a software update that affects the text
- **QuickBooks Video links**
- **QuickBooks Help and Support links**
- **Other QuickBooks Resources** to make learning QuickBooks easier and more effective
- **QuickBooks Issue Resolution** offers a guided approach to troubleshooting QuickBooks

> **Troubleshooting QuickBooks and Correcting Errors** are crucial QuickBooks skill to acquire. See www.My-QuickBooks.com > QB Issue Resolution for Troubleshooting QuickBooks tips. See Chapter 17, Quick Review Guide, for tips on Correcting Errors.

EXERCISE 15.1: QuickBooks Apps

The Intuit App Center features apps that work with QuickBooks, including apps that permit you to access your QuickBooks company data on your mobile phone.

1. From the Accountant Menu, select **Online Accountant Resources**
2. From the QuickBooks Accounting Software for Accountants window, select **3rd Party Apps.** From the Apps featured, select your favorite.
3. Summarize for your accounting clients why you consider your choice a worthwhile app for QuickBooks.

EXERCISE 15.2: Accountant Center

A QuickBooks feature designed for accounting professionals is the Accountant Center. To learn more about this feature:

1. To open the Accountant Center, from Accountant Menu, select **Accountant Center.**
2. From the Tools section of the Accountant Center window, select two Accountant tools and write a short email to send to your accounting firm staff summarizing information about how these tools can be used.

PROJECT 15.1

Germain Consulting

Project 15.1 is a continuation of Project 11.1.
To start Project 15.1, either:

- Open your Project 11.1 QuickBooks Company file (YourName Project 11.1.QBW) or
- Restore your Project 11.1 Backup file (YourName Project 11.1 Backup.QBB)

If you have issues with your QuickBooks file, contact your instructor for assistance.

QB SatNav

The focus of Project 15.1 is mastery of QuickBooks Desktop budgets, a type of report.

QB SatNav

1 QB SETTINGS

- Company Settings
- Chart of Accounts

2 QB TRANSACTIONS

> Money in *Money out >*

- Banking
- Customers & Sales
- Vendors & Expenses
- Employees & Payroll

3 QB REPORTS

- Reports

P15.1.1 Update Company Name

Update the QuickBooks Company name to **YourName Project 15.1 Germain Consulting.**

P15.1.2 Create a Profit and Loss Budget

Create a Profit and Loss Budget for Germain Consulting for the year 2024.

1. Enter the following budget items and amounts for January 2024.

Account No.	**47900**
Account	**Sales**
January 2024 Budget Amount	**$5,000**

Account No.	**64900**
Account	**Office Supplies (Expense)**
January 2024 Budget Amount	**$350**

Account No.	**67100**
Account	**Rent Expense**
January 2024 Budget Amount	**$900**

2. Use a **1%** monthly increase for each budget item. Enable compounding
3. Export to **Excel** the Profit and Loss Budget Overview report for 2024

P15.1.3 Back Up Project 15.1

Save a backup of your Project file using the file name: YourName Project 15.1 Backup.QBB. See *Appendix B: Back Up & Restore QuickBooks Files* for instructions.

PROJECT 15.2

YourName Floral Design

BACKSTORY

On January 1, 2024, you establish a retail store that specializes in flower arrangements and floral services.

QB SatNav

Project 15.2 is a comprehensive project that facilitates your mastery of QuickBooks Desktop. As shown in the following QB SatNav, Project 15.2 covers all three processes: QB Settings, QB Transactions, and QB Reports. This project provides you with the opportunity to integrate your knowledge of QuickBooks Desktop through all three phases of QB SatNav.

QB SatNav

1 QB SETTINGS

- Company Settings
- Chart of Accounts

2 QB TRANSACTIONS

> Money in Money out >

- Banking
- Customers & Sales
- Vendors & Expenses
- Employees & Payroll

3 QB REPORTS

- Reports

P15.2.1 New Company Setup

Create a new company in QuickBooks using the following information.

1. Use the EasyStep Interview to set up a new QuickBooks company.

Company name	**YourName Project 15.2 Floral Design**
Federal tax ID	**12-1234567**
Address	**222 Main Street**
City	**Sanderson**
State	**CA**
Zip	**94355**
Main Phone	**415-258-1356**
Email	**< Enter your email address >**
Industry	**Retail Shop or Online Commerce**
Type of organization	**S Corporation**
First month of fiscal year	**January**
File name	**YourName Project 15.2**
What do you sell?	**Both products and services**
How will you enter sales?	**Record each sale individually**
Sales tax	**Yes**
Estimates	**Yes**
Sales orders	**No**
Billing statements	**No**
Progress invoicing	**Yes**
Track bills you owe	**Yes**
Track inventory in QuickBooks	**Yes**
Track time	**Yes**
Employees	**No**
Start date	**01/01/2024**
Use recommended accounts	**Yes**
Bank account name	**Checking**
Bank account number	**8945612307**
Bank account balance	**0.00 as of 01/01/2024**

2. Click **Start Working** to exit QuickBooks Setup
3. Set preferences as follows:
   - Accounting preferences to **Use account numbers** in the Chart of Accounts
   - Accounting preferences to **uncheck Warn if transactions are 30 day(s) in the future**
   - Checking preferences to Open the Make Deposits form with **10100 Checking** account

P15.2.2 Add Customer & Job

1. Add the following customers to the Customer List.

Customer	**Martini, Graziella**
Address Info:	
First Name	**Graziella**
Last Name	**Martini**
Main Phone	**415-555-1270**
Address	**13 Marco Drive** **Bayshore, CA 94326**
Payment Settings:	
Payment Terms	**Net 30**
Sales Tax Settings:	
Tax Code	**Tax**
Tax Item	**State Tax**

Customer	**TJ Ryan Interiors**
Address Info:	
First Name	**TJ**
Last Name	**Ryan**
Main Phone	**415-555-4545**

Address	**15 Scotch Drive** **Bayshore, CA 94326**
Payment Settings:	
Payment Terms	**Net 30**
Sales Tax Settings:	
Tax Code	**Tax**
Tax Item	**State Tax**

Customer	**Juckem, Ella**
Address Info:	
First Name	**Ella**
Last Name	**Juckem**
Main Phone	**415-555-1976**
Address	**18 Appleton Drive** **Bayshore, CA 94326**
Payment Settings:	
Payment Terms	**Net 30**
Sales Tax Settings:	
Tax Code	**Tax**
Tax Item	**State Tax**

2. From the Customer Center, export to **Excel** the Customer List.

   ! When exporting to Excel, remember to select Advanced Excel Options:

   - Uncheck **Space between columns**
   - Check **Row height**
   - Uncheck **Include QuickBooks Export Guide worksheet with helpful advice**
   - Select **On printed report and screen**

P15.2.3 Add Vendors

1. Add the following vendors to the Vendor List.

Vendor	**Joseph Leasing**
Opening Balance	**$0.00 as of 01/01/2024**
Address Info:	
Company Name	**Joseph Leasing**
Full Name	**Joseph Asher**
Main Phone	**415-555-0412**
Address	**13 Appleton Drive** **Bayshore, CA 94326**
Payment Settings:	
Account No.	**2700**
Payment Terms	**Net 30**
Tax Settings:	
Vendor Tax ID	**37-1726354**
Additional Info:	
Vendor Type	**Service Providers**

Vendor	**Flowersbyweb**
Opening Balance	**$0.00 as of 01/01/2024**
Address Info:	
Company Name	**Flowersbyweb**
First Name	**Michael**
Main Phone	**415-555-4567**
Address	**63 Web Lane** **Bayshore, CA 94326**
Payment Settings:	
Account No.	**6300**
Payment Terms	**Net 30**

Tax Settings:	
Vendor Tax ID	**37-3571667**
Vendor Type	**Suppliers**
Vendor	**Baskets Galore**
Opening Balance	**$0.00 as of 01/01/2024**
Address Info:	
Company Name	**Baskets Galore**
Contact	**Alicia**
Main Phone	**415-555-8900**
Address	**678 Summers Avenue** **Bayshore, CA 94326**
Payment Settings:	
Account No.	**8100**
Payment Terms	**Net 30**
Tax Settings:	
Vendor Tax ID	**37-3527667**
Vendor Type	**Suppliers**

2. From the Vendor Center, export to **Excel** the Vendor List

P15.2.4 Add Items

1. Add the following items.

Item Type	**Inventory Part**
Item Name	**Basic Floral Kit**
Description	**Basic Floral Kit**
Cost	**20.00**
COGS Account	**50000 – Cost of Goods Sold**
Sales Price	**50.00**

Income Account	**46000 – Merchandise Sales**
Asset Account	**12100 – Inventory Asset**
Tax	**Tax**
Qty on Hand	**0 as of 01/01/2024**

Item Type	**Inventory Part**
Item Name	**Deluxe Floral Kit**
Description	**Deluxe Floral Kit**
Cost	**28.00**
COGS Account	**50000 – Cost of Goods Sold**
Sales Price	**65.00**
Income Account	**46000 – Merchandise Sales**
Asset Account	**12100 – Inventory Asset**
Tax	**Tax**
Qty on Hand	**0 as of 01/01/2024**

Item Type	**Inventory Part**
Item Name	**Roses (per dozen)**
Description	**Roses (per dozen)**
Cost	**10.00**
COGS Account	**50000 – Cost of Goods Sold**
Sales Price	**35.00**
Income Account	**46000 – Merchandise Sales**
Asset Account	**12100 – Inventory Asset**
Tax	**Tax**
Qty on Hand	**0 as of 01/01/2024**

Item Type	**Service**
Item Name	**Floral Design**
Description	**Floral Design**

Income Account **48600 – Service Sales**
<Add new account if necessary>

Item Type **Service**
Item Name **Wedding Designs**
Description **Wedding Designs**
Subitem of **Floral Design**
Rate **25.00**
Income Account **48600 – Service Sales**

Item Type **Service**
Item Name **Funeral Designs**
Description **Funeral Designs**
Subitem of **Floral Design**
Rate **20.00**
Income Account **48600 – Service Sales**

2. From the Item List, enter the 7.75% sales tax rate as follows:
   - **Double-click** on **State Tax** in the Item List
   - Enter Tax Rate: **9.75%**
   - Enter Tax Agency: **California State Board of Equalization**
   - Click **OK**
3. Export to **Excel** or **print** the Item List as of January 1, 2024. (Use Report Center > List > Item Listing.)

   ! When exporting to Excel, remember to select Advanced Excel Options:
   - Uncheck **Space between columns**
   - Check **Row height**
   - Uncheck **Include QuickBooks Export Guide worksheet with helpful advice**
   - Select **On printed report and screen**

P15.2.5 Customize Chart of Accounts

Edit the Chart of Accounts and enter opening balances as follows.

1. Add the following information to the Chart of Accounts with the opening balances as of 01/01/2024.

Account	**Checking**
Account No.	**10100**
Opening Balance	**$0.00**

Account	**Industrial Refrigerator**
Account No.	**14400**
Opening Balance	**$0.00**
Account Type	**Fixed Asset**
Account Description	**Industrial Refrigerator**
Tax Line	**B/S-Assets: Buildings/oth. depr. assets**

Account	**Industrial Refrigerator Cost**
Account No.	**14500**
Opening Balance	**$5,000**
Account Type	**Fixed Asset**
Subaccount of	**Industrial Refrigerator**
Account Description	**Industrial Refrigerator Cost**
Tax Line	**B/S-Assets: Buildings/oth. depr. assets**

Account	**Industrial Refrigerator Acc Dep**
Account No.	**14600**
Opening Balance	**$0**
Account Type	**Fixed Asset**
Subaccount of	**Industrial Refrigerator**
Account Description	**Industrial Refrigerator Accumulated Depreciation**
Tax Line	**B/S-Assets: Buildings/oth. depr. assets**

2. From the Report Center, export to **Excel** the Chart of Accounts (Account Listing) report as of January 1, 2024
3. **Export** to Excel or **print** a Trial Balance report dated 01/01/2024. Verify your Trial Balance account balances are correct.
4. Transfer the Opening Balance Equity account balance to the Capital Stock account using a journal entry. Use Entry No.: **Open ADJ1.** Select **Save.** Export the opening balance adjusting entry to **Excel** by selecting the **Reports tab > Transaction Journal.**
5. Export to **Excel** or **print** the Adjusted Trial Balance (after opening adjustments) to verify that the Opening Balance Equity account balance was transferred to the Capital Stock account.

P15.2.6 Enter Transactions

YourName Floral Design entered into the following transactions during January 2024.

1. Record the following transactions.
   - Record all deposits to: **Checking.**
   - If necessary, change the Make Deposits default to **Checking.** (Select Edit Menu > Preferences > Checking > My Preferences > Open the Make Deposits form with 10100 Checking account).

Date	Transaction
01/01/2024	You invest $6,000 (Check No. 101) in Capital Stock of the business
01/01/2024	Floral Designs takes out a bank loan from City Bank for $12,000, to be repaid within 1 year. (Use Make Deposits window. Add new Account No. 26100 Note Payable.)
01/01/2024	Received the bill and paid one month's rental ($250) to Joseph Leasing. (Use Enter Bills and Pay Bills windows.)
01/01/2024	Ordered the following from Baskets Galore on account. • 10 Basic Floral Kits • 5 Deluxe Floral Kits
01/03/2024	Received all 10 Basic Floral Kits and all 5 Deluxe Floral Kits ordered on 01/01/2024 from Baskets Galore

Date	Transaction
01/06/2024	Ordered 5 dozen roses from Flowersbyweb
01/07/2024	Provided an estimate of 12 Wedding Design Arrangements for Ella Juckem
01/07/2024	Received bill from Baskets Galore for 01/01/2024 order
01/07/2024	Received order in full from Flowersbyweb
01/08/2024	Received bill from Flowersbyweb
01/09/2024	Sold 1 Funeral Design Arrangement to TJ Ryan Interiors on account
01/10/2024	Awarded job from Ella Juckem
01/13/2024	Sent Ella Juckem invoice for completing half of the job
01/13/2024	Paid the following bills: • Paid Baskets Galore in full for merchandise ordered on 01/01/2024 • Paid Flowersbyweb for goods ordered on 01/06/2024
01/14/2024	Received payment from Ella Juckem (Check No. 1015) and deposited funds
01/21/2024	Sent Ella Juckem invoice for completing the job
01/28/2024	Received payment from Ella Juckem for completing job (Check No. 1022) and deposited funds
01/30/2024	Sold 2 dozen roses to TJ Ryan Interiors on account
01/31/2024	Received payment in cash from TJ Ryan Interiors for 2 dozen roses from 01/30/2024 and deposited the funds
01/31/2024	Sold 25 Wedding Designs and 3 dozen Roses to Graziella Martini on account

2. Export to **Excel** the Deposit Detail report for January 2024
3. Export to **Excel** the Check Detail report for January 2024

4. Export to **Excel** the Transaction Detail by Account report for January 2024. (From the Report Center, select Accountant & Taxes > Transaction Detail by Account.)

P15.2.7 Adjusting Entries

1. Export to **Excel** the Trial Balance report at January 31, 2024
2. Make adjusting entries at January 31, 2024, using the following information.

   ADJ1: Industrial Refrigerator depreciation expense is $75 per month
3. From the Report Center, export to **Excel** the Adjusting Journal Entries for January 31, 2024
4. Export to **Excel** the Adjusted Trial Balance report at January 31, 2024

P15.2.8 Financial Reports

Create the following reports.

1. Export to **Excel** the Journal for the month of January 2024
2. Export to **Excel** the Profit & Loss, Standard for the month of January 2024
3. Export to **Excel** the Balance Sheet, Standard at January 31, 2024
4. Export to **Excel** the Statement of Cash Flows for the month of January 2024
5. Export to **Excel** the Customer Balance Detail report for January 1 - 31, 2024
6. Export to **Excel** the Vendor Balance Detail report for January 1 - 31, 2024
7. Create and export to **Excel** a Profit and Loss Budget for 2024 based on the following information.
   - January projected merchandise sales: $2000. Monthly expected sales increase: 3% (compounding).
   - January rent: $250. Monthly rent increase: 1% (compounding).

P15.2.9 Back Up Project 15.2

Save a backup of your Project file using the file name: YourName Project 15.2 Backup.QBB. See *Appendix B: Back Up & Restore QuickBooks Files* for instructions.

Chapter 16

QuickBooks Desktop Versus QuickBooks Online

Your QuickBooks consulting business continues to grow as satisfied clients refer new clients. While most of your clients need the added functionality and features of QuickBooks Desktop software, a few clients have asked you about anytime, anywhere QuickBooks Online. Your challenge is to find the best fit to meet your clients' needs while at the same time keeping your consulting service operations streamlined and efficient.

To make informed recommendations to your clients, you realize you need to learn more about the various QuickBooks options offered by Intuit.

Section 16.1

ASK MY ACCOUNTANT: WHICH QUICKBOOKS SHOULD I USE?

To meet different QuickBooks users' needs, Intuit offers several different versions of QuickBooks. If you are an accountant advising different clients on the best fit between their needs and QuickBooks version, then a general knowledge of the different types of QuickBooks available becomes vital to provide sound client advice.

In general, QuickBooks versions can be divided into two broad categories:

- **QuickBooks User.** Businesses and organizations that use QuickBooks to maintain their accounting and financial records.
- **QuickBooks Accountant.** Accountants who provide accounting and financial services to multiple clients who use QuickBooks.

Since QuickBooks offers several different options (summarized in the following table), QuickBooks users often turn to their accountants for recommendations about which QuickBooks to use. The QuickBooks version that the client uses dictates which QuickBooks version the client's accountant must use. As the accountant making recommendations, you will need to consider not only how the recommendation affects your client, but also how the recommendation will impact your client services operations.

Quickbooks Versions	QuickBooks Desktop (QBDT)	QuickBooks Online (QBO)
Client/User	QuickBooks Pro	QuickBooks Online
	QuickBooks Premier	
	QuickBooks Enterprise	
Accounting Firm	QuickBooks Desktop Accountant	QuickBooks Online Accountant

When making client recommendations, keep in mind the difference between client needs and wants. Needs are critical; wants are wishes. Stay focused on needs first, so you do not become distracted and sidetracked with client wants, which can keep you from meeting client needs. An easy way to do this is to make two lists with needs on one list and wants on another list. After needs are addressed, then wants can be considered. Prepare your client to face tradeoffs, such as tighter control over data security versus anytime, anywhere access. Your role is to summarize the features and tradeoffs, assisting clients with finding a good fit, even if they do not attain 100% of what they thought they wanted.

Section 16.2

HOW CAN OUR ACCOUNTING FIRM STREAMLINE OUR QUICKBOOKS CONSULTING?

Which QuickBooks version your clients use affects your consulting services operations. Some accounting firms relate war stories about clients using an array of QuickBooks Desktop software from the 2002 edition and every year to the present edition. This approach to QuickBooks consulting requires the accounting firm to maintain all the various versions of the client software and track which clients use which versions. This can become a logistical nightmare for an accounting firm since it must have not only all the QuickBooks editions operational but also staff trained on the multiple versions.

Other accounting firms take a more streamlined, proactive approach when working with multiple clients that use QuickBooks. These firms recommend to clients which QuickBooks edition to use based on the best fit for the client while still keeping it manageable for the firm. Some accountants move all their clients to the next edition of QuickBooks at the same time. For example, after the 2018 QuickBooks edition is released in fall of 2017 and the accounting firm has thoroughly tested the new edition, the firm moves all clients to QuickBooks 2018 on January 1, 2018. This approach permits the accounting firm to test the new software for possible issues, install updates, and create workarounds before moving clients to the new edition. Since many clients are on a calendar year starting January 1, this timeline permits a nice cutoff. Also, this approach streamlines firm operations since now all clients and the firm are in sync, using the same version of QuickBooks.

This proactive approach requires the accounting firm to communicate clearly with clients, working as a team with clients to prepare and transition them to the new version. Firms that use this proactive approach often state that it requires time and effort to do so, but much less time than trying to maintain multiple versions of QuickBooks for multiple clients. If clients start moving to the new edition as soon as it is released, clients may encounter unexpected issues that the accounting firm has not had time to thoroughly investigate and resolve. Some firms even provide training for clients as they transition them to the new version, summarizing differences and new features to proactively prepare clients for what to expect. This can minimize client errors in working with the new version and save the firm from unexpected disruptions and surprises.

Although features and functionality of QuickBooks options can be expected to change over time, the following sections summarize information about some of the QuickBooks options for clients and accountants. For additional updates about each of these options, see www.Intuit.com.

Section 16.3

WHAT ARE MY QUICKBOOKS USER OPTIONS?

A QuickBooks user is a business, entrepreneur, or not-for-profit organization that uses QuickBooks to maintain accounting and financial records for that entity. A QuickBooks user has two basic options:

- **QuickBooks Desktop**
- **QuickBooks Online**

> **QuickBooks is designed for business use, not personal finance.** For personal financial records of the business owners, personal financial apps should be used, such as Quicken (Intuit's predecessor to QuickBooks) or Mint (now owned by Intuit).

If the QuickBooks user selects the QuickBooks Desktop option, then there are several additional choices to consider that are summarized next.

QUICKBOOKS DESKTOP: PRO, PREMIER, OR ENTERPRISE

QuickBooks Desktop software can be installed on the hard drive of desktop computers, laptops, or servers controlled by the user (client). If QuickBooks is installed on a network, it can be accessed by multiple QuickBooks users. QuickBooks Desktop software can be purchased using three different approaches:

1. **CD.** QuickBooks software is installed from a CD.
2. **Software download.** Since new desktop computers and laptops increasingly do not have CD drives, users can purchase a QuickBooks software key code and download the QuickBooks software using an Internet browser.
3. **Subscription.** Instead of purchasing QuickBooks software, the user can choose to pay a monthly subscription fee to use the software. The QuickBooks software is still downloaded to the desktop computer or laptop, but when the user decides to stop paying the monthly fee, the user's access to the QuickBooks software is blocked.

In general, QuickBooks Desktop offers several advantages over QuickBooks Online including:

- Additional features and functionality not offered by QuickBooks Online
- User control over desktop computer access and security
- User control over backups and access to backup data files
- Portability of backup and portable QuickBooks files
- Remote access to QuickBooks Desktop
- Navigation features to streamline use, such as the My Shortcuts Icon Bar and the Home Page with flowcharts
- Intuit offers the following different editions of the QuickBooks Desktop software to meet specific user needs, including:
    - QuickBooks Pro
    - QuickBooks Premier
    - QuickBooks Enterprise

QuickBooks Pro is a good option for small businesses that do not require industry-specific features because it is less expensive.

QuickBooks Premier offers more advanced features than QuickBooks Pro and permits you to customize QuickBooks by selecting a version with industry-specific features. QuickBooks Premier has different industry versions from which you can choose including the following.

- Contractor
- Manufacturing and Wholesale
- Nonprofit
- Professional Services
- Retailers
- General Business

QuickBooks Enterprise Solutions is designed for mid-size companies that have outgrown QuickBooks Premier. QuickBooks Enterprise can be used to track inventory at multiple locations and consolidate reports from multiple companies.

QUICKBOOKS ONLINE

Accessed using a browser and the Internet, QuickBooks Online typically has fewer features and functionality than the QuickBooks Desktop version. With QuickBooks Online, there is no software to install on your computer hard drive or local server. The main advantage to QuickBooks Online is its anytime, anywhere use, so long as Internet access is available. Factors to consider when using QuickBooks Online include:

- Internet connection needs to be a secure connection with data in transit encrypted. Using an open WiFi at a café or a hotel when traveling to access QuickBooks Online, while convenient, places data in transit at risk. Your login, password, and confidential financial data could be viewed by others.
- Fewer features and functionality than QuickBooks Desktop with features that will continue to change as QuickBooks Online is dynamically updated.
- The convenience of dynamic updates that occur automatically without needing to download and install.
- Loss of control over when updates occur, which may result in the need to learn new updates at unplanned times.
- Convenience of not needing to remember to make backup files.
- Loss of control over backup files.

QuickBooks Online Mobile App permits you to access your QuickBooks Online financial records from your iPad®, iPhone® or Android™ device.

Section 16.4

WHAT ARE MY QUICKBOOKS ACCOUNTANT OPTIONS?

Designed for accountants serving multiple clients, Intuit offers two QuickBooks Accountant options:

- **QuickBooks Desktop Accountant**
- **QuickBooks Online Accountant**

Which option the accountant chooses is typically dictated by client use because QuickBooks Desktop files are not compatible with QuickBooks Online. For example, if all the accounting firm's clients use QuickBooks Desktop software, then the accounting firm would use QuickBooks Accountant Desktop version. If the clients use QuickBooks Online, then the accountant would need to use QuickBooks Online Accountant. Some accounting firms have clients using QuickBooks Desktop versions and other clients using QuickBooks Online, so those accounting firms must use both QuickBooks Accountant Desktop and QuickBooks Online Accountant to be able to work with both types of clients.

QUICKBOOKS DESKTOP ACCOUNTANT

QuickBooks Desktop Accountant is the software provided free with this text if purchased new. Like QuickBooks Desktop software, QuickBooks Accountant in the Desktop edition is installed on the hard drive of desktop computers, laptops, or network servers. The QuickBooks Accountant edition permits the accountant to toggle between different Desktop user editions of QuickBooks. This permits the accountant to view whatever edition of QuickBooks (QuickBooks Pro, QuickBooks Premier, and so on) that a particular client uses. For additional features of QuickBooks Accountant in the Desktop edition, see Chapter 15.

QUICKBOOKS ONLINE ACCOUNTANT

QuickBooks Online Accountant is designed for accounting firms that provide services to multiple clients who use QuickBooks Online. QuickBooks Online Accountant is accessed using the Internet and a browser and permits the accountant to collaborate with several different clients, viewing their QuickBooks Online company files. QuickBooks Online Accountant, at this time, does not use the Home Page navigational feature. In addition, there are fewer features and functionality with the QuickBooks Online

Accountant version than the QuickBooks Accountant Desktop version. The main advantage to QuickBooks Online Accountant is the anytime, anywhere access when an Internet connection is available. Of course, since the accountant is responsible for maintaining the confidentiality of client financial data, the Internet connection needs to be a secure connection with data in transit encrypted. Using an open WiFi connection risks data in transit (such as your login, password, and confidential client financial data) being viewed by others. Since accounting firms have a responsibility to maintain client data confidentiality and security, this is a serious concern.

For more information about QuickBooks Online, visit My-QuickBooks Online.com.

EXERCISE 16.1: QuickBooks Online Versus QuickBooks Desktop

Compare and contrast QuickBooks Online and QuickBooks Desktop.

1. What are the advantages of QuickBooks Online versus QuickBooks Desktop for the user?
2. What are the disadvantages of QuickBooks Online versus QuickBooks Desktop?

EXERCISE 16.2: QuickBooks Online Accountant Versus QuickBooks Desktop Accountant

Compare and contrast QuickBooks Online Accountant and QuickBooks Desktop Accountant.

1. What are the advantages of QuickBooks Online Accountant versus QuickBooks Desktop Accountant?
2. What are the disadvantages of QuickBooks Online Accountant versus QuickBooks Desktop?

EXERCISE 16.3: QuickBooks Client

If a client is using QuickBooks Online, what are the corresponding QuickBooks options for the accountant to use?

Chapter 17

Quick Review Guide

For your convenience, this Quick Review Guide is designed for you as:

- A user friendly review guide for frequently used QuickBooks tasks
- A review guide to enhance your prep for the QuickBooks User Certification examination

This Quick Review Guide contains step-by-step instructions for frequently used QuickBooks tasks, providing you with a convenient, easy-to-use resource that summarizes essential tasks. The chapters in *Computer Accounting with QuickBooks* are designed as tutorials for you to initially learn the accounting software, providing numerous screen captures and detailed instructions. To improve long-term retention of your software skills, exercises and projects are designed with fewer instructions to test your understanding and, when needed, to develop your skill at quickly locating additional information to complete the task. The ability to seek out information as needed is an increasingly important skill in the rapidly changing business environment, and the design of *Computer Accounting with QuickBooks* seamlessly facilitates your development of this crucial skill.

In addition, the Quick Review Guide is designed to enhance your preparation for the QuickBooks User Certification exam. Organized around the 10 domains covered on the QuickBooks User Certification exam, this Quick Review Guide is designed to guide you in quickly reviewing key material efficiently.

QUICKBOOKS USER CERTIFICATION EXAM REVIEW GUIDE

After you have completed prior chapters of *Computer Accounting with QuickBooks,* use this Quick Review Guide to review for the QuickBooks User Certification examination.

WHAT IS THE QUICKBOOKS USER CERTIFICATION EXAMINATION?

The QuickBooks User Certification exam is an online exam that is proctored at authorized testing centers. The exam consists of multiple choice questions or simulations. The QuickBooks User Certification examination is a certification focused on QuickBooks users. The QuickBooks ProAdvisor certification is a different certification that is focused more on accountants who provide advisory services to QuickBooks clients.

To learn more about the QuickBooks Certification exam, go to Certiport.com and search for QuickBooks Certified User. This text covers QuickBooks Desktop certification.

WHAT IS ON THE QUICKBOOKS USER CERTIFICATION EXAMINATION?

The QuickBooks User Certification exam covers 10 domains. The following table provides you with information about the QuickBooks User Certification exam domains, content and approximate coverage.

	QuickBooks User Certification Domain
1	QuickBooks Setup
2	QuickBooks Utilities and General Product Knowledge
3	List Management
4	Items
5	Sales
6	Purchases
7	Payroll
8	Reports
9	Basic Accounting
10	Customization and Saving Time

WHY CONSIDER TAKING THE QUICKBOOKS USER CERTIFICATION EXAMINATION?

Passing the QuickBooks User Certification examination can add another credential to your resume. Employers often look for credentials that indicate skill and knowledge level as a baseline for employment.

HOW CAN THE QUICK GUIDE HELP ME REVIEW FOR THE QUICKBOOKS USER CERTIFICATION EXAMINATION?

This Quick Review Guide is mapped to the 10 domains of the QuickBooks User Certification exam to streamline your review for the exam.

The Quick Review Guide domain mapping to the QuickBooks User Certification follows.

Quick Review Guide Section	QuickBooks User Certification Domain
17.1	QuickBooks Setup
17.2	QuickBooks Utilities and General Product Knowledge
17.3	List Management
17.4	Items
17.5	Sales
17.6	Purchases
17.7	Payroll
17.8	Reports
17.9	Basic Accounting
17.10	Customization and Saving Time

WHAT IS AN EFFECTIVE REVIEW ACTION PLAN?

Consider the following action plan to increase the effectiveness of your review. Note that simply reading the instructions assists your review but deeper learning occurs when you actually complete the steps using the QuickBooks software.

1. Complete prior chapters of *Computer Accounting with QuickBooks.*
2. Download the file: **CHAPTER 17 STARTER.QBB** from www.mhhe.com/kay2018.
3. Restore the **CHAPTER 17 STARTER.QBB** file following the instructions in Appendix B for restoring a file. When restoring, use the filename **YourName Chapter 17.QBW.**

   ! *Important Note: With the new 2018 version of QuickBooks, there are some changes with regard to passwords.*

   - *When restoring a QBB file if QuickBooks requires you to create a password in order to continue, create your own password and record the password in a secure location, such as the inside cover of your textbook*

- *When restoring QuickBooks QBB files, if a password is requested:*
    - *Try using User ID: Admin and leave the Password field blank*
    - *If you are using the QBB Starter files and QuickBooks requires a password and QuickBooks will not accept the password field blank, try User ID: Admin and Password: KayQB2018*
    - *If none of the above approaches permit you to restore the QBB file, see your instructor*

4. Read and then complete the steps contained in this Quick Review Guide using the **YourName Chapter 17.QBW** file. To practice some of the tasks, simply insert realistic data to complete the forms.
    - Consider reviewing the Quick Review Guide a minimum of three times to improve your retention of the material.
    - Mark any tasks that you found challenging for later practice.
5. Try a practice exam.
    - Ask your instructor to provide you with a Chapter 17 Exam as an opportunity to practice multiple choice questions.
    - If you register to take the QuickBooks User Certification exam at www.Certiport.com, you will be provided with a code that permits you to take practice exams before you take the certification examination. Take a practice exam and see how well you do.

HOW DO I OBTAIN MORE INFORMATION ABOUT THE QUICKBOOKS USER CERTIFICATION EXAMINATION?

For more information, see www.Certiport.com or go to www.My-QuickBooks.com and click on QB Certified User.

Section 17.1

QUICKBOOKS SETUP

INSTALL QUICKBOOKS SOFTWARE

To install QuickBooks software, follow the step-by-step directions provided at www.My-QuickBooks.com or Appendix A: Install & Register QuickBooks Software.

REGISTER QUICKBOOKS SOFTWARE

Register or activate QuickBooks software at the time you install the software, following the directions provided at www.My-QuickBooks.com or Appendix A: Install & Register QuickBooks Software.

Failure to register or activate QuickBooks software within the first 30 days may result in the software no longer functioning. To avoid this, register the software at the time you install it. If you fail to register QuickBooks software within 30 days and you are locked out from using the software, select **Help Menu** > **Register QuickBooks.**

START QUICKBOOKS SOFTWARE

1. Click the QuickBooks desktop icon or click **Start** > **Programs** > **QuickBooks** > **QuickBooks Premier Accountant Edition** (or **QuickBooks Pro**).
2. If necessary, close the QuickBooks Learning Center window to begin using QuickBooks.

SET UP NEW COMPANY

1. Select **File Menu** > **New Company.**
2. Select **Detailed Start.** Follow the onscreen instructions to complete the EasyStep Interview to set up a new company. Also see Chapters 11 and 13.
3. Complete the QuickBooks Setup to add bank accounts, vendors, customers, employees, and items. Also see Chapters 11 and 13.

SET UP NEW COMPANY FROM EXISTING COMPANY

1. Select **File Menu** > **New Company from Existing Company File.**
2. Select **Browse.**
3. Select **a company to copy from.**
4. Enter **a name for the new company.**
5. Select **Create Company.**
6. Select **Save.**

CUSTOMIZE HOME PAGE

1. Select **Edit Menu** > **Preferences** > **Desktop View** > **Company Preferences.**
2. Select feature icons to appear on the Home Page.

SET UP LISTS

1. Select **Lists Menu** > **Add/Edit Multiple List Entries.**
2. Select **List** (Customers, Vendors, Service, Inventory or Non-Inventory).
3. **Customize columns** to display.
4. Paste from Excel or type to add or edit the list.
5. Select **Save Changes.**

Section 17.2

QUICKBOOKS UTILITIES AND GENERAL PRODUCT KNOWLEDGE

HOW TO NAVIGATE QUICKBOOKS

There are three basic ways to navigate QuickBooks:

1. Home Page
2. Menus
3. Navigation or Icon Bar with My Shortcuts.

See Chapter 1 for information about the three ways to navigate QuickBooks.

BACK UP COMPANY FILE (.QBB)

Backup company files (.QBB) are compressed company files. Typically, you will want to back up your company at regular intervals. To save a QuickBooks backup company file:

1. Select **File Menu** > **Back Up Company** > **Create Local Backup.**
2. Select **Local backup** > **Next.**
3. If requested, select location of backup file. Click **OK.**
4. Select **Use this Location.**
5. Select **Save it now** > **Next.**
6. Select location and backup filename (.QBB). Click **Save.**

Also see Appendix B: Back Up & Restore QuickBooks Files and Chapter 1.

RESTORE COMPANY FILE (.QBB)

Typically you restore a backup company file when the QuickBooks .QBW file fails. For purposes of this text, you will restore a backup file when you use the QBB Restore approach. For more information, see Appendix B: Back Up & Restore QuickBooks Files and Chapter 1.

To restore a QuickBooks backup company file:

1. Select **File Menu** > **Open or Restore Company.**
2. Select **Restore a backup copy** > **Next.**
3. Select **Local backup** > **Next.**
4. Select location of backup file and backup file name. Select **Open** > **Next.**
5. Select location and name of restored file. If saving to the hard drive, try saving to your desktop to make it easier to find the .QBW file later. If QuickBooks will not recognize your desktop, then save to the location that QuickBooks defaults to automatically for restoring the file. Make a note of the path and directory.
6. Click **Save.**
7. Click **OK.**

SAVE PORTABLE COMPANY FILE (.QBM)

Portable company files (.QBM) permit you to move your QuickBooks company file from one computer to another. To save a portable QuickBooks company file:

1. Select **File Menu** > **Create Copy.**
2. Select **Portable company file** > **Next.**
3. Enter the location and filename, then click **Save.**
4. Select **OK** to close and reopen your QuickBooks company file.

OPEN PORTABLE COMPANY FILE (.QBM)

To open a QuickBooks portable company file:

1. Select **File Menu** > **Open or Restore Company.**
2. Select **Restore a portable file** > **Next.**
3. Select the location and portable company file name (.QBM) to open. Select **Open** > **Next.**
4. Enter the QuickBooks working filename (.QBW) and location.
5. Click **Save.**

CHANGE COMPANY NAME

1. Select **Company Menu** > **My Company.** Or select **My Company** from My Shortcuts Icon Bar.
2. Select **Edit** icon.
3. Update Company Name.
4. Click **OK.**

VIEW VERSION AND RELEASE NUMBER

1. With QuickBooks software running, press the **CTRL** and **1** keys at the same time (**CRTL + 1**).
2. In the Product field of the Product Information window, find the version and release. (Example: QuickBooks Accountant R3P indicates the version is QuickBooks Accountant. R3P indicates it is release 3.)

UPDATE QUICKBOOKS SOFTWARE

To update QuickBooks software, first download the updates and then install the updates. To download the updates:

1. Verify that you have an Internet connection.
2. Select **Help Menu** > **Update QuickBooks Desktop.**
3. Click the **Options** tab.
4. If you would like QuickBooks to automatically update each time you connect to the Internet, select **Yes** for Automatic Update.
5. In the Updates section of the Options screen, select Updates: **Maintenance Releases, Help, Accountant, Data Protect.** Ask your instructor if you should select Payroll updates to download. If you download payroll updates, your answers may not match the text answers for payroll assignments.
6. To download an update, select **Update Now** tab > **Get Updates.** If asked if you want to update QuickBooks, click **Yes.**

To install the QuickBooks update:

1. **Exit** QuickBooks software, then **reopen** QuickBooks software.
2. At the prompt to install the update, select **Yes.**
3. After the update completes, **restart** your computer.

UPDATE QUICKBOOKS COMPANY FILE

To update your company file created using a previous version of QuickBooks (for example, to update a QuickBooks company file created in QuickBooks 2016 to QuickBooks 2018):

1. **Back up** your company file.
2. Using the newer version of QuickBooks, such as QuickBooks 2018 software, select **File Menu** > **Open or Restore Company.**
3. Select **Restore a backup copy** > **Next.**
4. Select **Local backup** > **Next.**
5. Select location of backup file for prior version of QuickBooks and backup file name. Select **Open** > **Next.**
6. When asked if you want to update the file, enter **YES** and click **OK.**

USE SINGLE-USER AND MULTI-USER MODES

1. If you are in multi-user mode, to switch to single-user mode select **File Menu** > **Switch to Single-user Mode** > **Yes.**
2. If you are in single-user mode, to switch to multi-user mode select **File Menu** > **Switch to Multi-user Mode** > **Yes.**

OPEN COMPANY FILE (.QBW)

To open a QuickBooks company file (.QBW) that is on the hard drive (C:) or that has been restored to the C: drive:

1. After QuickBooks software is open, select **File Menu** > **Open or Restore Company.**
2. Select **Open a company file (.QBW)** > **Next.**
3. Select the company file and location. Click **Open.**

CLOSE QUICKBOOKS COMPANY FILE (.QBW)

1. Select **File Menu.**
2. Click **Close Company.**

EXIT QUICKBOOKS SOFTWARE

1. Select **File Menu.**
2. Click **Exit.**

PASSWORD PROTECT QUICKBOOKS

1. Select **Company Menu** > **Set Up Users and Passwords** > **Set Up Users.**
2. Select **Add User** (or Edit User).
3. Enter **User Name.**
4. Enter **Password.**
5. Confirm **Password.**
6. Select **Next.** Select the appropriate QuickBooks user access settings.
7. Click **Finish.**

CUSTOMIZE QUICKBOOKS WITH PREFERENCES

To customize QuickBooks to fit your accounting software needs, you can select preferences as follows:

1. Select **Edit Menu** > **Preferences.**
2. From the left scroll bar Preferences window, select the category:
    - Accounting
    - Bills
    - Calendar
    - Checking
    - Desktop View
    - Finance Charge
    - General
    - Integrated Applications
    - Items & Inventory
    - Jobs & Estimates
    - Multiple Currencies
    - Payments
    - Payroll & Employees
    - Reminders

- Reports & Graphs
- Sales & Customers
- Sales Tax
- Search
- Send Forms
- Service Connection
- Spelling
- Tax: 1099
- Time & Expenses

3. Select the **My Preferences** tab or the **Company Preferences** tab.
4. Enter the preference settings you desire to customize QuickBooks.
5. When finished selecting preferences, click **OK.**

Section 17.3

LIST MANAGEMENT

MANAGE QUICKBOOKS LISTS

QuickBooks uses lists to record and organize information about:

- Customers
- Vendors
- Items (such as services, inventory, and non-inventory)
- Employees
- Other

There are several different ways to manage lists in QuickBooks. For example, the Customer List can be accessed from the Customer Center and the Vendor List accessed from the Vendor Center. Another option is to manage lists using the Add/Edit Multiple List Entries window as follows.

ADD NEW ENTRIES

To add new entries using the Add/Edit Multiple List Entries window:

1. Select **Lists Menu** > **Add/Edit Multiple List Entries.**
2. Select a type of list (such as Vendor) from the **List** drop-down menu.
3. **Customize Columns** to display in the list.
4. Enter or paste from Excel to add to the list.
5. Click **Save Changes.**

DELETE ENTRIES

To delete entries from a list using the Add/Edit Multiple List Entries window:

1. Select **Lists Menu** > **Add/Edit Multiple List Entries.**
2. Select a type of list (such as Customer) from the **List** drop-down menu.
3. Select the entry to delete.
4. **Right-click** > **Delete Line.**
5. Click **Save Changes.**

Note that typically entries related to transactions, such as customer entries related to invoices, cannot be deleted.

EDIT ENTRIES

To edit entries in a list using the Add/Edit Multiple List Entries window:

1. Select **Lists Menu > Add/Edit Multiple List Entries.**
2. Select a type of list (Customer, Vendor, and so on) from the **List** drop-down menu.
3. **Customize Columns** to display in the list.
4. Enter changes to the list entries.
5. Click **Save Changes.**

MERGE ENTRIES

To merge or combine entries on a list:

1. Select type of list (Customer, Vendor, Employee, or Item) from the **List** drop-down menu.
2. If your list has two names for the same vendor, for example, but one is misspelled, select the misspelled vendor name on the list, **right-click** then select **Edit.**
3. Type the correct name.
4. Click **OK.**
5. Click **Yes** when asked if you would like to merge this entry with the other entry with the same name.

After merging, only the correct name will appear on the list. QuickBooks will also merge the transactions for the two entries. Note that when merging accounts for the Chart of Accounts, only accounts with the same type (Income, Expense, and so on) can be merged.

IMPORT LISTS FROM EXCEL

To import lists of customers, vendors, accounts, or items from Microsoft Excel into QuickBooks:

1. Back up the QuickBooks company file.
2. Select **File Menu > Utilities > Import > Excel Files.**

3. When the Add/Edit Multiple List Entries window appears if you select **Yes,** QuickBooks will take you to the **Lists Menu** > **Add/Edit Multiple List Entries** to add/edit multiple lists. Further instructions follow in the next section.
4. If you select **No,** the Add Your Excel Data to QuickBooks window will appear.
5. From the Add Your Excel Data to QuickBooks window, click **Advanced Import** button.
6. Select the **Set up Import tab** > **Select A File** > **Mappings.**
7. Click the **Preference** tab. Select how to handle duplicates and errors.
8. Click **Preview.** Make appropriate corrections.
9. Click **Import.**

Another way to import data into Excel is using the Add/Edit Multiple List feature:

1. Select **Lists** > **Add/Edit Multiple List Entries.**
2. Select List (Customers, Vendors, Service, Inventory or Non-Inventory).
3. **Customize Columns** to display.
4. Paste from Excel or type to add or edit the list.
5. Select **Save Changes.**

You can also import data from Excel from the specific center. For example, to import the Customer List from Excel:

1. From the **Customer Center,** click the **Excel** button.
2. Select **Import from Excel.**
3. When the Add/Edit Multiple List Entries window appears, if you select **Yes,** QuickBooks will take you to the **Lists Menu** > **Add/Edit Multiple List Entries** to add/edit multiple lists.
4. If you select **No,** the Add Your Excel Data to QuickBooks window will appear. From this window, select the appropriate **type of data you want to add to QuickBooks** button.
5. Follow the onscreen instructions to copy your data into a spreadsheet formatted to work with QuickBooks.
6. **Save** the Excel file.

EXPORT LISTS TO EXCEL

You can export data to Microsoft Excel for customers, vendors, inventory items, transactions, payroll summary, and reports. For example, to export customer data to a new Excel workbook:

1. Click **Customers** on the Icon Bar.
2. Display the **Customer List.**
3. Click the **Excel** button. Select **Export Customer List.**
4. Select **Create new worksheet** > **in new workbook** > **Export.**
5. When the Excel file opens, save the Excel file.

Section 17.4

ITEMS

HOW TO USE QUICKBOOKS ITEMS

The QuickBooks Item List is used to track items purchased and sold. Types of items include:

- Service
- Inventory Part
- Inventory Assembly
- Non-inventory Part
- Group
- Discount
- Sales Tax Item

USE DIFFERENT TYPES OF ITEMS

When adding items to the Item List, the appropriate type of item is selected. This cannot be changed later. The three main types of items frequently used are service, non-inventory part, and inventory part.

- **Service item:** Use this item type for services you purchase or sell, such as labor, consulting hours, or professional fees.
- **Non-inventory part item:** Use this item type for goods you buy but don't need to track the quantity, such as office supplies or materials for a specific customer job that you will charge back to the customer.
- **Inventory part item:** Use this item type for goods you purchase, track as inventory, and resell to customers.

ADD ITEMS

1. From the **Company** section of the Home Page, click the **Items & Services** icon.
2. **Right-click** to display the pop-up menu. Select **New.**
3. Enter item information.

4. To enter another item, click **Next.**
5. When finished, click **OK.**

EDIT ITEMS

1. From the **Company** section of the Home Page, click the **Items & Services** icon.
2. After selecting the item you would like to edit, **right-click** to display the pop-up menu. Select **Edit** Item.
3. Edit item information.
4. When finished, click **OK.**

ENTER AN ITEM SELLING FOR A SPECIFIED PRICE

When a specific item is typically sold at the same specified price, that price can be entered in the Item List. This specified sales price will automatically appear on invoices when this item is selected.

To enter an item that sells at a specified price:

1. From the **Company** section of the Home Page, click the **Items & Services** icon.
2. **Right-click** to display the pop-up menu. Select **New.**
3. Select **Item Type.**
4. Enter item information.
5. Enter **Sales Price.** When the Sales Price is entered in the Item List, then this sales price will automatically appear on invoices when this item is selected. Note that this automatic price can be changed on the invoice when needed for a specific sale.
6. To enter another item, click **Next.**
7. When finished, click **OK.**

ENTER AN ITEM SELLING FOR DIFFERENT PRICES

When a specific item is typically sold at different prices, the price for that item can be left blank in the Item List. When the item is selected for sale on an invoice, the sales price will automatically appear as $0.00. Then you enter the price required for the specific sale on the invoice.

To enter an item that sells for different prices:

1. From the **Company** section of the Home Page, click the **Items & Services** icon.

2. **Right-click** to display the pop-up menu. Select **New.**
3. Select **Item Type.**
4. Enter item information.
5. Enter **Sales Price: 0.00.** When a Sales Price of $0.00 is entered for an item in the Item List, then $0.00 will automatically appear as the sales price on invoices when this item is selected. You can enter whatever price is required for the specific sale on the invoice.
6. To enter another item, click **Next.**
7. When finished, click **OK.**

Section 17.5

SALES (CUSTOMER TRANSACTIONS)

USE THE CUSTOMER CENTER

1. Click **Customers** on the Icon Bar.
2. From the Customer Center, you can view your Customer: Job List, enter new customers, edit current customers listed, enter new transactions, print or export to Excel, view transactions and contacts.

ENTER CUSTOMER INFORMATION

1. Click **Customers** on the Icon Bar.
2. Select **New Customer & Job** > **New Customer.**
3. Enter customer information.
4. Click **OK** to save and close the window.

ADD NEW JOB

1. Select the specific customer from the Customer List in the Customer Center.
2. With the customer selected, **right-click** to display the pop-up menu. Select **Add Job.**
3. Enter the Job Name and other job information.
4. Click **OK** to save and close the window.

INVOICE CUSTOMERS

1. From the **Customers** section of the Home Page, click the **Create Invoices** icon.
2. Enter invoice information.
3. Click the **Print** icon to print the invoice or the **Email** icon to email the invoice.
4. Click **Save & New** to enter another invoice or **Save & Close** to close the window.

RECEIVE CUSTOMER PAYMENTS

1. From the **Customers** section of the Home Page, click the **Receive Payments** icon.
2. Enter receipt information.
3. Click **Save & New** to enter another receipt or **Save & Close** to close the window.

DEPOSIT CUSTOMER PAYMENTS

1. From the **Banking** section of the Home Page, click **Record Deposits.**
2. Select **Payments to Deposit,** then click **OK.**
3. Select **Bank Account.** Enter **Date** and deposit information.
4. Click **Print** to print the deposit summary.
5. Click **Save & Close.**

CREATE SALES RECEIPTS

1. From the **Customers** section of the Home Page, click the **Create Sales Receipts** icon.
2. Enter receipt information.
3. Click **Save & New** to enter another receipt or **Save & Close** to close the window.

CREATE STATEMENTS

1. From the **Customers** section of the Home Page, click the **Statements** icon.
2. Select Statement Date, Statement Period, and Customer.
3. If requested, in the Select Additional Options section you can choose to show invoice item detail on the statement.
4. Click **Print** to print the invoice or **Email** to email the invoice.
5. Click **Close** to close the window.

CREATE PROGRESS INVOICE

1. Select **Edit** > **Preferences** > **Jobs & Estimates** > **Company Preferences.** Select Do you create estimates? **Yes.** Select Do you do progress invoicing? **Yes.**

2. From the **Customers** section of the Home Page, click the **Create Invoices** icon.
3. Select Template: **Progress Invoice.**
4. Select appropriate Customer and Job.
5. When asked, select appropriate estimate.
6. Enter the quantity or percentage of work completed to be billed.
7. Click **Save & New** to enter another receipt or **Save & Close** to close the window.

RECORD A CUSTOMER CREDIT

1. From the **Customers** section of the Home Page, click the **Refunds & Credits** icon.
2. Select the appropriate Customer and Job.
3. Enter credit information.
4. Click **Save & New** to enter another receipt or **Save & Close** to close the window.

ACCOUNT FOR BOUNCED NSF CHECK

When a customer check is returned by the bank because the customer has insufficient funds to cover the check, you must account for:

- The returned check
- Any bank fees you are charged by the bank
- Any fees you charge the customer for the NSF check

How you account for an NSF check depends upon which QuickBooks version you use. If you are using a QuickBooks version that has a bounced check feature, complete the following steps to account for the NSF check.

1. From the **Customers** section of the Home Page, select the **Receive Payments** icon.
2. From the Receive Payments window, select the customer payment associated with the bounced check. For example, find the customer payment for **Abercrombie, Kristie: Remodel Bathroom** on **12/15/2022** for **$7633.28.**
3. The Pmt. Method must have **Check** selected for the **Record Bounced Check** icon to be active in the Receive Payments window.

4. With the customer transaction for the bounced check appearing in the Receive Payments window, select the **Record Bounced Check** icon. (Note: if your Receive Payments window does not display a Bounced Check button: (1) the Pmt. Method was not Check, or (2) your QuickBooks version may not offer this feature.)
5. In the What did the bank charge you for this bounced check? section of the Manage Bounced Check window, enter amount for **Bank Fee.**
6. Enter **Date.**
7. Enter Expense Account: **60600 – Bank Service Charges.**
8. In the How much do you want to charge your customer? section of the Manage Bounced Check window, enter amount for **Customer Fee.**
9. Select **Next.**
10. A Bounced Check Summary window should appear summarizing what will happen in QuickBooks when you record the bounced check. QuickBooks will perform a series of steps to account for the bounced check:
    - The original customer invoice is marked unpaid.
    - The customer payment is stamped: Bounced Check.
    - The customer's bounced check that was deposited in your account will be deducted from your bank account. (A journal entry is made to increase accounts receivable and decrease your Checking account.)
    - The fee the bank charges you for bounced checks will be deducted from your bank account. (A journal entry is made to increase the Bank Service Charge Expense account and reduce your Checking account by the amount you are charged for the bank's NSF fee.)
    - A new invoice is created to charge the customer for the bounced check fee.
11. Select **Finish.**
12. Select **Save & Close** to close the Receive Payments window.

To create a collection letter to send the customer regarding a bounced check:

1. From the Customer List in the **Customer Center,** select the customer to receive the bounced check collection letter.
2. At the top of the Customer Center, click the **Word drop-down arrow > Prepare Letter to [Customer Name].**

3. In the Choose a Letter Template window, select **Bounced Check.**
4. Follow the onscreen instructions in the Letter and Envelopes wizard to create the customer's bounced check letter.

If your version of QuickBooks does not have the bounced check feature, approaches to account for the NSF check include the following:

- Create a credit memo for the NSF check and offset it against the corresponding customer invoice
- Create a new invoice for the NSF check including the bounced check fee charged the customer

The following instructions are an example of how to use a new invoice to account for an NSF check if your QuickBooks version does not have the bounced check feature.

First, create an item for tracking bounced (NSF) checks:

1. From the **Company** section of the Home Page, select **Items & Services.**
2. Select **Item** button > **New.**
3. Select Type: **Other Charge.**
4. Enter Item Name/Number: **Bounced Check.**
5. In the Amount or % field, leave: **0.00.**
6. In the Account field, select: **Checking.**
7. Click **Next** to enter another item. Leave the New Item window open.

Next create an item to track bad check charges that you charge customers for bounced checks.

1. With the New Item window still open, select Type: **Other Charge.**
2. Enter Item Name/Number: **Bad Check Charge.**
3. In the Amount or % field, leave: **0.00.**
4. In the Account field, select: <**Add New**>.
5. Select Account Type: **Income.**
6. Enter Account Name: **Returned Check Charges.**
7. Select **Save & Close** to close the Add New Account window. The Account field should now display Returned Check Charges.
8. Click **OK** to close the New Item window.

The next task is to re-invoice the customer for the bounced check plus any returned check charges.

1. From the **Customers** section of the Home Page, select **Create Invoices.**
2. From the customer drop-down list, select the customer and job related to the bounced check.
3. Select Item: **Bounced Check.**
4. In the Amount field, enter the amount of the bounced check. Note that this will reduce your bank account by the amount of the bad check.
5. Move to the second line item. Select Item: **Bad Check Charge.**
6. In the Amount field, enter the amount of returned check charges you want to recover from the customer.
7. The rest of the invoice can be completed as you normally would.
8. Select **Save & Close.**

Another related task is to see that any NSF fees the bank charges your company are recorded when you reconcile your company bank statement.

Section 17.6

PURCHASES (VENDOR TRANSACTIONS)

USE THE VENDOR CENTER

1. Select **Vendors** on the Icon Bar.
2. From the Vendor Center, you can view your Vendor List, enter new vendors, edit current vendors listed, enter new transactions, print or export to Excel, view transactions and contacts.

ENTER VENDOR INFORMATION

1. Select **Vendors** on the Icon Bar.
2. From the **Vendor Center,** click the **New Vendor** button > **New Vendor.**
3. Enter vendor information.
4. Click **OK** to save and close the window.

ENTER ITEMS

1. From the **Company** section of the Home Page, click the **Items & Services** icon.
2. **Right-click** to display the pop-up menu. Select **New.**
3. Select type of item.
4. Enter item information.
5. To enter another item, click **Next.**
6. When finished, click **OK.**

CREATE PURCHASE ORDERS

1. After entering items into the Item List, to record the purchase of inventory, from the **Vendors** section of the Home Page, click **Purchase Orders.**
2. Enter purchase information.
3. To enter another purchase order, click **Save & New.**
4. When finished, click **Save & Close.**

RECEIVE ITEMS

1. From the **Vendors** section of the Home Page, click **Receive Inventory.**
2. Select **Receive Inventory with Bill** or **Receive Inventory without Bill.**
3. Select the vendor. If asked if you want to match against outstanding purchase orders, click **Yes.**
4. Enter the remaining information.
5. To enter another item received, click **Save & New.**
6. When finished, click **Save & Close.**

ENTER BILLS AGAINST INVENTORY

1. From the **Vendors** section of the Home Page, click **Enter Bills Against Inventory.**
2. Select the vendor and choose the Item Receipt that corresponds to the bill.
3. Enter the remaining information.
4. To enter another bill, click **Save & New.**
5. When finished, click **Save & Close.**

ENTER BILLS

1. From the **Vendors** section of the Home Page, click **Enter Bills.**
2. Select the vendor.
3. Enter bill information.
4. Select Expenses or Items tab and select the appropriate account.
5. To enter another bill, click **Save & New.**
6. When finished, click **Save & Close.**

PAY BILLS BY CHECK

1. From the **Vendors** section of the Home Page, click **Pay Bills.**
2. Select **Show all bills.**
3. Select bills to pay.
4. Enter **Payment Date.**

5. Select Method: **Check.** Select appropriate Checking account.
6. Click **Pay Selected Bills.**

PRINT CHECKS

1. Select **File Menu** > **Print Forms** > **Checks** (or click the **Print Checks** icon in the **Banking** section of the Home Page).
2. Select **Bank Account.**
3. Enter **First Check Number.**
4. Select checks to print.
5. Click **OK.**
6. Select **Check Style.**
7. Click **Print.**

WRITE CHECKS

1. From the **Banking** section of the Home Page, click **Write Checks.**
2. Select **Bank Account.**
3. Enter **Check Date** and remaining check information.
4. Enter **Account** and **Amount.**
5. Select **Print Later.**
6. Click **Print** to print the checks.

PAY WITH CREDIT CARD

1. From the **Vendors** section of the Home Page, click **Pay Bills.**
2. Select **Show all bills.**
3. Select bills to pay.
4. Enter **Payment Date.**
5. Select Method: **Credit Card.** Select appropriate account.
6. Click **Pay Selected Bills.**

PAY WITH DEBIT CARD

1. From the **Vendors** section of the Home Page, click **Pay Bills.**
2. Select **Show all bills.**

3. Select bills to pay.
4. Enter **Payment Date.**
5. Select Method: **Check.**
6. Select **Assign check number.**
7. Select appropriate Checking account.
8. Click **Pay Selected Bills.**
9. Assign check number **DC** for Debit Card. Click **OK.**

PAY WITH ONLINE BANK PAYMENT

1. From the **Vendors** section of the Home Page, click **Pay Bills.**
2. Select **Show all bills.**
3. Select bills to pay.
4. Enter **Payment Date.**
5. Select Method: **Online Bank Pmt.** Select appropriate account.
6. If appropriate, select **Include reference number.**
7. Click **Pay Selected Bills.**

RECORD VENDOR CREDIT

To record a vendor credit:

1. From the **Vendors** section of the Home Page, click **Enter Bills.**
2. Select **Credit** (instead of Bill) near the top of the Enter Bills window.
3. From the drop-down list, select the appropriate **vendor.**
4. Enter the **credit amount.**
5. Select the **account** used to record the initial expense or item.
6. To enter another vendor credit, click **Save & New.**
7. When finished, click **Save & Close** to save the credit memo.

To apply the credit memo against a specific bill:

1. From the **Vendors** section of the Home Page, click **Pay Bills.**
2. Select the bill that you would like to apply the credit to.
3. If the amount of the credit needs to be adjusted, select **Set Credits.**
4. Enter amount of credit in the **Amount To Use** column for the bill(s).
5. Click **Done** to close the Discount and Credits window.

6. Select any other bills to pay.
7. Click **Pay Selected Bills.**
8. Select **Done** or **Print Checks** to close the Payment Summary window.

HOW TO SET UP, COLLECT AND PAY SALES TAX

To set up sales tax:

1. Select **Edit Menu** > **Preferences** > **Sales Tax** > **Company Preferences** (or from the **Vendors** section of the Home Page, select **Manage Sales Tax** > **Sales Tax Preferences**).
2. Select Do you charge sales tax? **Yes.**
3. Select **Add sales tax item.** Enter and save sales tax item information for each county or sales tax district where you collect sales tax.
4. Select your most common **sales tax item** from the drop-down list.
5. Select **Accrual** or **Cash Basis** as appropriate for When Do You Owe Sales Tax?
6. Select appropriate answer for When Do You Pay Sales Tax?
7. Click **OK** to close the Preferences window.
8. When entering customer information into the Customer List, select the appropriate sales tax settings for the specific customer from the New/Edit Customer window by selecting **Sales Tax Settings** tab > **Tax Code** > **Tax Item.**

To collect sales tax:

1. When using the Create Invoices or Create Sales Receipts windows, enter the customer information and items sold. The Tax column should automatically reflect the sales tax settings entered in the Customer List for the specific customer.
2. If necessary, select the appropriate sales tax item from the Tax drop-down list on the Create Invoices or Create Sales Receipts windows.

To pay sales tax:

1. From the **Vendors** section of the Home Page select **Manage Sales Tax** > **Pay Sales Tax.**
2. From the Pay Sales Tax window, enter the **Pay From Account.**
3. Select **Check Date.**
4. Select **Show sales tax due through** date.
5. Check the sales taxes to pay.
6. Click **OK,** then print checks to pay sales taxes.

RECONCILE BANK STATEMENT

1. From the **Banking** section of the Home Page, click **Reconcile.**
2. Select **Bank Account.**
3. Enter **Statement Date** and **Ending Balance.**
4. Enter **Service Charges** and **Interest Earned.**
5. Click **Continue.**
6. Check deposits and checks that appear on the bank statement.
7. Click **Reconcile Now.**

Section 17.7

PAYROLL (EMPLOYEE TRANSACTIONS)

WAYS TO PROCESS PAYROLL WITH QUICKBOOKS

There are two general ways that a company can process payroll using QuickBooks:

- Manually calculate payroll taxes.
- Use a QuickBooks payroll service.

QuickBooks offers three different levels of payroll services:

1. **Basic Payroll.** Basic payroll service creates paychecks using automatic calculation of payroll tax deductions. Tax forms for filings are not automatically prepared so the entrepreneur must complete the tax forms or work with an accountant on payroll tax filings.
2. **Enhanced Payroll.** Enhanced payroll service creates paychecks using automatic calculation of payroll tax deductions and generates payroll tax forms for filings automatically.
3. **Full Service Payroll.** Full service payroll automatically calculates payroll tax deductions and processes payroll taxes and filings for the entrepreneur.

HOW TO SET UP PAYROLL

1. Select **Edit Menu** > **Preferences** > **Payroll & Employees** > **Company Preferences** > **Full Payroll.**
2. Enter **Employee Defaults.**
3. Click **OK** to close the Preferences window.
4. Select **Employees Menu** > **Payroll Setup.**
5. Complete the QuickBooks Payroll Setup.

See Chapters 8 for more information about payroll setup.

ADD PAYROLL ITEM

1. Select **Employees Menu** > **Manage Payroll Items** > **New Payroll Item.**
2. Select **EZ Setup** > **Next.**

3. Select type of payroll item, such as Insurance Benefits. Click **Next.**
4. After the Payroll Setup Interview loads, select the appropriate payroll items, such as Health Insurance. Click **Next.**
5. Answer any remaining questions about the payroll item(s).
6. Select **payees,** appropriate **accounts,** and **payment frequency.**
7. Click **Finish.**

EDIT PAYROLL ITEM

To edit a payroll item:

1. Select **Employees Menu** > **Manage Payroll Items** > **View/Edit Payroll Item List** to open the Payroll Item List.
2. Select the specific payroll item you would like to edit. **Right-click** and select **Edit.**
3. If necessary, edit the name of the payroll item. Click **Next.**
4. Answer the questions regarding the payroll item, then click **Next.**
5. Click **Finish.**

Next, enter employee information as needed for payroll item deductions.

ENTER EMPLOYEE INFORMATION

1. Select **Employees** on the Icon Bar.
2. From the **Employee Center,** click the **New Employee** button.
3. Enter employee information.
4. Click **Next** to enter another employee or click **OK** to save and close the window.

TRACK TIME FOR PAYROLL

1. From the **Employees** section of the Home Page, select **Enter Time** icon > **Use Weekly Timesheet.**
2. Select **Employee Name.**
3. Select **Week.**
4. Enter time worked (if needed, select customer and service item).
5. To enter another timesheet, click **Save & New.**
6. Click **Print** to print the timesheets.
7. When finished, click **Save & Close.**

TRACK TIME FOR INVOICING CUSTOMERS

See the preceding Track Time for Payroll for instructions on entering time using the weekly timesheet.

To transfer time worked to customer invoices:

1. From the **Customers** section of the Home Page, select **Create Invoices.**
2. Select the customer and job from the Customer:Job drop-down list.
3. If necessary, select **Add Time/Costs.**
4. When the Billable Time/Costs window appears, click: **Select the outstanding billable time and costs to add to this invoice?** Click **OK.**
5. Select **Time** tab. Select time to transfer to the invoice and appropriate options. Click **OK.**
6. Complete the rest of the invoice.
7. When finished, click **Save & Close.**

TRACK SICK AND VACATION TIME

To track sick and vacation time for employees, when setting up payroll, select the appropriate options for sick and vacation time. To adjust sick or vacation time for a specific employee:

1. Select **Employees** on the Icon Bar.
2. From the Employee List, double-click on the employee's name to open the Edit Employee window.
3. Select **Payroll Info** tab.
4. Select Sick Hourly, Sick Salary, Vacation Hourly or Vacation Salary from the Item Name drop-down list.
5. Choose the **Accrual period** from the drop-down list.
6. Select other sick and vacation options as needed.
7. When finished, click **OK** to close the Sick and Vacation window.
8. Click **OK** to close the Edit Employee window.

SET UP PAYROLL SCHEDULES

1. From the **Employees** section of the Home Page, select **Payroll Center.**
2. If this is the first scheduled payroll, from the **Pay Employees** section, select **Start Scheduled Payroll > Set up Now.**
3. If a payroll schedule already exists and you are adding another payroll schedule, from the **Pay Employees** section, select **New** from the Payroll Schedules drop-down.

4. In the New Payroll Schedule window, enter the name for the payroll schedule.
5. Enter how often you will pay employees on this schedule.
6. Select what date should appear on paychecks for this pay period.
7. Click **OK.**

PAY EMPLOYEES

1. From the **Employees** section of the Home Page, click **Pay Employees.**
2. In the **Pay Employees** section of the Employee Center: Payroll Center window, select **Start Scheduled Payroll** or **Start Unscheduled Payroll.**
3. In the Enter Payroll Information window, enter **Pay Period Ends** and **Check Date.**
4. Select **Employee name.** Select **Open Paycheck Detail.**
5. Enter withholding and deduction amounts. Select **Save & Close.**
6. Continue until all employee paychecks are completed. Then click **Continue.**
7. Click **Create Paychecks.**
8. Click **Print Paychecks** to print the paychecks.

PAY PAYROLL LIABILITIES

1. From the **Employees** section of the Home Page, select **Pay Liabilities.**
2. In the **Pay Liabilities** section, select payroll liabilities you would like to pay.
3. Select **View/Pay.**
4. Select **E-payment** or **Check.**
5. When finished, click **Save & Close.**

PREPARE PAYROLL FORMS

1. From the **Employees** section of the Home Page, select **Process Payroll Forms.**
2. Select **Federal form** or **State form.** Click **OK.** (Forms available to select depends upon the payroll service.)
3. Choose the form you want to use.
4. Click **OK.**

Section 17.8

REPORTS

USE THE REPORT CENTER

You can access the Report Center in the following ways:

1. Select **Reports** from the Icon Bar, My Shortcuts.
2. Select **Reports Menu** > **Report Center.**

After opening the Report Center to display a report:

1. Select the report type.
2. Select the report.
3. Select **Date.**
4. Click **Run.**

CUSTOMIZE REPORTS

1. From the **Report Center,** display the desired report.
2. Select **Customize Report** near the top of the report window.
3. Select from **Display, Filters, Header/Footer,** and **Fonts & Numbers** tabs to customize your report.
4. Select **OK.**

EXPORT REPORTS TO EXCEL

To export reports to Microsoft Excel:

1. Using the **Report Center,** display the desired report.
2. Click the **Excel** button at the top of the report window.
3. Select **Create New Worksheet** or **Update Existing Worksheet** as appropriate.
4. If you are replacing a worksheet in an existing worksheet, select **Replace Existing Worksheet.** Select the appropriate workbook and sheet.
5. If you would like to add Auto Outline or Auto Filtering to your Excel worksheet, select **Advanced.** Select **Auto Outline** and/or **Auto Filtering.** Select **OK.**

6. Click **Export.**
7. When the Excel file opens, save the Excel file.

MEMORIZE REPORTS

1. From the **Report Center,** display the report that you wish to memorize.
2. Select **Memorize** at the top of the report window.
3. In the Memorize Report window, enter the **Name** you wish to use for the report.
4. Select **Save in Memorized Report Group** and specify the group.
5. Click **OK.**
6. Close the report window.

PRINT TRIAL BALANCE

1. From the **Report Center,** select **Accountant & Taxes** > **Trial Balance.**
2. Select **Dates.**
3. Click **Run** icon.
4. Click **Excel** or **Print.**

PRINT GENERAL JOURNAL

1. From the **Report Center,** select **Accountant & Taxes** > **Journal.**
2. Select **Dates.**
3. Click **Run** icon.
4. Click **Excel** or **Print.**

PRINT GENERAL LEDGER

1. From the **Report Center,** select **Accountant & Taxes** > **General Ledger.**
2. Select **Dates.**
3. Click **Run** icon.
4. Select **Customize Report** > **Advanced.** Select to show only accounts **In Use.**
5. Click **Excel** or **Print.**

PRINT INCOME STATEMENT

1. From the **Report Center,** select **Company & Financial.**
2. Under the **Profit & Loss (Income Statement)** section, select **Profit & Loss Standard.**
3. Select **Dates.**
4. Click **Run** icon.
5. Select **Customize Report** > **Display** tab. Select the type of Report Basis needed for your income statement: **Accrual** or **Cash.** Click **OK.**
6. Click **Excel** or **Print.**

PRINT BALANCE SHEET

1. From the **Report Center,** select **Company & Financial.**
2. Under the **Balance Sheet & Net Worth** section, select **Balance Sheet Standard.**
3. Select **Dates.**
4. Click **Run** icon.
5. Click **Excel** or **Print.**

PRINT STATEMENT OF CASH FLOWS

1. From the **Report Center,** select **Company & Financial.**
2. Under the **Cash Flow** section, select **Statement of Cash Flows.**
3. Select **Dates.**
4. Click **Run** icon.
5. Click **Excel** or **Print.**

Section 17.9

BASIC ACCOUNTING

BASIC FINANCIAL STATEMENTS

Three basic financial statements often used when evaluating an organization's performance are:

1. Income statement (also called Profit and Loss or P & L). The income statement measures revenues and expenses over a period of time, such as one year.
2. Balance sheet (also called a statement of financial position). The balance sheet measures assets (items with future benefit), liabilities (obligations), and owner's equity (the residual left when liabilities are subtracted from assets).
3. Statement of cash flows. The statement of cash flows has three main sections: cash flows from operations, cash flows from financing activities, and cash flows from investing activities.

To create these three main financial statements, see preceding Section 17.8 Reports.

DIFFERENCE BETWEEN CASH AND ACCRUAL

The cash basis and accrual basis are two different ways of measuring revenues and expenses. The cash basis uses cash inflows and cash outflows. For example, an income statement on the cash basis measures cash inflows received for revenues and cash outflows paid for expenses.

The accrual basis uses the matching principle to measure revenues and expenses. In general when the accrual basis is used, revenues are recorded when the goods or services are provided to the customer (earned). Expenses are matched against revenues earned.

To select Accrual basis for a report:

1. From the **Report Center,** open the desired report, such as the income statement.
2. Select **Customize Report** > **Display** tab.
3. Select Report Basis: **Accrual.**
4. Select **OK.**
5. **Print** or **export** the report to Excel.

To select Cash basis for a report:

1. From the **Report Center,** open the desired report, such as the income statement.
2. Select **Customize Report** > **Display** tab.
3. Select Report Basis: **Cash.**
4. Select **OK.**
5. **Print** or **export** the report to Excel.

ENTER NEW ACCOUNTS

1. From the **Company** section of the Home Page, click the **Chart of Accounts** icon.
2. **Right-click** to display the pop-up menu. Select **New.**
3. Enter **Type of Account, Account Number, Name, Description,** and **Tax Line.**
4. Click **Save & New** to enter another account.
5. Click **Save & Close** to close the Add New Account window.

ENTER BEGINNING ACCOUNT BALANCES

1. If the account has a beginning balance, when entering the new account, from the Add New Account (or Edit Account) window, select the **Enter Opening Balance** button.
2. Enter the **Opening Balance** and the **As of Date** for the beginning balance.
3. Click **OK.**

PRINT CHART OF ACCOUNTS

1. From the **Report Center,** select **Accountant & Taxes** > **Account Listing.**
2. Enter **Date,** select **Run,** then **Excel** or **Print.**

JOURNAL ENTRIES

1. Select **Accountant Menu** > **Make General Journal Entries.** (For QuickBooks Pro, select **Company Menu** > **Make General Journal Entries.**)

2. Enter **Date, Entry Number, Accounts,** and **Debit** and **Credit** amounts.
3. Click **Save & New** to enter another journal entry.
4. Click **Save & Close** to close the Make General Journal Entries window.

ADJUSTING ENTRIES

1. Select **Accountant Menu** > **Make General Journal Entries.** (For QuickBooks Pro, select **Company Menu** > **Make General Journal Entries.**)
2. Enter **Date, Entry Number (ADJ#), Accounts,** and **Debit** and **Credit** amounts.
3. **Check** the **Adjusting Entry checkbox.**
4. Click **Save & New** to enter another journal entry.
5. Click **Save & Close** to close the Make General Journal Entries window.

CORRECTING ENTRIES

To correct an error, make two correcting entries in the Journal:

1. Eliminate the effect of the incorrect entry by making the opposite journal entry.

For example, assume the Cash account should have been debited for $200.00 and the Professional Fees Revenue account credited for $200.00. However, the following incorrect entry was made for $2,000.00 instead of $200.00.

Debit	*Cash*	*2,000.00*
Credit	*Professional Fees Revenue*	*2,000.00*

To eliminate the effect of the incorrect entry, make the following entry:

Debit	*Professional Fees Revenue*	*2,000.00*
Credit	*Cash*	*2,000.00*

2. After eliminating the effect of the incorrect entry, make the following correct entry that should have been made initially:

Debit	*Cash*	*200.00*
Credit	*Professional Fees Revenue*	*200.00*

In addition to correcting entries, QuickBooks provides a number of additional ways to correct errors. For more information about correcting errors in QuickBooks, see My-Quickbooks.com, QB Issue Resolution.

CLOSING

Before closing a fiscal period, prepare adjusting entries and print all reports needed. To close the fiscal period:

1. Select **Edit Menu > Preferences > Accounting > Company Preferences.**
2. In the Closing Date section, select **Set Date/Password.**
3. Enter the **Closing Date.** If desired, enter and confirm the **Closing Date Password.**
4. Click **OK.**

Section 17.10

CUSTOMIZATION/SAVING TIME AND SHORTCUTS

MEMORIZE TRANSACTIONS

1. Enter the transaction into the appropriate form (Enter Bill, Create Invoice, and so on).
2. Select the **Memorize** icon.
3. Enter **Name** for the memorized transaction.
4. Select **How Often.**
5. Select **Next Date.**
6. Click **OK.**

SET UP MULTIPLE USERS WITH ACCESS

1. Select **Company Menu** > **Set Up Users and Passwords** > **Set Up Users.**
2. Select **Add User** (or **Edit User**).
3. Enter **User Name.**
4. Enter **Password.**
5. Confirm **Password.**
6. Select **Next.** Then complete the following QuickBooks user access settings.
7. Click **Finish.**

CREATE CUSTOM FIELDS

1. Open the appropriate list, such as customer, vendor, or employee list.
2. With your cursor over the list, **right-click** and select **New** or **Edit.**
3. Select the **Additional Info** tab > **Define Fields.**
4. In the Label column of the Setup Custom Fields for Names window, enter the name you wish to use for the custom field.

5. Select Use for: **Customer, Vendor** and/or **Employee.**
6. Click **OK** to close the Set up Custom Fields for Names window.
7. Click **OK** to close the customer, vendor, or employee window.

CUSTOMIZE AN INVOICE

First, create a copy of an existing invoice template:

1. From the **Customers** section of the Home Page, select **Create Invoices.**
2. Select the **Create a Copy** icon near the top of the Create Invoices window.
3. If a QuickBooks Information window appears informing you that a duplicate invoice has been created, click **OK** to close it.

Next, customize the layout of the duplicate invoice template:

1. Select the **Template** that you wish to customize.
2. Select the **Formatting** tab near the top of the Create Invoices window.
3. Select the **Customize Data Layout** icon.
4. Select Basic Customization, Layout Designer, or appropriate tabs (Header, Columns, Prog Cols (Progress Invoice Columns), Footer, or Print) to customize your invoice.
5. When finished, click **OK.**

Chapter 18

QuickBooks Consulting Project

Chapter 18 provides an opportunity to apply the knowledge and skills you have acquired thus far to an authentic QuickBooks project. You will assume the role of a consultant providing QuickBooks consulting services to a client. This project provides an opportunity for realistic, valuable practical experience to better prepare you for professional employment as well as enhance your resume.

The chapter contains a project management framework to guide you through the development of an accounting system for entrepreneurs or not-for-profits using QuickBooks Desktop accounting software. The system development approach provided in this chapter can be used with various types of organizations, allowing for flexibility to customize the system to meet the specific needs of the entrepreneur or not-for-profit.

Consistent with a sound project management approach, the consulting project is divided into seven milestones. Each milestone should be reviewed by your instructor before you proceed to the next milestone. In addition, the QuickBooks Consulting Project Approval form should be signed by the client as each step is completed and approved.

The project management framework for developing a real QuickBooks accounting system consists of the following seven milestones.

Milestone 1. Develop a proposal. In this milestone, you will identify a real-world client (either a small business or a nonprofit organization) that needs assistance in establishing an accounting system using QuickBooks. After identifying the client, gather information from the client and develop a plan for a QuickBooks accounting system that will meet the client's needs.

Milestone 2. Develop a prototype or sample QuickBooks accounting system for the client. Set up a company in QuickBooks with a sample Chart of Accounts for the client to review. After obtaining approval of the Chart of Accounts from the client and your instructor, enter beginning balances for the accounts.

Milestone 3. Develop sample QuickBooks lists for customers, vendors, items, and employees. Obtain client and instructor approval for the lists and enter the list information.

Milestone 4. Enter sample transactions to test the prototype and then memorize the transactions in QuickBooks.

Milestone 5. Identify the reports that the client needs and then create memorized reports using QuickBooks.

Milestone 6. Develop documentation for the project including instructions for future use.

Milestone 7. Present the final project first to your class and then to the client.

This project can be completed individually or in teams. Ask your instructor which approach you will be using.

Section 18.1

MILESTONE 1 PROPOSAL

For Milestone 1, you will create a project proposal. The purpose of the proposal is twofold. First, it forces you, the consultant, to plan the project from start to finish. Second, the proposal serves to improve communication between you and your client. When the client reads your proposal, there is an opportunity for the client to further clarify any misunderstandings. Furthermore, the client may think of additional information or user requirements that were not mentioned earlier.

Complete the following steps to create a project proposal:

1. Identify a real QuickBooks project.
2. Gather project information and user requirements.
3. Write the project proposal.

IDENTIFY QUICKBOOKS PROJECT

The first step is to identify an actual client who needs a QuickBooks accounting system. The client can be an entrepreneur, small business, or not-for-profit organization. For example, the client can be a friend or relative who operates a small business and needs an updated accounting system. Some colleges have Service Learning Coordinators who assist in matching student volunteers with charitable organizations needing assistance.

> **! Note:** It is important to inform the client that this is a class project and all work should be reviewed by his or her own accountant to verify appropriateness. Check with your instructor to see if your instructor or college requires a client waiver, indicating that the client will have all work reviewed and approved by an appropriate professional.

GATHER QUICKBOOKS PROJECT INFORMATION AND USER REQUIREMENTS

After identifying the client, the next step is to interview the client to determine specific accounting needs and user requirements. Communication is extremely important to the process of designing and developing a successful accounting system. Listening to the client's needs and then communicating to the client the possible solutions are part of the ongoing development process. If clients are not familiar with accounting or QuickBooks, they may not be able to communicate all of their needs. This requires you to gather enough information from the client to identify both the need and the solution. To make the most effective use of your client's time during the interview, prepare in advance. Before the interview, review all seven milestones of the project to identify the types of information you need to collect. For example, when gathering information for the Customer List, what customer fields does the client need? Also review the QuickBooks New Company Setup (see Chapters 11 and 13) to make certain you ask your client the questions you will need to answer when setting up the new company QuickBooks file for your client.

When collecting information about the Chart of Accounts, first identify the tax return filed by the enterprise. This will help you determine the accounts that are needed for tax purposes. Then, collect information about the assets, liabilities, equity, revenue and expense accounts that the company currently uses. Also, collect information about the beginning balances for accounts with opening balances.

> ! **Note:** All information the client shares with you is confidential and should not be shared with anyone else. If you need to share information of a confidential nature with your instructor, first ask the client's permission.

Prior to your interview, create your own User Requirements Checklist for gathering information from the client. A sample checklist follows.

Milestone 1 User Requirements Checklist

- Organization name
- Type of business (industry)
- Chart of Accounts information
- Type of Tax Return Filed: Schedule C, Form 1120 or Form 1120S
- Beginning account balances
- Customer List information
- Vendor List information
- Employee List information
- Item List information
- Types of transactions to be recorded
- Types of reports needed

- Users of the QuickBooks system and security access
- Other user requirements

PREPARE QUICKBOOKS CONSULTING PROJECT PROPOSAL

After gathering information from the client, write a proposal that describes your plan for designing and developing your project. The proposal is a plan of what you intend to accomplish and how you will accomplish it.

Your proposal should have a professional appearance and tone that communicates to your client your competency and your enthusiasm for his or her project. Components of the proposal include:

1. **Cover Letter.** In the cover letter, you can thank the client for the opportunity to work together on this QuickBooks project, provide a brief introduction about yourself, summarize the main points in your proposal, and provide your contact information if the client has questions.
2. **Executive Summary.** The Executive Summary should include the following.
   - The project name, your name, client name, and the date.
   - Project objectives and initial feasibility assessment.
   - Possible solutions that would meet project objectives.
   - Your recommendation for the project and supporting rationale.

   See the following Executive Summary Template for more information.

	Executive Summary Template
Company Name	[Your consulting name and logo]
Contact Name	[Your name]
Date	[Date of proposal]
Client	[Client name]
Project Name	[QuickBooks project name]
Objectives	[Paragraph 1 contains a concise summary of the project objectives and the initial feasibility assessment.]

	Executive Summary Template
Possible Solutions	[Paragraph 2 briefly summarizes possible solutions that satisfy the project objectives.]
Recommendation	[Paragraph 3 contains your recommendation and supporting rationale.]

3. **Proposal Report.** Include the following headings and sections:
   - **Overview and Objectives.** Briefly describe the client organization and operations. Identify the client's user requirements for an accounting system. For example, the client needs accounting records for tax purposes. Evaluate the feasibility of meeting the organization's needs with QuickBooks and the objectives of this project.
   - **Scope of Services.** Outline the services that you will provide for the client. What accounting features of QuickBooks will be implemented? Accounts receivable? Accounts payable? Specify the services you will provide the client. Will you provide implementation and setup? Conversion assistance?
   - **Client Responsibilities.** Clearly specify any responsibilities or information that the client will need to provide.
   - **Cost/Benefit Analysis.** Provide a summary of the costs associated with the project that the client might expect to occur. Provide information about the benefits that might be expected, including financial and nonfinancial benefits. For example, estimated time that the client might save in maintaining accounting records.
   - **Timeline.** Identify and list the major tasks involved in completing the project. Include a timeline with completion dates for each task. See the sample format below.

Task	Projected Completion Date
1. ____________________	___/___/_____
2. ____________________	___/___/_____
3. ____________________	___/___/_____
4. ____________________	___/___/_____

Task	Projected Completion Date
5. ______________________	___/___/_____
6. ______________________	___/___/_____
7. ______________________	___/___/_____

- **Recommendation.** State your recommendation and provide a short summary including any disclaimers or remaining challenges. End the proposal on a positive, upbeat note.

Submit the proposal to both the client and your instructor. Obtain approval from both the client and your instructor. Ask the client to sign off on the proposal using the approval form that appears at the end of Chapter 18.

Section 18.2

MILESTONE 2 COMPANY SETUP

In this milestone, you will set up a prototype or sample company for the client to review and revise.

1. Based on the information collected from the client, set up a new company and customize the Chart of Accounts for the company.
2. Submit the Chart of Accounts to your instructor for review and recommendations.
3. Have the client review the Chart of Accounts and make recommendations. Ask the client to sign off on the Chart of Accounts using the approval form.
4. After obtaining approval from both the client and instructor, enter beginning balances for the accounts.

Note: Nonprofits use fund accounting. Use sub accounts or the class tracking preference for fund accounting. In addition, Intuit offers a fund accounting version of QuickBooks.

Section 18.3

MILESTONE 3 CUSTOMER, VENDOR, EMPLOYEE AND ITEM LISTS

After the Chart of Accounts has been approved, develop lists (customer, vendor, employee, and item) for the client.

1. After consulting with the client, list the customer information (fields) needed for each customer. If necessary, create user-defined fields in QuickBooks to accommodate the client's needs.
2. List the information needed by the organization for each vendor. Create any user-defined fields that are needed for vendors.
3. List the employee information needed by the organization for each employee. Determine any payroll items needed to accurately record payroll. If applicable, collect payroll year-to-date information.
4. Determine the items (inventory, non-inventory, and service items) required to meet the organization's needs. List the information needed for each item.
5. After obtaining approval for the lists from the client and your instructor, enter information for the following:
   - Customer List
   - Vendor List
   - Employee List
   - Item List
   - Payroll year-to-date information

Section 18.4

MILESTONE 4 MEMORIZED TRANSACTIONS

Complete the following steps for Milestone 4.

1. Determine the types of transactions the client will enter in QuickBooks (for example: cash sales, credit card sales, purchase orders).
2. Enter test or sample transactions in QuickBooks. Obtain client and instructor approval of the results.
3. Modify forms as needed to meet the client's needs. For example, if the client needs a Date column on the invoice, customize the invoice by following the instructions in Chapter 11.
4. After obtaining the client's approval for transactions, create memorized transactions for the transactions that will be repeated periodically.

Customizing the Chart of Accounts. As you develop the accounting system, you may find that further customization of the Chart of Accounts is needed to meet specific business needs. In your final project, highlight any new accounts added.

It is important that you and the client reach an agreement regarding what you will complete before you turn the project over to the client. Discuss with the client whether you will be entering only a few sample transactions or entering all transactions for the year to date. For example, if entering all transactions is too time consuming, you may agree that you will enter only sample transactions and the client will enter the real transactions after you submit the final project.

Section 18.5

MILESTONE 5 MEMORIZED REPORTS

Complete the following steps for Milestone 5.

1. Determine which reports the client needs. Review Chapters 5 through 10 to obtain information about the different reports that QuickBooks can generate. You may need to make the client aware of the reports that are available in QuickBooks and then let the client select the reports that would be useful.
2. Obtain client and instructor approval for the reports.
3. After obtaining approval concerning the reports, create and memorize the reports using QuickBooks.

Section 18.6

MILESTONE 6 DOCUMENTATION AND CLIENT INSTRUCTIONS

Create documentation for the client. Include a history of the project development as well as instructions that the client will need. For example, instructions regarding how and when to back up and restore company files are essential. Providing instructions on how to use memorized transactions and memorized reports is also advisable.

An easy way to provide the client with adequate instructions is to recommend existing training materials to the client and then simply reference pages in the training materials. For example, if the client obtains a copy of this book, you may wish to reference pages of the text for each task the client will be performing.

Other documentation that the client might find useful is the QuickBooks Year-End Guide. To view the Year-End Guide, select **Help** menu > **Year-End Guide.**

QuickBooks Help. Provide the client with instructions for using QuickBooks Help feature.

Be prepared for clients to ask if they may call if they need your assistance in the future. Adequate user instructions (Milestone 6) are essential in reducing the client's future dependence on you.

Section 18.7

MILESTONE 7 PRESENTATION

There are three parts to this milestone:

1. Make any final changes to your project.
2. Make the project presentation to your class.
3. Make a project presentation to the client.

The presentation to your instructor and classmates is practice for the final presentation to the client. You may want to ask your classmates for suggestions you can incorporate into your final presentation for the client.

A suggested outline for the project presentation follows:

1. **History and Overview.** Provide background about the client and the client's needs as an introduction for your presentation.
2. **Demonstration.** If the room has projection equipment, demonstrate your QuickBooks project. Display memorized transactions, memorized reports, and lists for the class and/or client to view. Remember to use test/sample data for the class presentation instead of actual client data that is confidential.
3. **Examples.** Present examples of the documentation and client instructions you are providing the client (see Milestone 6).
4. **Cost/Benefit and Advantages/Disadvantages.** Briefly present advantages and disadvantages of using QuickBooks for this particular project as well as associated costs and benefits.
5. **Summary.** Present concluding remarks to summarize the major points of your presentation.
6. **Questions and Answers.** Provide classmates or the client an opportunity to ask questions about the project. In preparing for your presentation, you will want to anticipate possible questions and prepare appropriate answers.

QuickBooks Consulting Project Approval			
Milestone	**Notes**	**Approved**	**Date**
1. Proposal		____________	___/___/_____
2. Company Setup & Chart of Accounts		____________	___/___/_____
3. Lists: Customers, Vendors, Employees & Items		____________	___/___/_____
4. Memorized Transactions		____________	___/___/_____
5. Memorized Reports		____________	___/___/_____
6. Documentation		____________	___/___/_____
7. Final Presentation		____________	___/___/_____

Appendix A

Install & Register QuickBooks Software

INSTALL QUICKBOOKS SOFTWARE

To install your QuickBooks trial version software that accompanies *Computer Accounting with QuickBooks:*

1. Go to **www.My-QuickBooks.com**
2. Select **QB2018** link
3. Scroll down to **Download and Install QuickBooks Software**
4. Follow the instructions to download and install the QuickBooks software
5. **Register/Activate the QuickBooks software following the instructions provided**

For more accountant resources, select **Help menu** > **Ask Intuit** > **Download & Install.**

If you already have another version of QuickBooks software installed on your computer, you can select to replace it with the newer version or to install both versions. If your QuickBooks software fails to install, try uninstalling any prior versions of QuickBooks and then reinstalling QuickBooks 2018 software.

! **QuickBooks Accountant** software comes with new texts. If you purchase a used text, be aware that the QuickBooks software codes may already have been used and expired.

REGISTER QUICKBOOKS SOFTWARE

You can use the QuickBooks trial version for 30 days without registering. Three ways to register your QuickBooks trial version are:

1. Register the software when you install it
2. Select **Help menu** > **Register QuickBooks**
3. Register your QuickBooks software by phone at 888-246-8848 or 888-222-7276 and select the appropriate menu option

If you are locked out from using the software, select **Help menu** > **Register QuickBooks.** If that is unsuccessful, try uninstalling and reinstalling the QuickBooks software.

> **! Register your QuickBooks software!** Failure to register your QuickBooks trial version software will result in the software no longer functioning.

Appendix B

Back Up & Restore QuickBooks Files

QuickBooks File Versions

QuickBooks software uses a company file to store information about a specific enterprise. Thus, you can use the QuickBooks software installed on your computer with many different company files. This is similar to using Microsoft Excel software, for example, with many different Excel data files.

The different versions of QuickBooks company files are summarized in the following table.

Extension	QuickBooks File
.QBW	**QuickBooks for Windows.** You can think of this file as a QuickBooks working file. This is the file version that you use to enter transactions and data. It is usually saved to the hard drive of your computer.
.QBB	**QuickBooks Backup.** A QuickBooks Backup file should be created at regular intervals in case your .QBW file fails or is destroyed. The .QBB file version is a compressed file and cannot be opened directly. Furthermore, you cannot enter transactions directly into a .QBB file. Instead, you must unzip the file first by restoring the file into a .QBW file version.
.QBM	**QuickBooks Mobile.** A QuickBooks Mobile file, also called a QuickBooks Portable file, is used to move a QuickBooks file to another computer. Like the .QBB backup file version, the .QBM file version is compressed and must be unzipped and restored into a .QBW file version before it can be used to enter data.

.QBX	**QuickBooks Accountant.** A QuickBooks Accountant Copy is identified with a .QBX extension. This version of the company file is given to the accountant. The accountant can make changes, such as adjusting entries, to the .QBX version of the company file while the .QBW company file is used to continue entering transactions.

QuickBooks File Management

QuickBooks file management involves managing your QuickBooks company files to ensure the security and integrity of your QuickBooks accounting system.

In a typical business workflow, you use the same .QBW computer file on the same computer. Sound file management includes making backups as part of a disaster recovery plan. A good backup system is to have a different backup for each business day: Monday backup, Tuesday backup, Wednesday backup, and so on. Then if it is necessary to use the backup file and the Wednesday backup, for example, fails, the company has a Tuesday backup to use. Furthermore, it is recommended that a business store at least one backup at a remote location.

If a company's .QBW file fails, then you must restart by restoring your most recent .QBB file version. The backup file (.QBB) is compressed and must be converted to a working file (.QBW) before you can use it to enter data or transactions.

The following diagrams illustrate when you will back up and restore for purposes of this text. Note that we will be using a new QBB Starter file provided with the text for each chapter (except Chapters 11, 12, 13, 14, 16, and 18). For the projects, instead of restarting each project by restoring a Starter file, we will continue to use our QBW file.

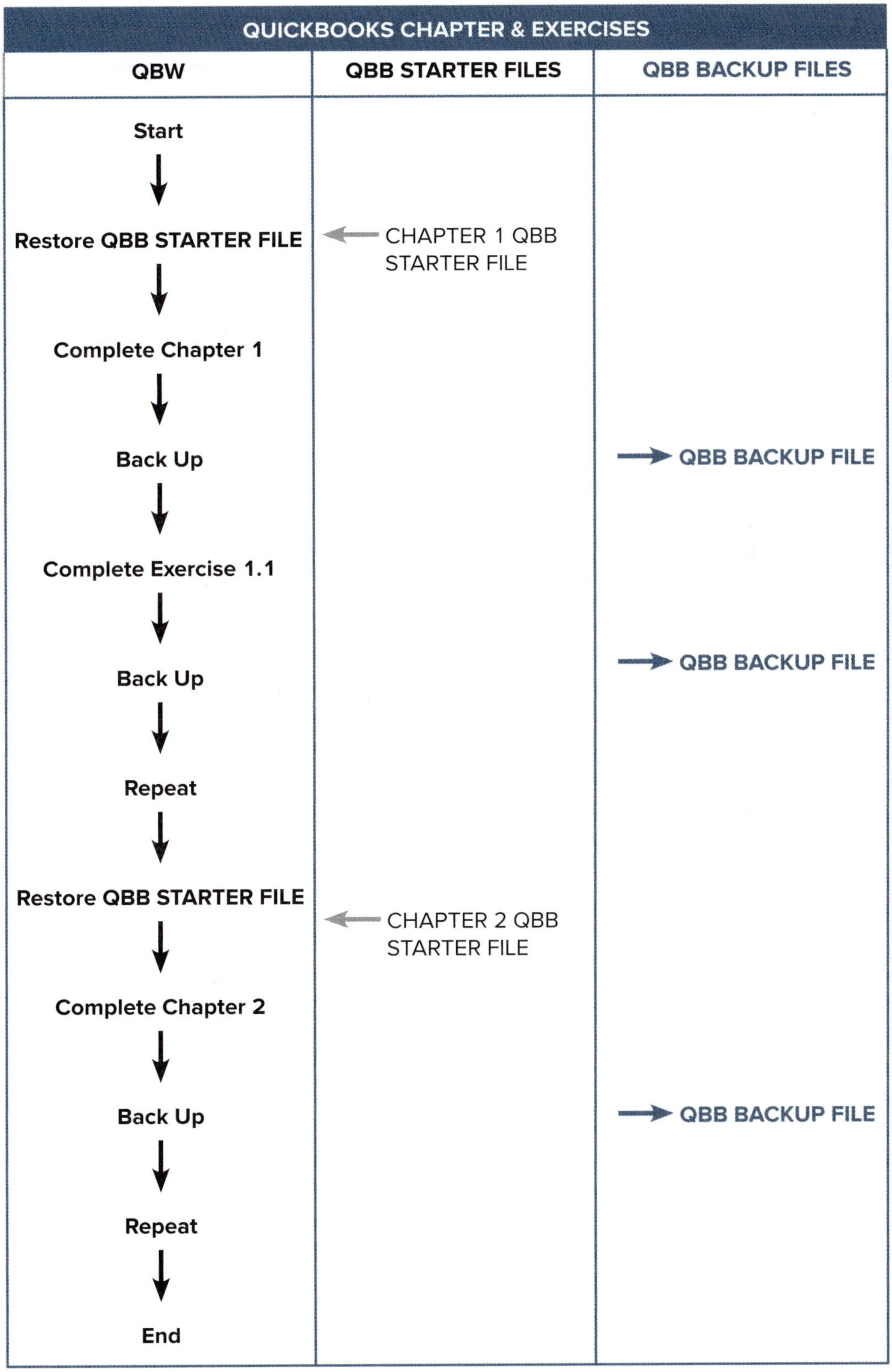
QUICKBOOKS CHAPTER & EXERCISES
QBW
QBB STARTER FILES
QBB BACKUP FILES
Start
Restore QBB STARTER FILE
CHAPTER 1 QBB STARTER FILE
Complete Chapter 1
Back Up
QBB BACKUP FILE
Complete Exercise 1.1
Back Up
QBB BACKUP FILE
Repeat
Restore QBB STARTER FILE
CHAPTER 2 QBB STARTER FILE
Complete Chapter 2
Back Up
QBB BACKUP FILE
Repeat
End

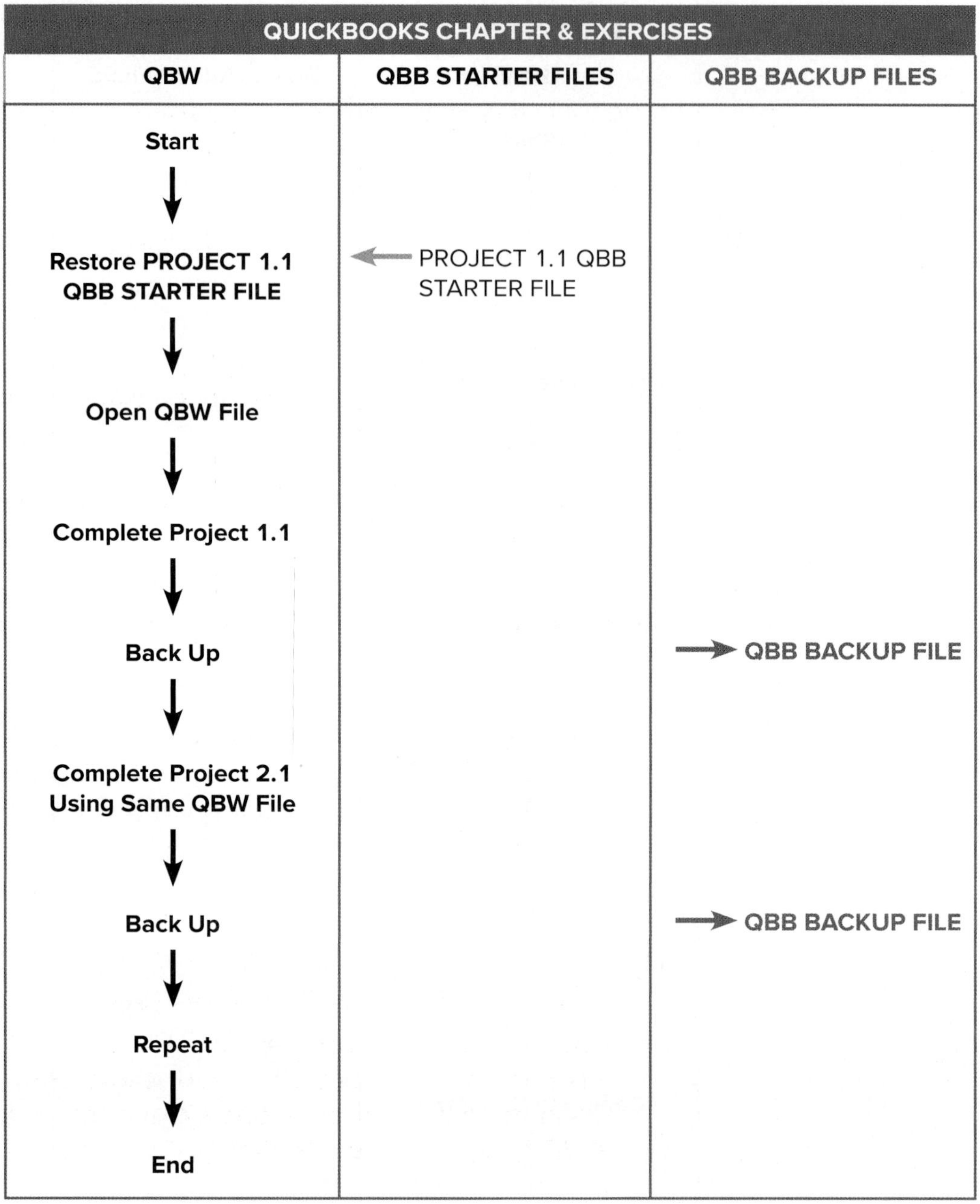
QUICKBOOKS CHAPTER & EXERCISES
QBW
QBB STARTER FILES
QBB BACKUP FILES
Start
Restore PROJECT 1.1 QBB STARTER FILE
PROJECT 1.1 QBB STARTER FILE
Open QBW File
Complete Project 1.1
Back Up
QBB BACKUP FILE
Complete Project 2.1 Using Same QBW File
Back Up
QBB BACKUP FILE
Repeat
End

Back Up QuickBooks Files

Throughout the text you will be instructed when to back up your QuickBooks file.

To save a backup (.QBB) file:

1. With your QuickBooks file (*.QBW) open, select **File**
2. Select **Back Up Company**
3. Select **Create Local Backup**
4. When the following window appears, select **Local backup**
5. Select **Next**
6. If asked where to save your files, to make it easier to find your backup files, click the **Browse** button
7. To make it easier to find your backup files, select **Desktop.** To organize your backup files, consider creating a QBB Backup folder on your desktop and then saving your QBB files to that desktop folder.
8. Click **OK** to close the Browse for Folder window. Click **OK** again to close the Backup Options window. If a QuickBooks Warning window appears, select **Use this Location.**
9. Select **Save it now**
10. Select **Next**
11. When the Save Backup Copy window appears, the Save in field should automatically show: **Desktop**
12. Update the File name field. For example, as shown below the File name field is updated to **YourName Chapter 1 (Backup).** Depending on your operating system settings, the file extension .QBB may appear automatically. If the .QBB extension does not appear, ***do not type it.***
13. The Save as type field should automatically appear as **QBW Backup (*.QBB)**
14. Click **Save.** If a QuickBooks Information message appears, click **OK.**

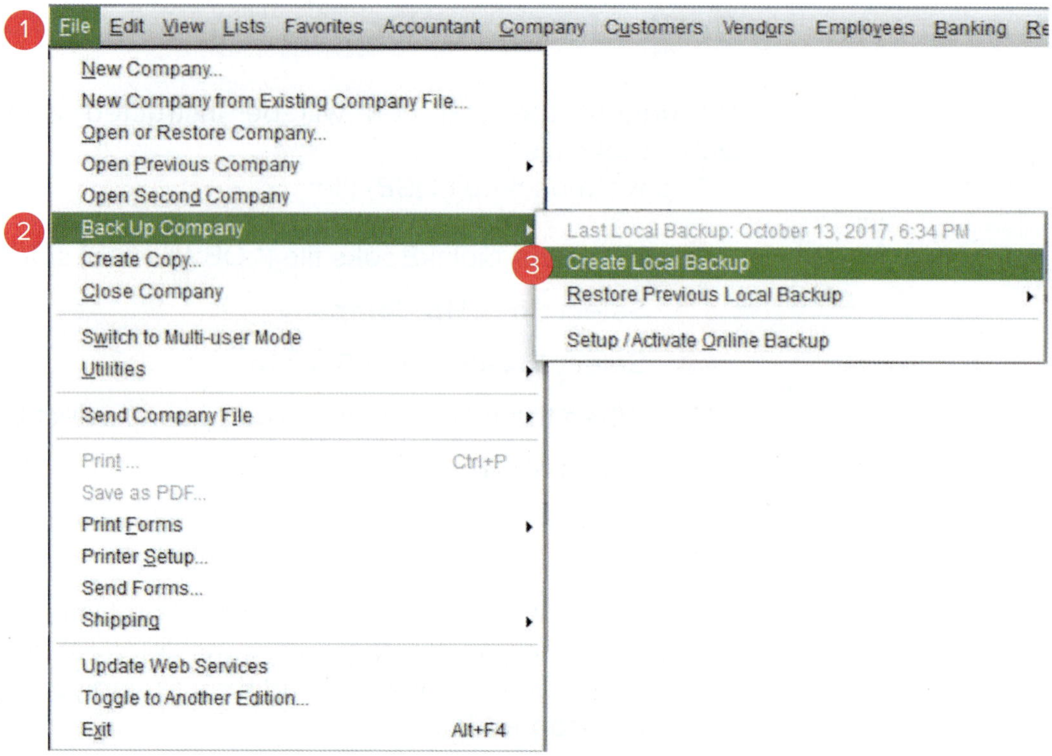
File Edit View Lists Favorites Accountant Company Customers Vendors Employees Banking
New Company...
New Company from Existing Company File...
Open or Restore Company...
Open Previous Company
Open Second Company
Back Up Company
Create Copy...
Close Company
Switch to Multi-user Mode
Utilities
Send Company File
Print ... Ctrl+P
Save as PDF...
Print Forms
Printer Setup...
Send Forms...
Shipping
Update Web Services
Toggle to Another Edition...
Exit Alt+F4
Last Local Backup: October 13, 2017, 6:34 PM
Create Local Backup
Restore Previous Local Backup
Setup / Activate Online Backup
1
2
3

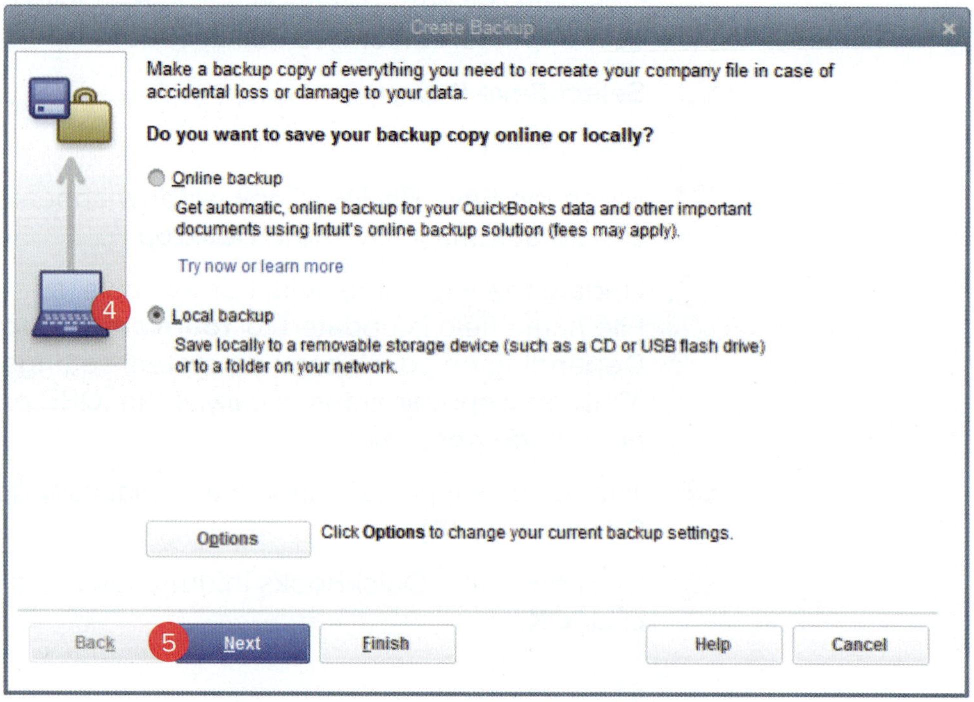
Create Backup
Make a backup copy of everything you need to recreate your company file in case of accidental loss or damage to your data.
Do you want to save your backup copy online or locally?
Online backup
Get automatic, online backup for your QuickBooks data and other important documents using Intuit's online backup solution (fees may apply).
Try now or learn more
Local backup
Save locally to a removable storage device (such as a CD or USB flash drive) or to a folder on your network.
Options
Click Options to change your current backup settings.
Back
Next
Finish
Help
Cancel
4
5

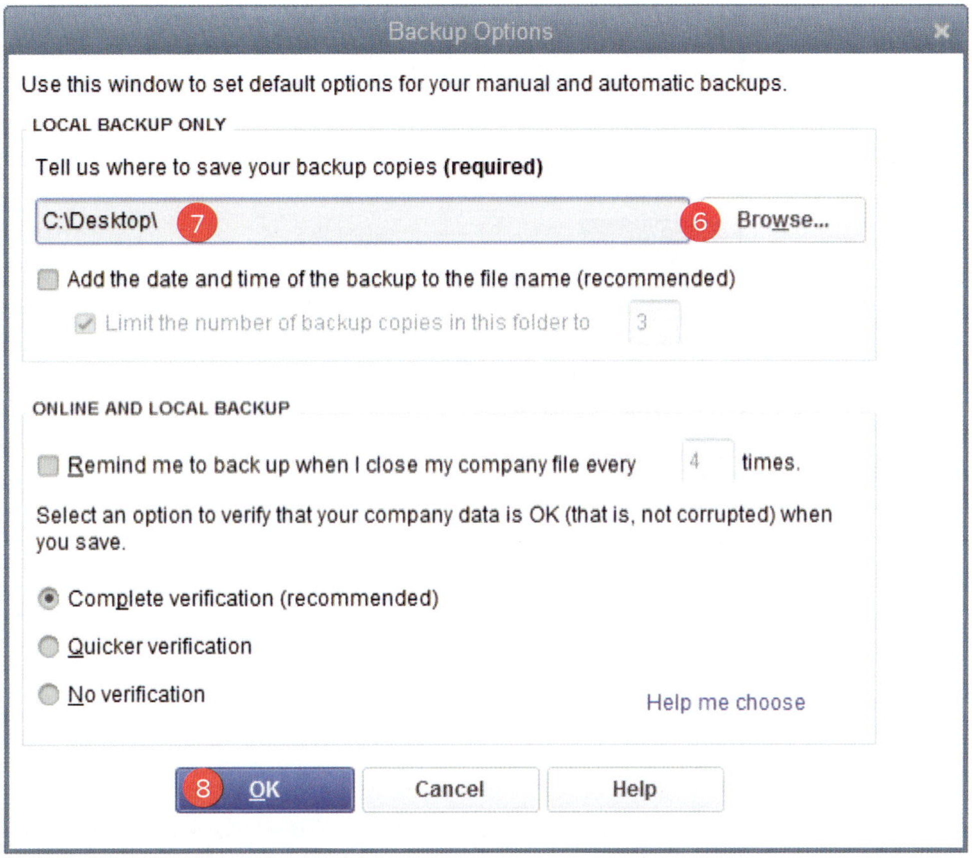
Backup Options
Use this window to set default options for your manual and automatic backups.
LOCAL BACKUP ONLY
Tell us where to save your backup copies (required)
C:\Desktop\
7
6
Browse...
Add the date and time of the backup to the file name (recommended)
Limit the number of backup copies in this folder to
3
ONLINE AND LOCAL BACKUP
Remind me to back up when I close my company file every
4
times.
Select an option to verify that your company data is OK (that is, not corrupted) when you save.
Complete verification (recommended)
Quicker verification
No verification
Help me choose
8
OK
Cancel
Help

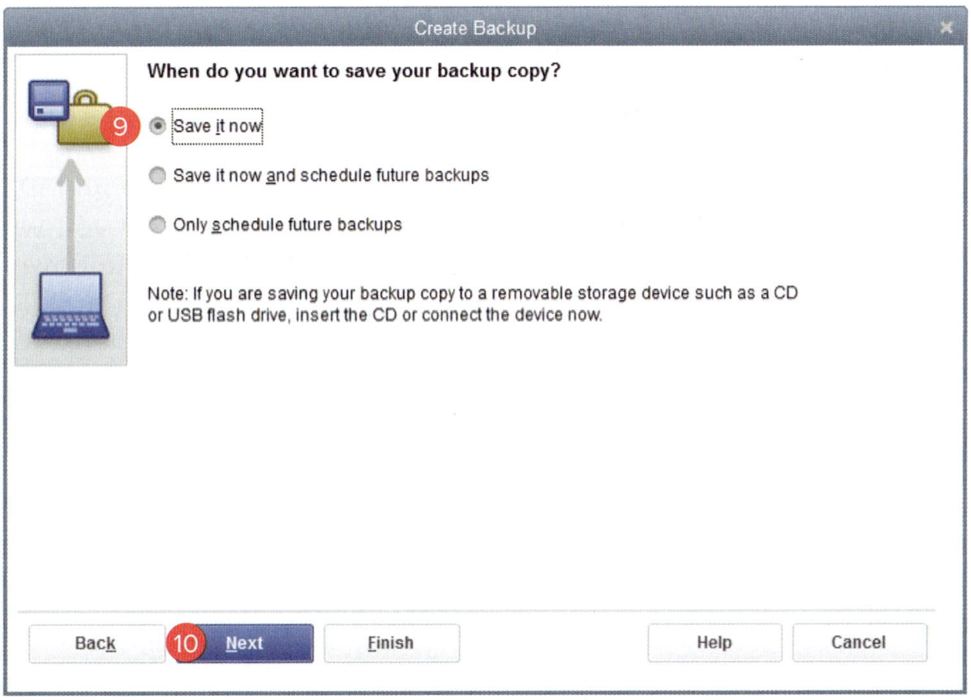
Create Backup
When do you want to save your backup copy?
9
Save it now
Save it now and schedule future backups
Only schedule future backups
Note: If you are saving your backup copy to a removable storage device such as a CD or USB flash drive, insert the CD or connect the device now.
Back
10
Next
Finish
Help
Cancel

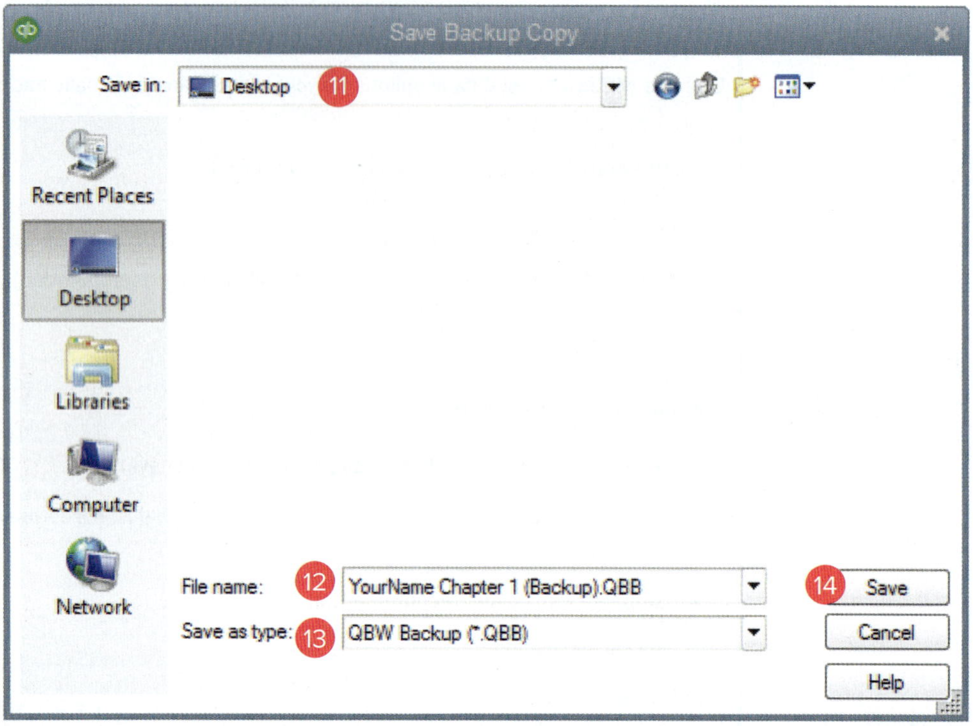

You can schedule a backup every time you close a QuickBooks company file or at regular intervals. Backup files can also be saved using QuickBooks Online Backup service.

Restore QuickBooks Files

At the beginning of chapters 1 through 10 and 15 and 17, you will be asked to restore a Starter file provided for you with the text. Ask your instructor for the location of the Starter files to download.

Another time you might need to restore a QuickBooks file is if you need to switch computers. Then you will back up your .QBW file and then restore the .QBB backup file you created to another computer.

A third reason you might need to restore a QuickBooks file is if you realize you have an error that you are unable to track and fix. In this case if you have a .QBB file, you would roll back to the most recent .QBB file and restore it.

! *Important Note: With the new 2018 version of QuickBooks, there are some changes with regard to passwords.*

- *When restoring a QBB file if QuickBooks requires you to create a password in order to continue, create your own password and record the password in a secure location, such as the inside cover of your textbook*
- *When restoring QuickBooks QBB files, if a password is requested:*

  1. *Try using User ID: Admin and leave the Password field blank*
  2. *If you are using the QBB Starter files and QuickBooks requires a password and QuickBooks will not accept the password field blank, try User ID: Admin and Password: KayQB2018*
  3. *If none of the above approaches permit you to restore the QBB file, see your instructor*

To restore a backup .QBB file:

1. From the No Company Open window, select **Open or restore an existing company.** (Or select **File** > **Open or Restore company.**)
2. Select **Restore a backup copy**
3. Click **Next**
4. When the Open or Restore Company window appears, select **Local backup**
5. Click **Next**
6. Identify the location for the QBB file to restore.
   - If you are restoring a QBB Starter file that you copied to your desktop, select the **Look in field** to find the location of the .QBB Starter file on your desktop.
   - If you are restoring one of your QBB Back Up file that you created, select the **Look in field** to find the location where you saved your .QBB Back Up file.
7. Select the **QBB file to restore,** such as Chapter 1 STARTER.QBB or YourNameChapter 1.QBB
8. The Files of type field should automatically display: **QBW Backup (*.QBB)**
9. Click **Open**
10. When the Open or Restore window appears, click **Next**

11 Identify the file name and location of the new company file (.QBW) file. You can save the .QBW (working file) on your desktop or create a folder on your Desktop for your QuickBooks files. Select the location to save in: **Desktop.** (Another option is to save your QBW files to Users > Public > Public Documents > Intuit > QuickBooks > Company Files. Be sure you have permissions to save to a folder or you may receive an error message.)

12 Enter the QBW File name, such as **YourName Chapter 1.** Insert your name in the file name so you can identify your files.

13 The Save as type field should automatically appear as **QuickBooks Files (*.QBW)**

14 Click **Save**

15 Click **OK** if the QuickBooks Desktop Information window appears notifying you that **You're opening a QuickBooks sample file**

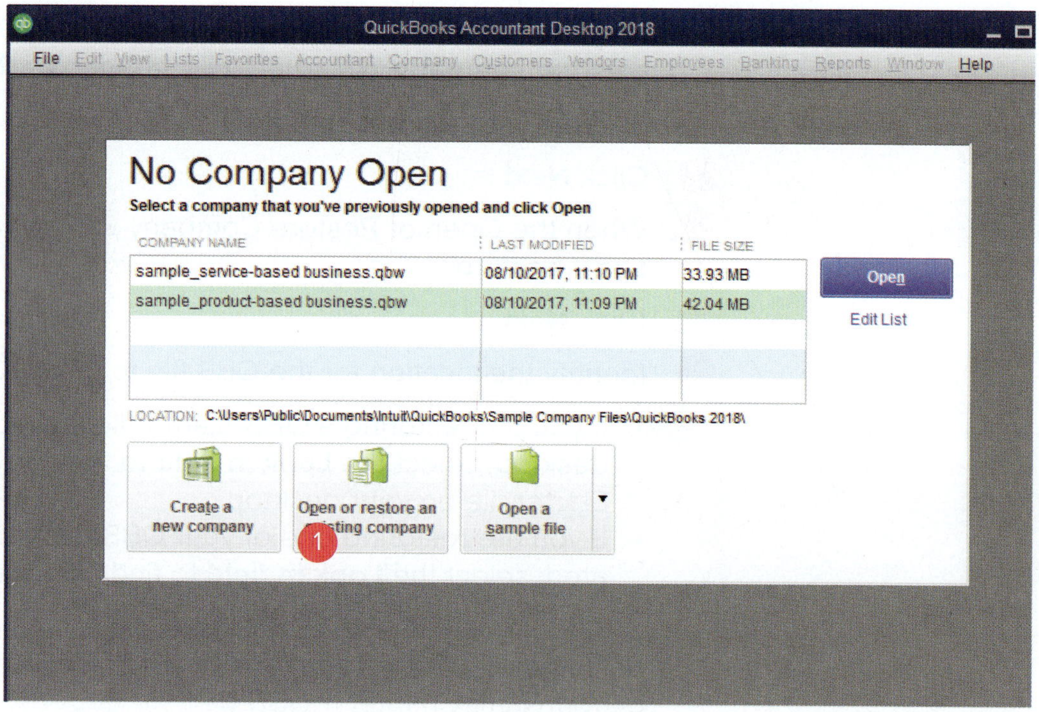

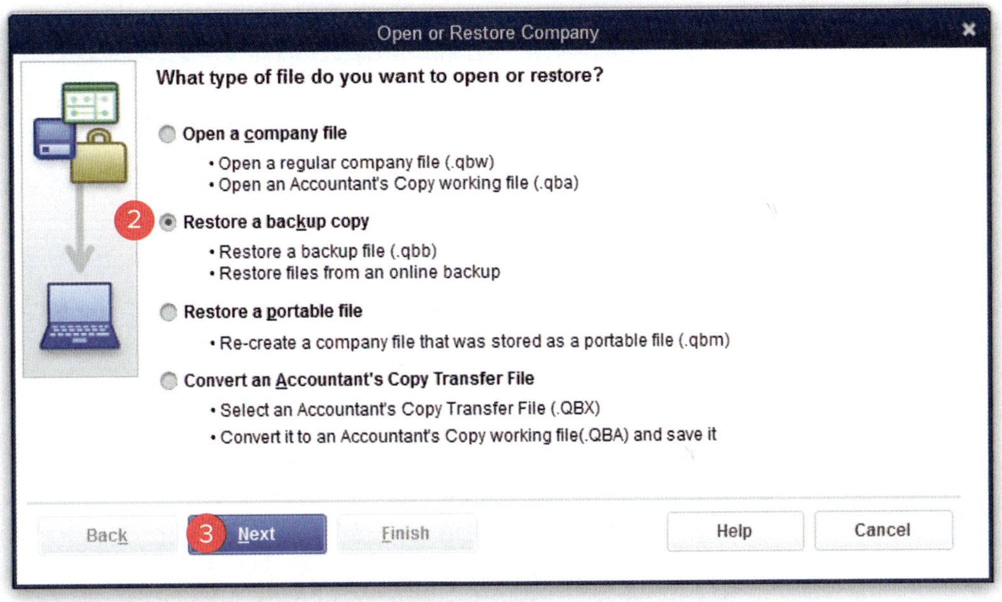
Open or Restore Company
What type of file do you want to open or restore?
Open a company file
• Open a regular company file (.qbw)
• Open an Accountant's Copy working file (.qba)
2
Restore a backup copy
• Restore a backup file (.qbb)
• Restore files from an online backup
Restore a portable file
• Re-create a company file that was stored as a portable file (.qbm)
Convert an Accountant's Copy Transfer File
• Select an Accountant's Copy Transfer File (.QBX)
• Convert it to an Accountant's Copy working file(.QBA) and save it
Back
3
Next
Finish
Help
Cancel

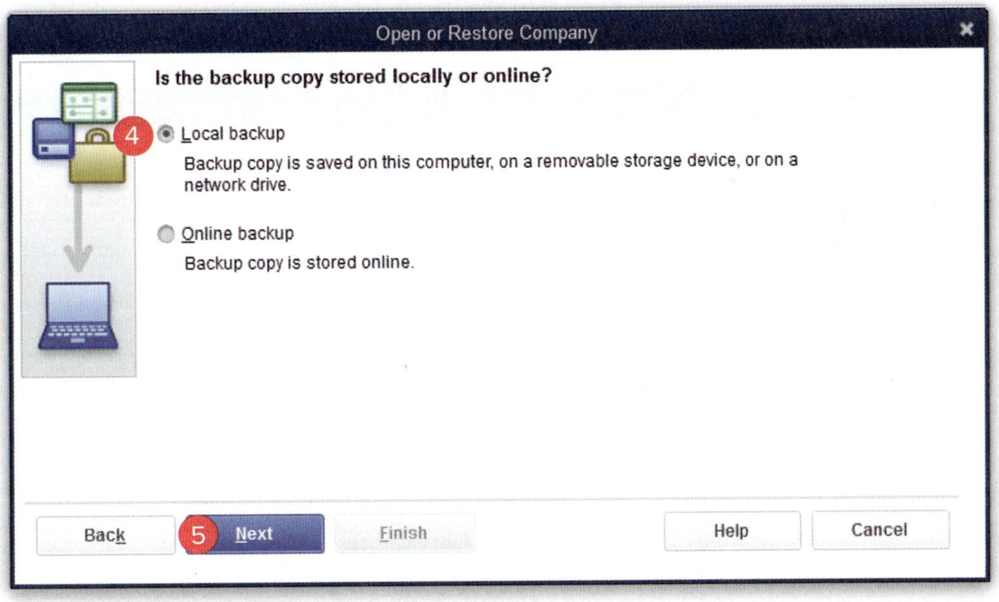
Open or Restore Company
Is the backup copy stored locally or online?
4
Local backup
Backup copy is saved on this computer, on a removable storage device, or on a network drive.
Online backup
Backup copy is stored online.
Back
5
Next
Finish
Help
Cancel

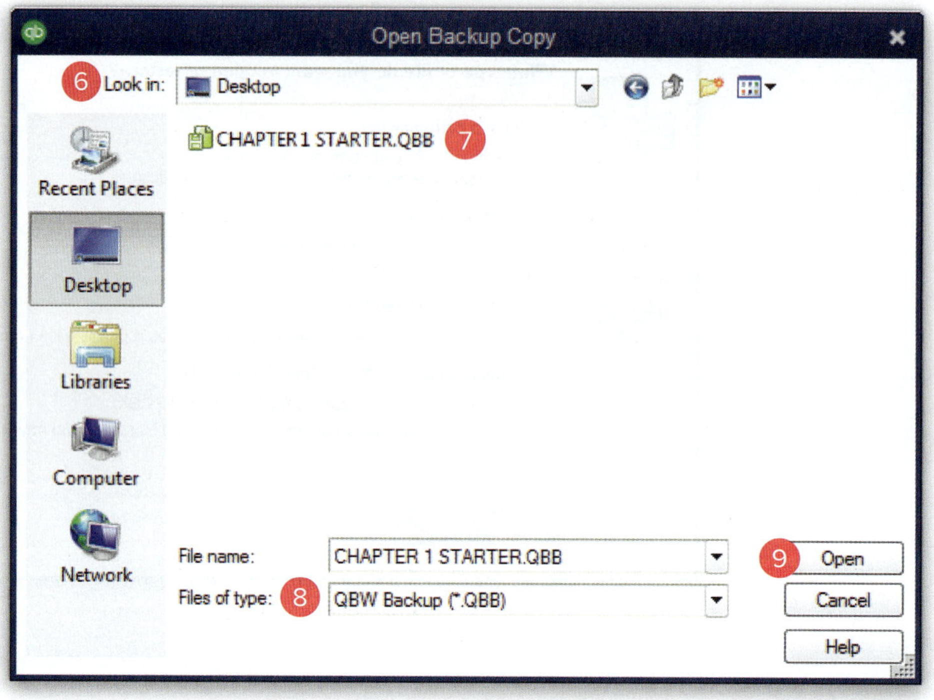
Open Backup Copy
6
Look in:
Desktop
CHAPTER 1 STARTER.QBB
7
Recent Places
Desktop
Libraries
Computer
Network
File name:
CHAPTER 1 STARTER.QBB
9
Open
Files of type:
8
QBW Backup (*.QBB)
Cancel
Help

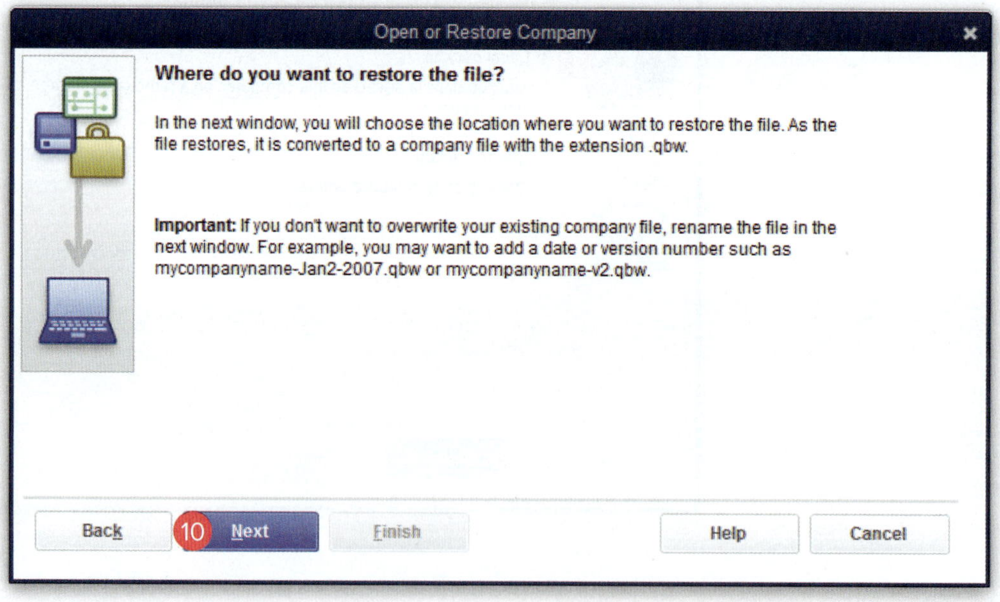
Open or Restore Company
Where do you want to restore the file?
In the next window, you will choose the location where you want to restore the file. As the file restores, it is converted to a company file with the extension .qbw.
Important: If you don't want to overwrite your existing company file, rename the file in the next window. For example, you may want to add a date or version number such as mycompanyname-Jan2-2007.qbw or mycompanyname-v2.qbw.
Back
10
Next
Finish
Help
Cancel

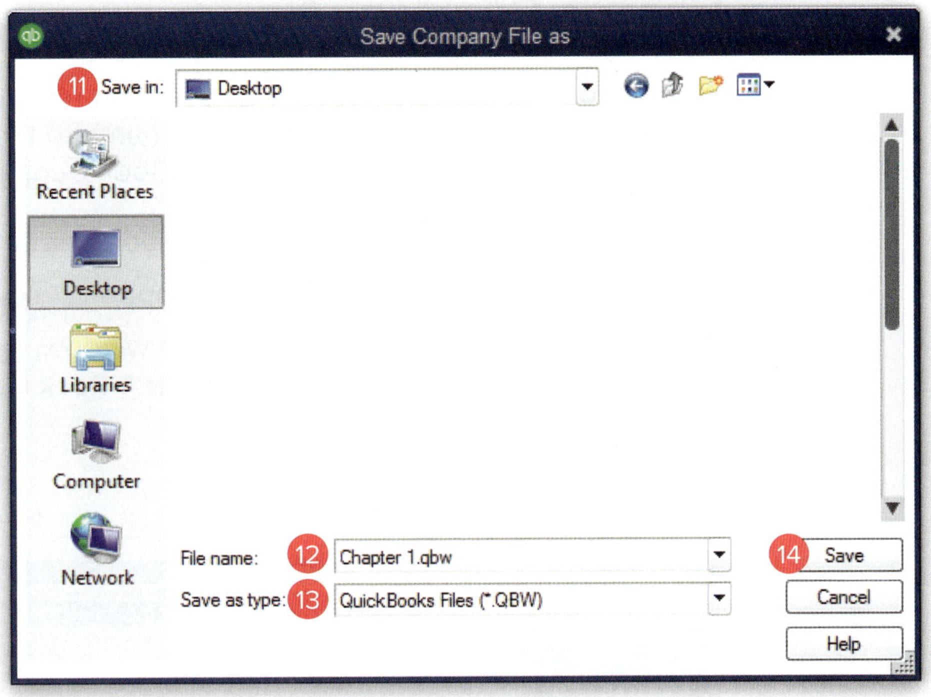
Save Company File as
11 Save in: Desktop
Recent Places
Desktop
Libraries
Computer
Network
File name: 12 Chapter 1.qbw
Save as type: 13 QuickBooks Files (*.QBW)
14 Save
Cancel
Help

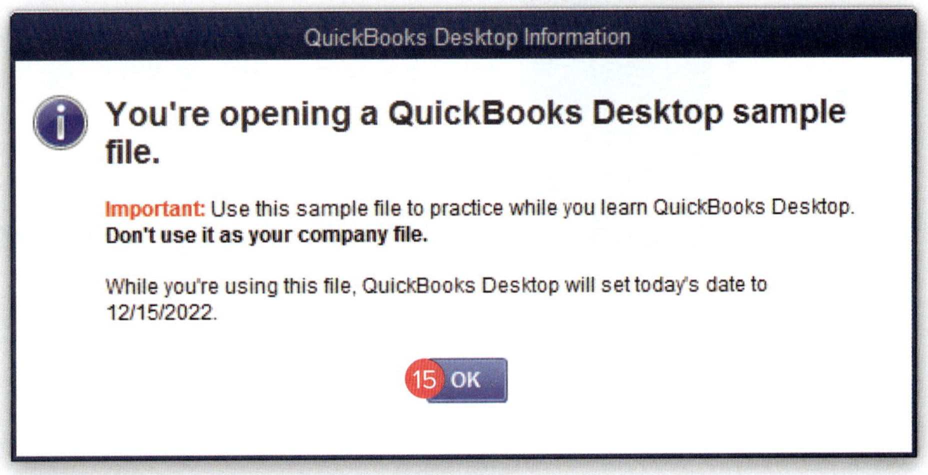
QuickBooks Desktop Information
You're opening a QuickBooks Desktop sample file.
Important: Use this sample file to practice while you learn QuickBooks Desktop. Don't use it as your company file.
While you're using this file, QuickBooks Desktop will set today's date to 12/15/2022.
15 OK

Change Company Name

So that your name automatically appears on reports and checks, update the Company Name setting to add your name to the company name.

To change a company name in QuickBooks, complete the following:

1. From My Shortcuts on the Navigation Bar, select **My Company**
2. When the My Company window appears, select **Edit**
3. Update the Company Information window, update Company Name field to: **YourName Chapter 1 Rock Castle Construction**
4. **Close** the My Company window

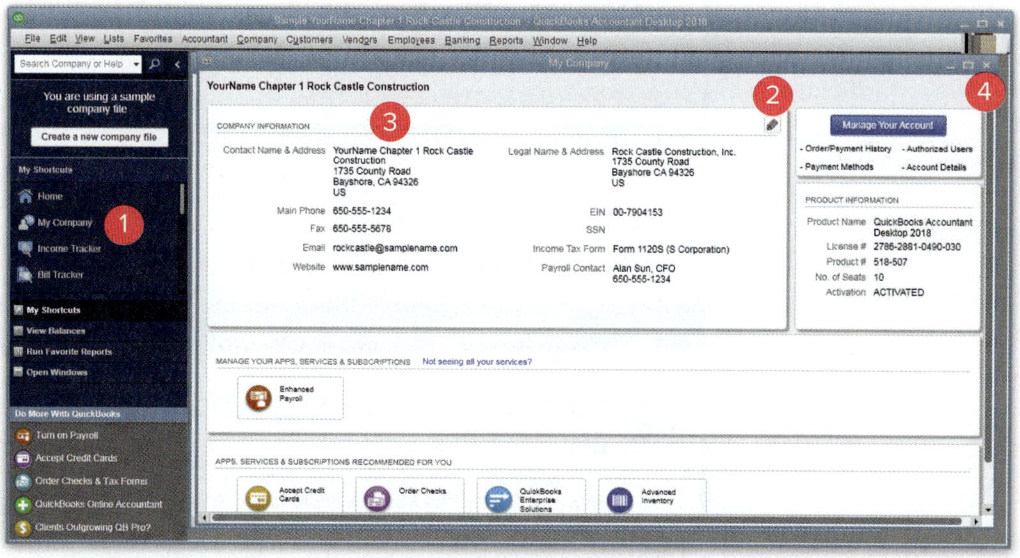

Appendix C

www.My-QuickBooks.com

Go to www.My-QuickBooks.com to view the QuickBooks website to accompany *Computer Accounting with QuickBooks.*

www.My-QuickBooks.com includes:

- **Excel Report Templates.** Use the Excel report templates to create digital QuickBooks reports instead of paper printouts for your assignments.
- **QuickBooks Videos.** View videos on QuickBooks topics such as back up, restore, and much more.
- **Computer Accounting with QuickBooks Updates.** Check out updates to stay current with the latest updates for QuickBooks software and this text.
- **QuickBooks User Certification Information.** Learn more about how you can obtain the QuickBooks User Certification.
- **QuickBooks and My Mac.** Explore different approaches and ideas for using QuickBooks with your Mac.
- **QuickBooks Issue Resolution and Troubleshooting Tips.** Provides you with information about the following frequently asked questions (FAQs) and issue resolution tips, including a QuickBooks Issue Resolution Strategy, QuickBooks Help and Live Community information, and tips on how to track and correct errors.
- **And More. . . .**

Index

B

C

F

S

T

U

V

W

Y